MEDIAEVAL STUDIES

Volume *XXXVII*
1975

PONTIFICAL INSTITUTE OF MEDIAEVAL STUDIES
TORONTO, CANADA

Editor:

Professor Virginia Brown

Pontifical Institute of Mediaeval Studies
59 Queen's Park Crescent East
Toronto, Ontario M5S 2C4
Canada

ISBN 0-88844 638-1

Printed by
UNIVERSA — WETTEREN — BELGIUM

CONTENTS

MEDIAEVALIA

THE FELLOWS AND ASSOCIATES

OF THE

PONTIFICAL INSTITUTE OF MEDIAEVAL STUDIES

DEDICATE

THIS VOLUME

TO THE MEMORY OF

VINCENT LORNE KENNEDY

Vincent Lorne Kennedy

VINCENT LORNE KENNEDY
1899-1974

VINCENT Lorne Kennedy was born 24 January 1899 in Kinkora, Ontario. He received his early education in Stratford, Ontario, schools and at Assumption College in Windsor, Ontario. On 1 August 1917 he entered St. Basil's Novitiate, Toronto, where on 10 August 1918 he made his religious vows as a member of the Congregation of Priests of St. Basil. He was ordained priest on 20 December 1924. His studies for the priesthood included Theology at St. Basil's Scholasticate, an honours degree in Classics from the University of Toronto (1923), a teacher's specialist certificate at the Ontario College of Education, Toronto (1924), and an M.A. in Classics from the University of Toronto (1925). Following ordination Father Kennedy was asked to assume a series of administrative duties that left him little time for teaching and scholarship: registrar of Assumption College (1925-27), principal of St. Michael's College School, Toronto (1927-28), and president of Assumption College (1928-31).

Meanwhile, St. Michael's College and the Basilian Fathers had established (1929) the Institute of Mediaeval Studies, Toronto, which was going to need a professor of liturgy. Etienne Gilson who was director of the newly founded Institute insisted that the professorship required some one already trained in Classics. Father Kennedy undertook with enthusiasm to prepare himself for the post. He went to the Université de Strasbourg (1931-33) to study under the direction of Michel Andrieu of the Faculté de Théologie Catholique. On the advice of Msgr. Andrieu he transferred to the Pontificio Istituto di Archeologia Cristiana, Rome, where he completed his doctoral dissertation, *The Saints of the Canon of the Mass*, in 1935 under Dom L. C. Mohlberg. That autumn Father Kennedy began his teaching career at the Pontifical Institute of Mediaeval Studies as professor of Christian Archaeology and Hagiography, a post he held until 1960.

Inevitably administrative work was added to his lectures and seminars. He served as secretary of the Institute (1935-43), as managing editor of *Mediaeval Studies* (1941-43), and as an associate editor of *Worship* (1938-57). In addition to his academic duties Father Kennedy served the Basilian Fathers as a general councillor (1942-60) and as procurator general at the Holy See (1937-42, 1952 in a temporary capacity, and

1961-67). During his student years in Rome and in his first term as procurator general he played an important role in obtaining for the Institute the papal charter (1939) empowering it to grant degrees. In 1960 he was appointed a consultor to the Historical Section of the Sacred Congregation of Rites and was named a consultor to the Pontifical Commission for the Sacred Liturgy in Preparation for the Second Vatican Council. He was made (1964) a consultor to the Revising Committee of the Commission for the carrying out of the Liturgical Constitution of the Second Vatican Council.

Father Kennedy was appointed in 1963 an extraordinary professor at the Pontificio Istituto di Archeologia Cristiana where he lectured until 1967. During these years he also taught a course at the Regina Mundi Institute for Sisters. Ill health and the burden of administrative duties had several times interrupted Father Kennedy's scholarly work. In the late sixties poor health seriously handicapped his academic career. He died of leukemia in St. Joseph's Hospital, Houston, Texas, 25 March 1974.

BIBLIOGRAPHY OF VINCENT LORNE KENNEDY

1. Review of Fidelis Boeser, *The Mass Liturgy* (Milwaukee, 1932), trans. Charles Cannon, in *Ephemerides liturgicae* 48 (1934) 274.
2. Review of Charles F. Curran, *The Eucharistic Life* (Milwaukee, 1930), in *Ephemerides liturgicae* 48 (1934) 274.
3. "The Pre-Gregorian *Hanc igitur*", *Ephemerides liturgicae* 50 (1936) 349-358.
4. *The Saints of the Canon of the Mass*, Vatican City, 1938. (Pontificio istituto di archeologia cristiana: Studi di antichità cristiana 14).
5. "The *De officiis divinis* of MS. Bamberg Lit. 134", *Ephemerides liturgicae* 52 (1938) 312-326.
6. "The Offertory Rite", *Orate fratres* 12 (1938) 193-198, 244-249, 294-298.
7. "The *Summa de officiis ecclesiae* of Guy d'Orchelles", *Mediaeval Studies* 1 (1939) 23-62.
8. "The Franciscan *Ordo Missae* in the Thirteenth Century", *Mediaeval Studies* 2 (1940) 204-222.
9. "The Corpus Christi Procession", *Orate fratres* 14 (1940) 297-301.
10. "The Handbook of Master Peter, Chancellor of Chartres", *Mediaeval Studies* 5 (1943) 1-38.
11. Review of Walter Lowrie, *The Lord's Supper and the Liturgy* (London, 1943), in *Theological Studies* 4 (1943) 631-634.
12. "The Moment of Consecration and the Elevation of the Host", *Mediaeval Studies* 6 (1944) 121-150.

13. Review of The Liturgical Conference, *1943 National Liturgical Week* (Ferdinand, Ind., 1944), in *Theological Studies* 5 (1944) 245-246.

14. "Robert Courson on Penance", *Mediaeval Studies* 7 (1945) 291-336.

15. Review of Gregory Dix, *The Shape of the Liturgy* (Westminster, 1945), in *Theological Studies* 6 (1945) 554-560.

16. "The Date of the Parisian Decree on the Elevation of the Host", *Mediaeval Studies* 8 (1946) 87-96.

17. "The Content of Courson's *Summa*", *Mediaeval Studies* 9 (1947) 81-107.

18. "The Two Collects of the Gelasian", *Miscellanea liturgica in honorem L. Cuniberti Mohlberg* 1 (Rome, 1948), pp. 183-188.

19. Review of Henry G. J. Beck, *The Pastoral Care of Souls in South-East France during the Sixth Century* (Rome, 1950), in *Speculum* 26 (1951) 703-705.

20. "The Lateran Missal and Some Allied Documents", *Mediaeval Studies* 14 (1952) 61-78.

21. Review of F. X. Arnold and B. Fischer, eds., *Die Messe in der Glaubensverkündigung* (Freiburg, 1950), in *Theological Studies* 13 (1952) 142-144.

22. Review of Robert Folz, *Etudes sur le culte liturgique de Charlemagne dans les églises de l'empire* (Paris, 1951), in *Speculum* 27 (1952) 217.

23. Review of Guy d'Orchelles, *Tractatus de sacramentis ex eius Summa de sacramentis et officiis ecclesiae*, eds. D. Van den Eynde and O. Van den Eynde (St. Bonaventure, N. Y., 1953), in *Speculum* 28 (1953) 575-576.

24. Review of Francis Wormald, *The Miniatures in the Gospels of St. Augustine* (Cambridge and New York, 1954), in *Speculum* 30 (1955) 133-134.

25. "For a New Edition of the *Micrologus* of Bernold of Constance", *Mélanges en l'honneur de Monseigneur Michel Andrieu* (Strasbourg, 1956), pp. 229-241.

26. "The Calendar of the Early Thirteenth-Century Curial Missal", *Mediaeval Studies* 20 (1958) 113-126.

27. *The Saints of the Canon of the Mass*, 2nd ed. rev., Vatican City, 1963. (Pontificio istituto di archeologia cristiana: Studi di antichità cristiana 14).

MEMORANDA AND SERMONS OF ETIENNE AUBERT (INNOCENT VI) AS BISHOP (1338-1341)

Daniel Williman

Concealed among the fiscal records of the Avignonese papacy in the Vatican Archives lies a small memorandum book, apparently the autograph of Etienne Aubert, the future Pope Innocent VI ; it contains notes of the personnel and possessions of his household and the texts of six occasional sermons, dating from his first year as bishop of Noyon to his first year as bishop of Clermont.[1]

Etienne Aubert was the son of Adhémar Aubert, lord of Monts in the diocese of Limoges. Alumnus of Toulouse with the doctorate of laws, canon of Paris from 1335, *juge-mage* of the seneschal's court of Toulouse and counsellor in Parlement to Philip VI, and ambassador between the royal and papal courts, he was inducted into the double office of bishop and count of Noyon in January 1338, translated to Clermont in mid-1340, created cardinal in 1342 and elected pope in 1352.[2] The pontificate of Innocent VI is marked chiefly by his appointment of the legate Gil Albornoz in Italy and his defense of Avignon against the Free Companies. His predecessors at Avignon left behind them a more colorful memory, and a small collection of writings — sermons and scrip-

ent VI is marked chiefly by his appointment of the legate Gil Albornoz in Italy and his defense of Avignon against the Free Companies. His predecessors at Avignon left behind them a more colorful memory, and a small collection of writings — sermons and scrip-

1 For their valuable advice in the preparation of this article, the author wishes to thank Leonard E. Boyle, Pierre Gasnault, Jacques Monfrin, Bernard Peebles, Richard Rouse, and Norman Zacour. The research was carried out under Doctoral and Killam grants from the Canada Council.

2 For the ecclesiastical careers in this article, see Conrad Eubel, *Hierarchia catholica medii aevi I (1196-1431)*, 2nd ed. (Regensburg, 1915; rpt. Passau, 1960); for Etienne Aubert as bishop, *Gallia Christiana*, 2nd ed. (Paris, 1870-1874) 9.1015D and 2.287C-D; Etienne Baluze, *Vitae paparum avenionensium*, ed. Guillaume Mollat, 4 vols. (Paris, 1914-1927); Guillaume Mollat, *Les papes d'Avignon (1305-1378)*, 10th ed. (Paris, 1964), pp. 104-115; Bernard Guillemain, *La cour pontificale d'Avignon 1308-1376: étude d'une société* (Paris, 1966).

tural theology — as well;[3] until now, Innocent VI has been known as the author only of papal letters.

His notebook may have entered the cameral archives on his death in 1362, when his nephew Arnaud Aubert, papal Camerarius, was gathering information for the execution of his testament by Cardinal Audoin Aubert, also a nephew (see the text and its notes below: [A17], [A14], and [D]). In any case, the booklet is preserved in the Vatican Archives with the mark *Collectoriae* 220, a place to which it has no intrinsic right, and which has concealed it so far from historians of the Avignonese papacy and of Valois France.[4] The index to the *Fondo camerale* in the Vatican Archives, the work of Monsignor Pietro Guidi (*Indice* 1036), attributes the booklet to an earlier bishop of Noyon; his later *Inventari di libri nelle serie dell'Archivio Vaticano, 1287-1459*[5] correctly attributes the lists of books on fols. 24[r] and 26[r], but is not concerned with the other contents of the volume. No other study of the document is mentioned in the four volumes so far published of the *Bibliografia dell'Archivio Vaticano*.

The memoranda and sermons were written into a small blank book of 96 paper folios, each 115 × 141 mm. The maker cut sixteen sheets of Tuscan paper,[6] each about 23 × 43 cm., into thirds, each about 23 × 14 cm. He then folded them, three at a time, in half; the irregular pattern in which fragments of the watermark appear in the different ternions (fols. 1 and 4, 9 and 12, 22 and 23, 26 and 27, etc.) proves that the cutting preceded the gathering and folding of each ternion. Finally, he sewed the sixteen ternions together, trimmed the edges, and covered the booklet with white parchment, leaving the cover full enough on one side to fold over the opening edge, with a parchment tie of which a fragment remains. There seems to have been no subsequent trimming. The book bears no external mark except the Archives labels, the old Avignon Archives shelf-number 1137, and an identification of the diocese mentioned in the memoranda: "Francia. Noviomen."

As pope, Innocent VI signed his approval to supplications in the form

---

3 Guillemain, pp. 21-23.

4 Leonard E. Boyle, *A Survey of the Vatican Archives and of Its Medieval Holdings* (Toronto, 1972), pp. 43, 165-168, for the *Collectoriae*; that series includes some informal notes of the property of bishops, claimed by right of spoil, which superficially resemble the present notebook.

5 Studi e Testi 135 (Vatican City, 1948), p. 27.

6 The watermark, cut in two in each ternion, is a hammer, mushroom, or pestle 38 × 46 mm., similar to Vladimir A. Mošin and Seid M. Traljić, *Filigranes des XIIIᵉ et XIVᵉ siècles*, 2 vols. (Zagreb, 1957), no. 6188 or 6189, found with dates of Bologna, 1300-1306; Lucca, 1311; Pistoia and Florence.

"Fiat. G.", too small a sample to use as a definitive comparison with the hand of *Collectoriae* 220;[7] and I know of no other extant autograph. But our booklet was a very private record of the affairs of "dominus Noviomensis" from 1338, the first year of Etienne Aubert's prelacy. The bishop is the grammatical first person in sections [B 1-5], [J], [L], and [M]; and where he is mentioned in the third person, in [A], [C], and [E], the language echoes the original instruments that stood behind the present record. One hand did all the writing, and made changes of substance and style: the bishop's own hand, or that of an incredibly confidential and self-effacing secretary. A secretary would presumably keep legal records in the form of notarial instruments, not as informal memoranda; he would use the third person consistently; and in referring to the bishop, he would use a more circumstantial title than *dominus* — likely *reverendissimus pater et dominus, dominus*. The hand is a regular and legible Gothic, not much abbreviated, but compressed in the small pages. The inks are somewhat pale, one grey and one brown. Fewer than half the pages are used.

These memoranda reveal a churchman of substance and power, the leader of his own family, closely connected to the king and to influential prelates, capable enough in preaching out of the basic texts of canon law and theology. Here is a brief account of the contents of his notebook.

[A] from 7 October 1338, a list of 137 liveried retainers (eight of them grouped together in [96]). The names are listed according to their rank and its appropriate attire: familiars and chaplains [1-34], squires [35-99], clerks [100-104], officials [105-117], and body-servants [118-130]. The original distribution of liveries was to 133 men, of whom 15 were stricken from the list [42, 46, 47, 51, 56, 68, 69, 70, 88, 98, 102, 106, 108, 113, 124], many because they became knights and wore their own arms; and four names were added between the lines of the original list and in a different ink [33, 34, 54, 55]. At least eighteen members of the household were the bishop's relatives by blood or marriage [14-19, 31, 35, 39, 46-48, 55, 59, 64, 65, 74, 86], and many of the rest represent exchanges of favor and information with the powerful, especially with Pierre Roger, archbishop of Rouen and soon-to-be Pope Clement VI [30, 61, 72, 76], and with Cardinal Elie Talleyrand de Périgord [96, 105]. The importance of these contacts for Etienne Aubert's future career is

7 Pierre Gasnault indicates such fiats in Bibliothèque Nationale MS. Nouv. acq. lat. 1887, 54[r] and 86[r] and MS. Nouv. acq. lat. 2481, 6[r], 7[r], and 8[r]. A facsimile of the second example above is in Alain de Boüard, *Manuel de diplomatique française et pontificale* 1 (Paris, 1929), Album, plate IV, 1.

illuminated by a survey of the conclave that elected him pope in 1352: of the twenty-four cardinals present, not counting himself, three had worn his livery [10, 30, 72], eight more were related to members of his household,[8] and the critical one, Talleyrand, had exchanged squires with him [96, 105].[9] His entourage was a center for the Limousins on the eve of their first papal election, and it included five future cardinals, among them a future master-general of the Dominicans and a future pope, Gregory XI [10, 14, 18, 30, 72]. Fols. 3^r-8^r.

[B] 5 July 1340-October 1341. Five memoranda of debts: payments to quit debts to the brothers Gaucelme and Guillaume de Simon and Jean des Moulins, possibly contracted in 1338 to pay the Services for Noyon [1, 2]; cash transferred by the brothers Simon to Noyon [3, 4]; a note of the balance of a debt to them, outstanding in October 1341, possibly for the Services for Clermont [5]. Fol. 10^r.

[C] 30 May 1338. Inventory of the bishop's silver, stored at St. Victor in Paris, by Gaucelme de Simon; 378 marks, 4 $^1/_2$ ounces by the reckoning given, this treasure would be worth at least 1500 florins if it were sold by weight.[10] Fols. 18^r-22^r.

[D] 6 May 1339. The list of his study-library, likely in his house at Carlepont, to judge by the date. The size and content of the library are not surprising for the period:[11] the *Corpus juris civilis* in five volumes [1-5] and the contemporary *Corpus juris canonici* in four [6-9]; the *Summa aurea* of Henricus de Segusio (Ostiensis), *Summa* of Goffredus de Trano, and commentary of Innocent IV, all on the *Decretales* [11, 13, 15]; the *Summa* of Azo and commentary of Cinus Pistoriensis on the *Codex* [14, 12]; the *Speculum judiciale* of Guillelmus Durandus the elder [10]; and Jacobus de Bellovisu on the civil *Liber feudorum* [19]; a small borrowed Bible [22]; glossed Gospels in two volumes [16]; the *Sententiae* of Petrus Lombardus [17], an anonymous large *De vitiis et virtutibus* [18]; one of the *Chronica* of Bernardus Guidonis, likely that of the popes [20]; an alphabetized collection of the sayings of the Fathers, *Flores sanctorum* [23]; the *Summa confessorum* of Joannes de Friburgo [24], and the sermons of Jacobus de Lausana [25]. Fol. 24^r.

8 Pierre Desprez, Guillaume Court, Hugues Roger, Bertrand de la Tour, Guillaume de la Jugie, Pierre Bertrand, Nicolas de Besse, and Guillaume d'Aigrefeuille.

9 Norman P. Zacour, "A Note on the Papal Election of 1352: The Candidacy of Jean Birel," *Traditio* 13 (1957) 461-462.

10 *Vatikanische Quellen zur Geschichte der päpstlichen Hof- und Finanzverwaltung (1316-1378)* (hereafter cited as *VQ*) 1 (Paderborn, 1910), p. 45*.

11 My unpublished Ph.D. thesis, *The Books of the Avignonese Popes and Clergy: A Repertory and Edition of the Book-Notices in the Vatican Archives, 1287-1420* (Toronto, 1973), pp. 107-108.

[E] 28 April 1339-c. 24 June 1339 (the first date is given as '29 on 25^r, the other is found on 31^r). Inventory of the furnishings of the bishop's house at Carlepont (Oise, canton of Ribecourt): the chapel [1-16] and its books [17-23], the bishop's bedchamber [24-40], hall [41-50], kitchen [51-60], beds and bedding [61-67]. Fols. 25^r-31^r.

[F] 28 April 1339. Inventory of the house at Noyon, furnished for brief stays. Fol. 33^r.

[G] Tables and benches at Ercheu (Somme, canton of Roye); no furnishings listed for the houses at Sempigny and Mauconseil (both Oise, canton of Noyon), only blank pages headed with their names.[12] Fols. 35^r, 37^r, 39^r.

[H] Untitled address, planned for the bishop's first visit to Reims after his consecration, expressing respect to his metropolitan, Jean de Vienne (1334-1351), and based largely on canonical texts. Fols. 41^r-41^v.

[I] "A conference to be made in the chapter of Noyon", upon his arrival in his see, promising the canons that he would reside in the diocese and defend their rights. Fols. 64^r-66^r.

[J] "A sermon made by me in synod", to the effect that good preaching requires good living and true doctrine. Fols. 67^r-67^v.

[K] "A conference made in the abbey of St-Eloi-Fontaine" (OCanSA, Aisne, canton of Chauny), on the occasion of the episcopal visitation. The abbot was Jean Moyset.[13] Fols. 69^r-70^r.

[L] "A conference to be made on my departure, in the chapter of Noyon", expressing goodwill and appreciation. In the summer of 1340, leaving behind the fortification of Noyon and the litigation attached to it,[14] the bishop was departing for the richer see of Clermont, on the edge of his native Languedoc. These circumstances, which might mar the formal sorrow of the occasion, are not mentioned in the sermon. Fols. 71^r-72^r.

[M] "A sermon made by me at the conferring of Orders", likely at Clermont, because one of its texts is the Languedoc saying "Qui no es be garnitz es amutz": "He who is not well armed is silenced". Fols. 72^v—74^v.

Here is the text in full:[15]

---

12   A. Lognon, *Pouillés de la province de Reims* (Paris, 1908) for identifications of these houses of the episcopal *mensa*.

13   L. H. Cottineau, *Répertoire topo-bibliographique des abbayes et prieurés* 1 (Mâcon, 1939) 748; *Gallia Christiana* 9.1127D.

14   Etienne Aubert saw to the repair of the fortifications of Noyon as bishop and count of the city; the mayor and jury then claimed that the walls belonged to the king, but Aubert made the bishop's claim good in Parlement (16 September 1340): P.-C. Timbal *et al., La Guerre de cent ans vue à travers les registres du Parlement* (Paris, 1961), pp. 175-179.

15   Following François Masai, "Principes et conventions de l'édition diplomatique," *Scriptorium* 4

[A]

3^r In nomine domini amen. Anno domini M^{o}CCC^{o}XXXVIII°, die sep-
tima mensis Octobris, Galterus Alberti de Monte fuit factus serviens armorum ad verbum domini Noviomensis episcopi avunculi sui,[16] apud
Sanctum Christoforum in Halata, ubi dominus rex tunc erat.[17]

Item prefatus dominus Noviomensis die veneris sequenti, videlicet
nona die dicti mensis incepit dare libratam suam, et distribuit personis
infrascriptis. Primo sociis et cappellanis [---de re] ac aliis de rebus
sociorum et cappellanorum, dominis et magistris:[18]

[1] Bernardo de Nexonio vicario
[2] Johanni de Suessione officiali   } Noviomensibus
[3] Petro de Castro Villani baillivo
3^v [4] Roberto de Lauduno promotori
[5] Stephano de Rua sigillifero   } Noviomensibus
[6] Geraldo la Franchilha receptori
[7] Hugoni de Arsiaco

(1950) 190-193, the following signs are used: [[   ]] = illegible; [[et ab]] = illegible, reading presumed; [-----] = suppressed by lining out; [---Alano] = suppressed but legible, reading given;
\domini Helie∕ = inserted from above the line; \\de hospitio domini regis∕∕ = inserted from the
margin. The author's own textual citations are enclosed in parentheses unless they are grammati-
cally incorporated into his sermons. For citations of canon law, see A. Friedberg, *Corpus juris canonici*, 2 vols., 2nd ed. (Leipzig, 1879-1881; rpt. Graz, 1955): D[istinctio] or C[ausa], q[uaestio], c[anon]
in the *Decretum*; X (*Decretales*) followed by numbers for *liber, titulus*, and *capitulum*. Spelling follows
the manuscript, except that *ti*, not *ci*, is given where standard orthography demands it, and *j, v* are
distinguished from *i, u*. The punctuation is the editor's.

16   See [A 35]; on 23 May 1341, part of Etienne Aubert's Services for the see of Clermont were
paid to the papal Camera "per manus Gauterii Alberti nepotis sui et servientis armorum domini
regis Francie": *VQ* 4.90; *cave* Guillemain, pp. 161-162, nn. 345 and 359, where Gautier is given as
the bishop's brother; cf. Baluze-Mollat 2.434-438.

17   The Clunaic priory of St-Christophe-en-Halatte, diocese of Beauvais (Cottineau 2 (Mâcon,
1937) 2633), a royal retreat where Philip VI had met Edward III in 1331; see Jules Viard, "Itiné-
raire de Philippe VI de Valois," *Bibliothèque de l'Ecole des Chartes* 74 (1913) 528.

18   Many members of the household had long futures in the church or the papal court, which
the editor has tried to trace; where the identifications are most hazardous, they are qualified.

[1] Clerk of the papal Camera 1348-1361: Guillemain, p. 286, *VQ* 7.357.
[3] Papal sergeant in 1372, 1377: Guillemain, p. 428 n.
[5] Priest of Clermont, he paid part of Etienne Aubert's Services for that see to the Camera:
VQ 4.95.
[6] Rector of Laurac, diocese of Mirepoix, and attached to the papal treasury in 1354: *VQ* 7.21,
60.
[7] Dean of Beauvais, 1339: Baluze-Mollat 2.248.

[8] Reginaldo de Molinis
[9] Geraldo de Chan
[10] Johanni de Molinis
[11] Guillelmo de Albusacco
[12] Guidoni la Chame
[13] Guillelmo Ademarii
[14] Audoyno Alberti
[15] Seguino Helie
[16] Arnaldo de Lyeuron
[17] Arnaldo Alberti
[18] Petro de Monturuco
[19] priori Carcassone
[20] Petro Andree
[21] Fulconi de Chanaco
4^r [22] Petro de Braco officiali Parisiensi
[23] Johanni de Segurano socio
[24] Nicolao cappelano ⎫
[25] Johanni Munerii   ⎬ cappellanis
[26] Petro ʹde Montoulon ⎭
[27] Hugoni clerico
[28] Guidoni Piccarini

[8] Cf. [A 10]; Reginald died elect of Nevers in 1360; the executor of his testament was Audoin Aubert's [A 14] camerarius: *VQ* 7.302.

[9] Secular abbot of St. Gènes in the diocese of Béziers and canon of Clermont in 1354: *VQ* 7.70.

[10] Found below [E 22] as de Molendino. Under royal patronage in 1336: J.-M. Vidal, *Benoît XII ... lettres communes...*, 3 vols. (Paris, 1903-1911), nos. 2597-4271 ; master general of the Dominicans in 1348: R. P. Mortier, *Histoire des maîtres généraux de l'ordre des frères prêcheurs* 3 (Paris, 1907), pp. 275-277; then cardinal, 1350-1353.

[11] Papal treasurer, 1342: Guillemain, p. 281; bishop of Fréjus 1343-1346.

[13] *Custos cerae* of the papal palace, died 1353: *VQ* 7.14, 30.

[14] Nephew of Etienne Aubert, died cardinal bishop of Ostia in 1363.

[15] Of the family d'Elie de Pompadour, related to Etienne Aubert's uncle and namesake; see Baluze-Mollat 2.434 f.

[16] Related to Etienne Aubert's sister-in-law Marguerite de Livron: *ibid.*, p. 434.

[17] Etienne Aubert's nephew, elect of Agde, then bishop of Carcassonne in 1354, archbishop of Auch in 1357, papal Camerarius in 1361, died 1371.

[18] Etienne Aubert's nephew, died cardinal in 1385.

[19] An unnamed nephew of Etienne Aubert [B 1], possibly the one who died in 1348, prior of the Augustinian convent of Bénevent, Limoges (Cottineau 1.344): *VQ* 5.415.

[20] Canon of Paris; later bishop of Noyon, Clermont, Cambrai; died 1368.

[21] Doctor of both laws, died bishop of Paris, 1349.

[22] Auditor sacri palatii under Innocent VI and papal chaplain, author of a poem, *Repudium ambitionis*, against cardinals' followers, found in Vat. lat. 3989, *inter alia*.

[23] Cf. [B 3].

[29] Vitali de Prinhaco cantori Parisiensi
[30] Petro de Croso doctori in theologia
[31] Ranulpho Helie canonico Lemovicensi
[32] Johanni Lame procuratori in parlamento
[33] Johanni de Cameraco capellano
[34] Symoni clerico

4^v   Item scutiferis infrascriptis

[35] Galtero Alberti de Monte
[36] Goulferio
[37] Rigaldo Guicardi
[38] Petro de Jauseux
[39] Stephano de Monturuco
[40] barberio
[41] Loyseto coquo
[42] [---Alano] marescallo
[43] Stephano de Solonno
[44] Petro Stephani
[45] Aymerico Bertini
[46] [---Ademaro Helie] ⎫ militis
[47] [---Gaufredo Helie] ⎭
[48] [---ipsius] Gaufrido \domini Helie∕ filio
[49] Guidoni Vigerii
[50] Helie de Chanaco
[51] [---Guidoni Serragrici]
[52] Othenoco de Brevo
[53] Bernardo Francisci

[30] Cousin of Clement VI, died as cardinal in 1361.
[31] D'Elie de Pompadour; cf. [A 15, 46, 47], and see [D 22].
[33] and [34] were added after the completion of the original list.
[35] Etienne Aubert's nephew, lord of Monts, cleric after the death of his wife; in 1341 canon and chancellor of Metz, counsellor in Parlement: Baluze-Mollat 2.434 f.
[37] Papal castellan of Pont-Sorge near Avignon, died in 1361: *VQ* 7.371 f.
[39] Etienne Aubert's nephew, brother of Cardinal Pierre de Monteruc [A 18]: Baluze-Mollat 2.450.
[42] As knight-marshal of the bishop's house, he wore his own arms; cf. [A 128].
[44] Possibly the Pierre Etienne Jordan who died in 1349 as prior of Orville in the diocese of Toulouse: E. Déprez *et al.*, Clement VI, *Lettres closes, patentes et curiales se rapportant à la France*, 3 vols. (Paris, 1910-1961), no. 4270.
[46] and [47] D'Elie de Pompadour; cf. [A 15, 31].
[50] Married Galiène de Ventadour in 1338: Baluze-Mollat 2.609.
[53] He paid part of Etienne Aubert's Services for Noyon in 1338, and was identified as "mercator Claromontis": *VQ* 4.71.

[54] Bernardo Baralhi
5ʳ [55] Guidoni Alberti
[56] [---Galtero Malibernardi]
[57] Ymberto de Beychaco
[58] Gaucelmo Symonis
[59] Johanni Gorsa
[60] Stephano de Vassinhaco
[61] Asturgono nepoti domini Rothomagensis
[62] Petro de Sancto Martiale
[63] Guidoni de Vassinhaco
[64] Petro de Rouffinhaco
[65] Ademaro la Ribiera
[66] Guidoni de Fayu
[67] Petro Sibois scutifero cancellarii
[68] [---Reginaldo de Turre] miles
      [---Gaucelmo Symonis] [58]
[69] [---Roberto de Bontemvillier] de hospitio domini regis miles
[70] [---Helie de Sancto Juliano] quia miles
[71] Mahieto Ravenel \de hospitio domini regis//
[72] Petro Rogerii nepoti domini Rothomagensis
[73] vigerio
[74] Audoyno filio Stephani de Raffinhaco
[75] generi baylivi Noviomensis
5ᵛ [76] Guillelmo Rogerii nepoti domini Rothomagensis
[77] Geraldo de Mathias

[54] Added after the original list had been completed.
[55] Grand-nephew of Etienne Aubert, son of Gautier Aubert des Monts [A 35]; added after the
     list had been completed.
[58] Cf. [B 1, 5] and [C].
[59] Grand-nephew of Etienne Aubert, nephew of cardinal Pierre de Monteruc.
[60] Prior of St-Saturnin-du-Port, Cluniac, in the diocese of Uzés, in 1359: *VQ* 7.265.
[61] Nephew of Pierre Roger, archbishop of Rouen, the future Clement VI.
[62] Died as archbishop of Toulouse in 1397.
[63] Died as abbot of St. André, Villeneuve-lès-Avignon, in 1380: ASV *Collectoriae* 359, 53ʳ-54ʳ.
[64] Relative of Bertrand de Ruffignac, husband of Etienne Aubert's niece Valérie: Baluze-
     Mollat 2.434.
[65] Lord of St. Bonnet and husband of Etienne Aubert's niece Agnes: *ibid.*
[72] The future Pope Gregory XI, at this time less than eight years old, unless Pierre Roger had
     two fraternal nephews with the same name.
[74] Cf. [A 64].
[75] Cf. [A 3].
[76] The heir of Pierre Roger's brother the count of Beaufort.

[78] Geraldino nepoti domini Hugonis de Arsiaco
[79] +Johanni Anglici de Noviome
[80] +majori Karolipontis
[81] +preposito d'Erchiensi
[82] +preposito Noviomensi
[83] +preposito Pontis Episcopi
[84] +firmario de Villa
[85] +Johanni de Nappes [---ad requisit] pro domino de Vincenis
[86] +pueri de Monte
[87] Matheo Gayte
[88] [---Petro de Sancto Georgio] miles
[89] Arnaldo de Saleres scutiferi domini Albani
[90] nepoti domini Albiensis \\videlicet Raymundo Curti//
[91] item cuidam alio qui consuevit habere de raubis officiarioris
[92] Hugoni Oliverii
[93] nepoti domini Penestrinensis
[94] et socio suo
[95] nepoti domini Eduensis cardinalis
[96] item in domo domini Petragoricensis VIII
[97] item Gaufrido nepoti officialis Noviomensis
[98] [---Raymundo Caveti]
[99] item preposito de Lachinhi

6[r]   Item clericis infra nominatis

[100] Bernino cubiculario
[101] Guillelmo de Cappella
[102] [---Bertrando pedagiario Pontis Episcopi]
[103] Hugueto Raffi de Cappella
[104] clerico receptoris

---

[78] Cf. [A 7].
[85] The patron was Pierre Aubert, Etienne's brother, prior of Vincennes; see [B 2].
[86] Son of Gautier Aubert des Monts [A 35].
[89] The cardinal bishop of Albano was Gaucelme de Jean (died 1348), nephew and vice-chancellor to John XXII.
[90] Guillaume Court "of Albi", cardinal bishop of Tusculo, was the nephew of Benedict XII; he died in 1361.
[93] The cardinal bishop of Palestrina was Pierre Desprez (died 1361).
[94] Pierre Bertrand "of Autun", cardinal of San Clemente, died in 1361.
[96] Elie Talleyrand, the cardinal "of Périgord" (1331-1364).
[97] Cf. [A 2].
[104] Cf. [A 6].

7^r   Item officiariis infra nominatis

[105] messagerio domini cardinalis Petragoricensis
[106] [---messagerio domini Albiensis]
[107] Martino   ⎫
                     ⎬ palefrenariis
[108] [---Pascaleto] ⎭
[109] Johanni porterio
[110] Bidoni messagerio
[111] Perreto buticulario
[112] Perrino de Nemore
[113] [---Johanni Gougane]
[114] item Andree cisori raubarum de Tholosa dedit unam raubam de
      librata officiariorum
[115] item Bochardo qui moratur apud Karolipontem
[116] item Nichasio venatori
[117] item Richardo le Velu

8^r   Famulis infrascriptis

[118] dicto Gobillot
[119] dicto le Paage
[120] dicto le Bidaut
[121] famulo magistri Johannis de Segurano
[122] famulo domini Nicolai
[123] famulo domini Petri
[124] [---famulo Galteri]
[125] famulo Goulferii
[126] famulo Rigaldi
[127] famulo Petri de Jauseux
[128] famulo marescalli
[129] famulo de coquina
[130] dicto le Sarrasin
      [---Bouchardo apud Karolipontem] [115]

[105] Cf. [A 96].
[106] Cf. [A 90].
[114] "By appointment couturier to my lord of Noyon"?
[121] Servant of one of the bishop's *socii* [A 23].
[122] Servant of the chaplain Nicolas [A 24].
[123] Servant of the chaplain Pierre de Montoulon [A 26].
[124] Servant of the squire Gautier Aubert [A 35].
[125] Servant of the squire Goufier [A 36].
[126] Servant of the squire Rigaud Guicard [A 37].
[127] Servant of the squire Pierre de Jauseux [A 38].
[128] Servant of the marshal Alain [A 42].
[129] Cf. [A 41].

[B]

10[r] [1] Memor sit quod restam quam debebamus Gaucelmo et Guillelmo Symonis[15] solvimus dicto Guillelmo, sic quod remansimus de omnibus que unquam eis debueramus, vel ipsi nobis, quieti et liberati, exceptis quod dicebat dictus Guillelmus, quod dictus Guillelmus tradiderat pro nobis in partibus nostris de novo priori Carcassonensi nepoti nostro[16] XXX libras Turonenses que adhuc restant si fuerunt tradite. Actum apud Sanctum Marcellum[17] V die Julii, anno domini M°CCC°XL°.

[2] Item eadem die solvimus magistro Johanni de Molinis dicto Beatus[18] II[c]L florenos ad scutum, de quibus habebat litteras nostras et fratris nostri prioris tunc de Vincenis, nunc abbatis Grandimontis,[19] quas litteras nobis reddidit, et remansimus quieti et liberati; nec aliquid debemus eidem magistro Johanni.

[3] Item post, videlicet ante festum sancti Jacobi[20] per IIII vel V dies, tradidi[---mus] fecimus per magistrum Johannem de Seguirino[21] Guillelmo Symonis IIII[c]IIII[xx]II Parisienses, quas aportaverat receptor noster.[22]

[4] Item in die dicti festi, III[c] libras Parisienses quas eidem Guillelmo tradidit sigillifer noster Noviomensis.[23]

[5] Quando tamen ultimo de Parisiis recessimus, videlicet mense Octobris anno M°CCC°XL primo, computavimus cum Guillelmo Symonis, et omnibus receptis et traditis computatis, debuimus eidem et fratri suo II[c] libras Parisienses tantum, de quibus habuit a nobis litteram nostro sigillo sigillatam.

18[r]   [C] Vasa argentea

Item anno XXXVIII° predicto, die penultima mensis Maii, prefatus dominus fecerat ponderari vassellam suam argenteam infrascriptam per Gaucelmum Symonis[24] apud Sanctum Victorem juxta Parisius.

15   See [A 58].
16   For the prior of Carcassonne, see [A 19].
17   The modern successor of this collegiate church stands on the Boulevard de l'Hôpital in the 13th *arrondissement* of Paris.
18   See [A 10].
19   Pierre Aubert, prior of Ste. Marie de Bois de Vincennes, diocese of Paris; then abbot of Grandmont, 1337-1347: *Gallia Christiana* 2.655D-E.
20   25 July 1340.
21   See [A 33].
22   Gerard la Franchilha [A 6].
23   Etienne de la Rue [A 5].
24   See [A 58] and [B].

[1] Et fuit ponderata una duodena scutellarum factarum Parisius XXII marcharum et duarum onciarum.

[2] Item due alie duodene scutellarum factarum etiam Parisius ponderis XXXI marcharum et VII^{tem} onciarum.

[3] Item una alia duod'ena scutellarum factarum Tholose ponderis XV marcharum, VII^{tem} onciarum cum dimidio.

[4] Item una alia duodena scutellarum factarum Tholose ponderis XXI marcharum et VI onciarum.[25]

[5] Item sex platelli de opere Tholose ponderis XVII marcharum et parum minus.

[6] Item duo majores platelli de opere Tholose ponderis VII^{tem} marcharum, IIII^{or} onciarum cum dimidio.

[7] Item sex alii platelli de opere Parisis ponderis XVI marcharum, V onciarum.

[8] Item duo platelli de opere Parisis ponderis VII^{tem} marcharum IIII^{or} onciarum cum dimidio.

[9] Item duo platelli ad lavandum ad arma episcopatus Noviomensis ponderis XI marcharum, VI onciarum.

[10] Item alii duo majores ad eadem arma ponderis XI marcharum, VII^{tem} onciarum cum dimidio.

[11] Item alii duo minores ad eadem arma pro capella ponderis VIII marcharum I oncie et XV sterlingorum.

[12] Item duo candelabra argentea pro cappella ponderis VI marcharum et VI onciarum.

[13] Item potus seu vas pro aqua benedicta ponderis VI marcharum V onciarum cum dimidio.

[14] Item potus pro elemosina ponderis VI marcharum V onciarum et dimidia.

[15] Item due quarte magne de opere Parisis ponderis decem marcharum, trium onciarum.

[16] Item bacinus ad barberium ponderis VI marcharum, XV sterlingorum.

[17] Item due pinte de opere Tholose ponderis X marcharum II onciarum.

[18] Item sex chopine seu aquarie de opere Parisis ponderis XII marcharum I oncie cum dimidio.

[19] Item due alie aquarie impares de opere Tholose ponderis IIII^{or} marcharum IIII^{or} onciarum cum dimidio.

---

25 Marginal signs indicate that the order of [3] and [4] should be reversed.

[20] Item duodecim ciphi plani de opere Parisis ponderis XI^{cim} marcharum VI onciarum et XV sterlingorum.

[21] Item sex ciphi minores de opere Parisis ponderis trium marcharum VI onciarum V sterlingorum.

[22] Item duodecim alii plani de opere Tholose ponderis XI marcharum.

[23] Item IIII^{or} magni ciphi operati de opere Tholose ponderis V marcharum VI onciarum.

19^v [24] Item duo alii minores operati de opere Montispessulani ponderis duarum marcharum et dimidia oncie.

[25] Item duo alii ciphi esmaillati ad arma Francie in fundo de opere Parisis ponderis II marcharum III onciarum XV sterlingorum.

[26] Item quinque pedes argenti ad ciphos murreos de opere Parisis ponderis IIII^{or} marcharum, quinque onciarum.

[27] Item unus ciphus deauratus et esmaillatus cum pede et copersculo ponderis quinque marcharum II onciarum cum dimidio.

[28] Item unus alius ciphus deauratus cum pede et coopersculo ponderis III marcharum, quinque onciarum cum dimidio.

[29] Item unus parvus ciphus deauratus cum pede sine coopersculo ponderis VII^{tem} onciarum cum dimidio.

[30] Item unus gobeletus cum coopersculo sine pede deauratus ponderis II marcharum V onciarum cum dimidio.

[31] Item dragerium esmaillatum et deauratum in bordis ponderis IIII^{or} marcharum II onciarum XV sterlingorum.

[32] Item unus calix cum patena et par cocleari de opere Parisis ponderis II marcharum quinque onciarum.

[33] Item unus alius calix de opere Tholose ponderis II marcharum III onciarum.

20^r [34] Item una naveta pro incenso ponderis I marcharum [sic] VI^{tem} [sic] onciarum.

[35] Item due parve pinteole pro cappella ponderis I marche XV sterlingorum.

[36] Item baculus pastoralis ponderis I marche II onciarum cum dimidio.

[37] Item una aquaria in qua includuntur sex gobeleti de opere Tholose, ponderis cum dictis sex gobeletis IIII marcharum VII onciarum cum dimidio.

[38] Item unum aliud dragerium de opere Tholose ponderis II marcharum VI onciarum XV sterlingorum.

[39] Item incensarium cum cathena ponderis V marcharum.

[40] Item una duodena coclearium ponderis I marche V sterlingorum.

Summa omnium usque hic III^cLXXVIII marche IIII oncie cum dimidio, de quibus serviunt in cappella LXVII marche VI oncie XV sterlingi.[26] De premissis fuerunt dati Avinione unus ciphus et una aquaria qui ponderabant V marche vel circa ... nepti domini Penestrinensis[27] fuerunt dati [sic].

24^r

[D] Libri legales theologie et juris
Die Ascensionis domini anno XXXIX[28]

[1] Digestum vetus [2] Digestum novum [3] Codex [4] Infortiatum [5] parvum Volumen [6] Decretales [7] Decretum [8] Sextus liber decretalium cum apparatu Archidiaconi [9] Clementine cum apparatu Johannis Andree [10] Speculum judiciale [11] Innocentius [12] Sinus [13] Summa Ostiensis [14] Summa Azonis [15] Summa Gaufridi [16] Evangelia glosata in duobus voluminibus [17] liber Sententiarum [18] liber de vitiis et virtutibus in quatuor voluminibus [19] Jacobus de Bello visu super libro feudorum [20] Cronice domini Bernardi Guidonis [21] quedam Biblia in parvo volumine [22] et quedam major Biblia que est domini Ranulphi Helie[29] [23] Flores sanctorum [24] Summa confessorum [25] Sermones dominicales et festorum de Lausania in parvo volumine.

25^r

[E] Cappella

Item anno domini M°CCC°XXIX° [sic] die XXVIII^a Aprilis in loco de Karoliponte fuit factum inventarium de rebus infrascriptis existentibus in dicto loco, et primo de illis que in cappella serviebant et serviunt, sine argento, quia utensilia argentea in isto quaterno sunt prescripta. [1] Et primo, cappella alba habens pecias que sequuntur, videlicet, pro corpore dicti domini rochetum, amictum, albam, cingulum, stolam, manipulum, tunicam, damaticam, duas infulas albas, unum colarium,

---

26   The items as given total really 317 marks, 4 ounces, 5 pennyweight sterling (1 mark = 8 ounces = 160 sterling). The list may be in error, or added wrong. Of its items, [11, 12, 35] are "pro cappella", and [13, 14, 32, 33, 34, 36, 39] may well have been used there; but their weight together is only 52 marks, 4 ounces.

27   See [A 93].

28   6 May 1339. The legal books in the present list correspond closely to the fourteen titles which Audoin Aubert, the pope's nephew, executor, and successor as cardinal bishop of Ostia and curator of the Collège de St.-Martial at Toulouse, received for the college as goods which Etienne Aubert had owned "antequam fuisset ad apicem summi apostolatus assumptus": Marcel Fournier, "Les bibliothèques des collèges de l'université de Toulouse," *Bibliothèque de l'Ecole des Chartes* 51 (1890) 453-455.

29   See [A 31].

unam cappam, cendalia pro pedibus, cooperturam cathedre; item, pro
diacono de eadem cappella, amictum, albam, stolam, manipulum,
damaticam et colarium; item pro subdiacono de eadem cappella, amictum, albam, manipulum, tunicam et colarium; item unam capam pro
cappellano administrante circa dominum; item de eadem cappella duos
parvos albos ad parandum altare; item tres mitre sive magna [?] una
videlicet operata et due albe. [2] item cappella rubea habet tantas et
similes pecias per omnia sicut alba, excepto quod nullum cingulum
habet pro domino nec pro aliis, et quod non habet etiam nisi unam in-
25ᵛ fulam. /[3] Item cappella ynda habet tantas et similes pecias sicut alba,
excepto quod nullas habet stolas, manipulos, neque cingula, et quod
non habet etiam nisi unam infulam. [4] Item cappella de defunctis est
omnino integro sicut alba exceptis cendalliis que non sunt necessaria, et
excepto quod nullum habet cingulum nec habet nisi unam infulam. [5]
Item cappella cotidiana pro cappellanis habet amictum, albam,
cingulum de filo, stolam, manipulum et infulam. [6] Item tres pannos ad
lilia parantes cotidie altare, et unum parvum de eadem forma pro
leterno. [7] Item sunt due mappe parate, videlicet una pro diebus
solempnibus et alia pro cotidiano. [8] Item sunt tres alie mappe non
parate. [9] Item sunt duo superpelicia, et due almicie pro domino, una
videlicet de griso et alia de calabria fourrate de minutis variis. [10] Item
pro domino duo manutergia linea, et unum paratorium pro ipso
26ʳ sedente in cathedra, et una mappa paratoria quando celebrat. /[11]
Item sunt tres almicie pro cappellanis et quinque superpelicia, [12] item
duo manutergia pro cappellanis et unum coissinum pro Missali. [13]
Item duo panni deaurati pro parando et unum celum pro altari. [14]
Item due cathedre, una ferrea et una de ligno. [15] Item duo marchipedes, unus ante altare continens diversa arma et alius in oratorio
cum duabus coissinis yndis. [16] Item quatuor coffri ferrati in quibus
premissa indumenta reponuntur.

Libri cappelle

[17] Primo unum parvum Missale ad usum Romanum. [18] Item
unum Breviarium ad eundem usum. [19] Item ad usum Noviomensem
unum Missale in duobus voluminibus. [20] Item ad eundem usum unum
Breviarium in duobus voluminibus et [21] unum Graduale similiter in
duobus voluminibus. [22] Item duo Pontificalia, unum majus et aliud
minus. [23] Item volumen Breviarii pro tempore yemis, nam aliud
volumen pro tempore estatis fuit ammissum per dominum Johannem
Molendinarii.[30] Anno XXXIX et die predictis.

30 See [A 10].

27^r

Camera domini

In camera domini reperta fuerunt apud Karolipontem die XXVIII dicti mensis Aprilis, que sequuntur: [24] Primo in camera paramenti una culcitra plumea cum coissino, una culcitra puncta alba, quatuor pecie [---ynde] sargie adurate. [25] Item tres marchipedes circumcirca, lectum et chevetellum bordatum de armis domini et episcopatus Noviomensis. [26] Item quatuor banquerii de dicto colore adurato cum dictis armis. [27] Item unus pulcher pannus ad ymagines operatus. [28] Item sex carrelli circa lectum de velvello viridi. [29] Item tres magni cappelli pro domino. [30] Item unus bancus et tres fourmule quarum due sunt de cappella. [31] Item in gardarauba una culcitra plumea cum coissino in lecto quo jacet dominus, una culcitra puncta. [32] Item coopertorium viride fourratum de grossis variis. [33] Item una sargia ynda pro chencello. [34] Item due marchipedes viridi barrati quilibet de duabus barris rubeis. [35] Item duo coffri ferrati pro sommerio camere. [36] Item due candelarie longe pro cereis. [37] Item una magna culcitra puncta cooperta de cendallo viridi. [38] Item unum coopertorium de

27^v

perso adurato fourratum de griso. /[39] Item quatuor banquerii virides barrati de rubeo qui erant positi in aula. [40] Item una duodena carrellorum ad arma domini et episcopatus Noviomensis huc et illuc per domum.

29^r

Aula Karolipontis anno XXXIX et die predictis

[41] In aula est unus magnus bancus pro mensa domini. [42] Item unus alius minor. [43] Item quatuor fourmule. [44] Item quatuor mense cum trescellis. [45] Item una mensa sine trescellis pro officiariis. [46] Item drecoerium. [47] Item in camera inferiori ubi pauperes comedunt est una mensa cum trescellis, et una parva fourmula. [48] Item sunt tres arche magne, una videlicet in fourreria, alia in camera superiori turris, et alia in camera cappellanorum. [49] Item sunt tres coffri, unus in dicta foulreria, alius in parva camera subtus cappella, et alius in camera supra portam. [50] Item duo siculi ferrati quibus ministratur vinum in buticularia.

30^r

Coquina Karolipontis anno XXXIX° et die predictis

[51] in qua sunt septem poti cuprei, duo videlicet magni, duo mediocres, et tres minores. [52] Item tres magne pelves et una minor quelibet ad duos ansos ferreos. [53] Item una magna calderia ad quatuor anulos ferreos. [54] Item tres magni tripodes. [55] Item unus magnus caviculus dupplex. [56] Item tria magna verna ferrea. [57] Item due craticule ferree. [58] Item una patella ferrea. [59] Item sunt sex

caviculi ferrei, duo videlicet in aula, duo in camera domini, et duo in magna camera inferiori. [60] Item sunt tres bacini et tres calferie ad lavandum.

31r Lecti et lingium existenti in Karoliponte anno et die predictis

[61] Primo sunt XXVII culcitre plumee, et XXVII coissini computatis illis qui sunt in lectis domini. [62] Item sunt XXXVI paria lintheaminum. [63] Item XV^cim cooperture foulrate de griso. [64] Item due simplices sine foulraturis. [65] Item decem [---coopertorie] cooperture pro famulis et una culcitra puncta parva. [66] Item XXXII pecie mapparum, et XV pecie manutergiorum. [67] Item fuerunt empti apud Novionium circa festum nativitatis beati Johannis Baptiste anni XXXIX predicti[31] XII^cim culcitre plumee et XII^cim coissini, VI culcitre puncte, et VI nigre floceie et XII^cim paria lintheaminum que omnia sunt delata apud Karolipontem exceptis una culcitra plumea cum coissino et duobus lintheaminibus et una culcitra puncta.

33r [F] Infrascripta sunt apud Novionium anno et die predictis

[1] Videlicet septem culcitre plumee et XII^cim coissini. [2] Item sexdecim paria lintheaminum tam magna quam parva. [3] Item quatuor coopertoria foulrata. [4] Item duo coopertoria nigra sine foulraturis et una culcitra puncta. [5] Item IIII^or magna auricularia et tria parva. [6] Item XII^cim capitegia. [7] Item sex mappe, sex doublerie et tria manutergia. [8] Item XII^cim magni poti stannei, duo poti ad lot, sex poti ad demilot, due pinte, sex aquarie et quatuor salverie stamine. [9] Item duo bacini et due calserie ad lavandum. [10] Item sex caniculi ferrei et duo cenailli. [11] Item due anderie. [12] Item tres poti cuprei. [13] Item una pelia ferrea. [14] Item XXXV scutelle, duo magni platelli, octo platelli mediocres et quatuor parvi platelli stannei. [15] Item una culcitra plumea cum coissino, duobus lintheaminibus et una culcitra puncta, empta apud Novionium circa festum nativitatis beati Johannis baptiste anno XXXIX predicto.

35r [G] Infrascripta apud Erchieu

Videlicet unus magnus bancus, due mense cum trescellis et quatuor fourmule in aula.

31 24 June 1339.

37ʳ   Item in domo de Sempeigny

39ʳ   Item in domo de Malo Consilio

41ʳ   [H]

Laudabile discretumque est majoribus honorem et reverentiam exhibere (ii q.vii *Sicut inquit*).[32] Et sunt verba beati Gregorii suffraguaneos cujusdam episcopi alloquentis, et quomodo ipsum tractare debeant instruentis. Videmus secundum ordinem nature, quod omnia etiam irationabilia ordinantur ad unum capud unde apes unum habent principem, grues unam sequuntur ordine literato, et si sic obtineat in ratione carentibus, multo fortius obtinere debet in personis rationabilibus, et maxime ecclesiasticis; et ideo singularium ecclesiarum cathedralium singuli sunt episcopi, qui omnes ad unam metropolitanam ecclesiam et ad unum provincie judicem ordinantur secundum quod hec optime describuntur vii q.l *In apibus*.[33] Et ideo Gregorius recte in verbis premissis inducit subfraganeos ad impendendum honorem et reverentiam ecclesie metrapolitane, dicens *laudabile discretumque est, etc.* In quibus quidem verbis tria nobis per ordinem ostenduntur: primo ad exibendam per nos reverentiam prefertur [----] exitatio commendabilis cum dicit *laudabile discretumque est*; secundo ad ipsam exibendam infertur ratio inconvincibilis, quia *majoribus*; tertio ad ipsam exibendam subinfertur exequtio propta et humilis cum dicit *honorem et reverentiam exibere*. Pro primo, quod est exitatio comendabilis facit quod ait papa Johannes, *Humani enim more est, illum vereri cujus judicio et voluntate nunc quis erigitur nunc vere deprimitur* (xvi q.ii *Visis*).[34] Certum est autem quod ecclesia metropolitana et erigere et deprimere potest subfraganeos cum in multis ei subsint (x q.iii *Quis cognovimus*; Ex. de offi. ord., cum ibi *Nec*).[35] Et est etiam istud comendabile, quia sic est de more antiquo quod non est alicujus civis vel peregrini libidine violandum (vii d. *Que contra mores*).[36] Pro secundo, quod est ratio inconvincibilis, quia de justitia et ratione naturali est ut serviat minor majori (xxxiii q.v *Est ordo*),[37] unde et alibi dicitur quod ordo ecclesiasticus confunditur si sua jura cuilibet non serventur (xi q.i *Pervenit*).[38] Pro tertio, quod est exequtio propta et

32   C.2, q.7, c.46.
33   C.7, q.1, c.41.
34   C.16, q.2, c.1.
35   C.10, q.3, c.6; X 1, 11, 31.
36   D.8, c.2.
37   C.33, q.5, c.12.
38   C.11, q.1, c.39.

humilis, quia obedientia seu reverentie exibitio, debet esse prompta, unde in psalmo dicitur, *in auditu auris obedevit mihi*,[39] et beatus Petrus dixit *Nolite expectare ut ipse vobis dicat* (xciii di.c),[40] unde dicit beatus Bernardus, *Verus et obediens nescit moras, mandata non procrastinat sed parat aures auditui, oculos visui, pedes gressui, manus operi et totum se interius recollegit ut exterius mandatum adimpleat imperantis.*[41] Debet etiam esse humilis et sine

41[v] vocis contradictione, unde/ Ozee iiii,[42] *Populus omnis sicut hii qui contradicunt sacerdotibus et corues hodie.* Et potissime in episcopo debet esse humilitas quia secundum beatum Gregorium, *Nichil in episcopali cornice fulget spiritu didius quam humilitas* (c d. *Contra morem*).[43] Et Ecclesiastici iii,[44] *Dum quanto major est, humilia te in omnibus et invenies gratiam coram Deo.*

Quia quidem comendabile et rationabile et consuetum est, et quia est etiam ad hoc naturalis et inconvincibilis ratio me compellit [*sic*], veni ad reverentiam huic venerabili ecclesie debitam exibendam, et ad recomendandum me et sponsam meam Noviomensem ecclesiam vobis, et ad offerendum me et mea vobis et vestrum singulis, pro quibus sine dubio [---facerem] juxta posse facerem que velletis, et supplico ex spirituali dono ut me in vestris orationibus recomendatum habere velitis, ut eis coadjurantibus me et gregem mihi comissum taliter regere valeam ut recipere merear mercedem boni pastoris, de qua I Petri v c.,[45] *Cum approverit princeps pastorum percipient immarcessabilem glorie coronam*, et gloriam sempiternam quam vobis et nobis prestare dignetur qui est benedictus in secula seculorum amen.

64[r]   [I] Collatio facienda in capitulo Noviomensi

Letare filia Syon quia ecce venio et habitabo in medio tui, et scies quia dominus exercituum misit me ad te (Zacharie secundo capitulo).[46] \Carissimi, quamquam secundum doctores sanctos Jeronimum et alios／ verba ista prefata ystorialiter sunt dicta de Deo plebem Judaycam de captivitate ad statum pristine libertatis in Jerusalem reducente, quamquam etiam allegorice seu spiritualiter loquendo, sunt de Christo Dei filio benedicto ad nos secundum incarnationis misterium veniente et in medio nostri et

---

39 Ps. 17:45.
40 D.93, c.1.
41 Bernard of Clairvaux, Sermo 41 *De virtute obedientiae* (PL 183.657B), not *verbatim*.
42 Os. 4:4-5.
43 D.100, c.8.
44 Eccli. 3:20.
45 1 Pe. 5:4.
46 Zach. 2:10-11.

hominum corporaliter et presentaliter habitante, moraliter tamen et satis proprie, verba predicta possunt et debent accipi in persona boni episcopi et prelati ad suam ecclesiam et diocesim, et presertim ad congregationem venerabilis capituli ecclesie sue venientis, ipsamque congregationem venerabilis capituli in adventu novo sui episcopi congaudentis. In cujus figura etiam Jerusalem fuit mirabiliter jocundatum in adventu Christi cui multum honorifice [---exadierunt] obviam precesserunt, ut patet Mathei xxi,[47] ita ut possim \merito/ dicere isti ecclesie et congregationi hujus venerabilis capituli [---hic presentis] verba predicta, *letare filia Syon etc.*

Circa quod est sciendum quod homines letari consueverunt generibus circa tria seu de tribus, secundum quod est triplex bonum, bonum scilicet utile, bonum delectabile, bonum honestum. Circa bonum utile letantur homines, propter quod filii Israel per illam sanctam mulierem Judit utiliter liberati dixerunt ei Judith xv,[48] *Tu gloria Jerusalem, tu letitia Israel, tu honorificentia populi nostri, ideo eris benedicta in eternum.* Circa bonum delectabile homines letantur ut in Salmo,[49] *Adimplebis me letitia cum vultu tuo et delectationes in dextera tua usque in finem.* Letantur etiam

64[v] homines circa bonum/ honestum et virtuosum, ut in Salmo,[50] *Domine in virtute tua letabitur rex etc.* Et quia quilibet episcopus et prelatus debet suis subditis procurare bonum utile providendo in spiritualibus et anime salutaribus, bonum delectabile quoad temporalia subveniendo indigentibus, bonum honestum et virtuosum in bonis exemplis et operibus, in figura cujus triplicis boni dixit dominus beato Petro pastori ecclesie et rectori, cujus vices gerunt episcopi et prelati, *Pasce oves meas* (Johannis ultimo capitulo).[51] Ideo verus episcopus et prelatus ad exitandum letitiam in adventu suo novo spiritualiter et corporaliter ecclesie sue, que est filia Christi spiritualis et sponsa episcopi, potest in predicto suo adventu novo prorumpere spiritualiter in hec verba, *Gaude et letare filia Syon etc.*

In quibus quidem verbis sic aliqualiter introductis, duo breviter tangi possunt, primo nobilis ecclesie Noviomensis, et per consequens totius dyocesis, et presertim congregationis venerabilis capituli hic presentis in adventu sui prelati, letitia et exaltatio gaudiosa, cum dicitur *letare filia Syon; Syon* (secundum glosa [*sic*] Eronimia, ecclesia)[52] *letare etc.* Secundo

47 Mt. 21:8-11.
48 Jdt. 15:10-11.
49 Ps. 15:11.
50 Ps. 20:2.
51 Jo. 21:17.
52 *Commentarium in Zachariam* 1:2 (PL 25.1434B; CCL 76A.768, line 211).

tangitur hujus gaudii et excitationis causa multiplex et ratio fructuosa, cum subadditur *et inhabitabo in medio tui et scies quia dominus exercituum misit me ad te*; glosa ibi *ad te*, id est ad ecclesiam nobilem Noviani. De predicto sciendum quod Syon interpretatur speculatio seu speculum, et significare potest istam congregationem, et ecclesiam Noviomensem, in qua sunt et esse debent viri ecclesiastici in speculatione vite contemplative, pro tanto sunt divino servitio deputati, et per consequens sunt et esse debent Syon, id est speculum, id est forma exemplaris, et spirituale speculum aliorum totius diocesis in quo speculo spirituali ipsorum secundum honestatem sancte vite et bonorum morum alii valeant se mirari, ita ut in eis veridice dictum salvatoris impleatur, 65ʳ *Vos / estis lux mundi* (Mathei v),[53] et ibidem, *Luceat lux vestra coram hominibus ut videant bona opera vestra et glorificent patrem vestrum qui in celis est.* O *Syon*, glosa, id est O ecclesia Noviomensis, filia spiritualis Christi et sponsa mea licet indignum [*sic*], *gaude et letare*, id est gaudeant et letentur venerabiles fratres mei hic presentes de adventu prelati sui, juxta illud Thobie xiii,[54] *Ego autem et anima mea etc.* Et gaudeant, dico, interius et exterius : interius in corde et exterius in operatione, ut de adventu veraciter compleatur quod dicitur in Salmo,[55] *Sicut letantium omnium nostrum habitatio est in te*, dicendo O episcope Noviomensis hic [---presens et] veniens et presens, omnium nostrum de adventu tuo letantium habitatio est in te, quia quando prelatus in sua ecclesia habitat assidue et moratur, et non hinc inde discurrens et evagans se absentat ad altiora, ulterius, licet non secundum animam, interdum utilius, havelando, tunc omnes de dyocesi habent occasionem et materiam rationabiliter quod sint leti, et hec de primo membro in quo, ut dixi, vocabatur ecclesie et capituli letitia et exaltatio gaudiosa ibi, *Gaude et letare filia Syon.*

Dico secunde quod tangitur in hiis verbis hujus gaudii et exaltationis tam multiplex et ratio fructuosa, ibi, quia *ego venio et habitabo* etc., ubi, circa causam hujus letitie habende de adventu episcopi seu prelati, occurrit primo prelati venientis personalis [---residen] presentia, ibi cum dicit *ecce ego venio*;\ secundo, ipsius presentia, assidua residentia ibi ⁄ , *et habitabo in medio tui etc.*; tertio, ipsius bene docentis et unientis certa experientia, ibi *scies* (scilicet experimento) *quod dominus exercituum misit me ad te etc.* De primo, qui dicit *quia ecce ego venio: ecce* inquam in evidentia, *ego* in persona propria *venio* ad deffendendum jura ecclesie et deneria,

53 Mt. 5:14-16.
54 Tob. 13:9.
55 Ps. 86:7.

semper cum Dei gratia propitia et mihi previa. Et dico *ecce ego venio*; *venio* inquam, et veniam ad ecclesiam istam ad tria: primo ad amandum in spiritu concordie et caritatis, secundo ad non gravandum in effectu injustitie et crudelitatis seu rapacitatis, tertio ad juvandum in/ profectu misericordie et pietatis. *Venio* igitur primo, et semper venire propono, ad vos in spiritu concordie et caritatis, ita ut de adventu meo dignus sim dicere illud verbum Christi (Johannis xiiii),[56] *Veniam et accipiam vos ad me ipsum ut ubi ego sum et vos sitis*, et quia verba sunt Christi et ad propositum meum facientia, pondero verba ista, et ponderanda sunt, et rogo suppliciter et ex corde quod semper vestris cordibus sint impressa. *Veniam* igitur *ad vos* semper favorabiliter, non proterve, *et accipiam vos ad me ipsum* precordialiter et interne, *ut ubi ego sum*, scilicet amicabiliter et paterne, *et vos sitis*. Utique mecum concorditer et fraterne, et sic, propter istum spiritum concordie et caritatis quem in me reperietis, nunc merito sitis leti; nec credere velitis aliquibus discolis et bricosis, qui utinam non sint inter vos, et si sint, secundum optatum Apostoli abscindantur,[57] pro quo Jeremie xv capitulo.[58] Secundo, dixi quod debet venire prelatus ad non gravandum in effectu iniustitie et crudelitatis, et tertio quod debet venire in profectu misericordie et pietatis, et de hiis duobus, causa brevitatis, simul: Secunda ad Corinthos xiii [*sic*],[59] *Ecce ego paratus sum venire ad vos et non ero vobis gravis* (glosa, scilicet accipiendo vestra); *non enim quero vestra* (scilicet divitias in auro et argento, secundum glosam), *sed vos*, id est salvare vos secundum glosam; sequitur, *parentes enim debent filiis suis thesaurisare*; glosa ibi, id est divitias eterne glorie, et cum habent, temporalia impendere. Sequitur de secundo principali secundi membri, ubi notatur prelati venientis assidua residentia, ibi *et habitabo in medio tui*; et dicit verbum *in medio tui* quia non dextera, prosperitatis, divitibus et potentibus parcendo, nec in sinistra, adversitatis, pauperes opprimendo, sed in medio justitie et equitatis quod suum est omnibus reddendo, et de isto medio equitatis dicitur Ecclesiastici x;[60] *In medio fratrum rector illorum in honore et qui timent Deum erunt in oculis ejus*. Unde igitur dicit scriptura *habitabo in medio ejus*. De ista habitatione et residentia prelati in dyocesibus suarum dicitur pulcre Secunda ad Corinthos vi capitulo,[61] *Inhabitabo in illis et inambulabo inter [---illis] eis et ipsi erunt mihi populus. Inhabitabo in illis*, id est corporaliter et

56 Jo. 14:3.
57 Gal. 5:12.
58 Jer. 15:1.
59 2 Cor. 12:14.
60 Eccli. 10:24.
61 2 Cor. 6:16.

66ʳ spiritualiter habitabo, *in/ eis* dicit, non *super eos* subiciendo, nec *contra eos* adversando et resistendo, sed *in eis* equaliter quandiu unde fecerunt convivendo, quod secundum Gregorium in Registro v,[62] *Omnes bene facientes sumus pares.* Sequitur, *et ambulabo inter eos*, scilicet dyoceses visitando et exempla bonorum operum demonstrando sicut Johannes x dicit,[63] *bonus pastor ante eos* (scilicet oves) *vadit*; sed glosa ibi, ipsos per bona opera precedendo, faciens facto quod docet verbo, dicitur ibi, *et oves sequntur ipsum*, scilicet extraniter operantem.

Sequitur tertium membrum, sed et principale: *et scies quia dominus exercituum misit me ad te. Scies*, dicit glosa, ex literis, quod premisi; si enim placet, venit ad ecclesiam suam personaliter et residet ibidem utiliter modis superius expressatis; signum et experientia est infallibiliter quod Deus omnipotens misit eum, ita ut veraciter, querens non que sua sunt, sed que Jesu Christi, possit dicere illud Genesis xlv,[64] *Pro salute enim vestra me misit dominus in vos*, id est in presentia vestra; nec mirum, quia secundum Apostolum ad Ebreos primo,[65] *Omnes prelati sunt administratorii spiritus*, id est sociales et non carnaliter venientes, et *in ministerium missi, ministerium* utique episcopatus, *propter eos*, scilicet subditos, *qui hereditatem capiunt salutis*, scilicet eterne. Unde et episcopus superintendens dicitur Latine, sicut Johannes in quadam epistoleta,[66] superintendens utique saluti perpetue subditorum, quorum saluti ac proprie donet mihi intendere salvator noster Jesus Christus, qui secundum Apostolum primum ad Thimoteum secundo[67] *vult omnes salvos fieri*. Qui cum patre et spiritu sancto regnat Deus benedictus in secula amen.

67ʳ   [J] Sermo per me factus in synodo

Attendite vobis et universo gregi: Actuum xx; xxxviii di. c.[68] Et prothema: *Attende tibi et doctrine*, idest ad Thimoteum iiii.[69] Duo sunt predicatori verbi Dei necessaria, que in verbis secundo propositis describuntur, scilicet bona vita, quod nota cum dicitur *Attende tibi*, scilicet ut bene

---

62 The *Epistolae* of Gregory I were called his *Registrum* by analogy to the chancery practice of later popes. This quotation is not to be found among the extracts incorporated into the *Decretum*.

63 Jo. 10:4.

64 Gn. 45:5.

65 Heb. 1:14.

66 Not in the Epistles of St. John the Evangelist, nor in the *Decretum* extracts from the letters of Popes John I, III, or VIII; possibly an echo of Jerome, *Ep.* 46, c.1 (PL 22.1193).

67 1 Tim. 2:4.

68 Act. 20:28; and D.38 of the *Decretum*, devoted entirely to priests as preachers and the learning which they should possess.

69 1 Tim. 4:16.

vivas; secundo, exigitur sana et vera doctrina, quod tangitur cum dicit *et doctrine*, scilicet attende ut sanam et veram doctrinam habeas. Bona ergo vita requiritur, quia secundum Gregorium,[70] *Cujus vita despicitur, restat ut ejus predicatio comptenatur* [sic], unde Johannes Crisostomus,[71] *Bene docendo et male vivendo Deum instruis quomodo te debeat condempnare*; unde et Ceneca,[72] *Magna miseria est nescire et nolle discere, major scire et nolle docere, maxima docere et nolle operari*; ibidem per Guidonem, per quem illi versus,[73]

> Tres infelices in mundo dicuntur esse:
> Infelix qui pauca sapit spernitque doceri,
> Infelix qui multa sapit spernitque docere,
> Infelix cujus nulli sapientia prodest,

unde in Salmo[74] etiam dicitur, *Dixit pecatori: Deus tu enarras justitias meas et assumis testamentum meum per os tuum.* Doctrina etiam sana exigitur ut non de proprio capite, sed de sacris scripturis, arripiat quod predicat, unde Gregorius in Moralibus,[75] *Qui ad vere predicationis verba se preparat, necesse est ut causarum origines a sacris paginis sumat ut omne quod loquitur ad divine auctoritatis fundamentum revocet, atque in eo edifficium sue loqutionis firmet.* Debet etiam esse vera, quia secundum Augustinum,[76] *Sicut melius est habere prudentiores quam formosiores amicos, sic utilior est sermo verior quam desertior.* Item secundum ipsum Augustinum,[77] *Ad sempiternam salutem nullus nullus* [sic] *est ducendus opitulante mendacio.* Et quia tam bona vita quam sana et vera doctrina veniunt ex munere gratie Dei ideo in principio nostri sermonis, ad ejus gratiam recurramus; ut autem eam facilius impetremus, dicamus more solito Ave Maria etc.

Attendite vobis et universo gregi ut supra. Sicut dicit beatus Gregorius,[78] et hoc fuit figuratum Genesis xli,[79] quia quando Josep fuit per Faraonem prelatus toti terre Egypti circuivit omnes Egypti regiones, et blada in area cum summa diligentia congregavit, et si cum omni honoris augmento crecere [sic] debet sollicitudo, multo magis cum

70 C.3, q.7, c.2.

71 D.40, c.12.

72 Likely from the moral letters of Seneca the Younger.

73 A commonplace: Hans Walther, *Proverbia sententiaeque latinitatis medii aevi* 2 (Göttingen, 1964), nos. 12299 and 12306; 5 (Göttingen, 1967), no. 31559.

74 Ps. 49:16.

75 *Moralia* 18, 26 *in Job* 28, 1 (PL 76.58A-B).

76 D.38, c.12.

77 C.22, q.2, c.8.

78 D.10, c.9.

79 Gn. 41:45-49.

67^v honore rectorie seu gubernationis ecclesiastice, quia ubi/ majus periculum vertitur ibi cautius est agendum (xvii di. *Quiescamus*).[80] Et ad hec nos ortatur apostolus in verbis preassumptis dicens *Attendite etc*. In quibus quidem verbis duo tanguntur que in qualibet persona ecclesiastica requiruntur.

69^r [K] Collatio facta in abbatia Sancti Eligii Fontis

Vade et vide si cuncta prospera sunt erga fratres tuos et pecora et renuntia mihi quid agendum (Gen. xxxviii capitulo).[81] Carissimi, sicut dicitur Ecclesiastico xvii,[82] *Deus mandavit hominibus unicuique de proximo*, scilicet adjuvando, et hoc fecit quando dixit Exodi xx, *Diliges proximum sicut teipsum*, et Mathei xxii.[83] Mandavit igitur Deus unicuique de proximo suo utpote mandavit de paupere sustentando, de afflicto consolando, de peccante corrigendo, de justo in melius promovendo, et licet hoc sit omnium in omnes ex caritate generali, tamen hoc est prelatorum in subditos ex officio pastorali et debito spirituali, secundum quod inuitur in verbo preassumpto *Vade etc*. Quod literaliter et secundum ystoriam fuit illius magni patriarche Jacob ad filium suum [---Job] Joseph quem misit ad visitandum fratres suos. Pro spiritualiter, potest esse verbum Christi ad me, licet immeritum, et quemlibet alium prelatum, vel potest esse verbum prelati superioris, scilicet domini pape, vel alterius ad alium, ut super fratres suos in Christo, id est super collegia seu conventus sibi subditos et comissos per visitationem et presentiam personalem habeat diligentiam pastoralem.

Ubi breviter tria tangit: primo prelati visitantis a Deo missi operationis fidelitatem, ibi *Vade et vide*; secundo eorum, scilicet subditorum ad quos mittitur visitans, intenta vendicatio ibi *si cuncta prospera sunt erga fratres tuos et pecora*; tertio tangit ejus a quo prelatus visitans mittitur, scilicet Dei, excellentem auctoritatem ibi *renuntia mihi quid agatur*.

Circa primum notatur fidelitas prelati visitantis, notabiliter in duobus, primo in promtitudine laborandi, secundo in sollicitudine conciderandi. Primum tangitur ibi *Vade*: non jaceas per pigritiam, non dormias per somnolentiam, sed vadas vel vade per sollicitudinis diligentiam et caritatis fraterne exuberantiam, et filiis dicitur Mathei (Mathei xxi):[84]

80 D.40, c.2.
81 Gn. 37:14.
82 Eccli. 17:12.
83 Lv. 19:18; Mt. 22:39.
84 Mt. 21:29.

Vade hodie opereris in vineam meam, id est in religionem talis abbatie etc.,
69ᵛ et dicit unde *hodie*, id est in lumine gratie, boni operis luminosi/ et
exemplaris juxta illud Mathei v:[85] *Luceat lux vestra coram hominibus ut
videantur bona opera vestra et glorificent patrem vestrum qui in celis est*: dixit
etiam *opereris*, non *epuleris*. *Vinea* est collegium quodlibet vel conventus in
quo quot sunt bone persone quot sunt palmites, secundum Gregorium
in Omelia super dicto verbo.[86] Bene ergo dicit *vade*, quia nobis prelatis
dixit Christus (Johannis xv),[87] *Posui vos ut eatis* per dioceses visitando, *et
fructum afferatis*, scilicet boni operis, *et fructus vester maneat*, scilicet in
memoriam subditorum ad faciendum bona. Sed sequitur et additur
vide, ubi tangitur sicut dixi fidelitas prelati visitantis in sollicitudine
considerandi. Prelatus enim est sicut oculus in corpore, principes sicut
brachia, et ideo oculis istis, scilicet prelatis, dicitur (Mathei xiii)[88] *Videte,
vigilate et orate*. *Videte*, inquam, subtiliter investigando; *vigilate* subtilius et
dyutius discernendo et judicando; *orate* Dei adjutorium devotius im-
plorando, ne in predictis duobus defficiatis errando; sed pro dolor
multi ex nobis, qui palpant et pertranseunt, sumus correctione et
reprehencione digni, quia coniventibus oculis deffectus et insolentias
subditorum,[89] juxta illud quod dicitur in Salmo,[90] *Oculos habent et non
videbunt, aures habent et non audient, etc.*

Circa secundum, patet ut dixi subditorum ad quos visitando prelatus
mittitur intenta utilitas, ibi *si cuncta prospera sunt erga fratres tuos*, scilicet
intelligentiores, *et pecora*, scilicet simplices, et primo in provectorum et
perfectorum confirmatione, secundo in simpliciorum et imperfectorum
eruditione, ibi *et pecora*. De primo, xx Paralipomenon:[91] *Credite profectis
ejus*, id est scripturis divinis et preceptis eorum et doctrinis, *et cuncta
eveniunt vobis prospera*, juxta illud Salmi primi,[92] *Beatus vir, etc., sed in lege
domini, etc., et folium, etc.*; et subdit *et omnia quecumque faciet* (scilicet talis
vir) *semper prosperabuntur*, juxta illud Luce,[93] *Querite primo regnum Dei et
omnia* (scilicet necessaria) *adicientur vobis*. De secundo, Proverbiorum

---

85 Mt. 5:16.
86 *Homiliae* 19 and 31 on the Gospels identify the vineyard as the universal church.
87 Jo. 15:16.
88 Mt. 26:41.
89 The required sense can be made by eliminating *quia*, winking at the change of person, and
rearranging: *multi ex nobis qui palpant et pertranseunt, coniventibus oculis, defectus et insolentias subditorum,
sumus correctione et reprehensione digni, juxta...*
90 Ps. 113:5-6.
91 2 Par. 20:20.
92 Ps. 1:1-3.
93 Lc. 12:31.

xxvii[94] dicitur cuilibet prelato et curato, *Diligenter agnosce vultum pecoris tui*, et Jeremie xii,[95] *Ubi est grex qui datus est tibi*, scilicet ad regendum, dicet dominus in die judicii. Sed heu, dicitur Jeremie L capitulo,[96] *Grex perditus factus est populus meus et seducerunt eos*, unde talis grex, / id est populus et conventus nobis commissus, a nobis requiretur in extremo examine judicii magni Dei, et dicitur cuilibet nostrum (tertii Regum xx),[97] *Custode virum istum qui si lapsus fuerit*, scilicet in pecatum per negligentiam tuam, *erit anima tua pro anima ejus*, et est valde verbum terribile nobis.

70[r]

Circa tertium ut dixi tangitur mittentis, scilicet Dei, precellens actoritas, ibi *et renuntia mihi quid agatur*. Habemus enim, carissimi, de vobis et aliis nobis subditis ut supra pretactum est Deo reddere rationem (ad Ebreos capitulo ultimo),[98] *et renuntiare* seu referre facta vestra sive bona sive mala, bona ad cumulum nostre glorie et corone, mala, quod absit, ad cumulum et tormentum nostre miserie et verecundie, secundum quod dicitur Ecclesiastis ultimo capitulo,[99] *Cuncta que fiunt* per subditos *adducet Deus in judicium pro omni errato sive bonum sive malum sit*. Donet igitur nobis omnipotens Deus unde et vos et alios visitare ut de vobis et aliis nobis subditis bona et non mala domino renuntiare possimus quando dicetur nobis illud (Luca xvi)[100] *Redde rationem villicationis tue*, sic quod pro vestra salute valeamus feliciter coronari ac ad vitam eternam pervenire, quam nobis et vobis concedat qui est benedictus in secula seculorum amen.

71[r]   [L] Collatio facienda in recessu meo
                         in capitulo Noviomensi

Nunc comendo vos Deo (Actuum xx capitulo).[101] Carissimi, dicitur Actuum i capitulo[102] quod Jesus salvator noster cepit facere et postea dicere, propter quod beatus Gregorius dicit in quadam omelia[103] quod omnis Christi actio nostra est instructio. Ipse siquidem salvator noster fuit totius humane vite quedam inobligabilis regula et exemplar, secun-

---

94   Prv. 27:23.
95   Jer. 13:20.
96   Jer. 50:6.
97   3 Rg. 20:39.
98   Heb. 13:17.
99   Eccle. 12:14.
100 Lc. 16:2.
101 Act. 20:32.
102 Act. 1:1.
103 *Homiliae in Evangelia* 1.17 (PL 76.1139A).

dum quam regulam et exemplar debemus facere actus nostros et actiones nostras et etiam laudabiliter et meritorie regulare. Legimus autem Luce ultimo capitulo[104] inter ceteras actiones domini salvatoris nostri quod ipse proponens de mandato Dei patris recedere corporaliter a suis apostolis et discipulis, quos dilexerat et rexerat in hoc mundo, *elevatis manibus benedixit eis* benedictione vocali (scilicet, glosa ibi, oris mentalis) unde et bonum gratie eis imprecando ac etiam pro eis orando; hoc enim est benedicere, id est bonum dicere, ac etiam bonum alicui non solum vocaliter, sed ore mentis cordialiter imprecare. Et dicit Theophilus Grecus sanctus doctor[105] quod fecit Christus ad nostram instructionem moraliter ut quotiens recedimus benedictionibus Deo nostros subditos vel amicos comendemus benedictionibus inquam mentalibus et orationibus eos comendando. Unde in figura hujus et doctrina dicebat Christus Deo patri a discipulis recessurus (Johannis xvii capitulo),[106] *Pater sancte serva eos in nomine tuo quos dedisti mihi; serva* inquam per gratiam tuam finalem et subditos istos. Cum essem cum eis, ego servabam eos *in nomine tuo quos dedisti mihi*, et ideo rogo ut serves eos a malo in mea absentia, scilicet corporali. Et quia, carissimi, locum Christi et prelati, licet indignus et immeritus, tenui hic inter vos spiritualiter et universaliter in tota dyocesi Noviomensi et nunc de mandato patris nostri domini pape sum in proximo a vobis recessurus, volens me pro posse Christi actioni, quantum Deus per suam gratiam annuerit, conformare, possum vestre caritati proponere et pro imminenti recessu meo assumere verbum superius introductum, *Nunc vos*
71[v] *comendo Deo*; et sunt verba Pauli apostoli gloriosi a suis amicis/ et discipulis recedentis. In quibus quidem verbis sic aliqualiter introductis, tria sunt notabiliter et memorabiliter intuenda: primum, respectu mei recedentis exclamatio seu desolatio [---doloso] dolorosa, cum dicitur *nunc*, scilicet in meo recessu; secundum, respectu capituli seu collegii hic presentis, ymo respectu totius dyocesis Noviomensis, dilectio amorosa vere vicerosa et conversatio gratiosa, cum dicitur *vos*; tertium, respectu Dei, non recedentis nec absentis, ymo universaliter presentis, protectio viviosa et consolatio gaudiosa et fructuosa.

De primo, videlicet mei recedentis vel in proximo recessurus etc., possum dicere ad litteram illud [---quod] Christi dum a discipulis recedebat,[107] *Nunc turbata est anima mea, et quid dicam?* Super quo verbo

---

104 Lc. 24:50.
105 Unidentified in the writings of Theophilus of Alexandria and Theophilus of Antioch.
106 Jo. 17:11.
107 Jo. 12:27.

dicit beatus Augustinus in Origenum[108] quod anima Christi fuit turbata dispensative et condescentive ex operatione ejus a corpore quod naturaliter diligebat, unde sicut Christus unionem anime et corporis sancti naturaliter diligebat, ita separationem horum duorum per mortem fiendam naturaliter ut verus homo horrebat et refugiebat, quamquam secundum rectum judicium rationis contrarium judicabat, dicens patri *non sicut ego volo sed sicut tu fiat*, et ideo ut homo turbabatur dicens *nunc turbata est anima mea*. Sic, carissimi, moraliter et suo modo loquendo, ego debeo in anima turbari et dolere sicut Christus suo modo, et debet esse ista turbatio naturalis et quodammodo me cogens, quia sicut naturaliter et veraciter et non ficte [---dileb] dilexi mei et istius capituli et totius dyocesis unionem spiritualem, ita refugio et horresco separationem corporalem; spiritualiter enim, numquam ab ista nobili et sancta ecclesia potero separari. Ymo dico vobis ex corde in generali et cuilibet vestrum in speciali, illud quod dicitur Mathei ultimo capitulo,[109] *Ecce vobiscum sum omnibus diebus* vite mee, licet non corporaliter, tamen spiritualiter et interne, licet enim non maneam vobiscum secundum corporalitatem, vobiscum tamen manere volo secundum proptam ac \ad vos semper/ benivolam voluntatem, ut veraciter vobis dicam illud apostoli Pauli ad Corinthos v capitulo,[110] *Ego*
72ʳ *quidem* a vobis *absens* a corpore scilicet/ de cetero, *presens autem spiritu* ero. Resumo verbum supradictum pro imminenti recessu meo, et dico *Nunc anima mea turbata est* propter separationem a vobis corporaliter non spiritualiter nunc fiendum [*sic*], et sequitur verbum Christi, *Quid dicam pater*, scilicet de vobis? Certe ego possum dicere et etiam solvere isti questioni secundum illud quod dicitur Mathei viii capitulo,[111] *Amen dico vobis non inveni tantam fidem in Israel*, et in aliquo capitulo, quod est Israel, videns Deum et totam bonitatem et fidelitatem erga suum episcopum, ita ut dicam vobis illud Apostoli ad Galatas iiii capitulo[112] dicentis *non sprevistis nec respuistis me sed sicut angelum suscepistis me sicut Christum Jesum*. Quippe qualiter minister ejus et vices ejus gerens fui inter vos, licet immeritus et indignus, et hoc de primo principali membro.

Sequitur secundum membrum principale, ibi *vos etc.*, ubi tangitur, respectu venerabilis capituli etc., de quo vel de quibus possum dicere illud Christi etiam a discipulis recessurus,[113] *Vos estis qui permansistis*

---

108 Unidentified; but consonant with Augustine's treatment of the suffering of Christ.
109 Mt. 28:20.
110 1 Cor. 5:3.
111 Mt. 8:10.
112 Gal. 4:14.
113 Lc. 22:28.

mecum in temptationibus meis, id est in necessitatibus meis relevandis et in bonis consiliis condonandis ubi requirebam vos, et dicitur *Benedictus qui permansistis*, quo contradicitur Ecclesiastici vi,[114] *Est amicus secundum tempus suum et non permanebit in die tribulationis ... et est amicus qui odium et rixam et convitiam denudabit et est amicus socius mense et non permanebit in die necessitatis.* Non sic vos. Ymo quilibet vestrum fuit mihi verus et fidelis amicus et permanens mecum corde et voluntate, ut sic cuilibet vestrum possit dici illud Ecclesiastici vi,[115] *Amicus si permanserit fixus, erit tibi coequalis et in domesticis tuis negotiis fiducialiter aget*, et subdit, *amico fideli nulla est comparatio et non est digna ponderatio auri vel argenti contra bonitatem fidei illius*, et ut ibi dicit sapiens, invenire fidelem amicum est medicamentum vite et donum Dei singulare.

Sequitur de tertio unum verbum et brevissimum et concludo. *Comendo Deo*, ubi glosa dicit sic: Comendo vos Deo ut Deus vos custodes aliorum custodiat, quia *vos estis lux mundi* (Mathei v),[116] et ideo debetis alios custodire per bonam doctrinam et opera luminosa sicut Deus per suam gratiam vos protegit et custodit. *Comendo* igitur *vos Deo* et dico cuilibet vestrum in recessu meo ipsum Deo comendando illud Psalmi[117] *Dominus custodit te ab omni malo*, scilicet culpe, *custodiat animam dominus*, scilicet per gratiam in presenti et per gloriam in futuro, quam nobis concedat etc.

72[v]   [M] Sermo per me factus in ordinibus

Tabernaculum factum est primum (ad Hebreos ix capitulo).[118] Carissimi, vulgariter dicitur *Qui no es be guarnit es amutz*;[119] quod patet dupliciter: primo in opere arduitatis, secundo in officio dignitatis. In opere ardui[ta]tis ad primum, si comes habeat debellare contra alium fortem et potentem et timeat quod castrum per adversarium impugnetur nisi bene munitum fuerit etc., hoc prolatat; primo Petri v,[120] *Sobrii estote et vigilate, etc.* et Paulus,[121] *Scutum fidei et galeam salutis accipite ut possitis resistere contra telam nequissimi inimici*; et quare? *Qui no es be guarnit etc.*

---

114 Eccli. 6:8-10.
115 Eccli. 6:11-16.
116 Mt. 5:14.
117 Ps. 120:7.
118 Heb. 9:2.
119 "He who is not well armed is silenced"; cf. the French "Qui n'est garni si est honny": J. Morawski, *Proverbes français antérieurs au XIᵉ siècle* (Paris, 1925), p. 74.
120 1 Pe. 5:8.
121 Eph. 6:16.

Hoc patet etiam in officio dignitatis, in figura Numeri xvi capitulo,[122]
secundum istoriam Core, Datan et Abiron, qui contra Aron electum a
domino ut sacerdotio fungeretur insurrexerunt, dicentes *Cur elevamini
contra populum domini?* Moyses respondit, Cras notum faciet dominus
quem elegerit ad sacrificium celebrandum; et notum fecit dominus
sicut dixit, quia terra aperuit os suum, et absorbuit eos vivos et quos ad
eos pertinebant, et vivi descendunt in infernum, et hoc quia sacerdotali
dignitate indigni sunt inventi, et ideo dicit Apostolus ad Ebreos v
capitulo,[123] *Non assumat quisquis honorem, sed qui vocatus est a Deo tamquam
Aron.* Et sic lucide patet quod *qui no es be garnitz etc.*, et per oppositum,
qui es be garnitz no es amutz.

Igitur, carissimi, vos qui estis ad sacros ordines promovendi, si bene
vos purgaveritis rimando bene conscientias vestras, juste potestis dicere
73[r] mihi presidenti verbum suprascriptum allegorice/ in collecto, *Tabernaculum etc.* ubi supra. Ubi duo tanguntur brevissime, primum fundamentum abile ad recipiendum quod probat Gregorii baptismalis
prima collatio,[124] cum dicit *Tabernaculum primum est, secundum com-
plementum stabile ad permanendum*, quod probat condonante Gregorio
collata receptio, cum dicit *factum est.*

Ut de primo sumatur, illud Salmi,[125] *In sole posuit tabernaculum suum*, id
est, in divina magestate posuit corpus et animam; et ut de secundo
sumatur, illud Psalmi,[126] *Factum est cor meum tamquam cera liquescens in
medio ventris mei*, ad modum cere ardore caloris naturalis liquefacientis,
cor meum, dum est divina gratia repertum et tactum est [[et ab]] ipso
liquefactum, primo gratia tangitur in verbo, *pertactus sum [[divina]] etc.*,
sicut eum vidimus sencibiliter, quod in terra sabulosa et bullienti
solidum edifficium non construitur nisi ad fundum solidum per-
tingatur, sic spiritualiter, in terra sabulosa, id est in corpore humano
calore libidinis vel alterius criminis bullienti, solidum spirituale edifficium construi non potest, nisi prius motus tales quietentur et sic
spirituale edifficium construetur; et hoc est sententia Aristotelis,[127]
dicentis *Sedendo et quiescendo anima fit prudens.* Et ideo dicit Job v
capitulo,[128] *Visitans speciem tuam non pecabis, et habeat pacem tabernaculum*

---

122   Nm. 16:1-30.
123   Heb. 5:4.
124   Unidentified; possibly from Gregory Nazianzen.
125   Ps. 18:6.
126   Ps. 21:15.
127   Unidentified, and problematic: contemplation, not active wisdom (*prudentia*), is fostered by
quietness; the distinction is plain in the *Nicomachean Ethics.*
128   Job 5:24.

tuum. In quibus verbis duo ad propositum valde bene facientia con-ciderantur: primo, concideratio singularis asserens quietationem con-scientie, cum dicitur *visitans etc.*; secundo, compositio sive convicio salutaris, asserens adminicula concordie, cum dicitur *habeat etc.*

Circa primum est sciendum quod ista dispositio singularis quadrupliciter habet fieri: primo per carnis macerationem, secundo per mentis inordinate represionem, tertio per cibi potusque subjectionem, 73ᵛ quarto per maligni actus accusationem, / et per omnes veram et sin-ceram confessionem. Et hoc est quod scribit Ozee profeta iiii capitulo profesie sue:[129] *Visitabo per eos quatuor species, id est gladium ad occisionem, canes ad lacerandum, volatilia celi et bestias terre ad devorandum et dissipandum. Visitabo* insuper debet dicere juste desiderans promoveri *super eos,* hoc est sensus meos qui me ad male operandum insitarunt et impugnarunt, id est per *gladium ad occisionem,* hoc est per carnis macerationem, ut im-pleam in me ipso quod dicit David pro se,[130] *Accingere gladio tuo super femur tuum potentissime,* hoc est ut sis precinctus gladio super femur, id est carnem tuam, que sit spiritui subjecta, ut compleas quod dicitur Ezechielis v capitulo,[131] *Sume tibi gladium acutum radentem pilos, et sumes et duces per capud et barbam,* id est per omnia tui corporis loca super-fluitatem emitentia. Secundo habet facere dispositio singularis per men-tis inordinate represionem quod necatur per *volatilia*; Job xii capitulo,[132] *Interroga volatilia celi, et indicabunt tibi* si habundant tabernacula predonum, et si audacter Deum provocant, et certe dicent tibi quod non, quia *qui se exaltat humiliabitur.*[133] Tertio habet fieri ista consideratio per cibi potusque subtraxionem, quod datur intelligi per *bestias devoran-tes,* quod pulcre figuratur Josue iii capitulo,[134] *Ex ore principum et regum, homines et jumenta, boves et pecora cibum non gustent nec pascantur, nec aquam bibant*; supple, donec mitigetur ira Dei quam per cibi et potus habun-dantiam incurristi. Quarto habet fieri concideratio ista per maligni [---sp] actus accusationem etc., quod datur intelligi per *canes,* quia secun-dum sanctos in sacra scriptura predicatores designantur quia sicut canes fures\in noctis silentio/ ad hostia dominorum venientes per \latrusus/ manifestant, sic per predicatores mali actus cognoscuntur 74ʳ et postea expelluntur, ut in Salmo:[135] *Linga canum/ ex inimicis ab ipso.*

---

129 Really Jer. 15:3. The word *visitabo* also occurs in Os. 4:9, and so the error is clearly a slip of the eye in a concordance.
130 Ps. 44:4.
131 Ez. 5:1.
132 Job 12:7.
133 Luc. 14:11.
134 Jon. 3:7, likely misread as Jos. in a concordance.
135 Ps. 67:24.

Secundo, sequitur in verbis predictis compositio salutaris etc., ut *pacem habeat etc.* Circa quod est sciendum quod ista compositio in rite ordinando habet quadrupliciter[136] reperiri: primo, conversationis pulcritudo per castitatis candorem; secundo, educationis certitudo per veritatis splendorem; tertio, subjectionis promptitudo per humilitatis tenorem; quarto, contemplationis altitudo per caritatis ardorem. Primus titulus est conversationis etc., et iste primitus debet in quocumque promovendo relucere et ob hoc figurative pulcre dicebat Exodus xxx capitulo,[137] *Sume tibi aromata mirre prime electe, synamonum, calamum et cassiam et oleum de olivetis faciesque inde unctionis oleum sanctum et ex eo unges tabernaculum testimonii. Sume tibi mirram*; talis nature confertur quod etiam corpora mortua ex ea condita non putrescant, per quod datur intelligi carnis mortifacio et mentis candidatio, queque maxime debent in clerico relucere, secundum quod habetur xxii distinctione capitulo *Hiis igitur,*[138] quia clerici *sint a vita vulgari seclusi, a mundi voluptatibus se abtineant, spectaculis et pompis non intersint, convivia publica fugiant, privata non tamen pudica sed sobria colant, ... non oculis vani, non effreni linga, ... viduarum et virginum frequentationes effugiant, ... castimoniam inviolati corporis studeant observare*; item alibi, episcopi non presumant subdiaconum facere nisi prius se promisit caste victurus, quia nullus debet ad altare misterium accedere nisi prius ejus castitas fuerit aprobata (xxviii distinctionis *Nullus*).[139] Item nullus missam audiat presbiteri quem scit concubinam aut aliam mulierem introductam habere (xxxii distinctionis *Cum*),[140] ut alibi habetur [---corda] castitas sit ordini clericali anexa. Igitur tu qui avelas ad sacros ordines promoveri, *sume tibi mirram* carnem mortificantem et mentem a putredine preservantem, ut

74[v] possis/dicere juxta illud Canticorum v,[141] *Manus mee distillaverunt mirram,* id est, corpus et anima mea sunt per meam sollicitudinem a fetore libidinis reservata, *et digiti mei,* id est V sensus mei, sunt *pleni mirra probatissima,* lucidissima et candidissima venutaste [*sic*], *et ideo quasi mirra electa dedi suavitatem odoris* (Ecclesiastici xxiiii capitulo).[142] *Summe etc. symamannum,* quod est parvum quantitate sed magnum virtute, et est cynerei coloris et subnigrum, quia caste vivere cupiens debet mundo pallidus esse, cum et habet accuratus celestibus disciplinis juxta illud

---

136 But the sermon develops only the first title of this division.
137 Ex. 30:23-26.
138 D.23, c.3.
139 D.28, c.1.
140 D.32, c.1.
141 Ct. 5:5.
142 Eccli. 24:20.

Cantica i,[143] *Nolite me considerare quod fusca sim quia decoloravit me sol.* Summe etiam tibi *calamum et cassiam et oleum de olivetis* [---et facies ungen-tum], que omnia sunt odorifera, ceteris virtutibus pulcritudinis [[pullulan]]tia et inde *facies unguentum ad unguendum tabernaculum testimonii*, id est conscientiam tuam, O ordinande; ista castitate debes relucere pre ceteris, non sicut monstruosum et quasi deforme esset [---ut] si in corporis humani nobiliorem locum membrum vilius poneretur, sed recte, quasi monstruosum et deforme esset in ecclesiastico ordine, si quis lubricus aut immundus in tante dignitatis statu ponetur, cum medius inter Deum et peccatores habeatur. Ergo *sume tibi aromata prime mirre*, et si custoderis, vitam eternam possidebis, ad quam etc.

State University of New York, Binghamton

143   Ct. 1:5.

THE CONSTABULARY OF BORDEAUX:
THE ACCOUNTS OF JOHN LUDHAM (1372-73)
AND ROBERT DE WYKFORD (1373-75)
Part II*

Timothy Runyan

Compotus magistri Roberti de Wykford, constabularii Burdegale, cui
rex per litteras suas patentes de magno sigillo dat' 7 die Maii anno
47 super hunc compotum liberatas et per alias litteras suas patentes de
eodem sigillo dat' 12 die Aprilis eodem anno irrotulatas in originalia de
anno predicto commisit custodiam castri Burdegale et officium constabularii[1] ibidem habendo cum omnibus ad officium illud pertinentibus quamdiu regi placuerit; ita quod de exitibus inde provenientibus regi respondeat et in officio illo feodum percipiat consuetum:
videlicet de dictis exitibus a 20 die Augusti dicto anno 47, ante quem
Johannes Ludham, thesaurarius et constabularius ibidem, alias inde
computavit rotulo quarto rotulo compotorum, usque 23 diem Julii
anno 49 per visum et testimonium Guillelmi de Holcombe,[2] con-

  * For Part I see *Mediaeval Studies* 36 (1974) 215-258. The author wishes to thank Dr. Mary
Rechenbach for providing information on mints and money. She is presently completing a work on
the money of Bordeaux. I am also indebted to the work of Dr. Elizabeth A. R. Brown, especially
her "Gascon Subsidies and the Finances of the English Dominions, 1315-1324," *Studies in Medieval
and Renaissance History* 8 (1971) 33-163, which includes a table of place-names and a helpful map.
  1 MS. *constabularie*.
  2 William Holcombe (Wolcombe), master, notary and burgess of Bordeaux, succeeded Fillong-
ley as controller by commission dated 8 March 1373 (C. 61/ 86, m. 7). One week later he was given
the power *de cartulariis faciendis* (C. 61/ 86, m. 6). He was replaced in 1376 by Thomas Myton (C.
61/ 89, m. 4). Holcombe's Particulars are partially printed in *AHG* 12. 328-41. For his account book
see E. 101/ 179/ 15 covering 47-49 Edward III, 48 pp., listed in P.R.O. List XXXV, p. 134. For the
books relating to customs see E. 101/ 180/ 3 covering 48-49 Edward III, 84 pp.

trarotulatoris ibidem, a quo die Ricardus Rotour,[3] constabularius ibidem. Immediate post dictum magistrum Robertum inde computavit dicto rotulo quarto rotulo compotorum.

REDDITUS ASSISUS:

Idem reddit compotum de 786 *li.* 12 *s.* 4 *d.* monete *nig.* currentis, unde 7-$\frac{1}{2}$ *d.* valentibus *st.* Anglie receptis de redditu assiso diversorum tenencium in civitate Burdegale et alibi infra ducatum predictum pro diversis domibus, terris et feodis et aliis rebus que de rege tenentur de terminis Decollacionis Sancti Johannis Baptiste, Sancti Michaelis, Sancti Severini, Sancti Martini, Natalis Domini, Sancti Thome Martiris et Prime Dominice Quadragesime, Pasche, Nativitatis Sancti Johannis Baptiste et Assumpcionis Beate Marie, accidentibus infra tempus huius compoti sicut continetur in libris de particulis predicti constabularii ac eciam predicti Guillelmi de Holcombe contrarotulatoris in thesauro liberatis.

SUMMA: 786 *li.* 12 *s.* 4 *d.* Dicte Monete Currentis.

EXITUS BALLIVARUM, PREPOSITURARUM, ET ALIORUM:[4]

Idem reddit compotum de 5,348 *li.* dicte monete *nig.* currentis receptis de exitibus prepositure Umbrarie Burdegale cum scribania eiusdem, sigilli et contrasigilli quibus utitur in Burdegala ad contractus, parvi sigilli hostagiorum,[5] defectuum curie Vasconie, ballive ad aulas et salavine (*sic*), custume vinorum venditorum in tabernis vocate issak', prepositure Aquensis,[6] ballive de Hastyngs,[7] ballive de Capbreton,[8] ballive de la Borde,[9] prepositure Sancti Seueri,[10] assensatis diversis ad

---

3   Little of the personal life of Richard Rotour is known. He followed Wykford as constable by letters dated 16 April 1375 (C. 61/ 88, m. 6), serving until October 1379. He received power of general attorney for going to "partes Vasconie" on 12 May following (C. 61/ 88, m. 4). On this same date, two men were granted his power of attorney (C. 61/ 88, m. 4). On 17 August protection was granted to him for one year (C. 61/ 88, m. 2). He is spoken of in his accounts as *defunctus*, so it can be assumed that he died before 1381, when his account was rendered by executors (E. 364/ 15). His accounts are excellent examples of a finely trained fourteenth-century hand and have been highly praised by Eleanor Lodge who laments the lack of revenues received while lauding the calligraphic style of the register (Lodge, *EHR* 50 (1935) 236).

4   The heading for this section was absent and the present one has been reconstructed from similar ones in other constables' accounts.

5   MS. *hogast'*.

6   Dax, dép. Landes.

7   Hastingues, dép. Landes, arr. Dax, cant. Peyrehorade.

8   Capbreton, dép. Landes. Capbreton was an important seaport near the mouth of the Adour until the river's lower course shifted to Bayonne in 1579.

9   Bordes, dép. Tarn-et-Garonne, arr. Moissac, cant. Valence-d'Agenais, com. Pommevic.

10   Saint-Seurin, dép. Gironde, arr. Bordeaux.

terminos Sancti Michaelis, Natalis Domini, Pasche et Nativitatis Sancti
Johannis Baptiste, accidentes infra idem tempus sicut continetur
ibidem. De exitibus omnium prepositurarum et ballivarum in partibus
Landarum de termino Sancti Michaelis anno 47 accidentibus infra idem
tempus seu de exitibus prepositure Vasati et Vasadesie, ballivarum de
Monte Sturnge, Samnesano, Montepellano et Bogolomo, herbagii Landarum, guydonagii vaccarum,[11] ballive de Tholoseto,[12] ballive Sancti
Mauricii,[13] castellanie Malleonis,[14] exitibus pedagii seu aliorum pro-
ficuorum ville Marmande seu de exitibus custume Montis Andro-
nis,[15] piscarie cuiusdam nasse in aqua de la Dore[16] prope Bayon',[17] de
exitibus comitatus Bigorr'[18] seu de exitibus comitatus Agennesii per totum tempus huius compoti non respondet eo quod nichil inde recepit
nec recepisse potuit propter guerram inimicorum Francie quia occu-
pabantur per dictos inimicos ut dicit per sacramentum suum et per
breve regis de magno sigillo thesaurario et baronibus suis de scaccario
directum dat' 16 die Julii anno 50 quod est inter communia de termino
Sancti Hilarii anno 51, per quod rex inter cetera mandavit eisdem quod
de possessionibus per inimicos regis occupatis que in manibus regis esse
solebant per sacramentum ipsius constabularii inde exonerari et
quietum esse faciant et de quibus dictus constabularius nichil recepit ut
dicit per sacramentum suum et prout testificatur per dictum contrarotulatorem sicut continetur ibidem. De exitibus porte castri Burdegale et de turri dicti castri, scribanie curie Vasconie, prepositure Inter Duo Maria,[19] castri et ballive Peillon',[20] ballivarum de Montford[21] et
de Bone Garde,[22] ballive de Sorde,[23] ballive Montifferuri, molendini
Montessecury, pedagii de Longonio, ballive de Sancto Liberto, ballive
et castellanie Sancti Macharii et pedagii ibidem, ballive de Bogio[24]
<de> honore Briggeraci cum pertinenciis, bladagio seu aliis proficuis

11 Guidagium was a payment made on the passage of cows to the different pastures.
12 Toulouzette, dép. Landes, arr. Saint-Sever, cant. Mugron.
13 Saint-Maurice, dép. Landes, arr./cant. Saint-Sever.
14 Mauléon, dép. Basses-Pyrénées.
15 Montendre, dép. Charente-Inférieure, arr. Jonzac.
16 The Adour River.
17 Bayonne, dép. Basses-Pyrénées.
18 Bigorre, dép. Hautes-Pyrénées.
19 Entre-Deux-Mers, district at the confluence of the Dordogne and Gironde Rivers.
20 Pouillon, dép. Landes, arr. Dax.
21 Montfort, dép. Landes, arr. Dax.
22 Bonnegarde, dép. Landes, arr. Saint-Sever, cant. Amou.
23 Sordes, dép. Landes, arr. Dax, cant. Peyrehorade.
24 Buch, dép. Gironde.

ville Blavie[25] non respondet eo quod dictus Edwardus Princeps Wallie dedit predictas ballivas, preposituras, honorem et alia proficua diversis magnatibus et aliis personis quorum quidem magnatum et aliorum nomina annotantur in particulis huius compoti et per dictum breve regis de magno sigillo dictis thesaurario et baronibus directum dat' 16 die[26] anno 50, in quo inter cetera continetur cum rex nuper de avisamento consilii sui per litteras patentes revocari mandavit omnimodas donaciones factas in ducatu Aquitanie cuicumque persone facte fuerint si per regem facte et confirmate non fuissent et postea de avisamento dicti consilii ordinatum fuisset quod, non obstante quod dictum mandatum regis extitit generale, predictus constabularius permitteret aliquas personas uti et gaudere donacionibus eis factis absque impedimento prout videbatur dicto constabulario necesse fore in adventu suo in dictis partibus per avisamentum consilii regis apud Burdegalam pre timore maioris dispendii et ad evitandum diversa pericula et dampna que inde evenire potuerunt, rex vellet ipsum constabularium exonerari iubere de revencionibus et proficuis castrorum, villarum, prepositurarum, ballivarum et aliorum consimilium datorum et concessorum per Edwardum nuper principem Wallie aut per Johannem regem Castelle et Legionis, ducem Lancastrie nuper locum tenentem regis in partibus Aquitanie sive per Thomam de Felton, senescallum regis Aquitanie; ultra hoc quod idem constabularius de huiusmodi revencionibus per testimonium contrarotulatoris castri Burdegale recepit, rex mandavit eisdem thesaurario et baronibus quod demanda quam eidem constabularius pro revencionibus seu proficuis castrorum, villarum, prepositurarum, ballivarum, et aliorum consimilium datorum per prefatum principem seu per dictum regem Castelle aut per prefatum Thomam que eis constare poterit ipsum constabularium per sacramentum suum ac per testimonium predicti contrarotulatoris non recepisse, fieri faciant supersederi et ipsum constabularium inde ad dictum scaccarium exonerari quietum esse faciant, revocacione predicta non obstante, et de quibus exitibus dictus constabularius nichil recepit causa predicta ut dicit per sacramentum suum et per testimonium predicti contrarotulatoris sicut continetur ibidem. De exitibus custume ollarum, lutearum et thede,[27] quam custumam dictus dominus princeps

25 Blaye, dép. Gironde.
26 Month is missing; a space appears for it in manuscript.
27 *Olla* is a type of earthenware pot, and *lutea*, a type of earthen jar. *Tede* is usually grouped with *barrillage* as it is described by M. Trabut-Cussac as a custom, "sur les pins amenés à Bordeaux pour le chauffage." At the end of the reign of Edward I it was valued at 16 *li. bord.* per year when

dedit Johanni Pemburgg',[28] garderobario suo ad terminum vite sue, non respondet per breve regis Ricardi de privato sigillo suo thesaurario et baronibus de scaccario suo directum dat' 15 die Junii anno tercio quod est inter communia de termino Sancti Hilarii anno quarto, in quo brevi inter cetera continetur quod cum idem dominus princeps concesserit dicto Johanni, garderobario suo, dictam custumam ollarum et thede in Burdegala ad terminum vite sue, virtute cuius concessionis predictus constabularius permisit ipsum Johannem habere et percipere custumam predictam, rex mandavit eisdem thesaurario et baronibus quod de eadem custuma predicto constabulario pro tempore quo idem Johannes illam percepit per sacramentum ipsius constabularii et per testimonium predicti contrarotulatoris debitam faciant allocacionem et per sacramentum ipsius constabularii et per testimonium predicti contrarotulatoris sicut continetur in dictis rotulo et contrarotulo de particulis; et nec respondet de exitibus quarte partis fori seu mercati Burdegale quos Johannes Colomb', miles, tenuit et percepit per tempus huius compoti per idem breve, in quo inter cetera continetur quod pro eo quod per totum tempus quo dictus magister Robertus extitit constabularius ibidem predictus Johannes Colomb' tenuit dictam quartam partem prepositure mercati Burdegale in prejudicium dicti domini regis Edwardi avi et dictus constabularius non audebat per totum dictum tempus distringere dictum Johannem causa potencie sue in villa predicta pro firma regi pertinente pro quarta parte antedicta, que firma solebat esse 80 *li.* monete currentis per annum, ita quod ob causam predictam dictus constabularius nichil levare potuit de dicto Johanne de firma predicta per idem tempus prout dictus constabularius dicit, rex mandavit quod per sacramentum ipsius constabularii et per testimonium dicti contrarotulatoris exonerare faciant dictum constabularium de firma quarte partis predicte pro tempore predicto et per sacramentum ipsius constabularii et testimonium dicti contrarotulatoris sicut continetur in dictis rotulo et contrarotulo de particulis. De exitibus parve custume Roiani[29] quos dominus Amanenus de

---

combined with barrillage. (Trabut-Cussac, "Les coutumes," 148.) In October of 1375 this custom was granted to Pierre Mercier for life (C. 61/90, m. 3).

28 John Pemburgge, wardrober, is mentioned as the recipient of a grant dated 24 November 1372 (C. 61/85, m. 1; repeated at C. 61/86, m. 4 and lined out).

29 Royan, dép. Charente Maritime. This wine tax is in the main classification with the great custom and issac'. Although in theory all paid the custom, there were many granted immunity, as in the case of the other customs. *Roiani*, though, was even paid by the diocese of Bordeaux: *Item habet dominus rex magnam custumam vinorum de qua custuma cives Burdegale commorantes sunt liberi et franqui de omnibus vinis suis provenientibus de vineis suis quas tantum habent in diocesi Burdegale ..., excepta custuma*

Burgo,[30] miles, tenet ad terminum vite sue vel 200 *li*. monete currentis percipiendis de dicta custuma per annum ex concessione dicti domini principis non respondet per idem breve regis Ricardi de privato sigillo thesaurario et baronibus de scaccario directum dat' 15 die Junii anno tercio, in quo inter cetera continetur quod dictus dominus princeps concessit dicto Almaneno 200 *li*. dicte monete currentis percipiendas per annum de dicta parva custuma Roiani apud Burdegalam ad terminum vite ipsius Amaneni, virtute cuius concessionis dictus Amanenus habuit et percepit 200 *li*. per annum de custuma predicta, rex mandavit eisdem thesaurario et baronibus quod allocacionem faciant eidem constabulario de 200 *li*. predictas per sacramentum suum et per testimonium contrarotulatoris predicti et que quidem custuma non se extendit ad dictam summam 200 *li*. per annum prout plenius patet per papiros tam ipsius constabularii quam predicti contrarotulatoris sicut continetur in dictis rotulo et contrarotulo de particulis. De exitibus ballive Salve Terre non respondet eo quod dictus dominus Thomas de Felton', senescallus Aquitanie, dedit illam ballivam cum proficuis et pertinenciis suis quamdiu placuerit regi et dicto Thome Johanni Savage, scutifero, capitaneo dicte ville, ad gubernandum et custodiendum illam contra potenciam inimicorum circumquaque illam existencium prout per copiam seu vidimus litterarum dicti senescalli sub sigillo autentico super hunc compotum liberatam et per dictum breve regis de magno sigillo dat' 16 die Julii anno 50 pro huiusmodi donacionibus allocandis et per aliud breve regis Ricardi de privato sigillo suo thesaurario et baronibus de scaccario suo directum dat' 15 die Junii anno tercio quod est inter communia de termino Sancti Hilarii anno quarto, in quo brevi inter cetera continetur quod de parcellis et rebus istum compotum tangentibus rex vult quod per copias litterarum et mandatorum ipsius regis Edwardi avi dicti regis Ricardi, Johannis ducis Lancastrie et aliorum loca eorum tenencium, predicti senescalli et consilii ipsius regis avi constabulario predicto inde factorum super dictum compotum exhibitas sub sigillo autentico et per sacramentum ipsius magistri Roberti constabularii cum testimonio dicti contrarotulatoris debitam faciant allocacionem eidem magistro Roberto adeo plene et integre

---

Royani, scilicet 2-1/2 *d. pro dolio, quam solvent omnes, tam cives Burdegale quam extranei, sive sunt privilegiati, sive non.* The sum of 2-1/2 *d.* was fixed by ordinance of Edward I in 1285, making it a good source of revenue, though a *petit coutume*. It is also imperative to distinguish this custom from the *petit coutume de Royan*, of the same name but of less value. See Trabut-Cussac, "Les coutumes," 135-50.

30   Amanenus de la Mota was given the *parva custuma Roiani* as a gift of the Black Prince (value 200 *li. Burd.*) which custom was "as a rule let out at farm or given in reward for service" (Lodge, *EHR* 50 (1935) 228).

prout facerent per originalia litterarum et mandatorum predictorum et de quibus exitibus dictus constabularius nichil percepit ut dicit per sacramentum suum et per testimonium predicti contrarotulatoris sicut continetur ibidem; seu de exitibus ballivarum de Caudirot[31] et de Longonio, que nuper fuerunt Arnaldi de Guanareto, nichil recepit quia dominus Petrus de la Mota, dominus de Roguataillada,[32] tenet et percipit omnia proficua dictarum ballivarum pro custodia dicte ville de Longton' ex assignacione dicti senescalli ut idem constabularius dicit per sacramentum suum ac per testimonium dicti contrarotulatoris ac eciam per dictum breve regis de magno sigillo pro huiusmodi donacionibus allocandis sicut continetur ibidem. De exitibus et proficuis prepositure de Comperiano,[33] pedagii de Medulco,[34] prepositure de Blankadesio, castellanie de Burgo, prepositure Leybourne, ballive et prepositure Sancti Emiliani,[35] castellanie Podii Normanii cum bastida ville Franchie,[36] terre de Pessaco,[37] loci de Pellagrua,[38] prepositure Baion' et custodie castri ibidem, ballive Sancti Edwardi,[39] prepositure Abbatie Sancti Seueri[40] et temporalitatum eiusdem abbatie, ballive de Guos et Seuhas,[41] ballive de Putos, ballive de Brussaco cum bastida Montis Astruci,[42] Montis Pesarii[43] et loci de Sabros, ballive Herbe Fanerie, terre de Condaco, ballive Auri Vallis,

---

31   Caudrot, dép. Gironde, arr. la Réole, cant. Saint-Macaire.

32   La Mothe, dép. Lot-et-Garonne, arr. Villeneuve-sur-Lot. Roguataillada, dép. Gironde, arr. Bordeaux, cant. Langon, com. Mazères. This apparently powerful noble was granted the prévôté of the city and castle of Bazas with all appurtenances for life as shown in a letter of inspeximus and confirmation dated 3 December 1374 (actual grant was made 6 March 1373). The enrolment letter is unusual: it begins in Latin and ends in French (C. 61/ 87, m. 3). The present grant of Langon is recorded in the Gascon Rolls for 7 December 1374. He was to receive a custom of 4 d. per pound on merchandise: *pro bono servicio ... concessimus prefato Petro dictam custumam 4 d. de libra percipiendo pro salva custodia dictorum locorum quamdiu custodiam eorundem habuerit et guerra duraverit* ... (C. 61/ 87, m. 1).

33   Comparrian, dép. Gironde, arr. Bordeaux, cant. Pesac.

34   Medoc, dép. Gironde.

35   Saint-Emilion, dép. Gironde, arr. Libourne.

36   Puymormand, dép. Gironde, arr. Libourne, cant. Lussac. Villefranche-du-Queyran, dép. Lot-et-Garonne, arr. Nérac, cant. Casteljaloux.

37   Pessac, dép. Gironde, arr. Bordeaux.

38   Pellegrue, dép. Gironde.

39   St. Edouard, dép. Landes, arr. Saint-Sever, cant. Mugron.

40   St. Sever, dép. Landes, arr. Mont-de-Marsan. The Abbot of St. Sever was a member of the Court of Sovereignty, shown by writs of appointment on 17 April 1372 (*Foedera* 3.ii, 940) and on 15 June 1378 (*Foedera* 4.44).

41   Sos, dép. Lot-et-Garonne, arr. Nérac, cant. Mézin.

42   Montastruc, dép. Lot-et-Garonne, arr. Villeneuve-sur-Lot, cant. Monclar.

43   Monpazier, dép. Dordogne, arr. Bergerac.

ballive de Menisano et prepositure de Buru', nichil recepit eo quod diversi magnates ducatus predicti et alii omnia exitus et proficua predicta perceperunt et occupaverunt per predictum tempus huius compoti pretextu diversarum concessionum regis et suorum loca tenencium et senescallorum eiusdem ducatus certis de causis inde factarum et que quidem concessiones plenius annotantur in compoto magistri Johannis de Stretle,[44] nuper constabularii Burdegale, de anno 35 et de aliis annis precedentibus rotulo 36 rotulorum compotorum ubi dicti exitus excusantur causis supradictis et de quibus exitibus dictus Robertus de Wykford nichil recepit vel recepisse potuit ut dicit per sacramentum suum et sicut testificatur per dictum contrarotulatorem sicut continetur ibidem. De exitibus piscarie magne nasse infra castellaniam Sancti Macharii nichil recepit quia tempore alterius guerre fuit dirupta et totaliter desolata ut patet in dicto compoto precedente nec usque finem huius compoti reperata ut dicit per sacramentum suum sicut continetur ibidem. De exitibus cuiusdam chaii[45] in parochia Sancti Michaelis Burdegalensis,[46] per tempus huius compoti non respondet quia fuit combustus longo tempore elapso et nullus voluit placeam dicti chaii affirmare ut dicit per sacramentum suum et per testimonium predicti contrarotulatoris sicut continetur ibidem.

SUMMA: 5,348 *li.* Monete Predicte.

MAGNA CUSTUMA VINORUM:

Idem reddit compotum de 6,294 *li.* 6 *s.* 11-$^1/_2$ *d.*[47] que monete currentis receptis de magna custuma vinorum infra predictum castrum Burdegale custumatorum inter predictum 20 diem Augusti anno 47 et eun-

---

44 John de Streatley was appointed constable on 28 April 1348 and served until 12 September 1350, and again from 18 January 1353 to 1 July 1361 (Lodge, *EHR* 50 (1935) 341). He attended Oxford and received his doctorate in laws by 1343. He seems to have served as king's clerk until his appointment to the constabulary. He was a member of the Black Prince's council and a frequent envoy to foreign lords and kings. He served as chancellor of Guyenne after the Black Prince took possession (1362) until 1364 (Emden, *A Biographical Register of the University of Oxford to A.D. 1500* 3.1804). The Black Prince tried to get him appointed to the bishopric of Bath and Wells and recommended him for the position to the Pope, but to no avail (Chaplais, "Chancery of Guyenne," 85). He was back in England in 1364 where he stayed as Dean of Lincoln Cathedral. He died in either 1368 or 1369 (Emden, *loc. cit.*). In a letter by the king in 1368, requesting an audit of Streatley's accounts, it was found that he was nearly 94 *li.* in arrears to the crown. The king pardoned him of the sum by writ of privy seal on hearing his plea (*CPR* [1367-70], p. 161).

45 Chaii (chai), a cave, or warehouse for wines.

46 The parish of St. Michel was located just south of Bordeaux on the Gironde and above the Estey Sainte-Croix. For a map of the area see Higounet, *Bordeaux pendant le haut Moyen Age*, p. 113.

47 MS. *dimidio.*

dem diem anno revoluto, scilicet per unum annum, sicut continetur in dictis particulis constabularii et contarotulatoris ac eciam in papiris ipsorum constabularii et contrarotulatoris de particulis eiusdem custume hic in thesauro liberatis. Et de 4,080 *li*. 8 *s*. 4 *d*. dicte monete currentis receptis de consimili magna custuma vinorum infra castrum predictum custumatorum inter predictum 20 diem Augusti anno 48 et 23 diem Julii proximo sequentem sicut continetur ibidem. De custuma 39 doleorum vini[48] que Dux Britannie eduxit de Burdegala in Britanniam, seu vinorum Archiepiscopi Burdegalensis ad ecclesiam suam Burdegalensem pertinencium, seu de aliqua custuma contra privilegium prioris et fratrum Hospitalis Sancte Juliane Burdegale; habitatorum ville regis de Sancto Machario; Hospitalis Sancti Johannis Jerusalem' magistrorum, fratrum et hominum suorum; conventus monasterii Sancte Crucis Burdegalensis;[49] burgensium et habitatorum ville de Reula; prioris, fratrum et conventus hospitalis Sancti Jacobi Burdegalensis et capituli et canonicorum ecclesie Burdegale non respondent per dictum breve regis Ricardi thesaurario et baronibus suis de scaccario suo directum dat' 15 die Junii anno tercio, in quo quidem brevi inter cetera continetur quod cum Johannes rex Castelle et Legionis, dux Lancastrie tempore quo extitit locum tenens regis Edwardi avi dicti regis nunc in partibus ultra mare mandaverit dicto constabulario per litteras suas quod permitteret ipsum ducem Britannie educere de Burdegala in Britanniam predicta 39 dolea vini absque solucione custume pro eisdem ac eciam concesserit per litteras suas Archiepiscopo Burdegalensi qui tunc fuit non solueret custumam pro vinis suis ad ecclesiam suam Burdegalensem pertinentibus et quod diverse alie persone fuerunt privilegiate per cartas et litteras ipsius regis avi dicti domini principis et aliorum progenitorum regis essensi (*sic*) quiete de custuma pro vinis suis et quod virtute mandatorum litterarum et concessionum predictorum idem constabularius permisit predictos ducem Britannie, Archiepiscopum Burdegalensem et alias personas privilegiatas quietos esse de custuma pro dictis vinis suis, rex[50] volens ipsum constabularium debitam habere allocacionem in hac parte, mandavit quod de dicta custuma vinorum, de qua permisit ipsos ducem Britannie, Archiepiscopum Burdegalensem et alias personas privilegiatas esse quietos secundem tenorem mandatorum, concessionum et

---

48   The *doleum* was a cask or tun for carrying wine.

49   Sainte-Croix was a very large and important Benedictine abbey with many possessions along the Garonne; for fuller details, see Higounet, *Bordeaux*, pp. 126-29.

50   MS. sown here, *rex* repeated.

privilegiorum predictorum, allocacionem faciant eidem constabulario in dicto compoto suo per sacramentum suum et per testimonium predicti contrarotulatoris sicut continetur in predictis particulis ipsorum constabularii et contrarotulatoris et que quidem littere ipsius regis Castelle et Legionis cum 9 copiis seu vidimus dictorum privilegiorum sub sigillis autenticis super istum compotum liberantur.[51]
SUMMA: 10,374 *li.* 15 *s.* 3 *d.*

PARVA CUSTUMA:

Idem reddit compotum de 505 *li.* 22-$^1/_2$ *d.* dicte monete receptis de exitibus gaugati vinorum proveniencium de 24,244 tonellis et 1 pipa vini gaugatis infra castrum predictum per tempus huius compoti, videlicet pro quolibet tonello 1 *d. st. g.* valenti 5 *d.* monete currentis, sicut continetur in dictis particulis constabularii et contrarotulatoris ac eciam in papiris predictis in thesauro liberatis. Et de 42 *li.* receptis de exitibus custume killagii provenientibus de 56 navibus, videlicet de qualibet navi nova vel cui nova killa fuit apposita pro primo introitu dicte navis in portu Burdegale 15 *s.* monete currentis per idem tempus sicut continetur ibidem. Et de 44 *li.* 5 *s.* 5 *d.* dicte monete receptis custume mellis provenientibus de 425 tonellis custumatis ibidem per idem tempus, videlicet pro quolibet tonello 2 *s.* 1 *d.* monete currentis sicut continetur ibidem. De exitibus parve custume Roiani, videlicet de quolibet tonello vini custumato apud Burdegalam tam per burgenses Burdegale quam per extraneos 2-$^1/_2$ *d.* monete currentis, per tempus huius compoti nichil recepit quia dominus Amanenus de la Mote, miles, castellanus de Burgo, tenet eam ad terminum vite sue vel 200 *li.* monete currentis percipiendo de dicta custuma per annum ex donacione dicti domini principis ut idem constabularius dicit per sacramentum suum et per testimonium predicti contrarotulatoris ac eciam per supradictum breve regis de magno sigillo dat' 16 die Julii anno 50 pro huiusmodi donacionem allocando et que quidem custuma non se extendit ad dictas 200 *li.* per annum prout in dictis papiris de custuma vinorum plenius annotatur sicut continetur ibidem.
SUMMA: 591 *li.* 7 *s.* 3-$^1/_2$ *d.*

51 For more on the "privileged" merchants see above n. 29.

Custuma composicionis vinorum Leybornie cum gaugato, killagio[52] et custuma mellis ibidem:

Idem reddit compotum de 173 *li*. 5 *s*. dicte monete currentis receptis de exitibus custume vinorum exeuncium portum Leybornie et custumatorum in dicto castro Burdegale per tempus huius compoti provenientibus de 346 tonellis vini custumatis ad custumam composicionis, pro quolibet tonello 10 *s*. monete currentis, prout continetur in dictis papiris constabularii et contrarotulatoris ac eciam in dictis parcellis in thesauro liberatis. Et de 7 *li*. 4 *s*. 4-$^1/_2$ *d*. dicte monete receptis de gaugato dictorum 346 tonellorum per idem tempus, videlicet pro quolibet tonello 5 *d*. dicte monete, sicut continetur ibidem. De killagio seu custuma mellis ibidem non respondet quia nullus proficuum inde accidebat per idem tempus ut idem constabularius dicit per sacramentum suum et per testimonium predicti contrarotulatoris sicut continetur ibidem.
Summa: 180 *li*. 9 *s*. 4-$^1/_2$ *d*.

Decima vinorum:

De exitibus decime vinorum descendencium de obediencia regis Francie usque Burdegalam nichil recepit quia nulla huiusmodi vina descenderunt ibidem per tempus huius compoti ut per sacramentum suum et per testimonium dicti contrarotulatoris sicut continetur ibidem.
Summa: nichil.

Monetagium auri et argenti:

De exitibus monetagii auri et argenti non respondet quia nulla moneta fuit fabricata Burdegale seu aliquibus aliis locis de obediencia regis per tempus huius compoti ut constabularius dicit per sacramentum suum et per testimonium contrarotulatoris sicut continetur ibidem.
Summa: nichil.

Burdenagium peregrinorum:

Idem reddit compotum de 15 *li*. 3 *d*. monete currentis receptis de exitibus burdenagii peregrinorum apud pontem Sancti Johannis Bur-

---

52 MS. *Killiagio*.

degale, videlicet de quolibet peregrino unum *tur.*, per tempus huius compoti sicut continetur ibidem.

SUMMA: 15 *li.* 3 *d.*

VENDITA ET REVENDITA:

Idem reddit compotum de 177 *li.* 19 *s.* 3 *d.* receptis de vendita et revendita in villa Leybornie per tempus huius compoti sicut continetur in dictis particulis constabularii et contrarotulatoris in thesauro liberatis.

SUMMA: 177 *li.* 19 *s.* 3 *d.*

FORISFACTURE ET BONA REBELLIUM:

Idem reddit compotum de 1,527 *li.* 15 *s.* monete currentis receptis de forisfacturis et bonis rebellium in diversis locis infra ducatum predictum per tempus huius compoti sicut continetur in predictis parcellis constabularii et contrarotulatoris.

SUMMA: 1,527 *li.* 15 *s.*

FINES ET CONDEMPNACIONES ET PERQUISITA:

Idem reddit compotum de 799 *li.* dicte monete receptis de diversis finibus, redempcionibus et aliis proficuis curie Vasconie per tempus huius compoti sicut continetur in parcellis predictis.

SUMMA: 799 *li.*

RECEPTA FORENCECA:[53]

Idem reddit compotum de 527 *li.* 8 *s.* 8 *d. st.* Anglie valentibus 3,955 *li.* 15 *s.* dicte monete currentis receptis de thesaurario et camerariis ad receptam scaccarii Anglie 16 die Marcii termino Michaelis anno 47 per manus Roberti Rous,[54] militis, maioris ville Burdegale, in denariis eidem

---

53 *Forenceca* (foreign) here means those receipts that where not a part of the usual income. The same applies to expenditures. See below p. 75.

54 The office of mayor of Bordeaux was considerably changed under Edward I when he began appointing these officials himself (Lodge, *Gascony under English Rule*, p. 50). Under Edward III this became the normal procedure, with Englishmen usually receiving the office. The mayor was the main source of authority in the town and a force to reckon with. He had his own court which had jurisdiction over all the burgesses of the community. His position was very respectable and in the event of his violating a town rule, he was forced to pay four times the normal fine (*ibid.*, p. 163).

Robert Rous was appointed mayor on 8 March 1373 (C. 61/ 86, m. 7). His background is uncertain, though he appears as an agent of the king in 1371 (Rous took miners to Gloucester, then held in farm on 12 July; see *CPR [1370-74]*, p. 124). He appears as at least a partial rebuilder of

Roberto Rous liberatis per manus Guillelmi de Tyryngton'[55] et Simonis
Ayllesham super vadiis guerre et regardo 20 hominum ad arma et 15
sagittariorum moraturorum in obsequio regis in partibus Vasconie per

the walls of Bordeaux (*Cal. Pap. Reg. [1362-1404]*, p. 114). On 9 March 1373 he was granted
100 *marks* yearly at the Exchequer, though this was later changed to a grant of the same amount
from proceeds of the farm of Cambridge (*CPR [1370-74]*, pp. 263, 288). On the 14th and 16th of
March 1373 he was allowed wages for 20 men-at-arms, 3 knights and 15 archers (C. 61/ 86, mm. 5,
8). His grant of a license to transport grain from Weymouth or Plymouth is recorded for 6 December of the same year (C. 61/ 86, m.1). His replacement as mayor, John Multon, was appointed
on the 5th (and 10th) of May 1375 (C. 61/ 88, m. 6). In June 1377 he mainprized himself, along with
Guy de Brien and John de Montegut, to arrange the release of Edmund of Arundel, king's prisoner
in the Tower of London (*CPR [1377-81]*, p. 551). Next September he was envoy to Flanders to
help continue the alliance between her and England (*Foedera* 4.20). On 1 April 1383 he treated with
the king of Castile for a truce, and then the kings of Aragon and Navarre (*Foedera* 4.165-67). Part of
his account for the embassies may be found in Leon Mirot and Eugene Deprez, *Les ambassades
anglaises pendant la guerre de Cent Ans: Catalogue chronologique, 1327-1450* (Paris, 1900), no. cdxvi.

55   William de Tyrington was an important clerk of the Privy Seal who served the king in
several capacities. He was educated (probably at Oxford) before entering the royal service, and
made great use of his clerical privileges in obtaining benefices (Emden, *A Bibliographical Register of the
University of Oxford to A.D. 1500* 3.1925). He was rector of Moulton, Suffolk, by 1354, obtained a
benefice in the diocese of York the same year, and was master of St. Leonard's Hospital, Derby, by
1355 (*Cal. Pap. Reg. [1362-1404]*, p. 547; *Cal. Pap. Reg. Petitions [1342-1419]*, p. 284). He was presented to the church of Pullerbache, d. Hereford, on 23 March 1359 (*CPR [1358-61]*, p. 191). In 1358
he received the church of Shipdham, Norfolk, and was forced to establish his claim on it in a legal
suit settled in 1362 (*CPR [1358-61]*, p. 191; *Cal. Pap. Reg. Petitions [1342-1419]*, p. 378; date of vacation, November 1369, *CPR [1377-81]*, p. 362). His pluralities continued as he received four grants
in 1361: church of Barnack, Northants (*CPR [1361-64]*, p. 61); prebend of collegiate church of
Abrygwilly (*CPR [1361-64]*, p. 80); a canonry of St. Paul's, London (*CPR [1361-64]*, p. 96; *Cal. Pap.
Reg. [1362-1404]*, p. 1750); a prebendary of Sneating, held till 1394 (*CPR [1394-96]*, pp. 209, 226).
In addition to the receipt of benefices, Tyrington also was involved in the writing of the Treaty of
Bretigny — 1360 (Tout, *Chapters* 3.225-226). His work along this line continued in 1362 when he
reduced the Treaty of Castile to public form (Tout, *Chapters* 5.38 n. 1). Tyrington's profits from his
benefices were in arrears from the *curia* at Rome. He was absent for three years, which was permissible in the office of Privy Seal as long as he did not demand pay (Tout, *Chapters* 5.88; for appointment of attorneys in his absence see *CPR [1361-64]*, p. 303). In 1366 he was granted power of
attorney to go abroad with the earl of Hereford to treat with Galeazzo, lord of Milan, concerning
the possibility of marriage between Galeazzo's daughter, Violanta, and Lionel, duke of Clarence
(*CPR [1364-67]*, p. 304); letters of protection to travel were granted on 4 June 1371, but were addressed to William Tyrington, esquire (*CPR [1370-74]*, p. 93). On 20 June 1367 he was appointed
warden of the king's free Chapel in Shrewsbury Castle (*CPR [1364-67]*, p. 419). He requested the
pardon of a murderer in 1369 (*CPR [1370-74]*, p. 319). A sour note to his holdings came in 1371
when he was charged at the *curia* with having obtained the canonry and prebend of Lincoln (granted 3 December 1370, *CPR [1370-74]*, p. 26) by false suggestion (charged on 21 February 1371,
Cal. Pap. Reg. [1362-1404], p. 92). He appears to have managed the maintenance of the office,
though, as he exchanged it in September 1394 (*CPR [1389-92]*, p. 104). It must be remembered
that all during this period, except in cases of absence, Tyrington was a clerk of the Privy Seal.
Perhaps his relationship to this office stems from his kinship to John Welwick, B.C.L., King's Notary,
a senior and most distinguished clerk of the Privy Seal (Tout, *Chapters* 5.37). Tyrington held office
from 17 November 1350 until 3 December 1370, and his accounts are extant: Particulars of

dimidium annum sicut continetur in pelle memorandorum[56] ad eandem receptam de eisdem termino et anno ac eciam in parcellis predictis. Et de 260 *li.* 6 *s.* 1 *d. st.* Anglie valentibus 1,952 *li.* 5 *s.* 7-¹/₂ *d.* dicte monete currentis receptis de eisdem thesaurario et camerariis ad receptam predictam 11 die Aprilis dicto termino Sancti Michaelis anno 47 per manus proprias ipsius constabularii super vadiis suis guerre et regardo 9 hominum ad arma et 10 sagittariorum secum morancium in obsequio regis in partibus Vasconie per unum dimidium annum sicut continetur in pelle memorandorum ad eandem receptam de eisdem termino et anno et eciam in particulis predictis. Et de 1,392 *li.* 6 *s. st.* Anglie valentibus 10,442 *li.* 5 *s.* dicte monete currentis receptis de eisdem thesaurario et camerariis 27 die Maii termino Pasche dicto anno 47 per manus proprias ipsius constabularii super vadiis guerre unius baneretti ad 6 *s.*, 9 militum quilibet ad 3 *s.*, et 60 sagittariorum quilibet ad 9 *d.* per diem moraturorum in obsequio regis in partibus Vasconie per dimidium annum sicut continetur in pelle memorandorum ad eandem receptam de eisdem termino et anno et eciam in particulis predictis. Et de 50 *li. st.* Anglie valentibus 375 *li.* dicte monete currentis receptis de eisdem thesaurario et camerariis dicto termino Pasche eodem die et[57] anno 47 per manus Guillelmi Forest'[58] super regardo dicti constabularii speciali prefecturi[59] in obsequio regis ad partes Vasconie sicut continetur in pelle memorandorum ad eandem receptam de eisdem termino et anno ac eciam in particulis predictis. Et de 545 *li.* dicte monete currentis receptis de domino Johanne de Ludham, nuper thesaurario Aquitanie, predecessore dicti constabularii, ut in diversis particulis eidem Johanni debitis de remanenciis dicti officii per dictum constabularium levatis per indenturam inde factam sicut continetur ibidem.

SUMMA: 17,270 *li.* 5 *s.* 7-¹/₂ *d.*

Tyrington, E. 101/ 509/ 1 for 34-42 Edward III and E. 101/ 509/ 15 for 43-44 Edward III (cited in P.R.O. List XXXV, p. 309; Tout, *Chapters* 5.87, n. 3). He received custody of the king's jail in York Castle for life in a grant dated 5 October 1377, but it was cancelled with his assent in 1386 (*CPR [1377-81]*, p. 27). He is said to have made a grant to New College, Oxford, before his death (Emden, *Register* 3.1925).

56 *Pelle memorandorum* is a reference to the Issue Rolls which record issue of crown monies. These rolls are classified at the P.R.O. as E. 403 and are continuous from 25 Henry III to 19 Edward IV. See *Issues of the Exchequer; Being a Collection of Payments Made out of His Majesty's Revenue, from King Heznry III to King Henry VI Inclusive*, ed. F. Devon (London, 1837), and *Issue Roll of Thomas de Brantyngham (44 Edward III, 1370)*, ed. F. Devon (London, 1835).

57 A certain William Forester, chaplain, received letters of protection to sail in the company of Wykford in the king's service, dated 11 May 1373. He could be the deliverer of this sum (C. 61/ 86, m. 3).

58 MS. *eodem die et*, interlinear.

59 MS. *profecturi*.

Onerata super compotum:

Et oneratur de 5,174 *li*. 13 *s*. 4 *d*. monete currentis in precio 689 *li*. 19 *s*. 1 *d*. qua *st*. Anglie receptis de Roberto Rous, milite, nuper maiore civitatis Burdegale, de mutuo super solucionem vadiorum et regardorum eiusdem Roberti et retinencie sue et unde habet billam sub sigillo dicti constabularii sigillatam sicut continetur ibidem.
Summa: 5, 174 *li*. 13 *s*. 4 *d*.

Summa receptarum: 42,245 *li*. 17 *s*. 7-$^1/_2$ *d*. dicte monete currentis.

Expense capelle castri burdegale:

Idem computat in torcheis cereis, minutis candelis et aliis diversis necessariis emptis pro divino servicio in capella predicta castri regis Burdegale una cum vadiis et robis Johannis de Plompton', capellani in eadem capella divina celebrantis, a predicto 20 die Augusti anno domini 1373 et regni dicti regis Edwardi 47 usque predictam 23 diem Julii dicto anno 49, 114 *li*. 16 *d*. dicte monete currentis unde 7-$^1/_2$ *d*. valent *st*. Anglie, dicto capellano capiente pro vadiis suis 3 *d*. *st*. Anglie, 22-$^1/_2$ *d*. dicte monete currentis, per diem et pro roba sua 20 *s*. *st*. Anglie valentes 7 *li*. 10 *s*. dicte monete currentis per litteras Thome de Felton', senescalli Aquitanie, de waranto pro predictis vadiis et roba solvendis et per breve dicti regis Edwardi de magno sigillo thesaurario et baronibus de scaccario directum dat' 16 die Julii anno 50 quod est inter communia de termino Sancti Michaelis anno 51, in quo brevi inter cetera continetur quod quia predictus magister Robertus de Wykford, nuper constabularius regis Burdegale, diversas soluciones denariorum fecit diversis personis de mandato Johannis regis Castelle et Legionis, ducis Lancastrie, ac dicti Thome de Felton', senescalli Vasconie, ac de mandato domini de La Sparre et Roberti Rous, nuper maioris Burdegale, rex mandavit eisdem thesaurario et baronibus quod omnes soluciones denariorum per mandata predicta rationabiliter factas per sacramentum ipsius magistri Roberti ac per testimonium predicti contrarotulatoris in compoto[60] ipsius magistri Roberti allocent et per testimonium contrarotulatoris predicti sicut continetur in predictis particulis ipsorum constabularii et contrarotulatoris et prout consimiles expense, vadia et roba allocantur in compoto magistri Johannis de Stretle, nuper constabularii Burdegale, rotulo 36 rotulo compotorum.
Summa : 114 *li*. 16 *d*.

---

60 MS. *in compoto*, repeated.

FEODA, VADIA ET ROBE MINISTRORUM:

Et in vadiis ipsius magistri Roberti, constabularii pro dicto officio suo, capientis 4 *s. st.* Anglie valentes 30 *s.* dicte monete currentis, per diem per dictum tempus huius compoti 1,053 *li.* dicte monete currentis per breve ipsius regis Edwardi patens indentatum sub privato sigillo suo dat' 8 die Marcii dicto anno 47 super hunc compotum liberatum, in quo continetur quod idem magister Robertus percipiet in officio suo predicto talia vadia per diem et tantum pro robis suis et clericorum suorum prout alii clerici constabularii percipere solebant in officio predicto sicut continetur in particulis predictis et prout huiusmodi vadia allocantur magistro Johanni Stretle, nuper constabulario, in dicto compoto suo, dicto rotulo 36 rotulo compotorum, et eidem pro robis suis per idem tempus, percipienti 14 *li. st.* Anglie pro huiusmodi robis suis per annum, 201 *li.* 19 *s.* dicte monete currentis per idem breve sicut continetur ibidem et prout huiusmodi robis allocantur eidem magistro Johanni Stretle dicto rotulo 36 rotulo compotorum. Et magistro Guillelmo de Holcombe, contrarotulatori regis in castro suo Burdegale, percipienti pro vadiis suis 2 *s. st.* Anglie, valentes 15 *s.* dicte monete currentis per diem, et pro robis suis et clericorum suorum 8 *li. st.*, valentes 60 *li.* dicte monete currentis per annum, in persolucionem dictorum vadiorum et robarum per dictum tempus huius compoti 641 *li.* 17 *s.* 10 *d.* dicte monete currentis per copiam brevis dicti regis Edwardi sub sigillis autenticis quibus utitur in Burdegala ad contractus super hunc compotum liberatam, dat' eiusdem brevis 8 die Marcii dicto anno 47, in quo continetur quod cum idem dominus rex concesserit dicto magistro Guillelmo officium contrarotulatoris castri sui Burdegale habendum[61] quamdiu regi placuerit percipiendo in officio illo prout alii hactenus dictum officium habentes in eodem percipere consueverunt, mandavit constabulario suo ibidem qui pro tempore fuerit quod eidem Guillelmo talia feoda sive vadia qualia alii dictum officium hactenus habentes in eodem percipere consueverunt de exitibus et proficuis castri predicti de tempore in tempus quamdiu steterit in officio predicto solvat eidem, recipiens litteras suas acquietancie in hac parte, et per 2 litteras acquietancie ipsius magistri Guillelmi super hunc compotum liberatas et per predictum breve regis Ricardi de privato sigillo thesaurario et baronibus directum dat' 15 die Junii anno tercio et superius in onere in parcella exitus ballivarum et prepositurarum plenius annotatum, pro huiusmodi copiis sub sigillo autentico exhibitis,

---

61 MS. *habendum*, interlinear, with caret.

allocando sicut continetur in particulis predictis et prout huiusmodi vadia et robe allocantur in dicto compoto magistri Johannis Stretle dicto rotulo 36 rotulo compotorum. Et magistro Johanni de Ecclesia,[62] baculario in legibus, judici appelacionum tam civilium quam criminalium et aliarum causarum quarumque ad curiam Vasconie interpositarum auditori, percipienti pro feodis et vadiis suis racione officiorum suorum 250 *li.* dicte monete currentis per annum, in persolucionem dictorum feodorum et vadiorum suorum a predicto 20 die Marcii dicto anno 47 per quod rex mandavit constabulario suo[63] Burdegale quod dicto magistro Johanni feodum seu vadium consueta pro tempore[64] quo steterit in officio predicto solvat et per litteras acquietancie[65] ipsius magistri Johannis super hunc compotum liberatas sicut continetur in particulis predictis et per dictum breve pro huiusmodi copiis allocandis et prout huiusmodi vadia allocantur consimili judici in dicto compoto magistri Johannis Stretle dicto rotulo 36 rotulo compotorum. Et magistro Bernardo Mauryn, consimili judici ibidem post dictum magistrum Johannem de Ecclesia, pro consimilibus feodis et vadiis suis racione officiorum suorum predictorum a predicto 20 die Augusti anno 48 usque predictum 23 diem Julii tunc proximo sequentem 230 *li.* 3 *s.* 4 *d.* dicte monete currentis per litteras dicti Thome de Felton' senescalli de mandato prefato constabulario directas et per dictum breve regis Edwardi de magno sigillo datum 16 die Julii 50 superius in parcella de expensis capelle annotatum de allocando mandata ipsius senescalli[66] sicut continetur in particulis predictis. Et magistro Elie de Brolio, procuratori et consiliario domini regis in Burdegalesia, percipienti pro feodis et vadiis suis 100 *li.* monete currentis per annum; magistro Reymundo Guillelmi de Podio, baculario in decretis uni judici curie superioritatis Aquitanie ac consiliario domini regis; et magistro Reginaldo Desclaus,[67] licenciato in legibus uni judicum dicte curie

---

62   Jean d'Eglise (Ecclesia, de la Glyse) was appointed to the Court of Gascony on 8 March 1373 by letter patent followed by a note to the constable of Bordeaux to pay him his wage (C. 61/ 86, m. 8). He is described as *judex majoris civitatis nostrae Burdegalensis*, and empowered to treat with Peter, king of Aragon, on 15 March (*Foedera* 3.ii, 972-73). His family was granted a safe conduct, presumably to travel, on 2 April following (C. 61/ 86, m. 5). The only other reference I have found concerning him is the record of his payment of a fine on 20 May 1376 (*CPR [1374-77]*, p. 277).

63   MS. *suo*, interlinear.

64   MS. *pro tempore*, repeated (underlined).

65   MS. *acquitancie.*

66   *Respice in dorsa rotulo* occurs 2 cm. below the main text, centered and at the foot of the pell. The text following is from the dorsal side.

67   There is a reference to a Reginald de Claus, canon of Bordeaux, requested to hear appeals in Gascony, probably as a member of the Court of Sovereignty (C. 61/ 86, m. 3; dated 12 April 1373).

superioritatis Aquitanie ac consilliario dicti domini regis; utroque
eorum percipiente pro feodis et vadiis suis racione officiorum suorum
300 g.[68] *aur.* per annum valentes 375 *li.* dicte monete currentis, in persolucionem dictorum feodorum et vadiorum per totum tempus huius
compoti 1,634 *li.* 12 *s.* 9 *d.* dicte monete currentis per tres litteras ipsius
Thome de Felton' senescalli de mandato dicto constabulario pro dictis
feodis et vadiis solvendis directas et per 6 litteras de recepcione ipsorum
magistrorum Elie, Reymundi et Reginaldi et per dictum breve regis Edwardi de allocando mandata ipsius senescalli sicut continetur in particulis predictis.
SUMMA: 4,011 *li.* 12 *s.* 9 *d.*

EXPENSE NECESSARIE:

Et in magnis et diversis papiris ligatis officia dictorum constabularii
et contrarotulatoris in scaccario castri Burdegale et alibi in domino
Aquitanie tangentibus ac eciam in papiris pro litteris ac aliis memorandis dictum scaccarium et negocia regia tangentibus scribendis et
memorari faciendis et in pergameno, incausto, cera et aliis minutis in
dicto castro necessariis emptis per diversas vices infra tempus huius
compoti, 50 *li.* dicte monete currentis per dictum breve regis Ricardi
thesaurario et baronibus de scaccario suo Anglie directum dat' 15 Junii
dicto anno tercio, in quo inter cetera continetur quod allocari faciant
eidem constabulario per sacramentum suum et per testimonium dicti
contrarotulatoris expensas appositas in empcionibus papiri legati pro
custumariis et alterius papiri et pergameni pro indenturis et acquietan-
ciis et aliis memorandis tangentibus tam officium constabularii quam
contrarotulatoris ibidem usque ad summam 10 marcas *st.* Anglie et per
sacramentum ipsius constabularii et per testimonium dicti contrarotulatoris sicut continetur in particulis predictis. Et solucionem
magistro Gyles Aurifabro pro argento et factura unius sigilli magni[69]

---

68 MS. *gyan'*.

69 The seal of the Court of Gascony was created primarily for judicial reasons and first appears
in an order given 26 October 1255, when a three man tribunal was established. The custody of the
seal was entrusted to the constable of Bordeaux, one of the three men sent to relieve the seneschal
of his growing problems in litigation. It seems that the seal was, by name, created to ratify acts of
the *curia Vasconie*, but it was soon found to be convenient for other purposes. It was used by the
seneschal for sealing administrative documents of all varieties. By 1278 it became the official seal of
the seneschal, and replaced the seneschal's sealing of papers by personal seal. In the Gascon Ordinance of 1289 the same seal is referred to as the *sigillum ducatus*, which it continued to be called as
late as the fourteenth century. By this ordinance Edward also fixed the Court at Bordeaux, and it
no longer followed the seneschal about. The keeper of the seal was originally a judge, as mentioned

ordinati pro curia superioritatis Aquitanie[70] infra tempus huius compoti, 29 *li.* 6 *s.* monete currentis sicut continetur in particulis predictis,
de quo quidem sigillo dictus constabularius respondet inferius. Et in
uno cipho argento cum coopertorio deaurato empto et presentato
domino Johanni Colomb, militi, pro bono gestu suo ad sustentandum
jura et comoda domini regis in villa Burdegale, 32 *li.* 12 *s.* 6 *d.* monete
currentis per litteras dicti Thome de Felton' senescalli de mandato dicto
constabulario inde directas et per dictum breve regis Edwardi de
magno sigillo de allocando mandata ipsius senescalli sicut continetur in
particulis predictis. Et solucionem magistro Marco Barendario Beri et
Johanni Tortoza cum quattuor valettorum suis venientibus de Aragon
ordinatis et assignatis per dictum constabularium[71] et maiorem Burdegale et per alium consillium regem morari et esse Burdegale ad
faciendum unum artificium vocatum canon' ad sagittandum et jac-
tandum lapides et querellos pro inimicis gravandis tam in vadiis et expensis suis existentibus ibidem per 38 dies quam in plumbo, ferro,

above, but later the custody went to a *clericus* or *scriptor curie Vasconie.* This man was also head of the
seneschal's secretariat and keeper of the rolls of his sénéschausée. At this point the court and the infant chancery were operating under the same seal, but with the increasing amounts of litigation
and administrative work in their respective areas, the two groups split. The *scriptor* (or registrar) lost
the seal to the seneschal permanently by 1327. With this change it is interesting to note that the seal
was now referred to as the *sigillum officii senescallie Aquitanie* by at least 1390. In changing hands it has
also changed names. Since the seal remained with the seneschal it could not ratify any of the judicial pronouncements of the Court, and thus lost some of its purely legal function. This slack was
soon taken up by the seal of the Judge of Gascony. Though the seal's limits were narrowed by acts
of 1320, its physical dimensions continued to grow. The one-sided oval seal bearing the three
leopards of England measured 30 mm. in 1313, 34 mm. in 1328, 54 mm. in 1377 and 73 mm. in
1390. The enlargement of 1377 came at the instigation of Thomas Felton as the old seal made of
lead was so worn that he ordered a new silver seal to replace it (Tout, *Chapters* 5.304-305, n. 6,
citing E. 101/ 180/ 1, m. 23). The increase of the seal in size should also be noted as a possible indication of increased activity and authority. Earlier acts by the seneschal were often sent to the palace
at Westminster to be resealed in a perhaps more authentic and meaningful way. After all, the Black
Prince's seal, measuring 88 mm., made the Court's seal look diminutive. It is instructive to note that
the seal was used very little during the tenure of the Black Prince (1362-1372), but flourished when
there was no lieutenant to override the seneschal. Thus the seal is useful, to some degree, as a
barometer of administrative governance.

　　This seal was usually impressed upon red wax and applied with a tongue or a tag to the document, though green wax and a silk cord might be utilized for special occasions. There appear to be
no survivors of the seal for the period of the Principality, though copies from earlier and later
periods exist. Its prominence is attested by the references to it as the royal or great seal of Gascony.
It was referred to by the chancery of Edward III as *le sceau dont se servait le roi dans son duchie.* For
further details see Dr. Sharp in Tout, *Chapters* 5.302-306 and notes; Chaplais, "Chancery of
Guyenne"; Chaplais, "Le sceau de la cour de Gascogne ou sceau de l'office de Seneschal de
Guyenne," *Annales du Midi* 67 (January, 1955) 19-29.

　　70　MS. *Aquitannie.*
　　71　MS. *constabularium,* repeated.

ligno, focali, pulueribus et aliis diversis necessariis emptis ad faciendum canon' infra tempus huius compoti, 141 *li.* 11 *s.* 3 *d.* monete currentis per litteras dicti Thome de Felton' senescalli de mandato dicto constabulario inde directas et per dictum breve regis Edwardi de allocando mandata ipsius senescalli sicut continetur in particulis predictis. Et in expensis et costagiis magistri Reymundi Guillelmi de Podio, unius judicum curie superioritatis Aquitanie,[72] et duorum sociorum suorum de consilio regis existente Burdegale tam ipsorum et gencium suarum quam plurimorum et diversorum marinariorum et hominum armatorum pro sua conductione secum existencium, assignatorum et ordinatorum per totum consilium regis Burdegale ad visitandum, providendum et roborandum castra et villas de Ryons, Cadelac,[73] Sancto Makario[74] et Langon ac alia loca existencia super aquam Gerundie, ita quod fierent bene ordinata parata ad resistendum contra adventum ducum Dangeo et Burbon; Bertrandi de Claykyn, constabularii Francie;[75] domini de la Breto et aliorum magnatum dominorum de regno

72   MS. *Aquitannie.*

73   Cadelac, dép. Gironde, arr. Libourne, cant. Fronsac.

74   MS. *Sancti Makarii.*

75   Bertrand Du Guesclin (Claylin, Clayquin — c. 1320-1380), was constable of France and probably the ablest French warrior of his time. Only a few points relative to this account will be mentioned here. In the war between Charles of Blois and John de Montfort for the duchy of Brittany, he headed a band of adventurers that sided with Blois. He fought brilliantly, but left the field for a number of years. He fought against the duke of Lancaster in 1356 and served the servant of the king of France. His greatest exploit to date was the capture of Jean de Grailly, the famous Captal de Buch, at the battle of Cocheral, on 16 May 1364. This encounter reduced the king of Navarre to a mere conspirator for some time and no longer a major threat to the French throne. For his efforts he was made count of Longueville and lieutenant of Normandy. Soon afterward he was taken prisoner at the battle of Auray by Sir John Chandos. His ransom brought 100,000 crowns. On release he partially resolved the problem of the *routiers* or *compagnies* that were ravaging France. He led them into Spain where he supported Henry of Trastamara and exiled Pedro the Cruel. By 1366 he was constable of Castile and count of Trastamara. This situation did not endure long though, as the Black Prince supported the exiled Pedro and met Trastamara's forces at Nájera, a total English victory. Du Guesclin was captured, though soon released on receipt of another heavy ransom. He fought again for Trastamara and won the battle of Montiel in 1369, being rewarded with the title of duke of Molina. The next year he was back in the service of the king of France, who appointed him constable. He faced the fresh English thrust led by Robert Knowles, who had marched on Paris itself. Du Guesclin made him pay heavily in his forced retreat to Brittany with the use of rear-guard actions. While Gaunt was visiting his sick brother, the Black Prince, in Bordeaux, a new French offensive was launched with Du Guesclin at the head. All of the Agenais, including Agen and Moissac, and most of Limousin submitted. The Garonne was crossed and Bazas fell also. The English response was the Black Prince's sack of Limoges, his most infamous act. In 1372 Du Guesclin again led and helped direct the taking of Poitou, Saintonge and Angoumois (though the English were not completely ousted until 1375). When Gaunt went on his famous chévauchée from August to December 1373, marching from Calais to Bordeaux, Du Guesclin helped in the harrying of his flanks which nearly reduced his numbers by half (*Froissart*, [ed. Lettenhove], 8.307-21, 17.546-50 and

Francie de die in diem descendencium, existencium in illa visitacione, eundo, morando et redeundo per 10 dies infra tempus huius compoti, 60 *li*. monete currentis per litteras ipsius Thome de Felton' senescalli de mandato dicto constabulario inde directas et per litteras acquietancie ipsius Guillelmi et per predictum breve regis Edwardi de allocando mandata ipsius senescalli sicut continetur in particulis predictis. Et in expensis unius spynacus[76] et marinariorum in ea existencium serviencium constabularium Burdegale ad portandum se, homines suos et harnacia sua de Burdegale usque villam de Cadelac[77] ad loquendum ibidem cum domino senescallo Aquitanie[78] de certis et onerandis negociis dominum regem et suam patriam Aquitanie tangentibus, existencium in illo viagio per quattuor dies infra tempus huius compoti, 11 *li*. 5 *s*. dicte monete currentis per litteras ipsius senescalli dicto constabulario inde directas dat' 8 die Decembris anno 47 super hunc compotum liberatas, per quas mandavit eidem quod solvat dictis marinariis pro dicto cariagio faciendo et de huiusmodi solucionibus eis factis per testimonium contrarotulatoris ibidem allocacionem percipiet in compoto suo et per testimonium predicti contrarotulatoris ac eciam per dictum breve regis de allocando mandata ipsius senescalli sicut continetur in predictis particulis. Et solucionem Gayhardo de Miraville, burgensi Burdegale, pro locacione trium equorum quolibet (*sic*) ad 8 *s*. monete currentis per diem per tres dies locatorum et ordinatorum per consilium regium Burdegale ad serviendum pro tribus nunciis venientibus de rege Francie pro treuga habenda cum dicto domino rege Castelle et Legionis et locum tenente Aquitanie tunc existente apud Aquensem per tempus huius compoti, 72 *s*. dicte monete currentis et Gailhardo Roberto servienti regio deputato et ordinato per consilium regis ad ducendum dictos nuncios de Burdegala usque Aquensem ad

for details of the march, 17.280-96). For an analysis of the army's size, see James W. Sherborne, "Indentured Retinues and English Expeditions to France, 1369-1380," *EHR* 79 (1964) 718-46. In 1375 the peace negotiations began at Bruges and military actions were curtailed. Du Guesclin was kept in relative inactivity by these negotiations and was only able to return to the game of war in 1377 with the expiration of the truce. Here he encountered a new foe in John Neville, who proved to be a better match than Gaunt or his lieutenants had been and stifled the French conquests. Unable to mount a major offensive, Du Guesclin contented himself with sweeping Auvergne and chasing *routiers*, who were plentiful in the area. He died besieging the fortress of Châteauneuf-de-Randon on 13 July 1380. His life has been heralded by the *Chronique de Bertrand Du Guesclin par Cuvelier*, ed. E. Charrière (Paris, 1839). For fuller details see Delachenal, *Histoire de Charles V*, especially vol. 4.

76   A spinace, small ship.
77   MS. *Cadelalac*.
78   MS. *Acquitannie*.

dictum dominum locum tenentem existentem ibidem pro vadiis et expensis suis ad 10 *s.* monete currentis per diem per quattuor dies infra tempus huius compoti, 40 *s.* dicte monete currentis per litteras ipsius senescalli de mandato dicto constabulario inde directas et per dictum breve regis de allocando mandata ipsius senescalli sicut continetur in particulis predictis. Et solucionem magistro Johanni Crispyn,[79] clerico, scriptori et ordinatori litterarum et aliorum memorandorum per consilium regis existente Burdegale deputato, percipienti pro vadiis suis racione laboris sui 15 *li.* dicte monete currentis pro quarterio anni, videlicet pro tribus quarteriis infra tempus huius compoti, 45 *li.* monete predicte per litteras ipsius senescalli de warranto dicto constabulario inde directas et per dictum breve regis de allocando mandata ipsius senescalli et per litteras ipsius Johannis de recepcione sicut continetur in particulis predictis. Et solucionem magistro Elie Lamberti, notorio, pro scriptura et extractis cuiusdam processus facti coram constabulario et marescallo excercitus domini Johannis, regis Castelle et Legionis, ducis Lancastrie, inter dictum Henricum del Hay,[80] militem, et Yvonem Beaustayng, scutiferum Britannie, 100 *s.* dicte monete currentis per litteras Florimondi, domini de Le Sparre et Roberti Rous, maioris Burdegale, loca tenencium regis in ducatu predicto de mandato dicto[81] constabulario inde directas et per litteras recognicionis ipsius magistri Elie super hunc compotum liberatas et per predictum breve regis de allocando mandata ipsorum domini de Lesparre et Roberti sicut continetur in particulis predictis. Et in expensis et custagiis Reymundi Guillelmi de Podio, unius judicum curie superioritatis Aquitanie ac consiliarii domini regis et duorum sociorum suorum de consilio regis una cum gentibus suis assignatorum et ordinatorum per totum consilium regis existentem Burdegale ad eundum in comitiva domini de Le Sparre[82] versus villas de Royan, Sancti Makarii et Langen et alia loca super aquam Gerundie ad tractandum ibidem de diversis negociis statum patrie Aquitanie tangentibus, eundo, morando et redeundo infra tempus huius compoti, 20 *li.* dicte monete currentis per litteras dicti Thome de Felton' senescalli de mandato dicto constabulario inde direc-

---

79 The only reference I found concerning him is a letter presenting him to the chantry of the Holy Trinity, Christ Church, Oxford, dated 10 November 1376 (*CPR [1374-77]*, p. 373).

80 Henry del Hay, knight, appears in the Patent Rolls (28 October 1374) as the subject of a legal hearing. He had been captured by a squire of Brittany, who claimed he was being illegally kept from him. It is not stated whether Henry was returned to the squire or not (*CPR [1374-77]*, pp. 57-58).

81 MS. *dicti.*

82 MS. *delsparre.*

tas et per testimonium predicti contrarotulatoris et per dictum breve regis de allocando mandata ipsius senescalli sicut continetur in predictis rotulis de particulis. Et in expensis et custagiis domini officialis Burdegale et locum tenentis domini senescalli Aquitanie ordinatorum et rogatorum per totum consilium regis existentem Burdegale eundo versus villam de Lasparr' ad loquendum et tractandum ibidem cum domino de Lesparre de et super deliberacione domini Johannis Columb', capti et arestati ex certis causis[83] per predictum dominum de Lesparr', eundo, morando et redeundo per tempus huius compoti, 20 *li.* dicte monete currentis per supradictum breve regis Ricardi de privato sigillo suo thesaurario et baronibus suis de scaccario directum dat' 15 die Junii anno tercio, in quo inter <cetera> continetur quod allocent dicto constabulario per testimonium contrarotulatoris ibidem soluciones per ipsum factas <de> dictis duobus nunciis missis versus dictum dominum de Lasparre ad tractandum cum eo super deliberacione ipsius domini Johannis et litteras ipsius senescalli super hunc compotum exhibitas ad solvendas 20 *li.* predictas per testimonium predicti contrarotulatoris sicut continetur in particulis predictis.
Summa: 420 *li.* 6 *s.* 9 *d.*

Opera et reparaciones castrorum:

Idem computat in maeremio, tegulis, plumbo, ferro, clavibus, bordis, lathis[84] et aliis necessariis emptis et expenditis in operacionibus regis infra dictum castrum suum Burdegale et super domos extra dictum castrum ad idem castrum pertinentes una cum stipendiis carpentariorum, cementariorum, coopertorum, et aliorum operariorum conductorum reperancium defectus diversorum domorum, murorum et edificiorum infra dictum castrum et domorum extra dictum castrum ad idem castrum pertinencium per diversas vices infra tempus predictum, 272 *li.* 5 *s.* 9 *d.* dicte monete currentis per litteras dicti senescalli de warranto dicto constabulario inde directas et per predictum breve regis de allocando mandata ipsius senescalli sicut continetur in particulis ipsorum constabularii et contrarotulatoris supra dictis.
Summa: 272 *li.* 5 *s.* 9 *d.*

83 See above, Ludham's account, Part I, n. 45 for information concerning his treason.
84 MS. *lathes.*

EXPENSE NUNCIORUM ET CURSORUM:

Idem computat solucionem Guillelmo Motheley, clerico, Henrico Sturmyn, clerico, Johanni Esmere et aliis diversis nunciis et cursoribus tam equitibus quam peditibus pro expensis suis per Johannem regem Castelle et Legionis, ducem Lancastrie, locum tenentem Aquitanie, senescallum Aquitanie, constabularium, dominum de Lasparre, maiorem Burdegale, loca tenentes ibidem missis ad diversas partes ducatus predicti et extra dictum ducatum ad regem et reginam de Arragon et alios pro diversis negociis regis expediendis per diversas vices infra tempus huius compoti, 489 *li.* 18 *s.* dicte monete currentis per quattuor litteras ipsius senescalli de mandato pro dictis expensis solvendis et per predictum breve regis de huiusmodi mandati allocanda et per tres litteras de recepcione predictorum Guillelmi, Henrici et Johannis sicut continetur in predictis particulis.
SUMMA: 489 *li.* 18 *s.*

MUNICIONES CASTRORUM ET VILLARUM CAUSA GUERRE:

Idem computat liberacionem juratis, bonis hominibus et habitatoribus ville de Montesecuro pro diversis victualibus per eosdem emptis, et receptis pro diversis hominibus armatis et sagittariis assignatis et ordinatis per senescallum Aquitanie et consilium regis Burdegale ad custodiendum predictam villam contra inimicos regis et eorum potenciam existentes prope illam circumquaque, 113 *li.* 2 *s.* 6 *d.* dicte monete currentis. Domino Bertrando Frank, militi, castellano dicti castri Regule, super garnistura victualium dicti ut in precio 15 quarterii pri,[85] precii quarterii 100 *s.* monete currentis, 75 *li.* dicte monete currentis, eidem Bertrando Frank, militi, castellano dicti castri Regule, pro garnistura dicti castri contra adventum ducum Dangeo et Burbon, Bertrandi Claykyn, constabularii Francie, domini de la Breto, et aliorum dominorum de regno Francie cum magno excercitu descendencium versus villam Regule in precio diversorum victualium 491 *li.* 11 *s.* monete currentis.[86] Guillelmo Wayte, constabulario de Podio Guillelmo, super garnistura dicti loci, 30 *s.* monete currentis et Guillelmo

---

85 I am unable to identify this produce.
86 La Réole was the object of a concerted attack by Anjou and Du Guesclin in August 1374. It was located about 28 miles south-west of Bordeaux on the right bank of the Gironde. The town yielded on first request, but the castle held out. It was agreed that it should surrender if no aid came before 8 September. The day came and as no help had arrived, the agreement was kept. While Anjou continued ravaging the country, Du Guesclin remained at La Réole and maintained the castle (Delachenal, *Histoire de Charles V* 4.512-15 and notes).

More, custodi porte de La Vent de Montesecuro, in precio duorum cordarum pro bridis et duas libratas de filo pro arbalistis pro defensione et
tuicione dicte porte, 8 *li.* 12 *s.* dicte monete currentis per 5 litteras ipsius
senescalli de warranto dicto constabulario directas pro dictis summis
eisdem seperaliter liberandis et predictum breve regis de dictis warran-
tis allocandis et per 5 litteras dictorum juratorum, Bertrandi, Guillelmi
Wayte et Guillelmi More recepcionem dictarum summarum testifican-
tes sicut continetur in particulis predictis. Et de quibus summis predicti
jurati et boni homines ville de[87] Montesecuro, Bertrandus, Guillelmus
Wayte et Guillelmo More seperaliter sunt responsuri. Et respondent infra. Et liberacionem dicto Bertrando Franc' super garnistura dicti castri
Regule in precio diversorum victualium, 331 *li.* 12 *s.* dicte monete
currentis; Johanni Russell, castellano castri Sancti Macharii, in precio
diversorum victualium pro garnistura dicti castri, 249 *li.* dicte monete
currentis per 3 litteras dominorum Florimundi, domini de la Sparre et
Roberti Rous, loca tenencium regis ibidem de warranto dicto constabulario directas pro predictis summis eis liberandis et per dictum
breve regis de dicto warranto allocando et per 3 litteras ipsorum Bertrandi et Johannis Russell de recepcione sicut continetur in particulis
predictis. Et de quibus summis predicti Bertrandus et Johannes
seperaliter sunt responsuri. Et respondent infra. Et liberacionem juratis
et bonis hominibus ville Sancti Macharii tam pro garnistura et
provisione dicte ville quam ad solvendum vadia hominum armatorum
et sagittariorum ibidem existencium pro tuicione et defencione dicte
ville ad resistendum[88] contra adventum ducum de Angeo et Burbon,
Bertrandi de Claikyn, domini del Brete et aliorum dominorum de Francia existencium cum magno excercitu in obsidione castri et ville Regule,
895 *li.* dicte monete currentis; Johanni Russell castellano Sancti Macarii
pro garnistura et provisione victualium dicti castri Sancti Macarii ad
sustendendum gentes armatorum et sagittariorum ibidem ad resistendum adventum dictorum dominorum de Francia existencium cum
magno excercitu apud Regulam ut in precio diversorum victualium 263
li. 10 *s.* predicte monete currentis; domino Reymundo Isarne, abbati de
Cystres, pro garnistura et victualibus dicte abbatie ut in bladis et aliis
necessariis, 154 *li.* dicte monete currentis; et domino Arnaldo Rampnol
militi, comendatori hospitalis Sancti Johannis de Salabrunean,[89] pro
garnistura et victualibus dicti loci de Salabruenean ad sustendendum

---

87   MS. *de*, interlinear, with caret.
88   MS. *resitendum*.
89   Salabrunean, located in Entre-Deux-Mers.

gentes ibidem pro tuicione et defensione dicti loci, 168 *li.* monete currentis per quattuor litteras predicti domini Thome de Felton' senescalli de warranto dicto constabulario directas pro dictis summis eisdem seperaliter liberandis causis supradictis et per dictum breve regis pro dictis mandatis senescalli allocandis et per quattuor litteras ipsorum juratorum et aliorum de recepcione sicut continetur in particulis predictis. Et de quibus summis predicti jurati et boni homines ville Sancti Macharii, Johannes Russell et alii seperaliter sunt responsuri. Et respondent infra.

SUMMA: 2,596 *li.* 17 *s.* 6 *d.*

VADIA GUERRE:

Idem computat solucionem domino Bertrando de Pomeriis, militi, capitaneo ville Makarii, pro vadiis suis ad 20 *s.* et trium scutiferorum quolibet ad 10 *s.* monete currentis per diem[90] existentibus super custodia et defensione dicte ville Sancti Makarii a predicto 20 die Augusti dicto anno 47 usque 22 diem Julii anno 49, ultimo die computato, scilicet per unum annum 337 dies, per tempus huius compoti in persolucionem dictorum vadiorum per idem tempus, 1,755 *li.* dicte monete currentis per litteras dicti senescalli de warranto eidem constabulario inde directas pro dictis vadiis solvendis et per dictum breve regis pro mandata (*sic*) ipsius senescalli allocanda (*sic*) et per duas litteras predicti Bertrandi de recepcione sicut continetur in particulis predictis. Et solucionem Willelmo More et Johanni Leg, scutiferis, quolibet ad 8 *s.*, et octo sagittariorum, quolibet ad 4 *s.* monete currentis per diem, existencium in custodia et tuicione porte[91] de La Vent de Montesecuro a festo Sancti Michaelis dicto anno domini 1373, videlicet dicto anno 47, usque dictum 22 diem Julii anno 49, utroque die computato, in persolucionem dictorum vadiorum per tempus supradictum, 1,586 *li.* 8 *s.* dicte monete currentis per duas litteras predicti senescalli de mandato pro dictis vadiis solvendis et per dictum breve regis pro huiusmodi litteris allocandis ac eciam per duas litteras ipsorum Guillelmi et Johannis de recepcione sicut continetur in predictis particulis. Et solucionem dicto domino Thome de Felton', baneretto, senescallo Acquitanie, super vadiis suis guerre ad 6 *s.*, 9 militum quilibet ad 3 *s.*, 50 armigeriorum quilibet ad 18 *d.*, et 60 sagittariorum quilibet ad 9 *d. st.* Anglie per diem, moraturorum in obsequio domini regis in partibus

---

90 Here the parchments are sown together.
91 MS. *portis.*

Vasconie per dimidium annum ut in precio 1,392 *li.* 6 *s. st.* Anglie per
prefatum constabularium in recepta regis pro dictis vadiis regis solvendis 27 die Maii termino Pasche dicto anno 47 receptarum, de quibus
idem constabularius superius oneratur, 10,442 *li.* 5 *s.* dicte monete
currentis per supradictum breve regis[92] Ricardi de privato sigillo suo
thesaurario et baronibus de scaccario suo directum dat' 15 die Julii
anno tercio, in quo inter cetera continetur quod receptis litteris
acquietancie dicto constabulario per dictum dominum Thomam de
summa predicta factis, penes ipsos thesaurarium et barones per
testimonium predicti contrarotulatoris allocari faciant eidem constabulario summam predictam, ipsum dominum Thomam de summa
predicta versus regem onerando, et per dictas litteras acquietancie
super hunc compotum liberatas et per testimonium predicti contrarotulatoris sicut continetur in particulis predictis. Et de quibus
quidem 1,392 *li.* 6 *s. st.* Anglie predictus dominus Thomas est regi
responsurus. Et respondet infra. Et in vadiis debitis Roberto Rous,
maiori civitatis Burdegale, pro 3 militibus quilibet ad 3 *s.,* 17 scutiferis
quilibet ad 18 *d.* et 15 sagittariis quilibet ad 9 *d. st.* Anglie per diem, de
retenencia sua existentibus ibidem per ordinacionem domini regis
Anglie per avisamentum consilii sui pro securitate et tuicione eiusdem
civitatis Burdegale ac eciam pro bono regimine officii maiorie eiusdem
civitatis ac eciam pro regardo dictorum 20 hominum ad arma juxta
ratam 222 *li.* 4 *s.* 5 *d. st.* Anglie per annum, videlicet pro huiusmodi
vadiis et regardis a 24 die Aprilis dicto anno 47 usque 27 diem Septembris anno 48, utroque die computato, per unum annum et 158 dies,
deductis de eisdem vadiis et regardis 127 *li.* 3 *s.* 3 *d. st.* Anglie pro vadiis
et regardis hominum ad arma et sagittariorum vacancium in tempore
predicto, 1,384 *li.* 16 *s.* 9 *d.* qua *st.* Anglie, valencium 10,386 *li.* 5 *s.* 9 *d.*
dicte monete currentis per tria brevia sub magno sigillo dicti regis Edwardi eidem constabulario pro huiusmodi vadiis et regardis eidem
Roberto Rous solvendis directa et super hunc compotum liberata sicut
continetur in predictis particulis. Et eidem constabularium pro vadiis
10 hominum ad arma, quilibet ad 18 *d. st.* Anglie per diem, secum
existencium in servicio domini regis per ordinacionem ipsius regis et
consilii sui pro securitate et tuicione dicte civitatis Burdegale ac pro
bono et securo regimine officii constabularii ibidem ac eciam pro
regardo dictorum 10 hominum ad arma per annum 111 *li.* 2-$^{1}/_{2}$ *d.* qua
st. Anglie, videlicet de parte vadiorum et regardorum predictorum pro

92 MS. *regi.*

dictis vadiis et regardis per totum tempus huius compoti 493 *li.* 6 *s.* 2-$^1/_2$
d. qua *st.* Anglie, valencium 3,699 *li.* 16 *s.* 8 *d.* qua dicta[93] monete currens
per dictum breve regis Ricardi de privato sigillo suo dictis thesaurario
et baronibus directum dat' 15 die Junii anno tercio, in quo inter cetera
continetur quod cum virtute unius indenture facte inter dominum
regem Edwardum avum regis nunc et dictum constabularium, idem
constabularium secum habuit de retenencia sua durante tempore quo
stetit in officio predicto 10 homines ad arma et 10 sagittarios predictos,
super quo per concordiam inter consilium regis et dictum constabularium inde factam rex vult et mandavit quod dicti thesaurarius et
barones allocari faciant dictos 493 *li.* 6 *s.* 2-$^1/_2$ *d.* qua in plenam satisfactionem vadiorum et regardorum pro dictis 10 hominibus ad arma et 10
sagittariis pro tempore quo stetit in officio predicto, que quidem vadia
et regarda ad 926 *li.* 5 *s.* 9-$^1/_2$ *d.* qua *st.* Anglie per parcellas ipsius nuper
constabularii se extendunt sicut continetur in particulis predictis. Et
eidem constabulario pro speciali regardo suo proprio pro primo
dimidio anno tempus huius compoti in valore 50 *li. st.* Anglie, 375 *li.*
monete currentis per idem breve regis Ricardi de privato sigillo, in quo
inter cetera continetur quod supplicavit regi idem constabularius quod
cum tempore quo per dictum regem avum et consilium suum idem
magister Robertus constitutus fuit in officio predicto 100 *li. st.* Anglie
per annum sibi concesse fuerunt per dominum regem avum et consilium suum de regardo speciali pro tempore quo steterit in officio illo,
unde habuit solucionem ad receptam scaccarii ipsius regis avi de 50 *li.*
pro dicto primo dimidio anno de quibus dictus constabularius superius
oneratur, rex mandavit quod allocari faciant eidem constabulario in
dicto compoto suo de dictis 50 *li.* in plenam satisfactionem dictarum 50
li. pro dicto primo dimidio anno sicut continetur in particulis predictis.
Et eidem constabulario in plenam solucionem dicti regardi sui specialis
per tempus huius compoti post dictum primum dimidium annum in
precio 142 *li.* 6 *s.* 2 *d. st.* Anglie, valencium 1,067 *li.* 6 *s.* 3 *d.* dicte monete
currentis per breve ipsius regis Edwardi avi de privato sigillo suo dicto
constabulario inde directum dat' 20 die Junii dicto anno 47, per quod
rex mandavit eidem quod inito[94] dicto primo dimidio anno de tempore
quo idem constabularius stabit in officio predicto secundum tenorem
indenture inter ipsum regem et dictum constabularium, percipiet ad
usum suum proprium de exitibus predicti dominii Aquitanie 100 *li.* per

---

93   MS. *dicte.*
94   MS. *pinito.*

annum de regardo speciali de dono regis pro tempore steterit in officio predicto et quod virtute brevis predicti in compoto suo perciperet allocacionem de eisdem sicut continetur in particulis predictis. SUMMA: 29,312 *li.* 20 *d.* qua.

DONA:

Idem computat solucionem domino Matheo de Gurney,[95] militi, cui dictus dominus princeps dedit et concessit 300 *li.* dicte monete currentis per annum super exitibus et proficuis et emolumentis prepositure Aquensis cum pertinenciis habendas pro tempore quo idem domino principi placuerit ad solvendum vadia gentium armorum et sagittariis existentibus in castro Aquensis pro custodia et tuicione eiusdem castri prout patet per copiam seu vidimus litterarum dicti domini principis sub sigillo autentico hic liberatam, videlicet in persolucionem dicti certi sui per dictum tempus huius compoti, 576 *li.* 18 *s.* 7 *d.* dicte monete currentis per litteras tam dicti regis Castelle et Legionis ducis Lancastrie locum tenentis ipsius avi in partibus Aquitanie, quam dicti Thome de Felton' senescalli Aquitanie dicto constabulario directas pro dicto certo predicto Matheo vel eius in hac parte attornato causa predicta solvendo et per supradictum breve dicti regis Edwardi avi de huiusmodi litteris allocandis et per duas litteras de recepcione sicut continetur in particulis predictis. Et domino Reymundo de Monte Alto, militi, domino de Mussydano, cui dictus dominus princeps dedit et concessit per annum super exitibus magne custume vinorum infra castrum Burdegale primo custumandorum 600 *scut. vet. aur.*, videlicet in partem solucionis dicti sui

---

95 Matthew Gournay came from a family which provided him with a background of intrigue. His father was one of the murderers of Edward II. Matthew himself served time in the Tower of London for his activities with the Companies. He was a veteran of both Crécy and Poitiers, serving the English well. In 1365 he was one of the *routiers* led across the Pyrénées by Du Guesclin, driving out Pedro the Cruel. At one time he was capable of lending 11,000 florins to Enrique toward campaign expenses, on promise of an annuity of 1,000 florins, which he never received. His attachment to key political figures in Spain seemed to continue, for in the next few years he befriended the king of Aragon and received a grant of 2,000 florins per year. This was in defiance of an order of Edward III to stay out of Spanish affairs. He bought a castle in Aragon from his old captain, Hugh Calverley, in 1371 while both were in Bordeaux. He was the uncle of Sir Thomas Trivet, whose services he borrowed in 1378 when Trivet was leading a force to relieve the siege of Pamplona. Gournay was then commander of the garrison at Dax and used his nephew's aid to reduce some small local castles held by brigands. Edmund of Cambridge employed him as one of his chief commanders in his expedition to Portugal in 1381. At this juncture he was described as: "Pere III's old friend and vassal, Sir Matthew Gournay, who had campaigned in Castile in 1366 and 1367 and must have been ranked as something of an expert on Peninsular warfare and politics" (P. E. Russell, *The English Intervention in Spain and Portugal at the Time of Edward III and Richard II* (Oxford, 1955), pp. 39-40, 70, 189 n. 2, 271, 302).

per dictum tempus huius compoti, 838 *li.* 15 *s.* dicte monete currentis per litteras ipsius Thome de Felton' senescalli de mandato pro dicto certo annuo solvendo et per dictum breve regis de allocando mandata ipsius senescalli et per 5 litteras de recepcione sicut continetur in particulis predictis. Et domino Johanni Colomb, militi, cui dictus dominus princeps dedit et concessit 200 *li.* dicte monete currentis per annum ad totam vitam ipsius Johannis ad terminos Sancti Michaelis et Pasche equaliter <solvendas> super exitibus custume vocate issac, vinorum ad tabernam in predicta civitate Burdegale venditorum prout patet per copiam seu vidimus litterarum dicti domini principis sub sigillo autentico hic liberatam, videlicet in persolucionem dicti certi sui pro eisdem terminis infra tempus huius compoti accidentibus 400 *li.* dicte monete currentis per litteras ipsius senescalli de mandato et per dictum breve regis de allocando mandata ipsius senescalli et per duas litteras de recepcione sicut continetur in particulis predictis. Et domino Petro de Landirano, militi, cui idem dominus princeps dedit et concessit 200 *li.* dicte monete currentis per annum ad totam vitam suam super exitibus dicte custume vocate issac, vinorum ad tabernam in dicta civitate Burdegale venditorum ad terminos Michaelis et Pasche equaliter prout per copiam seu vidimus litterarum dicti domini principis sub sigillo autentico liberatas plenius declaratur, videlicet in persolucionem dicti certi sui pro eisdem terminis accidentibus infra tempus huius compoti, 400 *li.* per consimiles litteras ipsius senescalli[96] de mandato et per dictum breve regis de allocando mandato dicti senescalli et per duas litteras ipsius domini Petri de recepcione sicut continetur in particulis predictis. Et Johanni de Cantirano, scutifero suo, idem dominus princeps dedit et concessit 200 *li.* dicte monete currentis quolibet anno ad terminum vite ipsius Johannis super exitibus custume predicte ad dictos terminos Sancti Michaelis et Pasche equaliter ut patet per copiam seu vidimus litterarum dicti domini principis sub sigillo autentico hic liberatam in persolucionem dicti certi sui pro eisdem terminis accidentibus infra idem tempus 400 *li.* per consimile mandatum dicti senescalli pro dicto certo solvendo et per dictum breve regis de allocando mandata ipsius senescalli et per duas litteras ipsius Johannis de recepcione sicut continetur in particulis predictis. Et domino Reymundo de Pelegrua, militi, cui idem dominus princeps dedit et concessit 120 *li.* dicte monete currentis per annum ad totam vitam suam super exitibus et redditibus domorum, placearum et aliorum locorum ville Leyborn' ac eciam super

---

96 MS. *senascalli.*

exitibus vendita et retrovendita ibidem dicto regi pertinencium prout
patet per copiam seu vidimus litterarum dicti domini principis sub
sigillo autentico hic liberatam, in persolucionem huius certi sui per dictum tempus huius compoti, 230 *li.* 15 *s.* 10 *d.* dicte monete currentis per
consimiles litteras ipsius senescalli de mandato et per dictum breve regis
de allocando mandata ipsius senescalli et per 2 litteras ipsius Remundi
de recepcione sicut continetur in particulis predictis. Et domino
Stephano Day, militi, cui idem[97] dominus princeps dedit et concessit 100
li. dicte monete currentis per annum ad terminum vite sue super
exitibus proficuis et emolumentis ballive de Capbreton ad terminos
Sancti Michaelis et Pasche equaliter prout per copiam seu vidimus litterarum dicti domini principis sub sigillo autentico hic liberatam
plenius declaratur, in partem solucionis dicti certi sui de dictis terminis
accidentibus infra dictum tempus huius compoti, 150 *li.* dicte monete
currentis per consimiles litteras ipsius senescalli de mandato et per dictum breve regis pro huiusmodi mandatis allocandis et per 2 litteras ipsius Stephani de recepcione sicut continetur in particulis predictis. Et
Petro Reymundo Fulcher,[98] quondam burgensi de Montalba, cui idem
dominus princeps dedit et concessit 50 *li.* dicte monete currentis per annum ad terminum vite sue super exitibus et proficuis prepositure Umbrarie Burdegale ad terminos consuetos ut patet per copiam seu
vidimus litterarum dicti domini principis sub sigillo autentico hic
liberatam, in persolucionem dicti certi sui pro dictis terminis infra tempus huius compoti accidentibus, 100 *li.* predicte monete currentis per
litteras predicti regis Castelle et Legionis ducis Lancastrie de mandato
et per dictum breve regis pro[99] huiusmodi mandatis allocandis et per 2
litteras ipsius Petri de recepcione sicut continetur in particulis predictis.
Et domino Johanni de Causade,[100] militi, cui dictus dominus Edwardus
rex avus dedit et concessit 50 *li.* dicte monete currentis per annum ad
totam vitam suam super exitibus et proficuis et emolumentis dicti castri
Burdegale per manus constabularii eiusdem castri qui pro tempore fuit,
in persolucionem dicti certi sui per dictum tempus huius compoti, 192
li. 5 *s.* 2 *d.* dicte monete currentis per breve ipsius regis avi dat' 16 die
Marcii dicto anno 47 cuius copia sive vidimus sub sigillo autentico
super hunc compotum liberatur et per supradictam aliud breve dicti

97   MS. *idiem.*
98   He appears as co-holder of the prévôté of the Umbraria and Scribania from 1372-74 (Ludham's Particulars, E. 101/ 179/ 8 fol. 3 dorse; Wykford's Particulars E. 101/ 179/ 14 fol. 3 recto).
99   MS. *per.*
100   He is recorded as being the recipient of a grant of 100 *li. Burd.* for one year, dated
16 March 1373. A note to the constable ordering payment follows the entry (C. 61/ 86, m. 7).

regis Ricardi de privato sigillo dat' 15 die Junii, anno tercio pro huiusmodi copiis allocandis et per 2 litteras dicti Johannis de recepcione sicut continetur in particulis predictis. Et domino Bertrando domino de Monteferando, cui dominus rex Edwardus avus regis huius dedit et concessit per litteras suas patentes 204 <*li.*> *st.* Anglie per annum super exitibus et proficuis castri Burdegale sibi et heredibus suis quousque eidem Bertrando vel heredibus suis ad 200 marcatas terre et redditus per annum in locis competentibus in predicto ducatu Aquitanie in feodo et hereditate habendas per ipsum regem vel heredes suos fuerit provisum, in partem solucionis dicti certi sui de tempore huius compoti, 350 *li.* dicte monete currentis per breve ipsius avi dat' 13 die Marcii anno 48, cuius copia seu vidimus sub sigillo autentico super hunc compotum liberatur et per dictum breve regis Ricardi pro huiusmodi copiis allocandis et per litteras ipsius domini Bertrandi de recepcione sicut continetur in particulis predictis. Et domino Isarno de Rothford', cui dictus dominus Johannes rex Castelle et Legionis, dux Lancastrie ac locum tenens[101] regis avi in partibus Aquitanie et alibi ultra[102] mare, dedit et concessit de gratia sua speciali 200 *fr. aur.* super exitibus custume vinorum primo proveniencium per aquam de Dordogne[103] et custumatorum in castro Burdegale, una vice tantum modo solvendos, in persolucionem dictorum 200 *fr. aur.*, precio 25 *s.* dicte monete currentis, 250 *li.* eiusdem monete currentis per litteras ipsius ducis Lancastrie de mandato et per dictum breve ipsius regis[104] avi de huiusmodi mandatis allocandis et per litteras ipsius domini Isarni de recepcione sicut continetur in dicto rotulo et contrarotulo de particulis. Et domino Emerico, domino de Monteferando de Peregor', militi, cui idem dominus rex Castelle et Legionis dedit et concessit per litteras suas patentes 200 *fr. aur.*, super exitibus prepositure Umbrarie Burdegale et super exitibus sigilli et contrasigilli quibus utitur in Burdegala ad contractus, in persolucionem 200 *fr. aur.*, precio pecii ut supra, 250 *li.* dicte monete currentis per litteras ipsius regis Castelle et Legionis de mandato et per dictum breve regis Edwardi avi regis <de> huiusmodi mandatis allocandis et per litteras ipsius domini Emerici de recepcione sicut continetur in dicto rotulo et contrarotulo de particulis.[105]

---

101 MS. *tenens*, interlinear, with caret.
102 MS. *ulta*.
103 MS. *Dordoyne*.
104 MS. *regis*, repeated.
105 MS. indicates, *Quere registrum huius compoti post "Item compotus magistri Roberti de Wykford, constabularii Burdegale a 20 die Augusti anno 47 usque 23 diem Julii anno 49."* This last sentence appears as a separate line in the manuscript, 2 cm. below the text and centered on the pell.

ITEM COMPOTUS MAGISTRI ROBERTI DE WYKFORD, CONSTABULARII BURDEGALE,
A 20 DIE AUGUSTI ANNO 47 USQUE 23 DIEM JULII ANNO 49.[106]

Et domino Bertrando, domino de Gavaston, cui dictus dominus
Johannes rex Castelle et Legionis et dux Lancastrie dedit et concessit de
gratia sua speciali 200 *li.* dicte monete currentis super exitibus et
proficuis et emolumentis receptarum Landarum quarumcumque in
persolucionem dicti certi sui, 200 *li.* monete predicte per copiam seu
vidimus litterarum ipsius ducis Lancastrie de mandato sub sigillo autentico liberatam et per dictum breve regis Edwardi avi de mandato ipsius
ducis allocando et per supradictum breve regis Ricardi de huiusmodi
copiis seu vidimus allocandis et per litteras ipsius domini Bertrandi de
recepcione sicut continetur in dicto rotulo et in contrarotulo de particulis. Et Petro Arnaldi de Tatyn alias dicto Petri, cui dictus dominus
princeps dedit et concessit 12 *d. st.*[107] per diem ad terminum vite sue per-
cipiendos per manus thesaurarii Aquitanie sicut per copiam seu
vidimus litterarum ipsius domini principis sub sigillo autentico hic
liberatam plenius declaratur, in partem solucionis dictorum vadiorum
de tempore huius compoti, 43 *li.* 8 *s.* dicte monete currentis tam per litteras ipsius Johannis regis Castelle et Legionis quam predicti Thome de
Felton' senescalli de mandato et per dictum breve regis Edwardi avi pro
dictis mandatis allocandis et per litteras ipsius Petri de recepcione sicut
continetur in dicto rotulo et contrarotulo de particulis. Et domino
Florimundo domino del Sparre pro magnis laboribus, custagiis et expensis que fecit, expendidit (*sic*) et supportavit in diversis partibus Landarum et Bayon' et in illo viagio predictus dominus del Sparre posuit ad
manus dicti domini regis totam terram de Marensium[108] cum pertinenciis suis propter rebellionem vicecomitis de Castellon'[109] in recom-
pensacionem dictarum expensarum per ipsum factarum in viagio
predicto, 640 *li.* dicte monete currentis per litteras ipsius Thome de
Felton' senescalli de mandato et per dictum breve regis Edwardi avi de
allocando huiusmodi mandata et per litteras aquietancie ipsius domini
Florimundi sicut continetur in dictis rotulo et contrarotulo de particulis.
SUMMA: 5,022 *li.* 2 *s.* 7 *d.*

---

106 This first line appears in well-defined majuscule script across the top of this pell (m. 49).
107 MS. *gr.* appears here.
108 Marennes, dép. Charente-Maritime.
109 Castillon, dép. Gironde, arr. Libourne.

EXPENSE FORINCECE:

Idem computat solucionem frectagio unius navis portantis artillariam domini regis ordinatam pro garnistura Vasconie de la Pole[110] usque Waymouthe[111] et abinde usque Plumoth'[112] ac eciam pro expensis factis et appositis ad extrahendum dictam artillariam de navi et pro una domo locata pro salva custodia earundem et pro reportacione usque navem tam apud Waymouth' quam Plumuth' in Angliam per tres vices propter timorem inimicorum existencium in galleys et pro frectagio duarum navium pro passagio ipsius constabularii et hominum suorum cum artillaria[113] predicta de Plumuth' usque Burdegalam, in valorem 20 *li. st.* Anglie, 150 *li.* dicte monete currentis per supradictum breve regis Ricardi de privato sigillo suo thesaurario et baronibus et scaccario suo directum dat' 15 die Junii dicto anno tercio, in quo inter cetera continetur quod rex, de avisamento consilii sui et per concordiam predicatam cum dicto constabulario per dictum consilium regis, vult quod allocari faciant eidem constabulario per sacramentum suum expensas per ipsum constabularium factas super predicta eskipiamentum,[114] frettagium, cariagium et portagium usque ad dictam summam 20 *li.* et per sacramentum ipsius constabularii sicut continetur in dictis rotulo et contrarotulo de particulis.
SUMMA: 150 *li.*

SUMMA EXPENSARUM: 42,389 *li.* 6 *s.* 6 *d.* qua. Et habet de superplusagio 143 *li.* 8 *s.* 10-^{1}/$_2$ *d.* qua. dicte monete currentis valentes 19 *li.* 2 *s.* 6 *d. st.* Anglie.

RECEPTA ORNAMENTORUM CASTRI BURDEGALE ET ALIORUM RERUM IBIDEM:

Idem respondet de uno vestimento continenti 2 amictas, 2 albas, 2 stolas, 2 fanulas,[115] 1 casulam, 1 capam, 2 dalmaticas de panno serico cheketto lineatas cum carde serul', unde capam et dalmaticam quasi novam; et alio vestimento quasi perusitato: item 1 corporali vetere, 2 tuallis veteribus bonis ad cooperiendum altare, 2 manicis parvis, 1 frontelli ante altare et 1 frontali supra altare de panno serico vetere, 1 capa de panno adaurato vetere sine linura, 1 pulvinari ad ponendum sub

---

110 Refers to the "pool" of London.
111 Weymouth, co. Dorset.
112 Plymouth, co. Devon.
113 MS. *artellaria.*
114 *Eskipiamentum* is the equipment of ships, or a shipment; manning a ship.
115 MS. *fanilas.*

libro; item duo missalibus, 1 legendario de temporali, 1 legendario
sanctorum de usu curie Romane, 1 graduali parvo vetere, 1 antiphonario vetere; item 2 coffris grossis coopertis et ligatis de ferro
albo, 1 coffra ligata de ferro albo et nigro cum serura et clavibus, 1 coffra ligata de ferro vetere, 1 coffra sine ligatura et serrura pro libris imponendis, 1 cista cum coopertura plana et cum serrura et clavibus, 1
cista rubea de Flandria, et 2 cistis veteribus grossis de Flandria; item 1
libro scripto de pergameno vocato le livre noir; item 1 libro scripto de
pergameno vocato le livre rouge; item 4 libris extractis de thesauria
Anglie de diversis memorandis tangentibus ducatum Acquitanie
titulatis A.B.C.D. et 22 quaternis de pergameno extractis pro copia libri
titulati per A. facienda; item 1 registro de pergameno continenti 11
quaternos et dimidium de diversis libertatibus, donacionibus et concessionibus factis per reges Anglie; item 2 cavillis grossis de ferro pro
magnis enginiis; item 3 lapidibus magnis de alabaustro;[116] item 7 balistis
grossis et 420 quarellis grossis receptis de Johanne de Ludham nuper
thesaurario Acquitanie per indenturam inde inter eos factam dat' 20
die Augusti anno domini 1373 super hunc compotum liberatum sicut
continetur in dictis particulis ipsorum constabularii et contrarotulatoris. Et de uno magno sigillo argenteo ordinato pro curia appelacionum superioritatis Aquitanie empto et proviso per dictum constabularium sicut supra continetur in particulis predictis, quod quidem
vestimentum et omnia alia predicta, excepto uno[117] lapide magno de
alabaustro,[118] computat <se> liberasse prefato Ricardo Rotour, succedenti constabulario ibidem ad opus regis custodiendum per breve
dicti regis Edwardi avi dicto magistro Roberto de Wykford, nuper constabulario Burdegale, vel eius locum tenenti directum dat' 16 die Aprilis
dicto anno 49, in quo continetur quod cum rex commiserit dicto
Ricardo Rotour custodiam dicti castri Burdegale et officium constabularii Burdegale habenda cum omnibus ad officium illud pertinentibus quamdiu regi placuerit, mandavit quod eidem Ricardo
custodiam et officium predicta cum clavibus, rotulis, papiris, memorandis et omnibus aliis officium illud tangentibus que in custodia sua
existunt per indenturam inde inter eos conficiendam liberet et per indenturam inter dictum Ricardum Rotour et Johannem Farewey, locum
tenentem dicti nuper constabularii[119] inde factam dat' 23 die Julii anno

116 MS. *alabaustre.*
117 MS. *excepta una.*
118 MS. *alabaustre.*
119 The constables of Bordeaux had regular lieutenants to help them with their duties, which

domini 1375 super hunc compotum liberatam sicut continetur in particulis predictis, de quibus quidem rebus idem Ricardus Rotour debet respondere. Et respondet infra. Et remanet 1 lapis magnus de alabaustro.[120] Et respondet in rotulo 11 in London'.

RECEPTA ARTILLARIARUM:

Idem reddit compotum de 1,500 arcubus, 5,000 garbis sagittarum et 60 grossis cordis pro arcubus crussatis in 22 pipis et 1 barella receptis de Johanne de Sleford,[121] nuper clerico private garderobe regis infra turrim London', super garnistura castri et ville Burdegale per indenturam inter eos inde factam dat' 6 die Marcii dicto anno 47 super hunc compotum liberatam sicut continetur in particulis predictis. SUMMA: 1,500 arcus; 5,000 garbe sagittarum; 60 grosse corde pro arcubus. [De quibus.[122]]

Idem computat ipsum liberasse Thome de Melbourne, thesaurario ducis Britannie,[123] pro defencione et rescursu castri de Brest[124] 100 arcus, 200 garbas sagittarum et 200 cordas pro arcubus[125] per breve dicti regis Edwardi avi regis huius thesaurario et baronibus de scaccario suo directum dat' 25 die Julii anno 50, quod est inter communia de termino Sancti Michaelis anno 51, in quo continetur quod cum nuper ordinatum fuisset per bonam deliberacionem per Guillelmum comitem

---

were considerable. The oddity in this office seems to be that they were never promoted to the actual position of constable. It would seem that they were well suited for the task, as they were often important persons (Lodge, *EHR* 50 (1935) 239). Farewey appears in 1382 as the collector of customs and farmer of a subsidy at Bristol (*CFR* [1377-83], pp. 300, 315). In 1392 he is noted as a tenant for life on a manor in Devon, *CCR* [1389-92], p. 452.

120 MS. *alabaustre*.

121 Sleford received the grant of a prebend in the collegiate church of Ripon on 16 January 1374 (*CPR* [1370-74], 385). He is also mentioned in a payment on the Issue Roll for 43 Edward III as "clerk of the king's private wardrobe" (*Issues of the Exchequer, Henry III - Henry VI*, ed. Fredrick Devon (London, 1837), pp. 191-92).

122 MS. *de quibus* appears in the right margin at the center of the lines with the preceding sums.

123 Thomas Melborne served prominently in the service of the duke of Brittany and was commissioned to treat with the king of England for the receipt of the duchy of Richmond and the marches between Brittany and Poitou (dated 25 February 1372, *Foedera* 3.ii, 936; regranted 20 July 1372, *C. Chart, R.* [1341-1417], 224). He was in charge of procuring the supplies with which Brest castle was defended and was addressed as the treasurer of the duke of Brittany (see *CCR* [1374-77], p. 385; the dates for the release of arms by the constable for Brest are given as 6 March 1373 - 22 July 1375, in E. 101/ 179/ 14, fol. 13[r]; *AHG* 12.328 for the amounts released to him; *Froissart, Chroniques*, ed. Luce, 8.lxxxi. Note his frequent appearance in Michael Jones, *Ducal Brittany, 1364-1399* (Oxford, 1970), pp. 30 ff. See also below p. 79.

124 Brest, dép. Finistère.

125 A record of these amounts may be seen in *AHG* 12.328.

Sarum',[126] nuper capitaneum flote regis supra mare existentis et locum regis tenentem pro rescursu dicti castri de Brest, per Johannem Nevill,[127] tunc locum tenentem ducis Britannie, quod dictus nuper con-

126 Montacute (Montagu), William de, second earl of Salisbury (1328-97). Succeeding to his father's honors as a minor in 1344, he quickly contemporized himself with events by joining the king on an expedition to France two years later. On arrival at La Hague he was knighted by the Black Prince, and participated in the campaign there. In 1350 he was chosen as a member of the original Knights of the Garter. He fought in the battle of L'Espagnols-sur-Mer. In 1354 he was made constable for the king's army in France. He sailed to Bordeaux with the Black Prince on 30 June 1355, having received a two year respite for debts he might obtain in Gascony. At Poitiers he commanded the rear of the Prince's army with the earl of Suffolk and fought in routing the attack of the French constable, Jean de Clermont. He continued to serve in France and assisted in the negotiations for the Treaty of Brétigny (Foedera 3.i, 483, 493). As an appointee to the king's council, he encouraged the efforts of Gaunt in Spain. He journeyed to France again, this time in the service of Gaunt. It was the king's intention that Salisbury would lead the relief of La Rochelle when that town was under attack, but the plan changed. He did see service in the abortive attempt to relieve Thouars in September 1372. His fortunes improved with a promotion to commander of an expedition to patrol the coast. Collaborating with the admirals of the northern and western fleets, he burned seven Spanish ships at the port of St. Malo. He then ventured on to Brest, under siege by Du Guesclin. The city had promised to surrender and had given hostages in the event of no reinforcement by the English. Froissart relates how he challenged the French constable to meet him in the field, but his offer was refused. Supplies were ordered for the maintenance of the garrison from the constable of Bordeaux, to be delivered to Thomas Melbourne, the treasurer of the duke of Brittany (CPR [1374-77], p. 385, and above n. 123).

His actions were strongly praised in parliament by Sir John Knyvet, chancellor (Rot. parl. 2.316). In 1375 Salisbury took part in the conferences at Bruges and continued diplomatic duties as a commissioner to France (notably: 1377, 1379, 1389 and 1391). He held a brief appointment to the admiralty of the western fleet from July-November 1376. The fear of French invasion caused him to be sent to his estates on the Isle of Wight to muster all the help he could for its defense (Foedera 3.ii, 1073). At the death of Edward III, Salisbury had just returned from negotiations in France which produced only a one-month truce. He attended Richard's coronation wearing a royal vestment. Continuing to serve abroad and at sea, he was active with Gaunt in France and in 1379 was captain of Calais. He had an opportunity to counsel the young king at the outbreak of the Peasants' Revolt in 1381, accompanying him in the Tower at London and also at Smithfield. He is said to have urged moderation in the handling of the affair and the meeting with Wat Tyler. He received the captaincy of the Isle of Wight for his efforts with the king in Scotland (1385). He also held the Isle of Man which he sold in 1393 for lack of an heir (his only son, William, was killed in a tilting). See May McKisack, The Fourteenth Century, 1307-1399 (Oxford, 1959), pp. 474, 479, and, for a fuller account of his life, DNB 13.661-62.

127 John, 5th Baron Neville de Raby, was the son of Ralph Neville de Raby and the brother of Alexander, archbishop of York. His call to foreign shores came early as he voyaged to Gascony in 1349 with the earl of Lancaster. He was knighted by Edward III in 1360 while campaigning near Paris. He appears to have accompanied the Black Prince in his expedition to Spain in 1367. In the following year he attended parliament as Baron Neville, since his father had died. He pledged himself to serve in France with 4,000 men in 1370 in a new capacity as admiral of the North Fleet. He became one of Gaunt's retainers the same year, though still indentured to serve in France. As a strong supporter of Gaunt, he was responsible for several loans to him (E. C. Lodge and Robert Somerville [eds.], John of Gaunt's Register, 1379-1383, Camden Third Series, vols. 56-57 [London, 1937], 56.75, 78; 57.15, 93, 134, 187, 190). He was made Steward of the Royal Household in 1371 (Tout, Chapters 5.279), and served until 1376 when he was removed by the Good Parliament. His association with Gaunt and Latimer caused him to receive their wrath, resulting in his impeach-

stabularius de artillaria regis quam habuit in custodia sua deliberaret predicto Thome de Melbourne, thesaurario predicti ducis Britannie, pro defensione et rescursu eiusdem castri 100 arcus, 200 garbas sagittarium et 200 cordas pro arcubus sicut per litteras patentes ipsorum comitis et Johannis in cancellaria regis ostensas et liberatas plene liquet, que quidem nuper constabularius arcus, sagittas et cordas predictos prefato Thome juxta ordinacionem predictam ut asserit liberavit, rex mandavit quod si ita est, tunc eidem nuper constabulario arcus, sagittas et cordas predictos prefato Thome pro defensione et rescursu predictis sic liberatos in compoto suo ad dictum scaccarum allocent, et per indenturam ipsius Thome de recepcione dat' 7 die Augusti anno domini 1373 super hunc liberatam et per testimonium predicti contrarotulatoris sicut continetur in dictis[128] particulis huius compoti; de quibus quidem 100 arcubus, 200 garbis sagittarum et 200 cordis pro arcubus idem Thomas est responsurus. Et respondet infra. Et liberat Ricardo Rotour, succedenti constabulario, 7 arcus, 2,761 garbas sagittarum et 391 duodenis cordarum per dictum breve regis Edwardi avi dat' 16 die Aprilis anno 49 superius in parcella de exitibus ornamentorum capelle plenius annotatum et per dictam indenturam inter dictum Ricardum et predictum Johannem Farewey, locum tenentem ipsius nuper constabularii, inde factam et in dicta parcella annotatam sicut continetur in particulis predictis, de quibus quidem 7 arcubus 2,761 garbis sagittarum et 391 duodenis cordarum pro arcubus idem Ricardus Rotour debet respondere. Et respondet infra. Et liberat domino Ameneno de Balsada, militi, castellano de Burgo, et aliis diver-

---

ment on several counts. He was ordered to redress all he had injured and to pay a fine of 8,000 marks. With the reactionary events of 1377 this penalty was reversed and he received Bamborough castle on the Scottish border. In 1373 he played a part in the relief of Brest castle. On 20 June 1378 he was appointed lieutenant in Aquitaine in an effort to stiffen the resistance against the increasingly victorious French armies (for letter of appointment dated 10 June, see C. 61/ 91, m. 1; letters of protection and power of attorney, C. 61/ 91, mm. 2, 3 and C. 61/ 93, mm. 7, 10; sailing orders, C. 61/ 91, m. 10). His actions in the war were very commendable for he was credited with taking as many as 83 towns, castles and fortresses from the French. His service continued throughout the next two years, after which he appeared again in England. There he arranged a protective escort for Gaunt (returning from the Scottish Marches) against possible attack by the revolting peasants (CPR [1377-81], p. 26). For the remainder of his life he remained in the Marches in various capacities as warden. He was embittered during the last days of his life by his brother's removal from the See of York and expulsion from England (1387), and the Appelant's refusal to subsidize the defense of the border. He died at Newcastle-upon-Tyne on 17 October 1388 and was buried in the family chantry in the south aisle of Durham cathedral. The great stone screen behind the high altar was erected primarily at his expense and so bears his name. For more details of Neville's life see DNB 14.262-65.

128 MS. *dictis*, interlinear, with caret.

sis personis per diversas vices inter 6 diem Marcii anno 47 et 22 diem
Julii anno 49, 1,393 arcus, 2,039 garbas sagittarum, 3,596 cordas pro arcubus per 52 litteras dicti senescalli et 35 litteras Florimundi domini de
Lesparre et Roberti Rous, maioris Burdegale, loca tenencium regis in
ducatu Aquitanie de mandato dicto nuper constabulario directas pro
dicta artillaria liberanda et per dictum breve regis Edwardi de magno
sigillo dat' 16 die Julii anno 50 pro dictis mandatis allocandis et per dictum breve regis nunc de privato sigillo dat' 15 die Junii anno tercio, per
quod rex mandavit dictis thesaurario et baronibus de scaccario quod
de dicta artillaria sic liberata diversis <personis> pro garnistura et
defensione castellorum et fortaliciorum regis in partibus predictis per
mandata predicta allocacionem faciant eidem constabulario per
sacramentum suum ac eciam per testimonium contrarotulatoris
predicti et quod inde exonerari faciant illos qui dictam artillariam
receperunt pro eo quod datum est regi, intelligi pro certo quod dicta
artillaria expendebatur in guerra ipsius avi ibidem et defensione patrie
contra inimicos regis et per 94 indenturas et per litteras de recepcione
simul cum predictis litteris de mandato super hunc compotum liberatas
sicut continetur in dictis particulis huius compoti ac eciam in rotulo et
contrarotulo de nominibus personarum recipiencium dictam artillariam et de[129] parcellis seperaliter cuilibet illorum liberatis.

SUMMA EXITUUM: 1,500 arcus, 5,000 garbe sagittarum, 8,488 corde pro
arcubus.

ET REMANENT: 152 corde pro arcubus.

ET RESPONDET IN ROTULO 11 IN LONDON'.

Juratores,[130] boni homines et habitatores ville de Montesecuro debent
respondere de 113 *li.* 2 *s.* 6 *d.* dicte monete currentis *nig.* valentibus 15 *li.*
20 *d. st.* Anglie videlicet, 7-$\frac{1}{2}$ *d.* dicte monete currentis pro 1 *st.* Anglie,
receptis de predicto Roberto de Wykford, constabulario, pro diversis
victualibus per eos emptis et receptis et pro diversis hominibus armatis
et sagittariis assignatis et ordinatis per senescallum Aquitanie et consilium regis Burdegale ad custodiendum et defendendum predictam
villam contra inimicos regis sicut continetur in rotulo principis. Et
respondet in rotulo 11 in London'.

Dominus Bertrandus Frank', miles, castellanus castri Regule in tribus
parcellis debet respondere de[131] 893 *li.* 3 *s.* monete predicte valentibus

---

129   MS. *de*, interlinear.
130   This list appears at the end of the roll and is a tabulation of the sums already recorded. The
first letter of each heading is a majuscule protruding into the left marginal column.
131   MS. *de*, interlinear.

119 *li*. 15 *s*. 1 *d*. *st*. Anglie receptis de predicto constabulario super garnistura victualium dicti castri sicut continetur ibidem. Et respondet in
rotulo 11 in London'.

Willelmus Wayte, constabularius de Podio Willelmi, debet respondere de 30 *s*. dicte monete valentibus 4 *s*. *st*. Anglie receptis de predicto
constabulario Burdegale super garnistura dicti loci ibidem. Et respondet in rotulo 11 in London'.

Willelmus More, custos porte de La Vent de Montesecuro, debet
respondere de 8 *li*. 11 *s*. monete predicte valentibus 22 *s*. 11 *d*. qua *st*.
Anglie receptis de predicto constabulario pro garnistura dicte porte
sicut continetur ibidem. Et respondet in rotulo 11 in London'.

Johannes Russell, castellano (*sic*) castri Sancti Macharii, in duobus
parcellis debet respondere de 512 *li*. 10 *s*. monete predicte valentibus 68
li. 6 *s*. 8 *d*. *st*. Anglie receptis de predicto constabulario pro garnistura
eiusdem castri ibidem. Et respondet in rotulo 11 in London'.

Jurati et boni homines ville Sancti Macharii debent respondere de
895 *li*. monete predicte valentibus 119 *li*. 6 *s*. 8 *d*. *st*. Anglie receptis de
predicto constabulario pro garnistura sicut continetur ibidem. Et
respondent in rotulo 11 in London'.

Dominus Reymundus Isarne, Abbas de Cistres, debet respondere de
154 *li*. monete predicte valentibus 20 *li*. 10 *s*. 8 *d*. *st*. Anglie receptis de
predicto constabulario pro garnistura abbatie sue sicut continetur
ibidem. Et respondet in rotulo 11 in London'.[132]

Dominus Arnaldus Rampnol, miles, comandator hospitalis Sancti
Johannis de Salabrunean debet respondere de 168 *li*. monete predicte
valentibus 22 *li*. 8 *s*. *st*. Anglie receptis de predicto constabulario pro
garnistura eiusdem loci sicut continetur ibidem. Et respondet in rotulo
11 in London'.

Dominus Thomas de Felton', banerettus, debet respondere de 10,442
li. 5 *s*. dicte monete currentis valentibus 1,392 *li*. 6 *s*. *st*. receptis de
predicto constabulario super vadiis suis guerre ad 6 *s*., 9 militum
quilibet ad 3 *s*., 50 armigerorum quilibet ad 18 *d*., et 60 sagittariorum
quilibet ad 9 *d*. *st*. Anglie per diem, moraturorum in obsequio regis in
Vasconia per dimidium annum ibidem. Et respondet in rotulo 9 regni
<regis> Ricardi in adhuc item Eboricum.

Ricardus Rotour, constabularius Burdegale, debet respondere de uno
vestimento continenti 2 amictas, 2 albas, 2 stolas, 2 fanulas, 1 casulam, 1
capam, 2 dalmaticas de panno serico cheketto lineatas cum carde serul',

132 The parchments are sown here and partially cover the first entry which follows.

unde capam et dalmaticam quasi novam; et alio vestimento quasi perusitato; item 1 corporali vetere, 2 tuallis bonis ad cooperiendum altare, 2 manicis parvis, 1 frontali ante altare et 1 frontali supra altare de panno serico vetere, 1 capa de panno adaurato vetere sine linura, 1 pulvinari ad ponendum sub libro; item duo missalibus, 1 legendario de temporali, 1 legendario sanctorum de usu curie Romane, 1 graduali parvo vetere, 1 antiphonario vetere; item 2 coffris grossis coopertis et ligatis de ferro albo, 1 coffra ligata de ferro albo et nigro cum 1 serura et clavibus, 1 coffra ligata de ferro vetere, 1 coffra sine ligatura et serrura pro libris imponendis, 1 cista cum cooperturo plano et cum serura et clavibus, 1 cista rubea de Flandria et 2 cistis veteribus[133] grossis de Flandria; item 1 libro scripto de pergameno vocato le livre noir; item 1 libro de papiro vocato le livre rouge; item 4 libris extractis de thesauria Anglie de diversis memorandis tangentibus ducatum Aquitanie titulatis per A.B.C.D. et 22 quaternis de pergameno extractis pro copia libri titulati per A. facienda; item 1 registro de pergameno continenti 11 quaternos et dimidium de diversis libertatibus, donacionibus et concessionibus factis per regem Anglie; item 2 cavillis grossis de ferro pro magnis enginiis; item 3 lapidibus magnis de alabaustro; item 7 balistis grossis, 420 quarellis grossis et uno magno sigillo argenteo ordinato pro curia appelacionum superioritatis Aquitanie de predicto constabulario per indenturam in duabus parcellis sicut supra continetur. Et respondet inde compoto suo[134] rotulo precedente rotulo compotorum.

Thomas de Melbourne, nuper thesaurarius ducis Britannie, debet respondere de 100 arcubus, 200 garbis sagittarum et 200 cordis[135] pro arcubus receptis de predicto nuper constabulario Burdegale pro defensione et rescursu castri de Brest sicut continetur ibidem. Et respondet in rotulo 10 in adhuc item London.

Idem Ricardus Rotour, constabularius Burdegale, debet respondere <de> 7 arcubus, 2,761 garbis sagittarum, 391 duodenis cordarum, receptis de Roberto de Wykford, nuper constabulario ibidem. Et respondet inde compoto suo[136] rotulo precedente rotulo compotorum.

133 MS. *et 2 cistis veteribus* is underlined, repeated.
134 MS. *compoto* and *suo*, interlinear, with caret.
135 MS. *cordibus*. This is a variation of the preferred form.
136 MS. *compoto suo*, interlinear.

Debita per billam:

Debentur predicto Roberto Rous, militi, nuper maiori civitatis Burdegale, de supradictis vadiis suis a 24 die Aprilis anno 47 usque 28 diem
Septembris anno 48 non ad plenum solutis, unde habet billam predicti
constabularii et de qua billa idem constabularius superius oneratur 689
li. 19 *s.* 1 *d.* qua *st.* Anglie, de quibus allocantur prefato Roberto alibi in
hoc rotulo in <item> Somerset, 123 *li.* 10 *s.* Et remanent: 566 *li.* 9 *s.* 1
d. qua.

APPENDIX

*Westminster, 12 April 1373. Edward III empowers Thomas Felton, seneschal, and
Robert Wykford, constable, to administer the transfer of holdings in Gascony.*
Public Record Office, Rotuli Vasconie, C. 61/86, m. 2.
De civitatibus, etc., in partibus Vasconie in manum regis capiendis.
Rex dilectis et fidelibus suis Thome de Felton', senescallo nostro Aquitanie
et magistro Roberto de Wykford, constabulario nostro Burdegale salutem.
Sciatis quod cum Edwardus, carissimus primogenitus noster in quinto die Octobris proximo preterito principatum Aquitanie et Vasconie ac omnia
civitates, castra, villas, loca, terras, comitatus, patrias et provincias et
quecumque alia que idem primogenitus noster habuit vel tenuit ad terminum
vite sue ex dono et concessione nostris una cum omnibus insulis adjacentibus,
homagiis, ligeanciis, honoribus, obedienciis, vassallis, feudis, retrofeudis, ser-
viciis, recognicionibus, juribus, mero et mixto imperio et cum jurisdictionibus
altis, mediis atque bassis, salvis gardiis, advocacionibus et procuratoribus ecclesiarum metropolicitarum et cathedralium tam secularium quam regularium
et aliorum ecclesiasticorum beneficiorum quorumcumque, de variis censibus,
redditibus, proventibus, confiscacionibus, emolumentis et reversionibus
universisque juribus et pertinenciis suis sursum reddiderit in manus nostras et
omne jus et clamencem que idem progenitus noster habuit vel habere potuit in
eisdem vel eorum aliquo, nobis et heredibus nostris remiserit, relaxaverit et
quietum clamaverit, adeo plene et integre sicut ea tenuit vel habuit pretextu
donacionis et concessionis nostrarum predictarum; nos de fidelitate et cir-
cumspectione provida vestris plenam fiduciam reportantes assignavimus, vos
conjunctimus et divisimus ad omnia supradicta civitatis (*sic*), castra, villas, loca,
terras, comitatus, patrias et provincias una cum omnibus insulis adjacentibus,
homagiis, ligeanciis, honoribus, obedienciis, vassallis, feudis, retrofeudis, ser-
viciis, recognicionibus, juribus, mero et mixto imperio et cum jurisdictionibus
altis, mediis atque bassis, salvis gardiis, advocacionibus et procuratoribus ecclesiarum metropolicitarum et cathedralium tam secularium quam regularium
et aliorum ecclesiasticorum beneficorum quorumcumque, de variis censibus,
redditibus, proventibus, confiscacionibus, emolumentis et reversionibus
universisque juribus et pertinenciis suis in manus nostras resumenda, capienda

et seisienda ac ad opus nostrum retinenda et occupanda, aliquibus donacionibus seu concessionibus ante hec tempora per quoscumque factis que per nos ratificate et confirmate non existunt non obstantibus, ita quod vos prefati constabularii[137] nobis de exitibus, proficuis et emolumentis quibuscumque inde provenientibus a predicto quinto die Octobris et exnunc ad scaccarium nostrum Anglie respondeatis et fidelem compotum inde reddatis. Et ideo vobis committimus et mandamus quod circa premissa omnia et singula sollerter intendatis et ea faciatis et fideliter expleatis in forma predicta. In cuius, etc., Dat' apud Westmin' 12 die Aprilis.

Per ipsum regem.

Cleveland State University

137 MS. *prefate constabularius.*

TWO MIDDLE ENGLISH TRACTS ON THE CONTEMPLATIVE LIFE[1]

P. S. Jolliffe

Two fifteenth-century manuscripts deposited in the British Museum, Additional MSS. 37790 and 37049, of Carthusian provenance,[2] contain tracts on the contemplative life with almost identical descriptions of the threefold way. The shorter tract in MS. Add. 37790 (fols. 234r-

1   The writer is deeply indebted to Miss Joy Russel-Smith for communicating to him her identification of the Latin source, Hugh of Balma's *Mystica theologia*, and of two passages from Middle
English sources together with her views on the relationship between the two compilations and their
dependence upon their sources. He also acknowledges with gratitude the assistance of Professor
T. J. Brown in providing information about the two manuscripts and a transcript of passages from
the British Museum MS. Harley 6579 text of *The Scale of Perfection*; of Dr. A. I. Doyle in providing
information about English manuscripts of the *Mystica theologia*, and the provenance and dating of
the two manuscripts containing the tracts; and of the Revd E. Colledge, O.S.A., and the Revd
J. Walsh, S.J., for their very helpful comments on an early draft of this article and the information
which they have provided.

He assumes, however, full responsibility for the opinions and conclusions set forth in this article.

The research has been aided by a grant from the Central Research Fund of the University of
London.

2   MS. British Museum Additional 37790, written in several hands of the mid-fifteenth century,
is annotated by James Grenehalgh, the Carthusian of Shene: see E. Colledge, "*The Treatise of Perfection of the Sons of God*: A Fifteenth-Century English Ruysbroek Translation," *English Studies* 33
(1952) 49-66, esp. 59-61 where Colledge has discussed the Carthusian provenance of the manuscript;
but he informs me that he does not now consider the manuscript to bear a 'JS' monogram, a fact
important for dating and provenance. It contains, among other items on the spiritual life: the Misyn
translations of Rolle's *De emendatione vitae* and *Incendium amoris* (fols. 1r-95r); portions of Rolle's *Ego
dormio* and *The Form of Living* (fols. 132r-135v); a text of Julian of Norwich's *Revelations of Divine Love*
(fols. 97r-115r); chapter 4 of Suso's *Horologium sapientiae* in English (fols. 135v-136v); the 'M.N.' version of *The Mirror of Simple Souls* (fols. 137r-225r); the text printed in this study (fols. 234r-236r); and
a note on St. Bridget's visions (fol. 236v). (See J. Bazire and E. Colledge, *The Chastising of God's Children* (Oxford, 1957), pp. 9-10).

The inclusion of *The Mirror of Simple Souls* and the annotations by James Grenehalgh support the
likelihood of Carthusian provenance.

See M. Doiron (ed.), "Margaret Porete, 'The Mirror of Simple Souls': A Middle English Trans-

236r) deals only with the purgative, illuminative and unitive ways; the longer one in MS. Add. 37049 (fols. 87v-89v), entitled *Of Actyfe lyfe & contemplatyfe declaracion*, distinguishes between the active and contemplative lives, describes the active life, principally in verses which have not been recorded elsewhere but seem to be derivative,[3] and incorporates in the description of the contemplative life much of the material in the shorter tract.

A great deal of the material has been traced to its sources. The two tracts contain borrowings from *The Cloud of Unknowing* and its related writings, combined with material taken from Walter Hilton's *The Scale of Perfection*. Additional borrowings from the *Scale*, Rolle's *Form of Living* and *A Tretyse of þe Stodye of Wysdome þat men clepen Beniamyn* occur in the longer tract. Moreover, the treatment of the threefold way owes its structure and some of its content to Hugh of Balma's *Mystica theologia*. For these reasons the two tracts are printed below, with such sources as have been identified.

I

Where possible, the texts of the two tracts and the source of each borrowing are printed concurrently. When the point is reached at which the tract on the threefold way begins, this text is used as the basis of comparison, for it will be shown to be closer to the sources than *Of Actyfe lyfe & contemplatyfe declaracion*. The texts of the sources which are

---

lation," *Archivio italiano per la storia della pietà* 5 (1968) 241-355, esp. 244-245.

MS. British Museum Additional 37049, written by one hand in the second quarter of the fifteenth century at the earliest and quite probably later in the century, was made for, or in, a Charterhouse and contains drawings of Carthusians on several pages. Among other items it contains: a poem on the Carthusian order (fol. 22r); passages from Richard Rolle's writings (fol. 30v); chapters 4 (fols. 43v-44v) and 5 (fols. 39r-43v) of Suso's *Horologium sapientiae* in the same translation as that in Additional MS. 37790; the *Desert of Religion* (fol. 46r); the second Middle English version of *De remediis contra temptaciones* (fols. 91v-94r) included in a longer tract *Agayne despayre* (fols. 89v-94r); and the text printed in this study (fols. 87v-89v). There are also many religious lyrics, of which Rosemary Woolf has made extensive use in her study, *The English Religious Lyric in the Middle Ages* (Oxford, 1968), esp. pp. 185-186, 374-375.

See B. Hackett, E. Colledge, and N. Chadwick, "William Flete' *De remediis contra temptaciones* in Its Latin and English Recensions: The Growth of a Text," *Mediaeval Studies* 26 (1964) 210-230, esp. 224-226; E. Colledge and N. Chadwick, "'Remedies against Temptations': The Third English Version of William Flete," *Archivio italiano per la storia della pietà* 5 (1968) 203-240; T. W. Ross, 'Five Fifteenth-Century 'Emblem' Verses from Brit. Mus. Addit. Ms. 37049," *Speculum* 32 (1957) 274-282, esp. 275; F. Wormald, "Some Popular Miniatures and Their Rich Relations," in *Miscellanea pro arte: Festschrift für Hermann Schnitzler* (1965), pp. 279-285 and pls. CLV-CLVIII.

3   This text is listed in C. Brown, *Register of Middle English Religious Verse* 2 (Oxford, 1920), no. 512, p. 85, and C. Brown and R. Robbins, *Register*, no. 804.

printed here can only be a guide: we cannot know the form of the texts from which the first compiler borrowed. The uncertainty is increased by the absence of critical editions of *The Scale of Perfection*,[4] *The Form of Living*,[5] and the *Mystica theologia*.[6] Nevertheless a comparison of this kind between the tracts and the texts of sources from which borrowings have been made is useful if this reservation is borne in mind.[7]

While other agreements in teaching between unidentified passages in the tracts and these sources can be traced,[8] only verbal agreements have been recorded in this study. Although it is not possible to identify borrowings from the *Mystica theologia* so exactly because of the difference in language, an attempt has been made to confine the identification of borrowings to those passages which seem to agree closely in thought and expression. Nevertheless, passages from the *Mystica theologia* are recorded below which are less certainly identifiable as sources than those reproduced from the Middle English treatises.

For convenience, the tract in MS. Add. 37790 is denoted by "X" and that in MS. Add. 37049 by "Y", and this usage is retained in the ensuing discussion. The sources are identified as follows:

    BM: *A Tretyse of þe Stodye of Wysdome þat men clepen Beniamyn* (referred to hereafter as *Beniamyn minor*)
    CU: *The Cloud of Unknowing*
    DS: *A Pistle of Discrecioun of Stirings*
    FL: *The Form of Living*
    MT: *Mystica theologia*
    PP: *A Pistle of Preier*
    SPI: *The Scale of Perfection*, Book I
    SPII: *The Scale of Perfection*, Book II

The texts are printed in the order: source of borrowing, X and Y. Each unit of text, or of parallel texts, is numbered for convenient reference,

---

4   MS. British Museum Harley 6579, the manuscript upon which Evelyn Underhill based her edition of *The Scale of Perfection* and Dr S. S. Hussey his edition of book II, has been used for comparison with borrowings from that source.

5   The text in H. E. Allen (ed.), *English Writings of Richard Rolle Hermit of Hampole* (Oxford, 1931) is used here.

6   The text in St. Bonaventure, *Opera Omnia*, ed. A. C. Peltier, 8 (Paris, 1866), pp. 1-53 is used here, with the reservation that it is not necessarily reliable.

7   Professor Hodgson's editions of the *Cloud* tracts have been used: *The Cloud of Unknowing and the Book of Privy Counselling*, EETS 218 (London, 1944); *Deonise Hid Diuinite and Other Treatises on Contemplative Prayer related to 'The Cloud of Unknowing'*, EETS 231 (London, 1955).

8   For instance, Y. ll. 76-81, resembles the *Cloud*, c.35, p. 71/ 11-14 and c. 36, p. 73/ 1-2, and the *Scale*, I, 15, fol. 9r-v.

and the number listed at every multiple of 5. Folio and line references
for each text are recorded in notes.

Contractions have been expanded in both texts, and in the *Scale*
passages from MS. Harley 6579.[9] A consistent treatment of "ℍ" and all
flourishes to final "h," "r" and "t," and of all suspension marks has not
proved to be practicable in X and MS. Harley 6579: where expansions
are clearly intended, they have been transcribed; but where there has
been reasonable uncertainty as to how the marks should be treated in
transcription they have been omitted.

The bottom edges of the folios in MS. Add. 37049 are worn and some
of the text has been lost. This has been indicated as follows: <...>.

Y: of Actyfe lyfe & contemplatyfe declaracion   1

Y: I beseke þe reuerent doctour to informe me þe way of goode
    lyfyng

Y: & how I sal dispose me to cum to euerlastyng lyfe þe whilk is

Y: ordand for þaim þat here dewly lufs & serfys almyghty god.

Y: þe doctor awnsvers[10]   5

CU: þou schalt wel vnderstonde þat þer ben two maner of liues in
    Holy
Y: Thou sal vndyrstande þat þer ar two lyfes in holy

CU: Chirche. þe tone is actiue liif, & þe toþer is contemplatiue
    liif.[11]
Y: kyrke. þe tone is Actyfe. and þe toþer is contemplatyfe.[12]

FL: Til men or wymen þat takes þam til actife lyfe, twa thynges
    falles.
Y: To men & women þat takes þaim to Actyfe lyfe. twoo þinges
    falles.

FL: Ane, for to ordayne þair meyne in drede and in þe lufe of
    God,
Y: One for to ordand þair meyne in þe dred & þe luf of god.

---

9 The exception, "&", has been retained as it has in the editions of the *Cloud* tracts which are
used here.

10 Fol. 87v/ 1-6.

11 P. 31/ 3-5. *Cf. The Scale of Perfection*, I, 2: "þou schalt understonden. þat þer ben in holy kirke
to manere of lyues. as seint Gregorie seyth: in wihlke cristen men schullen ben saf. On is clepid Ac-
tif. þat other contemplatif." (fol. 2v).

12 Fol. 87v/ 7-9.

FL: and fynd þam þaire necessaries, and þamself kepe enterely þe

Y: & fynde þaim þaire necessares. And þaim selfe kepe interly þe   10

FL: comandementes of God, doand til þar neghbur als þai wil þat
þai do

Y: commawndments of god. doyng to þair neghbours as þai wald
þai dyd

FL: til þam. Another es, þat þai do at þar power þe seven werkes
of mercy

Y: to þaim. Ane oþer is þat þai do at þair power þe seuen warkes
of mercy

FL: ... þai wil have þe benyson on domes day, þat Jhesu sal til al
gyf

Y: þat þai may hafe þe blyssyng on domes day þat Ihesus Crist sal
gyf to al

FL: þat dose þam; or els may þai drede þe malysoun þat al mon
have

Y: þat dos þaim. or els may þai drede þe malyson þat alle mon
hafe

FL: þat wil noght do þam, when þai had godes to do þam wyth.[13]

Y: þat dos þaim noght. When þai[14] had godes to do þaim with.[15]   15

Y: Alle þat may & is of power. þai may not be whytte with one or
twoo

Y: of þaim. bot þaim behofes to do þaim alle. And to þi more
opyn

Y: declaracion take gode hede to þies þat folowes.[16]

Y: Fyrst þou sal make knawlege to god of heuen

Y: How þou has synned dedly in þe synnes seuen   20

Y: And to þe preste gods vicar þou sal þe schryfe

Y: And take þi penaunce here[17] in þi lyfe

13 P. 117/ 19 - p. 118/ 25; p. 118/ 31-34.
14 Interlinear addition.
15 Fol. 87v/ 9-20.
16 Fol. 87v/21-24.
17 Interlinear and marginal addition.

Y: For & þow to heuen wylle wyn

Y: þou must kepe þe oute of dedly syn

Y: þat is to say pryde & fals inuy. 25

Y: Couetyce. slewthe. glotone & lychery

Y: And ire. þat many man dos woo

Y: þe whilk to helle makes many one go.

Y: þow must þe ten commawndments kepe also

Y: þat is worschip o god & no mo 30

Y: þe secunde in vayne gods name þou not swere

Y: And þi fader & moder þou worschip here

Y: Also in gode warkes kepe þi haly day

Y: Nor sla þou no man ne his godes take away

Y: Ber þou no fals witnes on þi lyfe 35

Y: Take not þi neghbour catelle lande ne wyfe

Y: Ne his seruand ne no woman þou fyle

Y: Desyre not þi neghbour gode nor hows with frawde or gyle

Y: Al so þe fyfe inwyttes þou awe to kepe & lere

Y: <..........> ee. syght and heryng of ere. 40

Y: <..........> mowthe taste speche & nose smellynge

Y: <..........>e goyng & myshandyllynge

Y: <..........> t thynkynge for þi folye

Y : <..........> cy to <.....>r kynge mekely þou crye/

Y: Also to þi power behofes þe in hy 45

Y: To fulfylle þe seuen warkes of mercy

Y: þat is þe hongry & þirsty to gyf drynke & feede

Y: And clethe þe nakyd þat has nede

Y: And help & vyset þaim þat ar in prison sette

Y: And to comforthe þe sorowful & seke loke þou not lette 50

Y: Harbar þou þe howsles & bery þou þe dede

Y: To do þies warkes þou haste þe I rede.

Y: þe fourtene artykyls of trowthe withouten heresy

Y: Awe þou with trewe fayth to trowe stedfastly

Y: And þe seuen sacraments as I þe say   55

Y: Awe þou to trowe & worschip ay

Y: Kepe also þe seuen princypal vertews in euere chawnce

Y: þat is faythe. hope. charyte & temporaunce

Y: And trewe strenthe. with wisdom. also

Y: Thynke on þies wer so þou go.   60

Y: For & þou wil þies vertews trewly. kepe

Y: þai saule þai wil safe fro schame & schenschepe.

Y: Alle þies forsayd thynges must þe kepe with alle þi myght

Y: If þou wil in actyfe lyfe. lyf right

Y: And also pray & do penaunce for þi syn.   65

Y: And to do gode werkes loke þou not blyn

Y: And if þou do þus or þou hence wende

Y: þow gos to blys wythouten ende.[18] Contemplatyfe lyfe

SPI: Contemplatif lif
Y: The secunde is contemplatyfe lyfe. þis lyfe contemplatyfe

SPI: lith in perfect loue. and charite. felid inwardli. bi
Y: lygges mykil in perfyte luf & charyte felyd inwardly be   70

SPI: gostly vertues. & bi sothfast cnowynge: and siȝte of god: in
     gostly
Y: gostly vertewe & be sothfast knawyng & syght of god & gostly

SPI: þinges. þis lif longeth specialy to hem. whilk forsaken for
Y: thynges. þis lyfe langes specially to þaim. þe whilk forsakes for

---

18   Fol. 87v/ 25 - fol. 88r/ 24. The triteness of these verses on the active life would suggest that Y was compiled for a simple, uninstructed and perhaps illiterate audience, if they had not been combined with the teaching on the contemplative life which follows.

SPI: þe loue of god. alle worlthli richesse wurschipes and outward
bysinesses.
 Y: þe luf of god al warldly rytches. worschps & outeward
besynes.

SPI: and holly ȝiuen hem body and soule vp here might in here
 Y: & hooly gyfes þaim body & saule in þair myght & þair

SPI: connynge. to seruise of god bi gostly occupacion[19]
 Y: connynge to þe serues of god be gostly occupacion.[20]   75

 Y: þe menes to þis lyfe be gods grace. is lesson. meditacion. &

 Y: prayer. þat is redyng of holy writt & specially wher it styrs

 Y: to þe luf of god & myndyng of þine awne wretchydnes with

 Y: repentance & also of þe passion of criste with compassion

 Y: pyte & lofyng. And prayng besily with deuocion for to exclude   8o

 Y: al syn. & purches þe perfyte luf & lofyng of god.

 Y: Thre ways þer ar to cum by þe mercy & grace of god. þe fyrst
is

 Y: purgatyfe. þe secunde Illmynatyfe. & þe thyrd vnatyfe.[21]

*
* *

 X: Via ad contemplacionem capiat qui potest capere quia

 X: gracia est ductrix.[22]   8,

MT: Triplex est igitur via ista ad Deum, scilicet:
 X: Triplex est via ad deum veniendi Prima

MT: purgativa, qua mens ad discendam veram sapientiam
 X: purgatiua qua mens ad veram sapienciam discendam

---

19 Fol. 2v - fol. 3r.
20 Fol. 88r/ 24-31.
21 Fol. 88r/ 31-38. The passage from X, which precedes the point at which Y continues, is inserted next.
22 Fol. 234r/ 1-2. Cf. Y, fol. 89v/ 14: "capiat qui potest capere quia gracia est ductrix", with
which Y concludes (l. 283).

MT: disponitur; secunda vero illuminativa dicitur, qua mens
X: disponitur. Secunda est Illuminatiua qua mens

MT: cogitando ad amoris inflammationem accenditur: tertia
X: ad perfectam amoris Inflammacionem accenditur. Tercia

MT: unitiva, qua mens super omnem intellectum, rationem
X: vnitiua qua mens supra omnem intellectum racionem   90

MT: et intelligentiam, a solo Deo sursum actu dirigitur ...
X: et intelligenciam a solo deo sursum acta[23] dirigitur.

MT: Sic enim quilibet novus discipulus ad perfectionem hujus
X: Therefore Euere new discipull Ascende to the perfeccioun

MT: scientiae gradatim ascendat[24]
X: of this scyence fro degre to degre[25]

*

* *

MT: ut primo in via purgativa, quae est via puerilis et
X: Fyrste he schall ascende by the waye the whilke is
Y: Fyrst þou sal ascende by þe way þat is

MT: incipientium, studiosissime se exerceat.[26]
X: callyd purgatiue. And he schalle do on this wise.[27]
Y: purgatyfe. þat is clensyng.   95

Y: þat is þou be lawfully amendyd of þi mysdedys be þe forme

Y: & lawe of holy kyrk with trewe confession contricion &

Y: satisfaccion to þi power.[28]

MT: ut primo recolat peccata sua in aliquo loco occultissimo,
X: he schalle do in the nyght or in the day in a Secrete place.
Y: And in þe day or in þe nyght þou sal in som secrete & preuy
place

---

23 MS. thus.
24 P. 2b - p. 3a.
25 Fol. 234r/ 2-9.
26 P. 3a. Notice the link between the "via purgativa" and the "via incipientium" which X and Y
ignore. Both the *Cloud* (pp. 71/ 17 - 72/ 22) and the *Scale* (fols. 106v-107r) introduce the distinction
between beginner, proficient and perfect which can be identified in the writings of the Victorines.
27 Fol. 234r/ 9-11.
28 Fol. 88r/ 38-41.

MT: et maxime in secreto noctis silentio ...[29]
  X: liggynge prostrate or knelynge remembyr the synnys and the
  Y: rememyr þe offence & trespes þou has done agayne þi lord
     god with þi   100

  X: grete offence the whilke he hase done agayns Allemyghty
     god.[30]
  Y: synfulle lyfyng be many synnes doyng & lyg prostrate or knele
     deuoutly[31]

MT: faciem suam dirigendo in coelum ... dicendo: Domine Jesu
     Christe ...
  X: lyftynge vp his face to heuene sayinge thus Lorde Ihesu Cryste
  Y: & [cry] hym mercy. Also þou sal rememyr how he myght hafe

MT: ego sum ille peccator nequissimus ... nequissimis abo-
     minabilior,
  X: I am the moste synner and most abhomynabull of all oþer the
  Y: dampned þe in to þe pytte of helle & <..> his gret mercy ȝit has

MT: qui tuam majestatem in tot et tantis criminibus offendi,
  X: whilke hase offendyd agayns þi maiesty in this and þes synnes
  Y: spard þe & abydes of/ þine amendment[32]

MT: ut illa enumerare non sufficiam, sicut nec arena
  X: þe whilke I am not sufficiant to tell. Lyke vnto the grauell 105

MT: maris prae multitudine numerari potest. Et ibi
  X: of the see that may noȝt be nowmbryde for multytude. And
     þan

MT: suspiret vel gemat, prout efficacius poterit:[33]
  X: schalle he sighe and sorowe as affectuously as he maye

  X: And when he hase sorowede thus. and sighyde. than schall he
     thynke[34]

MT: quod ipsum quoad speciem suam tam nobilem creaturam de
     nihilo
  X: howe nobull a creature god hase made hym of nought. And
     whate

29 P. 5a.
30 Fol. 234r/ 11-14.
31 Fol. 88r/ 42-44.
32 Fol. 88r/ 45 - fol. 88v/ 1.
33 P. 5a.
34 Fol. 234r/14-22.

MT: sic creavit ...[35]
   X: benyfice and goodnes god hase schewid vnto hym. And than
     schall   110

MT: beneficium incarnationis recordetur[36]
   X: he remembyr howe allmyghty god wolde of his grete mercy
     be come

   X: man and take flesch and blode of the blyssyd virgyne Oure
     lady

MT: De secundo ... percurrat
   X: saynte marie to safe[37] man kynde.[38] And aftyr this he schall

MT: ad tertium, scilicet ad recordationem Dominicae passionis ...
   X: thynke of the passion off oure lorde Ihesu Criste in his

MT: tam innumerabilia vulnera tolerasti,
   X: ymagynacion consyderynge whate Innumerabyll paynys he
     suffryd   115

MT: ut a planta pedis usque ad verticem
   X: for hym So that fro the crowne of his hede. vnto the sole

MT: non esset membrum in corpore tuo quod non
     sanguine
   X: of his fete þer was no membyr bot it was write with his
     precyous

MT: tuo sacratissimo spargeretur ... Et ibi cogitet de passione
     Domini
   X: blode. And thynke than deply of þe wounde in his syde

MT: aliquantulum, ut per vulnus lateris usque ad contactum
     divinitatis
   X: þat wente vnto his herte. And streyne hym in all that he may

MT: occultae latentis interius, per experimentum amoris, attingere
   X: for to haue compassion of Cristis passion ouer all thyngis
   Y: Also rememyr Cristes passion deuoutely & hafe sorow & com-
     passion   120

35 P. 5b.
36 P. 5b. This may be echoed in X.
37 MS. *hafe*.
38 Fol. 234r/ 22-27.

MT: mereatur.[39]   in quantum humilius,
  X: for it relesis the paynys of purgatory.[40] and ȝif he do thus
  Y: þerof with gret lofyng & thankyng of hym for al his benefyces

MT: in tantum etiam citius et abundantius gratiam divinae
  X: owre lorde/ when he woll Aftyr bittyr terys and mekyll wepynge
  Y: & godenes schewyd to þe & oþer.[41]

MT: misericordiae provocabit[42]
  X: schalle helde downe his grace and his comforth to his herte

  X: For whi it semys noȝt so worthy alorde to won in any stede bot

  X: yf it be made ryght clene and well weschyn with terys of compunccion.[43]   125

MT: Sed si etiam dolorem non poterit quoad effectum consequi, per ea
  X: And þofe a man may noȝt hafe so verrey sorowe as he walde ȝit

MT: quae dicta sunt, in qualibet nocte succinte hoc teneat, quod dictum
  X: latte hym vse euery nyght or ellys in the day as is before sayde

MT: est: quia Creatori sufficit, quando homo fecit quod in se est,
  X: for it is sufficiante tyll oure lorde that a man do that in hym ys.

MT: nec non ipse Dominus, rei exitum expectans, quandoque se subtrahit,
  X: At þe laste when oure lorde seys his perseueraunce and his

MT: ut et ista faciens, dolorem nullum ad consolationem inveniat, ut ejus
  X: laboure than when oure lorde likys   130

MT: patientia ad tempus per divinam sustinentiam comprobetur, et ut sibi
  X: of his hy grace he will sende hym

39   P. 5b.
40   Fol. 234r/ 27-35.
41   Fol. 88v/ 1-3.
42   P. 6b. This may be echoed in X.
43   Fol. 234r/ 35 - 234v/ 4.

MT: postea amplior consolatio, et de peccatis contritio divinitus
conferatur.[44]

X: verrey ande trewe compunccion.[45]

MT: Sed quia ista inter sanctos alios, in superlativo gradu
X: Also turne he hym than to oure lady saynte marye besekynge hyr
Y: And also for a special aduocate & helper to þe þou sal incal

MT: excellentissime in beata Virgine reperiuntur, ad ipsam con-
fugiat ...
X: that scho will beseke hyr mercifull sone
Y: our lady saynt Mary to be þi socoure & helpe þat þou may hafe

MT: rogo ... ut sic per te de peccatis meis propriam purgationem
X: Swete Ihesu. to sende hym trewe sorowe and compunccion
Y: forgyfnes of þi synes. & for a special homage þou sal   135

MT: obtineam, ut tandem ipsum in isto amore constringam, quem
X: for his synnys so that he may be purgyd and lufe hyr
Y: say dayly a certayne Aues vn to hyr as fyfty or als many

MT: tu totis visceribus dilexisti. Et tunc dicat ei:
X: blyssyde sone Ihesu. And euere day in wyrschipe of hyr as for an
Y: as þe lykes þat sche wil be þi helper & mere to hir blissed son

MT: *Ave, Maria*, quadraginta vicibus, vel quinquaginta, sub certo
X: homage say[46] fowrty or fyfty Aues knelynge or liggynge prostrate
Y: Ihesu þat þou may be trewly purged & clensed in þi saule

MT: numero, si voluerit ... Hoc quasi in signum dilectionis et
X: As he can hafe the moste deuocion. No dowte of ȝif a creature
Y: fro al fylth of syn.[47]

MT: spiritualis homagii reddens ei quotidie pro tributo ...[48]
X: vse this deuoutly before sayde bott he schall fynde grete grace 140

---

44 P. 6b. This may be echoed in X.
45 Fol. 234v/ 4-10.
46 Marginal and interlinear addition.
47 Fol. 88v/ 3-8.
48 P. 8a.

X: with in schorte tyme. Also saynte hyllary says. who so will

X: hafe god mercyfull vnto hym saye he before A Crucifix this psalme

X: Vsquequo domine and Ad te domine[49] leuaui and Deus misereatur nostri.[50]

MT: Via enim purgativa respondet ordini Thronorum: nam ibi tunc
X: This way purgatife answers to the Ordure of Angels the whilke is
Y: þis way purgatyfe awnswers to þe ordyr of thrones when þe saule

MT: primo purgatur anima ad hoc, quod primo Deus in ipsa veluti in
X: callede trones. for A man that is purgede in his saule is
Y: is þare[51] purged to þat þat fyrst in hyr god as in a clene   145

MT: loco mundo resideat[52]
X: the trone of Allemyghty god[53] Via illuminatiua the lightnynge way
Y: place is resident & sittes.[54] The way Illumynatyfe

MT: Per viam purgativam
X: The Secunde waye illuminatyfe   For be the way the whilke is
Y: cummes aftyr purgatyfe   For by þe way

MT: mens ad illuminativam
X: callyde purgatife Anone aftyr the mynde is raysid vp to the
Y: Purgatyfe onone after þe mynde is raysed vp to þe

MT: immediate erigitur .../ ... quia per gemitus et lacrymas anima
X: waye that is lightnede For why be sorowe and wepynge the sawle
Y: way þat is lightynd. For why be sorow & wepyng þe saule

---

49 Marginal addition.
50 Fol. 234v/ 10-20. The psalms suggested are Vulgate 12, 24 and 66 respectively.
51 Interlinear addition.
52 P. 9b.
53 Fol. 234v/20-23.
54 Fol. 88v/8-11.
55 Cf. *Cloud*, p. 43/16 where the same figure as in the *Mystica theologia* is employed.

MT: a rubiginibus peccatorum[55] abluitur, et per hoc immediate ad
  X: is clensyd fro the ruste of syn. And be that it is Ordande
  Y: is clensed fro þe rust of syn. And by þat it is ordand   150

MT: susceptionem divini radii praeparatur ... Unde oportet
  X: to receuynge of the light of the godlye beme. wharefore it
  Y: to receyfyng of þe light of þe godly beme. Wherfore it

MT: primo quod mens sit quasi speculum sine macula;
  X: behofes that the mynde be fyrste a morow with outen spotte
  Y: behofes þat þe mynde be fyrst as a morrow with outen spotte

MT: et statim ad suscipiendum lucis splendores divino radio
     disponitur,
  X: and sone disposyd to receyfe the schynynge of the godly light.
  Y: & sone disposed to receyfe þe schynyng of þe godly lyght

MT: et sic, cum fuerit curata, aeternae sapientiae conformetur.[56]
  X: And conformede to euerlastynge wysdome.[57] And be cause a
     sawle
  Y: & conformed to euerlastyng wisdom.[58] And because a saule

  X: is lightly inclynyd to vayne thoghtys therefore it
  Y: is lightly inclyned to vayne thoghtes þerfore it   155

  X: is necessary to sette the mynde to one thynge[59]
  Y: is necessary to sett þe mynde to o þinge[60]

*
*   *

  X: and that is this blyssyd name of Ihesu. For ȝif it be

  X: ryght kepyd in mynde it purges the sawle fro synne and chasys

  X: the feynde and puttys owte vanytese and makys A sawle abyll

  X: to receyfe grete grace.[61]   160

MT: Ista autem, ut dictum est, respondet Cherubim: Cherubim
     plenitudo
  X: This way illumynatyfe answers/vnto the Ordure of Angels the

---

56   P. 8a-b.
57   Fol. 234v/ 23-31.
58   Fol. 88v/ 11-17.
59   Fol. 234v/ 31-33.
60   Fol. 88v/ 17-19. At this point X and Y diverge and each is printed separately.
61   Fol. 234v/ 34-37.

MT: scientiae interpretatur. Tantum autem per artem hujus
    theoricae scientiae

X: whilke is callede Cherubyn For Cherubyn is as mykyll to saye
   as fulnes

MT: lumen acquiritur, et tanta sapientiae dilatatio in Scripturis
    ...[62]

X: of kunnynge. For the sawle is lightnede to vndyrstande holy
   scripture[63]

*

* *

BM: in þis maner. þou schalt clepe togeders þi þou3tes
Y: in þis maner of wyse. þou sal calle togedyr al þi thoghtes

BM: & þi desires, and make þee of hem a chirche, & lerne þee þerin
    for to
Y: & þi desyres & make of þaim a kyrk & lerne þer in for to   165

BM: loue only þis goode worde Jhesu, [so þat alle þi desyre & þi
    þou3t
Y: luf onely þis gode worde Ihesu so þat al þi desyre & þi þoght

BM: be onely sette for to loue Jhesu] and þat vnsesyngly, as it may
Y: be onely set for to luf Ihesu. And þat vncessyngly as it may

BM: be here, so þat þou fulfille þat is seyde in þe psalme:
Y: be here in þis lyfe so þat þou fulfylle þat is sayd in þe psalme.

BM: 'Lorde, I schal bles þee in chirches,'
Y: In ecclesiis benedicam te domine. In kirkes I sal blys þe lord

BM: þat is in þou3tes and desires of þe loue of Jhesu. And þan, in
    þis
Y: þat is in thoghtes & desyres of þe luf of Ihesu. & þan in þis   170

BM: chirche of þou3tes & desires, & in þis oneheed of studies & of
    willes,
Y: kyrk of þoghts & desyres & in þis onehede of stodyes & of
   wylles

---

62 P. 9b.
63 Fol. 234v/37-fol. 235r/3. v. Y: fol. 89r/7-10 (ll. 211-217).

BM: loke þat alle þi þouȝtes & þi desires & þi studyes & alle þi
Y: loke þat al þi þoghtes & þi desyres & al þi stodyes & al þi

BM: willes be only set in þe loue & þe preisyng of þis Lorde Jhesu,
Y: wills be onely set in þe luf & þe praysynge of þi lord Ihesu

BM: wiþouten forȝetyng, as fer forþ as þou maist by grace & as þi
Y: withouten forgyttyng als farforth as þou may be grace & as þi

BM: freelte wil suffre, euer more mekyng þee to preier & to coun-
    sel,
Y: frelte wil suffer euer more mekyng þe to prayer & to cownsel 175

BM: pacyently abidyng þe wille of oure Lorde, vnto þe tyme þat þi
Y: paciently abydyng þe wylle of our lord vnto þe tyme þat þi

BM: mynde be rauischid abouen itself to be fed wiþ þe feire
Y: mynde be raueschyd abowue it selfe to be fedde with þe fayr

BM: foode of aungelles in þe beholdyng of God & godly þinges. So
    þat
Y: foode of angels. in behaldyng of god & godly thynges. so þat

BM: it be fulfillid in þee þat is wretyn in þe psalme: 'Ibi
Y: it may be fulfyld in þe þat is written in þe psalme. Ibi

BM: Beniamyn adolescentulus in mentis excessu.' þat is 'þere is
Y: beniamyn adolescentulus in mentis excessu. þer is beniamyn 180

BM: Beniamyn, þe ȝonge childe, in raueschyng of mynde.'[64]
Y: þe ȝonge chylde in raueschyng of mynde.[65]

*
* *

X: Therefore þou schalle desyre the perfytte loue of god
Y: luf þerfore þi lord Ihesu & desyre alway þe perfyte luf of god

SPII: For contemplacion is not ellis bot a
X: in contemplacione[66] For contemplacion is nouȝt ellys bot a
Y: in contemplacion[67]   for contemplacion is noght els bot a

64 P. 45/ 13 - p. 46/ 14.
65 Fol. 88v/ 19-34.
66 Fol. 235r/ 3-4.
67 Fol. 88v/ 34-35.

SPII: siȝt of Ihesu whilk is verrey pes ... for trust
  X: sight of Ihesu the whylke is verreye pees. For trust[68]
  Y: syght of Ihesu. þe whilk is vere pees. For trest

SPII: sikirly þawȝ þu haue synned here ... bifore if þu be now
  X: sykyrly þough þou hafe synnede herebefore ȝif þou be nowe
  Y: sykyrly þof þou hafe synned herebefore If þou be nowe   185

SPII: reformed bi þe sacrament of penaunce aftir þe lawe of holi
  X: reformede by the sacramente of pennaunce eftyr the lawe of
        holy
  Y: reformed by þe sacrament of penannce aftyr þe lawe of haly

SPII: kirke þat þu art in þe riȝt weie. Now þan siþen þu art in þe
  X: kyrke that þou erte in þe ryght way. Now sen þou erte in the
  Y: kyrke þat þou art in þe right way. &

SPII: siker weye ... þe behouiþ to holden þese two þinges often in
  X: ryght way. the behofes to holde the two thynges often[69] in
  Y: þe behofes to halde þies twoo thynges oftyn in

SPII: þi mynde. meknes & luf. þat is. I am noȝt I haue noȝt
  X: thy mynde that is mekenes and lufe. that is I Am noȝt. I hafe
        nouȝt
  Y: þi mynde. þat is meknes & luf/ þat is I am noght. I hafe noght.

SPII: I coueite noȝt. bot on þou schalt hafe þe menynge
  X: I couet nought bot on. Thowe schall hafe the menynge
  Y: I couet noght bot one. þou sal hafe þe menyng   19ᴄ

SPII: of þese wordes in þin entent & in habite of þi soule
  X: of these wordys in thyne entente and in habite of thy sawle
  Y: of þies wordes in þine intent & in habyt of þi saule

SPII: lastendly: þawȝ þu hafe noȝt specialy þese wordes ay formed
  X: lastandly þof þou hafe not specially thes wordes ay formyd
  Y: lasttyngly. þof þou hafe not specially þies wordes ay formed

SPII : in þi þouȝte. for þat nediþ not: Meknes saiþ I am noȝt
  X: in thy thought for that nedys nought. Mekenes says I am
        nouȝt.
  Y: in þi þoght for þat nedes not. Meknes says I am noght.

68 MS. *criste*.
69 MS. *eftyr*.

SPII: I hafe noȝt. lufe saith I coueite noȝt bot on. & þat is Ihesu[70]
   X: I hafe noȝt lufe says. I couet not bot on. and that is Ihesu.
   Y: I hafe noght. And luf says I couet noght bot one. & þat is
      Ihesu.

SPII: And þat is. þu schalt setten in þin herte holly & fully. þat
   X: And þus sall þou set fully in thy herte that þou wolde no
      thynge
   Y: And þus sal þou sett in þi hert fully þat þou wald no þinge 195

SPII: þu woldest no þinge hafe bot þe luf of Ihesu. & þe gostly
   X: hafe bot the lufe of Ihesu. and the gostely
   Y: hafe bot þe luf of Ihesu & þe gostly

SPII: siȝt of him. as he wile schewe hym. for to þat only þu art
   X: sight of hym as he woll schewe hym. for vnto that only arte
   Y: syght of hym as he wyll schewe hym for <   > þat onely art

SPII: made & boȝte[71]... Now be war of enmys þat wilen be
   X: þou made and boȝt[72] Nowe be ware with thyne Enmyes that
      wille be
   Y: þou made/ & boght.[73] And if it hapyn be þine enmys gostly or

SPII: bisy. for to lette þe if þei mown ... Bot ... what so it be þat þei
   X: besy for to lette the yf thay may. bot what so thay say belefe
   Y: bodely to be sayd vn to þe in þi þoght or oþerways[74]

SPII: saien. trowe hem not bot holde forþ þi wey. & only desire þe
   X: tham nouȝt. bot holde furth and desyre the   200

SPII: luf of Ihesu: Answere ay þus I am noȝt I hafe noȝt
   X: love of Ihesu And answere ay thus and say. I am noȝt. I hafe
      noȝt

SPII: I coueite noght bot only the luf of Ihesu ... Also if þei sey[75]
   X: I couet noȝt. bot the love of Ihesu. Also ȝif thay say[76]

70 Fol. 85r.
71 Fol. 86r.
72 Fol. 235r/ 4-19.
73 Fol. 88v/ 35 - fol. 89r/ 1.
74 Fol. 89r/ 1-2.
75 Fol. 86v - fol. 87r.
76 Fol. 235r/ 20-24.

SPII: þat þu art not worþi to hafe þe luf of god: ... trowe hem not
   X: þat þou arte noȝt worthy to hafe the love of god. trowe þaym
       noȝt.
   Y: þat þou art not worthy to hafe þe luf of god. trow þaim not

SPII: bot go forþ. & say þus. Not for I am worþi but for
   X: bot hold furth and saye thus. Noȝt for I am worthy bot for
   Y: bot hald forth & say þus. Noght for I am worthy. bot for

SPII: I am unworþi. þerfore wolde I luf god. for if I had it:
   X: I Am vnworthy therfore wolde I lufe god. for yf I had it.
   Y: I am vnworthy. þerfore wald I luf god. for if I had it.   205

SPII: þat schulde make me worþi. And siþen I was made þer to:
       þawȝ
   X: it schulde make me worthy. And sen I was made þer to þof
   Y: It suld make me worthy. And sen I was made þer to. þof

SPII: I schuld neuer hafe it: ȝit wil I coueite it[77]...
   X: I schulde neuer hafe it. ȝit wyll I covet it[78]
   Y: I suld neuer hafe it. ȝit wil I couet it.[79]

SPII: And þan if þin enmys seeþ þat þu bigynnist to wexen bolde &
   X: And eftyr this. when thyne enmyes seys þat þou erte so

SPII: wel willed to ... kepe þi þouȝte & þi desire hol to þe
   X: wele willyd to kepe thy desyre and thy lufe hole to

SPII: luf of god. þan are þei mikel abasched[80]
   X: god than ar thay mekyll Abayschyd. Via vnitiua. The Oned
       Waye.[81]   210

*
* *

   Y: And þus be gods grace sal þou cum to þe way Illumynatyfe.

MT: Ista autem, ut dictum est, respondet Cherubim:
   Y: þis way Illumynatyfe awnsswers to þe ordyr of angels þe whilk

MT: Cherubim plenitudo scientiae interpretatur.
   Y: is cald cherubyn. for cherubyn is als for to say. as

77 Fol. 87r.
78 Fol. 235r/ 24-29.
79 Fol. 89r/ 2-6.
80 Fol. 87r & fol. 88r.
81 Fol. 235r/ 29-32.

MT: Tantum autem per artem hujus theoricae scientiae lumen
acquiritur,
  Y: fulnes of connyng for þe saule is lightynd to vndirstand holy

MT: et tanta sapientiae dilatatio in Scripturis, ... quot creaturae
  Y: scripture & þai þat ar in þis way   215

MT: in mundo, tot habeat anima intelligentias, vel sermones,
  Y: has mony lightnynges of grace in þair saule as god wil

MT: totum ad Deum ad punctum amoris omnia referendo.[82]
  Y: vouche safe to gyf to his lufers[83]

*
*   *

MT: Dicto de via
  X: The thyrde waye is vnatife. For be this waye that is callyd
  Y: þe thyrd way is vnatyfe. For by þis way þat is cald

MT: illuminativa, et quomodo actualiter per ipsam ad unitivam
  X: illumynatyfe. it is ascendit to that way the whilke is callyd
  Y: Illuminatyfe. It is ascendyd to þat way þat is cald

MT: ascenditur, sequitur de via unitiva ...[84] saltem aspiret
  X: vnatyfe. A sawle awe with all his strengthis to take and aspyre
  Y: vnatyfe. A saule awe with al hir strenthe to take & aspyre 220

MT: ad amorem[85]
  X: that it may be onede to þe Spowse and that it may receyfe in
this
  Y: þat it may be oned to þe spowse. & þat it may receyfe in þis

  X: presente life þe erles of euerlastynge ioye. And þerfore A man
  Y: present lyfe þe erls of euerlastyng ioy. And þerfore a man

  X: awe to make oure lorde/ Ihesu Criste Euer presente before
the
  Y: awe to make our lord Ihesu Crist euer present be fore þe

---

82 P. 9b - p. 10a.
83 Fol. 89r/ 6-12.
84 P. 21a.
85 Perhaps X and Y echo *aspiret* on p. 21a.

X: sight of his sawle and covet no thynge forto hafe bot only hym
Y: sight of his saule & couet no thyng for to hafe bot onely hym.

X: and desyre to lufe hym with A reuerente affeccion[86]
Y: And desyre to luf hym with a reuerent affeccion[87]   225

PP: and acordaunce of wile. After þe worde of Seint Poule
X: and Acordance of wille eftyr the worde off Saynte Paule
Y: & acordaunce of wil aftyr þe wordes of Saynt Paule

PP: seiing þus: 'Qui adheret Deo, vnus spiritus est cum illo.'
X: sayinge thus. Qui adheret deo vnus spiritus est cum illo.
Y: sayng þus Qui adheret deo vnus spiritus est cum illo.

PP: þat is to sey: 'Whoso draweþ nere to God,' as it is bi soche
X: That is who so drawys nere vnto god. that is be swylke
Y: þat is to say Who so drawes nere to god. as it is by swylk

PP: a reuerent affeccioun touchid before, 'he is o sperit with
    God'; þat is
X: a reuerente[88] affeccion he is O Sperit with god. that is.
Y: a reuerent affeccion he is o spyrit with god. þat is

PP: þof al þat God & he ben two and sere in kynde, neuerþeles
X: þough all þat god and he er two and sere in kynde. Neuerþeles
Y: þof al þat god & he ar twoo & sere in kynde. ner þe les 230

PP: ȝit in grace þei aren so knitte togeders þat þei ben
X: ȝit in grace þay ar so knytt to gedyr. that thay er
Y: ȝit in grace þai ar so knytt to geder. þat þai ar

PP: (bot) o sperit. And alle þis is for onheed of loue and
X: bot one in speritt. And all this is for onede of lufe and
Y: bot one in spyrit. And al þis is for onehed of luf &

PP: acordaunce of wile. And in þis oonheed in þe mariage maad
    bitwix
X: acordance of wille. And in this onede is the mariage made
   betwyx
Y: acordaunce of wylle. And in þis onehede is þe maryage made
   betwyx

---

86 Fol. 235r/ 33 - fol. 235v/ 3.
87 Fol. 89r/ 12-19.
88 MS. *reuerence*.

PP: God and þe soule, þe whiche schal neuer be broken, þof
  X: god and the sawle. the whilke schalle neuer be brokyn. þough
  Y: god & þe saule. þe whilk sal neuer be brokyn. þof

PP: al þe hete & þe feruour of þis werk ceese for a tyme, bot by a
  X: all þat the hete and the feruour cese for atyme. bot be a
  Y: al þat þe hete & þe feruour cese for a tyme. bot be a   235

PP: deedly sinne[89]
  X: dedely synne[90]
  Y: dedly syn.[91]

MT: Tertia autem, scilicet unitiva, respondet
  X: This way vnatyfe answers vnto the ordur of Angels þe whilke
    is

MT: Seraphim, qui interpretatur ardens ...[92]
  X: calde Seraphyn that is to saye brynnynge in lufe.[93]

CU: Lift up þin herte vnto God wiþ a meek steryng
  X: Therfore lyfte vp thy herte vnto god with a meke sterynge
  Y: þerfore lyft þi hert vnto god with a meke styrryng

CU: of loue; & mene him-self, & none of his goodes, & þerto loke
  X: of lufe. and mene hym selfe. And þerto luke
  Y: of luf. & mene hym selfe. And þerto loke   240

CU: þee loþe to þenk on ouȝt bot on hym-self, so þat
  X: þat the lothe for to thynke on oȝt bot on hym selfe. so þat
  Y: þat þe lothe for to thynke on oght bot on hym selfe. so þat

CU: nouȝt worche in þi witte ne in þi wille bot only him-self.
  X: noȝt worke in thy witte nor in thy wylle bot only hym selfe.
  Y: noght wyrk in þi wytt ne in þi wylle bot onely hym selfe.

CU: & do þat in þee is to forȝete alle þe creatures þat euer
  X: And do that in the is to forgitte all the creatures that euer
  Y: And do þat in þe is to forgytt al þe creatures þat euer

CU: God maad & þe werkes of hem, so þat þi þouȝt ne þi
  X: god made and the workys of thaym. So that thy thouȝt nor þy
  Y: god made & þe warkes of þaim. so þat þi thoght nor þi

89   P. 56/ 14-23.
90   Fol. 235v/ 3-13.
91   Fol. 89r/ 19-27.
92   P. 10a.
93   Fol. 235v/ 14-16. V. Y: fol. 89v/ 10-13 (ll. 279-282).

CU: desire be not directe ne streche to any of hem, neiþer
  X: desyre be nouȝt dyrecte ne reche vnto ony of thaym. nouþere
  Y: desyre be not direct ne reche vnto any of þaim. nowdyr   245

CU: in general ne in special. Bot lat hem be, & take no
  X: in generall nor in specyall. bot latt thaym be. and take no
  Y: in general nor on specialle. bot lat þaim be. & take no

CU: kepe to hem. þis is þe werk of þe soule þat moste plesiþ
  X: kepe to thaym. this is the worke of the sawle that moste plesis
  Y: kepe to þaim. This is þe warke of the saule þat moste pleses

CU: God. Alle seintes & aungelles han ioie of þis werk, & hasten
  X: god. All sayntes and Angels hafe ioy of this worke and hastis
  Y: god. Alle sayntes & angels has ioy of þis werke & hastes

CU: hem to helpe it in al here miȝt. Alle feendes ben wood whan
  X: thaym to helpe it in all þer myght. All feyndis ar wode when
  Y: þaim to helpe it in al þair myght. Alle fendes are woode when

CU: þou þus doste, & prouen for to felle it in alle þat þei kun.
  X: þou dose thus and profes for to fell it all þat þay kan.
  Y: þou dos þus. And profes for to felle it in al þat þai can.   25c

CU: Alle men leuyng in erþe ben wonderfuli holpen of þis werk,
  X: All men lyfynge in erthe are wondyrfully helpyd of this
    worke.
  Y: Al men lyfyng in erthe ar wondyrfully helpyd of þis warke.

CU: þow wost not how. ȝe, þe soules in purgatori ben esed of þeire
  X: þou wote not howe. ȝa the sawles in purgatorye ar esyd of þer
  Y: þi selfe art clensed & made vertewos be no wark so

CU: peine by vertewe of þis werk. þi-self arte clensid & maad ver-
    tewos
  X: paynes be vertewe of this worke thy selfe ar clensyd and made
    vertews
  Y: mykil. ȝe þe saules in purgatóry ar esed of þaire paynes be

CU: by no werk no mochel.[94]
  X: be none worke so mykyll[95]
  Y: vertewe of þis warke.[96]

---

94 P. 16/ 3-16.
95 Fol. 235v/ 16-31.
96 Fol. 89r/ 27-39.

SPI: Soþeli I hadde leuere felen and han a soþfast disir and a clene
 X: Sothely I had leuer fele and hafe a sothefaste desyre & A clene
 Y: Sothely I had leuer fele & hafe a sothfast desyre & a clene 255

SPI: [97]   in myn herte to my lord Ihesu Crist þouȝ I see
 X: lufe longynge in my herte to my lord Ihesu Criste þough I se
 Y: luf langyng in my hert to my lord Ihesu Criste. þof I se

SPI: riȝt[98] litel of hym wiþ my gostli eiȝe þanne for to han wiþouten
 X: ryȝt lityll of hym with my gostelye eye. Than to hafe with outyn
 Y: right lytel of hym with my gost<ly> ee. þan for to hafe with outen

SPI: þis disir alle bodili penaunce of alle men lifende. ore visions ore
 X: this desyre All bodely pennance or visiouns or revelacions
 Y: þis desyre alle bodely penaunce oɪ visions <.....> reuelacions

SPI: reuelacions of angeles apperende songes and sounes sauours and
 X: of angels or sangis or soundys. or smellys.
 Y: of angels or sanges or sowndes. smelles.

SPI: smelles brennynges and oni likynges bodili felende, and schortli
 X: or brennynges and ony lykyngis bodely felynges And schortly
 Y: or byr<nyn>ges. & <....> lykynges bodely felyng. And schortly 260

SPI: forto seyen or al þe ioye of heuene and of erþe wilk I miȝte
 X: forto say. all þe ioye of heuen and of erthe. whilke I myght
 Y: to say al þe ioy of he <..........> whilk I myght

SPI: haue wiþouten þis disir to mi lord Ihesu.[99]
 X: have withouten this desyre to my lord Ihesu.[100]
 Y: hafe withouten þis desyre to my lord Ih<esu>[101]

DS: For ȝif God be þi loue and þi
 X: Therfore lyfte vp thy herte for yf god be thy love and thy
 Y: <..........> þi hert. For if god be þi luf & þi

---

97 MS. Harley 2387 reads *loue-longynge*.
98 MS. *rist*.
99 Fol. 32r.
100 Fol. 235v/ 31 - fol. 236r/ 1.
101 Fol. 89r/ 40-45.

DS: menyng, þe cheef and þe pointe of þin herte, it suffiseþ to
X: menynge. the choyse and þe poynte of thy herte it Suffice to
Y: menyng <..........> þe ch<..........> suffice to

DS: þee in þis liif, þof al þou se neuer more of him wiþ þe iȝe
X: the in this lyfe þough all þou se neuer more of hym with the eye
Y: þe in þis lyfe. þof þou se neuer <..........   265

DS: of þi reson alle þi liif tyme. Soche a blinde schote with
X: of thy reson alle þy lyfe tyme. Swylke a blynde schote with
Y: ....>/ al þi lyfe tyme. Swilk a blynde schote with

DS: þe scharp darte of longing loue may neuer faile of þe
X: the scharpe darte of longynge lufe. may nouȝt defayle of the
Y: þe scharp darte of longyng luf may neuer defayle of þe

DS: prik, þe whiche is God; as himself seiþ in þe *Book of Loue*
X: prike. the whilke is god. As hym selfe says in the boke of lufe.
Y: prykke þe whilk is god as hym selfe says in þe boke of luf.

DS: where he spekiþ to a langwisching soule and a louyng, seiing þus:
X: where he spekys to A languyschynge saule and A lufynge thus
Y: wher he spekes to a langwyschyng saule & a lofyng sayng þus

DS: 'Vulnerasti cor meum, soror mea, amica mea, sponsa mea,
X: Vulnerasti cor meum Soror mea. amica mea. et sponsa mea. 270
Y: Vulnerasti cor meum Soror mea. amica et sponsa mea.

DS: vulnerasti cor meum in vno oculorum tuorum';
X: Vulnerasti cor meum in vno oculorum tuorum. that is to say.
Y: et cetera

DS: 'þou hast wounded myn hert, my sistre, my lemman, & my spouse,
X: Thowe hase woundyd my herte, my Sister my lemman and my Spowse
Y: þou has wounded my hert. my systyr. my luf & my spowse[102]

DS: þou hast woundid myn herte in one of þin iȝen'[103]
X: þou hase woundyd my herte in on of thyne eyne Deo Gracias. Amen.[104]

---

102 Fol. 89r/ 46 - fol. 89v/ 5.
103 P. 72/ 10-19.
104 Fol. 236r/ 1-13.

*
* *

SPI: þe knittynge and þe fastning
  Y: þus sal þou knyt þi hert to Ihesu. þe knyttyng & þe festynyng

SPI: of Ihesu to a mannes soule is bi a good wil and by a gret disir
  Y: of Ihesu to a mans saule is be a gode will & a gret desyre 275

SPI: to hym. only forto haue hym. and see hym in his blis gostly.
  Y: to hym onely for to hafe hym & se hym in his blys gostly.

SPI: þe more þat þis disir is: þe faster is Ihesu knitt to þe
  Y: þe more þat þis desyre is þe faster is. Ihesu knytt to þe

SPI: soule: þe lesse þat þe disir is: þe loslyer is he knitt.[105]
  Y: saule. & þe les þat þe desyre is. þe lowslyer is he knytt.[106]

MT: Tertia autem, scilicet unitiva, respondet Seraphim, qui
  Y: þis thyrd way vnatyfe awnswers to þe ordyr of seraphyn þe
     whilk

MT: interpretatur ardens: ibi enim in tanto ardore fertur anima
  Y: betokens byrnyng. For þer is þe saule in so mykyl luf borne 280

MT: in Deum, ut maxime corpus per extensionem affectuum
  Y: vp in to god. þat gretly þe body be þe extendyng of affeccions

MT: et motuum quandoque mirabiliter affligatur.[107]
  Y: & of mefynges is sumtyme mervelosly afflicte.[108]

  Y: Capiat qui potest capere quia gracia est ductrix.[109]

II

The subject matter of Y is more extensive than that of X; but in the
description of the threefold way of the contemplative life, which is common to both, the tracts agree very substantially.

In the treatment of the purgative way verbal parallels from only one

105 Fol. 8r.
106 Fol. 89v/ 6-10.
107 P. 10a.
108 Fol. 89v/ 10-13.
109 Fol. 89v/ 14, v. X: fol. 234r/ 1-2 (ll. 84-85).

source, Hugh of Balma's *Mystica theologia*,[110] can be identified. X borrows from it much more extensively than Y,[111] and the two tracts differ in their development of other teaching. There are two short passages independent of the source in which Y agrees with X, but the agreement is much less exact than in similar passages in the treatment of the illuminative and unitive way; and whereas in X each passage establishes continuity between material derived from the *Mystica theologia* this does not occur in Y.[112]

The treatment of the illuminative and unitive way reveals much closer agreement. There are only two major differences between X and Y in the presentation of the illuminative way. First, after an introductory section derived from the *Mystica theologia*,[113] and a warning against vain thoughts,[114] the tracts diverge: X employs a brief passage on the virtue of the Holy Name,[115] whereas Y borrows a longer treatment of that theme from *Beniamyn minor*.[116] Second, Hugh of Balma's comparison between the illuminative way and the order of cherubim is placed differently in the tracts.[117] In two passages derived from book II of *The Scale of Perfection* Y differs significantly from X.[118] Both texts agree in six minor variations from the Peltier text of the *Mystica theologia*,[119]

110 It must be stressed that only direct verbal borrowings are being identified here (see above p. 87). Close resemblances to aspects of the teaching given on the purgative way in the *Mystica theologia* can be found in the *Cloud* writings (esp. *Privy Counselling*, p. 158/ 17 - p. 160/ 3) and the *Scale*, I, 91 (esp. fols. 61v-62r), as well as in other treatises on the spiritual life.

111 There are ten passages which can be traced with certainty to the *Mystica theologia*: ll. 86-91; 92-93; 94-95; 99-100; 102-107; 109-110; 115-119; 133-139; 139-140; 144-146.

Five of these (ll. 86-91; 92-93; 109-110; 115-119; and 139-140) occur in X alone; and one (ll. 144-146) appears in a more extensive form in Y. Although the form in which the latter appears in X is an improvement in style, this may not have been intended.

In four other passages (ll. 111-114; 119-121; 121-123; and 126-132) X may be related to the *Mystica theologia*.

112 Ll. 99-101; 120-121.

113 Ll. 146-154.

114 Ll. 154-156. Similar warnings occur in *Privy Counselling* (p. 136/ 9 and 14), the *Scale* II, 22 (fol. 87r) and elsewhere.

115 Ll. 158-160.

116 Ll. 164-181.

117 Ll. 161-163 and ll. 212-217. Y employs the passage at the end of the description of the illuminative way and uses a fuller form.

118 In the first, Y briefly summarises the first part of a longer extract in X and agrees with X in the rest of it (ll. 198-202); and in the second, Y entirely omits the sentence which concludes the description of the illuminative way in X (ll. 208-210).

119 L. 148: add *anone*; l. 150: omit *immediate*; l. 151: add *of the light*; l. 152: omit *primo*; l. 153: modify *lucis splendores divino radio*; l. 154: omit *cum fuerit curata*.

These variations could be due to the different Latin text from which the compiler worked.

and in two others Y agrees with the Peltier text against X.[120] In the two short connecting passages apparently introduced by the compiler, Y agrees with X, exactly in the first and very substantially in the second.[121]

X and Y agree very closely in the treatment of the unitive way. They place the reference to the order of seraphim differently, and Y concludes with a quotation from book I of the *Scale* which is not in X.[122] Where minor variations have been noted, X and Y agree much more frequently against the source[123] than either agrees with it against the other.[124] In the two short passages which apparently have been introduced in this section by the compiler, X and Y appear to agree exactly.[125]

Thus there is a significant relationship between X and Y. Both employ the same sources in the same order.[126] They agree very closely verbally with their source and each other in material on the illuminative and unitive way, and too closely on the purgative way for the similarities to be coincidental.[127] They frequently agree when they differ from their source, or when apparently original passages occur. Clearly neither extant text derives immediately from the other;[128] and there are four reasons why Y appears to depend upon an earlier form of X.

First, Y is a loose collection of material derived from demonstrably different and varied sources: the crude, unsophisticated verses on the active life, prose extracts from Rolle's *Form of Living*, book I of the *Scale* and probably the *Cloud*,[129] as well as the material also in X. Although its

---

120 Ll. 147-148: X adds *the whilke is callyde*; l. 152: X omits *as*.

121 Ll. 155-156; 182-183.

122 Ll. 271-282. Y also omits the. last few words in X from *A Pistle of Discrecioun of Stirings*.

123 X and Y agree against the text of the source in fourteen instances: e.g. l. 235 omit *of þis werk*; and l. 258 omit *of alle men lifende*.

124 X agrees with the source against Y in two instances: Y omits *up* l. 239; and Y omits *al* l. 265.

Y agrees with the source against X in two instances: X omits *to sey* l. 228; and X reads *that* for *as it* l. 228.

In addition Y omits one sentence from the *Cloud* and several words also from the preceding sentence (ll. 252-254) - an eye slip?

125 Ll. 221-225, 263. The imperfect state of the Y manuscript makes this uncertain.

126 Except for the instances already noted.

127 Contrast, for example, the borrowings from the *Mystica theologia* in X and Y with the two quite independent translations of *þe pistill of saynt Machari þe Ermyte* in MSS. U.L.C. Ff.6.33, and in B.M. Add. 33971, Bodl. Rawlinson D 913 and Huntington Lib. HM 148, on which the writer is preparing a study.

128 The instances already noted in which Y agrees with the source against X, or X agrees with the source against Y, together with the differences noted in passages common to X and Y, suffice to justify this statement. X contains a number of careless errors which do not occur in Y.

129 See n. 9, where the alternative, a passage from book I of the *Scale*, is printed.

The sentence which in Y introduces the exposition of the threefold way could be a summary of the Latin passage from the *Mystica theologia* with which X begins (ll. 82-83).

teaching on the active and contemplative lives is clear and ordered, and some attempt has been made to impose unity on the tract by using the device of the disciple and the doctor,[130] casting the borrowings into the second person, and perhaps by altering the position of the angel passages, there is no unity of style. It seems more likely that the compiler incorporated a tract on the threefold way into his exposition of the two lives than that the teaching on the threefold way was isolated and expanded to become X. Second, whereas in X the exposition of each way is of approximately the same length, in Y the purgative way is discussed in a passage only one third the length of those devoted to the others.[131] As the compiler of Y has already given considerable attention to active purification in the verses on the active life, it seems more likely that he has condensed the treatment of passive purification in the purgative way than that the compiler of X has expanded it for stylistic reasons.[132] Third, it would seem pointless to remove the references to cherubim and seraphim from their positions in Y to those in X, whereas considerations of style might have led a compiler to place them in positions corresponding to the reference to thrones in the description of the purgative way. Fourth, where X and Y differ significantly in a borrowed passage, X appears generally to be closer to the source than Y. None of these arguments is decisive; but each increases the likelihood that Y depends upon some form of X.

Although X is generally closer to its sources than Y, the differences between X and Y indicate that Y does not depend directly upon the extant text of X. Thus, Y uses the passage from *Beniamyn minor* where X uses the short Holy Name passage;[133] and Y follows the *Mystica theologia* more closely and extensively in the angel comparison.[134] There are also

---

130   *Cf.* Additional MS. 37049, fol. 89v, where the same device is employed at the beginning of *Agayne despayre*, which includes the second Middle English version of *De remediis contra temptaciones*: "Worthy doctour I beseke þe to declare vnto þe ese and to exclude þe heuynes of my herte...".

131   If we exclude the introductions to the threefold way, the number of words in each section for X and Y is approximately:

> X: Purgative — 570; Illuminative — 520; Unitive — 650.
> Y: Purgative — 260; Illuminative — 770; Unitive — 710.

132   There is little evidence that the compiler of X gave thought to questions of style.

133   This passage on the Holy Name could have been found in any spiritual writing of the period; but it need not be a borrowing.

134   These two variations are probably a deliberate revision by the compiler of Y or another hand. In both tracts the context demands some explanation of "one thynge". Again, the more extensive borrowing in the angel passages does add to the teaching of the tract. Thus Y refers to "mony lightnynges of grace" in the illuminative way; and to the afflictions of the body through "þe extendyng of affeccions & of mefynges" in the unitive way. The compiler develops neither.

minor variations, even in borrowings from the *Mystica theologia*,[135] where Y is closer than X to the source. Therefore the compiler of Y probably used for his treatment of the threefold way a text very similar to the extant text of X. He condensed and freely modified its description of the purgative way; and be modified the descriptions of the illuminative and unitive way by adding passages from *Beniamyn minor* and book I of the *Scale*,[136] and by placing the angel passages differently.

The passages referring to thrones, cherubim and seraphim merit separate consideration. In his discussion of the illuminative way, Hugh of Balma compares the threefold way and the orders of angels.[137] The comparison is in no way essential to the argument of his treatise and he does not develop it further, yet it appealed sufficiently to the first compiler for him to use it in the English exposition of the threefold way. It adds nothing material to the content of X or Y: where it does introduce new teaching, this is not developed sufficiently to warrant the introduction, and its reference to "fulnes of kunnynge" is quite alien to the English description of the illuminative way.[138]

The use of this comparison throws some light on the development of the two Middle English tracts. If, as one might expect, the reference to each order was originally placed in the same relative position in each section, then X would represent a later development. There is no evidence to suggest that the passage on thrones has been displaced, and there is no other position in the description of the purgative way where it could properly have been placed. If the Middle English accounts of

---

135 It has been assumed here that the compiler who included the material on the threefold way in the account of the contemplative life in Y is the same person who brought ll. 1-83 to their present form. The use of the *Cloud* and *Scale* material in the same way as in the Y passages in the rest of the tract makes this a plausible assumption. It is quite possible, however, that others have been at work on the tracts also.

136 In view of the relationship between X and Y and the sources, it seems much more probable that these passages were added later than that they were originally in the compilation, were then omitted, and the Holy Name passage and ll. 271 and 273 were then added.

137 "Via enim purgativa respondet ordini Thronorum: nam ibi tunc primo purgatur anima ad hoc, quod primo Deus in ipsa veluti in loco mundo resideat. Ista autem, ut dictum est, respondet Cherubim: Cherubim plenitudo scientiae interpretatur. Tantum autem per artem hujus theoricae scientiae lumen acquiritur, et tanta sapientiae dilatatio in Scripturis, ut quot verba in Novo et Veteri Testamento, quot creaturae in mundo, tot habeat anima intelligentias, vel sermones, totum ad Deum ad punctum amoris omnia referendo, ut postea apparebit. Tertia autem, scilicet unitiva, respondet Seraphim, qui interpretatur ardens: ibi enim in tanto ardore fertur anima in Deum, ut maxime corpus per extensionem affectuum et motum quandoque mirabiliter affligatur." (p. 9b - p. 10a).

138 Perhaps the Y compiler or some other person, aware of the difference between Hilton's meekness and love and "fulnes of kunnynge", added l. 211, which suggests that persistence in these dispositions will lead to "fulnes of kunnynge" of the illuminative way.

the illuminative and unitive way ended originally where the angel passages stand in X, the proportion of borrowings from the *Mystica theologia* in these two accounts would have been much higher originally than it is now, and in the account of the illuminative way would approach more closely that in the purgative way.[139] Furthermore there would not have been any borrowings from the *Scale*, all of which now follow the angel passages. The attractiveness of this possibility diminishes when one considers how trivial the treatment of the illuminative way must then have been, and how disproportionate to that of the purgative way.[140] Possibly the passages were displaced in X and retain their original position in Y; but more probably the first compiler did not care enough about questions of style to bother placing the three passages in the same relative position in each section when he borrowed them, and the compiler of Y altered the position of the second and third.

How significant are the differences between X and Y? Some changes in Y, notably the briefer account of the purgative way and the insertion of the long extract from *Beniamyn minor*, have slightly modified its teaching, but no change is of major importance.[141] By introducing the material on the active life and the distinction between the active and contemplative lives, the compiler of Y has produced a tract which, however crudely, treats the whole range of Christian life and sets the threefold way in this perspective. Moreover, although he has significantly reduced the borrowings from the *Mystica theologia*, he has turned with correspondingly greater frequency to the *Cloud* tracts,[142] and in earlier material has borrowed more from book I of the *Scale* and used an extract from Rolle's *Form of Living*.[143] While the differences between X and Y are noteworthy, they do not alter significantly the teaching both tracts give on the threefold way.

---

139 Even then the proportion of material from the *Mystica theologia* in the illuminative way would be just over one half, compared with over two thirds in the purgative way. In the unitive way the proportion would still be well under one quarter of the material.

140 The illuminative way would be less than one third its present length, and the unitive way just over one third.

141 For instance, Y entirely omits the teaching in X on the Lord's will to reward perseverance with true compunction; and the change to the *Beniamyn minor* extract omits from Y the assertion that the Name "purges the sawle fro synne and chasys the fende and puttys owte vanytese and makys A sawle abyll to receyfe grete grace", but adds the teaching that by it the mind will be ravished to behold God and godly things.

142 See below, pp. 118-19.

143 Ll. 8-15, 69-75.

III

The extent to which the tracts incorporate borrowings from other writings is remarkable: for instance, almost five sixths of X can be traced to the sources identified. Approximately one third of X, and two thirds of its exposition of the purgative way, has been traced to the *Mystica theologia*. Approximately one fifth of Y, and only half the much shorter description of the purgative way, has been traced to the same source. More material has been borrowed from the *Mystica theologia* than from any other source. Against this, however, must be set the fact that much of the derivative material is only generally related to the Latin, often with no exact correspondence;[144] and the fact that a significantly greater proportion of borrowings is copied exactly from the *Scale* and the *Cloud* tracts.[145]

Does such extensive borrowing mean that the compilers also depended for their own teaching on the spiritual life upon the treatises from which they borrowed? There is abundant evidence that they[146] knew the treatises which provided the borrowings, and were presumably influenced by them. Unless it could be shown that the tracts X and Y contain teaching which is peculiar to the treatises from which the borrowings come, there can be no conclusion that these treatises directly influenced the teaching of the tracts.

X and Y certainly rely upon the *Mystica theologia*[147] for their outline of the threefold way; but that treatise is not unique in its division of the contemplative life according to a threefold pattern, for the *Cloud*, the *Scale* and the *Formula noviciorum* among other writings employ the

144   See above, p. 87.

145   In X, just over one third of the tract depends on the *Mystica theologia*, and almost one half upon the English spiritual writings. In Y, less than one fifth of the threefold way depends on the *Mystica theologia*, and about three fifths upon the English spiritual writings. About one eighth of the whole tract depends upon the *Mystica theologia*, and about two fifths on the English writings.

146   This can be stated less certainly of the compiler of Y.

147   For an account of the conclusions of recent scholarship on the treatise, and an outline of its teaching see "Hugues de Balma," *Dictionnaire de Spiritualité*, cols. 859-873. *Cf.* A Benedictine of Stanbrook, *Medieval Mystical Tradition and St. John of the Cross* (London, 1954), pp. 92-100; and J. Leclercq, F. Vandenbroucke, and L. Bouyer, *The Spirituality of the Middle Ages* (London, 1968), pp. 421, 457.

It seems unlikely that the popularity accorded to the *Mystica theologia* on the continent was as great in England. Dr. Doyle notes only two extant manuscripts of English provenance which contain the Latin text: MSS. Trinity College Cambridge B.14.25 and Caius College Cambridge 353. Syon Abbey had the treatise in MS. M.116. See also n. 166.

classification of beginners, proficients and perfect,[148] the *Scale* identifies
three parts of contemplation and three manners of prayer,[149] and
Bonaventure's *De triplici via* distinguishes the purgative, illuminative and
unitive way.[150] The tracts are most closely related to the *Mystica theologia*
in their teaching on the purgative way: most of their teaching on it can
be identified in some form in the treatise, although only minor details
are peculiar to it.[151] Their description of the illuminative way differs
significantly from that in the *Mystica theologia*[152] and that of the unitive
way relies much more heavily upon the *Cloud*,[153] so that any dependence
here is indirect.[154] The two areas in which the *Mystica theologia* and the
Cloud have most in common, the *cognitio per ignorantiam* and the loving
aspirations, receive less prominence than might be expected, and when
they do appear, the words and teaching of the English writers are
used.[155]

While it is true, therefore, that both tracts describe the contemplative
life in terms of the threefold way which the *Mystica theologia* helped to
popularise and used words partly borrowed from that treatise, there is
little evidence to establish that the compilers depended on it for their
teaching. Significantly they borrowed most from it to describe the
purgative way, which it treats least distinctively and to which it devotes
least attention.

Nearly all the identifiable borrowings in the exposition of the
illuminative and unitive way come from the *Scale* and the *Cloud* writings.
To describe the illuminative way, the compiler of X has combined brief
borrowings from the *Mystica theologia* with roughly three times as much

148   See n. 26. For the treatment in the *Formula noviciorum* see Queens' College Cambridge MS.
31, fols. 44r-48r.

149   Book I, 4-9 (fols. 3r-6r); 27-32 (fols. 17r-19v).

150   "Thes ben the preisinges to oure lord God" in MS. U.L.C. Add. 3042, fols. 116r-125r. I am
indebted to Miss Russell-Smith for drawing this to my attention.

151   *E.g.* the prayer for forgiveness; the recommended considerations; the number of Aves; and
the order of thrones. Of these, probably only the last is clearly derivative in that it could hardly
have come from elsewhere; and the use which is made of it in the compilations is different from
that made by Hugh of Balma.

152   *Cf.* "Hugues de Balma," *Dictionnaire de spiritualité*, cols. 861-862 with the outline of the
illuminative way in the tracts.

153   See below, pp. 118-19.

154   Walsh has shown that there is evidence of a relationship between the *Cloud* and the *Mystica
theologia*; so it might be possible to argue that some of the teaching on the unitive way depends indirectly upon the *Mystica theologia*.

155   See below, p. 119.

material reproduced almost exactly from the early stages of the journey to Jerusalem described in book II of the *Scale*. He has used no *Cloud* material in this description, but the compiler of Y has introduced the long extract from *Beniamyn minor*. Three significant points in Hilton's teaching occur: his definition of contemplation as "a sight of Ihesu the whylke is verreye pees";[156] the simple aspirations recommended to express settled dispositions to meekness and love;[157] and his advice against the temptation to desist because of a sense of unworthiness.[158] It is as arguable that the compiler chose the passages because they expressed his own teaching well as that he derived his teaching from them; for much of Hilton's teaching is omitted.[159] The passage from book I which is incorporated in the description of the unitive way and the other two passages borrowed by the compiler of Y do not express Hilton's distinctive teaching: each is an effective expression of a commonly held understanding of the contemplative life.

To describe the unitive way, the compiler of X has relied very heavily upon the *Cloud* tracts, with a short borrowing from book I of the *Scale* and a shorter one from the *Mystica theologia*. The compiler of Y has a somewhat greater proportion of material from the *Scale*. The extracts include elements which are characteristic of the *Cloud* writings: notably teaching on the effect of "þe werk of þe soule þat most plesiþ God",[160] and phrases like "a meek steryng of loue" and the striking "a blinde schote with þe scharp darte of longynge lufe" which are more distinctive than the advice they express.[161] Some teaching in the extracts from these writings might as readily have been conveyed in extracts from the *Scale*.[162] Distinctive elements in the *Cloud*'s teaching like the cloud metaphor, and direct reference to "unknowing" are absent; and the specific teaching about the loving aspirations associated with the *Mystica theologia* and the *Cloud* occur in words borrowed from the *Scale*.[163]

156 Ll. 183-184.
157 Ll. 188-194.
158 Ll. 204-207.
159 There is no reference, for instance, to reformation in faith and feeling; to the image of sin and the image of Jesus; or to the fourfold work of Jesus based on Romans 8:29-30.
160 Ll. 247-254.
161 These phrases derive their significance from the teaching in the *Cloud* tracts: for instance, in the context of the *Cloud*'s teaching, the "scharp darte" is a striking expression of the Dionysian "extensio". Divorced from their full context, they can only carry such meaning as X and Y give them, except to the reader who identifies them and accords them the meaning they carry in the *Cloud* writings.
162 The extract from *A Pistle of Preier* (ll. 226-236), for instance, conveys the same teaching as in the *Scale*, I, 8 (fol. 5r-v). See n. 11.
163 Ll. 188-194.

The evidence does not indicate that the compilers of X or Y derived their teaching from the *Scale* or the *Cloud* writings any more than from the *Mystica theologia*. The teaching which could most plausibly be attributed to the Middle English writings is Hilton's practical advice on the dispositions of meekness and love, and, perhaps, the *Cloud*'s insistence on the value of the work of love in God's purpose for others. On the other hand, as the teaching of the tracts is consistent within itself,[164] the extracts presumably were borrowed to express that teaching.

The tracts are valuable in the study of Middle English spiritual writings for a number of reasons.

First, only these two tracts and one other extant in Middle English describe the contemplative life in terms of the purgative, illuminative and unitive way.

Second, they provide evidence that the *Mystica theologia* was known in fifteenth-century England, at least among the Carthusians. Walsh has shown that Richard Methley, in his Latin translation of the *Cloud*, indicates his knowledge of the treatise[165] and that the Latin treatise, *Exposicio super quedam verba libri beati Dionisii de mistica theologia*, which occurs with the *Cloud* and associated tracts in Bodleian MS. Douce 262 (another manuscript of Carthusian provenance), is a long extract from book III of the *Mystica theologia*.[166] The existence of extensive borrowings from it in the same compilations with extracts from the *Cloud* writings provides further evidence to support his findings, although these tracts do not themselves demonstrate that the author of the *Cloud* depended upon the *Mystica theologia*.

Third, they contain borrowings from the *Cloud* writings. Compared with the *Scale* and the more popular writings by Rolle, the *Cloud* and its associated epistles occur in few extant manuscripts. Whereas extracts by Hilton and Rolle have been copied to stand independently or in combination with other material,[167] there is only one other instance yet

---

164 If there is any inconsistency of teaching, it occurs in the presentation of the illuminative way which does not develop the suggestion borrowed from the *Mystica theologia* that it is the way of "fulnes of kunnynge" in which "the sawle is lightnede to vndyrstande holy scripture", but rather introduces the response of meekness and love.

165 He presents this in the edition of Methley's Latin version of the *Cloud* and the *Mirror of Simple Souls* (Pembroke College Cambridge MS. 221) which he and Colledge have prepared for publication in the *Archivio italiano per la storia della pietà*.

166 J. Walsh, "The Ascent to Contemplative Wisdom," *The Way* 9 (1969) 243-250.

167 An extract from Rolle's *Form of Living* stands independently, for instance, in Additional MS. 37049, fol. 35v, and another is combined with other material in U.L.C. MS. Ff.5.40, fols. 113v-116r. An extract from the *Scale* stands in B.M. MS. Harley 6615, fols. 100v-103v, and passages from Hilton's writings are combined with extracts from Julian's *Revelations of Divine Love* in a Westminster

identified of material from the *Cloud* having been borrowed; and that, occurring in a *Cloud* manuscript and being little more than an extract isolated for instruction on one topic,[168] is less significant than these tracts.

Finally, it is noteworthy that the *Cloud* material occurs in conjunction with extracts from the *Scale*, and that, particularly in the description of the unitive way, material from both sources is combined to teach the union of the soul with God. Although it would be unwise to draw from this any conclusion as to the relationship between the *Scale* and the *Cloud* epistles, particularly as these sources, like the *Mystica theologia*, appear to have been used to express the compilers' teaching rather than to determine it, nevertheless it suggests that there may have been a fairly settled tradition of teaching on the contemplative life to which both writers were seen by their successors and admirers to have contributed.[169]

Further study of the spiritual teaching in lesser-known Middel English writings in this fiels is desirable before other conclusions are drawn.

Cheltenham, Victoria, Australia

Cathedral manuscript (see J. Walsh and E. Colledge, eds., *Of the Knowledge of Ourselves and of God* (London, 1961)).

168   In the University Library Cambridge MS. Kk.6.26, which contains the seven *Cloud* tracts, there is a short piece on fols. 28r-31r with the heading *Howe þe myȝtes of mans saule stonden in þe noumbre of fyfe* which consists of the material contained in chapters 63 to 66 of the *Cloud* prefaced by a brief introduction and concluded by a short sentence using material from chapter 67. It can be seen even from this short description that the use of the *Cloud* material in this piece is not comparable with the use of the borrowings in the tract under discussion.

I have identified the piece (Item D.1) only since the publication of P. S. Jolliffe, *A Check-List of Middle English Prose Writings of Spiritual Guidance* (Toronto, 1974).

169   Far too little is yet known of the spiritual guidance extant in Middle English writings of the fifteenth century. The writer is preparing for publication a study of this subject.

FIFTEENTH- AND SIXTEENTH-CENTURY ENGLISH VERSIONS OF "THE GOLDEN EPISTLE OF ST. BERNARD"

Edmund Colledge, O.S.A.

I<small>N</small> the "Amherst MS.", British Museum Additonal MS. 37790,[1] fols. 95ᵛ-96ᵛ contain a brief prose item, an English translation of what is known in Latin sometimes as *Varia et brevia documenta pie seu religiose vivendi*,[2] sometimes as *Notabile documentum*,[3] and which in the late Middle Ages was often, as here, attributed to St. Bernard. A Latin text is in PL 184. 1173-4; Migne reprinted it from Mabillon,[4] who took it from Horstius.[5] The ascription to Bernard is spurious; Cavallera lists it among "ouvrages apocryphes d'auteurs inconnus".[6] In English it is often given the title, *The Golden Epistle*. Though Richard Whitford in the preface to his version rejects the attribution to Bernard, the frequency with which it was translated and the printed versions reissued shows that it was, none the less, esteemed as spiritually helpful.

In editing this Amherst version, notes have been supplied indicating how the English varies from the Latin; but it will be understood that, in the lack of any critical text, such judgments as "not in the Latin", "the English omits", can be only provisional.

This pistill made saynt Barne*r*de vnto his cosyn*n*, the whiche is calde a goldyn*n* pystill, for the grete abundan*n*ce of gostely fruyte that is contynede.

---

1 The contents have been variously described. What it is hoped will be a comprehensive description will appear in the forthcoming critical edition of Julian of Norwich's *Revelations* by Edmund Colledge and James Walsh.

2 This is the Mabillon-Migne title.

3 This is the Latin title given to it by Whitford. See below.

4 1690 (Paris), 2.797-9; 1719 (Paris), 2.814-6; 1727 (Venice), 3.887-8.

5 1642 (Paris), 5.272-4, where it is printed as a mere appendage of *De honestate vitae*.

6 "Bernard, apocryphes attribués" (DSAM 1.1501).

My frende, yf ye will come perfitely to tho thynges the whiche ye
desire, two thyngis be in all wyse to yowe necessarye. The fryste is that
ye sett no more by transitory and erthely thynges than yf þay were not.
The seconnde is that ye gyf youre selfe so interly to god that ye say ne do
5   ony thynge bot syche as ye deme schulde trewly plese hym. Ye may
come vnto the fyrst by this mene: euer dyspyse youre selfe and holde
youre selfe as no nothyr, and juge all oþer persons gude and better than
youre selfe, for so schall ye best plese god.[7] And whate so euer ye here or
see of ony religiouse or famouse[8] personne, what soo euer it be, deme
10 the beste þerof, yff all it seme to yow oþerwyse and contrarye, for by
suspecion mann[9] is ofte dysceuyd. Ye schall displese no creature by
youre will ne say no thynge in praysynge of youre selfe vnto only personne, be he neuer so famyliar with you, bot laboure euer to hyde youre
vertues more thann youre vices. Say no thynge of ony personn detrac-
15 ciously, yf all the dede be trewe and oppenn, bot elles it (be) so þat ye
maye no oþer wyse oppenn youre synne, and thann þat ye do it in youre
confessionn. Euer be gladder to here ony personn preysed þann dis-
presed. When ye schall speke let youre wordes be fewe, witty[10] and of
god; and yf a worldly mann speke with you and begynne to tell yow
20 vayne thyngis, alsonn as ye may breke his tale and turne it[11] to suche
thyngis as fallis to god. Whate sum euer happenn vnto yow or vnto ony
of youre frendes in þis worlde, set not gretly þer by. And it be
prosperouse be not to glad þerof, and if it be aduersite be not to sory
þerfore, bot sett all sych thyngys at noght, and euer preyse god. Be oc-
25 cupied als mekyll as ye maye, and euer intende diligently to þat whiche
shall be euerlastyngly wele for youre saule.[12] Flee mykyll spech as fer-
forth als ye may, for it is better for you to holde youre pease þan to
speke (f. 96ʳ) mekill. After complynn speke not till þe messe of þe next
day be done withoute right a grete cause make it. And yf ye se ony
30 thynge þat displesis you, take goode hede yf ye kanne fynde þe same
thynge in youre selfe; and yf ye do, amende it, I pray you. Yf ye see or
here ony thynge þat plese you, take hede yff it be in you, and yff it be,

15   be: om. MS.

7   for so schall ye best plese god: "magisque placere deo" ("and that they are more pleasing to God").
8   or famouse: not in the Latin.
9   for by suspecion mann: "humana suspicio".
10 fewe, witty: "rara, vera, ponderosa".
11 and turne it (sc. "his tale"): "et transferas te".
12 to þat which shall be euerlastyngly wele for youre saule: "vilitate" (and cf. Mabillon 1690, 2.798, etc.).
The English clearly derives from a corrupt "utilitate".

kepe it sourly, and if it be not in you, gett it *and* ye may.[13] And so schall all thynge be vnto you als a myrro*ure*. How heuely þ*at* ye here[14] ony
35 man*er* of thynge, lat no man vnd*er*stonde þ*at* ye groche þ*er* w*ith*, olesse tha*nn* ye see þ*at* it schall pr*of*et you. Affe*r*m or deny neu*er* ony thynge obstinatly, bot lat yo*ure* yees *and* nayes be als dowtys. Be ye no mollere,[15] lawith seldome *and* emonge fewe *and* schortly. Behaue yo*ure* selfe in alle yo*ure* sayng*es* þ*at* þ*er* be no selfe will fone in thame.[16] Vnto þe
40 secunde parte of my co*n*nsell ye cume by þis meane. Gyff tent vnto yo*ure* pr*a*yers w*ith* grete deuocio*nn*, and to say þa*m*m in dewe tyme. Whate so ye rede,[17] reme*m*bre it wele in yo*ure* herte, *and* fest it in yo*ure* mynde,[18] and reme*m*br*e* oft þe estate of þame for who*m*m ye pr*a*y. Thre thyng*es* all way haue in yo*ure* mynde, þ*at* is to saye whate ye haue bene, whate ye
45 er*e and* what ye schalle be. Whate were ye bot stynkynge seed of ma*n*n,[19] what er*e* ye bot a seke full of filth, whate schalle ye be bot wormes mete? Also ymagy*n*n whate payne þay haue þ*at* be i*n* hell and howe it schall neu*er* haue ende, and for a litill dilectacio*n* and plesa*n*nce how gret payne þay suffre. In like wyse ymagyne þe joye of hevyn, and howe
50 it schalle neu*er* haue ende, and how sone[20] it may be gette*nn*; and þay may sorowe *and* co*m*pleyn*n* þe which losis it for litill lust of þe fals worlde, which is so schorte in co*m*pariso*nn* of þ*at* whiche neu*er* schall haue ende.[21] And when ye haue or dredys ony thyngis þ*at* displesis you,

---

13 *and ye may*: not in the Latin.

14 *þat ye here*: "quod habes". This looks like English scribal error, "haue here".

15 *Be ye no mollere*: "Acachinnis semper abstineas". The etymology seems to be OFr *moiller* <Lat. *mulier*, and the meaning "chattering woman". *Cf.* NED *Mulier*; this sense is not recorded, but the entry is inadequate.

16 *þat þer be no selfe will fone in thame*: "ut sint (*sc.* dicta sua) ita quae dubia dimittantur". Plainly there has been some corruption of the Latin text.

17 *Whate so ye rede*: "quod offers in oratione".

18 *and fest it in youre mynde*: not in the Latin.

19 *Whate were ye bot stynkynge seed of mann...*: "Quid fuisti quia sperma fetidum..."; this is a commonplace in late mediaeval ascetic literature. *Cf.* the Cleopatra text of the *Ancrene Riwle*: "Nart þu icumen of ful slim. Philosophus. sperma es fluidum, vas stercorum, esca vermium. Nart þu nu fulðe vette. Ne bist þu wurme fod" (ed. E. J. Dobson (London, 1972), pp. 202-3). The reading "fluidum" is found in other *Riwle* texts (*e.g.* Nero, ed. Mabel Day (London, 1952), p. 124); but "ful" presupposes "fetidum" in the autograph; and if, as Dobson suggests, the author himself revised Cleopatra, he failed to detect this error. He may have derived the saying from Giraldus Cambrensis, by whom it is attributed to Dionysius the Philosopher, speaking in reproof to Alexander the Great (*Gemma ecclesiastica* 2.4, ed. J. S. Brewer (London, 1862), p. 183, where there is the erroneous reading "spuma"; *De principis instructione liber*, ed. G. F. Warner (London, 1891), p. 5). George Cary evidently knew of no source earlier than Giraldus: *The Medieval Alexander* (Cambridge, 1956), p. 102.

20 *how sone*: "quam breuiter et cito".

21 *for litill lust of þe fals worlde, which is so schort in comparisonn of þat whiche neuer shall haue ende*: "pro parva re".

þann þynke þat and ye were in hell ye schulde haue þat same and all þat
55 euer ye wolde not haue; and so schall ye haue pacience to suffre all
þynge for þe luff of criste with gude will.[22] And when ye haue a thynge
þat plesis you,[23] thynke than and ye were in heven, ye schulde haue þe
same þynge with ony oþer þat ye wolde desyre, and if ye were in hell ye
schulde not haue þat ye desyre. When þer falles only haly day of ony
60 saynt, remembre you what he or scho sufferde for oure lorde, and ye
schall fynde þat his sufferannce was bot schort. Then remembre you
whate was his rewarde, and ye schall fynde þat it was euerlastynge life.
Also thynke howe þe tribulacions of good men passis (f. 96ᵛ) sone, and
the lykyng of ill menn makis sone ende, and good menn for þer
65 tribulacions paciently sufferde gettys euerlastynge joye, and euyll menn
for þer litill schorte lykynge[24] gose to euer lastynge payne. Þerfore when
ye haue leysere,[25] take this schorte wrytynge and remembre all thyngis
þer in, and considere whate tyme ye lose whenn ye myght be full wele oc-
cupyed in redynge, praynge or meditacion. For tymm y tell yow is ryght
70 preciouse;[26] and þay þat be in hell for so lityll tyme wolde gyf and thay
had it all þis worlde, so þat þay myght haue it at þer awne leysere to
repente þamm selfe in.[27] When ye haue ony tribulouse thynges, thynke
thann that thay þat be in hevenn lakys all suche tribuls;[28] and when ye
haue ony comforthis,than thynke þat alle þay that be in hell lakys alle
75 sich comfortes. When ye lay you downe to slepe, remembre whate ye
haue thoght, what ye haue saide and whate ye haue done[29] that day, and
howe[30] ye haue spendyd þe tyme þerof which was granntyd to you to
purchese þerby euerlastynge life, and yf ye haue spendit it wele preys and
thanke[31] god þerof, and yf ye spendit neclygently,[32] wepe and spende not
80 þe next day so febilly, bot confesse[33] you for youre defaute.[34] This I put
in the conclusionn of my wrytynge. I will þat ye oft tymes ymagynn ij

22 and so schalle ... with gude will: not in the Latin.
23 þat plesis you: the English omits "vel optas habere".
24 for þer litill schorte lykynge: "ex indebitis gaudiis".
25 whan ye haue leysere: "quandocunque te vincit accedia".
26 whenn ye myght be ... is ryght preciouse: not in the Latin.
27 so þat þay ... þamm selfe in: not in the Latin.
28 tribuls: NED records Tribul, v., first example a. 1325, but no corresponding noun; but cf.
Godefroy, Tribol, "tribulation".
29 and whate ye haue done: not in the Latin.
30 and howe: the English omits "utiliter".
31 and thanke: not in the Latin.
32 neclygently: the English omits "male".
33 and spende not ... but confesse: et sequenti die non differas confiteri.
34 The English omits: "Si aliquid cogitasti, dixisti vel fecisti quod tuam conscientiam multum
remordeat, non comedas antequam confitearis".

cytes, the tone full of all tormentys, whiche is hell, the toþer full of alle
joye, and that is hevenn. And thynke sadly[35] that to the tone of thies two
most you nedys goo. Therfore kepe wele all þies rehersyd afore, and
forgett none of thamm, and rede this lessonn oft, I pray you.[36] And if ye
85 fynde youreselfe that ye do als it techis you, than prays god, which is
euer mercyfull vnto synners, of the whiche I am þe moste. I pray you ten-
dyrly, pray to Jhesu for me, that he of my syns will haue mercye.
Amenn.[37]

Jhesu mercy. Lady helpe. J S/

This translation, which the single hand of most of the Amherst MS.
permits us to date ante 1450, is wholly independent of that which is
found in MS. St. John's College, Oxford, 173. This manuscript also is in
one chief hand of c. 1450, and the scribe signs himself on fol. 45ʳ as
"Johannes Colman". The contents are chiefly Latin, but several English
items occur; and one begins, fol. 141ʳ :

Saynte Bernarde to a newe begynner in relygion

If thou entende to playse god and woldest obteyne grace to fulfylle the
same two thynges ben to the necessari. Fyrste thou must wythdrawe thi
mynde from al transitori *and* erthly thynges ...

Fol. 143ᵛ, it ends:

Now for a conclusion, imagynge in thy mynde too citees, one ful of
trouble *and* myserye whiche is helle, a nother ful of joye and comfort
whiche is paradyse, and how to one of thyse two you muste nedes come.
Than thynke in thi self what thyng sholde cause the to do euyl or what
thinge sholde drawe the fro god, and I trow thou shalte fynde none suche.
I am certeyne yf þou kepe welle and thyse þat ben wryten here the holy
gooste wyl be with the and teche the to kepe theym parfitely. Wherfore
kepe wele al thise preceptes *and* commaundementes and leue none
behynde. Rede theym twys in the weke on Wensdaye *and* Saturdaye, and
as þou fyndest thou hast doon as it is wryten, geue praysyng to god whiche
is euer pyetous *and* merciful in worlde wythouten ende. Amen.

Comparison of this incipit and explicit with those of the Amherst text
show that they are independent, and that the St. John's version contains
features of the Latin not found in the Amherst.

---

35   *And thynke sadly*: not in the Latin.
36   *Therfore kepe wele ... I pray you*: this replaces: "Vide quid te possit trahere ad malum vel impedire a bono. Credo quod nihil invenies. Certus sum quod si bene servaveris ea quae sunt hic,
spiritus sanctus habitabit in te et perfecte docebit te facere omnia. Ergo bene serves ista, et nihil
negligas. Et lege ea in septimana bis, scilicet in die Mercurii et in die Sabbati".
37   *of the whiche ... Amenn*: not in the Latin.

During the sixteenth century two other versions of the text gained wide circulation as printed books. The first is by the celebrated Richard Whitford of Syon:[38] *A goodly treatyss and it is called a notable lesson otherwyse it is called the golden pystle.*[39] In his introductory paragraph, Whitford denies the ascription to Bernard: it was "put amonge his werkes I thynke by some vertuous man þat wolde it schulde therby haue the more auctorite and the rather be redde and better be borne awaye …".[40] At the end, Whitford writes: "This was brought vnto me in englysshe of an olde translacyon roughe and rude and requyred to amende it. I thought lesse labour to write newe the hole and I haue done vnto the sentence not very nere the letter and in dyuers places added some thinges folowyng upon the same to make the mater more sentencyous and full".[41]

Whitford's translation begins:

> If you intende to please god *and* wolde obtayne grace to fulfyll the same two thynges ben vnto you very necessary. The firste you muste withdrawe your mynde from all worldly and transytory thynges in suche maner as though you cared not wheder any such thynges were in this worlde or no …[42]

and it ends:

> And where you profyte gyue thankes laude and prayse vnto our lorde god and moste swete sauyour Jesu Christ who sende you his mercy and grace that alway lyeth god: In secula seculorum. Amen.[43]

Whitford has made two major additions in the text, a passage on the daily order of the canonical hours, and an explanation of how the six grammatical cases can serve as mnemonic and guide to different modes of prayer. Also, in the margin of f.B.ij[r], there is printed: "you may in the englysshe Martyloge breuely se the lyues of many sayntes for euery daye in the yere". This was evidently an afterthought, once the type has been set up. Whitford's work on the Martirology for the Syon nuns is well known,[44] and it may be that it was at their request that this new

---

38 There is a useful account of him in DNB by Ronald Bayne, though the bibliographical information concerning the "Golden Epistle" is inaccurate. Briefer but in this respect more reliable is F. R. Johnston, "Syon Abbey," *VCH Middlesex* 1 (Oxford, 1969), p. 187.

39 4⁰, Wynkyn de Worde, 1530; Pollard and Redgrave, 1912, who also notice, 1913, another edition, ?1531.

40 F.A. ij[r].

41 F.B. iij[v].

42 F.A. ij[v].

43 F.B. iij[v.]

44 *Cf.* Bayne.

version of the "Golden Epistle" was made. Which was the earlier English translation, "roughe and rude", which Whitford rejected, we do not know, tempting though it might be to suppose that it was this in the Amherst MS., which had at one time been in the hands of James Grenehalgh at Sheen, just over the river Thames from Syon.[45]

Very soon after the publication of the Worde version, a revision appeared above the imprint of Robert Wyre.[46] It is the same translation, but it has been carefully re-read, by Whitford, we need not doubt, so that Worde's *suspycious* > Wyre's *suspycyons, Flye* > *Fle, lowe* > *loude, or ensample* > *or any example, receyue* > *reygne*.

In contrast with this careful supervision of his work, the next printed edition offers evidence that Whitford no longer had control of it; for Thomas Godfray produced a volume which combines Whitford's well-known Englishing of *The Imitation of Christ* with a new version of the "Golden Epistle", hardly an arrangement of which Whitford would have approved. The reviser may have had Whitford's text before him, but a comparison only of the introductory sentences in the two versions shows how far apart they are:

> (Worde): If you intende to please god *and* wolde obtayne grace to fulfyll the same, two thynges ben vnto you very necessary. The firste, you muste withdrawe your mynde from all worldly and transytory thynges in suche maner as though you cared not wheder any such thynges were in this worlde or no. The seconde is that you gyue *and* aplye your selfe so wholy to god and haue your selfe in suche a wayte that you neuer do, saye ne thynke that you knowe, suppose or byleue shulde offende or displease god, for by this meane you may sonest and moste redyly obtayne and wynne his fauoure and grace. In all thynges esteme and accompte your selfe moste vyle and moste symple, and as very naught in respecte *and* regarde of vertue, and thynke, suppose and byleue that all persons ben good and better than you be, for so shall you moche please our lorde.[47]

> (Godfray): Therfore if thou wylt fynde his grace and be trewly solitarye, two thynges be necessary to the. The fyrst is that thou so withdrawe thy selfe fro al transitory thynges that thou care no more for them than if there were none such, and that thou sette thy selfe at so vyle a price in thyne owne syght that thou accompte thy selfe as nought, beleui(n)g al men to be better than thou arte, and (f.A.iii^r) more to please god.

---

45 E. Colledge, "*The Treatise of Perfection of the Sons of God*: A Fifteenth-Century English Ruysbroek Translation," *English Studies* 33 (1952) 49-66.

46 Pollard and Redgrave, 1914, who date it 1531.

47 *Ibid.*, 1915.

The British Museum Catalogue of Printed Books suggests that the presence in one volume of the *Imitation* and the 'Golden Epistle' is adventitious; but it is evident that Godfray or some patron set store by producing this revision of a text which, the new preface states, "is in some bokes imprinted in the later ende of the boke called in latyn Imitatio Christi". Pollard and Redgrave date this version tentatively 1535,[48] the year in which Syon's troubles came to a head with the arrest, trial and execution of St. Richard Reynolds, events which might account for Whitford's failure to exercise control over his work.

Godfray's revision is entitled "An epistell of saynt Bernarde which he sent to a yong relygious man whom he moche loued that is called the golden Epystell"; and it is furnished with a new prologue, inc.: "That the wyldernesse of thy relygion maye wexe swete and plesaunt vnto the ...".[49] A second edition was produced by Godfray; Pollard and Redgrave do not notice it, but by contrast the British Museum catalogue dates it 1530 and calls it the first edition. The same version was reissued by William Middleton[50] along with Whitford's *Imitation*; and this reissue was closely followed by John Cawood in his volume of 1556.[51] And this 1556 edition is the basis of the last, which was published, without imprint, overseas in 1585.[52]

Plainly, Whitford and his anonymous precursors had religious in mind in making their translations, as had the author of the Latin original; but the text's popularity, witnessed by these several English versions, shows that it reached a wider, lay public, to whom also its brevity, its sound common sense and its insistence on the primacy of charity for the proper conduct of the spiritual life would recommend it.[53]

Pontifical Institute of Mediaeval Studies

---

48   F.A. ij[v].
49   F.A. ii[r].
50   Pollard and Redgrave, 23965, where it is dated ?1545.
51   *Ibid.*, 23966.
52   *Ibid.*, 23968.
53   I am grateful to the Canada Council for a grant in 1974 which made possible the necessary investigations at the British Museum and in Oxford, and to Mr. Michael Sargent and Miss Linda Spear for their help in the preparation of this article.

JEAN DE RIPA O.F.M. AND THE OXFORD CALCULATORS

Janet Coleman

DURING the fourteenth century Paris and Oxford were the principal intellectual foyers of Western Europe. The traditional liaison between the centers, well-established by the mid-thirteenth century, was continued by the practice of sending English scholars abroad to do their theological studies at Paris. In the early decades of the fourteenth century there were Englishmen teaching or circulating their tracts abroad as well. By mid-century the reciprocal influence and activity make it a difficult period to describe briefly in terms of a few distinct controversies. But we shall not unjustly characterize the central years of the fourteenth century if we say they were less Christocentric than preceding decades. Not that the period leaned so much less towards eschatological ends; in fact, a great interest in the salvation of the viator and in the precise nature of the beatific vision had developed. But there was less direct discourse on the role of Christ in man's salvation and rather more elaborate attempts to affirm an overall theoretical order. Scholars enmeshed themselves in questions of possibility, change, contingency of the future, seeking definitions of the continuum. There was less continuity with the synthetic scholarship of an earlier generation than perhaps they cared to admit. To avoid official condemnation of the sort that riddled the late thirteenth-century university controversies, scholars with hazardous ideas sought refuge in probability.

Such concern for the uncertain future seems appropriate enough in retrospect — these were times when the plague gathered up an entire scholarly generation; the *Commentaries* on the *Sentences* got reduced to discussions of the first book with excessively long prologues, or to ad hoc arguments distantly related to the Lombard's accepted text; there was an on-off war between France and England; the papacy was displaced to Avignon and one pope was rather loudly criticized and his thesis on the beatific vision rejected outright.[1] In social terms there was a substantial rise in a literate middle class; in intellectual terms the efforts to argue for determinism against contingency were only momentarily championed by Bradwardine's *De causa Dei*. It is not surprising that the scholastic circles, in which Bradwardine was a pivotal influence, fostered the trend to seek 'laws' by which to describe minutely the workings of the determined natural order and its fixed relationship with the supernatural order that was heretofore acknowledged uncritically. One is tempted to see in the rise in the number of customs officials and shopkeepers[2] an analogy for a correlative rise in the number of attempts to structure precisely and geometrically the natural world as one might structure the monthly balance sheet of debits and credits. Possibly as a result of Ockham's discovery that God was, at best, a distant benevolence, the structured unity of things on all levels needed to be reaffirmed. In the abstract school discussions this developed into the theory of warring contraries. It was believed that the presence of contrary qualities explained how certain natures, certain species of qualities or accidents, submitted to alteration and could be said to become more or less intense — in whiteness, in warmth, in dearness to God — without denying that a species so altered yet remained identifiably the same species.[3] It thereby preserved its determined place in the order of created natures. The outrage that was caused by certain aspects of Ockham's terminism as applied to the Eucharist[4] and to *caritas*, had made popular those discussions concerning the unchanging essence of a thing that undergoes change — in its extension and in its

---

1   H. Denifle and A. Chatelain, *Chartularium universitatis Parisiensis* 2 (Paris, 1891), pp. 414-42 on John XXII and the state of the blessed souls prior to the Last Judgment.

2   Sylvia Thrupp, *The Merchant Class of Medieval London (1300-1500)* (Chicago, 1948).

3   The role of the alteration of contraries in intension is dealt with in Ockham's *Philosophia naturalis* (Rome, 1637), Lib. 3, chapter 22: "Sed de ista alteratione est una difficultas specialis, quae in aliis motibus et mutationibus non habet locum. Est autem difficultas haec: quando aliud alteratur de contraria qualitate in contrariam qualitatem an simul expellantur aut una qualitas introducatur in alia, ita quod illae qualitates secundum gradus remissos simul maneant." Cited by Herman Shapiro, "Walter Burley and the Intension and Remission of Forms," *Speculum* 34 (1959) 418-19.

4   Ockham, *De sacramento altaris* 1, q.3; IV *Sent*. q.4, O; q.6, J in Oxford, Merton College MS. 103, fols. 1-202v. Ockham identified substance with quantity. This was rejected by Francis de Marchia (*Comment. Sent.* c. 1319-20) and by Buridan (*Comment. Physics* c. 1328). See A. Maier, "Einige Probleme der Ockhamforschung," *AFH* 46 (1953) 174-77. The extensive information and clear discussion in Father James Weisheipl's unpublished Oxford D. Phil. dissertation (1956), *Early Fourteenth-Century Physics of the Merton School*, are still invaluable.

intensity. Very many thinkers with somewhat differing interests tried their wits in these arguments about warring contraries or, as it was then called, the problem of intension and remission of forms.[5] What was the nature of the process in which forms, qualities or essences could be said to be intensified or diminished in their intensity?

In the Oxford schools and primarily at Merton College the intension and remission of qualities was a topic of considerable importance by the 1330's. Alteration and augmentation had come to be discussed in rather technical natural science treatises[6] many of which circulated on the continent and were read at the University of Paris not more than a decade after they were written in England. Some were used as elementary introductions to the study of physics as the subject was pursued in the arts curriculum.[7] The tracts offered several explanations of intensification. Their divergence of opinion permits us to examine fruitfully the background to one influential Franciscan's 'vain curiosity in the workings of faith':[8] through a selective interpretation of his sources the theologian Jean de Ripa established his 'proprius modus ponendi' to explain intension and remission of *caritas*.[9]

Jean de Ripa was teaching in Paris during the 1350's.[10] In 1362 the Parisian theology faculty condemned a certain position which one of his followers presumably derived from his master: intrinsic *alteration* in

5   See A. Maier, *Studien zur Naturphilosophie der Spätscholastik* (Rome, 1949) 5 vols. See especially:

1. *Die Vorläufer Galileis im 14. Jahrhundert* (1949);
2. *Zwei Grundprobleme der scholastischen Naturphilosophie: das Problem der intensiven Grösse, die Impetustheorie* (3rd ed., 1968);
3. *An der Grenze von Scholastik und Naturwissenschaft* (2nd ed., 1952);
4. *Metaphysische Hintergründe der spätscholastischen Naturphilosophie* (1955).

See also the fundamental work of P. Duhem, *Le système du monde* 7 (Paris, 1954-58), chapters 5-7.

6   I am grateful to Dr. John Murdoch for obtaining permission for me to see the unpublished Harvard doctoral dissertation (1970) of Dr. Edith Sylla, *The Oxford Calculators and the Mathematics of Motion 1320-50, Physics and Measurements by Latitude.*

7   See the unpublished D. Phil. dissertation of J. Weisheipl *passim*, cited above, n. 4. His research on the arts curriculum at Oxford: *Mediaeval Studies* 26 (1964) 143-85; 28 (1966) 151-75; 31 (1969) 174-225.

8   Jean Gerson, *Contra vanam curiositatem in negotio fidei*, two lectures in 1402, cited by A. Combes, "Présentation de Jean de Ripa," *AHDLMA* 23 (1956) 147.

9   See the exposition of Jean de Ripa's understanding of the intension and remission of forms given by the late Mgr. A. Combes, "L'intensité des formes d'après Jean de Ripa," *AHDLMA* 37 (1970). Also P. Vignaux, "Note sur le concept de forme intensive dans l'œuvre de Jean de Ripa," in *Mélanges Alexandre Koyré* 1 (Paris, 1964), pp. 517-26.

10   See A. Combes, "Présentation," 145-242; 183-5. Also the introduction in his edition of the *Conclusiones* of Jean de Ripa (Paris, 1957). See his preface to his edition of Jean de Ripa, *Lectura super primum Sententiarum, prologi, quaestiones 1 et 2* (Paris, 1961).

the divine intellect. This event highlights the fact that de Ripa's writings stand as some of the most direct and critical examples of the relation between theological thought and the physics of motion during the mid-fourteenth century. His method is to return, via physical analyses of alteration and intension of forms, to the traditional core of distinction 17 in the first book of the *Sentences*, impressing on the text of the Lombard and the Augustinian tradition, aspects of the new physics. The Oxford natural science tracts collectively provide a reference point for determining the extent to which the English ideas were established in Paris as what de Ripa calls "the common opinion". As a result of seeing these ideas alongside de Ripa's elaboration, the mid-century relationship between Oxford and Paris can be further clarified and we can attempt an appraisal of the "modern" school.

Intension was understood as the movement of alteration in a subject by which a quality is acquired. In his *Commentary* on the *Sentences*, the second part of distinction 17,[11] Jean de Ripa offers the past opinions of the ancients on the subject so that he can show them to be inadequate explanations of the mode of alteration in intensity of those essences said to remain invariable forms. Then he presents the several views of the *moderni*, presumably his contemporaries or his recent teachers, on the same topic. Unfortunately he mentions few names[12] so that we are forced to speculate as to what tracts and which men he is using when he refers to "the common opinion". In the fourth and last article he selectively appropriates certain aspects of the modern doctrines to elaborate his own thesis. In the interests of establishing an orientation in the flow of these ideas as well as to affirm Gerson's later evaluation of de Ripa as a highly original and influential — if wrongheaded — thinker, we should like to know something about his actual forerunners.

Historians of fourteenth-century science have recently begun to refer to a group of Englishmen, comprising logicians and natural scientists, some of whom were also theologians, as the Oxford Calculators. Pursuing their interest in velocities and resistant forces they wrote treatises on first and last instants, on maxima and minima, on determining the relations of certain physical variables particularly forces and velocities, on alteration and susceptibility to more and less, and on the process of

---

11   The text that shall be cited is based on Z (MS. Paris, Bibliothèque Nationale Lat. 15369) chosen as the base text by Mgr. Combes. For a discussion of the MS. tradition we refer the reader to A. Combes, ed., *Jean de Ripa, Conclusiones*, pp. 15-20.

12   Gregory of Rimini is cited throughout the *Commentary*; Francis de Marchia and Burley are mentioned infrequently along with *alius doctor novus* or *alius magister modernus* (fol. 248vb).

intension and remission. Most of the Oxford theoreticians were at Merton College through the 1330's and the group included men of varied academic and political achievements.[13] They developed three different theories of alteration of forms: 1) Walter Burley's succession of forms theory where a new form was generated and the previous one destroyed;[14] 2) the addition of part to part or degree to degree theory favored by Scotus and by most of the Oxford theoreticians; 3) and the admixture theory in which a quality was more or less intense depending on its being more or less mixed with its contrary. This was a view most heavily relied on by one thinker, Roger Swineshead (fl. 1330),[15] and it was to be criticized by Burley and modified by the later Calculators. Each of these theories, plus a fourth older one espoused by earlier schoolmen, comes in for some lengthy criticism and evaluation by Jean de Ripa. What he presents as erroneous opinions we now can recognize to be aspects of the theories for which some of the Oxford thinkers became famous in their time. We ask, how close was de Ripa to the Oxford texts themselves? Which, if any, of the Oxford opinions is the common opinion to which he refers and to which he devotes at least two thirds of his distinction 17?

We must realize we are not dealing with arcane material, nor isolated idiosyncratic positions. The Calculators' tracts on local motion and alteration of intensive qualities are known to have considerably influenced continental writers who were also doing studies of natural science in the arts faculties. Their lectures and *summae* on Aristotle's *Physics* and on Averroes' *Commentary* on the *Physics* were jumping-off points for their views on the composition of continua and on alteration in local motion. Their measurements were applied to the more general areas of change — involving the categories of quantity and quality.

As a Franciscan, Jean de Ripa was an heir to Scotus' formalizing legacy. Of necessity he was familiar with his Order's particular line of thought concerning the augmentation of created forms like charity and, more basically, with its views on the composition of continua. It was believed that some understanding of the continuum was fundamental to further discussions of local motion and alteration. Gerard d'Odon, the

13   J. Weisheipl, "Repertorium Mertonense," *Mediaeval Studies* 31 (1969) 174-224.

14   Burley lectured in arts at Oxford c. 1300-10, and then went to Paris to become a master in theology (c. 1322). He was a fellow of Merton College by 1305. See A. B. Emden, *Biographical Register of the University of Oxford to A.D. 1500* 1 (Oxford, 1957), pp. 312 ff.

15   Weisheipl, "Roger Swynshed, O.S.B., Logician, Natural Philosopher and Theologian," in *Oxford Studies Presented to Daniel Callus* (Oxford, 1964), pp. 247 ff.

Minister General in 1329, and his follower Nicolas Bonetus were perhaps the most renowned of that group which held opposing views to the Oxford theoreticians. Consequently their tracts received a great deal of attention from contemporaries.[16] In speaking of Gerard d'Odon as opposed to, say, the Mertonian Bradwardine,[17] we mean to distinguish the former as an atomist in that he sought to show that continua could be composed of extensionless indivisibles or points. Bradwardine on the other hand, was a divisibilist who said that a continuum was composed of an infinity of divisibles; early in his academic career he believed he had proved this with Euclidean geometry.[18] He also denied that such "atoms" would be immediately next to one another. His ideas were heartily adopted by his and the next generation. All the Oxford treatises, beginning with Bradwardine's *De proportionibus*[19] and the *De continuo*, in some way sought to answer the atomists and establish their own opposing criteria for the composition of continua. In so doing, they developed the theory of latitudes or formal distances and moved beyond the problem of mathematical continua to problems of continuous alteration — of qualities and quantities, intensive and extensive magnitudes. Intension and remission were spoken of in terms of distances traversed and measured by degrees and latitudes.

On the part of the Oxford physicists the desire for a law that would describe all variations in velocities was paralleled by de Ripa's desire as a theologian for a law of intensive latitudes encompassing all possible variations in perfection of created natures. Such a law for de Ripa would define the relationship between the divine essence and the created intellect in terms of a special process of communication — by *immutatio vitalis*. In modern terminology we observe that he describes a "law" of infinite sets containing infinite subsets to link the infinite number of created perfections in the continuum of created being with the divine, infinitely immense perfection that stands as an extrinsic *terminus* to this continuum. He utilizes the analytic resources available in the

16   See John E. Murdoch, "*Mathesis in philosophiam scholasticam introducta*: The Rise and Development of the Application of Mathematics in Fourteenth-Century Philosophy and Theology," in *Arts libéraux et philosophie au moyen âge: Actes du quatrième congrès international de philosophie médiévale* (Montreal-Paris, 1969), pp. 215-54.

17   At Merton 1323-35 (Weisheipl, "Repertorium Mertonense," 177).

18   In his *De continuo*, edited in the unpublished doctoral dissertation of John Murdoch, *Geometry and the Continuum in the Fourteenth Century: A Philosophical Analysis of Thomas Bradwardine's "Tractatus de continuo"* (Wisconsin, 1957), p. 461.

19   *Thomas Bradwardine, Tractatus de proportionibus*, ed. and introd. H. Lamar Crosby (Madison, 1955).

new physics of intensified quality to fix the modality of all possibile continuous alteration in created natures seeking perfection of their species. By analogy between quantitative and qualitative change he can speak of degrees of forms and divisible continuous intensities of species. In this period when theological consideration of the contingent future and the all-embracing realm of the possible reached fantastic proportions, de Ripa seems to have been a conservative force trying to inscribe possibility within a law of change. Thus he employs these technical terms to discuss the capacities of species to achieve the determined *summum* of their latitude of perfection. This was also treated by *magistri* who were not specifically interested in the theological end of such discussion. The difference is one of perspective, for de Ripa begins his inquiry not by commenting on Aristotle's *Physics* or by discoursing on the implications of the *Categories* as did the Oxford natural scientists, but with the question that is central to his theology: whether *caritas* may be considered properly intensible; is it a form susceptible to intensification? He thus introduces *circa secundam partem istius distinctionis (17) in qua doctores communiter investigant de augmento caritatis create et aliarum formarum.*[20]

Some of the better known tracts written by the Oxford Calculators are the following:

Burley[21] — *De primo et ultimo instanti*
    Tractatus primus; tractatus de activitate, unitate et augmento formarum activarum habentium contraria et suscipientium magis et minus. (c. 1320-27).
    Tractatus secundus: de causa intrinseca intentionis et remissionis formarum accidentalium. (c. 1320)
Bradwardine — *De proportionibus* (1328)
    De continuo (c. 1328-35)[22]
Roger Swineshead — *Descriptiones motuum* (1328-38)[23]

20 *Conclusiones*, p. 145; Bibliothèque Nationale Lat. 15369, fol. 237vb.

21 See A. Maier, *Ausgehendes Mittelalter* 1 (Rome, 1964), p. 219; also *Studien* 2.337-46, 77 n. 8. Also Herman Shapiro, "Walter Burley," 413-27; *Tractatus secundus* (Venice, 1496), fols. 2ra-15vb; "*De primo et ultimo instanti* des Walter Burley," ed. H. Shapiro and C. Shapiro in *Archiv für Geschichte der Philosophie* 47 (1965) 157-73 from the MSS. Paris, Bibliothèque Nationale Lat. 16401, fols. 120r-125v, Vat. Lat. 4545, fols. 48v-57v, and Columbia University Plimpton MS. 171, fols. 7r-10r.

22 *De continuo*, MS. Toruń, Gymnasialbibliothek R4° 2, fols. 153-92; incomplete in Erfurt, Stadtbücherei Amplon. Q. 385, fols. 17r-48r; unpublished edition see n. 18; *De proportionibus*, ed. Crosby.

23 Erfurt, Amplon. F. 135, fols. 25va-47rb; fragments in Paris, Bibliothèque Nationale Lat. 16621. I have looked at the Columbia University photostat of the Erfurt MS. in Thorndike Collection 123.

Heytesbury — *Regulae solvendi sophismata* (1335)
                Termini naturales (1330-37)[24]
Dumbleton — *Summa logicae et philosophiae naturalis* (c. 1335)[25]
Richard Swineshead — *Liber calculationum* (c. 1350)
                       De intensione et remissione formarum[26]

Many of their somewhat specialized notions on the nature of movement came to be studied in Paris and elsewhere. We shall see how they were incorporated by de Ripa into a theological context in his *Commentary* on the *Sentences* which is believed to have appeared by 1357.[27] The concept of intensive latitude underwent certain modifications in the Oxford works. De Ripa is explicitly aware of these interpretations and his own arguments reflect the evolution of these ideas. Although he frequently refers to older theories like Burley's "destruction of the preceding form", de Ripa also speaks of the addition and admixture hypotheses as they are to be found in the tracts of Roger Swineshead and John Dumbleton. Then he rejects or selectively revises. We can determine with some precision the nature of de Ripa's debt to the Calculators if we know the extent to which his treatment of intension and remission of forms, his discussion of substances' susceptibility to more and less, his concern for infinitely divisible continua and simultaneously existing contrary qualities draw from the treatises of the times: Dumbleton's *Summa* (part 2), from Roger Swineshead's *Descriptiones motuum*, from Heytesbury's *Termini naturales*, from Burley's *Tractatus secundus* and the *De primo et ultimo instanti*. Their summaries of past opinions is of the greatest significance: Dumbleton discusses and chooses amongst them to construct his own theories and the whole presentation is a foreshadowing of de Ripa's in part two of distinction 17 of his *Commentary* on the *Sentences*. Is it to Dumbleton that de Ripa refers when he speaks of the common opinion he had been taught by the Franciscans,

24 *Regulae* (Venice, 1494), fols. 9v-52; *Termini naturales*: London, British Museum Royal 8 A XVIII (membr., xiv), fols. 69v-75. This is misprinted in Weisheipl, "Repertorium Mertonense."

25 Weisheipl, "Repertorium Mertonense," 210-11. I have looked at Cambridge, Gonville and Caius College 499/ 268 (membr., xiv), fols. 1-162v; Cambridge, Peterhouse 272 (membr., xiv), fols. 1-111; London, British Museum Royal 10 B XIV (membr., xiv), fols. 1-244; Oxford, Merton College 279 (membr., xiv), fols. 4-179; Paris, Bibliothèque Nationale Lat. 16146 (membr., xiv — English), fols. 2-141ra; Paris, Bibliothèque Nationale Lat. 16621 (chart., xiv), fols. 117v-123v; 169-180v.

26 Weisheipl, "Repertorium Mertonense," 220-21. For the *Calculationes* I have looked at Cambridge, Gonville and Caius College 499/ 268, fols. 165r-203v; Paris, Bibliothèque Nationale Lat. 6558 (membr., xiv), fols. 1-70va and (Venice, 1520); the *De intensione* (*In primo de celo*) is in Gonville and Caius 499/ 268, fols. 204-211v.

27 16 December 1357; see Combes, "Présentation," 170.

presumably in the 1340's? The arguments of distinction 17 show that he hardly had need of more information about the varied modern opinions than what Dumbleton or even Richard Swineshead provided (in an intension treatise[28] earlier than his *Liber calculationum*) and for the most part rejected. If summaries like the *Termini naturales* and Dumbleton's *Summa* were already in use in Paris, it is very likely the Franciscans used them as well, and if at Oxford and Cambridge, then certainly at Paris.[29] In this way they would constitute the direct rather than distant foundation for de Ripa's own construction of summarized past opinions.

We must say something about de Ripa's acquaintance with certain new views concerning intension which he presents as the arguments of a *doctor novus* or *modernus* before he refutes them. It is likely that this doctor represents certain "new" Parisian positions — those of Buridan or his followers. For Buridan a subject's essence remained unchanged despite any alteration in the extension of the subject; air remains essentially the same despite any changes in its volume. A distinct peculiarity of Buridan's conception of local motion, however, was that he took velocity to be an inherent quality of a moving body and so it could be described as an intensive magnitude.[30] Jean de Ripa and the Oxford theoreticians like Dumbleton recognized the analogy between intensive and extensive movements but did not confuse external distance covered with the internal latitude of intensity achieved. De Ripa, for example, is careful with his terminology, distinguishing intensive from extensive divisibility,[31] whereas his *doctor novus* applies to qualities what he does to

28   In Cambridge, Gonville and Caius 499/ 268, fols. 204-211v: "In primo de celo philosophus comm. 35 arguit corpus infinitum circumvolvi non posse." In his unpublished dissertation, pp. 101-2, Weisheipl believes this work antecedes Swineshead's larger tract, the *Liber calculationum*, following A. Maier who dates the *Liber* c. 1350: *Studien* 3.361.

29   The ordinance issued in the bull *Redemptor noster*, 28 November 1336, by Benedict XII indicates the same texts read at Paris were to be read in the English *studia*. P. Michael Bihl, in *AFH* 30 (1930) 324-5, summarizes as follows: "Tunc in n. 2-3 Papa idem principium provinciae Angliae applicat, ubi pari iure ac in studio Parisiensi venia legendi in s. theologia sive magisterium aut doctoratus acquiri poterat in duabus universitatibus Oxoniensi et Cantabrigiensi... Haec in praeiudicium Provinciae Angliae ordinabatur, cum eius Minister prov. tuncusque lectores horum studiorum assignavisset." The text of *Redemptor noster*, pp. 332-86; pars IX, *De studiis*, pp. 346-52.

30   Buridan, *Quaestiones super octo libros Physicorum*, lib. 1, q.4 (Paris, 1509), fol. 5ra; lib. 7, q.3. See also C. Michalski, "La physique nouvelle et les différents courants philosophiques au 14e siècle," in *La philosophie au 14e siècle*, ed. Kurt Flasch (Frankfurt, 1969), p. 262. Buridan, *Quaestiones Physic.*, lib. 3, q.11: "Notandum est quod hoc nomen motus non supponit pro mobili ut dictum fuit set pro dispositione secundum quam mobile se habet aliter et aliter." Cited by Michalski, "Les courants critiques et sceptiques dans la philosophie du 14e siècle," in *La philosophie*, p. 203.

31   See below; fol. 242va.

quantities. For reasons other than de Ripa's the *doctor novus* rejects the common addition thesis. This means that he too was familiar with this *modus ponendi* of the Calculators. So our concern will not be with Parisian developments of Oxford ideas just yet.[32] If Jean de Ripa was in a Franciscan *studium* in the 1340's, quite clearly he is closer in time and in view to earlier concepts like those emanating from across the Channel. To a large extent he draws upon the better known aspects of the Oxford physics which apparently were available to him and to others of his generation. Whether de Ripa actually used the English treatises as his textbooks within the Franciscan *studium*, at Paris or elsewhere, or whether he used abridged continental versions, leads us to ask another question, for which only a partial and preliminary answer can be suggested: what were the relevant texts in use in the mid-fourteenth-century Parisian circles, at the bachelor of arts level and in the theology program?[33] We know of a widely used introductory treatise on the terminology *secundum usum Oxonie*.[34] It is an important and revealing tract. But despite its apparent popularity and therefore its significance in estimating intellectual trends which de Ripa inherited, it is for the most part a greatly simplified reduction of the issues and proofs to be found in the Oxford treatises and in Jean de Ripa's *Commentary*. To us it shall be helpful in providing a series of rudimentary definitions. We also have the treatise attributed to Roger Swineshead, the *Descriptiones motuum*, that had been *datus Oxonie ad utilitatem studencium*.[35] And we have the MS. Paris, Bibliothèque Nationale Lat. 16408, an inventory that tells us who was teaching in Paris at mid-century and what texts it

32   Nor shall we discuss the ideas of de Ripa's contemporary Nicole Oresme, because his more geometric approach to intension of forms and the fact that he was contemporary prevent him from having exerted the kind of influence we seek.

33   See Weisheipl, "The Curriculum of the Faculty of Arts at Oxford in the Early Fourteenth Century," *Mediaeval Studies* 26 (1964) 143-85 and "Developments in the Arts Curriculum at Oxford in the Early Fourteenth Century," *Mediaeval Studies* 28 (1966) 151-75; P. Glorieux, "Jean de Falisca, la formation d'un maître en théologie au 14ᵉ siècle," *AHDLMA* 41 (1966) 23-104.

34   Weisheipl has provided a transcription in the appendix of his unpublished dissertation. The attribution to Heytesbury is in MS. Munich Clm 8997, fol. 167r.

35   Weisheipl, dissertation, p. 196. The heavy emphasis in the arts *quadrivium* at Oxford was on the natural sciences, giving evidence of a devotion to geometry and astronomy and to logic and mathematical physics. The corresponding Aristotelian texts were in uses, *i.e.* for the licence at the University of Paris, 1366, the major *libri naturales* were heard: *Physics, De generatione, De caelo, Parva naturalia, aliquos libros mathematicos* and the *Metaphysics*. All this was *less* than what was required to be considered for the degree of Master. See the statutes of 1366 in *Chartularium univ. Paris.* 3.143-48, no. 1319. See also the Oxford statutes of 1340 in Strickland Gibson, *Statuta antiqua univ. Oxon.* (Oxford, 1931), p. 32.

was likely that a student in theology would possess.[36] Lastly, we have the reforming Bull *Redemptor Noster*, issued in 1336 by Benedict XII, which established the appointment of foreign Franciscans to read the *Sentences* at Oxford, Cambridge, Paris and in other provinces of the Order. The books to be read in the *studium* at Paris were the same as those for Oxford and Cambridge — these were the three principal *studia* — and so they maintained parallel curricula, at least after 1336.[37] With these data we are able to construct a tentative appreciation of the milieu in which the problem of intension and remission of forms got carried over from discussions of natural science to those of supernatural *scientia*.

In the thirteenth century the intension and remission of forms like *caritas* were discussed by theologians. But fourteenth-century thinkers, absorbed by their interest in velocities of motion, tended to probe the

---

36 P. Glorieux, "Jean de Falisca"; see below, n. 45.

37 Of the seven *studia*: "Cantabrigiensem cum universitate et studio Norwicensi; Oxoniensi cum universitate et studio Stanfordiensi; Vigorniensem (Worcester) cum studio Conventreiensi." The Cathedral Library at Worcester maintained contemporary copies of nearly all the texts we shall look at in addition to the collection of other contemporary lecture notebooks: Dumbleton's *Summa*, MS. F. 6 (membr., xiv), fols. 1-165 and F. 23, fols. 91-126v. Heytesbury's *Termini naturales*, F. 118 (s. xv), fols. 32rb-35rb. Burley, *Quaestiones quaedam physicae de anima et aliis*, F. 86 and Q. 38. Richard Swineshead, *Calculationes* (fragments), F. 35 (s. xv), fols. 27-65rb, 70ra-75v; and the *Tractatus de intensione et remissione formarum* (*in primo de celo*), F. 35, fols. 65va-69.

From Bihl's transcription of the bull *Redemptor noster*, *AFH* 30 (1930) pars IX, *De studiis*: "14. Nullus quoque frater dicti Ordinis ad legendum in prememoratis studiis sententias assumatur nisi prius legerit IV Libros Sententiarum cum scriptis approbatorum doctorum in aliis studiis quae in eodem Ordine dicuntur generalia, vel in conventibus infrascriptis, videlicet: ... Londoniensi, Eboracensi, Northwicensi, Novicastri, Stanfordiensi, Conventreiensi (p. 349). 19. Cum autem huiusmodi fratres assumpti fuerint ad magisterium et in universitate sua perfecerint cursum suum fiant lectores alibi in locis solemnibus ut in lectura valeant utiliter occupari. 20. Aliis autem conventibus habentibus ea studia quae in Ordine generalia nuncupantur, generalis minister in capitulo generali de idoneis lectoribus et baccalaureis provideat de consilio ministrorum et magistrorum, qui erunt in loco dicti capituli generalis (p. 350). 23. Praedicti vero magistri, lectores et baccalaurei legentes theologiam dictis philosophorum non multum insistant sed quae theologice possunt tractari, pertractent theologice (p. 350, n. 9: Statuta Parisiensia an. 1366 ap. *ChUP* 2.698 n. 6: Legentes Sententias non tractent quaestiones aut materias logicas vel philosophicas nisi quantum textus Sententiarum requiret.) et communibus antiquorum et approbatorum doctorum, prout secundum Deum et veritatem poterunt, se conforment. 25. Circa fratres siquidem tam ad Parisiense quam ad alia generalia studia Ordinis transmittendos provide duximus statuendum quod illi qui ad huiusmodi studia extra suas provincias de debito transmittuntur, per sua provincialia capitula eligantur... (p. 351). 34. Ne autem nova cuiusvis doctrinae opera per fratres ipsius Ordinis incaute et periculose communicari aut publicari contingat districte praecipimus quod novum opus theologicum iuridicum vel philosophicum (n. 5 Physicum prout Per.) scilicet librum seu libellum, summam, compendium, postillam, expositiones, glossas, tractatum vel collectionem seu compilationem quaestionum vel sermonum a quocumque fuerit editus vel edita seu editum, nullus frater sine subscripto examine ac ministri et capituli generalis prius obtenta licentia speciali, intra vel extra Ordinem publicare, communicare vel copiare praesumat. Si quis autem hoc attentare praesumpserit, omnibus scholasticis et legitimis actibus ac usu librorum se noverit ipso facto fore privatum (p. 352)."

physical aspects of quantities and push theological issues to one side and to other treatises. Any appraisal of the modern school of natural science must keep in mind that *intensio et remissio formarum* was being taken up with regard to the issue's geometric and physical aspects first. Elsewhere, in theological commentaries on the *Sentences*, it was treated ontologically. This is to say that in the mid-fourteenth-century arts faculty intension and remission of forms was not first broached as it had been by theologians at the time of St. Thomas — with reference to the form of charity increasing in man. Rather it referred to Aristotle's treatment of changes in quantified and qualified substances in the *Physics* and in Averroes' *Commentary* on it. The masters of arts dealt with the problem of intension at the same time that they tried to answer questions as to whether infinities could be compared and whether or not continua were composed of discrete indivisibles. These problems subsequently passed to the theological disputes where the language of latitudes and alteration was applied to certain traditional theological concerns. New facets of issues tended to be exposed as one can see from contemporary commentaries on the *Sentences* and from the lists of theological debate topics for this period:[38] one encounters definitions and comparisons of infinities, discussions about the distances of angels from the zero degrees of their species, treatises on the relative perfections of created species and their respective distances from their *summa* of the species, *in cuius fine de essentia beatitudinis*.[39] Continuity and infinitely divisible magnitudes were treated by the Augustinian Gregory of Rimini, who, armed with geometrical arguments, took a stand against the Franciscan radical atomism.[40] He is one of the few worthies de Ripa does cite throughout his *Commentary*, and we know he lectured on the *Sentences* at Paris in 1344. And in 1337 at the Franciscan *studium* of Norwich associated with Cambridge University,[41] Bartholemy de Repps[42] participated in a *determinatio* where the new physics principle of local motion was involved in the question whether the body of Christ *potest moveri localiter in altari*.[43] A contemporary quodlibet in a Worcester

---

38 See P. Glorieux, "Jean de Falisca," 46-47; MS. Paris, Bibliothèque Nationale Lat. 16408.

39 Gregory of Rimini (Glorieux, "Jean de Falisca," 48).

40 II *Sent.* d.2 a.1 (Venice, 1522). See Murdoch, "*Mathesis*," 223.

41 Bihl, "*Redemptor noster*," 329.

42 De Repps (Rippes) — 52nd master of the Franciscans at Cambridge, c. 1332; see *Eccleston, De adventu Fratrum Minorum in Angliam*, ed. A. G. Little (Manchester, 1908), pp. 73-4; see J. R. H. Moorman, *The Grey Friars at Cambridge* (Cambridge, 1952), appendix B, p. 204.

43 Cited by P. Doucet from MS. Chigi B. V. 66, fols. 126r-128v in "Le studium franciscain de Norwich en 1337 d'après le Ms Chigi B. V. 66 de la Bibliothèque Vaticane," *AFH* 46 (1953) 85-98.

Cathedral MS. asks *utrum spiritus creatus possit moveri localiter et successive*.[44]

The notebooks from the Paris faculty of theology, Bibliothèque Nationale Lat. 16408 and 16409, which contain references to the masters who taught at Paris *c*. 1360, cite de Ripa along with Nicolas Autrecourt and Oresme. They also mention certain English masters and their tracts, like Dumbleton, (Roger) Swineshead, Heytesbury, Bradwardine and Burley.[45] The MSS. reveal some of the studies and methods of work in the Parisian theology faculty for the formation of bachelors and masters within a 15 to 20 year period. Because de Ripa is mentioned along with Oresme and Buridan these MSS. can only provide information about which Englishmen and which of their treatises were known and disputed at Paris after the years of de Ripa's own formation, i.e. after the early 1340's. Included in the theological curriculum were disputes on the nature of infinities between two extremes,[46] the composition of lines, and a large place was held by instantaneous and local motion.

With the citations of the English *magistri* and the titles of their treatises, there is, in what Père Glorieux believes to be Jean de Falisca's compendium (preserved as Bibliothèque Nationale Lat. 16621) the text of Burley's *De primo et ultimo instanti*.[47] This is one of his earlier works in

---

44 This is the last *quaestio* in Worcester Cathedral Library MS. *162* (s. xiv); see J. K. Floyer, *Catalogue of the MSS* (Oxford, 1906).

45 Table J, Glorieux, "Jean de Falisca," 61 ff.; from MS. X (Paris, Bibliothèque Nationale Lat. 16408) identified as the table for the text of Bibliothèque Nationale Lat. 16621, a paper notebook given to the Sorbonne by Thomas of Cracow. Cahier 3: "Suincet, primi, de 1° motore in 4 quaternis cum tribus dubiis parisien." (fols. 14-25v); fol. 25r: mention of Suiset and de Ripa ending with: "opus suiset de 1° motore, 8 differenciis, distinguitur prout patet in processu eius." Fols. 26-92v: "de maximo et minimo"; Oresme: "Dulminton cum quodam sophismate forti de unitate difformi in sequenti cisterno." Fols. 129v-140v: "tres cisterni de dulminton..."; then Buridan, Bradwardine on propositions and Burley, *De ultimo instanti*. Fol. 222v of Bibliothèque Nationale Lat. 16408: inventory of the contents of two lost volumes: "De questionibus dulminton ... et sophismata dulminton et estybray; Suicet de primo motorum et dulminton" (Glorieux, "Jean de Falisca," 66). The above inventories and cahiers cover the period from 1348-1357 according to Glorieux, "Jean de Falisca," 69. The table of MS. 16408 which presumably identifies works in MS. 16621 also includes (fols. 78 ff.) two *quaestiones* of M. R. Barbe ("Utrum divina voluntas est cuiuslibet actionis nostre regula ductiva et de necessitate divini auxilii ad quodlibet nostrum bene agere vel judicare contra pelagium" etc.) and a second question ("Utrum Deus sit omnium aliorum a se primum principium seu causa ubi multa de divinis influxibus ... et materia et forma ... juxta ymaginationem de Ripa in speciali de incarnatione..."). H. Schwamm (*Magistri Johannis de Ripa doctrina de praescientia divina* (Rome, 1933)) notes a secular priest, Richard Barba, as one of the Ripien school of the later fourteenth century. See Glorieux, "Jean de Falisca," 26, Table A of MS. X (16408).

46 Gregory of Rimini (*ibid.*, 58).

47 Beyond fol. 180 and before 261. Tables H and J in Glorieux, "Jean de Falisca," 61-2; table K, 66. Text ed. H. Shapiro and C. Shapiro, *Archiv für Geschichte der Philosophie* 47 (1965) 157-73.

which he uses the concept of latitude in a philosophical context. He describes the latitude of the species of a quality as a formal distance, a range, comprised of indivisible degrees. This latitude provides a static basis, a grid, for possible alteration in intensity within the particular species while the species remains the same. Burley speaks of first and last instants to define a range of instrinsic being. As a temporal beginning of a thing's existence we assign either a first instant of being (*primum instans rei*) or a last instant of non-being which is an extrinsic boundary (*ultimum instans non esse rei*). Either one or the other suitably defines something; both as definitions are incompatible. This may be seen as one means of treating what was then an important current problem — that of denomination. It is also an incipient argument for the later descriptions of a latitude of alteration from the extrinsic non-being or zero degree of a species to some intrinsic positive degree,[48] as we find it in the writings of Jean de Ripa.

In another work, the *Tractatus secundus*,[49] which is Burley's famous treatise on intension, the question to be answered was the following: how do forms or qualities increase or decrease in intensity? When Burley was writing two theories of intensification had been proposed — by addition and by admixture. Scotus and others suggested that qualitative increase occurred by the addition of a new, real and distinct qualitative part, similar to its antecedents, which joined them to create a whole, single, determined, intensified, qualitative degree *per se*.[50] The admixture thesis suggested that qualitative intensification depended on the degree to which a quality was mixed with its contrary. Burley argued against admixture and also insisted that forms do not augment by the addition of part to part because illumination does not augment by the addition of illumination to illumination.[51] Instead, he proposed

---

48 Shapiro, "*De primo*," 169: ... for positive things whose perfection consists in indivisibles or of things having a latitude in perfection or in degrees of perfection ("de re positiva que consistit in indivisibili, aut de re habente latitudinem in perfectione, sive in gradibus perfectionis"), I say we give an ultimate, last instant in which the thing has being. The reason is that perfection, consisting in indivisibles, if destroyed, is not made less by something of it being destroyed because what remains as indivisible is the same perfection ("cuius ratio est quia perfectio consistens in indivisibili si corrumpatur, non aliquid eius corrumpitur vel minuitur, remanente eadem perfectione"). See below de Ripa, fol. 248ra.

49 *De causa intrinseca intensionis et remissionis formarum accidentalium* (Venice, 1496), fols. 2ra-15vb: see chapter 4.

50 Scotus, I *Sent.* d.17 q.2 (Venice, 1597-1598). Also see Scotus' favorite student, Jean de Bassols, I *Sent.* d.17 q.2 (Paris, 1517) and François de Meyronnes I *Sent.* d.17 q.2 a.2 (Venice, 1520); Duhem, *Le système* 7.507-8; *Dictionnaire de théologie catholique* 6 (Paris, 1924) under 'Frères Mineurs,' cols. 809 ff.

51 Chapter 1, proof 1, fol. 2ra: "... quia intensio luminis non est per additionem luminis ad lumen utroque lumine remanente..."

three conclusions, the first and third of which were already held by most additionists:

1. in every movement that pertains to a form (*motu ad formam*) something new is acquired which is either a form or part of a form;
2. in every movement with regard to form the whole preceding form, from which the *per se* motion (like intensification) occurs, is destroyed and a totally new form is acquired of which nothing preexisted;[52]
3. no form is intended or remitted but the subject of the form is intended and remitted with respect to the form so that the form we say is that according to which the subject is increased or decreased.

The second conclusion constitutes his succession theory. In intension, the preceding form is destroyed and succeeded by a totally new form of which nothing preexisted. The addition, the admixture and Burley's succession theory are treated in Jean de Ripa's four arguments *quod non*, fol. 237vb-238ra, to the central question whether the created form *caritas* is properly susceptible to intensification.[53] Burley's statement of purpose is significant in this later context, for his presentation of the problem of intension of forms seems to have been the base text for the revisions and manipulations of subsequent generations:

> Intendo perscrutari de causa intrinseca susceptionis magis et minus. In 1° declaratur quod forma non suscipit magis et minus per additionem partis ad partem utraque parte remanente. In 2° ostenditur quod forma non accipit magis et minus per admixtionem contrarii.

In chapters 4-6 he proposes the succession of forms theory, and he clearly affirms the currency of the additionist and admixturist theses in his day:

> In primis duobus capitulis destruuntur duae opiniones quae istis temporibus magis sunt famosae.[54]

---

52 Chapter 4, fol. 10va.

53 This question was asked by older schoolmen: "Utrum caritas sive quicumque habitus possit augeri per essentiam"; in Godfrey of Fontaines, *Quodlibetum* 2, q.2 (M. de Wulf and A. Pelzer, *Les quatre premiers quodlibets de G. de Fontaines* (Les philosophes belges 2 (Louvain, 1904)); also Henry of Ghent, *Quodlibeta* 5, q.3 (Paris, 1518); and Durand de St. Pourçain, I *Sent.* d.17 q.5 (Paris, 1508): "Utrum caritas possit augeri"; Jean de Bassols, I *Sent.* d.17 q.2.

54 Fol. 2ra.

For Burley qualities are not infinitely divisible as are quantities. Nor is it possible for two accidental forms of the same genus to be so comprised that one would infinitely exceed the other in perfection.[55] He feels this would have to be concluded if a form were increased by part-to-part addition. He argues that finite forms are proportional to one another; that contraries are of different species; that two species cannot be equal in perfection. In arguing from perfection he notes that the attainment of perfection occurs when more of it is acquired than was first possessed, and this means acquiring something which at first it did not have.[56] In the same way something is made more hot by acquiring more heat than it first possessed. It is necessary, by analogy, that in intension something new be acquired.[57] In the process of intension the same quality does not remain under the same mode in two different instants; *sequitur quod in quolibet instanti temporis mensurantis motum est alia et alia qualitas numero, quod est propositum.*[58] Thus the succession theory.

The *gradus vel modus* is an intrinsic form made successively more perfect through the acquisition of a new form or part thereof. If the degree (*gradus*) is really intrinsic to the subject then it actuates and informs the subject and thereby is its form; hence the subject is the *materia* in which is such a *gradus* or form of the subject. If we expand this statement we confront the mid-century ramifications of these arguments: that the intrinsic cause of intension and remission is a latitude of a species, and the same species can be preserved in a form more perfect and in a form less perfect. Thus one form of a species can be more intense than another of the same species and this via the possession of the *gradus* as form which actuates and informs the individual of the species.[59]

We shall return to such an understanding of latitude in the *Commentary* of Jean de Ripa. His first of four articles in the second part of distinction 17 concentrates most specifically on the older theses of intension held by the scholastics of an earlier generation. The distinction between forms increasing with regard to being and separately with regard to essence — the existence-essence two-sidedness of the question — was vital to this earlier discussion as Burley indicates in the *Tractatus*

---

55 Fol. 3rb.
56 "Sed quidquid acquirit maiorem perfectionem quam prius habuit acquirit aliquam perfectionem quam prius non habuit" (chapter 4, fol. 10va).
57 "Ergo necesse quod in intensione caloris acquiritur aliquid novum quod est calor vel pars caloris."
58 Fol. 10va.
59 Fol. 11va.

secundus. Burley devotes chapter 4 to *ista opinio que ponit formam intendi secundum esse et non secundum essentiam.*[60] The distinction was not unusual.[61] In the Quaestiones (MS. Tortosa 88) of the Mertonian Thomas Wylton,[62] disputed *c.* 1315, precisely this opinion is considered: that intension occurs *secundum esse non secundum essentiam,* and it is known that Burley and Wylton were in contact. Wylton objected to the succession theory in the augmentation of *caritas.* Instead, a quality was to intensify by taking on new material parts educed *de potentia materia quam perfecit gradus imperfectior.*[63] Burley argues that since the form, which is first, gives the subject its being, such that it is susceptible to more and less, this shows that the form first and naturally had *in se magis,* or intension and remission. It follows that if the form with regard to the *esse in subiecto* is susceptible to more and less, then the form in its essence also possesses more and less.[64] De Ripa also denies the existence/essence distinction. He tackles the issue in much the same way as Burley, but his purpose is to get it out of the way in order to treat the more modern approaches to the problem of intension.

Lastly, Burley concludes that there is a succession of qualities in movement measured through time and that the motion of alteration is not continuous. Here de Ripa will part company with him; but many other aspects of the problem that he will discuss turn on issues treated by Burley, in chapters 5 and 6: on moral, philosophical and theological approaches to intension.[65] The later Oxford treatises and even more so

---

60   Fol. 11rb.

61   See Duhem, *Le système* 7.490-91 on Aegidius Romanus distinguishing between existence and essence; Master of Theology, Paris, 1314-1320.

62   Chancellor of St. Paul's London, 1320-1327 and Fellow of Merton College, 1288-1301; see A. Maier, *Ausgehendes Mittelalter* 1.87-92, 219-26; also A. Maier, "Handschriftliches zu Wilhelm Ockham und Walter Burley," *AFH* 48 (1955) 234-43. Weisheipl, dissertation, p. 65.

63   MS. Tortosa 88, fol. 4vb.

64   "... ita si forma secundum esse in subiecto magis et minus, sequitur quod forma in essentia sua habeat magis et minus ... imo mihi videtur quod causa intrinseca intentionis et remissionis est latitudo forme specifice, ut quod eadem species forme potest salvari in forma magis perfecta et in forma minus perfecta."

65   Fol. 12va: "... ex parte caritatis arguitur sic secundum istam opinionem": if the intense *habitus* of *caritas* is to be increased, it is shown (they say) that God creates *caritas* more perfect and greater than He did at first, which is *inconveniens.* Thus it is proved that if He created *caritas* which is lesser along with the whole preceding *caritas* which is destroyed (in the process of intension) there would be no increase of *caritas.* Instead there would be a diminution of *caritas.* Yet if there were created *caritas* equal to that which preceded, then there would be no increase but also no decrease in the amount of *caritas.* We say, therefore, that God increases *caritas* in the instant in which He elicits the act by which *caritas* merits to be increased and this act which merited the increase in *caritas* is thus meritorious. Thus the subject is said to increase not according to the *habitus* which was destroyed; it increases with regard to the *habitum perfectiorem quem generat* (fol. 14vb). This perfect

Jean de Ripa take up where Burley left off. De Ripa will not agree with Burley on the succession of forms theory, nor with Burley's understanding of the mechanics of local motion as an acquisition of an infinite number of indivisible different places per instant, to which correspond separate qualitative forms gained successively in each instant of alteration.[66] Burley had also discussed this non-homogeneous continuum in his earlier *De primo et ultimo instanti*. There he said that each individual form, newly produced and succeeding the previous existing form, is indivisible and possesses an ultimate instant of being intrinsic to it. The *forma speciei* includes an infinite number of these individual forms and the entire *forma* can be terminated extrinsically as well, by a first instant of non-being. Echoes of this view will be found in Dumbleton and in de Ripa's interpretation of latitudes terminated extrinsically by the *non gradus* or zero degree of a species' being or by God's infinite immensity as the other possible extrinsic boundary.[67]

Evidently Burley's influence was enormous in his time so that it is not surprising to find extensive borrowing in de Ripa's *Commentary*. But much of de Ripa's familiarity with the issues comes from an additional knowledge, somehow acquired, of the other Oxford Calculators — specifically from the group in which the ideas of Roger Swineshead, Heytesbury and Dumbleton flourished. What is indeed startling is that in rejecting some of Burley's and Roger's arguments, de Ripa seems to follow much of the argumentation as presented in Dumbleton's *Summa*, part 2, from chapter 25 to the end. It is in the Dumbleton text that we can discern most of what de Ripa will later speak of as the commonly held views that were current in the schools.[68]

The physical basis of the modern thesis is conveniently summarized in an Oxford tract on the *termini naturales*, ascribed to Heytesbury and to the 1330's.[69] The series of definitions in this treatise, *secundum usum*

habit is not acquired by means of one act completely but rather through several preceding acts leading to the perfect *habitus* ("... nullus habitus perfectus acquiritur per unum actum totaliter sive tamquam per causam totalem sed per plures actus prececentes et disponentes ad habitum perfectum").

66 Chapters 4 and 6.

67 De Ripa, concl. 3, a.1, proof 3.

68 Richard Swineshead's proofs in the earlier intension tract (*In primo de celo*), MS. Gonville and Caius 499/ 268, fols. 204-11, and the more comprehensive *Liber calculationum* also are of interest, if not as sources for de Ripa — the *Liber* is dated by Maier around 1350 — then as summaries of the earlier conclusions of the Calculators. See n. 28.

69 Weisheipl transcribed the text in his dissertation, pp. 369 ff.; the attribution to Heytesbury is made in the fourteenth-century Munich MS. Clm 8997, fol. 167r. For this study I have looked at London, British Museum Royal 8 A XVIII (membr., xiv), fols. 69v-75r and Paris, Bibliothèque Nationale Lat. 6673 (s. xv), fols. 14-18.

Oxonie, indicates that the general problem in discussions of alteration was that of quantified substance, quantified first matter, which would remain the same both in substantial changes and in augmentation-diminution or condensation-rarefaction. Specifically, the summary of Oxford ideas corresponds to what one finds elaborated at greater lengths in Dumbleton's *Summa* and even later in Richard Swineshead's *Calculationes*, which in turn chiefly correspond to the first six books of the *Physics*, and less to the *De generatione et corruptione* and the *Praedicamenta* (chapter 8 on quality). What was sought was a uniform law describing relative speeds of change. Much emphasis was placed on rarefaction for example. One wanted a statement relating the dependence of the velocity of alteration on the proportion of quantity uniformly acquired, to the original volume in a given time. Heytesbury defines rarefaction as the separation of parts of matter subsequently occupying an increased volume without any addition of a new body; condensation is a constriction, a compression of parts without any loss of a body.[70]

Father Weisheipl has called this summary of Oxford ideas a beginner's text and cites numerous variations and commentaries based on it which "came into use later on the continent."[71] In fact, its frequent reference to the notion of rarefaction and condensation serves to characterize a mode of argument often used in the modern school from the time of Ockham. Jean de Ripa freely avails himself of such notions.[72] They were common enough that he need not have relied solely on Alphonsus Vargas[73] who cites a similar discussion in the works of Thomas of Strassburg. Dumbleton also extensively treats rarefaction and condensation in part 3 of his *Summa*[74] in conjunction with augmentation and diminution and also in part 2[75] in relation to the manner in which qualities are said to increase and decrease in intensity.

But the larger issue for the *Termini naturales* and for the other more elaborate tracts, was to define suitably the various kinds of movement: *motus subitus* and *motus successivus*, thereby relating the processes of *alteracio* and *augmentacio* involving respectively change in quality and in

---

70   British Museum Royal 8 A XVIII, fol. 69vb.

71   Weisheipl, dissertation, p. 198; p. 160.

72   *Conclusiones* (2), pp. 145 f., 14-17.

73   Mgr. Combes has suggested Alphonsus Vargas as the likely source for such a discussion ("L'intensité," *AHDLMA* 37 (1970) 40).

74   Vat. Lat. 6750, fol. 47vb (chapter 19).

75   Cambridge, Peterhouse 272, fol. 17va (chapter 25).

quantity. Successively we find definitions for *punctus* — *est quóddam indivisibile in linea ad quod copulantur partes linee*; for extrinsic and intrinsic points; for lines being composed of an infinite number of points, and the statement that no infinite thing is any more or less infinite than another.[76] Then we move on to a discussion of local motion relating to a *corpus simplex* (that not composed of contraries, *ut elementum*) and *corpus mixtum*. As such, these issues are treated by Dumbleton who found them in Aristotle and the Commentators. But even more useful is the subsequent treatment of the *gradus summus*, the use of the concept of latitudes of qualities, and the discussion of the *gradus intensi vel remissi* in relation to the distance from its zero degree — *a suo non gradu*. The value of the *Termini naturales*, then, lies in its brief and clear presentation of the many definitions that are found at the core of Jean de Ripa's later conclusions. From the *Termini naturales* we should keep the following in mind:

> the concept of a maximum degree of intensity;
> the concept of the *gradus* of certain qualities resulting from the mixture of contraries;
> the concept of both the *summum* and *non gradus* of one quality as the privation of the quality's contrary;
> the definition of a latitude of a quality as a range comprised of degrees of uniform disposition of intensity and remissness from zero to the maximum degree;
> that there is an infinite number of degrees in such a range or latitude because of the infinite divisibility of degrees;
> the intensity and remissness of a degree (*gradus*) depends on greater or lesser participation of its contrary qualities;
> the alternative of describing intensity and remissness as distance from zero degree;
> explanations of modes of intensification, that is, the process of intensification is the acquisition of the *gradus* of perfection via some latitude;
> definitions of uniform and difform modes of intensification and remission;
> that things may be described and therefore denominated either with respect to a part or the whole;
> uniform and difform qualities are defined;
> qualities are called great and small *per accidens* not *per se*, just as we call quantities great and small;
> the parallel between extension and intension is drawn and yet they are distinguished;

---

76 "Nullum infinitum est alio infinito maius neque minus, nec aliqua infinita aliis infinitis sunt plura aut pauciora" (British Museum Royal 8 A XVIII, fol. 7ora).

distinction of internal and external extremes at which qualities (uniformly difform) are terminated, i.e. the extremes within the latitude (inclusive) or outside the latitude (exclusive);[77]

the equating of a uniformly difform quality with the latitude which
corresponds to its mean degree's intensity.

This treatise can serve us as a necessary introduction to the
vocabulary of the moderns. It is highly significant that Jean de Ripa's
arguments and conclusions take place on an even more sophisticated
level; as we shall see, his treatment of the complicated ontological issue
of created and uncreated essences susceptible to increase is matched by
his ability to manipulate the complicated physics of the modern school.

ROGER SWINESHEAD

De Ripa affirms that he was taught a theory of contraries by the
Franciscans to explain the intensification of forms. The more a form is
composed the more it is intense, the more attenuated or remiss, then
the more the form is simple.[78] The decisive distinction between intension by coextended contraries and intension by addition of part to
part is made time and again throughout articles 2 and 3. It is evident
from our own summaries that intension by simultaneous coextended
contraries was one of the primary theses presented in full and only in
part rejected by Burley and Dumbleton. It was one of the key
arguments of the treatise *Descriptiones motuum (tractatus ... datus oxonie ad
utilitatem studencium)* attributed to Roger Swineshead and read in Paris
at mid-century. If de Ripa, writing around 1355-57, objected formally
to the admixture explanation of intension, he is indirectly informing us
not only that Roger's ideas were considered among the Franciscans, but
that additionists were also forced to acknowledge the role of contraries
in the common opinion. Either he is directly using the later Oxford additionist tracts which illustrate this fact, or he has heard them as lectures in the *studium*. This means they were in Paris 10 to 15 years after
they were enunciated in Oxford circles, as Glorieux's research seems to
show. From what he tells us in article 3 it was not the admixture but
the additionist theory that was taught by the Franciscans — that of intension of a form resulting from the addition of a new degree of being
to the precedent producing a third new, more intense degree.[79] We shall

---

77 See de Ripa below, argument 4, fol. 239ra.
78 See below, fol. 246ra.
79 *Conclusiones* a.2, p. 148, 2-4.

present Roger's thesis in brief not only because it was one of the English tracts mentioned in Falisca's inventory, but to understand how interacting admixed contraries were also acceptable to the Oxford additionists.

Weisheipl has suggested that Roger wrote his tract sometime between 1328-1338. It is "the work of a young but ambitious master in arts (which) seems to reveal no awareness of Dumbleton's *Summa* nor even of Heytesbury's *Regulae*. Hence it may have been 'datus Oxonie' well before 1335."[80] The tract is variously known as *De motibus naturalibus* and *Descriptiones motuum*.[81] In eight parts it is, as its titles indicate, a work devoted to a physical analysis of different kinds of movement.[82] Part 4 describes intensive alteration as the admixture of simultaneously existing contrary qualities.[83] A double measure of intensity and of remission is thereby set up to correspond to the admixed qualities. Intensity is defined as the distance from zero degree; a remiss degree is defined in terms of its distance from the *summum*.[84] De Ripa shall align himself with Dumbleton and Richard Swineshead in rejecting such measurement from the supreme degree. For these three, intension and remission are both determined by means of their intensive distances from the zero degree of the species.

Roger approaches his subject by establishing proofs (against three erroneous positions) that intension and remission through local motion *is* applicable to qualities. One can define a formal range for each species of quality comprising indivisible degrees.[85] The term of perfection for each qualitative species discussed is never far from his actual argument.[86] And that latitudes are formal distances adds to his position that it is not things but modes of things that are susceptible to intension and remission. So it is with de Ripa. But Roger says that we imagine that intensive change occurs through degrees disposed continuously throughout, and something intends *proprie* because at the same time remission of a contrary is occurring. He concludes that contrary qualities are simultaneously mixed and, despite changes in intension and extension, the composite contrary qualities remain at the same degree of intensity or remissness (for the species). Such composite ad-

---

80 Weisheipl, dissertation, pp. 99-100, n. 216.
81 Erfurt, MS. Amplon. F. 135 (a. 1337); incomplete Bibliothèque Nationale Lat. 16621.
82 Erfurt, MS. Amplon. F. 135, fol. 25vb: sets out the eight *differentiae*.
83 Fols. 35rb-38rb.
84 Fol. 38rb; Roger lists his own ten *suppositiones*.
85 Fol. 33vb.
86 Fol. 36rb.

mixture means that a quality increases in degree only when it is less mixed with its contrary. In fact, there can be qualities coextended at the maximum degree, where one might be remitted but not the other, so that to describe the process accurately there must be two manners of measuring intension — distance from *non gradus* or zero degree, and remission — as distance from the *summum*. The composite subject that undergoes intension and remission apparently already possesses the necessary contraries, the subsequent relative alteration of which results in the alteration of the whole. Dumbleton was to modify this and say that each contrary was intended or remitted by a part to part or degree to degree addition of something new, while the summation of all the coexisting contrary degrees would remain constant for the species. He has a single mode for measuring loss and gain in that both intension and remission are determined from the zero degree of the species.

JOHN DUMBLETON

We are returned to the Aristotelian context of intension and remission when we look at Dumbleton's *Summa*. If substantial forms were to be considered susceptible to more and less, even when spoken of abstractly, then one needed to know the properties of contraries of primary and secondary qualities for these were the principles by which one could say a substantial form was more or less. The intension problem was conceived directly along Aristotelian lines where the Philosopher, in the *Categories, Physics* and *Metaphysics*,[87] had presented a systematic analysis of primary and derivative contraries as principles in process.[88] As *termini*, these principles delimit the life process of an individual substance, marking the movement or change in a substance.[89] The current *modus loquendi*, as Dumbleton saw it, linked the susceptibility to *maius et minus* with the capacity to become more remiss or more intense, thereby reinforcing the parallel between the characteristics of the extension and intension processes. The modern discussions were the result of Ockham's controversial doctrine of quantity as applied to the Eucharist.[90] The capacity to be made more in-

---

87 *Categories* 2 (1a16-1b9); *Metaphysics* Δ.10 (1018a25-37).

88 Not generated or caused by another.

89 See John P. Anton, *Aristotle's Theory of Contrariety* (London, 1957), p. 9: "The fundamental role of contrariety is the formal demand for the determinateness in 'process'." Contrariety is the basis on which distinctions are made and having a physical counterpart, it provides the criterion for the intelligibility of process.

90 *De sacramento altaris* 1, q.3, ed. T. B. Birch (Burlington, Ia., 1930).

tense, in turn, was related to the perfectibility of an individual of a species through the acquisition (or loss) of more (or less) of its whole species' latitude. For Dumbleton such a susceptibility to more and less was the direct consequence of forms possessing real qualitative distances. Such latitudes could be acquired *partibiliter*. While extension time and again is shown to be an analog of intension, he treats each separately.

Previous studies of his *Summa logicae et philosophiae naturalis* have been primarily interested in what he has to say about velocities of moving bodies.[91] In the third part of the *Summa* he is most specifically interested in an accurate general description of diverse velocities of alteration within moving bodies that are diversely quantified. Certainly here lies the novelty of the modern school's physics. But all this is prefaced by part 2 where Dumbleton treats motion that pertains to qualities. Summaries of the arguments in this second part find their way into de Ripa's treatment. Chapters 25 to 43 in the Peterhouse manuscript[92] cover the numerous aspects of the process of intension and remission; Dumbleton presents some of the reasoning behind four current opinions "quibus (?) moderna disputatio maxime versatur". We shall outline these here.

The first erroneous opinion — that of the older schoolmen (Aquinas, Albert the Great) — states that qualities may be increased and decreased through the action of an agent. The quality itself remains unchanged during alteration. The agent simply moves it through an imaginary distance from a less to a more intense degree; as in rarefaction and condensation. Each qualitative degree is intensively indivisible. It contains no latitude *in se*.

The second position — (that of Burley) — says that in alteration a new quality is induced which is more intense *per seipsum* than the preceding quality which now is destroyed and replaced by the indivisible quality of greater intensity.

The third position — (that of Roger Swineshead) — argues that intension and remission of qualities occur only by greater or lesser coextension of contraries. Intension is therefore determined only in relation to its opposite and consequently there is no real movement in qualities.

The fourth opinion — (that of Dumbleton) — says that no quality submits to intension but the subject is intensible and remissible through the real acquisition or loss of qualities; the process is analogous to the in-

91 Weisheipl, dissertation, as well as Dr. Sylla's on the Oxford Calculators and the physics of motion (see n. 6).
92 Peterhouse 272, fols. 17va-22vb.

crease and decrease of quantity. The essence of the form remains unique; the subject alone takes on or dismisses superadded form. Coextension plays a part but a different one from that in Roger's hypothesis. Coextension is here an infinite superaddition of divisible form which, as part of the species, is generated in the movement of alteration. At the end of the alteration, the state of coextension determines the degree of intensity at which the subject rests. The movement is real in qualitative change and it is additive, successive, divisibly acquired and measured by the attainment or the loss of qualitative distance from the zero degree up to some intensified state. A qualitative maximum degree is understood as containing *sub se* the whole latitude or range of less intense states. When we speak of some contrary quality like blackness being acquired by a subject that possesses whiteness, we say the following: all contraries are of the same substance but are in diverse species (e.g. whiteness is in something white). For a subject to receive the quality of whiteness it, as recipient, must somehow have any contrary forms destroyed. Aristotle said that (1 *Physics*) the recipient is denuded of all form in order that it may receive form. Contraries may be received by a single subject but not immediately. Aristotle and his commentators say that two different forms of the same species of quality (e.g. two different intensities of warmth) can be received by a subject and from them a single degree of intensity results. We say these are homogeneous; they can be continuous because a single qualitative distance results from their unification. Now if contraries are superadded they cannot be acquired simultaneously unless they create a third quality, for one form cannot result from the acquisition of the forms of earth and fire. They say that a unique distance is not had as a result. So we must inquire first how difform qualities, i.e. latitudes, are intense and remiss; next how a latitude is itself intense, and lastly, whether a single intrinsic degree corresponds to a latitude. There are three prevalent opinions: 1) a latitude is either intense or remiss depending on the coextension in its subject of degrees, all of which are of equal intensities; 2) the latitude *proprie et per se* corresponds to its middle degree; 3) all qualities in the same species, whether possessed in a uniform or difform manner, contain the same (equivalent) latitude when seen as an intensive qualitative distance.

Among the conclusions we say that intensive qualities are not to be confused with their extension throughout a subject. Extension of whiteness causes no variation in the degree to which a subject may be intensely white. Nor can we say that a difform quality, i.e. the divisible latitude as a whole, is as intense as any one of its diversely intense parts. Certainly motion of the whole is not as intense as that in any of its moving parts; although the distance covered by the whole may be the same as that covered by a part, the opposite is not true. As no extensive quantity is understood as equal to its half, no latitude or intensive distance in quality equals its half or its mean degree. The third opinion is therefore most valid. A latitude is properly said to be a qualitative distance between degrees pertaining to the intensive movement of alteration in a subject. A given whole latitude is therefore the maximum degree of its species and all qualities in the same species contain the same latitude which is designated by this maximum degree. They may possess the latitude in various difform or uniform ways. It is only in an improper manner of speaking that we say a qualitative latitude has quantitative parts of diverse and unequal intensities.

Intension is caused by the qualitative distance between degrees, given the latitude of a species of quality. This is real intensive movement. The degrees are *termini* of movement; no *terminus* is more intense than another — they are merely endpoints of change. The latitude is placed between the degrees; it is the latitude which is successively more and more intense, not the terminating degrees themselves. Is this intensive latitude, then, infinitely divisible? And is there an infinitely remiss degree in every alteration in a latitude? It is said that no maximum degree, whether finite or infinite, is also remiss. Some also say that any degree is as intense as it is remiss. Intension and remission must be understood in two ways: intension is described positively and remission is described privatively. Every intensible quality is infinitely divisible. It can be said that the zero degree never is reached by a quality. Instead, the degree of intensity is measured from zero as a limiting extreme — just as a surface ends at a line. The intensity is infinitely divisible and in theory is limited at zero. We can speak of remiss degrees in several ways. We can say something is absolutely intense and so refrain from opposing it to what is remiss. Some say that all degrees of a finite latitude are equally remiss since they are all at an infinite distance from the infinitely intense degree. Or some say that a degree is remiss when, in the same latitude, there is something more intense. This is to measure the state of intensity in relation to the maximum degree attainable. Another, preferable, position states that one degree is more remiss than another when one contains proportionally less intensity or less qualitative distance than another. This is to measure intensity from the zero degree. Lastly, we say a latitude that is terminated at zero is infinitely remiss, for nothing more remiss can act as an extreme or *terminus*. Although modes of movement may be compared positively and privatively, we must not, however, compare degrees of species. We must remember that intension in qualities does not vary the species, although qualities (like colors) may be remiss and less perfect in their species.

We next investigate how qualitative mixtures are intense. Some say no mixture can be more intense than its mean degree. Others say a mixture is as intense as the dominating element in it. A third view is that a mixture is as intense as some maximum which is had with regard to the diverse qualities contained in it. A fourth opinion says that a mixture is as intense as a *simplex* having an excess *per se*. The modern third opinion, where a mixture is intense as though it were a *simplex* at a maximum degree, assumes that there is one latitude for each of the component qualities in the mixture — a separate latitude for warmth, one for coldness, one for dryness and one for moistness. This means that a body would have to be infinitely long to accommodate the infinite number of separate, non-communicating qualities, which is absurd. The fourth opinion is acceptable. The excess *per se* by which a more intense quality intensively exceeds its contrary is what makes any mixture intense. Contraries impede one another so that in a mixture, whether it is uniformly or difformly qualified, the quality that is most intense is that which is had in excess over its contrary. Properly we say that a subject is more intense than another if it absolutely contains more intensity or a greater latitude. The subject is unique in its nature as species — it is qualified by a certain quality to the amount that its species determines by its capacity. The species is invariable, indivisible.

Thus there is no more of the *form* of *humanitas* in one man than in another ...

It is in the above context that we place de Ripa's analysis of intension.

JEAN DE RIPA

Although it may be regarded as scholastically dense, we cannot deny that de Ripa has effected a difficult and subtle synthesis of the varied trends of thought that were pursued in the different scholarly camps of natural scientists and theologians, at Oxford and at Paris.

As a theologian, Jean de Ripa is primarily concerned with salvation through the communicability of God's Essence. But before the relation of the viator's soul to the divine persons can be discussed, he must take up the relation of the created soul to the uncreated essence and this through the communication of form. In distinguishing between the two ways that form may 'be' and in proposing an opposition between information and *immutatio vitalis*, he speaks of a non-inherent form capable of increase and decrease. The latitude alone is said to change, not the form,[93] and extensive change has no bearing on the intensive state of the subject.

Being, as susceptible to quantification, is accepted by natural scientists and de Ripa. The consequent *latitudo entium* is understood as composed of degrees that are naturally and specifically distributed in a species. De Ripa deals early in his *Commentary* with the question whether they are comparable to discrete or continuous quantity.[94] He sees

---

93 *Conclusiones* (6), p. 149, 23-25.
94 *Conclusiones*, distinction 2, q.4, a.3, p. 74.

degrees as continuous and indistinct. He understands intension to be a continuous process, a degree by degree movement towards God. He imagines the bridging of the gap between infinity and immensity, between the end of the infinite series of intensities and God who transcends the series in His *immensitas* as a *terminus exclusivus*, an *immensitas* which is not susceptible to quantification.

To admit degrees of intensity in forms is to introduce problems of infinite processes in the qualities of being, i.e. into accidents (created charity) and into substances. It also introduces discussions of infinite series related to the essential order of being and of terms existing outside the series, beyond the latitude of created being. This is the scope of the discussion to which de Ripa addresses himself. In the four negative arguments to the question which he answers in the affirmative — whether *caritas* is itself susceptible to intensification —, we face what was for de Ripa the range of current opinions.[95] Because *caritas*, as commonly understood, is susceptible to increase and decrease since some can be dearer to God than others, de Ripa concludes that to *caritas* there must be attributed an intensive movement. The problem with which he has begun is the traditional one: whether an essence can be numerically the same and yet be varied intensively. From the four arguments *quod non* to this first article, he selects his issues and sets them out distinguishing the *positio antiquorum, ista vetusta positio*[96] from that of the moderns. Not only are we immediately confronted with the vocabulary associated with the problem of essential variation, but also with the discussion of increase by addition of superadded being, or through a new degree. We learn that an essence may vary accidentally but not essentially.

De Ripa outlines the negative arguments to intension as follows: 1) No essence that remains one and the same in number is properly said to be susceptible to increase or decrease, because no essence increases in intensity unless by acquiring a specific latitude, and if such is acquired, then the essence varies essentially. 2) No essence that remains substantially unvaried can exist as more or less intense, and therefore at a more or less intense degree no essence remains numerically the same; thus, the necessity of essential variation in intensification. This was the opinion of Giles of Rome.[97] 3) There is no increased intensity except where some new *esse* or new degree of being is superadded to its essence. If the new degree is essential to the essence, then its addition

95   "Utrum caritas creata sit forma proprie intensibilis?" (fols. 237vb-238ra; *quod non*).
96   Fol. 238va.
97   Combes. "L'intensité," 22.

means that a substantial variation has occurred in the essence and so it does not remain substantially the same in such augmentation. It does not therefore increase in its own intensity. If the new degree is not essential to the essence, then the change that occurs is only accidental and there has been no essential increase. 4) In every intensive latitude the more intense degree is more perfect. Either there is a coexistence of posterior and anterior degrees and then such intension is infinite for all degrees, each degree being more intense than any degree that has been given; or else each preceding degree is destroyed and it follows that no such form is increased since the form does not remain in the totality of the movement of intension.[98]

At least two important mid-fourteenth-century issues are here linked directly: the issue of intensive latitude and the relative perfection within the latitude of the species. The above four arguments to explain intension can be condensed to two theories which we have already encountered: either there is coexistence of superadded posterior degrees to the preceding degrees, or there is corruption of the antecedent. Coexistence is argued by Dumbleton and other additionists; destruction of the precedent is Burley's thesis of succession. In accepting that *caritas* is susceptible to *motus intensionis* de Ripa here borrows from the current physical analyses of intensive variation to fill up more than 14 folios in the base Z MS. Paris, Bibliothèque Nationale Lat. 15369, fols. 237vb-251va. In article 1, de Ripa rejects the general thesis that a form or essence, remaining numerically identical, can become either more or less intense.[99] And he presents two unsatisfactory positions: the ancient

98 "Et quod non, arguo quadrupliciter: 1° Nulla essentia eadem in numero manens est proprie intensibilis: igitur nec caritas. Consequentia patet, et antecedens probo: nam nulla talis essentia potest intendi, nisi vel acquirendo latitudinem specificam nel numeralem, quocumque istorum modorum essentialiter variatur. 2° Nichil per eandem essentiam numero potest reddi intensius vel remissius: igitur nulla talis essentia substantialiter invariata potest manere eadem numero sub gradu intensiori et remissiori. Prima consequentia patet: nam per prius aliquid est sic variabile quam subiectum per ipsius inexistentiam possit esse magis vel minus tale. Et antecedens patet ex hoc: nam aliter aliqua forma posset remissius esse actus alteri quam sit actus in sua natura. 3° Nichil potest intendi essentialiter, nisi per aliquod novum esse superadditum sue essentie, sive novum gradum essendi. Talis autem gradus aut est essentialis substantialiter variatur et non manet eadem substantialiter in tali augmento, et per consequens non intenditur. Si secundum: igitur talis essentia tantummodo accidentaliter transmutatur, et per consequens non intenditur in suo esse essentiali. 4° In omni latitudine intensiva, gradus intensior est perfectior: igitur si .a. intenditur, gradus posterius acquisitus est perfectior precedenti. Vel ergo gradus posterior manet cum precedenti — et sequitur quod quelibet talis forma in quolibet instanti intrinseco talis intentionis est infinita, pro quolibet in tali instanti habet infinitos gradus, quorum quilibet est intensior certo dabili — vel quilibet prior gradus corrumpitur — et sequitur quod nulla talis forma intenditur, cum nec maneat in toto isto motu intensionis: et habetur intentum."

99 *Conclusiones* (6), p. 146, 32-33.

and the modern. According to the former, it is the existence not the essence which varies in intensification. The modern thesis rejects this distinction and says that variation in quantitative extension has its parallel in intensive variation.

> Ymaginantur quod sicut idem potest rarefieri et condempsari et habere alium gradum quantitativum et extensivum, ita alium intensivum sine varietate sue essentie.[100]

Six conclusions on the *positio antiquorum*[101] and three *de positione modernorum*[102] are formulated. If it is said, de Ripa argues, that the essence has the same act throughout the process of continuous intension, then I ask, in what manner is the form increased? It must be through the intrinsic mutation of its intrinsic being and by means of a new *formal* act; and the process must be an infinite one.[103] If this is so, then intension is alteration. Alteration is some manner of being the same essence throughout the process of change, without any substantial mutation occurring. Consequently, in such manner of being, change is accidental and if such increase is caused by a natural agent, then such change, such *actus essendi*, this mode of existential being, must be drawn from the power of the essence. The position of the ancients *non potest stare*.[104] For de Ripa, then, growth in existential being means acquisition of a new formal act which the subject previously did not possess. Burley's *Tractatus secundus*, conclusion 1 says much the same: that in every motion with respect to form something new is acquired which is either a form or part of a form.[105] And as this is the concept at the core of the additionist thesis as well, we find it in Dumbleton[106] and later in Richard Swineshead's *Liber calculationum*.[107]

According to de Ripa the *moderni* suggest that the process of intension and remission is analogous to rarefaction and condensation; the essence

100   Fol. 238ra.

101   Fol. 238ra-va.

102   Fols. 238vb-239rb.

103   Proof 3: "quero quomodo ille intenditur, et oportet quod ponatur per mutationem eius intrinsecum et per novum actum et erit processus in infinitum" (fol. 238va).

104   "Preterea si sic est: igitur talis intensio est alteratio: est enim aliqualiter esse eiusdem essentie sine mutatione substantiali ipsius et per consequens tale esse existere est accidens. Et si talis intensio fiat per agens naturale tale esse existere educitur de potentia essentie: et infinita sequuntur inconvenientia que non oportet ultra deducere. Sic ergo patet quomodo ista vetusta positio non potest stare."

105   Burley, *Tractatus secundus*, fol. 10va. However, de Ripa places greater emphasis on the formal aspect of the acquisition.

106   Dumbleton, fol. 18va, chapter 30, quarta opinio.

107   Richard Swineshead, *Liber calculationum*, fol. 2vb: "... caliditas componitur ex partibus qualitativis..."

remaining constant without preventing intension. The analogy was a
common one as we have seen from Dumbleton and the *Termini naturales*.
A distinction is drawn, not between essence and existence as in the
earlier disputes, but between intensity as such and some mode of intensification. De Ripa establishes conclusions to suit the latter distinction: first, that if an essence is susceptible to intension, it cannot be at
the zero degree of its species' intensity nor at the degree of infinite
decrease (which would also be the maximum degree of its species' intensive latitude).[108] He goes on to say that every entity susceptible to intension has an imaginary latitude. It is possessed in a continuous manner (*contra* Burley). The latitude, he says, is the very matter of the intensive movement. There cannot be a form at the zero degree (*non
gradus*) of intension that still maintains the numerically identical being
that it first had, the zero degree being an extrinsic bound of the species
(Dumbleton; see above p. 155). *Caritas* cannot be such a form: indivisible
and yet at zero degree. So de Ripa rejects the concept of a continuum or
a continuous latitude comprised of infinite indivisibiles. He notes, further, that an intensive degree of some subject is *ex habitu* accidental to
the intensible subject, just as an extensive mode is an *habitus* to an extensible subject. But all things possessing the quantitative mode may
possess, through God, the power to be at zero degree of extension. This
is said, for example, of Christ's non-extensive body in the sacrament of
the altar.[109] So it may be for intensible things, as for extensible ones;
they can be at the zero degree of intensity *per dei potentiam*, but only in
this way.

The third conclusion clarifies that an intensive mode, i.e. a latitude
possessed by a subject susceptible to intension, is yet not sufficient to
cause variation.[110] If the mode of intensification is distinguished formally from the fact of intensity, then, according to de Ripa, the intensity

108 *Conclusiones* (1) a.1, p. 146, 40-54: "Nulla essentia intensibilis et remissibilis potest esse sub
non gradu intensionis, vel infinite remissionis. Probatur: nam omnis entitas sic intensibilis et
remissibilis habet ymaginariam latitudinem per modum continui que est materia talis motus intensionis" (fol. 238vb).

109 *Conclusiones* (2) a.1, p. 146, 42-44. (Ockham wrote controversially on this.) "Non stat intensionem precise esse modum variabilem — stante unitate rei numerali — et talem rem non posse
esse sub non gradu intensionis. Probatur: nam talis gradus intensivus — quoad propositum — eandem habitudinem habet ad rem intensibilem sicut modus extensivus ad rem extensibilem — secundum istam positionem — igitur, sicut omnis res habens modum quantitativum habet per Dei potentiam esse sub non gradu extensionis — sicut patet de corpore Christi in sacramento altaris — ita
omnis res intensibilis et remissibilis potest esse sub non gradu intentionis" (fol. 238vb).

110 Concl. 3, a.1, fol. 238vb: "Impossibile est rem intensive variari ex sola acquisitione huiusmodi intensivi modi essendi. Probatur: nam impossibile est aliquam rem intensibilem manere sub
eodem esse numerali et esse sub non gradu intensionis."

can include the zero degree as the *terminus* of the range of the essence's variation. But at zero, the essence is no longer the same; the species itself has undergone change. If we must maintain the essence, then the mode of intensity, the latitude, must be other than that which includes beginning at zero. The problem has become one of measuring intensity by means of at least one of the *termini* of the species' precise latitude. We have seen how this was treated as a physical problem by Dumbleton, analogous to extension in quality. Following the tradition, in his second argument de Ripa proposes *caliditas* as an example of a quality subject to intension. The subject possesses its numerical being, its essential denomination, — we might say it possesses its fixed range, a latitude peculiar to its species. It then possesses its degree of intensity, the accidental form to be seen as a point attained by the specific individual of a species in its species' range. God concurs, as the primary cause, with the natural agent in conferring a being, a specific latitude, to a species, but God does not concur in the individual's intensive mode of being, i.e. God does not concur as a cause when it is a question of the individual degree attained in the range of perfection within a given species.[111] The quality, here *caliditas*, is thereby altered through a latitude from its theoretical existence at the zero degree of intensity to some positive intensity. The *caliditas* as a species of quality is never really altered; only its intensive mode undergoes change.[112] And so de Ripa distinguishes between an alteration in heat and an alteration in the intensity of heat "just as an alteration in the thing is not the same as an alteration in its extensive mode." He further describes such continuous increase from zero degree as divisible, *partibiliter*.[113] And just as an initial change, a *primum mutatum esse*, is necessary in intension to mark the point where the thing begins to 'be' at some intensity, so it is necessary to give an ultimate being, or a last (point) of change in remission. Movement in intension is thereby defined as the giving of the first and last instants.[114] We have already said that Burley's *De primo et ultimo instanti*, a text cited and reproduced in the Falisca notebooks, is entirely devoted to this subject. Both Burley and de Ripa characterize the con-

---

111   Concl. 3, a.1, proof 1, fol. 238vb: "Pono ergo quod Deus concurrat cum .b. agente naturali precise ad suum esse non concurrendo ad illum modum intensive essendi."

112   Concl. 3, a.1, proof 2: "Sequitur quod talis alteratio est alterius speciei ab alteratione secundum modum intensivum et per consequens non est eadem alteratio ad calorem et ad intensionem caloris sicut nec ad rem et ad modum extensivum rei."

113   Concl. 3, proof 3, fol. 238vb: ".a. calor incipiat intendi a non gradu per agens naturale et partibiliter intendatur."

114   Concl. 3, proof 3: "et eodem modo in remissione est dare ultimum esse rei; et tunc cuilibet motus est dare primum et ultimum instans."

tinuum by its divisibility to a specific limiting minimum. De Ripa affirms, however, that it is impossible for every species with regard to its essential being to be indivisible *and* immediately at the zero degree of absolute being. This would mean that every species, with regard to its essential being, would be equally perfect with all others with regard to their essential being, and as such, each would be equally indifferent to all degrees of intensity.[115] Instead, de Ripa accepts with Dumbleton's fourth opinion (which is his own)[116] that the essence of the species is unique and therefore indivisible for the species. Because the essence is invariable the essential being is said to be indivisible for each species, in fact, incomparable. So it is impossible for one species to be changed into another by intension.[117]

It is the *specific latitude* that is communicated to a creature through the divine essence; it corresponds exactly to the mode of intensity.[118] The acquisition of such an intensive mode causes no essential variation. Speaking of the uncreated as well as the created essence, de Ripa concludes that the divine essence is also indivisible with respect to its essential perfection, the distinction being that the divine essence is absolutely, simply, indivisible, and as such, stands as a *terminus exclusivus* beyond the continuum of infinite indivisible essences of the infinite created species in the natural order. Likewise, the divine immensity, a special term to describe God's special infinity outside all infinite series, does come from a most perfect mode of intensity, from a latitude specific to divinity. The divine essence is not more life or essence or wisdom than the creature, but is only greater with respect to these *modes* of intensity. Just as a thing is not called more substantial from the fact that it is of greater quantity, so God is not called more essential or

---

115 Fol. 239ra: "et sequitur tunc quod omnis species quoad esse essentiale est eque perfecta cum altera et eque indifferens ad omnem gradum intensionis."

116 Peterhouse 272, chapter 30, fol. 18va.

117 "Patebit in 4° Sententiarum distinctione 10ª ubi ostendetur quod mutatio unius speciei in alteram speciem sit impossibilis."

118 "2° sequitur quod tota latitudo perfectionis communicabilis creature per divinam essentiam correspondet precise illi modo intensivo."

119 "3° sequitur quod divina essentia est simpliciter indivisibilis quoad perfectionem essentialem sed sua immensitas provenit tantum modo illo quantitativo. Consequentia patet: nam si divina essentia sit immensa in esse essentie in esse vite et huiusmodi cum ipsa sit communicabilis sub remissiori gradu citra plenitudinem secundum quamcumque talem denominationem, sequitur quod creatura non solum quoad modum intensivum sed etiam quoad esse essentiale vite et huiusmodi potest esse intensior et remissior: igitur per oppositum sicut ponis huiusmodi intensionem esse solum quoad modum huiusmodi intensivum in creatura et non quoad esse essentiale ita habens dicere consequenter sic esse in Deo: et per consequens immensitas divina in esse vite, sapientie et huiusmodi, non dicit immensitatem divine essentie secundum aliquod esse essentiale sed solum modum quemdam variabilem in re, cum omnimoda ydemptitate essentiali: et per con-

more in life from the fact that He has (quantitatively) a more perfect intensive mode. It follows that God is not more absolutely perfect than the creature but only *secundum quid*, according to such an intensive mode, a formal measure, is He more perfect.[119] Different species, therefore, ought not to be compared because essentially each has a granted, invariable perfection. Any extensive change in a creature has no repercussion in the essential order.[120] With Dumbleton, de Ripa concludes that no identity exists between intension and extension, but a parallel remains between quality and quantity. This is because de Ripa sees a degree of intensity as a divisible quantitative mode of the indivisible essence.[121]

While it is not of any value to compare essential perfections of different species, yet within the variation open to an individual of a given species, an infinite degree of intensity of such an essence can be attained. Thus de Ripa concludes that in some species, just as some soul can be infinitely alive, there can be an infinite intensive latitude of being that terminates exclusively in God.[122] Implied here is a great chain of perfected being, a continuous infinite series of perfected species, indivisible in their perfection and yet infinitely intense at the *summum* of each species. The picture is one of infinite subsets within an infinite set, all within an infinite "immense" set, the latter serving as an exclusive term beyond all infinite created intensities. This concept is expressed in perfection treatises of the fourteenth century,[123] but nowhere is it employed as clearly and with such a specifically theological purpose as by de Ripa.

Granted that there is this intensive mode, this latitude, an intrinsic

---

sequens divina essentia non est magis vita vel essentia vel sapientia quam creatura, sed solum maior quoad modum huiusmodi intensionum; ita quod sicut res non dicitur magis substantia ex hoc quod est magis quanta, ita Deus non dicitur magis essentia vel vita ex hoc quod habet modum illum intensiorem perfectiorem. Deus non est magis perfectus simpliciter quam creatura, sed solum secundum quid — puta secundum talem modum intensivum."

120 "Igitur, quantumcumque Deus extendat .a. quoad talem modum extensivum, dummodo non sit simpliciter magis vita, non est perfectior simpliciter in esse vite quam .a." (fol. 239ra).

121 "Ideo sicut quelibet substantia sub non gradu intensionis et quantificabilis potest esse eque quanta extensive cum alia, ita quelibet essentia indivisibilis simpliciter in esse vite — cuiusmodi est Deus, et creatura secundum esse essentiale — potest eque quantificari quoad modum intensionis ... ex quo talis gradus intensionis est quidam modus quantitativus essentie indivisibilis quoad esse essentiale talis denominationis; sequitur propositum" (fol. 239ra).

122 "Quelibet anima potest esse infinita vita infinita intelligentia intensive et sic de aliis: et ita in qualibet specie potest esse latitudo intensiva infinita et terminata exclusive ad Deum" (fol. 239ra); see Dumbleton, fol. 19va, chapter 32 and fol. 20va, chapter 37. In *Calculationes 2* Richard Swineshead speaks of infinite intensities in the same and in diverse species. It is imaginable that a subject may have infinite qualities of various degrees (*Calculationes* 1, fol. 3ra).

123 For example, Anon. Paris, Bibliothèque Nationale Lat. 6752, fols. 34r (chapter 14)-37r.

change cannot possibly come about if there is no new acquisition or loss, says de Ripa. Intension is simultaneous with intrinsic, positive change. De Ripa concludes that such additions are accidental rather than substantial.[124] We are given this essential being of any creature, and the creature varies specifically in acquiring, degree by degree and continuously, the whole possible latitude of its species up to the first. As such, an intensity can only be considered the accidental mode of the thing that is susceptible to increase. We recall the same thesis in the *Termini naturales*: that a quality is called great or small not *per se* but *per accidens*, as one says of quantities. Dumbleton treats this even more extensively in chapters 29 and 30.

In brief, de Ripa believes that only the intensive latitude of a form and not its essence is susceptible to intension and remission. This intensive latitude can be acquired or lost *partibiliter*. The continuous process of intension produces a new form that is divisible with regard to its own intensity, although the essence of the species remains invariable no matter what may be the intensive variation in its latitude whose range runs from zero degree to the *summum* of the given species. As Dumbleton said before him, the subject is only said to increase and decrease via accidental latitudinal intensity, its essence remaining constant. Dumbleton drew an analogy between the qualitative acquisition or loss of infinite intensities and the "apposition" of parts by which a quantity is made more or less. The resulting intensible quality is comprised of coextended parts generated in the motion of alteration that altogether (coextensively) make up the degree just as quantitative parts make up the quantity. Dumbleton merely seems to imply in chapter 30 that such qualitative parts are not really distinct degrees concurring in intensification.[125] De Ripa is clear that his degrees are only formally, not really distinct, and all these formally distinct degrees are essential to the form to which they intrinsically correspond.

Article 2 begins de Ripa's most systematic dealings with the modern opinion. He asks whether it is conceivable that the same essence formally denominates its subject with more or less intensity.[126] We are presented with three false opinions[127] and we learn that these comprise the common opinion that Jean de Ripa was taught:

---

124 "Cum talis intensio sit solum modus accidentalis ipsi rei que intenditur" (fol. 239rb).
125 Fol. 18va, fourth opinion.
126 Fol. 239rb-va.
127 Fol. 239rb-va: "Ista difficultas inducitur propter multa: primo quia multi ymaginantur quod nulla essentia habet latitudinem in sua natura, sed omnis intensio est subiecti per maiorem vel minorem existentiam per informationem. Alii vero ymaginantur quod intensio potest fieri per

Ego autem — quamvis in isto modo ponendi fueris a principio nutritus, cuius fundamentum pro maxima reputabam et nullam indigere probationem — non recolo tamen me pro isto modo ponendi audivisse probabilem rationem ...[128]

We are told that this has been a difficult problem for many thinkers, primarily because they imagine that no essence has a latitude in its own nature. Dumbleton gave this as his first rejected opinion. They say, continues de Ripa, that it is rather the subject that has intension, and the essence, by means of a process of information, has a greater or lesser existence in the subject. Following Duhem, Mgr. Combes identified this as the position held by the Dominicans (Aquinas) and by the Hermits of St. Augustine following Giles of Rome's second manner.[129] Others imagine that intension is caused solely through the decrease of contraries, the essence remaining the same. We can immediately identify this as the admixturist thesis against which Burley argued in chapter 2 of the *Tractatus secundus*. It was espoused by Roger Swineshead[130] and argued *contra* by Dumbleton in chapter 28 — the rejected third opinion.

De Ripa's third opinion imagines that, as the same degree can denominate the part more intensely than the whole, so the same part can denominate the whole with more or less intensity, while the degree of being is totally indivisible. The *Termini naturales* dealt with the description of things either with regard to parts or the whole, and Dumbleton spoke of it in chapter 33. It relates to what was a familiar logical problem during this period: the valid conditions of denominating the whole subject by one of its parts. It was commonly held that in a subject that did not possess a quality uniformly throughout, the intensity of one of its parts could not denominate the whole subject. In the following arguments de Ripa thoroughly examines the various situations where subjects are diversely qualified, and he considers what this does to the denomination of the whole subject. Such consideration of uniform and difform qualification of a subject was the hallmark of the natural science tracts we have looked at. De Ripa posits six conclusions *ad excludendum istos modos ponendi*.

Given that the degree of being of the intensive form is indivisible for each species, it is not possible for the same form to exist divisibly under

solam remissionem contrarii. Tertii vero ymaginantur quod sicut idem gradus potest intensius denominare partem quam totum ita eandem partem intensius et remissius cum omnimoda indivisione sui gradus essendi. Et ideo, ad excludendum istos modos ponendi, ponam aliquas conclusiones."

128 Fol. 240rb.
129 Combes, "L'intensité," 35.
130 *Descriptiones motuum*, chapter 4.

an informative mode. *A fortiori* no form having an indivisible degree of being (*entitatis*) that is communicable can be informed with a divisible intrinsic act.[131] Secondly: necessarily the form first has *in se* an intensive latitude of being (which is indivisible) before it has the latitude with the power to inform (divisible).[132] This is the fourth opinion offered and confirmed by Dumbleton, chapter 30. Thirdly: it is not possible for a subject to be increased by a form when the form is not communicated according to more and more of the latitude of its being, that is, when the form is not communicated divisibly. In other words, intensification must occur *partibiliter*, for only thus can a latitude be acquired. From an indivisible intensive form there cannot result a latitude of intensity in a subject, so that we must conclude that in the same continuous form there is (divisible) *applicatio* and *informatio*, according to more and more of the latitude of its being. Nor is it possible for some form to be more attenuated and less than it is, when it is informed in another subject, than it is in the whole of its own latitude of intensive essence.[133] In the communication of a form, the form's essence must remain, otherwise, another species would be communicated at some degree other than that which was *proprie*. This argument serves as the precursor of the larger issue whereby the form *caritas*, when informed in a subject, is informed to its own specific latitude, to its own characteristic essential power. Thus, it is not changed essentially in the information of whatever subject although the variation in the *caritas* range within the indivisible latitude of the species is susceptible to infinite divisibility. This accounts for some men being "more or less in *caritas*" than others. That *caritas* remains essentially identical, that it informs according to its ultimate degree of being, is supremely important for de Ripa's understanding of the divine manner of informing creation — by *immutatio vitalis*. But speaking *de modo informationis* and excluding the *modum vitalis actuationis*, de Ripa concludes that the same invariable form cannot continuously vary any subject intensively.[134] Thus the informing *form* must vary somehow through its existence in its subject. All that can be said to be

131 Concl. 1, fol. 239va.

132 Concl. 2, fol. 239va.

133 Concl. 4, fol. 239va.

134 Concl. 5 and 6, fol. 239va: "Non stat aliquod subiectum per eandem formam variari continue intensive. Et loquor semper de modo informationis, excludendo modum vitalis actuationis. Patet: nam precedenti articulo non stat eandem essentiam numero manere et acquirere latitudinem intensivam secundum aliquam denominationem essentialem; igitur non stat aliquod subiectum per huiusmodi formam variari quomodolibet intensive secundum intensionem et remissionem. 6ª conclusio: necessario ex omni forma informativa et variata per inexistentiam suo subiecto, invariabilis consurgit denominatio intrinseca in eodem qualiscumque fiat alia variatio."

invariable is the intrinsic denomination of that subject susceptible to such information by the varying form.

The problem that remains for de Ripa is to determine how we choose this invariable denomination; does it correspond to the most intense degree or to the middle degree of the individual subject of a given species? De Ripa says that any subject that has been made newly white, for example, has undergone an intrinsic change, from which this new whiteness necessarily results. He continues by arguing against *adversarii* who say that a contrary (quality) impedes the formal denomination of another more intense contrary (quality);[135] because of this they must concede that the contrary is denominated at some degree as is its opposite. We see here an indirect reference to Roger Swineshead's double mode of measure for two contraries in a single subject.

The main import of this second article, then, is that the process of intensification consists of an intrinsic positive change which reflects the fact that some new being exists to render the subject more white or more intensely possessed of a quality measured from zero degree intensity. Positive and privative possession of a single quality is meant here, rather than simultaneously warring contraries. The coextended contraries in a single composite subject affect the formal denomination not only of the whole subject but of the one so-called dominating quality concerned. But de Ripa carefully argues against the opinion that intension of the whole occurs by means of a decrease in the contrary quality. That he so frequently returns to counter this admixturist theory seems to indicate that it was still being maintained in some quarters.[136] This argument is that no contrary, like black, can impede the formal denomination of another more intense contrary, such as white. De Ripa says, however, that a positive change involving blackness does not necessarily mean that any new whiteness has been acquired.[137] No contrary can impede the formal denomination of another more intense contrary.

In his third proof Burley[138] had provided de Ripa with a model

---

135 Dumbleton rejected the third opinion, chapter 41 (Peterhouse 22ra); de Ripa, fol. 240ra: "correlarium; quod nulla intensio vel remissio potest fieri per maiorem vel minorem admixtionem contrarii."

136 Buridan supported admixture to some extent: *Quaestiones super octo libros Physicorum* 1 q.4, fol. 5rb-va (Paris, 1509).

137 Fol. 239vb: "3° Non stat aliquid noviter esse album sine mutatione intrinseca positiva ex qua necessario consurgat hoc esse album. Sed ex nulla mutatione positiva circa nigredinem sequitur necessario aliquem esse album; talis enim potest esse absque hoc quod nulla albedo sit."

138 *Tractatus secundus*, proof 3, fols. 6vb-7ra.

argument countering admixture. He also provided support for de Ripa in his chapter 4 where intension is said to occur by means of the acquisition of a new form: in every movement with respect to form something is acquired which is either a form or a part of a form.[139] We have seen that Dumbleton also presented powerful arguments against admixture. Remission of one contrary, say black, does not mean a subject necessarily has newly acquired the other contrary, say white. And like Dumbleton, de Ripa has chosen to understand remission as privation of intensity rather than acquisition of a contrary which has the power to impede. The qualitative change in intensity is, therefore, some manner of intrinsically informing a being with a new form which causes a positive change that is reflected in the being's concrete denomination.[141] The following statement in chapter 38 of Dumbleton's ˙Summa, part 2 serves as a fitting epitome of de Ripa's meaning:

> Ex quibus patet quod sicut dicendum est de qualitate intensa et remissa sic tendendum est in aliis que ratione positiva et privata considerantur.[142]

Against the admixture thesis de Ripa has proved that the activation of a subject through the communication of a form produces a corresponding intensive latitude to the amount pertaining to the communicated form. The form must be divisibly intensible for the subject to intend through the activation of this form, and yet the form with its properties is understood as essentially invariable. The subject to which it is communicated is similarly invariable and at the same latitude of intensity that is proper to the form.[143] Once again de Ripa's conclusion is

---

139 *Ibid.*, fol. 10va, concl. 1: "in omni motu ad formam acquiritur aliquod novum quod est forma vel pars forme."

140 Fol. 239vb: "... cum nullum contrarium possit impedire denominationem formalem alterius contrarii intensioris... Preterea, non stat .c. noviter esse album nisi per novam mutationem positivam in .c. Igitur non stat .c. per qualemcumque remissionem .b. fieri noviter album, vel magis album, cum remissio .b. sit mutatio deperditiva ipsius .c."

See Dumbleton, *Summa* 2, chapter 38, fols. 20vb-21ra. Also Richard Swineshead, *Liber calculationum* 1, fol. 2vb: "... quod remissio se habet privative respectu intensionis et privatum acquiri non est aliud quam positivum deperdi..."

141 Fol. 239vb: "Preterea contradictio esset quod aliqua res mutaretur essentialiter in .a. et talis res non noviter denominatur abstractive; igitur contradictio est quod alicui noviter communicetur esse albedinis et tamen tale non noviter sit album concretive; et per consequens non stat albedinem inexistere alicui per informationem et tale non denominari album concretive."

142 Fol. 21rb.

143 Fol. 240ra: "... ex quibus concluditur quod necessario cuilibet actuationi subiecti per aliquam formam tanta precise correspondet latitudo intensiva, quanta est latitudo huius forme et e converso; et ideo impossibile est aliquam formam esse indivisibilem intensive et ipsam divisibiliter actuare; et e converso impossibile est aliquod subiectum intendi ex actuatione alicuius forme, et huiusmodi formam non intendi. Ex eisdem quoque conclusionibus patet quod impossibile est per

the same as Dumbleton's: that a species (form) is unique, possessing an invariable, indivisible latitude susceptible to continuous intensive division, communicated as that unique latitude to the subject. It is impossible for something to increase solely through the remission or loss of its contraries, although the *moderni* commonly hold this position.[144]

"These *moderni* imagine that no quality can denominate a subject except by the excess over its contrary quality; for them the denomination of the total intensity corresponds to the excess.[145] And on this sort of reasoning do they base *multa sophismata et fantastica argumenta*."[146] This correspondence of excess and denomination is what de Ripa insists he was taught. We need refer only to Dumbleton's *Summa* 2, chapters 40-43, the third and fourth opinions, to corroborate that this was indeed a common opinion, but one against which Dumbleton also argues.[147] Dumbleton takes the position that denomination is by means of excess, not over a contrary, but an excess *per se* of the mixture viewed as a *simplex*.[148] If we assume that de Ripa was in school ten years before he issued his *Commentary*, then by 1346 the ideas expressed and refuted in Dumbleton's *Summa*, written in the mid-1330's had somehow reached Franciscan *studia*, presumably in Paris.

De Ripa returns to a more complete refutation of the admixed contraries thesis. Indeed, he says, "it was seen by me and by others that this *modus ponendi* was unacceptable; in the nature of things there cannot be something that is simultaneously white and black, hot and cold; and yet *iuxta communem inter nos* (Franciscans?) *modum ponendi*, we say that contraries at a remiss degree are alternately coextended so that only the maximum degree of calidity in the whole latitude would naturally exclude frigidity and *e contra*."[149] Thus two latitudes are imagined as coextended whereby the maximum degree of heat is also the *non gradus* of frigidity; in the latitude the more intense heat has a coextended half

---

eandem formam diversa subiecta difformiter actuari sed necessario ex eadem forma idem gradus actuationis consurgit dum in eodem in diversis temporibus sive in diversis substantiis."

144 Fol. 240ra: "ex eodem gradu actuationis in forma necessario idem gradus denominationis formalis consurgit; et ideo impossibile est aliquid intendi per solam remissionem vel deperditionem contrarii cuius oppositum ponunt moderni communiter."

145 Fol. 240ra: "Ymaginantur enim quod nulla qualitas potest denominare subiectum nisi ex excessu super aliam qualitatem contraria, ita quod tota intensio talis denominationis correspondent excessui."

146 Fol. 240ra.

147 See also Richard Swineshead, *Calculationes* 4.

148 In chapter 36, fol. 20va Dumbleton notes that it is the net quality or excess in a compound or mixture that points to the dominant quality present.

149 See Gregory of Rimini, I *Sent.* d.17 q.3 a.2.

that is more remiss: at the mean degree we say that the subject would
be at the *non esse calidi*, not being warm and not being cold, and yet not
at the zero degree of warmth or coldness. Something can begin to increase from not being warm or cold and nevertheless begin from a certain degree of warmth or coldness. Some of the moderns, however, say
that the act induces its own latitude proportionally in the patient and
decreases the latitude of the contrary form; the precise amount of the
latitude induced is the same as that of the contrary form. "The only
case for which we do not reject this by absolute necessity is with regard
to some remiss subject that is not mixed with contraries."[150] De Ripa
will therefore accept this for a uniformly qualified subject, not for mixtures.

He further separates himself from those who *multum inconsequenter
loquuntur circa istam materiam* because it is admitted in these discussions
that there can be a lack of harmony between formal denomination and
certain forms themselves. But one cannot affirm something concretely
and then say that formally the opposite is true.[151] In addition, they say
that the degree of intensity of one part is not extended to the intensity
of the whole. Thus the quality of a part denominates that part but not
the whole. De Ripa however understands that a quality, communicated
by information to the part, is, in virtue of this same communication, a
formal act of the whole.[152] Not only is there the same information in the

---

150 Fol. 240rb: "Ego autem — quamvis in isto modo ponendi fuerim a principio nutritus, cuius
fundamentum pro maxima reputabam et nullam indigere probationem — non recolo tamen me
pro isto modo ponendi audivisse probabilem rationem, nisi quod supponebamus sic esse. Videbatur enim michi cum aliis quod repugnantia esset in rerum natura idem simul esse album et
nigrum, calidum vel frigidum, et quia — iuxta communem inter nos modum ponendi — contraria
dicebamus sub gradibus remissis ad invicem coextendi ita quod solus summus caliditatis totam latitudinem frigiditatis excluderet naturaliter et e contra, et illas duas latitudines sic ymaginarie coextendi quod summus caliditatis esset non gradus frigiditatis et latitudo intensior caliditatis — puta
medietas — haberet coextensam medietatis remissiorem latitudinis frigiditatis et e converso, et
medius medium; et ideo consequenter dicebamus quod subiectum existens sub medio gradu caliditatis propter coextendum medium frigiditatis esset sub non esse calidi, et sub non esse frigidi,
licet non sub non gradu caliditatis vel frigiditatis; et ideo, cum concedebamus aliquid posse incipere
intendi a non esse calidi vel frigidi et tamen a certo gradu caliditatis vel frigiditatis; et quamvis iste
modus ponendi fundaretur in hoc, quod agens naturale ex aliquali proportione in passum inducit
latitudinem propriam et remittit latitudinem forme contrarie — et ideo, quantam latitudinem
forme proprie inducit precise, tantum remittit de latitudine forme contrarie — tamen hoc non
reputabamus simpliciter necessarium — propter aliqua subiecta remissa et tamen non admixta suis
contrariis."

151 Fol. 240va.

152 Fol. 240va: "Sed talis albedo actuat .a. non est ex modo ponendi istius ymaginationis —
puta quod intensio partis sic confert ad intensionem totius —: ymaginantur enim isti quod qualitas
partis in ea proportione plus denominat partem quam totum, in qua proportione totum se habet
ad partem."

whole as in the part but also the same degree of intrinsic denomination is applicable. Intension of a part thus confers intension to the whole.[153] He says that this is particularly true for a quality that is *equo intense* (uniformly intense) throughout the subject. For a part is a partial entity of the whole and thus all which is newly formal act of the part is such for the whole. In whatever manner the part may be altered or increased, *consimiliter* the whole increases and is altered, and in a continuous manner.

One of the positions he gives against his own argument says that every uniformly difform subject corresponds to the mean degree;[154] thus some part would be more intense than the whole. To de Ripa and Dumbleton[155] this is untenable. De Ripa says that he does not have to repeat the demonstrations of this proof since they are so numerous in the current tracts related to this material! The fourth and last argument against his own thesis also argues that the mean degree denominates the uniformly difform subject.[156] It is in fact a qualitative application of the famous Merton mean speed theorem. This fourth position expresses it in quantitative terms: the latitude of uniformly difform local motion, uniformly acquired in time, does not correspond to the most intense but to the mean degree. Thus, *conformiter loquendo*, any latitude of quality uniformly extended through the subject corresponds to the mean degree. Dumbleton only accepts this when dealing with uniform extension as is here the case for de Ripa.

To argue for the part denominating the whole and the part, de Ripa insists he will follow the mode of argumentation of his very adversaries.[157] Their first fundamental argument is in fact one which Dumbleton also presents and rejects:[158] that something difformly intense can

153 Fol. 240va: "Sed ex hoc quia medietas totius est quedam entitas partialis totius et ideo omnis qualitas medietatis per informationem est per eandem communicationem actus formalis totius et eque intensio, et ideo ex tali qualitate sicut eadem informatio, ita idem gradus denominationis consurgit in parte et toto. Et loquor hic semper de denominatione intrinseca qualis est in proposito, et hoc signanter propter multas alias denominationes, que possunt ... nam pars est quedam entitas partialis totius et ideo quidquid noviter est actus formalis partis est noviter actus totius: igitur qualitercumque alteretur vel intendatur pars, consimiliter intenditur et alteratur totum."

154 "Tertio argui sic: quodlibet subiectum uniformiter difforme correspondet medio gradui, igitur aliqua pars est intensior toto" (fol. 241ra).

155 See chapter 34, fol. 19vb against the second opinion.

156 Fol. 241ra: "Ultimo arguo sic: latitudo motus localis uniformiter difformis sive uniformiter acquisita secundum tempus non correspondet gradui intensissimo sed medio gradui: igitur — conformiter loquendo — quelibet latitudo qualitatis uniformiter per subiectum extensa correspondet medio gradui."

157 Fol. 241ra: "ex modo ipsorum ymaginandi."

158 A subject is not as intense as it is remiss. Dumbleton, fol. 19va, first *contra*.

correspond to a certain uniform degree. The proof of this, says de Ripa, is *ex communi assensu ipsorum* as well as *ex ratione fundata in ymaginatione eorum*.[159] "For they say that however more intense or more remiss a uniform degree may be, so it is as intense or remiss or can be uniformly. I prove this to be impossible. They argue that it is impossible for a subject to be made difform throughout the same latitude and yet for it continuously to increase in intensity. According to them, intension occurs by a degree to degree addition (i.e. uniform degrees superadded) so it is not imaginable that any subject throughout its whole latitude be continuously difform (diverse) and yet be continuously made more and more intense. I, however, affirm that subject .a. continuously will be intense at the same latitude, from say 8 to zero degree, and yet .a. will increase from zero degree of intensity to 8 exclusively so that through the same whole latitude, .a. is continuously qualified."[160] We see that his understanding of intensive latitude is very much like Dumbleton's: that a given latitude is invariably the same and yet susceptible to internal alteration whether by intension or remission.

The moderns say that a latitude with regard to its coextensive variation in the subject can correspond to some *in*trinsic degree and so they have to propose the mode of intension that was rejected in article 1, the last opinion (coexistence of posterior and anterior degrees in a single resulting degree). "But I say that in the case of induction to the maximum degree, which is an external *terminus*, the subject .a. increases by continuous alteration, continuously acquiring a new quality and a new qualitative being.[161] And whatever is acquired by the part is acquired by the whole and at the same velocity. But I deny that a uniformly uniform subject will correspond to the mean degree because, in fact, it corresponds to the most intense degree if such a degree exists.[162] If it does not, there is no determined degree to which it

---

159   Fol. 241ra.

160   Fol. 241ra: "Preterea, non solum hoc sequitur sed stat quod .a. subiectum continue erit intentum in eadem latitudine ab 8 usque ad non gradum, et tamen .a. intendetur a non gradu intensionis usque ad gradum sicut 8 exclusive, ita quod per eandem omnino latitudinem .a. continue qualificabitur et tamen acquiret latitudinem esse calidi a non gradu usque ad gradum sicut 8 exclusive."

161   Fol. 241rb: "Ad aliam rationem dico quod in casu inductionis talis gradus summi .a. per nullum tempus intendetur. Et ad probationem dico quod .a. continue alterabitur: continue enim acquiret novam qualitatem et novum esse quale."

162   Fol. 241rb: "... nego quod subiectum uniformiter uniforme correspondeat medio gradui, ymo intensissimo gradui, si aliquis talis sit, vel si non, nulli determinato gradui correspondet."

corresponds." We recall that a uniformly uniform degree is a qualified subject not mixed with its contrary. Its degree throughout is at uniform intensity and, as Richard Swineshead points out in his *Calculationes*, chaper 2 is as intense as any of its parts and therefore equals its maximum degree. An earlier statement of this was made by Heytesbury who, in speaking of uniform motion, said that as a whole the velocity of a given magnitude or subject is measured by the linear path traveled by a point in most rapid motion if such a point exists. De Ripa has, therefore, provided the qualitative expression of Heytesbury's quantitative uniform velocity theorem.[163]

But to the other argument on movement, that is, where qualification is difform corresponding to uniformly accelerated motion, de Ripa (like Dumbleton) concedes that something will cross a given amount of space as if it were moved through some length in time at the velocity of the mean degree. He thereby accepts Heytesbury's mean speed or uniform acceleration theory. What is perhaps most important is that he has considered both the Merton velocity theories. Uniform and difform qualification were topics that characterized the Oxford discussions.

From article 2 it is so far evident that an accidental or substantial form cannot make a subject more or less intense via any of the three following ways: 1) by its existence being more or less in the same subject, for this is impossible; 2) nor by the more or less admixture of contraries; 3) nor through a more intense denomination of one part and not the whole.

Can we generally say, asks article three, that intension in a form is caused by the addition of some new degree of being to the preceding degree, from which a more intense degree then results?[164] De Ripa will finally concede that in all intensive form there is a latitude of essential degrees which concur unitively and which intensively quantify this form. We recall that Dumbleton had defined a unique latitude per

163   The mean speed theorem of acceleration was derived from calculations pertaining to the latitude of movement, *i.e.* velocity lost or gained. The uniform acceleration or mean speed theorem said that in uniformly accelerated motion there was an infinity of parts of the latitude of motion involved. Those with the same mean degree as the whole latitude will traverse the same space as will the whole latitude traveling at its mean speed in a given time. Heytesbury's uniform velocity theorem says that in uniform motion the velocity of a magnitude taken as a whole is in all cases measured by the linear path traversed by the point which is in most rapid motion if there is such a point; *Regulae solvendi sophismata* (Venice, 1494), fol. 39v. See document 4.4 in Marshall Clagett, *The Science of Mechanics in the Middle Ages* (Madison, 1959).

164   Fol. 242ra: "Utrum generaliter intensio forme fiat ex additione alicuius novi gradus essendi ad precedentem unde consurgat gradus intensior?"

species. For de Ripa, intension does not result from really distinct degrees concurring but from degrees that are indistinct. According to him, the common opinion says that intension generally is had from the addition of new degrees to the pre-existing degrees (*ad gradum prehabitum*) and from these two degrees there results a third more intense degree.[165] According to this opinion the pre-existing degree is not itself increased but remains identical in its essence; nor is the new degree increased. Rather the resultant degree is produced from the union of one degree with another. In fact, they say that no form can be said to be increased. Instead, any being that is invariable in its essence can contain a latitude of really distinct degrees, and these degrees pertain to the essence of the whole *gradus*. They believe that only the subject, susceptible to alteration (*alterabile*), can be intended and remitted. In this manner, intensity is had in itself from the fact that a new degree in the same species exists in it already and from this degree, along with the precedent, comes a third, unique degree.[166] This kind of intension does not propose there be acquisition of a new degree by the same "adequated" subject (*non ponit acquisitionem novi gradus eidem subiecto adequato*) but it does propose union with other pre-existing degrees so that from them there results another that newly exists in the subject, and then the subject is increased. Of course this *modus ponendi* perfectly preserves the continuity of alteration in motion by placing within a form a continuous latitude of distinct degrees, says de Ripa, and this latitude is the very *materia* of such movement.[167] But if one asks them about the divisible acquisition of each successive divisible future degree, they say that such acquisition always begins at the zero degree (not from the preceding degree). If one then asks whether the later degree is more perfect than the preceding, they say that such a degree is

165 "... quod communis positio ... ponit quod generaliter intensio forme fit ex additione novi gradus ad gradum prehabitum ex quibus duobus resultat intensior" (fol. 242ra). See Dumbleton above pp. 153-54.

166 Fol. 242ra: "... ita quod ymaginantur in huiusmodi intensione gradum prehabitum in se non intendi, sed uniformiter manere in sua essentia nec etiam gradum novum intendi sed de novo produci, nec etiam totum resultans intendi, sed de novo produci ex unione unius gradus ad alterum: et ideo nullam formam dicunt ipsi de vi vocis intendi sed quamlibet invariabilem esse in sua essentia, licet contineat latitudinem graduum distinctorum realiter: nam illi gradus sunt de essentia gradus totalis. Sed dicunt solum subiectum alterabile posse intendi et remitti, et huiusmodi intensio fit in ipso ex hoc quod novus gradus eiusdem speciei sibi inexistit, ex quo cum prehabito fit unus gradus — aliter non intenderetur."

167 Fol. 242ra: "Et iste modus ponendi videtur perfecte salvare continuitatem motus alterationis, ex hoc quod ponit in forma latitudinem continuam graduum distinctorum, que est materia talis motus."

acquired divisibly from zero (not from some positive degree) and so it is added divisibly to the preceding degree. The addition is thus a continuous process from zero degree; indeed the future degree is not more perfect than the precedent except from the fact that it really includes the precedent and really communicates with it.[168] The resulting degree really contains some preceding *gradus*. Briefly, then, we see that they apply to intensification the same *modus* used for augmentation, with the difference, that in augmentation the newly acquired quantity does not come to the same part (to the fastest moving part, for example) as it does in alteration.[169]

All of the foregoing, says de Ripa, once seemed rational to me, but now it appears unlikely:

> In isto autem modo quamvis quasi semper fuerim connutritus, nec alius michi fuerit visus modus rationalis salvandi modum intensionis habitum cum aliis fundamentis iam per me prius positis, iste modus apparebit penitus improbabilis.[170]

"I say that every sort of intension occurs in a like manner, i.e. by means of the same mode which is via a latitude.[171] Now it is possible that in the same species one form may be more intense than another and yet neither has *in se* a latitude of really distinct degrees.[172] Take, for instance, the species of rational soul or created intelligence. It has an indivisible latitude by which one individual is as intense — being of the same species — as another, and yet neither contains a latitude of really distinct degrees. So if we see that no rational soul is more intense than another of the same species, and if this is not through either being composed of really distinct degrees nor from the continuation of a latitude with more of the same degrees superadded, then surely it is clear that the mode of intension does not consist in this kind of (distinctly divisible) latitude, nor does it consist in degree to distinct degree addition."[173]

---

168   Fol. 242ra: "Gradus enim adveniens non est perfectior precedenti nisi ex hoc quod includit realiter precedentem et cum ipso realiter communicat."

169   Fol. 242ra: "... hoc dempto quod quantitas noviter acquisita in augmentatione non advenit eidem parti quante sicut in alteratione..." See Dumbleton, fol. 20rb, chapter 36.

170   Fol. 242ra.

171   Concl. 1: "Generaliter omnis intensio forme fit per eundem modum intensionis" (fol. 242ra).

172   Concl. 2, fol. 242ra: "Stat in eadem specie unam formam esse intensiorem alia et tamen neutram habere in se latitudinem graduum realiter distinctorum."

173   Concl. 2, proof 1, fol. 242rb: "... clare videbit quod modus intensionis non consistit in huiusmodi latitudine nec in additione gradus ad gradum modo premisso."

Here we have de Ripa alone and original on this matter, sifting the
modern opinions, in particular Dumbleton's belief that species are not
to be compared. He selectively appropriates ideas from current
discussions and concludes with the following picture, creating important repercussions in the ontological order. In no matter what
denomination of absolute perfection there can be an infinite latitude
communicated to the creature. This latitude is a certain portion (*partitio*) of the immense degree of the similar (divine) denomination. We
can say then that the whole latitude of possible life (for the creature)
can be terminated exclusively in immense life (of God) and this whole
latitude is, by the same reason, *in* the 'being of life'. Its intrinsic degrees
differ only with regard to greater and lesser. So in the whole latitude
where one superior degree precedes and exceeds the inferior, either we
say that every degree contains really distinct intensive degrees by which
it may exceed some one degree designated as inferior; or it cannot be
thus stated. Rather, we would say that none of the degrees contains
really distinct degrees.[174] There is no degree possible in the *habitus* of life
that is really divisible in many degrees and consequently no intelligence
is really divisible if it is essentially life; nor is any intelligence really
divisible in being alive (*in esse vite*). We say, therefore, that we can
designate in this latitude a degree that is more intensively alive or in life
than another, and yet neither degree is really divisible. De Ripa has
described a latitude denominated by a unique, invariable mode of intensification, continuous throughout, where the indistinct degrees of
the latitude participate with respect to more and less. This he proves for
any intensive latitude that is called a denomination of absolute perfection. The proof is therefore applicable to the indivisible created
mind. In the same way we can designate a whole latitude, say of
wisdom, that is terminated exclusively in immense (divine) wisdom.
Since he believes it impossible for some individual species to be really

---

174 Concl. 2, proof 2, fol. 242rb: "In quacumque denominatione perfectionis simpliciter, est
possibilis latitudo infinita creatura communicabilis, que latitudo est quedam partitio immensi
gradus denominationis consimilis: igitur, signata tota latitudine vite possibilis terminata exclusive
ad vitam immensam, tota ista latitudo est eiusdem rationis in esse vite: gradus enim intrinseci solum
differunt secundum magis et minus: igitur in tota ista latitudine eo modo quod unus gradus
superior precedit inferiorem et quilibet suum inferiorem excedit: igitur vel oportet dicere quod in
tota ista latitudine omnis gradus continet gradus realiter distinctos intensive per quos excedat
quamcumque signabilem inferiorem vel quod nullus, sed eo modo quo unus excedit inferiorem et
quilibet. Sed primum non potest dari ... igitur oportet quod detur secundum: et per consequens,
sicut in ista latitudine est signabilis gradus vite intensior altero, et tamen neuter est realiter
divisibilis."

divisible in many intense degrees, he must say that no intension can be had in a species with respect to specific or individual being (*secundum esse specificum vel individuale*) by this kind of degree to degree addition (*per huiusmodi additionem gradus ad gradum*).[175] Certainly a material form is always extensively divisible, but this is not so for immaterial form like intellect.[176] In all intensible form, whether it be accidental or substantial, intension *infra* the individual or specific latitude consists in a greater approximation to and participation in the first being according to some essential divine perfection.[177] All intension therefore occurs by means of the same mode.

If, as the common opinion supposes, from two degrees there can be created a third more intense degree, this would mean that every degree is itself comprised of two really distinct half-intense degrees.[178] This is rejected. Furthermore, if one accepts the mode of distinct degree to degree addition, then one must deny that in every intelligent species there is a single specific or numerical latitude. So de Ripa concludes it is philosophically and theologically ridiculous to propose that a rational soul or angel contains infinite individuals of the same species that are yet really distinct: *quod nedum theologice, sed philosophice ridiculosum est ponere*.[179] We must concede, he says, that every separated intelligence in every denomination of absolute perfection is absolutely intensively indivisible and one cannot be more intensively perfect than another with respect to such intensity of perfection.[180] Their mutual separation is a formal one. Now, if the intelligence or essence is indivisible, we have a special case because it cannot be denominated at some latitude that is distant from zero degree or from the non-being of such denomination. Every degree that *is* distant from non-being through some intensive latitude really does contain the whole latitude of distinct degrees and

175 Fol. 242va.

176 See Aristotle, *Metaphysics* Δ; fol. 242va: "quoniam quod una forma materialis sit divisibilis extensive et non forma immaterialis est ex hoc quia forma materialis est educibilis de potentia materia divisibilis realiter sed non forma immaterialis."

177 Fol. 242va: "sed omnis forme intensibilis — sive substantialis sive accidentalis — intensio infra latitudinem individualem vel specificam consistit in maiori appropinquatione et participatione primi esse secundum aliquam perfectionem essentialem divinam."

178 Concl. 3, fol. 242va.

179 Concl. 4, proof, fol. 242vb.

180 Concl. 5, fol. 242vb: "Quilibet huiusmodi modum ponens habet consequenter concedere quamlibet intelligentiam separatam in omni denominatione perfectionis simpliciter esse simpliciter indivisibilem intensive nec unam posse esse perfectiorem altera intensive in quacumque tali perfectione."

thus has to be divisible. But this is not a situation that is applicable to indivisible intelligences.[181]

We see here the necessary distinction between material and non-material form reiterated; de Ripa is careful not to disturb the continuity in the created order because he has relegated denominations of perfections, i.e. intelligences alone, to the realm of indivisibles. Those individual instances of different species yet contain divisible latitudes by which their relation to their specific denominated perfection can be determined as to completeness. One might phrase this in the form of an evaluation: does the individual live up to its unvarying name? Thus the terminology of latitudes is led beyond the discussion of perfection in created species to the communication of the divine essential denomination, presumably to those indivisibles which denominatively participate in the immense perfection.

If we were to say that intension is by part to part addition of distinct degrees in this case, then we would have to say that the divine essence cannot be communicated *ad extra* by means of any essential denomination.[182] But if the divine essence is communicable in essential life (*sit communicabilis in esse vite*), then every possible creature at the degree of its essential life (*sub esse vite*) is intensively indivisible in essential life. If we say it is intensively divisible, then the degree (*gradus*) that is superior in life must contain more really distinct degrees than the inferior degree.[183] But if the creature is intensively indivisible, then essential life is communicable to it only *sub unico tantum gradu*. If however, the creature is divisible or can receive divisibly, then as much as the intelligence is intensively more perfect, to the same amount does it contain a greater latitude of really distinct degrees. Because perfections *can* be distinguished one from another, the point is made that something can have a latitude or a degree of "being" that is absolutely and really distinct from, say, a degree of "being in life". In an angel for example, a whole latitude of simple, indivisible, absolute being is distinguished from a similar latitude in life, and a latitude in life is distinct from a latitude in intelligence.

181   Concl. 5, proof, fol. 242vb: "nam omnis gradus distans per aliquam latitudinem intensivam a non esse continet realiter gradum subduplum et totam huiusmodi latitudinem graduum distinctorum: igitur nulla essentia realiter indivisibilis distat a non esse cuiuslibet essentialis denominationis per aliquam talem latitudinem intensivam."

182   Concl. 6, fol. 242vb.

183   We note that de Ripa is using a double meaning of "gradus" here: as the latitude or range or maximum degree attained, and as individual *termini* within that range. This double use was common in the tracts of the Calculators.

De Ripa encloses these distinctions in a formal system; he says that one distinguishes these degrees in life and intelligence as one distinguishes other formal reasons.[184] The common opinion, however, harbors contradictions according to him because it says that the latitude which separates the angel from non-being comprises *really* distinct degrees, and that *esse vite* is *really* distinct from absolute being. This would, of course, totally destroy the continuity in created and un-created order in a real sense. Maintaining the Scotist tradition, de Ripa affirms that such a separation of absolute being or divinity from created beings must be limited to a formal distinction.

Returning by way of summary to his modification of the common ad-dition theory, he says that were it the true way to describe the intension process, then we would have to say that in any intensible species there can be an infinite latitude of indivisibles due to the addition of a new degree to that which already is possessed.[185] But we cannot admit that forms which are unitable extensively are also unitable intensively in the same manner that quantities are conjoined.[186] On the other hand, something can be intensified without being extended. He sees a dif-ference in a form or quality being at a certain distance from absolute non-being and a form being distant from the non-being of its species,[187] here, *caritas*. This difference is only formal. If a quality .a. is intensively distant from absolute non-being (a kind of negativity of God who is ab-solute being) through some latitude up to the zero degree of its own species, and the whole of this kind of latitude by necessity is given as a latitude of degrees which by no means are really distinct from one another, then the essential denomination of quality .a. is a much greater latitude in itself than the latitude of another, and is more immaterial.[188]

---

184 Fol. 242vb: "Confirmatur: nam in angelo quicumque duo gradus in esse vite com-municantes solum distinguntur intensive secundum eandem rationem formalem participatam et gradus vite distinguitur a gradu essendi simpliciter sicut gradus alterius rationis formalis."

185 Concl. 7, fol. 243ra.

186 Fol. 242vb: "quod .a. et .b. sunt forme unibiles non tantum intensive quod resultet, sed ex-tensive solum." See Dumbleton, rejected opinion 3.

187 Dumbleton, chapter 22, fol. 17ra-rb: diverse species cannot be validly compared as to their perfection; even comparisons within the same species are *in abstracto* (fol. 17rb).

188 Fol. 243va: "3° principaliter arguo sic: Si aliqua forma sit isto modo intensibilis, sit ergo talis ipsa caritas creata supra: nam talis qualitas que sit .a. per maiorem latitudinem distat a non esse simpliciter et .a. non esse qualitatis quam a non esse sue speciei vel a non esse caritatis..., si enim .a. distat intensive a non esse simpliciter per aliquam latitudinem citra non gradum proprie specie et tota huiusmodi latitudo, necessario est ponenda latitudo graduum nullo modo realiter distinctorum, multo magis latitudo denominationis essentialis in propriam, que est magis species, que est magis immaterialis, et ideo magis accedens ad divisibilitatem realem. Et eodem modo potest argui de omni qualitate materiali vel immateriali de omni forma substantiali vel accidentali, inten-sibili vel remissibili."

The measurement is being made primarily in relation to absolute being, not to the being or non-being of the particular species. This manner of describing intension can be argued for all material or immaterial quality, for all substantial or accidental form, whether intensible or remissible.

What de Ripa has done, then, in order to counteract the really distinct degrees of the common opinion is to understand that the more a being is perfected (which one determines by its denomination in perfection), the less it is really divisible. Evaluation is made in terms of the *terminus exclusivus* of absolute perfection. In this way he can place the intellectual species closer to absolute divine perfection by recognizing its essential indivisibility. And he can say that with regard to all the species inferior to a certain denomination there is a 'really' divisible latitude or distance up to but not quite at the designated species at its own zero degree. These distinctions *infra* a latitude that is not yet attained may be infinite in number, but none of them singly or when added together ever *is* the species *caritas* or whatever designated quality.

One exception remains: if ever we may say that from such addition there *is* intension, then every uniform quality that qualifies some material subject can be made *per Dei potentiam* infinitely intense.[189]

This long series of deductions proves that no extensive quality can in any manner be made more intense through the loss of extension.[190] Intension must not be conceived of as a kind of extension; this is irrational. And yet, de Ripa says, we see such an argument put forth in a tract *De intensione formarum*:

> Quamvis autem rationibus nunc factis satis michi evidentibus sit destructa, multi tamen contra ipsam retroactis temporibus sunt conati, quorum tamen rationes vel sunt ex toto sophistice et eque concludentes contra omnem positionem, vel apparentiam nullam in se habent, sicut patere potest respicientibus quemdam tractatum de intensione formarum.[191]

Here Jean de Ripa begins his analysis and rejection of the arguments put forth by *quidam alius doctor novus*; he too, says de Ripa, has inveighed against the views found in the *Tractatus de intensione formarum* with *prima facie* quite pretty (*satis pulchras*) arguments but which are not *in se* con-

---

189 Fol. 243vb: "5° principaliter arguo sic."
190 Fol. 244ra: "Ex ista deductione tam longa evidenter apparet quod nulla qualitas extensiva potest quomodolibet fieri intensior deperdendo extensionem."
191 Fol. 244rb.

clusive.[192] This *alius doctor novus* professes the second opinion rejected in article 1, that all form is, via its essence, susceptible to intension and remission without any addition or subtraction.[193] First he argues that two forms of the same species can inform the same subject without intension and remission of any of its form, — without some form resulting from their combined presence, making the subject more intense than at first. If two bodies can be in the same place without being more extended than at first, then it is possible for there to be greater extension without addition of body to body, and this is so because two forms can inform the same subject without a third form being made from them.[194] It is in this manner that the *doctor novus* proves that intension does not come from the addition of qualities. He also argues that in any subject there can be a more intense form than at first without the subject being a more composite form. He is thus arguing against the addition thesis.

But de Ripa argues not only against distinct degree addition but also against the *doctor novus*, particularly because the latter draws too close a parallel between extension and intension. According to him some quantity could be extended without being composite and so some form could be more intense than another without being more composite, for *consimiliter*, form with respect to intension can be had just as quantity with respect to extension. This he tries to prove by reference to rarefaction. He also believes it possible for the same being to be absolutely simple as to its quantitative parts, i.e. having no such parts, and nevertheless be intense at some degree of latitude.[195] The latitude of form, according to him, is comprised of divisible parts and is a quantity of continuous quantity,[196] a view worthy of the Buridan school which de Ripa finds unacceptable. He further rejects the idea that if some subject, informed by some form, loses another similar form throughout at the same time in which the informing takes place, then the subject undergoes no alteration.[197] That which is altered with respect to form of the same species principally is altered by reason of quantity as much as it is by reason of the form, since, according to the *doctor novus*, form can be quantity, in its relationship to more and less.

---

192 *Ibid.*

193 Fol. 244rb: "Due forme eiusdem speciei possunt informare idem subiectum absque intensione vel remissione alicuius forme absque hoc quod aliqua forma intensior quam prius informet idem subiectum."

194 Fol. 244va; see Dumbleton, chapters 29 and 36, fourth opinion.

195 See Dumbleton, chapter 40, fourth opinion.

196 Fol. 244va: "3º arguit sic."

197 Fol. 244vb: "6º arguit sic."

The *doctor novus* devotes his last two positions (as de Ripa presents them) to rejecting the common *modus ponendi*,[198] the addition theory, which, as he understands it, says that a more intense form is necessarily more composed. De Ripa says his reasons are insufficient. De Ripa proposes his own conclusions which reiterate the proofs first set out. It is his concession to the last point, *contra* the *doctor novus*, that a form which is more intense *is* in one sense the more intensively composite, that points to de Ripa's general agreement with the Oxford additionists, except where he rejects their distinct degrees. He emphasizes that greater intensity means greater perfection.[199] Through intension there is acquired in a continuous manner some perfect condition but also another, in a negative sense, that is imperfect. His example is taken from the physics of light.[200] Light that is increased in a luminous body continuously acquires a latitude of light. It also loses a latitude of negative or non-light. Thus he affirms latitudes are measured positively in terms of acquisition, even acquisition of the negative or contrary of the qualities, acquisition of imperfection that is simultaneous with the achievement of perfection. His scale of measure is consistently from zero to some determined degree. The reverse of considering an intense quality in a positive manner is to consider a remiss quality privatively.[201]

In article 4 Jean de Ripa understands "really distinct degrees" to be like points: extensively indivisible. Any increase in intension will not come about through the adding together of such extensively indivisible and really distinct degrees. Intension will occur by the concourse of indistinct degrees. Dumbleton said earlier that degrees are intensively divisible but not really distinct like points.[202] Article four, the last of the second part of distinction 17, is devoted to de Ripa's own theory. It is here that he considers Burley's succession theory without mentioning

---

198   "... ex quo per additionem forme ad formam fit gradus maior sicut ex additione corporis ad corpus fit quantitas maior. Sed consequens dicit esse falsum ex communi scola et per rationem" (fol. 246ra).

199   Fol. 246vb: "Ad ultimam rationem concederetur quod forma quantum est intensior tantum est compositior intensive, et licet ista compositio ut compositio est dicat aliquam imperfectionem tamen ut intensiva est aliquam ponit perfectionem; et quanto magis intensiva maiorem."

200   Fol. 246vb: "Et tunc per intensionem acquiritur continue quedam conditio perfectiva et alia imperfectiva sicut — secundum omnem opinionem — lumen, si intenditur a corpore luminoso, continue acquirit latitudinem luminis et latitudinem dependentie a luminoso."

201   Dumbleton, fol. 21ra, chapter 38. In chapter 20: the three ways of discussing *maius et minus* (fol. 16vb).

202   Fol. 17vb: "causa deceptionis ponentium istam positionem..."

the author by name.[203] Although he will agree that in all intensive movement the preceding form is destroyed when the following one is produced,[204] he prefers a theory that takes into account the diversity in the form and the diversity in the concourse of continuous degrees comprising the latitude. His primary objection to the succession theory is that it requires that nothing be acquired or lost divisibly. He testifies that the topic was much discussed.[205] But all these erroneous opinions must be replaced.

De Ripa describes intensive latitudes in the following manner: first, any degree that is at a certain degree of intension from its species' own non-being is distant (from zero) by means of an imaginary latitude.[206] Let us recall that there is a latitude of each created species at a set distance from Absolute Being. This may be distinguished from the imaginary latitude running from a species' own zero degree to a certain intension achieved by some individual of a single species. Any such form *formally* contains the whole of this latitude which is distant from the zero degree of its own species. Any such form at a certain degree of intension contains indistinctly yet really the entire intensive latitude which is distant from its non-being.[207] Since no intension is had from the addition of distinct degree to degree, then no intensive latitude has a real variety of distinct intense degrees. Furthermore, the intensive mode of every intensive imaginary latitude is uniform because the mode of every form that is susceptible to intension and remission is continuous. Any rational soul is really indivisible, and yet the soul of Christ is *essentially* more intense than that of Judas.[208] It is through the latitude of acquirable or losable accidental form in some subject that a subject is

203 "... primo videndum est de illo modo ponendi — quod gradus precedens corrumpitur in huiusmodi intensione — cuiusdam qui circa hoc tractatulum quemdam scripsit. Et quia superfluum est circa hoc ipsius rationes discutere que in multitudine multe sunt sed in valore modicum ponderantes ymo quasi omnes sine aliqua radice deducte et superflue indagate..." (fol. 247rb).

204 Concl. 10, fol. 248rb: "necessario in omni intensione huiusmodi vel remissione forma precedens corrumpctur ex adventu posterioris."

205 Fol. 247rb; see n. 203.

206 Concl. 1, fol. 247rb: "Quelibet forma sub certo gradu intensionis a non esse proprie specie distat per aliquam ymaginariam latitudinem."

207 Concl. 2, fol. 247va: "Quelibet talis forma continet formaliter totam huiusmodi latitudinem qua distat a non gradu proprie speciei."

208 "2° arguo sic: aliqua est latitudo intensiva graduum non realiter distinctorum, igitur nulla est latitudo intensiva graduum realiter distinctorum. Consequentia patet, nam uniformis est modus intensivus omnis ymaginarie latitudinis intensive sicut omnis forme intensibilis et remissibilis — sicut patuit ex precedenti articulo — et antecedens patet ex hoc: nam quelibet anima rationalis est realiter indivisibilis; sed anima Christi est intensior essentialiter anima Iude."

itself intended or remitted.[209] The latitude is indivisible and yet intensive so that in some finite species of creature, there is possible an infinite number of individuals really distinct and communicating according to more and less communication in the fixed latitude.[210] This is like designating a maximum degree as a certain whiteness which is the maximum degree possible in a certain species, and yet allowing for something to be white at the mean degree of this same latitude or at any other degree which the species formally contains.[211] Dumbleton spoke in the same way of the maximum degree as that which denominated and therefore contained the whole intensive latitude of the species. In number the same form is constant and so it is not remitted or increased; while formally and intensively there is divisible alteration in an indivisible latitude of a species.

The immediate issue here is the philosophical one concerning the perfection of species. Inevitably it leads to theological considerations on perfectibility. All the arguments seeking to clarify the nature of intension have perfectibility as their underlying concern, because through the communication of essential perfection is some creature established in its determined relationship with divine perfection. With this in mind, de Ripa says that all essential perfection that is communicable to a creature naturally prior to any other perfection, however unitively it concurs in some thing, can still be communicated at a designated degree to an entity.[212] This can occur without the communication of any lesser, *infra* or prior perfection which is also at some designatable degree. It is stated in the same way of absolute being and being in life, that really indistinct perfections correspond to an angel, and all the prior, lesser perfections also correspond, but to some other entity and without any posterior degree — say in a stone. This is how each entity can par-

---

209   Concl. 6, fol. 247vb; see Burley, *Tractatus secundus*, fol. 11va: "immo mihi videtur quod causa intrinseca intensionis et remissionis est latitudo forme specifice. Ut quia eadem species forme potest salvari in forma magis perfecta et in forma minus perfecta. Ideo una forma potest esse intensior alia eiusdem speciei et alia remissior."

210   Concl. 7, fol. 247vb: "in qualibet latitudine intensiva et indivisibili in quacumque specie creature finita, possibile est infinita individua realiter distincta communicare secundum maiorem vel minorem communicationem in huiusmodi latitudine."

211   Fol. 247vb: "Intelligo istam sic quod signata latitudine intensiva et totali in specie albedinis et signata certa albedine, que sit suprema possibilis in huiusmodi specie — et sic .a.—: .a. ergo continet formaliter totam latitudinem intensivam qua distat a non esse albedinis. Dico ergo quod possibilis est alia albedo que sit precise sub gradu medio eiusdem latitudinis."

212   Fol. 247vb: "2°: omnis perfectio essentialis creature communicabilis prior naturaliter alia, quantumlibet unitive concurrat in aliquam rem potest sub aliquo gradu communicari alicui entitati sine communicatione perfectionis posterioris sub quocumque signabili gradu."

ticipate unitively and indistinctly in the supreme possible perfect species of intelligence if there be such.[213] The whole latitude in being in life that is terminated at some intensive degree as well as at zero degree at the other exclusive extreme concurs unitively and as a really distinct maximum, denominative degree.[214]

There is an additional relation with the extensive term outside the particular latitude. Because de Ripa returns again and again to his fundamental positions, testing them against the opposition, we are not permitted to forget that it is the intensive latitude of a form and not the form itself which is distant from its degree of non-being. The intensive latitude has intrinsic divisibility, and each degree of the latitude can correspond adequately (tanquam adequatus) to some form that is really distinct from the subject. It is therefore possible to say that the subject can be called "decreased" with respect to some proportion of its latitude without the whole latitude ceasing to be. In this sense the whole latitude is said to intend and remit divisibly.[215] Thus the degrees in a latitude are identical to one another but are not identical to the latitude itself. De Ripa concludes with Dumbleton's additionist solution, that every intension or remission in an intensible and remissible subject is had through divisible acquisition or loss of an intensive latitude possessed through a continuous mode.[216] "I speak of intension and remission as movement, and I speak of divisible acquisition or loss not according to time but according to nature where an inferior degree naturally is acquired before a superior degree."[217] The form that is acquired or lost has no temporal duration because continuous

213 Fol. 247vb: "... igitur cum consimilis habitudo sit graduum intensiorum in aliqua latitudine eiusdem rationis et denominationis indivisibilis sicut rationis prioris ad posteriorem in eadem re indivisibili realiter, sequitur quod stat in angelo gradum remissiorem latitudinis quam formaliter continet, communicari sine intensiori: et habetur intentum."

214 Fol. 247vb: "Et ista ratio concludit quod dato gradu quo anima Christi vel quicumque angelus distat a non esse sue speciei, sub quolibet gradu inter illum et non gradum quem formaliter anima Christi continet, potest esse aliqua anima a Deo creabilis." Fol. 248ra: "Nam tota huiusmodi latitudo vite unitive et indistincte realiter concurreret in supremam speciem intelligentie possibilem, si esset: tota etiam latitudo vite terminata ad aliquem gradum intensive et ad non gradum in altero extremo."

215 Concl. 8, fol. 248ra: "Licet nullam formam possibilem alicuius intensionis in aliqua specie intendi partibiliter vel remitti, cuiuslibet tamen talis forme latitudinem intensivam, que distat a suo non esse, stat intendi partibiliter vel remitti."

216 Concl. 9, fol. 248rb: "omnis intensio vel remissio in subiecto intensibili et remissibili fit ex partibili acquisitione vel deperditione latitudinis intensive que se habet per modum continui."

217 Fol. 248rb: "Loquor autem hic de intensione vel remissione que sit motus: et si etiam velimus loqui de alia, voco partibilem acquisitionem vel deperditionem non secundum tempus sed naturam utpote si gradus inferior prius naturaliter acquiratur gradu superiori."

movement necessitates immediate successive and momentary forms; this
is something that Burley had originally discussed.[218] And once again it is
reiterated that while no intellectual created essence can be divisibly intended or remitted, nevertheless the latitude by which it is distant from
its non-being can be divisibly increased and decreased.[219]

One of the last positions to be discussed both by Dumbleton[220] and de
Ripa concerns the kinds of excess of one thing over another that permits one to compare created perfections.[221] De Ripa cites three modes of
excess: one where one thing contains another according to all essential
perfection just as a thing at the same time can be both intelligence and
life and it can exceed another which is only life. Two denominations
are involved. The excess perfection does not communicate with respect
to the denomination of a thing that is inferior to the superior species
which possesses this excess.[222] The second kind of excess is where any
two things in every single denomination of essential perfection *do* communicate although they differ with respect to greater or lesser closeness
to God in such being, just as the soul of Christ is life and the soul of
Judas is life; the soul of Christ is just *alia intelligentia*. Nevertheless in the
being of the soul of Christ there participates more of the being in life,
that is, there is more of the immense intelligence in Christ's soul than in
the soul of Judas. This second manner of excess supposes that the absolute excess and that which it exceeds do communicate in each
denomination.[223] A third manner of excess is when something exceeds

---

218   *Tractatus secundus*, chapter 6, fol. 2vb. De Ripa later mentions the contradictory opinion that
some natural agent is essentially the act of simultaneous contraries. He says that Francis de Marchia
in his *Commmentary on the Sentences* argued thus against Burley: (fol. 248vb) "Istis autem rationibus in
sententia — licet non sub eisdem verbis — innititur magister Franciscus de Marchia contra
Burleyum. Aliter autem contra eundem ad istum punctum arguit quidam alius magister modernus.
Alius doctor arguit primo sic: non est possibile naturaliter seu virtute agentis naturalis aliquid esse
tantum per instans; igitur huiusmodi intensio non potest fieri etc."

219   Fol. 248rb: "Probatur conclusio: nam nulla talis intensio potest esse stante eadem forma
nec eadem forma potest fieri intensior et remissior; igitur ex sola deperditione partibili vel acquisitione latitudinis talis forme, potest fieri talis intensio vel remissio."

220   Dumbleton, chapter 43, fol. 22rb.

221   Fol. 250ra, responsio; see Richard Swineshead, *Liber calculationum* 4, fol. 12va.

222   Fol. 250rb: "Advertendum est ergo hic quod triplex est modus excessus unius rei super
aliam in rebus creatis. Maximus est cum una continet aliam secundum omnem perfectionem essentialem et aliquid superaddit in quo non communicat res excessa secundum aliquem gradum
denominationis quomodo in essentiali ordine specierum species superior excedit inferiorem sicut
res que est simul intelligentia et vita excedit aliam que est precise vita."

223   Fol. 250va: "Secundus modus excessus est minor: puta quando alique due res in omni
denominatione perfectionis essentialis communicant sed differunt secundum maiorem vel minorem
appropinquationem ad Deum in esse tali sicut anima Christi est vita et anima Iude est vita et anima

another as much as a part exceeds its extension. Greatness in extension does not mean greater intensive access to some superior degree in the latitude of being, nor is there greater access to God in some perfection of being.[224] If white, at intensive degree 4 is infinitely extended, it yet does not accede any more towards a superior degree in the latitude of being if it is to remain white.

One can summarize these modes as follows:[225] the first kind of excess consists in the multiple *replicatio* in the divine unity. These replications are the multiple participations in the divine perfection by *other* separate denominations. The second mode is in the greater (and lesser) participation of something in the *same* divine perfection; and the third kind of excess has neither of the above aspects so that it does not move towards God. The second mode, moreover, consists in the concourse of any degrees of the same denomination, not really distinct but really indistinct, concurrently in the same thing. For, as the divine essence differs from all species that are created, since it in itself is absolutely simple unity, then any species up to it is constituted and formed in some numerical form.[226] By the first mode of excess, according to more and less replication in the divine unity, some species is considered more or less in its capacity to exceed another. This excess, therefore, consists in the concourse of greater noncommunicating replications in the divine unity successively replicated. In the second manner the divine essence alone is an immense degree of being with respect to an essential denomination.[227] It is indivisible in every manner of being in life (*omnimode in esse vite*), wisdom and so on. All created life is participative in

Christi est alia intelligentia, tamen in utroque esse anima Christi magis participat esse vite immense vel intelligentie immense quam anima Iude. Et iste modus est minor quam primus quoniam iste supponit excedens et excessum simpliciter communicare in omni denominatione tali."

224 Fol. 250va: "Tertius modus est cum aliquid excedit aliud tanquam partem sui extensivam: ita ex tali maioritate extensionis non sequitur maior accessus intensivus ad aliquem gradum superiorem in latitudine entis nec per consequens maior accessus ad Deum in esse alicuius perfectionis."

225 Fol. 250va: "Primus modus consistit in multipliciori replicatione unitatis divine, que est multiplicior participatio perfectionum divinarum alterius denominationis. Secundus modus est in maiori participatione eiusdem perfectionis divine. Tertius neutro modo se habet, et ideo per ipsum non acceditur versus Deum."

226 Fol. 250va: "Secundus autem modus consistit in concursu plurium graduum eiusdem denominationis non realiter distinctorum sed indistincta realiter, concurrentium in eandem rem; et ratio est: nam sicut divina essentia ideo per accessum primo modo differt ab omni specie creata quoniam ipsa in se est unitas supersimplex, quelibet autem species citra ipsam constituitur et formatur in aliqua forma numerorum..."

227 Fol. 250va: "... ita in secundo modo sola divina essentia est simplex et immensus gradus essendi secundum quamcumque denominationem essentialem."

the life of the first life and therefore is deficient in the fullness of life.[228]
So every degree of life through participation contains a formal latitude
in the being of life that can be measured with regard to such fullness of
being. Consequently, just as the greater perfection and excess of one
species over another and just as access towards God is from the
multiple replication of the divine unity, so the greater access to God in
esse vite comes from a greater participation of the formal degrees in the
first life and from the possession of a greater formal latitude in life that
is communicated by the first life.[229] In the constitution of superior
beings, there is required a multiple participation in the formal degrees
of the same cause which are at the same time concurrent with the
superior entity.[230]

   The intellective soul is assumed to be more sensitively perfect because
the intellect contains sensitivity and it can superadd something to it.
Nevertheless it must add to itself unitively and with real distinctions if
another *new species* is to be created in the essential order of all species
and not simply one which is more intense in its own latitude. In this
way is a ternary number above a binary number.[231] In proposing a
unitive concurrence of a less intense degree that is really indistinct we
can instead cause a degree to be constituted intensively. Of its kind it is
more perfect and yet it remains the same denominating degree of the
species in the essential order of species' degrees.

   We can imagine *caritas* to be a formally indivisible degree which per-
fectionally contains the whole latitude of its species up to itself. *Caritas*
at a certain degree 8 can be intense or remiss in this indivisible habit of
love, given a specific instance, an individual, at some status relative to
the whole latitude's formal indivisible degree. From the oneness, *ex
unico* and the same indivisible degree, there can be formally a resulting
latitude in vital act (*latitudo actuationis vitalis*). So, from the same degree
and the same formal latitude such a degree can result as more or less
intense in vital actuation. It is through the divine essence which is indivisible with respect to a formal degree that yet something is vitally ac-

---

228   Fol. 250va: "... quelibet vita creata est participative vita a prima vita et sicut deficit a
plenitudine vite, ita a plenitudine indivisibilitatis et simplicitatis in esse vite."
   229   Fol. 250va: "... maior accessus ad Deum in esse vite est ex participatione plurimum
graduum formalium participatorum a prima vita et ex maiori latitudine vite formali communicata
a prima vita."
   230   Fol. 250va: "ad constitutionem entis superioris alterius rationis multiplicior replicatio et
participatio divinarum perfectionum alterius rationis, ita ad constitutionem gradus superioris eiusdem rationis requiritur multiplicior participatio graduum eiusdem rationis simul concurrentium ad
entitatem superiorem."
   231   Fol. 250vb.

tuated intensively or remissly according to its own species' capacity to be actuated.[232] So it is possible for the will through the same degree in 'informed' *caritas* to begin at zero degree in *esse caram*, that is, in the habit of love, and to continue successively and intensively in the habit of love.[233] So the same form or *caritas*, in *esse caritatis* can be intended or remitted to zero, preserving the unity of its essence. *Explicit* the fourth article.[234]

* * *

The third part of distinction 17 provides further and even more conclusive evidence for Jean de Ripa's debt to the current ideas of the Oxford calculators concerning intension of forms. For the moment, our point has been made with the text of the second part of distinction 17 set against the background of Dumbleton's *Summa*, part 2, and the theses of Walter Burley and Roger Swineshead and the *Termini naturales*. Not only is de Ripa's use of the technical language of latitudes a further support for the belief that Oxford-Paris relations in the mid-fourteenth century were not severed by the continuous warfare; it is also a fascinating example of the creative use of a technical vocabulary having become widespread in the arts faculty and then having been taken over and fruitfully exploited by a theologian in the interests of clarifying the nature of the communication between God and man in general, between God and the blessed in particular.

That de Ripa or his followers were believed to have gone too far in positing formal but not essential variation in the divine intellect was not a necessary consequence of his ontological use of the "new physics". Rather it was a result of pressing the formalizing of Duns Scotus to extremes. De Ripa stands in an historical context as a bridge between what we would today call the "two cultures". In this, he is representative of his age for it was a time when the nature of infinities and continuity were not only of interest for knowledge and manipulation of the natural order, but were of use in discerning the specific and overriding relation of divine causality to an infinitely enlarged and fragmented cosmos. The physics of infinite space became the logical analogue of God's infinite immensity.

Cambridge University.

232 Fol. 251rb.

233 Concl. 4, fol. 251rb: "Possibile est eandem voluntatem per eundem gradum caritatis informantem incipere a non gradu esse caram, vel habitualiter diligentem et continue intensius et intensius habitualiter diligentem."

234 Concl. 5, fol. 251rb: "Possibile est eandem formam seu caritatem in esse caritatis intendi vel remitti usque ad non gradum stante unitate sue essentie."

MALORY'S KING MARK AND KING ARTHUR

Edward D. Kennedy

A LTHOUGH some critics have felt that Malory's Tale 5, the "Tristram", is largely irrelevant to *Morte Darthur*,[1] others have found ways in which the tale is related to other parts of Malory's book;[2] and while these ways have not always offered as much evidence of "unity" as some of the critics have claimed, they have nevertheless shown that Tale 5 is not as separate from the other tales as Eugène Vinaver maintains. In their discussion of Tale 5's relationship to the other tales, however, commentators have not given the villainous King Mark the attention he deserves. Although some have briefly mentioned his role as foil to Arthur, Mark needs to be more carefully contrasted with Arthur in order to show clearly his function in Malory's book. Most critics have seen him simply as a cuckold or a villain and have ignored the political implications of his role;[3] the one recent attempt to examine political ideas in Malory has given only brief consideration to Mark[4] and, like the

1 E. K. Chambers, *Sir Thomas Malory*, The English Association Pamphlet No. 51 (Oxford, 1922), p. 5; W. H. Schofield, *English Literature from the Norman Conquest to Chaucer* (London, 1906), pp. 211-2; Vida D. Scudder, *The Morte Darthur of Sir Thomas Malory and Its Sources* (New York, 1917), pp. 229-30; Eugène Vinaver, *Le roman de Tristan et Iseut dans l'œuvre de Thomas Malory* (Paris, 1925), pp. 16-7; Eugène Vinaver, ed., *The Works of Sir Thomas Malory*, 2nd ed. (Oxford, 1967), pp. xxxv ff.

2 D. S. Brewer, "'the hoole book'," in *Essays on Malory*, ed. J. A. W. Bennet (Oxford, 1963), pp. 41-63; Thomas C. Rumble, "'The Tale of Tristram': Development by Analogy," in *Malory's Originality: A Critical Study of Le Morte Darthur*, ed. R. M. Lumiansky (Baltimore, 1964), pp. 118-83; Charles Moorman, *The Book of Kyng Arthur* (Lexington, 1965), pp. 49-63; Edmund Reiss, *Sir Thomas Malory*, Twayne's English Authors Series (New York, 1966), pp. 110-20; Donald G. Schueler, "The Tristram Section of Malory's *Morte Darthur*," *Studies in Philology* 65 (1968) 51-66.

3 See, for example, W. H. Schofield, *Chivalry in English Literature: Chaucer, Malory, Spenser, and Shakespeare* (Cambridge, Mass., 1912), pp. 96-7; R. T. Davies, "Malory's Launcelot and the Noble Way of the World," *Review of English Studies* N.S. 6 (1955) 360-1; Nellie Slayton Aurner, "Sir Thomas Malory — Historian?," *PMLA* 48 (1933) 377-82.

4 Elizabeth T. Pochoda, *Arthurian Propaganda: Le Morte Darthur as an Historical Ideal of Life* (Chapel Hill, 1971), pp. 97-100.

other critical works, has not discussed the most significant aspects of his kingship. Yet a medieval reader or audience would have been more closely attuned than modern readers are to the responsibilities incumbent upon a king; by neglecting or only briefly examining medieval theories of kingship in their analyses of Mark, critics have ignored some of the most important ways in which he contrasts with Arthur and have thus overlooked some of the most important links between Tale 5 and other parts of *Morte Darthur*.

Another matter that needs reconsideration is Malory's contribution to the characterization of Mark since this has at times been presented inaccurately. Thomas C. Rumble compares Malory's Mark with the Mark of the source, but his investigation is restricted to the early parts of the "Tristram", and his conclusions do not give as accurate an impression of Malory's role in shaping Mark's character as would be desired; for although Rumble admits that "the blackening of Mark's character had ... largely been accomplished" for Malory by the French prose source, he places undue emphasis upon the changes Malory made in Mark. Rumble writes, "Malory's most successful deviations from the French prose tradition of the story have to do with his re-characterization of King Mark." Others have followed his lead: Charles Moorman observes, "Malory blackens Mark; he appears in the *Morte Darthur* as a cowardly, treacherous villain so as to make the adultery of Tristan and Isolde more human"; and Donald Schueler and Elizabeth T. Pochoda agree that Malory makes Mark more villainous.[5] Yet these critics have apparently not carefully examined Malory's sources; what should be emphasized is that the changes that Rumble cites are definitely minor,[6] and to label them "re-characterization" is to give a misleading impression of Malory's contribution to Mark's character. Malory presents Mark essentially as he found him in the prose *Tristan*; in the source, as in Malory, he is "le plus mescheant de tous les rois".

5 Rumble, p. 153; Moorman, p. 23; Schueler, pp. 54, 60; Pochoda, p. 98.
6 According to Rumble (pp. 153-60), Malory blackens Mark's character in the following ways: 1) Malory eliminates references to the barons' hostility toward Tristram in order to "center the hostility against Tristram completely in the character of King Mark"; 2) when Mark at one point attacks Tristram, he has two knights help him instead of attacking his nephew himself as he does in the source; and 3) Malory has Mark, not, as in the source, the jealous barons, send Tristram to Ireland in hope of his being killed. Only the second of these instances, however, indicates blackening, and it is hardly a major change; the treacherous attack upon Tristram is derived from the source (see n. 47 below). Rumble's first example is inaccurate since Malory retains from the source the hostility of Mark's villainous knight Andret. The third example, as the paragraphs below indicate, also gives an erroneous picture of Malory's handling of his source (see n. 49).

Malory's portrait of Arthur, moreover, has not always been clearly
represented and needs re-examining with reference to ideas that Malory
may have had about kingship and to changes that he made in the accounts he found in his sources. Mrs. Pochoda's study of Malory finds
that his Arthur is a weak king who fails to differentiate between his
public and his private roles; but as I have pointed out elsewhere, her interpretation is based upon some dubious evidence and she fails to consider carefully Malory's source changes and ignores those passages in
Morte Darthur that contradict her thesis.[7] In fact, although the Arthur
that Malory found in the sources of his last two tales, 7 and 8, has traits
that make him resemble in many ways the tyrannical Mark, Malory's
portrait of Arthur in these tales contrasts sharply with both his sources
and his earlier portrait of Mark in the "Tristram". In presenting Arthur
in Tales 7 and 8 Malory departs from his sources much more than he
does in those early tales, 1 and 2, in which Arthur is a central character,
and these departures indicate that while writing *Morte Darthur* Malory
had become interested in making his Arthur correspond to the medieval
concept of a good king.

II

Medieval theorists maintained that government was established for
the common good, the *bonum commune*, and that the king was morally
obligated to seek the welfare of his people and to be, according to
Aquinas, like a shepherd, "commune multitudinis bonum, et non suum
commodum quaerens". John of Salisbury wrote that a king derived his
power from God for the purpose of ruling his people well; and
similarly, Tholemy of Lucca drew a parallel between the rule of the
king and the divine rule of God: just as God governed not for himself,
but for man, kings had to govern not for themselves, but for their subjects.[8]

---

7 See my review in *Speculum* 48 (1973) 397 ff. Below I comment specifically upon her interpretation of Arthur. Although Mrs. Pochoda considers political ideas in Malory, her approach is
different from mine in that it is based to a great extent upon ideas found in Ernst Kantorowicz, *The
King's Two Bodies: A Study in Medieval Political Theology* (Princeton, 1957), ideas which in my opinion
are difficult to apply to *Morte Darthur* since Malory shows little interest in the concept of the immortality of kingship. For a fuller discussion of this, see my review.

8 Aquinas, *De regimine principum ad regem Cypri* 1.i in *Opera Omnia* 16 (New York, 1950), p. 226;
John of Salisbury, *Policraticus* IV.i, ii, ed. C. C. J. Webb, 1 (London, 1909), pp. 236, 238; Tholemy
of Lucca, *De regimine principum* 3.xi, in Aquinas, *Opera Omnia* 16, p. 260. (Tholemy of Lucca's
treatise was formerly attributed to Aquinas.) These ideas were commonplace and appear in many
other works.

Political commentators often contrasted the king with his antithesis, the tyrant. Aquinas and other theorists influenced by Aristotle's *Politics* noted that while kingship was the best of all types of government, tyranny was the worst. It was a government that existed not, like kingship, for the *bonum commune*, but only for the tyrant's *bonum privatum*, and it was therefore "regimen injustum atque perversum".[9] A tyrant ignored the fundamental justification for government and used his power only for his personal advantage.

One of the chief virtues that a good king had was love for his people, a virtue that was linked with his concern for the common good. According to Wyclif, no one should rule "sine titulo caritatis", and Hugh of Fleury remarked that the king "debet ... diligere ... populum sibi a Deo commissum tanquam se ipsum."[10] One of the best ways for a king to show this love was through generosity, and although he should avoid prodigality, he should reward subjects deserving gifts.[11] A king should also show concern for his people by preserving law and order, preventing robbery and violence, punishing the evil, and protecting the innocent, but to do these things he needed a strong military force to support him.[12] Both the *De regimine principum* of Aegidius Romanus and the *Secretum secretorum* stressed the importance of a king's soldiers; and Gower in *Vox clamantis* gave as one of the chief purposes of knighthood the obligation to defend the common good.[13] A tyrant, unlike a king, was not motivated by any interest in the welfare of his subjects; he was

9   Aquinas, *De regimine principum* 1.i, p. 226; also 1.iii, p. 227; similarly, Aristotle, *Politics* 4.ii, x, Latin translation of William of Moerbeke in Aquinas, *In libros politicorum Aristotelis expositio*, ed. Raymondo M. Spiazzi, O.P. (Turin, 1951), pp. 188, 217; Bartolus de Saxoferrato, *De tyrannia* in *Consilia, quaestiones et tractatus* (Venice, 1567), fol. 143ra; Aegidius Romanus, *De regimine principum* (Rome, 1482), 3.ii.vi, fol. 101vb; William of Ockham, *Octo quaestiones de potestate papae* 2.iv, ed. J. G. Sikes in *Opera politica* 1 (Manchester, 1940), p. 75.

10   Wyclif, *De civili dominio*, ed. R. L. Poole, 1 (London, 1885), p. 212; Hugh of Fleury, *De regia postestate et sacerdotali dignitate* 1.6, ed. E. Sackur, MGH, *Libelli de Lite* 2 (Hanover, 1892), p. 473.

11   See, for example, William Perrault, *De eruditione principum* 1.v, 6.vii in Aquinas, *Opera Omnia* 16.396, 469 (Perrault's treatise was once attributed to Aquinas); *Secretum secretorum*, ed. Roger Bacon in *Opera hactenus inedita Rogeri Baconi*, ed. Robert Steele, 5 (Oxford, 1920), pp. 41-43, 52; Wyclif, *De officio regis*, ed. A. W. Pollard and C. Sayle (London, 1887), pp. 96-7; Aegidius Romanus, 1.ii.xvii, iv.i, fols. 27rb, 47rb.

12   See John of Salisbury, V.xv, xvi, 1.344, 352; *Fleta*, ed. H. G. Richardson and G. O. Sayles, Selden Society No. 72, 2 (London, 1955), p. 38; Thomas Hoccleve, *Regement of Princes* ll. 2552-5 in *Hoccleve's Works*, ed. F. J. Furnivall, E.E.T.S., E.S. No. 72 (London, 1897); Tholemy of Lucca, 2.xv, p. 248.

13   Aegidius Romanus, 3.iii.i, fol. 121rb-va and more extensively in the thirteenth-century French translation of Aegidius, *Li livres du gouvernement des rois* 3.iii.i, ed. Samuel Paul Molenaer (New York, 1899), pp. 372-3; *Secretum secretorum*, p. 41; *Vox clamantis* 5.i in *The Complete Works of John Gower*, ed. G. C. Macaulay, 4 (Oxford, 1902), p. 201.

noted instead for his hatred and jealousy of others. Aquinas, for example, pointed out that a tyrant mistrusted anyone who was independent and respected, for such a person was apt to detract from the ruler's own glory, and that the tyrant would attempt to dispose of those men in the community whom the people might turn to as leaders.[14]

In instructing kings, political theorists occasionally mentioned a king's concern for his wife: John of Salisbury, for example, noted that a king should not be overly concerned with his wife and that the relationship between a ruler and his people is as important as, if not more important than, the relationship between a ruler and his wife; and Aegidius Romanus wrote that if a king were jealous of his wife, he would be apt to become involved with his own problems and neglect the more important ones, those of his kingdom.[15] John of Salisbury and Aegidius Romanus were here, of course, making a distinction between a king's concern as an individual and his concerns as a ruler; they believed that a king should place the problems of the realm above those of his private life.

A king, moreover, should above all else be just, for the maintenance of justice was the most fundamental task and the *raison d'être* of a political society. One of the most important medieval statements concerning justice and society appears in St. Augustine's *De civitate Dei*:

> Ubi ergo non est ista iustitia, profecto non est coetus hominum iuris consensu et utilitatis communione sociatus. Quod si non est, utique populus non est, si uera est haec populi definitio. Ergo nec res publica est, quia res populi non est, ubi ipse populus non est.[16]

When there was no justice, there was no commonwealth. Other writers concurred. Bracton, for example, noted that a king was given great power only so that he would be better prepared to be just, and Fortescue said that a king should treat his subjects as "he wolde ben done to hym self, yff he were a subget."[17] Such concern with justice was naturally enough linked with concern for law.

14 Aquinas, *Commentum in libros politicorum seu de rebus civilibus* 5.xi in *Opera Omnia* 21 (New York, 1949), p. 597; Aquinas, *De regimine* 1.iii, p. 227.

15 John of Salisbury, VI.xxvi, 2.78; Aegidius Romanus, 2.i.xxii, fol. 65rb. The relationship between a king and his wife was of great concern in England in the mid-fifteenth century; see my "Malory and the Marriage of Edward IV," *Texas Studies in Literature and Language* 12 (1970) 155-162.

16 Augustine, *De civitate Dei contra paganos* 19.xxiii, ed. J. E. C. Welldon, 2 (London, 1924), p. 444.

17 Henry de Bracton, *De legibus et consuetudinibus Angliae*, ed. G. E. Woodbine, 2 (New Haven, 1922), p. 305; Sir John Fortescue, *The Governance of England*, ed. Charles Plummer (Oxford, 1926), pp. 116-7.

Although many writers agreed that a king should not be forced to obey the law, they nevertheless tried to persuade him to do so willingly. Theorists such as John of Salisbury, Aquinas, Gilbert of Tournai, and the author of *Fleta* emphasized the king's moral obligation to obey the law, not because of the fear of penalty but because of his love of justice.[18] In England the king was generally considered to be under the laws of the land and like every other citizen was expected to obey them.[19] William of Ockham noted that the *bonum commune* was protected by the laws of the community. Bracton said that a king ceased to be a king when his own will instead of the law dominated and that the law was a bridle the king should have. Wyclif wrote that a king should obey the law in order to be a good example to the people. Similarly Gower reminded the king that he was "to lawe swore" and must uphold it.[20] The limitation on the power of the ruler in England was affirmed in the fourteenth century by the deposition of Richard II: the charges against him maintained that he had refused to abide by "les anciens Leyes & Estatuz" and had instead ruled according to his own will.[21] A ruler like Richard II who refused to submit to the law or custom and governed in accordance with his own whim instead of law was a tyrant. John of Salisbury noted that while the king was a servant to the law, the tyrant placed his own desires above it, and similarly Salutati in his *Tractatus de tyranno* warned that the tyrant attempted to destroy the laws that would restrain him.[22]

Concern with justice, of course, meant concern with punishment. According to Ockham, a king "videtur principalissime institutus ut corrigat et puniat delinquentes"; Gilbert of Tournai wrote that a ruler had to judge with equity and deal with rich and poor alike; Hoccleve advised, "Do right to grete and smale"; and George Ashby asked the king to be "to high and lowe Indifferent,/ For youre Lawe is to bothe equiuolent."[23] In punishing, a king should be moderate, neither too

18 John of Salisbury, IV.ii, 1.238; Aquinas, *Summa theologiae* 1-2, 96.5, vol. 2 (Ottawa, 1941), p. 1240a; Gilbert of Tournai, *Le traité 'Eruditio regum et principum' de Gilbert de Tournai*, ed. A. de Poorter, Les philosophes belges 9 (Louvain, 1914), p. 48; *Fleta*, p. 36.

19 See Walter Ullmann, *Principles of Government and Politics in the Middle Ages* (New York, 1961), pp. 117-211.

20 Ockham, *Breviloquium* 2.v in Richard Scholz, *Wilhelm von Ockham als politischer Denker und sein 'Breviloquium de principatu tyrannico'* (Leipzig, 1944), p. 60; Bracton, 2.33, 110; Wyclif, *Officio*, p. 94; Gower, *Confessio amantis* 7.3078 ff. in *Works* 3 (Oxford, 1901), p. 317.

21 *Rotuli parliamentorum* ([London], 1767-77), 3.434. Individual volumes are not dated.

22 John of Salisbury, VIII.xvii, xxii, 2.345, 397; III.xv, 1.232; Coluccio Salutati, *Tractatus de tyranno*, ed. Francesco Ercole, Quellen der Rechtsphilosophie 1 (Berlin, 1914), pp. xiv-v.

23 Ockham, *Octo* 3.viii, p. 113; Tournai, p. 26; Hoccleve, l. 2170, also 2822-8; Ashby, "The Ac-

merciful nor too vindictive. The commentators urged kings to show mercy[24] but were aware that kindness could be carried to extremes. Thus Giraldus Cambrensis noted that a king in considering offenses should forgive "non omnes ... sed multas"; and Bracton and Gower wrote that it was unjust to show mercy to the depraved.[25]

When a ruler had to punish subjects, however, the punishment was to be for the good of the state and with regard to the law, not to gratify personal enmity. Augustine made this point in *De civitate Dei*: "si eandem uindictam pro necessitate regendae tuendaeque rei publicae, non pro saturandis inimicitiarum odiis exerunt."[26] This notion also appeared frequently in writings of the later Middle Ages. John of Salisbury wrote that a king was not to seek personal vengeance and was to judge in accordance with the law. Giraldus Cambrensis warned rulers never to thirst for the blood of even an enemy. James Yonge emphasized that "prynces and Iuges" should not correct "men ... to whome they haue Envy, whos correccion nys not but an enemyly percecucione."[27] A king was, in short, to act as an impartial guardian of justice and of law and was to disregard personal animosities.

Kings were also to be noted for their truthfulness and wisdom. Gower considered truth the chief virtue for a ruler and stressed the importance of a king's good name; and William Perrault said that a "princeps mendax" was an abomination to God.[28] The *Secretum secretorum*, Perrault, John of Salisbury, and others stressed the importance of wisdom.[29] A quality generally associated with wisdom was *prudentia*: a wise king should, in effect, be a man with foresight and sound judgment; he should always look to the future, consider the effect his actions might have, and exercise due moderation in all his actions.[30] A

tive Policy of a Prince," ll. 656-7 in *George Ashby's Poems*, ed. Mary Bateson, E.E.T.S., E.S. No. 76 (London, 1899).

24 Tournai, pp. 34, 68-9; Aquinas, *De regimine* 1.xii, p. 235; Perrault, 1.xiv, pp. 404-5; Aegidius Romanus, 1.iv.i, iv, fols. 46va, 48rb.

25 Giraldus Cambrensis, *De principis instructione*, ed. George F. Warner in *Giraldi Cambrensis opera* 8, Rolls Series No. 21 (London, 1891), p. 22; Bracton, 2.306; Gower, *Confessio*, 7.3520 ff., *Works* 3.335.

26 *De civitate* V.xxiv, 1.240.

27 John of Salisbury, IV.ii, 1.239; Cambrensis, p. 22; Yonge, *Gouernaunce of Prynces* in *Three Prose Versions of the Secreta secretorum*, ed. Robert Steele, E.E.T.S., E.S No. 74 (London, 1898), p. 167, also p. 181.

28 Gower, *Confessio* 7.1722 ff., *Works* 3.280; Perrault, 1.vii, p. 398; similarly, 3.ii, p. 415.

29 *Secretum*, p. 47; Perrault, 1.ii, p. 392; John of Salisbury, V.vii, 1.308; also see Wyclif, *Officio*, p. 46; Bracton, 2.21.

30 *Secretum*, p. 48; Aegidius Romanus, 1.ii.vii, fol. 20ra; Ashby, "Active Policy," ll. 653-4, 828-32.

tyrant, on the other hand, was thought to act impulsively and violently and in so doing to harm his people.[31]

Courage was another attribute expected of a good king and commentators often stressed his abilities as a military leader. Although wars begun for vengeance, aggression, and *vana gloria* were evil and could lead to no good,[32] "warres emprysed by iuste cause be permysed & suffryd of god."[33] Just wars included wars against oppression and usurpation, wars to defend the church and realm, and wars of conquest if the invaders were interested in the welfare of the conquered people.[34] The king, as head of his army, needed "strong herte or grete corage", and some authorities maintained that he should be willing, if the need was great enough, to expose himself in battle since his presence could give his men "the better herte to fyghte".[35] A tyrant, on the other hand, instead of being noted for his valorous acts in war, was characterized as a trouble maker. He kept his subjects stirred up, either by starting a civil war among them or by starting a foreign war so that the best men would have to defend the realm against outside forces and would be unable to rebel at home. A tyrant tried, Aquinas said, to keep the subjects so busy that they would be unable to overthrow his government.[36] He had to live in fear, and therefore had many spies to keep him informed about what was going on in the kingdom and to find out what people were saying about him.[37]

Political theorists were frequently concerned with the problem of rebellion. The king, as "imago deitatis" and "dei vicarius" was to be honored, and to rebel against him was generally to sin against God. Medieval writers usually asserted the religious duty of obedience to the ruling powers and commonly quoted Romans 13: 1 ("Omnis anima potestatibus sublimioribus subdita sit"), 1 Peter 2: 17 ("Deum timete,

---

31   Cambrensis, pp. 18-9, 54; Perrault, 1.xiv, p. 404; Ashby, "Dicta philosophorum," ll. 251-2.

32   Christine de Pisan, *The Book of Fayttes of Armes and of Chyualrye*, trans. William Caxton, ed. A. T. P. Byles, E.E.T.S., O.S. No. 189 (London, 1932), p. 12; Ockham, *Dialogus de potestate papae et imperatoris* 3.ii.i.27 (Turin, 1959), p. 899; Wyclif, *Civili* 2.239, 242-4; Wyclif, *Officio*, p. 262.

33   Pisan, p. 9, also p. 11; similarly, Augustine, XIX.vii, 2.416; Aquinas, *ST.* 2-2, 40, 3 (Ottawa, 1942), pp. 1632b-1633a; Wyclif, *Civili* 2.241.

34   Pisan, p. 11; Wyclif, *Civili* 2.252-4, 260; Wyclif, *Officio*, p. 272; Aegidius Romanus, 1.ii.xxiii, fol. 31rb; Dante, *De monarchia*, ed. E. Moore (Oxford, 1916), pp. 354-6.

35   Hoccleve, l. 3901; Pisan, p. 18; also Aegidius Romanus, 1.ii.xxiii, fol. 31ra; Cambrensis, p. 50. Some believed, however, that the king should avoid battle since his death could harm the realm (Pisan, p. 19; *Secretum secretorum*, p. 152).

36   Aquinas, *Commentum in ... politicorum* 5.xi, p. 596; similarly, Aegidius Romanus, 3.ii.x, fol. 104rb-va; Bartolus, *De tyrannia*, fol. 143ra.

37   Aristotle, 5.xi, p. 293; Aegidius Romanus, 3.ii.x, fol. 104rb; Bartolus, *De tyrannia*, fol. 143ra.

regem honorificate"), and Matthew 22: 21 ("Reddite ... quae sunt Caesaris Caesari: et quae sunt Dei, Deo"). They frequently expressed their fear of civil war and noted the sinfulness of rebellion.[38] One of the king's primary functions was to check rebellion severely and destroy those who were a menace to order and hence to public safety;[39] one of the worst crimes a subject could commit was rebellion against the king, and such a subject, *Fleta* asserted, deserved the most severe punishment.[40] Kings had to be on their guard against rebellion which could be caused by "þe grete varyablenes of the peple" or by ambitious nobles who could, if they gained enough power, cause the king considerable trouble.[41]

To some commentators, however, rebelling against a tyrant was far different from rebelling against a king. Although some of the theorists condemned rebellion against any ruler, no matter how unjust, others maintained that if a king violated the laws of God and of nature and neglected his duties, people were obligated to resist him. John of Salisbury even stated that a subject had the right to kill a tyrant.[42] Few commentators went quite this far. Although Salutati believed that a tyrant could be executed, such action could, in his opinion, be undertaken only by the community, not by the individual. Aquinas warned against tyrannicide, for he feared the unscrupulous would be more apt to kill good kings than the good to kill a tyrant; he also felt that if tyranny were not excessive, it was preferable to civil war. Yet he noted that subjects have the right to oppose laws "quae ordinantur contra Dei mandatum" and that they are permitted to resist commands that inflict unjust hurt on subjects of a realm. William of Ockham and Aegidius Romanus maintained that the people have the right not only to resist those commands that seem to them unjust, but also to depose a tyrant.[43] Thus obedience to a ruler was, at least to some commentators,

---

38 John of Salisbury, VI.xxv, VIII.xxiii, 2.73-4, 403; Ockham, *Octo* 3.v, p. 109; Aquinas, *ST* 2-2, 42.2, 3.1640a.

39 John of Salisbury, VI.xxvi, 2.79; Wyclif, *Officio*, pp. 9, 13; Aegidius Romanus, 3.ii.viii, fol. 103ra.

40 *Fleta*, p. 56; also John of Salisbury, VI.xxvi, 2.80.

41 *Somnium vigilantis*, ed. J. P. Gilson, *English Historical Review* 26 (1911) 521; Aristotle, 5.iii,x, pp. 250, 285-9; Fortescue, *Gouernaunce*, p. 130; Hoccleve, ll. 5223-9; Ashby, "Active Policy," ll. 639-42.

42 John of Salisbury, II.xv, 1.232. John of Salisbury later says that no one should kill a tyrant if he is bound to him by oath or obligation (VIII.xx, 2.377-8).

43 Salutati, pp. xxv-vi, xxxiii-iv; Aquinas, *De regimine* 1.vi, pp. 229-30; and *ST* 1-2, 96.4-5, 2.1239a; 2-2, 104.6, 3.1971a; Ockham, *Octo* 2.viii, p. 86, and *Dialogus* 3.ii.ii.20, pp. 917-8; Aegidius Romanus, 3.ii.13, fol. 106rb.

a relative matter and depended upon whether or not the ruler deserved it.

III

Malory found in his source for Tale 5, the French prose *Tristan*,[44] a portrait of King Mark that epitomizes the most salient characteristics of a tyrant; in the source Mark's kingdom Cornwall is dependent upon Tristram's ability to defend it, and yet Mark continually disregards Tristram's value to his realm and tries to dispose of his nephew because of his jealousy over Tristram's love for his wife Isode. Mark appears as a ruler who lives for his *bonum privatum* instead of the *bonum commune*, who is dominated by feelings of hatred, envy, jealousy, and fear, who punishes according to his own whims, who acts treacherously, who starts a foreign war to keep his people from turning on him, and who, as a result of his actions, loses the best knight in his kingdom and faces a civil war.

44 No extant manuscript of the French prose *Tristan* can be identified as the text Malory used for Tale 5. Vinaver reconstructs the source from seven manuscripts of the prose *Tristan*: Bibliothèque Nationale Fr. 103 for *Works*, pp. 371-512; B.N. Fr. 334 for *Works*, pp. 512-615; B.N. Fr. 99, Chantilly 646 (formerly 316), fr. 41 of the Pierpont Morgan Library and F.V. XV.2 of the Leningrad Public Library for *Works*, pp. 615-846; and MS. B.N. Fr. 362 for the "Alexander the Orphan" section of Tale 5. My comparison of Malory's text with the prose *Tristan* is based upon the first five of these manuscripts and the edition of the relevant portion of MS. 362 in *Alixandre l'Orphelin: A Prose Tale of the Fifteenth Century*, ed. C. E. Pickford (Manchester, 1951); the Leningrad manuscript, which Vinaver first used in his 1967 edition of Malory, was not available to me. I also consulted the following Spanish and Italian versions: *Libro del esforzado caballero Don Tristan de Leonis* in *Libros de caballerías*, primera parte, ed. Adolfo Bonilla y San Martin, Nueva biblioteca de autores españoles 6 (Madrid, 1907); *El Cuento de Tristan de Leonis*, ed. G. T. Northup (Chicago, 1928); *La leggenda di Tristano*, ed. Luigi di Benedetto, Scrittori d'Italia No. 189 (Bari, 1942). On reasons for consulting the Spanish and Italian versions, see Rumble, *Malory's Originality*, pp. 122-44 and my "Arthur's Rescue in Malory and the Spanish 'Tristan'," *Notes and Queries* N.S. 17 (1970) 6-10. I have also used E. Löseth, *Le Roman en prose de Tristan, le roman de Palamède, et la compilation de Rusticien de Pise* (Paris, 1891), Vinaver, *Roman de Tristan*, and the notes to Vinaver's 1967 edition of Malory. I have based my comparison primarily upon the first five manuscripts recommended by Vinaver. When Malory's text agreed with the suggested manuscript, I checked only that manuscript; when Malory's text differed, I checked insofar as possible the corresponding sections of the other texts. The manuscripts, however, are not equal in length and events found in one may be absent in another. MS. 334, for example, does not carry the Tristan story nearly as far as MSS. 103 and 99; the Chantilly and Pierpont Morgan manuscripts do not include the early adventures of Tristan. Although details in Malory that appear in none of the above texts may represent Malory's contribution to the story, they might also represent changes that scribes made in manuscripts no longer extant; thus any attribution of these changes to Malory must be considered tentative. As will be seen, what is most significant about Malory's portrait of Mark is ways in which it agrees with the source.

Brief references will appear in the text and longer ones in footnotes.

In the early part of Malory's Tale 5 and in the corresponding section of the French *Tristan* Mark does not display his treacherous nature. Instead, like a good king he appreciates Tristram's value to his realm.[45] Tristram appears as a great champion of Cornwall: he becomes a hero when he saves the kingdom by mortally wounding Marhalte, the champion of Ireland. After Tristram is injured fighting Marhalte, "kynge Marke and all hys barownes" were "passynge hevy"; and when he recovers, King Mark was "passynge glad, and so were all the barownes."[46]

In both Malory and the source, however, personal animosity soon takes precedence over Mark's concern for the *bonum commune*: there arises "a jolesy and an unkyndenesse betwyxte kyng Marke and sir Trystrames", for they both fall in love with the same lady, the wife of Sir Segwarydes (p. 393; MS. Bibliothèque Nationale Fr. 103, fols. 44r-44v). Ignoring Tristram's defeat of Marhalte and overwhelmed by jealousy, Mark considers Tristram an enemy and unsuccessfully tries to kill him by treacherously attacking him at night.[47] He fails in his attempt, but "as longe as kynge Marke lyved he loved never aftir sir Trystramys" (p. 376; MS. 103, fol. 46v). Mark's actions display the selfish motives of a tyrant and foreshadow his later reactions to Tristram's love for Isode.

Disregarding Tristram's value to his realm, Mark persists in his attempt to dispose of him. He soon sends Tristram to Ireland to bring Isode back to become his queen because he knows that the relatives of Marhalte will attempt to avenge their kinsman and kill Tristram: "all this was done to the entente to sle sir Trystramys" (p. 403). This plan is taken with little change from Malory's French source; although Vinaver

---

45   The prose *Tristan* accounts begin with instances of Mark's villainy that do not appear in Malory; there Mark at the outset kills a younger brother, has assassins kill Tristram's father Meliodes, and attempts to dispose of Tristram (MS. 103, fols. 28v, 30r; similarly MS. 334, fols. 29v, 31rb-va; MS. 99, fols. 36v, 39r; also see Löseth, pp. 17-8). The Italian version and one of the Spanish versions tell of Mark's murder of the brother, but Mark is not involved in the death of Tristram's father (see Benedetto, pp. 2, 12; Bonilla y San Martin, pp. 340, 344; *Cuento de Tristan* lacks the first five folios). MSS. Pierpont Morgan and Chantilly begin their narratives at later points. In all of the above accounts, however, Mark appreciates Tristram when he first comes to court.

46   *Works*, pp. 384, 393; similarly in MS. 103, fols. 35v-36r, 44ra. Although Vinaver says that in the source the barons at this point are hostile to Tristram, according to MS. 103, "Quant le roy et les barons voient tristan si lui sont ... grant joye et aussi grant feste" (fol. 44ra).

47   *Works*, pp. 394-6; MS. 103, fol. 46rb. Rumble cites this an an instance of Malory's blackening of Mark; he notes that in the source Tristram was accompanied by two other knights and Mark attacks them, but that in Malory's account Mark is the one who has two helpers, not Tristram; thus the odds are reversed (*Malory's Originality*, p. 158). This is not, however, a major change and Mark's basic treachery is derived from the source.

and Rumble maintain that the plan in the French *Tristan* was developed by the barons,[48] the extant manuscript closest to Malory's text makes it clear that in the source as in Malory, Mark is the one who wants to kill Tristram.[49] In both Malory's version and the source, Tristram safely returns to Cornwall with Isode and gives her to Mark as a bride even though Tristram and Isode have by this time fallen in love.

Soon after the marriage Mark's role as a suspicious and jealous tyrant becomes more pronounced. He sees Tristram and Isode sitting together in a window, and taking "a swerde in his honde", he calls Tristram "false traytowre" and attempts to kill him. When Tristram takes the sword away from Mark, the king, ignoring in his rage Tristram's importance to the kingdom, orders his men to "sle this traytowre." But "there was nat one that wolde meve for his wordys" (p. 426; MS. 103, fol. 70ra). The men's inaction clearly illustrates the medieval political belief that a subject can disobey the unjust demands of a tyrant and forcibly resist him; and it foreshadows a more serious rebellion against Mark later. Tristram threatens to strike the king; Mark, lacking the courage a ruler was expected to have, flees, but Tristram pursues him, gives him "fyve or six strokys flatlynge in the necke", and rides into the forest with his men. In the source Tristram at this point also threatens to kill Mark (cf. MS. 103, fol. 70r), but Malory omits this to make Tristram less reprehensible. Mark asks his barons what he should do; they advise him to ask Tristram back, and Dynas the Seneschal warns Mark of the probable consequence if he does not:

> Many men woll holde with sir Trystrames and he were harde bestadde. ... sir Trystrames ys called peereless and makeles of ony Crystyn knyght, and ... we know none so good a knyght but yf hit be sir Launcelot du Lake. And yff he ... go to kyng Arthurs courte ... he woll so frende hym there that he woll nat sette by your malyce (p. 427).

Mark sees the advisability of this warning and asks that Tristram be sent for "that we may be frendys."[50] A comparison with the source account

48 *Works*, p. 1461; *Malory's Originality*, p. 159.

49 MS. 103, fols. 49v-50r: "il [Mark] cuide se porra de tristan deliurer ... car il amie mieulx sa mort que sa vie. ... les barons distrent au roy que moult se merueilloient quil ne prenoit femme. Et tristan dit que moult lui plairoit quil eust moullier." The king then asks for Iseult: "quant tristan entent ceste nouuelle si pense que son oncle lenuoye plus en yrlande pour mourir que pour yseult auoir. ne il ne lui escondire ... le roy ... plus desire son mal que son bien." Similarly, MS. 334, fol. 52r; MS. 99, fol. 64v.

50 *Works*, p. 427. The Spanish *Tristan* is here closer to Malory's account than the French. See Bonilla y San Martin, p. 385; Northup, pp. 149-50. In the French, Andret advises Mark to lure Tristan back in order to kill him (*cf.* MS. 103, fol. 70v).

shows that what is most original about Malory's version is the comparison of Tristram with Lancelot and the statement that a knight of Tristram's prowess would be welcome at Arthur's court.[51] The whole scene emphasizes both the support Tristram has among Mark's knights and Tristram's value to the realm; and it implies that if Mark alienates Tristram, "many men woll holde with sir Trystrames" and civil war will ensue. Mark in both Malory and the source wisely decides to forgive Tristram. This is one of the few occasions when Mark acts wisely as a ruler and places the good of his realm first. His kingly behavior here, however, is soon negated.

A later scene that occurs in both Malory's Tale 5 and the source further illustrates Tristram's value to the *bonum commune* and consequently focuses attention upon the distinction between Mark as a wronged husband who might justifiably hate Tristram and Mark as a king who should value Tristram's past service to Cornwall and judge him fairly and unemotionally for the good of the realm. Mark is the type of ruler that John of Salisbury and Aegidius Romanus warned against, the ruler who lets his concern for his wife take precedence over his concern for his kingdom. Tristram and Isode are found together in bed, and Tristram is condemned to death "by the assent of kynge Marke and of sir Andret and of som of the barownes". In both Malory's account and the French source, Tristram speaks of the past deeds he has done for Cornwall: "Remember what I have done for the contrey of Cornwayle, and what jouparté I have been in for the wele of you all. ... I was promysed to be bettir rewarded."[52] Tristram's speech stresses his value to the kingdom; and subsequent events show that Mark, as a king, should have remembered these deeds and ignored the adultery with Isode.

Although Tristram at this time escapes from Mark, he is later captured and taken back to court. Mark has a trial for Tristram, but his manner of judging is a travesty of the justice and equity that the political theorists expected of a king. Mark wants his barons to decide the case in a way that will gratify his desire for vengeance, and he does

---

51 The idea for this may have come from a later section of the French source that tells of Tristram's madness and exile. There Andret advises Mark not to release Tristram from prison "car il sen yra en royaume de logres et sacointera dez bons cheualiers du lignage le roy ban et du roy artu *pour* la bonne cheualerie qui en lui est. Et sachies quil ... vous honnira et toute cornoaille en sera destruite" (MS. 103, fol. 165v; similarly, MS. 334, fol. 192v; MS. 99, fol. 224r).

52 *Works*, p. 431; again the closest parallel is in the Spanish, not the French account. See Bonilla y San Martin, p. 286. In the French version the people of Cornwall praise Tristan, but he does not speak himself. See MS. 103, fol. 75vb.

not give them much choice; he "lete calle hys barownes to geve jugemente unto sir Trystramys to the dethe." The barons, however, "wolde nat assente thereto" and instead advise that Tristram be banished for ten years (pp. 502-3). Malory appears to have given Mark a more villainous role here; in the source instead of wanting to have Tristram killed, Mark ignores Andret's advice to kill Tristram and instead wants to have him exiled forever.[53] When Tristram is preparing to leave Cornwall, he again emphasizes his past services to the realm: his battle against Marhalte; the trip to Ireland to bring Isode to Mark; the battles against Bleoberys, Blamoure de Ganys, Lamarok, the King with the Hundred Knights, the King of North Gaul, the giant Tauleas, and the battle against Palomydes to save Isode. He adds, "And many othir dedys have I done for hym, and now have I my waryson . ... And telle kynge Marke that many noble knyghtes of the Rounde Table have spared the barownes of thys contrey for my sake" (pp. 503-4). Malory appears to have lengthened the list of heroic deeds that Tristram mentions in order to stress Tristram's value to Cornwall and to emphasize the folly of Mark's desire to execute him.[54]

Subsequent events illustrate the tyrant's fear and jealousy of others and the danger of placing desire for personal vengeance above the welfare of the kingdom. After Tristram leaves Cornwall he goes to Arthur's court and wins fame as a knight. When Arthur's nephew Gaherys comes to Mark's court and tells of Tristram's success, Mark "in hys harte ... feryd sore that sir Trystram sholde gete hym such worship in the realme of Logrys wherethorow hymselff shuld nat be able to withstonde hym" (p. 545; MS. 334, fol. 265v). When Sir Uwayne challenges all the knights of Cornwall, the king at first has no knight to answer the challenge; Mark's nephew Andret and Dynas the Seneschal finally accept but are defeated (pp. 545-6). As Gaherys points out, Mark's vengeance has deprived Cornwall of the one man capable of saving it from dishonor: "Sir kynge, ye ded a fowle shame whan ye flemyd sir Trystram oute of thys contrey, for ye nedid nat to have doughted no knyght and he had bene here" (p. 547; MS. 334, fol. 269ra). Uwayne's success, however, does not teach Mark anything, and he persists in his hatred in subsequent parts of the "Tristram". Malory begins the "King Mark" subdivision by reminding his readers of Mark's

53 MS. 103, fol. 165r; similarly, MS. 334, fol. 192r-v; MS. 99, fol. 224r.
54 In the source one finds only the battles against "morhoult ... roy de norgules ... roy des cent cheualiers ... taulat de la montaigne"—MS. 103, fol. 166r; similarly, MS. 334, fol. 199ra; MS. 99, fol. 225rb-va.

"grete dispyte" and "grete suspeccion unto sir Trystram bycause of his
quene ... for hym semed that there was much love betwene them
twayne" (p. 577; MS. 334, fol. 302va). A little later Lamarok condemns
Mark for driving Tristram, "the worshypfullyst knyght that now is
lyvynge" from Cornwall "for the jeleousnes of his quene" (p. 580).
Malory seems to have added Lamarok's statement about Mark's
"jeleousnes",[55] a statement which emphasizes Mark's concern for his
wife, his interest in his *bonum privatum*, and his lack of interest in the
bonum commune of the realm.

Another scene in both Malory's Tale 5 and his source further
illustrates Mark's treachery and selfish concern and illustrates a second
time the doctrine that the individual can resist the unjust decrees of a
ruler. Like the tyrants discussed by the theorists, Mark has spies who
keep him informed, and when they tell him of Tristram's heroic ac-
complishments in England, Mark, with no regard for the law or justice,
sets out to "destroy sir Trystram by some wylys other by treson." When
he tells two knights of his plan, one of them, Bersules, rebukes him: "sir
Trystram is the knyght of worshyp moste that we knowe lyvynge. ... I
woll not consente to the deth of hym, and therefore I woll yelde hym
my servyse and forsake you." Although Mark has been personally
wronged by Tristram, he acts "shamfully" as a king in seeking
vengeance on such a "knyght of worshyp". After Bersules rebukes
Mark, the king displays the impulsiveness for which tyrants were noted
by drawing his sword and killing Bersules. When the other knight
Amant and his squire see that "vylaunce dede", they say: "Hit was foule
done and myschevously, wherefore we woll do you no more servyse."
Mark then becomes "wondirly wrothe" and tries to kill Amant, but he
and the squire "sette nought by his malyce" (p. 578; MS. 334, fol.
303rb-va). Like the previously cited passage in which Mark's men refuse
to attack Tristram, this scene presents the individual's right to disobey a
tyrant's evil command: "I woll ... forsake you"; "we woll do you no
more servyse." Moreover, it also anticipates the later rebellion that
Mark has to face.

Arriving at Arthur's court, Mark exhibits the mendacity for which
tyrants were noted. Arthur rebukes him: "Ever ye have bene ayenste me
and a dystroyer of my knightes." Mark, however, falls "flatte to the
erthe at kynge Arthur's feete", promises to "make a large amendys",
and wins Arthur's trust. Mark, however, is "a fayre speker and false

---

55   Not in MS. 334, fol. 305va; MS. 99, fol. 331r; MS. 103, fols. 254v-255r; Chantilly, fol. 138vb.

thereundir".[56] Arthur tries to make peace between Mark and Tristram and asks Mark to be a "good lorde unto sir Trystram", and to "cherysh hym". Mark swears to do this and he and Tristram, supposedly reconciled, return to Cornwall. At this point, however, the narrator emphasizes Mark's tyrannous duplicity: "But for all this kynge Marke thought falsely, as hit preved aftir; for he put sir Trystram in preson, and cowardly wolde have slayne hym" (pp. 608-9; MS. 334, fol. 330vb).

Soon after Mark and Tristram reach home, an event occurs which again shows Tristram's value to the realm and Mark's inability to set aside personal enmity. An army from "Syssoyne" invades Cornwall, and Tristram is needed to defend the realm; at first, however, Mark "wold nat sende for sir Trystram, for he hated hym dedly." Because his council warns, "Ye muste sende for sir Trystram ... other ellys they woll never be overcome", Mark finally asks Tristram to fight for Cornwall, but he is still "full lothe thereto". After Tristram fights for the kingdom in battle (pp. 618-9; MS. 99, fol. 365vb), Elyas, the leader of the enemy, challenges Mark to send him a champion for single combat. Mark's other knights find this preferable to another full-scale battle: "To fyght in a fylde we have no luste, for had nat bene the proues of sir Trystram, hit hadde been lykly that we never sholde have scaped"; but none of the knights will volunteer to fight the champion of Syssoyne. Mark is forced to admit "then am I shamed and utterly distroyed, onles that my nevew Trystram wolde take the batayle uppon hym" (p. 623; cf. MS. 99, fol. 373r). Tristram does agree to fight Elyas and once again saves Cornwall. The narrator adds the comment, "Yett for all this kynge Marke wolde have slayne sir Trystram" (p. 626; not in source), thus implying that in spite of the affair with Isode, Mark should have considered Tristram's heroism and set aside his enmity.

Mark persists in his villainy, and his efforts to kill Tristram have serious consequences for both himself and the realm. Malory begins the "Joyous Garde" subdivision of Tale 5 by having Mark attempt to have Tristram killed in a tournament; this attempt on Tristram's life was apparently not in Malory's sources and is one of the instances in which Malory seems to have actually blackened Mark's character.[57] In both Malory's account and the source, Mark then drugs Tristram and puts him "in a stronge preson", an act which produces immediate political

---

56 *Works*, pp. 594-5; MS. 334, fol. 320rb-va; for comment on Mark, see fol. 330v.

57 *Works*, p. 675; the source does not have Mark attempt to have Tristram killed in this manner. See MSS. 99, fol. 397vb; Pierpont Morgan, fol. 95vb; Chantilly, fol. 231rb-va.

repercussions in the realm. Hearing what the king has done, one of Mark's knights first attempts to assassinate him (p. 676; MS. 99, fol. 398r), and, failing to do that, stirs up rebellion against him. Sir Dynas also defies "suche a kynge" and renounces loyalty to him; and "all maner knyghtes seyde as Sir Dynas sayde." The angry knights soon fortify towns and castles and raise an army to overthrow their king (p. 677; MS. 99, fol. 398va). The result of Mark's desire for personal vengeance against the best knight of his realm thus is civil war.

To solve the problem, Mark establishes a crisis; he tries to unite his people by calling them to war in the Holy Land. This is the type of deception that, according to the theorists, a tyrant frequently relied upon. Mark has "countirfete lettirs from the pope" written which order the army of Cornwall "to go to Jerusalem for to make warre uppon the Saresyns". He offers to release Tristram from prison if he will "go warre uppon the myscreauntes"; but Tristram is not deceived and says to Mark's clerk: "I woll nat go at his commaundemente! ... for I se I am well rewarded for my trewe servyse." When the clerk returns with a second group of counterfeit letters, he gets a similar rebuff (pp. 677-8). The main change that Malory appears to have made here is that in his version both sets of letters are counterfeit; in the French *Tristan*, the first ones are genuine, but Tristram does not believe that the pope would send letters to the "felon traitre roy marc".[58] Tristram's statement about his "trewe servyse" also seems to be original with Malory and further emphasizes Tristram's importance to the realm.

Mark's ruse fails and the rebellion continues; some of his men ask, "Kynge, why fleyste thou nat? For all this contrey ys clyerly arysen ayenste the" (p. 678; MS. 99, fol. 399rb). At this point Perceval arrives in Cornwall, and after freeing Tristram tells Mark that "he had done hymselff grete shame for to preson sir Trystram so, 'for he is now the knyght of moste reverence in the worlde. ... And yf he woll make warre uppon you, ye may nat abyde hit.'" Mark replies, "That is trouthe, ... but I may nat love sir Trystram, bycause he lovyth my quene, La Beall Isode" (p. 679). In the source Perceval reminds Mark of the services Tristram has done for him and of the danger of offending him, but Mark's reply appears to be original with Malory.[59] This addition is important, for it shows that Mark is more concerned about Tristram's love for Isode than about a potentially disastrous civil war, and he is more

---

58 MS. 99, fols. 398vb-399ra; Chantilly; fol. 233r; Pierpont Morgan, fol. 96vb.
59 *Cf.* MS. 99, fol. 399va; MS. 103, fol. 300r; Pierpont Morgan, fol. 95r; Chantilly, fol. 234r.

willing to risk the destruction of his kingdom than forget a personal wrong.

Although Mark promises Perceval "never by no maner of meanys to hurte sir Trystram", as soon as Perceval leaves, the king thinks "of more treson"; and, finding Tristram with Isode, "by treson Kynge Marke ... put hym in preson, contrary to his promyse that he made unto sir Percivale" (pp. 679-80; MS. 99, fol. 399vb). Isode, however, hearing of this, has Dynas capture Mark and imprison him; then she and Tristram escape to Arthur's kingdom.[60] Thus the story of Mark in Tale 5 ends with the king in prison as a just reward for his tyrannous acts.

The narrative in both Malory and the source shows that Mark and Cornwall need Tristram and that although Mark as a husband has ample reason for hating Tristram, as a king he is clearly wrong in trying to destroy him. Tristram's valor saves Cornwall from such enemies as Marhalte and Elyas; his forced absence results in disgrace for Cornwall because Mark has no champion to defend it; and his imprisonment causes a civil war. In his relationship with Tristram Mark clearly violates the political theorists' belief that a ruler must live solely for his kingdom.

Mark's unfitness as a king is revealed not only in his attacks upon Tristram but also in his relationship with other knights. He is reviled as a "grete enemy to all good knyghtes" (p. 580; similarly MS. 334, fol. 305v) and a "dystroyer of good knyghtes" (p. 582; similarly MS. 334, fols. 308vb-309r). At one point Mark secretly rides after Uwayne, smites him "allmoste thorow the body", and leaves him to die (p. 547; MS. 334, fol. 270r-v). Shortly after this, he and Sir Andret attack Kay and Gaherys; and Gaherys turns on them and says, "Ye ar false traytours, and false treson have ye wrought undir youre semble chere that ye made us. For hit were pité that ye sholde lyve ony lenger" (pp. 548-9; MS. 334, fol. 277ra); the political sentiments expressed here in both Malory and his source are the same: a king who is treacherous deserves to die. Mark's lack of chivalry and cowardice is emphasized by the knight Berluse: "ye slew my [fader] traytourly and cowardly ... ye ar the moste vylaunce knyght of a kynge that is now lyvynge, ... and all that ye do is but by treson" (p. 582; MS. 334, fols. 308vb-9ra). Later, after

---

60 *Works*, p. 680; MSS. 99 (fol. 399vb), Chantilly (fol. 234va), Pierpont Morgan (fol. 95rb) do not tell exactly how Isode saved Tristram. In some versions, including MS. 103, Tristram is rescued by the people of Leonis. (See Vinaver's note, *Works*, p. 1509; Löseth, p. 203 n. 5.) In some MSS. Mark is imprisoned before Tristram escapes in order to make the escape plausible.

Berluse has been overcome in combat by Dynadan, Mark tries to kill him; for "this kynge Marke was but a murtherer."[61] Mark elsewhere further shows that he lacks the courage that a king was supposed to have (pp. 585-6, 588; MS. 334, fols. 311v, 313v); and at one point Dynadan angrily tells him, "Ye ar full of cowardyse, and ye ar also a murtherer, and that is the grettyst shame that ony knyght may have."[62]

Mark epitomizes the tyrant's fear of others who might be more powerful or who might detract from his own glory. His jealousy is not restricted to sexual jealousy; some of his animosity toward Tristram, for example, is motivated by his fear of Tristram's prowess. Such fear is further shown in the story of Alexander the Orphan in Tale 5. In this story Mark has a brother, Bodwine, "that all the peple of the contrey loved ... passyng well." When Cornwall is invaded by Saracens, Bodwine raises an army and defeats the invaders. Hearing of his brother's heroism, Mark displays the jealousy characteristic of tyrants:

> he was wondirly wrothe that his brother sholde wynne suche worship and honour. And bycause this prynce was bettir beloved than he in all that contrey, and also this prynce Bodwyne lovid well sir Trystram, ... he thought to sle him.
>
> And thus, hastely and uppon hede, as a man that was full of treson, he sente for ... Bodwyne and ... his wyff, and bade them brynge their yonge sonne ... and all this he ded to the entente to sle the chylde as well as his fadir, for he was the falsist traytour that ever was borne.

When Bodwine comes to dinner, Mark asks him why he raised the army himself without calling the king:

> "Sir," seyde ... Bodwyne, "... and I had [taryed tyl that I had] sente for you, tho myscreauntes had distroyed my contrey."
>
> "Thou lyeste, false traytoure!" seyde kynge Marke, "For thou arte ever aboute to wynne worship from me and put me to dishonoure, and thou cherysht that I hate!"
>
> And therewith he stroke hym to the herte wyth a dagger, that he never aftir spake worde (pp. 633-4).

The only known version of the prose *Tristan* that comes close to this is the account given in MS. Bibliothèque Nationale Fr. 362.[63] Malory

---

61   *Works*, p. 583; remarks about Mark being a murderer not in MS. 334, fol. 309v; Chantilly, fol. 144v; MS. 103, fols. 258v-259r; MS. 99, fol. 335r.

62   *Works*, p. 585; in the source Dynadan does not seriously rebuke Mark (*cf.* MS. 334, fol. 310rb-va).

63   *Alixandre l'Orphelin*, p. 88.

seems to have added the statement about the brother being a friend of Tristram and he also seems to have given Mark a more specific and political reason for murdering his brother. Although in both cases the murder is caused by jealousy of the brother's popularity, in Malory's account the brother is a national hero who, like Tristram, saves the country from foreign invasion. Malory notes, moreover, that the Saracen invasion occurs "sone aftir the Sessoynes were departed" (p. 633). The Sessoynes were the invaders that Tristram had defeated after which Mark had tried to dispose of him. The Bodwine episode thus underlines Mark's disregard for those who work for the good of the country and further shows that Mark, thoroughly controlled by his passions, tries to destroy the men that Cornwall needs most. In the case of Tristram, Mark is motivated primarily by jealousy over Isode, but his anger when he hears of Tristram's success at Arthur's court also indicates his jealousy of Tristram's prowess and his fear of retribution. In the case of Bodwine, Mark is again angry that someone other than himself "sholde wynne suche worship and honour". What he overlooks is the "trew servyse" of these two men to Cornwall; his concern is only with his *bonum privatum* and not with the *bonum commune* of the realm.

Mark's treatment of Bodwine and Tristram shows disregard not only for two champions of his realm but also for two kinsmen, his brother and his nephew; Mark should have been loyal to both men, not only because of their service to his kingdom but because of the blood bond between them. Malory, in fact, at least twice emphasizes Mark's neglect of his blood bond with Tristram. The narrator says that Mark "chaced hym [Tristram] oute of Cornwayle (yette was he nevew unto kynge Mark)" (p. 577; not in source), and Perceval rebukes Mark for mistreating his nephew: "for shame ... for ar nat ye uncle unto sir Trystram?" [64] Later in the story of the King of the Red City in Tale 5 Malory added references that were not in his source to the importance of ties of kinship: a ruler is destroyed because he neglects the lords "of his owne bloode"; one of his subjects says, "And all kyngis and astatys may beware by oure lorde; for he was destroyed in his owne defaute; for had he cheryshed his owne bloode, he had bene a lyvis kynge."[65] Malory may have added the emphasis upon the blood bond to the story of the King of the Red City in order to draw a parallel between that

---

64 *Works*, p. 679; in the source Perceval does not place as much emphasis upon the relationship; he simply says, "comment es tu si desloyaulx que tu tiel chevalier comme est tristan ton nepueu metz en prison" (MS. 99, fol. 399v).

65 *Works*, pp. 711-2; not in the source; *cf.* account in MS. 99, fols. 431r ff.

king's fate and Mark's. As will be shown later, Malory placed great importance on blood ties and Mark was surely wrong to violate them.

Malory found most of Mark's villainy in his source; the additions that
Malory might have made — Mark's attempts to have Tristram executed,
his hope that Tristram would be killed in the tournament, his coun-
terfeiting both sets of letters from the pope, the comments of Lamarok
and Mark that emphasize Mark's love for Isode, the political reason for
his hatred of his brother Bodwine, and his failure to regard his blood
ties with Tristram and Bodwine — are not nearly as significant as the
tyrannical aspects of Mark's character that appear in the source. The
picture of Mark that the source provided must have suited Malory's
purposes, and he saw little reason to make drastic changes in Mark's
character. Of the changes that he did make, the most interesting are
those that emphasize Mark's love for Isode and his disrespect for blood
ties, for these changes suggest that while writing Tale 5 Malory was concerned with the political nature of Mark's role.

Malory found in the concluding section of the prose *Tristan* the
culminating instance of Mark's villainy: the king discovers Tristram and
Isode together and treacherously stabs Tristram in the back. Although
Malory ends his Tale 5 with Tristram and Isode together and omits
most of the final portion of his French source, he nevertheless works the
murder of Tristram into his narrative at three different points. He first
mentions it rather early in Tale 5, concluding the story of Alexander
the Orphan with a statement apparently not in his source: "this false
kynge Marke slew bothe sir Trystram and sir Alysaundir falsely and
felonsly."[66] But the most detailed accounts of the murder occur not in
Tale 5 but in the final tales, 7 and 8.

In the seventh tale Malory gives an account of the murder in his story
of Sir Urry for which there is no known source. Malory writes: "that
traytoure kynge slew ... sir Trystram as he sate harpynge afore hys lady,
La Beall Isode, with a trenchaunte glayve." Malory at this point also
tells of the fate of Mark: "Sir Bellynger revenged the deth of ... sir
Trystram, for he slew kynge Marke" (pp. 1149-50). Although Malory
would have found Tristram's murder in the prose *Tristan*, the account
of the retributive slaying of Mark is not found in any of the known versions of the *Tristan* and appears to be original with Malory.[67] Malory

---

66 *Works*, p. 648; not in MSS. 99, 362, Chantilly, Pierpont Morgan. MS. 334 ends before this;
MS. 103 does not contain the Alexander story.

67 Different accounts of Mark's death appear in a few other works: in a French MS. of the post-
Vulgate *Mort Artu*, MS. Bibliothèque Nationale Fr. 340, he is killed by Paulart; in an Italian poem of

thus lets his readers know that Mark's reward for his villainy is death, and he expresses no disapproval over the tyrannicide; Malory would apparently have agreed with theorists like John of Salisbury who approved of this means of disposing of a tyrant.

Malory adds the third account of the murder to Tale 8; this account is of interest because it leads to an explicit contrast between Mark and Arthur, a contrast that does not appear in Malory's sources. Lancelot's kinsman Bors, fearing that Guenevere will be burnt at the stake, suggests that Lancelot rescue her and take her back to Arthur when the king is no longer angry. Lancelot is reluctant to do this: "for by sir Trystram I may have a warnynge: for whan ... sir Trystram brought agayne La Beall Isode unto kynge Marke ... that false traytour kyng Marke slew hym as he sate harpynge afore hys lady." Bors replies: "All thys ys trouthe ... but there ys one thyng shall corrayge you and us all: ye know well kynge Arthur and kynge Marke were never lyke of cond[y]cions, for there was never yet man that ever coude preve kynge Arthure untrew of hys promyse" (p. 1173; not in source). Bors's faith in Arthur is justified, for after Guenevere's rescue by Lancelot, Arthur is willing to take the queen back and make peace with Lancelot (p. 1190). Mark reacts to the love affair by taking personal vengeance and killing his best knight; Arthur's attitude toward the affair between Lancelot and Guenevere shows willingness to forgive. Mark and Arthur, as Bors's comparison clearly shows, exemplify quite different types of kingship.

IV

Malory's Arthur has many of the best traits of the medieval ruler: interest in the common good, love of his men, courage, concern for law, a sense of justice. Although Malory found some of these traits in the Arthur of his sources, he added some to make Arthur appear in many ways a better king than he was in the source accounts. Arthur is a main character in only four of Malory's eight tales, 1, 2, 7, and 8; in the central tales he is in the background. But the portrait of Arthur in the final tales is considerably different from the portrait of Arthur in Malory's first two tales; moreover, this is not due merely to the different ways in which Malory's sources present Arthur, for Malory relied far less

the fourteenth century Lancelot kills him in combat; and in the Italian *Tavola Ritonda* he dies of overeating after having been kept in a cage and fed intensively. See Vinaver, *Works*, pp. 1503-4; C. E. Pickford, *L'évolution du roman arthurien en prose vers la fin du moyen âge* (Paris, 1960), pp. 197-8.

heavily upon his sources in presenting the Arthur of Tales 7 and 8 than he did in presenting the Arthur of Tales 1 and 2. In discussing Malory's freer use of his sources in the final tales, Vinaver comments: "If ... his progress [is] traced from beginning to end, it becomes obvious that there was ... a consistent, though somewhat slow, evolution towards a higher degree of independence in the interpretation of the narrative material, and even in the refashioning of that material for purposes of reinterpretation" (p. 1624). Development and reinterpretation of Arthur's role as king are especially important in Tales 7 and 8 and when he briefly appears in Tale 6. Although Malory derived some of his ideas from his sources, the Arthur of these final tales is more Malory's own creation than is the Arthur of the early tales. Malory seems, in fact, to have developed the conception of Arthur that appears in these final tales as he was writing *Morte Darthur*.

The different picture of Arthur that emerges in Tales 7 and 8 does not necessarily suggest that Malory originally intended to have Arthur develop into a better king as his book progressed. Malory apparently thought of Arthur as a good king in the early as well as the later parts of *Morte Darthur*. The Arthur of the early tales has traits that, according to the theorists, a good king should have: a sense of justice and chivalry, courage and wisdom; Malory at times added to the early tales to emphasize these traits. In 1, for example, the young Arthur shows that he is aware of the responsibility incumbent upon a king for he promises to rule with "true justyce" (p. 16; no source) and he charges his knights "never to do outerage nothir morthir and allwayes to fle treson, and to gyff mercy unto hym that askith mercy";[68] in this tale the narrator also notes, "hit was myrry to be under such a chyfftayne that wolde putte hys person in adventure as other poure knyghtis ded" (p. 54; no source); in 2, during his Roman campaign Arthur assures his men that he will do his "trew parte" in battle (p. 221; no source); and King Angwysshaunce exalts him above all kings for his "kyghthode" and "noble counceyle".[69] Instances of Arthur's regard for his men also appear in 1 and 2 in, for example, Arthur's generous giving of "rychesse

---

68 *Works*, p. 120. This charge does not appear in the primary source for Tale 1, the *Suite du Merlin*; it was suggested, however, by another work that Malory knew, the fifteenth-century *Chronicle* of John Hardyng. See my "Malory's Use of Hardyng's *Chronicle*," *Notes and Queries* N.S. 16 (1969) 167-70.

69 *Works*, p. 188; in the source of 2, Arthur is "the knyghtlyeste of counsaile that euer corone bare"— *Morte Arthure, or The Death of Arthur*, ed. Edmund Brock, E.E.T.S., O.S. No. 8 (London, 1961), l. 291.

and londys" to his knights[70] and his care of them during the Roman campaign.[71] These acts would have been praised by the political theorists.

Malory's concept of Arthur, however, was not as fully developed in his early tales as it was in his later ones. On the whole, the Arthur of Tale 1 is not very different from the Arthur of the source, the *Suite du Merlin*; and although in Tale 2 Malory makes Arthur less cruel than the Arthur of the source, the alliterative *Morte Arthure*,[72] he is nevertheless an epic conqueror whose portrait is largely derived from the source. Malory's dependence on his source in 1 is evidenced particularly by his failure to remove from Arthur's character a number of imperfections that are in his source but that are of a type that he usually removed in his later tales. One of these is linked with the story of the birth of Arthur's illegitimate son Mordred. The begetting of Mordred is, of course, one of the most important elements of the Arthurian story; and, assuming that Malory had at least the plan of his "hoole book" in mind when he was writing Tale 1, he would have retained this from the source;[73] he might not, however, have been expected to retain, as he did, Arthur's barbarous reaction to Mordred's birth: the king attempts to dispose of the baby by drowning all of the children in the realm that were born on May Day,[74] an act that recalls all too well Herod's slaughter of the Innocents. Malory also retains from the source other instances in which Arthur acts rashly and vengefully. The king unreasonably wishes, for example, to fight with Pelinore and "be avenged on hym"; and Merlin must warn, "nat so ... ye shall have no worship to have ado with hym" (p. 53; Huth, 1. 200). When after his fight with Accolon, Arthur learns that Morgan le Fay wants to kill him, he says, "I [shall] be sore avenged uppon hir, that all Crystendom shall speke of hit" (p. 146; Huth, 2. 209-10); and on another occasion he

70 *Works*, p. 120 (1); also pp. 113 (1), 245-6 (2). These are additions to the sources.

71 *Works*, pp. 211, 217, 222, 224 (2). Examples one and three have some basis in the source; *cf.* alliterative *Morte Arthure*, ll. 1573-4, 2197 ff.

72 See Helen Iams Wroten, *Malory's 'Tale of King Arthur and the Emperor Lucius' Compared with Its Source, the Alliterative 'Morte Arthure'* (Diss. Illinois, 1950); William Matthews, *The Tragedy of Arthur: A Study of the Alliterative Morte Arthure* (Berkeley, 1960), pp. 172-7; Mary E. Dichmann, "'Tale of King Arthur and the Emperor Lucius': The Rise of Lancelot," *Malory's Originality*, pp. 67-90.

73 *Works*, pp. 41, 44; *cf.* Huth MS. of the *Suite du Merlin*, published as *Merlin: Roman en prose du XIIIe siècle*, ed. Gaston Paris and Jacob Ulrich, S.A.T.F. 1 (Paris, 1886), p. 154.

74 *Works*, pp. 55-6; in the *Suite* the children are rescued; *cf.* Huth, 1.203, 207-9; also see other versions of the *Suite*: Cambridge manuscript (Camb. Add. 7071), fols. 233rb, 244vb, 245vb, 246v and *El baladro del sabio Merlin: primera parte de la demanda del Sancto Grial* in Bonilla y San Martin, pp. 56, 70-2.

similarly threatens to "be avengid on hir".[75] He also unjustly banishes
Morgan's son Uwayne because he holds him "suspecte" of being allied
with his mother (p. 158; Huth, 2. 230). Thus while Arthur in Tale 1 is
for the most part a good and just ruler he also has unkingly traits
derived from the source, traits of a type that Malory would have deleted
or altered in Tales 7 and 8.

In the final tales Malory's Arthur still has the good traits of a
medieval king that he had shown earlier. In 7 he is still the "floure of
chyvalry of [alle] the worlde" (p. 1161; no source); and in 8, in his final
battle against Mordred, Arthur conducts himself as bravely as he had in
the early tales: "ever kynge Arthure rode thorowoute the bat[a]yle ...
and ded full nobely, as a noble kynge shoulde do, and at all tymes he
faynted never" (p. 1236; no source). Traits such as his love of his men
and his sense of justice, however, receive more emphasis in the final
tales and are less dependent on the source accounts than they were in
the earlier tales.

One of Arthur's traits that becomes most prominent in the final tales
is love for his men, especially for Lancelot and Gawain. Mrs. Pochoda
feels that Arthur, in demonstrating such love, is subject to "personal
emotional ties" and is therefore unkingly.[76] But as theorists like
Aegidius Romanus and Gower noted, a ruler interested in the *bonum
commune* valued the knights who protected his realm. Such appreciation
enhances, rather than detracts from, Arthur's role as king; and this appreciation is nowhere so prominent as it is in Tales 6, 7, and 8. Arthur's
love for his men is not of nearly so much importance in the early tales:
1 is primarily concerned with the establishment of Arthur's kingdom
and the miscellaneous early adventures of his knights; 2, with Arthur's
conquest of Europe. The theme of the king's love for and loyalty to his
men becomes, however, of major importance in those tales that tell of
the deterioration and destruction of the realm.

Although Malory found in his sources instances of this love, in the
final tales he adds to these to give the reader an overwhelming impression of the bond between Arthur and his knights. The importance
of Arthur's relationship with his men appears emphatically at the beginning of 6 when the knights depart for the Grail Quest. Malory follows

---

75 *Works*, p. 157; in this case Arthur is more cautious in the source because he fears Morgan's
magic. See Huth, 2.250; also in a fragment, *Die Abenteuer Gawains, Ywains, und le Morhalts mit den drei
Jungfrauen (MS. B.N. fr. 112)*, ed. H. Oskar Sommer, Beihefte zur *Zeitschrift für romanische Philologie* 47
(Halle, 1913), p. 16; not in *Camb.* or *Baladro*.

76 *Arthurian Propaganda*, p. 107.

his source in having Arthur mourn the departure of the "trewyst of knyghthode that ever was sene togydir" and in having his king say, "I have loved them as well as my lyff";[77] when the knights leave, however, Malory adds to his account, "the kynge turned away and myght nat speke for wepyng" (p. 872). In 7 Malory, without source authority, has Arthur tell Gareth how to be a good knight: "ever hit ys ... a worshypful knyghtes dede to help and succoure another worshypfull knyght whan he seeth hym in daungere. ... and he that ys of no worshyp and medelyth with cowardise never shall he shew jantilnes nor no maner of goodnes where he seeth a man in daungere, for than woll a cowarde never shew mercy" (p. 1114). In Malory's final tale Arthur's comments show his concern for his men: "I am sure the noble felyship of the Rounde Table ys brokyn for evei" (p. 1174; no source); "Alas, that ever I bare crowne uppon my hede! For now have I loste the fayryst felyshyp of noble knyghtes that ever hylde Crysten kynge togydirs."[78]

Arthur's concern for his men and for the *bonum commune* is especially shown in Tales 7 and 8 by his love for Lancelot and his appreciation of Lancelot's service to the realm. Malory, to be sure, found some references to Arthur's love for Lancelot in the sources of the final tales, and he usually incorporates these instances into his account.[79] Malory, however, makes Arthur's love for Lancelot more pronounced than it is in the sources and also deletes references to Arthur's jealousy over the queen's relationship with Lancelot. The author of *Mort Artu* gives the affair much more emphasis than Malory does. In the beginning of this French romance, Agravaine warns Arthur of the adultery, but Arthur does not want to believe it: "Car ge sei bien veraiement que Lancelos nel penseroit en nule maniere" (p. 5); his fears are dispelled when Lancelot shows up at the tournament at Winchester instead of staying with the queen at Camelot as Arthur had suspected: "ge sei or bien que se Lancelos amast le reïne por amors, il ne se fust pas remuez de Kamaalot";[80] later, however, Morgan le Fay warns Arthur of the affair,

77 *Works*, pp. 866-8; similarly, *La queste del Saint Graal*, ed. Albert Pauphilet (Paris, 1923), pp. 16-25.

78 *Works*, p. 1183; similarly, *La mort le Roi Artu: roman du XIIIe siècle*, ed. Jean Frappier, 3rd ed. (Paris, 1964), p. 133; *Le Morte Arthur: A Romance in Stanzas of Eight Lines*, ed. J. Douglas Bruce, E.E.T.S., E.S. No. 88 (London, 1959), ll. 1968-77. These two works — the French prose *Mort Artu* and the English stanzaic *Morte Arthur* — are the sources for Malory's Tales 7 and 8.

79 *Cf. Works*, p. 1051 and stanzaic *Morte*, ll. 818-20; *Works*, p. 1092 and stanzaic *Morte*, l. 711; *Works*, pp. 1200, 1216 and stanzaic *Morte*, l. 2437, *Mort Artu*, p. 191.

80 *Mort Artu*, p. 29; Malory's allusions to the adultery in the tournament episodes are less explicit as far as Arthur is concerned; see *Works*, pp. 1065-6.

and he swears that if her warning is true, he will avenge himself "si cruelment qu'il en seroit a touz jorz mes parlé" (p. 65). Malory omits these early allusions to the adultery, and when he does tell of Arthur's reaction to it, his account is far different from that of the French source: in the French account, for example, when Arthur hears his knights discussing the affair, he threatens to kill Agravaine if he does not tell him the truth, and then threatens vengeance if Lancelot and Guenevere are taken together: "se ge n'en praing venchement tel com l'en doit fere de traïteur, ge ne quier jamés porter coronne" (p. 110); he then says that it would be better for Lancelot to die than for his shame to go unavenged (p. 111); from this point, in spite of a few references to Arthur's affection for Lancelot, the king is motivated largely by the desire to get vengeance on Lancelot and Guenevere or by his desire to win the queen again.

In Malory, on the other hand, when Arthur hears his knights discussing the affair, he simply asks "what noyse they made" and Agravaine willingly tells him. As in the source, Arthur wants proof of the affair, but Malory adds, without source authority, a statement about Arthur's love for Lancelot: "the kynge was full lothe that such a noyse shulde be uppon sir Launcelot and his quene; for the kynge had a demyng of hit, but he wold nat here thereoff, for sir Launcelot had done so much for hym and for the quene so many times that ... the kynge loved hym passyngly well" (p. 1163). In the events that follow, Malory plays down instances of Arthur's animosity. Although Lancelot feels that Arthur is his foe and says that Arthur has shown "hete" [anger] toward the queen (pp. 1171-7, 1188), Arthur's actions show, on the whole, love for Lancelot. When Arthur is told that Lancelot and Guenevere have been found together, he expresses regret that "sir Launcelot sholde be ayenste me" (p. 1174; no source); later he wants to take the queen back "to have bene accorded with sir Launcelot"; in the sources, on the other hand, Arthur is willing to make peace because of his love for Guenevere.[81] At one point Malory does follow his source in having Arthur show personal animosity toward Lancelot: during a battle after war has broken out between the king and Lancelot, "ever was kynge Arthur aboute sir Launcelot to have slayne hym, and ever sir Launcelot suffird hym and wolde nat stryke agayne". Lancelot, however, rescues Arthur and says in a speech original with Malory: "I pray yow remember what I have done in many placis, and now am I

<hr />

81 *Works*, p. 1190; similarly p. 1194; *cf. Mort Artu*, p. 153; stanzaic *Morte Arthur*, ll. 2272-3.

evyll rewarded." Arthur then "loked on sir Launcelot" and "the teerys braste oute of hys yen, thynkyng of the grete curtesy that was in sir Launcelot more than in ony other man."[82] Malory follows his source here in presenting an Arthur whose momentary vengefulness is replaced by affection for Lancelot and sorrow over the dissension between them. Arthur shows kingly appreciation for a knight who has been of great value to his realm.

Malory also places more emphasis upon Arthur's concern for his men and the *bonum commune* by deleting allusions in the sources that show Arthur's love for the queen. Although Malory's Tale 1 shows Arthur as a loving husband, Tales 2-8, particularly 7 and 8, present Arthur as a king who has more love for his knights than for his wife and who is more concerned with his role as monarch than his role as husband.[83] In 7 when Guenevere is falsely accused of killing one of Arthur's knights in the poisoned apple episode, both of Malory's sources place considerable emphasis upon Arthur's love for the queen and upon his emotional involvement in the case.[84] Malory, however, omits these allusions and instead presents in 7 a king who, though convinced that his wife has been unfairly accused, wishes to be a "ryghtfull juge" (p. 1050). The political theorists would have approved of Arthur's impartiality and concern with justice. Malory also omits references to Arthur's emotion when Guenevere is to be burnt at the stake, an affectionate parting scene between husband and wife when Arthur leaves to fight Lancelot, and references to the queen's fear of Arthur's jealousy (*Mort Artu*, pp. 122, 167, 217). Malory in fact presents an Arthur who clearly prefers his knights to his queen: "And much more I am soryar for my good knyghtes losse than for the losse of my fayre queen; for quenys I myght have inow, but such a felyship of good knyghtes shall never be togydirs in no company" (p. 1184). Mrs. Pochoda, in interpreting Arthur as a king dominated by personal ties, says nothing about Malory's treatment of the Arthur-Guenevere relationship; but the changes that Malory makes in this relationship indicate that he was cutting down Arthur's personal role as husband in order to build up his public role as king.

Although the Arthur of Malory's sources regrets the war that breaks

---

82 *Works*, p. 1192; *cf.* "ore a il passez de bonté et de cortoisie touz les chevaliers que ge onques veisse" — *Mort Artu*, p. 152; similarly, stanzaic *Morte*, ll. 2170-2205.

83 For a detailed discussion of the problem see my "The Arthur-Guenevere Relationship in Malory's *Morte Darthur*," *Studies in the Literary Imagination* 4 (1971) 29-40. The material in this paragraph is taken from that article.

84 See *Mort Artu*, p. 101; stanzaic *Morte*, ll. 957, 1521, 1544-5.

out between him and Lancelot,[85] he is often quite vengeful toward the
queen and her lover. The political theorists who inveighed against
rulers' using their positions of power to gratify personal enmity would
have had ample reason to criticize him. Malory, however, deletes
references in his sources to Arthur's vengeance toward Lancelot and
Guenevere and instead shifts more of the blame for the war in 8 to his
nephew Gawain's vindictiveness. Malory found in his sources instances
of Gawain's hatred for Lancelot and desire for vengeance because
Lancelot had accidentally killed his brothers; but he further emphasizes
both Gawain's hatred and his ability to influence Arthur. When, for
example, Arthur hears of Gareth's death, he says, "I am sure that whan
sir Gawayne knowyth hereoff that sir Gareth ys slayne, I shall never
have reste of hym tyll I have destroyed sir Launcelottys kynne and hym-
selffe bothe, othir ellis he to destroy me" (p. 1183). The hint for this in
Malory's source was "Lette no man telle Syr gawayne/ Gaheriet hys
brother is dede hym fro" (stanzaic MA, ll. 1978-9). Malory's Arthur
suggests that he and Gawain get revenge for the death of Gaheris and
Gareth, but the suggestion is much milder in Malory than in the source.
In Malory's account, Arthur tells Gawain, "Launcelot slew them in the
thyk prees and knew tham nat. And therefore lat us shape a remedy for
to revenge their dethys" (p. 1185). Gawain then tells Arthur:

> ... frome thys day forewarde I shall never fayle sir Launcelot untyll that
> one of us have slayne that othir. ... I requyre you, my lorde ... dresse you
> unto the warres, for ... I woll be revenged uppon sir Launcelot; ... I shall
> sle hym, other ellis he shall sle me (p. 1186).

There is no basis for this scene in the English stanzaic Morte Arthur; in the
French prose romance, Gawain says nothing at this point and Arthur is
the one who eagerly seeks revenge: "Ceste perte [of men] ... m'est ...
avenue ... par l'orgueill Lancelot ... ele nos est avenue par celui [Lance-
lot] que nos avons eslevé et escreü en nostre terre par meintes fois,
ausint come s'il fust estrez de nostre char meïsmes. ... Et vos estes tuit mi
home ... por quoi ge vos requier ... que vos me conseilliez ... en tel
maniere que ma honte soit vengiee" (pp. 133-4).

In a number of other instances Malory tones down Arthur's vengefulness as it appears in the sources, particularly the French prose
romance, and gives Gawain the major responsibility for the war against
Lancelot. In Mort Artu Arthur wants to go to war against Lancelot to
avenge his honor (p. 163); Malory omits this sentiment. At one point in

---

85 See, for example, Mort Artu, p. 195; stanzaic Morte, ll. 2205, 2394-5.

Mort Artu both Arthur and Gawain reject Lancelot's offer for peace (p. 142); Malory, however, follows the stanzaic *Morte Arthur* (ll. 2668 ff.) and has Gawain reject the offer (p. 1190). On a later occasion, before Lancelot is exiled, he reminds Arthur and Gawain of his service in "dyverce placis" (p. 1198; *Mort Artu*, p. 161); and in a speech largely original with Malory, he complains, "truly me repentis that ever I cam in thys realme, that I shulde be thus shamefully banysshyd, undeserved and causeles! ... in thys realme I had worshyp, and be me and myne all the hole Rounde Table hath bene encreced more in worshyp ... than ever hit was by ony of you all."[86] Malory modifies the source account of Arthur's role in sentencing Lancelot on this occasion. In *Mort Artu*, Arthur himself tells Lancelot: "Puis que Gauvains de velt ... il me plest bien. Laissiés ma terre par deça la mer et alés en la vostre par dela" (p. 158); he then threatens Lancelot with a great war: "bien fust Lancelos asseür que ja si tost ne seroit en son païs qu'il troveroit la guerre greignour qu'il ne porroit quidier" (p. 159). Malory has Gawain, not Arthur, do the talking: "in this londe thou shalt nat abyde paste fiftene dayes ... for so the kynge and we were ... accorded ar thou cam" (pp. 1200-1); and Malory's Arthur, by saying nothing, seems more appreciative than the king in *Mort Artu* of Lancelot's past deeds for the realm. In both Malory and the sources, Gawain pushes Arthur to resume the war against Lancelot, but in the French account Arthur promises Gawain that he will strike the lands of Lancelot so severely that not one stone will be left standing on another (pp. 165-6); this promise does not appear in Malory. Similarly, in the English poem Arthur eagerly prepares to attack Lancelot's lands "to brenne and sle and make all bare" (l. 2507); but such enthusiasm does not appear in Malory's account.

Malory incorporates instances from the sources which show Gawain's influence upon Arthur and he also adds some of his own. The narrator notes, "in no wyse he [Gawain] wolde suffir the kynge to accorde with sir Launcelot"[87] and Lancelot tells Gawain, "Ye wolde [cause] my noble lorde kynge Arthur for ever to be my mortall foo."[88] Several other comments that cannot be traced to the sources further show Gawain's responsibility for the war: Lancelot tells Gawain: "ye ... ar so

---

86 *Works*, p. 1201; *cf.* "Por moi le di ge qui esprové l'ai, car autant come g'i demorai m'i avint il toute boneürté plus abandoneement que ele ne feïst se je fuisse en une autre terre"— *Mort Artu*, p. 163.

87 *Works*, p. 1194; cf. stanzaic *Morte*, ll. 2274-7.

88 *Works*, p. 1199; *cf. Mort Artu*, p. 165.

myschevously sett. And if ye were nat, I wolde nat doute to have the good grace of my lorde kynge Arthure" (p. 1189); the narrator notes that Arthur would have made friends with Lancelot, but "sir Gawayne wolde nat suffir hym by no maner of meane" (p. 1190); Lancelot's knights warn him: "sir Gawayne woll nevir suffir you to accorde with kynge Arthur" (p. 1191); and sir Lucan says, "Alas ... my lorde Arthure wolde accorde with sir Lancelot, but sir Gawayne woll nat suffir hym" (p. 1213). Additions such as these emphasize Gawain's role in the war and also change Arthur into a king considerably different from the one who appears in the French source; while in *Mort Artu* the love affair is Arthur's chief motivation, in Malory's version Arthur's reason for beginning the war and persisting in it is clearly his loyalty to his nephew Gawain; the love affair itself is unimportant.

Malory emphasizes not only Gawain's influence upon Arthur in pursuing the war with Lancelot, but also Arthur's love for his nephew Gawain, a love that has greater importance in Malory's account than it does in the sources. Robert H. Wilson has pointed out that Malory's changes in the sources indicate that he wished to show an especially close relationship between Gawain and Arthur.[89] Although the sources suggest Arthur's affection for Gawain,[90] Malory adds to these references in Tales 7 and 8.[91] At the tournament at Winchester in 7, for example, "the kynge wold nat suffir sir Gawayne to go frome hym, for never had

---

89 *Characterization in Malory: A Comparison with His Sources* (Chicago, 1934), pp. 106-9.

90 See *Mort Artu*, pp. 13, 212, 221; stanzaic *Morte*, ll. 3132-5.

91 Wilson cites other examples from 1 and 5 that supposedly show Arthur's favoritism and indicate that Malory had this close relationship in mind from the beginning of the book (*Characterization*, pp. 106-7). None of these instances in the early tales, however, offers convincing evidence that in the early tales Arthur's love for Gawain is stronger than it is for any of the other knights. The first example Wilson cites from Tale 1 (*Works*, p. 99) demonstrates not love but the power of blood ties and will be discussed later. In the second, Gawain is set free by a lady who says, "I shall so speke for you that ye shall have <leve> to go unto kynge Arthure for hys love" (*Works*, p. 108); in the third, the narrator says, "Pelleas loved never aftir sir Gawayne but as he spared hym for the love of the kynge" (*Works*, pp. 179-80). Neither of these passages shows Arthur's special love for his nephew. In the first instance in 5, Lamarok tries to prevent Gawain from stealing a knight's lady, and Gawain says, "What woll ye do with me? I am nevew unto kynge Arthure" (*Works*, p. 449); this is another example of the power of blood ties, not of love, and it is spoken by Gawain, not Arthur. In the second instance in 5, Lancelot predicts that Gawain and his brother will kill Lamarok and Arthur says, "That shall I lette [prevent]" (*Works*, p. 613); but Arthur does nothing to punish Gawain and his brothers when they kill Lamarok. In not having Arthur punish his nephews, however, Malory was simply following his source, the prose *Tristan*. In the third and fourth instances, Lamarok says that he would have got vengeance on Gawain if it were not for his respect for Arthur (*Works*, pp. 664, 670); these last instances tell us about Lamarok's respect for the blood ties between Arthur and Gawain, but nothing about Arthur's love for his nephew.

sir Gawayne the bettir and sir Launcelot were in the fylde" (p. 1069); in the source Arthur's concern is not only for Gawain but for Gawain's brother Gaheriez too: "Mes messire Gauvains ne porta pas icelui jor armes ne Gaheriez ses freres, einz leur avoit li rois desfendu, por ce qu'il savoit bien que Lancelos i vendroit; si ne vouloit pas que il s'entreblefassent, se au jouster venist, car il ne volsist mie que mellee sorsist entr'eus ne mautalenz" (p. 13). Later when Gawain realizes that Lancelot had been fighting in the tournament, Arthur says, "All that knew I aforehande ... and that caused me I wolde nat suffir you to have ado at the grete justis" (p. 1080; no source). In 8 Arthur's love for Gawain becomes all the more striking when he yields to his nephew's desire for a war of vengeance against Lancelot. A notable instance of the king's partiality for Gawain after the war has begun occurs when Gawain challenges Lancelot to single combat. Malory found in his sources an account of Gawain's miraculous strength which increased until noon (*Mort Artu*, pp. 197-8; stanzaic *Morte*, ll. 2802 ff.); but he uses the information to emphasize Arthur's love for Gawain:

> Than had sir Gawayne suche a grace and gyffte ... that every day ... frome undern tyll hyghe noone, hys myght increased tho three owres as much as thryse hys strength. ... And for hys sake kynge Arthur made an ordynaunce that all maner off batayles for ony quarels that shulde be done afore kynge Arthur shulde begynne at undern; and all was done for sir Gawaynes love, that by lyklyhode if sir Gawayne were on tone parté, he shulde have the bettir in batayle whyle hys strengthe endured three owrys. But there were that tyme but feaw knyghtes lyvynge that knewe thys advauntayge that sir Gawayne had, but kynge Arthure all only (pp. 1216-17).

The reference to the "ordynaunce" made for Gawain's sake does not appear in the sources. Malory wished to show that Arthur's love for Gawain could lead him to give his nephew an advantage over other knights.

As indicated above, Malory did not in 1 and 2 make Arthur a perfect king, but most of the character flaws in these tales are the result of Malory's following his sources. In 7 and 8 two apparent weaknesses in Arthur's character seem to detract from his effectiveness as king: first, his favoritism to Gawain and his inability to resist Gawain's desire for vengeance and second, his condemnation of Guenevere without permitting trial by combat. Mrs. Pochoda emphasizes these points because to her they indicate that Malory was presenting Arthur as a king dominated by private will instead of concern for the common good.[92] A

92 Pochoda, pp. 134-6.

careful examination of Malory's text and sources, however, suggests that Malory probably had a quite different objective. These "weaknesses" differ from those of the early tales, for they do not result from Malory's repeating information he found in his source; instead, they result from Malory's deliberate attempt to change the portrait of Arthur that he found in his sources for the final tales and particularly to make Arthur less tyrannical than the Arthur of *Mort Artu*.

In discussing Arthur's relationship with Gawain, Mrs. Pochoda notes that Malory's Arthur cannot "stand apart from his personal ties" and he shows "unreasoned acquiescence to Gawain's influence".[93] There are, however, factors in the Arthur-Gawain relationship that Mrs. Pochoda overlooks. In waging the war against Lancelot Arthur is admittedly dominated by Gawain, and although he is unhappy about the war, he reluctantly fights Lancelot to satisfy his nephew. Gawain represents the type of advisor medieval rulers were warned against, the type who lacked prudence and was too emotionally involved to counsel wisely.[94] The reason that Malory chose to have the noble King Arthur influenced so strongly by Gawain is found partly in Malory's sources. Malory found in both his French and English sources the account of the destruction of the realm, a destruction that results partially from the wrath of Gawain and partially from the king's desire for vengeance. He wanted to retell the story of the fall of the Round Table and the changes he could make in this account were limited.[95] Malory apparently did not wish to present Arthur as the vengeful king he found in his chief source, the French *Mort Artu*; he consequently changed the character of Arthur and shifted most of the vengeance to Gawain. This change makes Gawain more directly responsible than Arthur for the destruction of the realm and removes from the king the fault of vengefulness. Yet in departing from his sources in this way Malory presents an Arthur who seems at times to be a weakling controlled by his wrathful nephew. Although Malory makes Arthur's deference to Gawain understandable by emphasizing the king's love for him in the final tales, Arthur's lack of independence surely seems to modern readers a flaw in his character. Malory, however, would probably not have considered Arthur's deference to his nephew as serious a flaw as

93 Pochoda, p. 136.
94 See, for example, Perrault, 4.ii, p. 423; John of Salisbury, V.vi, 1.300; Tournai, p. 58.
95 As Brewer notes, a medieval writer who based his narrative upon a source might "change the quality of personality of a given character ... or the interpretation of an event", but he could "hardly change a principal event completely" (*The Morte Darthur: Parts Seven and Eight* (London, 1968), p. 3).

the vengeance he found in his French source, for to Malory and his audience familial relationships were very important.

Malory emphasizes the importance of blood ties a number of times throughout *Morte Darthur*. In 1, for example, Malory adds a reference to the blood relationship between Arthur and Gawain: Arthur says he will make Gawain a knight because he is his "sistirs son", while in the source only the narrator mentions that Gawain is Arthur's nephew and the king himself says nothing (*Works*, p. 99; Huth, 2. 68-9). As noted earlier, the stories of Mark and of the King of the Red City in 5 clearly show that a good ruler "cheryshed his owne bloode." In 8 when Lancelot becomes ruler of France and distributes lands to his men, "firste he avaunced them off hys blood" (p. 1205; not in source); and Arthur appoints Mordred regent "bycause sir Mordred was kynge Arthurs son."[96] Similar respect for kinship would account for Arthur's loyalty to Gawain and alliance with him against Lancelot.

A. L. Morton has drawn parallels between the feuds of the "kindred and faction of Gawain and the kindred and faction of Lancelot" and the feuds of the Wars of the Roses. Gawain, Morton notes, represents "the ancient loyalty of the blood bond"; Lancelot, the "new loyalty of vassal for a lord", a loyalty that must give way when it conflicts with the blood bond.[97] Morton's point is well-taken; and the parallel between the "ancient loyalty of the blood bond" stressed by Malory and the ties of kinship adhered to during the Yorkist-Lancastrian disputes should be emphasized. Arthur's partiality toward Gawain would have been more sympathetically regarded in an age that understood the force of such ties. Although the Wars of the Roses would have shown Malory that allegiance to one's kin could have regrettable consequences, such allegiance was nonetheless a powerful fact of life. Loyalty to bonds of kinship was a part of the king's obligation, and ignoring them, as the King of the Red City did, could be a very serious offence. Edward IV, who was ruling when Malory wrote *Morte Darthur*, ignored blood bonds and civil strife resulted.[98]

Malory's Arthur finds himself in a dilemma in which he must choose between his two favorite knights, the one a nephew and the other the

---

96 *Works*, p. 1211; in stanzaic *Morte*, the barons, not Arthur, choose Mordred because they think he is the best man to rule the realm (ll. 2516 ff.); in *Mort Artu* Mordred volunteers to guard the queen, and Arthur lets him, but the fact that he is Arthur's son is not mentioned (p. 166).

97 Morton, "The Matter of Britain: The Arthurian Cycle and the Development of Feudal Society," *Zeitschrift für Anglistik und Amerikanistik* 8 (1960) 191.

98 See my "Malory and the Marriage of Edward IV," cited n. 15 above.

champion of the realm. This dilemma is implicit in Malory's sources, but its significance was diminished there by Arthur's great concern for the queen. In Malory, however, the enmity between Lancelot and Gawain, not the liaison between Lancelot and Guenevere, presents the difficulty for Arthur. Although the king decides to honor the blood bond, his choice is not an easy one since he loves both men. His affection for them is most dramatically illustrated by his lament as Gawain is dying:

> Here now thou lyghest, the man in the worlde that I loved moste. And now ys my joy gone! ... my nevew, sir Gawayne, ... in youre person and in sir Launcelot I moste had my joy and myne affyaunce. And how have I loste my joy of you bothe, wherefore all myne erthely joy ys gone fro me! (p. 1230)

These lines are based upon a passage in the French *Mort Artu*, but there Lancelot is given less emphasis.[99] Malory's version emphasizes Arthur's dilemma, a dilemma that Malory's audience would have been able to understand.

Although Arthur's decision to honor his blood bond with Gawain and with Mordred leads ultimately to Mordred's rebellion and the downfall of the kingdom, the decision is not presented as an irresponsible one, and the readers are clearly intended to sympathize with Arthur's predicament. This is indicated by the narrator's denunciation of the rebellion against Arthur and the fickleness of the English people:

> Lo ye all Englysshemen, se ye nat what a myschyff here was? For he that was the moste kynge and nobelyst knyght of the worlde, and moste loved the felyshyp of noble knyghtes, and by hym they all were upholdyn, and yet myght nat thes Englyshemen holde them content with hym ... And the moste party of all Inglonde hylde wyth sir Mordred, for the people were so new-fangill (p. 1229).

By Arthur, "the moste kynge and nobelyst knyght of the worlde", they "all were upholdyn", and they had no right to rebel against him.

Arthur's other apparent weakness occurs in 8. When Lancelot and Guenevere are found together, Lancelot escapes after killing thirteen of Arthur's knights and wounding Mordred. Guenevere, however, is captured and is to be sentenced by Arthur. The scene is largely Malory's invention, and it occurs before Gawain's brothers have been killed and before Gawain turns against Lancelot. Gawain, in fact, defends the

99 In *Mort Artu* Arthur tells Gawain: "Biax niés, grant domage m'a fet vostre felonnie, car ele m'a tolu vos, que ge amoie seur touz homes, et Lancelot après" (p. 212).

lovers in this case and says that Lancelot would fight for the queen in trial by combat: "peradventure she sente for hym for goodnes or for none evyll ... For I dare sey ... my Lady ... ys to you both good and trew. And as for sir Launcelot, I dare say he woll make hit good uppon ony knyght lyvyng that woll put uppon hym vylany or shame." Arthur replies, "That I believe well ... but I woll nat that way worke with sir Launcelot, for he trustyth so much uppon hys hondis and hys myght that he doutyth no man. And therefor for my quene he shall nevermore fyght, for she shall have the law. And if I may gete sir Lancelot ... he shall have as shameful a death" (p. 1175). According to Mrs. Pochoda, Arthur is here acting "not as king and judge but as a personal lord seeking revenge."[100] Arthur, one must admit, seems to be denying Guenevere her right to trial by combat and the passage thus seems somewhat inconsistent with two earlier occasions when Arthur as a "ryghtfull juge" (p. 1050) permitted such trials.[101] Medieval readers tolerated some inconsistencies within works of literature;[102] and in the source accounts of this scene trial by combat is not even mentioned although it had been used twice before. But this omission probably troubled Malory since he was careful to mention it at this time and justify Arthur for not using it.

The scene that Malory found in his sources presents a picture of Arthur that would have been quite unpalatable to him and which he would have felt a need to change. Mrs. Pochoda claims that in the source "Guenevere's death sentence is the baron's [sic] decision" and that Malory "assigns the responsibility for the whole episode to Arthur."[103] In fact, however, in the stanzaic *Morte Arthur* both the king and his knights take "there counselle" and decide to burn the queen (ll. 1920 ff.); in *Mort Artu* Arthur vindictively orders his barons to condemn the queen to death.[104] But in trying to ameliorate the picture of Arthur that he found in the sources, Malory still had to retain the essential features of the downfall of Arthur's kingdom. One might argue that if Malory wished to present a just king, he would have had Arthur give

100 Pochoda, p. 134.
101 The earlier occasions in which Guenevere is permitted trial by combat are in the "Poisoned Apple" and the "Knight of the Cart" episodes of 7; Malory found these trials in his sources.
102 See Brewer, *Morte*, pp. 4, 22-3; Elizabeth Salter, "'Troilus and Criseyde': A Reconsideration" in *Patterns of Love and Courtesy: Essays in Memory of C. S. Lewis*, ed. John Lawlor (London, 1966), pp. 90-1.
103 Pochoda, p. 134.
104 In the French source Arthur "se vengera de la reïne en tel maniere qu'il en sera parlé a toz jorz mes" (p. 120). Although the barons formally pass the sentence, Arthur does not give them much choice: "ge vos commant ... que vos esgardoiz entre vos de quel mort ele doit morir" (p. 120).

Guenevere a chance to escape, as he had on earlier occasions, by means of trial by combat. Here, however, Malory was bound by his source, for Lancelot's attempt to rescue the queen from the flames, the ensuing combat, Lancelot's accidental slaying of Gawain's brothers Gaherys and Gareth, and the subsequent downfall of the realm are all dependent upon the consequences of the condemnation of Guenevere. If Malory's Arthur had permitted trial by combat, Malory would have had two alternatives: either his hero Lancelot would have suffered defeat or Guenevere would have been proclaimed innocent and the whole course of the romance would have been changed. Since neither of these alternatives would have been acceptable to Malory, he could not include trial by combat at this point.

To make Arthur seem just, however, Malory gives him ample reason for not offering trial by combat. First, Arthur refuses to let Lancelot fight for the queen because "he trustyth so much uppon hys hondis and hys myght." Though inconsistent with Arthur's procedure in the earlier trials, this would probably have seemed reasonable enough to Malory's readers since there was great distrust of trial by combat in England in the later Middle Ages,[105] and this distrust is reflected elsewhere in *Morte Darthur*.[106] Second, Malory without source authority gives Arthur legal justification for the sentencing of Guenevere without trial by combat:

> So than there was made grete ordynaunce in thys ire, and the quene must nedis be jouged to the deth. And the law was such in tho dayes that whatsomever they were, of what astate or degré, if they were founden gylty of treson there shuld be none other remedy but deth, and othir the menour other the takynge wyth the dede shulde be causer of their hasty jougement. And ryght so was hit ordayned for quene Gwenyver: bycause sir Mordred was ascaped sore wounded, and the dethe of thirtene knyghtes of the Rounde Table, thes previs and experyenses caused kynge Arthure to commaunde the quene to the fyre and there to be brente (p. 1174).

---

105 See George Neilson, *Trial by Combat* (New York, 1891), pp. 147 ff.

106 At one point, for example, King Mark, though guilty of murder, wins the contest: "kynge Marke smote sir Amante thorow the body; and yet was sir Amaunte in the ryghtuous quarell"; no one believes that Mark is innocent and two maidens say, "A, swete Jesu ... Why sufferyst Thou so false a traytoure to venqueyshe ... a trewe knyght that faught in a ryghteuous quarell" (pp. 592-3; similarly in the source: *cf*. MS. 334, fol. 319 and Löseth, p. 163). Skepticism about this type of combat is also suggested by the narrator's statement "worshyp in armys may never be foyled. But firste reserve the honoure to God and secundly thy quarell muste com of thy lady" (p. 1119) and by statements such as Lancelot's: "never was I discomfite in no quarell, were hit ryght were hit wronge" (p. 896; similarly, pp. 897, 1052, 1058, 1166). Ernest C. York discussed some of the instances of trial by combat in "The Judicial Battle in *The Works of Sir Thomas Malory*," a paper read at the 1967 MLA meeting in New York and in "The Duel of Chivalry in Malory's Book XIX," *Philological Quarterly* 48 (1969) 186-91.

Arthur thus tells Gawain that the queen "shall have the law."[107] This sentiment is similar to that which the narrator expressed during Guenevere's earlier trial scene during the poisoned apple episode of Tale 7: "for such custom was used in tho dayes: for favoure, love, nothir affinité there sholde be none other but ryghtuous jugemente ... as well uppon a quene as uppon another poure lady" (p. 1055; not in source). These passages reflect the importance of law in medieval England; according to the theorists, the king obeyed the law while the tyrant disregarded it, and subjects of rich and poor were to be judged with equity. Though Mrs. Pochoda, in her discussion of medieval political theory, emphasizes the importance of law, in her condemnation of Arthur as a "personal lord seeking revenge", she ignores the politically significant passage that Malory added to his account of the final trial. Gawain assumes that Arthur could give the queen a chance to escape with trial by combat; but Arthur says nothing about a choice, and it is very doubtful that a medieval audience would have thought that he should have done anything other than what he did since "the law was such in tho dayes." In both the sources and in Malory's account the condemnation of Guenevere initiates the fall of the kingdom; Malory's Arthur, however, condemns her in accordance with the law while the Arthur of the sources is not bound by law and acts in accordance with his own whim. Gawain, when he defends Lancelot in this scene, tells Arthur, "oftyntymys we do many thynges that we wene for the beste be, and yet peradventure hit turnyth to the warste" (p. 1175). His statement is applicable to Arthur as well. In giving Guenevere the judgment prescribed by the law, Arthur takes the initial step that leads to the destruction of his kingdom.

Malory further mitigates Arthur's actions in this scene by minimizing his personal concern for the adultery and by giving him the concern a king should have, concern for the knights Lancelot has killed, the impending war with Lancelot, and the trouble it will cause his realm. When Arthur hears that Lancelot and Guenevere have been found together, he shows the same disregard for the adultery that he shows elsewhere in *Morte Darthur*. He says nothing about the love affair, but in-

107 Brewer mentions that Arthur is later ready to take Guenevere back and forget about the law (*Morte*, p. 30); this, however, is after Lancelot explains two things: 1) that he has slain Arthur's knights only because "I was forced to do batayle with hem in savyng of my lyff" ; and 2) that Guenevere "ys as trew a lady ... as ys ony lady lyvynge unto her lorde" (p. 1188). The second part of Lancelot's explanation is a conventional courtly defense of a lady's honor; the first, however, is worthy of special emphasis since this is the first time that Arthur learns that Lancelot was acting in self defense.

stead says, "me sore repentith that ever sir Launcelot sholde be ayenste me, for now I am sure the noble felyshyp of the Rounde Table ys brokyn for ever." Although Gawain assumes that Arthur is condemning the queen to death because of the adultery, Arthur says nothing about the queen. The "previs and experyenses" that, according to the passage on law, cause Arthur to condemn the queen are the wounding of Mordred and the "dethe of thirtene knyghtes of the Rounde Table." Guenevere is condemned to death because she is guilty of "treson", but "treson" seems to refer to the slaying of the thirteen knights instead of to the love affair.[108]

Thus, since the story that Malory found in his sources would not permit consistent use of trial by combat, Malory endeavors to put Arthur in a better light by noting that the law allowed "none other remedy but deth" in such a case, by showing Arthur's concern for such public problems as the war with Lancelot and the death of his knights, and by having Arthur show no concern for the adultery itself. These changes, like many others in 7 and 8, make Arthur into a better king than he was in the corresponding scenes in the sources.

Arthur's kingdom falls, but this was inherent in the story and was not, as Mrs. Pochoda claims, due to Malory's re-creation of Arthur as an inadequate king. As Vinaver has pointed out, the tragedy results from the conflict of loyalties of many people;[109] although Arthur's decisions to follow the law and to side with Gawain contribute to the fall, the decisions are not irresponsible. There is, however, no reason to believe that the war could have been prevented even if Arthur had not sided with Gawain. The hostility of Agravain and Mordred, Lancelot's fateful killing of the unarmed Gareth and Gaheris, and Gawain's subsequent hatred of Lancelot are matters over which a king, no matter how good or bad, could have little control. The fact that Malory makes Arthur into a better king then he was in the sources makes the destruction of his realm all the more regrettable.

108 Malory defines treason in different ways. At times it is indeed adultery: when Mellyagaunt believes Guenevere has been sleeping with a knight, he says: "I calle you of tresoun afore my lorde kynge Arthure" (p. 1132). At other times, however, it is murder: "All maner of murthers in tho dayes were called treson" (p. 405); "at that tyme ... all manner of [s]hamefull deth was called treson" (p. 1050).

109 Vinaver, Works, 1.xcv ff. and The Rise of Romance (Oxford, 1971), pp. 172 ff.

V

Malory's handling of the portrait of Mark that he found in the source of Tale 5 is, then, strikingly different from his handling of the portrait of Arthur that he found in the sources of Tales 7 and 8. Malory's Mark is essentially the same as he was in the source, a vengeful and jealous tyrant. The "blackening" of Mark that critics have emphasized amounts to only a few additions; Mark's villainy, including his hatred for Tristram and his jealous concern for Isode, is well developed in the source. Arthur, on the other hand, is in 7 and 8 far different from the king of the French *Mort Artu* and considerably different from the king of the stanzaic *Morte Arthur*; although *Mort Artu* was the primary source for his final tales, Malory presented the milder king of the English stanzaic poem, or more often, made changes of his own. Most signs of Arthur's jealousy and sentimental love for the queen are gone; most instances of the king's vindictiveness toward Lancelot have been transferred to Gawain. Malory's Arthur has less affection for the queen and greater affection for his knights, particularly for Gawain and Lancelot.

Arthur, like Mark, loses his wife and the best knight of his kingdom and must face a civil war, but while Mark is a tyrant, Arthur usually lives up to the medieval conception of a good king. Mark heads the court at Cornwall where the "false knyghtes" are "naught worth" and are "no men of worshyp as other knyghtes ar."[110] Arthur, on the other hand, heads the court of the "moste nobelest knyghtes of the worlde" (p. 1252). Mark is often reviled as a "murtherer", a "traytour", and "the falsyst knyght and kynge of the worlde."[111] Arthur is "the moste man of worshyp crystynde" (p. 1147), the "nobelyst knyght of the worlde" (p. 1229), and the "noble kynge" (p. 1237) whose "grete goodnes" made the pope want to end the war between him and Lancelot (p. 1194). In ruling, Mark is a slave to wrath, pride, and jealousy; Arthur rules in accordance with the law. While Mark is a liar, Arthur is known for keeping his word. Mark's chief concern is his wife and her lover; Arthur's is the welfare of the knights who are necessary to his realm. Mark is an enemy to all good knights and lives in fear and

---

110   *Works*, pp. 547, 581; similarly, pp. 398, 404, 504. References to the worthlessness of the Cornish knights also appear in the prose *Tristan*.

111   *Works*, pp. 583, 633, 592; *cf.* MS. B.N. Fr. 334, fol. 318ra: "le roy dolenz, le roy cheitis, le plus mescheant de touz les rois." Comments about the wickedness of Mark and the goodness of Arthur could have been suggested by the sources.

suspicion that someone will win more honor than he; Arthur loves his men and respects them for their service to the realm.

Since Mark's traits are derived from the source and Arthur's are to a much greater extent the result of Malory's changes in the sources, it seems likely that the differences between Arthur and Mark are partially the result of Malory's deliberate attempt to set one king off against the other. Some of Malory's additions to Tale 5 indicate that when he was writing this tale he realized that the story of Mark provided material for an excellent contrast with Arthur. Mark's statement that he cannot love Tristram "because he lovyth my quene", Lamarok's condemnation of Mark for chasing Tristram out of the realm for "jeleousnes", and Mark's failure to respect his blood ties with Tristram and Bodwine all suggest that Malory wished to emphasize Mark's contrast with the concept of Arthur as a good king that he was developing. Malory, moreover, adds to Tale 5 a statement that explicitly differentiates the two courts: Lamarok says that he had "lever stryff and debate felle in kyng Markys courte rether than in kynge Arthurs courte, for the honour of bothe courtes be nat lyke" (p. 443). Thus, although the major changes in Arthur do not occur until the final tales, these additions suggest that Malory, while writing his fifth tale, was looking ahead to the final ones.

The references in both Tales 7 and 8 to the murder of Tristram offer further evidence that Malory intentionally planned to have Mark contrast with Arthur. Although critics have suggested reasons for Malory's waiting until the final tales to give his most detailed accounts of Tristram's murder, they have concentrated upon the death of Tristram[112] and have ignored Mark's role. The reference to the murder in Tale 7 is important because, besides telling of Tristram's death, it also tells of the murder of Mark, and this provides an implicit contrast with the death of Arthur. Although the prose *Tristan* does not mention Mark's death, Malory's sources dictate Arthur's death in Tale 8; and Malory apparently did not want Arthur to die and Mark to remain alive. In his version both men die, and just as there has been a great dif-

---

112   Rumble and Moorman maintain that the death of Tristram was added to 7 and 8 to remind the readers of the adulterous relationship of Tristram and Isode and thus to show that such affairs were common in the declining days of Arthurian society (Rumble, pp. 146-7; Moorman, pp. 22-4). Malory's text, however, offers little evidence to support this interpretation. A more plausible explanation is implicit in Brewer's remarks on why Malory did not include the murder in Tale 5: the fifth tale is "devoted to the glory and success of the knights of the Round Table", and a tragic ending would have been inappropriate at this point ("hoole book", p. 46). One might add that the incorporation of the story of Tristram's death in the final tales adds to their gloom.

ference in the ways the two kings have lived, there is also a great difference in the ways the two kings meet death. Mark dies in a manner
appropriate for a tyrant: he is murdered by a knight who wants to
avenge the death of Tristram, and no one expresses regret. Arthur, on
the other hand, dies in a manner appropriate for a king: he tries to save
his kingdom and is mourned as "the f[lou]re of kyngis and [knyghtes]"
(p. 1252). Although this contrast between the two kings is implicit, the
one in 8 is explicit. In the description of Tristram's death in 8, Bors contrasts Mark and Arthur as being "never lyke of cond[y]cions" (p. 1173).
The account of the murder of Tristram in both tales shows, in fact, the
great difference in the two kings that is suggested by Bors's remark:
while Mark kills his best knight because he is jealous of his love for his
queen, Arthur wants to take Lancelot back and tries to ignore the
adultery.

These allusions to Mark show that while writing the final tales
Malory had Mark in mind. When this fact is considered along with the
ways in which Malory changed his source accounts of Arthur's character, the contrasts between Arthur and Mark seem to be at least in part
deliberate and Mark seems to have influenced Malory's conception of
Arthur in these final tales.

First, the story of Mark may have influenced Malory's handling of the
Arthur-Guenevere relationship in 7 and 8.[113] The contrast between the
two kings is best summed up in the statements, original with Malory,
that they make about their queens: in 5 Mark says, "I may nat love sir
Trystram, bycause he lovyth my quene, La Beale Isode" (p. 679); in 8
Arthur says, "more I am soryar for my good knyghtes losse than for the
losse of my fayre quene; for quenys I myght have inow, but such a

---

113   Whether Mark might have influenced the Arthur-Guenevere relationship in the earlier
tales is a moot point. The most prominent allusions to Tristram and Mark in 1 are in Malory's
source for this tale, the *Suite du Merlin* and not in the prose *Tristan* (*cf. Works*, pp. 71-3; Huth, 1.
230-2). Although Malory may have known the *Tristan* when he was writing this tale (see Robert
H. Wilson, "Malory's Early Knowledge of Arthurian Romance," *University of Texas Studies in English*
29 (1950) 36-7), there is no evidence in it that Mark influenced Malory's conception of Arthur's attitude toward the queen, for there Malory deliberately makes Arthur a more loving husband.
There also appears to be no influence in 3 or 4. When he was writing 2, however, Malory may have
been influenced by Mark's story; in any event Malory removes signs of Arthur's affection in this tale
(see my "Arthur-Guenevere Relationship," cited n. 83), and he also adds to his account references
to Tristram that are not in the source of 2, the alliterative *Morte Arthure* (see *Works*, pp. 185, 195).
Thus while writing 2, Malory may have seen in Mark's jealous love for Isode a contrast to his conception of the Arthur-Guenevere relationship. Aside from Arthur's indifference to his queen, however, there is little that could point to Mark's influence upon Arthur's character in 2; there are so
few parallels with Mark in this tale that it would be difficult to point to any direct influence of the
prose *Tristan*.

felyship of good knyghtes shall never be togydirs in no company"
(p. 1184). These statements show the difference between the tyrant and
the king; the one lives only for his *bonum privatum*, the other for the
bonum commune. Although the story of Mark's jealous concern for Isode
probably helped shape Malory's contrasting presentation of Arthur's attitude toward Guenevere, it may not be entirely responsible for it. The
story would, in fact, have confirmed what Malory learned from contemporary politics,[114] and while writing Tale 5 he would have found little reason to change what he found in the French *Tristan*. When he was
working on 7 and 8, however, he would have found in his sources signs
of love that would have made Arthur very much like the uxorious Edward IV and signs of jealousy that would have made him very much like
the tyrannous Mark. A desire to avoid both the uxoriousness of the
present Yorkist ruler and the villainy of Mark would have prompted
Malory's changes in Arthur's love for Guenevere as he found it presented in *Mort Artu* and the stanzaic *Morte Arthur*.

   Second, the story of Mark may have influenced Malory's presentation
of Arthur's affection for Gawain and Lancelot in 7 and 8. Throughout
Malory's book, to be sure, Arthur shows affection for his knights, and
such affection might have been inspired both by contemporary political
conditions and by Malory's own concept of the proper relationship between a king and his knights. Malory's emphasis in the final tales,
however, upon Arthur's love for both Gawain, his nephew, and Lancelot, the lover of his wife and champion of his realm, would have been
suggested, not only by his sources, but by Mark's very different attitude
toward Tristram who, like Gawain, is nephew to the king and, like
Lancelot, is lover of the king's wife and champion of the realm. In fact,
Malory's decision to remove the more aggressive, vengeful traits from
the Arthur of the sources and to emphasize instead Arthur's love for
and loyalty to Gawain may have been suggested by Mark's very different treatment of Tristram. Malory must have felt that such love for
his nephew offered motivation for the king's actions that was preferable
to the vengeance displayed by the Arthur of *Mort Artu*, who is too much
like Mark. The ways in which Arthur and Mark treat Lancelot and

---

   114   As I have suggested in another article (see n. 15), Malory's presentation of Arthur's attitude
toward his wife and his emphasis upon the king's love for his knights would probably have been influenced by contemporary indignation over the marriage of Edward IV to Elizabeth Wydville and
Edward's subsequent neglect of his nobility: a Lancastrian like Malory would surely have wished to
avoid presenting a King Arthur who was as uxorious as the Yorkist Edward IV; the rebellion of the
nobility that followed Edward's marriage would have impressed upon Malory an important
political lesson.

Tristram further emphasize the contrast between them. Both knights twice remind their kings of their "trew servyse" to their respective kingdoms, and both knights are banished; but the reactions of the kings are quite different. As indicated earlier, on two occasions Tristram tells of his service to Cornwall and his importance to the realm, but to Mark the affair with Isode is more important and he banishes Tristram for a personal reason, "for jeleousnes of his queen".[115] Lancelot also twice emphasizes the service that he has done for the realm, and Arthur's reaction indicates that he can look beyond the personal injury done to him. On the first occasion, after Lancelot complains that he is "evyll rewarded", Arthur weeps and thinks of the "grete curtesy that was in sir Lancelot"; on the second, Arthur says nothing and Gawain has the vengeful speech that was Arthur's in the source.[116]

Thus, at least by the time he was writing Tale 5, Malory planned to present in *Morte Darthur* two contrasting rulers, one a tyrant, the other a king, the vices of the one set against the virtues of the other; and he may have wished to present the contrast in order to give his book a better structure than it would otherwise have had. In his discussion of *Morte Darthur*, Larry D. Benson has suggested that in the fourth tale, the "Gareth", Malory's chief concern was presenting the theme of the education and vindication of the Fair Unknown, and to illustrate the theme Malory balanced events in the later part of the tale with those of the earlier part.[117] Benson notes that such symmetry might exist in other parts of *Morte Darthur*. I would suggest that Malory could well have been trying to achieve some symmetry between Tale 5 on the one hand and Tales 7 and 8 on the other in order to present more clearly the themes of kingship and tyranny. A desire to balance the events of the final tales with those of Tale 5 may have prompted some of Malory's additions to the final tales in Arthur's relationship with his nephew, his queen, and her lover, his presentation of Lancelot's banishment as a parallel to Tristram's, and the condemnation of the rebellion against Arthur as opposed to the approval of the rebellion against Mark.

Mark's function in *Morte Darthur* is, of course, related to the question of the unity of Malory's work. The story of Mark is not so organically related to the story of Arthur that it is essential to the whole; unlike a chapter of a novel or an act of a play, it could be omitted. Yet it does contribute to *Morte Darthur* in much the same way that the subplot of an

---

115 *Works*, pp. 431, 503-4, 580; see pp. 202-204 above.
116 *Works*, pp. 1192, 1200-1; see pp. 216-7, 219 above.
117 Benson, "*Le Morte Darthur*" in *Critical Approaches to Six Major English Works*, ed. Robert M. Lumiansky and Herschel Baker (Philadelphia, 1968), pp. 111-9.

Elizabethan play like *Volpone* or *The Changeling* contributes to the whole:
it is of value for the sake of contrast, and the work is a richer one if it is
retained. The scenes concerning Mark contribute to the whole of *Morte
Darthur* by presenting a king who acts in counterpoint to Arthur and
thus sets off more sharply Arthur's virtues as king. In this way the story
of King Mark contributes to the "connectedness" or "cohesion" of *Morte
Darthur*.[118]

The power of Malory's narrative in Tales 7 and 8 has often been
justly praised, and critics generally acknowledge that Malory's last tale,
in which he shows the most independence in the treatment of his sources, is his finest.[119] What has been overlooked is that the "Tale of
Tristram" was important to the development of Tales 7 and 8: it contributed markedly to Malory's greater independence in the use of his
sources by influencing his conception of Arthur in these final tales.

The University of North Carolina at Chapel Hill

118   These terms are more suitable for Malory's book than "unity" since the latter term too often connotes a tightly knit structure that *Morte Darthur* lacks. For objections to the term and alternatives, see Benson, pp. 97 ff.; Brewer, "hoole book", pp. 41-63 and *Morte Darthur*, p. 22; Reiss, pp.
26-30; Arthur K. Moore, "Medieval English Literature and the Question of Unity," *Modern Philology*
65 (1967-8) 296-9. For a general criticism of the concept of organic unity, see Catherine Lord,
"Organic Unity Reconsidered," *Journal of Aesthetics and Art Criticism* 22 (1963-4) 263-8.

119   See Vinaver's comments, *Works*, pp. xciii-xcix, 1623 ff.

THE PROBLEM OF INALIENABILITY IN INNOCENT III'S CORRESPONDENCE WITH HUNGARY: A CONTRIBUTION TO THE STUDY OF THE HISTORICAL GENESIS OF *INTELLECTO**

James Ross Sweeney

B Y the thirteenth century the doctrine of inalienability of the rights of the crown or of the realm had become a widely held European constitutional principle.[1] Legal collections and commentaries from this period attest to its acceptance as good law in Castile, England and Germany.[2] In some measure such wide acceptance is attributable to the influence of Honorius III's famous decretal *Intellecto*, which was included in the *Decretales* of Gregory IX in 1234, and which is now regarded as the canonical *locus classicus* of the inalienability principle.[3] This doctrine has attracted the considerable attention of historians of medieval law and constitutionalism largely because it placed a fundamental, theoretical limitation upon the free exercise of royal authority and because it is

---

* This essay is a revision of a paper delivered 19 May 1971 at the Sixth Conference on Medieval Studies sponsored by the Medieval Institute, Kalamazoo, Michigan. I am indebted to Brian Tierney of Cornell University and to Edwin C. Hall of Wayne State University for their helpful suggestions.

1 The *iura regis et regni* of the legists encompassed a complex of royal prerogatives, liberties and fiscal privileges, among which were numbered demesne estates, control of episcopal temporalities during a vancacy, and special tolls and monopolies. See Gaines Post, *Studies in Medieval Legal Thought* (Princeton, 1964), pp. 422-7. The best known passage which enumerates the imperial *regalia* of the twelfth century is in Rahewin's continuation of Otto of Freising, *Gesta Frederici I. Imp.*, ed. G. Waitz, MGH, *Scriptores in usum scholarum* (Hanover, 1884), p. 191 (IV, vii), where, *inter alia*, the alienation of fiefs without the consent of the overlord was forbidden.

2 For brief discussions with references to the pertinent passages of the *Siete Partidas* of Alfonso the Wise, the German *Schwabenspiegel*, and the English *Fleta*, consult P. E. Schramm, *A History of the English Coronation* (Oxford, 1937), p. 198; and P. N. Riesenberg, *Inalienability of Sovereignty in Medieval Political Thought* (New York, 1956), pp. 4-5, 15-7.

3 *Intellecto* was first included in the *Compilatio Quinta* of 1226 (II.15.3) and then in the *Liber Extra* (II.24.33).

thought that through an understanding of its relationship to the theory of kingship, the medieval concept of sovereignty might be further clarified.[4] In a characteristically medieval way, however, the application of this principle contributed to the strengthening of royal power by providing legal justification for the revocation of royal charters and for the refusal to make further grants from the royal demesne.[5]

The roots of the medieval principle of the inalienability of the rights of the crown have been shown in the light of current research to lie in the interaction of Roman law, feudal practice and canon law. We have learned recently that both the broad concept of inalienability and the familiar medieval terminology were present in the Roman legal tradition as early as the mid-fifth century.[6] The related principle of the inalienability of fiefs was expressly maintained by the Emperor Lothair III in a constitution of 1136 which was incorporated in the *Libri feudorum*.[7] It has also been shown that the principle of inalienability in the broad sense was to some degree recognized by the rulers of Germany, France and England by about the middle of the twelfth century.[8]

4   C. H. McIlwain, *The Growth of Political Thought in the West* (New York, 1932), pp. 376-82; Ernst Kantorowicz, "Inalienability: A Note on Canonical Practice and the English Coronation Oath in the Thirteenth Century," *Speculum* 29 (1954) 488-502; and Kantorowicz, *The King's Two Bodies* (Princeton, 1957), pp. 347-58; Riesenberg, *Inalienability*; Hartmut Hoffmann, "Die Unveräusserlichkeit der Kronrechte im Mittelalter," *Deutsches Archiv für Erforschung des Mittelalters* 20 (1964) 389-474. See also Marcel David, *La souveraineté et les limites juridiques du pouvoir monarchique du IXe au XVe siècle* (Paris, 1954), pp. 224-44; Ludwig Buisson, *Potestas und Caritas, die Päpstliche Gewalt im Spätmittelalter* (Cologne, 1958), pp. 270-347.

5   McIlwain, *Growth*, p. 378, cites the case of Edward III, who in 1341 revoked his own earlier grant on the grounds that it was "against our royal rights and prerogatives." For other examples from the late thirteenth and fourteenth centuries drawn from English, Aragonese and French sources see Riesenberg, *Inalienability*, pp. 164-7.

6   Gaines Post, "Early Medieval Ecclesiastical and Secular Sources of *Iura Illibata-Illaesa* in the Inalienability Clause of the Coronation Oath," *Collectanea Stephan Kuttner* in *Studia Gratiana* 11 (1967) 493-512. See also his earlier essay in *Studies*, pp. 415-33.

7   Post, *Studies*, pp. 422-3; *cf.* Riesenberg, *Inalienability*, pp. 11-2.

8   In 1154 Frederick Barbarossa declared that "regni utilitas incorrupta persistat et singulorum status iugiter servetur illesus"; MGH, *Legum sectio* 4 (Hanover, 1893) *Const.* 1, no. 148. For the sources and implications of this constitution see Post, *Studies*, pp. 422-4. Both Louis VII and Philip II of France swore not to alienate the lands recently taken under their protection. See J. R. Strayer, "Defense of the Realm and Royal Power in France" in *Medieval Statecraft and the Perspectives of History*, ed. J. F. Benton and T. N. Bisson (Princeton, 1971), pp. 292-3; and Riesenberg, *Inalienability*, pp. 105-6. The question whether Henry II of England swore to an inalienability clause as part of his coronation oath taken in 1154 is still unsettled. Both Schramm, *History*, pp. 180, 196-8, and Bertie Wilkinson, *Constitutional History of Medieval England, 1216-1399*, 3 (London, 1958), pp. 75-81, reject the possibility. H. G. Richardson not only asserts that such a clause was part of the English oath in 1154, but suggests that the responsibility for its inclusion lay with Nigel, bishop of Ely; "The Coronation in Medieval England: The Evolution of the Office and the Oath," *Traditio* 16

Within the Church certain bishops subject directly to Rome were forbidden by Pope Celestine III in the late twelfth century to diminish the substance of their sees by making grants from the episcopal demesne, which might be injurious to the rights of the Holy See.[9] Earlier, in 1185 Pope Urban III, employing the language of inalienability in a confirmation of privilege to Peter Chitiléni, the Hungarian archbishop of Spalato, declared that one of the obligations of a pontiff was so far as possible to preserve unimpaired the rights of his fellow bishops.[10] Innocent III, writing in the same vein to the bishop of Winchester in 1205, authorized this prelate to revoke any illegal alienations made by his predecessors from the episcopal *mensa*.[11]

The significance of *Intellecto* lies in part in the pivotal position it occupies in the evolution of the inalienability principle. The inclusion of this decretal among the laws of the Church virtually assured the recognition of the specific principle of the inalienability of the rights of the crown as applicable to all European monarchs, at least in the eyes of the canonists.[12]

(1960) 111-202, esp. 159-61. *Cf.* Richardson's earlier views in "The English Coronation Oath," *Transactions of the Royal Historical Society*, 4th series, 23 (1941) 129-58; and "The English Coronation Oath," *Speculum* 24 (1949) 44-75. A reasonable middle position was taken by R. S. Hoyt in "The Coronation Oath of 1308: The Background of 'les leys et les custumes'," *Traditio* 11 (1955) 235-57.

9   X.III.8.8. See Kantorowicz, "Inalienability," 496-98; also *The King's Two Bodies*, pp. 348-53.

10   "Fratres et coepiscopos nostros sincera debemus caritate diligere et utilitati honorique ipsorum propensioni cura intendere ac jura sua, quantum in nobis fuerit, illibata servare." *Historia Salonitana maior*, ed. Nada Klaić (Belgrade, 1967), pp. 123-4; Jaffé, no. 15480 (12 December 1185). For earlier twelfth-century examples of the *iura illibata* formula in papal documents see Post, *Studies*, pp. 425-6.

11   *Innocentii III Romani Pontificis regesta sive epistolae* 8.143 (PL 215.722; hereafter cited as *Reg.*), Potthast, no. 2595; C. R. Cheney and W. R. Semple, *Selected Letters of Pope Innocent III concerning England (1198-1216)* (London, 1953), p. 80, no. 24.

12   The decretal was placed in the title devoted to the swearing of oaths (*de iureiurando*) in the *Decretales*. Surprisingly, the noted decretalists of the thirteenth century paid scant attention to the question of inalienability, but focused instead upon the question of the validity of two contradictory oaths. See Innocent IV, *Apparatus super libros decretalium* (Strassburg, 1478) at II.24.33; Henricus de Segusio, *Summa* (Lyon, 1537; rpt. Darmstadt, 1962), fol. 107v; Bernardus Bottoni [Parmensis], *Casus longi super quinque libros decretalium* (Bologna, 1487) at II.24.33. In the fourteenth century the idea that kings ought to preserve the rights of the crown unimpaired and should swear to do so at their coronations was linked directly with *Intellecto*. For the well-known notation to the *Liber regalis*, see H. G. Richardson, "English Coronation Records; The Coronation of Edward II," *Bulletin of the Institute of Historical Research* 16 (1938) 11; and Kantorowicz, *The King's Two Bodies*, p. 357. Johannes Andreae declared that even if a king had not so sworn, he was still bound to preserve the rights of the kingdom, citing a parallel with clerical practice and Hostiensis' discussion of the decretal *Veritatis* (X.II.24.14): "Licet [*teneatur*] etiam si non iurauerit, sicut etiam clericus, licet non iurauerit obedientiam, tenetur obedire, de hoc, supra e. ueritatis, Hostien." *In primum ... sextum*

The canonical text of *Intellecto* is a slightly abridged form of a letter written to Archbishop Ugrinus of Kalocsa and his suffragans, which in turn was a copy of a letter dispatched to Prince Béla, heir to the Hungarian throne. Both letters, as W. H. Bryson has recently reaffirmed, were engrossed in the papal register *sub datum* 15 July 1225, not 1220.[13] Moreover, on 23 August 1225 the substance of the July letters was repeated almost verbatim in a second letter to Archbishop Ugrinus.[14]

In these letters the pontiff wrote that he understood that for some time King Andrew II of Hungary had made certain alienations in prejudice to his kingdom (*in praeiudicium regni sui*) and against the honor of the king (*contra honorem regis*). Honorius was desirous, as he explained, to manifest his paternal devotion; therefore, he directed that these alienations should be revoked despite an oath to the contrary, since this oath was given after the king had already sworn at his coronation to preserve the rights of his kingdom and the honor of the crown unimpaired (*iura regni sui et honorem coronae illibata servare*). The pope noted that if an oath not to revoke such alienations had been given, it was definitely illegal, and therefore the penalty for violating it ought not to be observed.[15]

In examining the background for *Intellecto*, scholars have largely overlooked or discounted the significance of two letters of Pope In-

---

decretalium librum novella commentaria (Venice, 1581; rpt. Turin, 1963), p. 200. Universal application of the principle was maintained by Baldus de Ubaldis in his commentary on *Intellecto*: "Nota quod omnes reges mundi in sua coronatione debent iurare iura regni sua conservare et honorem coronae." Cited in Kantorowicz, *The King's Two Bodies*, p. 357n. See also J. A. Wahl, "Immortality and Inalienability: Baldus de Ubaldis," *Mediaeval Studies* 32 (1970) 326-8.

13 P. Pressutti, ed., *Regesta Honorii papae III* 2 (Rome, 1895), p. 350, no. 5560. Pressutti struck all reference to a 1220 text in the "Addenda et Corrigenda", 2.494, 499. See W. H. Bryson, "Papal Releases from Royal Oaths," *Journal of Ecclesiastical History* 22 (1971) 26n. The text is printed in Augustin Theiner, *Vetera monumenta historica Hungariam sacram illustrantia* 1 (Rome, 1859), p. 60, no. 126; Potthast, no. 7443 and 7444. The recognition of a later date for the decretal naturally calls for a reappraisal of its historical background, a project which the present writer has already begun.

14 Pressutti, 2.361, no. 5611; Potthast, no. 7466. The text is printed in Theiner, 1.60, no. 127; and more recently in A. L. Tăutu, ed., *Acta Honorii III (1216-1227) et Gregorii IX (1227-1241)* (Vatican City, 1950), p. 188, no. 143. Pope Gregory IX restated the argument of *Intellecto* in a letter to King Andrew II of 31 January 1233; Theiner, 1.111, no. 188; Potthast, no. 9080.

15 Emil Friedberg, ed., *Corpus iuris canonici* 2 (Leipzig, 1881), p. 374: "Intellecto iamdudum, quod carissimus in Christo filius noster Hungariae rex illustris alienationes quasdam fecerit in praeiudicium regni sui et contra regis honorem, nos, *super hoc affectione paterna consulere cupientes*, eidem regi dirigimus scripta nostra, ut alienationes praedictas, non obstante iuramento, si quod fecit de non revocandis eisdem, studeat revocare, quia, quum teneatur, et in sua coronatione iuraverit *etiam*, iura regni sui et honorem coronae illibata servare, illicitum profecto fuit, si praestitit de non revocandis alienationibus huiusmodi iuramentum, et propterea penitus non servandum."

nocent III directed to Hungary in the spring of 1205.[16] On occasion, when one of these letters has been linked with *Intellecto*, its full significance has not been explored.[17] The antecedents of *Intellecto* most commonly cited from Innocent's reign are the letters which prohibited the dispersal of the royal demesne of the young Frederick II in Sicily[18] and which nullified Magna Carta on the grounds that that agreement diminished and impaired King John's rights and honor.[19] Both cases involved kingdoms widely known as papal fiefs, although in the English instance Innocent refrained from justifying his action on feudal grounds.[20] The purpose of this paper is to demonstrate the importance of the 1205 letters as a step toward the papal application of the inalienability principle to an independent secular monarchy.

I

On 30 November 1204, King Imre (Emeric) of Hungary died leaving his realm to his five-year-old son László (Ladislaus) III.[21] Shortly before his death Imre had released from prison his contentious and ambitious brother Andrew, the duke of Croatia and Dalmatia, and committed the young László to his brother's care.[22] As regent Duke Andrew was quick

16   *Reg.* 8.39 and 40; Potthast, no. 2476 and 2477.

17   *Reg.* 8.39 has been cited by R. W. and A. J. Carlyle, *A History of Medieval Political Theory in the West* 5 (Edinburgh and London, 1928), p. 164. See also Walter Ullmann's review of Ludwig Buisson, *Potestas und Caritas* in *EHR* 76 (1961) 326n.; Post, *Studies*, p. 431n. Both Riesenberg, *Inalienability*, p. 13, and Hoffmann, "Die Unveräusserlichkeit," 390-1, mention *Reg.* 8.39, but the former omits it as a precedent while the latter specifically rejects it. *Reg.* 8.40 is less well known; of the above writers, only the Carlyles noted it (5.164). But see also Fritz Hartung, "Die Krone als Symbol der monarchischen Herrschaft im ausgehenden Mittelalter" in *Corona regni*, ed. Manfred Hellmann (Weimar, 1961), pp. 55-6.

18   J. L. A. Huillard-Bréholles, *Historia diplomatica Frederici Secundi* (Paris, 1852-1861), 1.57; *Gesta Innocentii PP. III* 31 (PL 214.55). See Riesenberg, *Inalienability*, pp. 13-4, 114. *Cf.* Hoffmann, "Die Unveräusserlichkeit," 390, who links the Sicilian case with the Hungarian one of 1205 only to reject both.

19   Cheney and Semple, *Letters*, no. 82, pp. 212-6, esp. p. 215. Riesenberg, *Inalienability*, pp. 100-1, 114.

20   Walter Ullmann, *Medieval Papalism* (London, 1949), pp. 71-5; and Bryson, pp. 20-4.

21   Alexander Domanovszky, ed., *Chronici Hungarici compositio saeculi XIV* in *Scriptores rerum Hungaricarum*, ed. Imre Szentpétery, 1 (Budapest, 1937), p. 463. The most useful secondary authority on Hungarian history during this period is Bálint Hóman, *Geschichte des ungarischen Mittelalters* (Berlin, 1940-1943), although his treatment of the events of 1204-1205 is too brief to be satisfactory; see 2.11-2.

22   Thomas of Spalato, *Historia Salonitanorum pontificum atque Spalatensum*, ed. F. Rački in *Monumenta spectantia historiam Slavorum meridionalium* 26 (Zagreb, 1894), p. 82; *Continuatio Claustroneoburgensis secunda*, MGH, *Scriptores* 9 (Hanover, 1851), p. 620.

to use his position to reverse certain decisions of his brother and to set aside some provisions of the late king's will. One of his first acts was to recall his duchess, Gertrude of Merania, from Germany where she had been exiled by King Imre.[23] Next he refused to make proper dispersal of the royal treasure deposited at the Cistercian monastery of Pilis. Imre had directed that one third should be given each to the Templars and to the Hospitallers for the relief of the Holy Land, while the remaining third was to be given to László.[24] Andrew also refused to convey to his ward and the queen mother, Constance of Aragon, certain revenues which he had promised to them after his brother's death.[25] This precipitated a major political crisis in which the party of the regent was opposed by a faction loyal to the queen mother.[26] Sometime probably in the spring of 1205, Queen Constance together with the young king left Hungary to seek the protection of Duke Leopold VI of Austria in Vienna. The royal fugitives were accompanied by certain bishops and magnates who had sworn an oath of loyalty to László. They took with them a sizable treasure consisting of precious jewels and a royal crown.[27] One chronicler relates that along the way the queen and her partisans took by force several river ports and guard posts along the Hungarian frontier. The further evidence of border skirmishes between Andrew's forces and those of Leopold after the latter received Constance and László at Vienna indicates that the flight to Austria was probably undertaken by Queen Constance as a means of escaping from the regent's control and should not be viewed as the result of expulsion by Andrew.[28]

23 *Continuatio Admuntensis*, MGH, *Scriptores* 9.590, where the duchess's return is said to have taken place "cum gloria magna".

24 *Reg.* 8.37; Potthast, no. 2474.

25 *Reg.* 8.38; Potthast, no. 2475.

26 Andrew's supporters probably included the former palatine Count Mogh and Bishops Calanus of Pécs and John of Nyitra. László and Constance could rely upon Archbishops John of Kalocsa and Bernard of Spalato, perhaps also upon Bishop Catapanus of Eger. Their secular supporters would also have included some of the Aragonese nobles who settled in Hungary during Imre's reign.

27 *Continuatio Admuntensis*, pp. 590-1. Whether the crown mentioned here is identical with the much-discussed St. Stephen's crown cannot be determined with certainty. The chronicler seems to suggest that the crown's recovery was more important to Duke Andrew than the return of King László. See Josef Deér, *Die heilige Krone Ungarns* (Vienna, 1966), pp. 206-8.

28 *Continuatio Admuntensis*, p. 591. The usually reliable Admont account merely says the queen set out (*egressa est*) for Vienna. But *cf. Continuatio Claustroneoburgensis secunda*, p. 621, where Andrew is reported to have forced the departure (*terminos Austrie ... intrare coegit*) of Constance and László. For another view see Hóman, 2.12.

We do not know at what moment in this series of events Queen Constance appealed to Innocent III, but in view of the lack of any reference to the queen's flight in the papal correspondence, it is likely that her appeal antedated her departure for Vienna. According to the papal register seven letters were dispatched between 25 April and 27 April 1205 to Duke Andrew, the Hungarian princes and Hungarian churchmen. From them it is clear that Innocent was responding to Queen Constance's original letter of complaint.[29] The pope employed a combination of moral exhortation and legal directives in order to strengthen the political position of the young king and his mother. He urged Duke Andrew to be faithful to his responsibilities for the administration of the kingdom and for the care of László, so that "the boy might find a generous father in an uncle and a gracious protector in a patron." Innocent warned the duke against countenancing wicked designs against his nephew and to manage the affairs of the kingdom with diligence, so that when László reached adulthood, he would more readily recognize Andrew's great benefits to him.[30] In a similar spirit the pope also called upon the clergy and people of Hungary to show unwavering loyalty to László as Imre's heir and their king. By apostolic authority he strictly forbade anyone to contribute advice or assistance to any activity contrary to the interests of the crown.[31] He also wrote separately to the suffragan bishops of the province of Kalocsa commanding them to assist their metropolitan in everything that appertained to the defense of the king, his mother and the kingdom.[32] The pope in these letters was acting in his capacity both as a pastor and as the head of the spiritual hierarchy.

Innocent took legal cognizance of the duke of Croatia's refusal to carry out the terms of Imre's will. He commanded Andrew to make appropriate dispersal of Imre's treasure because, he said, it was fitting that Andrew implement his brother's last wish.[33] The basis for the pope's jurisdiction in this case rested upon the canonical theory of

29 *Reg.* 8.37 begins: "Accepimus autem, charissima in Christo filia ... regina Hungariae, referente...."

30 *Reg.* 8.36; Potthast, no. 2473 (25 April 1205). This is clearly Innocent's first letter to Andrew since he became regent. Andrew had written to Rome earlier assuring Innocent of his intentions to continue and complete Imre's policies and projects, and asking the pontiff to settle the disputed election to the see of Esztergom. See *Reg.* 7.226.

31 *Reg.* 8.40; Potthast, no. 2477 (25 April 1205).

32 *Reg.* 8.42; Potthast, no. 2478 (25 April 1205).

33 *Reg.* 8.37; Potthast, no. 2474 (25 April 1205).

testaments which by the beginning of the thirteenth century maintained that it was a bishop's duty generally to defend the integrity of wills. Those cases, moreover, involving bequests for religious purposes were considered subject to the competence of ecclesiastical courts.[34] Since two thirds of Imre's treasure was donated to the military orders for the relief of the Holy Land, the pope's right to judge a case involving a legacy in alms was established. Although Innocent did not inform Andrew in this letter, the customary penalty for failure to carry out testamentary provisions was excommunication.[35] Innocent also ordered the duke to hand over to Constance and László the revenues he had promised them after Imre's death.[36] The pope had a further obligation to help *miserabiles personae* — widows and orphans among others. He invoked this aspect of his office when he commanded Andrew and the Hungarian princes not to alienate the regalia in detriment to the boy king.[37] Finally, he informed the archbishop of Kalocsa and the bishop of Nagyvárad that he had placed the *familia* and clerks of King László and Queen Constance under his protection and that of the Holy See, and he ordered them to impose ecclesiastical penalties upon anyone who presumed to molest the possessions or revenues of the royal *familia* and clerks.[38] The extension of the protection of the Holy See to the retinue of László and Constance was a special favor which, however, did not have the connotation of feudal dependence.[39]

By far the most significant letters of this group are the fourth and fifth of the series found in the register. Taken together they contain clear references to the principle of inalienability and thereby provide a link with *Intellecto*. The fourth letter was addressed to the duke of

---

34   An excellent discussion of the evolution of this canonical doctrine is provided by Michael M. Sheehan, *The Will in Medieval England* (Toronto, 1963), pp. 119-35.

35   Andrew had once been excommunicated by Innocent III for his failure to discharge his obligations under the terms of his father's will. See Othmar Hageneder, "Exkommunikation und Thronfolgeverlust bei Innozenz III.," *Römische historische Mitteilungen* 2 (1957-1958) 9-50. In a parallel case involving John of England's refusal to grant Richard's bequest to their nephew, Otto of Brunswick, Innocent authorized the use of spiritual penalties if necessary. See Sheehan, p. 170.

36   *Reg.* 8.38; Potthast, no. 2475 (25 April 1205).

37   *Reg.* 8.39; Potthast, no. 2476 (25 April 1205).

38   *Reg.* 8.41; Potthast, no. 2479 (27 April 1205).

39   By extending the protection of the Holy See to the possessions of the attendants of a widow and a fatherless boy, Innocent seems also to have stretched the category of "miserable persons". On the non-feudal aspect of a papal grant of protection, see Helene Tillmann, "Zur Frage des Verhältnisses von Kirche und Staat in Lehre und Praxis Papst Innocenz' III.," *Deutsches Archiv für Erforschung des Mittelalters* 9 (1951) 176-8. *Cf.* Achille Luchaire, *Innocent III*, vol. 5 (Paris, 1908): *Les royautés vassales du Saint Siège*, p. 119.

Croatia and Dalmatia and to all the princes of Hungary. The central passage of this letter reads:

> Thus that the rights of the kingdom (*regni iura*) may be preserved intact (*integra*) for this same king, we, who are bound by the papal office to defend an orphan because although unworthy we act on earth in place of Him of whom it is said by the Prophet, "Thou art the helper of the fatherless," entreat [you] in Jesus Christ who shall come to judge the quick and the dead; and by authority of this present letter we strictly command under supplication of divine judgment that while this same king shall be a minor the regalia (*regalia*) shall not be alienated in detriment to him, but rather you should devote careful attention and efficient labor to the faithful preservation of it.[40]

Within this letter are combined both the concept and the customary legal terminology of inalienability. The pope here invoked the full weight of his office in defense of the integrity of the *iura regni*. The grounds on which he justified this unusual thrust into the temporal sphere were his responsibility to protect an orphan, Andrew's failure (by implication) to act as a diligent guardian, and the obligation of the papal office to render judgment as vicegerent of Christ. It is clear that Innocent believed that the *iura regni* must be preserved unimpaired. It is equally clear that he believed that in a special case such as this, where the secular government failed to maintain the *iura*, the papacy should act to guarantee their integrity. Thus the purpose of this exercise of supreme papal authority was to protect the temporal rights — and hence autonomy — of a secular monarch.[41]

The intent of this letter is reinforced by the text of the letter addressed to the prelates, princes, clergy and people of Hungary, which is the fifth letter of this series. Here Innocent recognized László as Imre's

---

40 *Reg.* 8.39. "Ut igitur eidem regi regni jura integra conserventur, nos, qui apostolatus officio tenemur tueri pupillum, cum illius, quamvis indigni, vices geramus in terris, cui dicitur per Prophetam: Pupillo tu eris adjutor, obsecramus in Christo Jesu qui venturus est judicare vivos et mortuos, et auctoritate praesentium sub obtestatione divini judicii districtius inhibemus, ne, dum idem rex fuerit in aetate minori, alienentur regalia in detrimentum ipsius, sed ad ea fideliter conservanda diligens studium impendatis et operam efficacem." *Cf.* Ps. 10:14 (A.V.).

41 Historians have recognized for some time that Innocent III advocated the independence of the *regia potestas*, rather than world-wide papal dominion in temporal affairs. See, for example, Sergio Mochi Onory, *Fonti canonistiche dell'idea moderna dello stato* (Milan, 1951), pp. 271-7; and Friedrich Kempf, *Papsttum und Kaisertum bei Innocenz III.* (Rome, 1954), pp. 253-70. The present case reveals not only Innocent's willingness to preserve that independence, but also his readiness to assert direct papal *auctoritas* within the secular order. In these circumstances the value of such terms as "dualist" or "hierocrat" is minimal. See Brian Tierney, "The Continuity of Papal Political Theory in the Thirteenth Century," *Mediaeval Studies* 27 (1965) 228-36.

heir and the legitimate king to whom all owed unfailing allegiance. He forbade anyone to participate in actions contrary to the interests of the crown (*contra coronam*) and urged instead that everyone defend the honor of the king (*honorem regis*).[42] Innocent's terminology connects this letter with the preceding one. The word *corona* clearly refers to the theoretical concept of the king's public authority rather than to a physical object. Similarly the *honor regis*, which the prelates and princes were exhorted to defend, was understood in the Middle Ages as considerably more than the king's personal dignity; rather it was the dignity and authority which were combined in the royal office.[43]

Despite the vigor of Innocent's intervention, these papal letters had no effect upon the Hungarian political situation, which was resolved in an unforeseen manner. On 3 May 1205, László III died in Vienna.[44] The bishop of Györ was sent from Hungary to escort his body for burial at Székesfehérvár. After a decent interval during which she was honorably treated by Duke Leopold, Queen Constance returned to her brother's court in Aragon.[45] The Hungarian throne passed to the duke of Croatia and Dalmatia who became Andrew II.

II

The points of convergence between the inalienability letters of 1205 and *Intellecto* are greater than the differences between them, although those differences are significant. The *iura regni* are mentioned on both occasions, and in the context of the 1205 letters these appear to be synonymous with the *regalia*.[46] On both occasions it is asserted that regalian rights should be preserved or maintained in their fullness. In 1205 the words are: *integra conserventur*; in 1225: *illibata servare*.[47] Moreover, the letter of 1205 which forbade participation in activities

---

42 *Reg.* 8.40. "... auctoritate vobis praesentium districtius inhibemus, ne cui contra coronam ipsius consilium vel auxilium impendatis, sed resistatis omnino, regis defendentes honorem, si quis forsitan contra eum agere tentaret."

43 Joseph Karpat, "Corona Regni Hungariae im Zeitalter der Arpaden" in *Corona regni*, ed. Hellmann, p. 312.

44 The correct date for László's death is provided by Imre Szentpétery in his edition of the *Chronicon Zagrebiense cum textu chronici Varadiensis collatum* in *Scriptores rerum Hungaricarum* 1.212 n. 3.

45 *Continuatio Claustroneoburgensis secunda*, p. 621; *Continuatio Admuntensis*, pp. 590-1; *Chronici Hungarici compositio saeculi XIV*, p. 211. Constance of Aragon later married the Emperor Frederick II; see *Reg.* 11.4; Potthast, no. 3306.

46 On "*regalia*" see Ch. DuCange, *Glossarium mediae et infimae latinitatis* 7 (Paris, 1938) 85-9.

47 I do not think the "positive" expression of the first phrase and the "negative" expression of the second is of any consequence. They are clearly synonymous.

directed *contra coronam* and which explicitly urged the prelates and princes to defend the *honor regis* is echoed in *Intellecto* where the Hungarian king is said to have sworn to preserve the *honor coronae*, but to have subsequently made alienations *contra regis honorem*.[48]

The principle invoked in both instances is identical. Regalian rights may not be alienated in detriment to the king or in prejudice to the kingdom. This doctrine is intellectually dependent upon the distinction between person and office, between the *rex* and the *corona*. Whereas the incumbent king was merely a temporary occupant of the office, the crown remained as an enduring entity above the individual ruler and served to strengthen his power.[49] The protection of the *iura regni* was therefore in the interests not only of the present occupant of the royal office but also of all those who in the future would enjoy the full exercise of royal authority. In 1205 the pontiff acted on behalf of a minor whose future authority appeared to be threatened. In 1225 papal action appears to have been taken in defense of the future rights of Prince Béla, the heir to the throne.[50] The intention of both papal actions was, therefore, to protect the *iura* by restraining the activities of a secular ruler, who, coincidentally, was the same man in each case.

The immediate grounds expressly given in justification for papal action in 1205 and 1225 appear to be distinct. Fundamentally, however, they were derived from a common source. Innocent declared that he was bound both by his office and by the concept of the *imitatio Christi* to defend an orphan.[51] Moreover, he invoked the image of Christ as the

---

48 It is not possible to say with any certainty that Honorius III consciously adopted the phraseology of Innocent's 1205 letters. The researches of Gaines Post have shown that these terms would have been found widely in other sources. Nonetheless, Innocent's registers would have been convenient for his successor. On Innocent's view of the importance of the registers see *Reg.* 1.540; *Die Register Innocenz' III.*, ed. O. Hageneder and A. Haidacher (Graz-Cologne, 1964), I/ 537; Potthast, no. 584 (30 January 1199). For the significance of the papal archives as a "veritable ideological storehouse", see Walter Ullmann, *Principles of Government and Politics in the Middle Ages* (London, 1961), pp. 30-31.

49 Hartung, p. 56. Karpat (pp. 271-289) has shown that in Hungary the first use of *corona* in the abstract sense dates from the end of the twelfth century in a document issued by the royal chancery (1197), and examples of this usage increase rapidly after the turn of the century. See also Kantorowicz, *The King's Two Bodies*, pp. 314-450.

50 This is inferred from the fact that the original letter was sent to Béla and the copy to his political ally the archbishop of Kalocsa. It would seem that they had requested papal intervention. On Ugrinus of Kalocsa's ties to Béla's circle see Hóman, 2.89-92. *Cf.* Vilmos Fraknói, *Magyarország egyházi és politikai összeköttetései a római szent-székkel* 1 (Budapest, 1901), p. 47, who asserts that Honorius III acted (in 1220) at the suggestion of Archbishop John of Esztergom. He provides no documentation.

51 Defense of orphans was a part of the broad episcopal responsibility to protect those who

Ultimate Judge in whose place on earth the pope acted.[52] Honorius
stated his desire to show paternal affection, but he acted in a judicial
capacity by ruling that the detrimental alienations were violations of
the Hungarian coronation oath.[53] In both instances the ultimate
authority for papal action flowed from the *plenitudo potestatis* of the vicar
of Christ, not, it should be observed, from any temporal feudal tie between Hungary and Rome.

A noteworthy difference between the 1205 letters and *Intellecto* is that
in the earlier case the pontiff restrained the activities of a regent, not a
reigning monarch; in the latter case the pope not only insisted upon the
limitation of the free exercise of power by a king, he revoked the
alienations as well. Although the distinction is important, it may be observed that if the applicability of the inalienability principle depended
in part upon the recognition of kingship as a temporary trust, it is just
at this point that the idea of regency simulates that of kingship. The
regent is the custodian or steward of royal political rights and power. In
both situations royal authority is seen to be held in trust, but the trust
of the regent grew out of particular historical conditions; it was
established with the intent that it be terminated at a specific date and
lacked the sanctification of anointing and coronation.[54]

Intellecto was concerned with purported violations of the Hungarian
coronation oath and for this reason entered the Decretals in the section
devoted to oaths. The correspondence of 1205 is completely silent on
the matter of a coronation oath. There can be little doubt that Andrew's violations of an alleged inalienability clause in the coronation

---

were legally regarded as *miserabiles personae*, a category which included widows, paupers and others:
see Brian Tierney, *Medieval Poor Law* (Berkeley - Los Angeles, 1959), pp. 15-9.

52   The phrases "vices [Christi] geramus in terris" and "obsecramus in Christo Jesu qui venturus
est iudicare vivos et mortuos" (*Reg.* 8.39) were intended to have more than rhetorical force. The
linking of Christ's role as supreme judge with the office of vicar of Christ refers directly to the concept of papal sovereignty, *plenitudo potestatis*. See John A. Watt, *The Theory of Papal Monarchy in the
Thirteenth Century* (New York, 1965), pp. 84-8.

53   The pope's right to judge the validity of oaths would have been acknowledged at the time.
By the beginning of the thirteenth century the imposition of penalties for the violation of oaths was
regarded as an expression of *auctoritas summa*. See Ullmann, *Medieval Papalism*, pp. 70-3; and David,
La souveraineté, pp. 190-6.

54   Innocent III would have been familiar with the canonical theory applicable to the administration of a diocese by a *curator* or *coadiutor* at a time when the ordinary bishop was in-
capacitated. Such an official was empowered to perform those functions which pertained to *ad-
ministratio*, but not those which flowed from the episcopal *dignitas* or *auctoritas*. See Edward Peters,
The Shadow King, Rex Inutilis in Medieval Law and Literature, 751-1327 (New Haven - London, 1970),
pp. 124-34.

oath facilitated Honorius III's intervention in Hungarian affairs, but the general principle of the inalienability of regalian rights is not dependent upon a coronation oath. Such a clause in the oath would be simply the most effective means of securing the integrity of the *iura regni*. Furthermore, the text of the Hungarian coronation oath for this period is uncertain.[55] If Honorius III was correct — and here the historian must weigh probabilities in the absence of evidence — then such a clause formed part of the oath sworn by Andrew II on 29 May 1205, the day of his coronation.[56] This event took place less than a year after the crowning of young László on 26 August 1204, during the lifetime of King Imre.[57] Conceivably, if an inalienability clause was included in the coronation ceremony of 1205, it may have been present in 1204 or even earlier. At László's coronation, if Innocent III's directives were observed, King Imre swore the customary oath on his son's behalf.[58] The reason for the silence regarding the coronation oath in the inalienability letters of 1205 is that even if we assume that László had been bound to such a clause by proxy, he had not violated it. But the principle of the inalienability of regalian rights was nonetheless vigorously defended by the pope in those letters.

55 No twelfth- or thirteenth-century text of the Hungarian coronation oath has as yet been found, although historians have assumed it to have been a version of the well-known *tria precepta*. For the Hungarian coronation *ordo* see Schramm, *The English Coronation*, p. 23; and the same author's "Die 'Stephanskrone' im Rahmen der ungarischen Staatssymbolik (11.-13. Jahrhundert)," *Herrschaftszeichen und Staatssymbolik* 3 (Stuttgart, 1956), pp. 752-3; also Magda von Bárányi-Oberschall, *Die sankt Stephans-Krone* (Vienna, 1961), pp. 16-7. Of particular importance is J. M. Bak, *Königtum und Stände in Ungarn im 14.-16. Jahrhundert* (Wiesbaden, 1973), pp. 165-90.

56 Pentecost, 1205; *Chronici Hungarici compositio saeculi XIV*, p. 464.

57 The coronation was performed by John, archbishop of Kalocsa, who was the royal candidate for the vacant archbishopric of Esztergom. See the complaint of the suffragans of Esztergom stated in *Reg.* 7.159; Potthast, no. 2328 (22 November 1204): "... quod memoratus archiepiscopus Colocensis, in grave Strigoniensis ecclesiae praejudicium ... filium praedicti regis [*Emerici*] coronavit in regem, cum non ad Colocensem ecclesiam, sed ad metropolim vestram coronatio regis Ungariae pertinere noscatur ...." For the date of László's coronation see *Chronici Hungarici compositio saeculi XIV*, p. 464.

58 *Reg.* 7.57; Potthast, no. 2196 (24 April 1204). Innocent directed that although László was a minor, no postponement of the crowning should be made ("quamvis minorem, non differas coronare"). King Imre acting for his son was to swear an oath to be obedient to the Holy See ("super apostolicae sedis obedientiam") and to maintain the liberties of the Church of Hungary ("super Ecclesiae Ungaricae libertate") just as his forebears had done ("sicut progenitores sui ... impenderunt"). No attempt was made by Innocent to provide the full text of the Hungarian coronation oath, but only to specify those clauses which pertained to the Holy See. On the non-feudal definition of *obedientia apostolicae sedis* see Karl Jordan, "Das Eindringen des Lehnswesens in das Rechtsleben der römischen Kurie," *Archiv für Urkundenforschung* 12 (1931-1932) 97; Helene Tillmann, "Zur Frage des Verhältnisses," 170-1.

III

Although some modern scholars, for example Walter Ullmann, Peter Riesenberg and Hartmut Hoffmann, while discussing the problem of inalienability have chosen to regard the kingdom of Hungary as a papal fief during the first half of the thirteenth century, there is no contemporary evidence for such a claim.[59] As early as 1924 R. W. Carlyle pointed to the absence of feudal terminology in Innocent III's letters to Hungary.[60] Karl Jordan and Johannes Haller have concurred in this, and my own recent examination of Innocent's relations with Hungary has confirmed this judgment.[61] Largely as a result of the misapprehension of the relationship between the Holy See and the Árpád monarchy, the significance of *Intellecto* and the antecedent letters of 1205 has been obscured.

In the eleventh century Pope Gregory VII had claimed that the king of Hungary was a papal vassal because the first Hungarian king, St. Stephen, had applied for and received a crown from Pope Sylvester II.[62] Gregory VII's feudal claim, however, did not receive permanent recognition in Hungary, in much the same way that his claim to England failed to find English support.[63] In the twelfth century when the Hungarian kings became kings of Croatia — a monarchy which had recognized the pontiff as its feudal overlord — feudal claims to

59 Ullmann, review of *Potestas und Caritas, loc. cit.*, p. 326 n. 1: "The king of Hungary (the subject of *Intellecto*) was a papal vassal and hence the tenor of the decretal should, historically anyway, be linked with this fact." Riesenberg, *Inalienability*, p. 114: "It is important that in both these cases [Frederick II and John Lackland], and in that of Andrew of Hungary, the Papacy was as much concerned to preserve its own feudal position as to protect or exalt the local ruler. For all three rulers were, at the moment in question, vassals of the Holy See." Hoffmann, "Die Unveräusserlichkeit," 390: "Und insofern ist die Massnahme mit entsprechenden Schritten zu vergleichen, die der Papst z.B. in Portugal und während der Vormundschaftsregierung Friedrichs II. in Sizilien in die Wege leitete, wobei er hier wie dort obendrein als Lehensherr Rechte geltend machen konnte." See also Luchaire, 5, esp. pp. 116-20, who has examined Innocent III's correspondence with Hungary in detail, but whose interpretation rests upon the *a priori* assertion of Hungarian feudal dependence upon the Holy See.

60 "The Claims of Innocent III to Authority in Temporal Matters," *Tijdschrift voor Rechtsgeschiedenis* 5 (1924) 134.

61 Jordan, pp. 96-7; Johannes Haller, *Das Papsttum, Idee und Wirklichkeit*, 2nd ed., 3 (Stuttgart, 1952), pp. 162, 435; and James Ross Sweeney, *Papal-Hungarian Relations During the Pontificate of Innocent III* (Diss. Cornell, 1971).

62 *Die Register Gregors VII.*, ed. Erich Caspar, MGH, *Epistolae selectae in usum scholarum* 2 (Berlin, 1955), pp. 144-6 (*Lib. 2, ep.* 13); Jaffé, no. 4886 (October 1074). See Walter Ullmann, *The Growth of Papal Government in the Middle Ages*, 2nd ed. (London, 1962), p. 334.

63 For the failure of Gregorian claims to Hungary see Jordan, p. 79. For William the Conqueror's rejection of similar claims to England, consult Z. N. Brooke, *The English Church and the Papacy* (Cambridge, 1952), pp. 140-4.

Hungary were not revived.[64] The major thirteenth-century canonical commentaries on *Intellecto* say nothing about a feudal bond between the papacy and Hungary.[65] It is true, however, that by the end of the thirteenth century Popes Nicholas IV and Boniface VIII revived the dormant Gregorian claims.[66]

If any doubt remains about the feudal status of Hungary at the beginning of the thirteenth century, a comparison of Innocent III's actions taken on behalf of Frederick II in Sicily with those on behalf of László III of Hungary should lay the question to rest. In Sicily the pope readily accepted personal responsibility for the regency in accordance with the wishes of the Empress Constance. He dispatched a legate to act as his representative in temporal affairs; he sent explicit orders for the political and fiscal administration of the kingdom; and when the need arose, he raised an army to enforce papal control and drive out his opponents.[67] Even when allowance is made for the strategic importance of Sicily and for the interconnection of papal Sicilian policy with the policy toward the Empire, the absence of any similar papal effort in Hungary is remarkable, if that kingdom also had been a fief of the Holy See. It is clear from the first letter addressed to Duke Andrew in the series outlined above that this was the first papal communication to the duke after King Imre's death. Yet in this letter Innocent neither ap-

---

64 The Croatian King Dimitar Zvonimir acknowledged his vassal status at his coronation at Spalato in 1076 conducted by a papal legate. Concerning Gregory's claims see Jordan, p. 80; and Ullmann, *Growth of Papal Government*, p. 333. At the end of the century when the papacy demanded that the Hungarian King László I swear a similar oath of homage for Croatia, which he had just successfully invaded, his response was to ally himself to the Emperor Henry IV and to recognize the anti-pope Clement III; Joseph Deér, *Die Anfänge der ungarisch-kroatischen Staatsgemeinschaft* (Darmstadt, 1970), pp. 27-8.

65 Riesenberg, *Inalienability*, p. 114, produces a gloss by Bernardus Bottoni in support of the idea that Hungary was regarded by the canonists as a papal fief. It appears, however, that he has drawn a false inference from the purely honorific words "domino pape" (the lord pope). The full text reads: "[I]ntellecto Rex ungarie fecit quasdam alienationes in praeiudicium regni sui et contra honorem regis iuramento interposito de ipsis non reuocandis: significatum fuit hoc domino pape." Bernardus Bottoni, *Casus longi* (Bologna, 1487) at X.II.24.33. See above, n. 12.

66 In the face of growing imperial influence, Pope Nicholas declared that it was well known that "the kingdom of Hungary pertained to the Holy See." Later, Pope Boniface maintained that "the kingdom of Hungary with all of its rights and authority had been devotedly offered and reverently granted to the Holy Roman Church by St. Stephen, as witnessed by numerous documents preserved in the archives of the Roman Church." See A. M. Cziráky, *Disquisitio historica de modo consequendi summum imperium in Hungaria* (Buda, 1820), pp. 43-5, where extracts are provided from the letters dated 2 January 1291 (Potthast, no. 23515) and 17 October 1301. *Cf.* Theiner, *Vetera monumenta hist. Hung.* 1.373, no. 500 and 388, no. 622.

67 *Gesta Innocentii PP. III* 23-40 (PL 214.38-73); Luchaire, *Innocent III* 1.153-92; Friedrich Baethgen, *Die Regentschaft Papst Innozenz III. im Königreich Sizilien* (Heidelberg, 1914), esp. pp. 9, 85-6. See also Thomas C. Van Cleve, *The Emperor Frederick II of Hohenstaufen* (Oxford, 1972), pp. 38-57.For a discussion of Innocent's equally strenuous efforts on behalf of his vassal James I of Aragon during his minority see Helene Tillmann, *Papst Innocenz III.* (Bonn, 1954), pp. 60-1.

proved nor confirmed Andrew in the regency, nor did he claim any right to do so. Rather, by taking note of the political changes in Hungary and addressing Andrew as regent (*gubernator*), the pontiff at most offered only tacit recognition of Andrew's regime. Despite the serious conflict between the duke and the party of the queen mother, no legate was dispatched even with the vague mission of "reforming the state of the Church", although such action was not without recent precedent.[68] Surely, if Innocent and the curia believed the Hungarian kingdom to be feudally dependent upon the Holy See, we should expect to find evidence of it in these circumstances. But there is none.

The relationship between the papacy and the Árpád monarchy, while free from the connotations of feudalism, was distinguished by a long history of close cooperation. Innocent III's correspondence contains references to the special esteem in which the Árpád dynasty was held from the time of St. Stephen to the reign of King Béla III. According to Innocent, papal-Hungarian relations were posited upon the reciprocal exchange of royal *devotio* and papal *dilectio*. In the papal view Árpád *devotio* was a continuing process through which the kings showed their loyalty to the Roman Church as, for example, when Béla III supported Alexander III against the rival German anti-popes.[69] In return the pope strove to show his affection through paternal solicitude in both temporalities and spiritualities as, for example, when Innocent, during a civil war, threatened to deprive the rebellious Duke Andrew of his right to inherit the throne.[70] This special relationship between the Roman pontiff and the Árpád kings unquestionably facilitated the intervention of the papacy in the kingdom's affairs.

In invoking the principle of the inalienability of the regalia in 1205, Innocent was exercising his authority as vicar of Christ. He had established the basis for intervention on grounds which few in the Middle Ages would question — the duty of a guardian to defend the inheritance of his ward, and the duty of a pope to protect *miserabiles personae* — but from them he shaped a new political doctrine.[71] The unique

---

68 In the spring of 1200, for example, Cardinal Gregory of S. Maria in Aquiro was dispatched to Hungary "super reformatione status Ecclesie Regni Ungarie"; Augustin Theiner, *Vetera monumenta Slavorum meridionalium historiam illustrantia* 1 (Rome, 1863), p. 47, no. 19; Potthast, no. 977. His real purpose, apparently, was to negotiate an end to the civil war between King Imre and Duke Andrew; *ibid.*, 1.51, nos. 156, 157.

69 *Reg.* 1.271 (Hageneder and Haidacher, *Register* I/ 271); Potthast, no. 285 (15 June 1198).

70 *Reg.* 1.10 (Hageneder and Haidacher, *Register* I/ 10); Potthast, no. 4 (29 January 1198). *Cf.* Hageneder, "Exkommunikation," 9-50.

71 This practice of employing clearly recognized legal precepts to support a particular action from which a new broad canonical doctrine might be extracted has been shown to be characteristic of Innocent III. See Brian Tierney, "'Tria quippe distinguit iudicia...' A Note on Innocent III's Decretal *Per Venerabilem*," *Speculum* 37 (1962) 54; and his "The Continuity of Papal Political Theory," 230-4.

tradition of mutual *devotio* and *dilectio* may well have assisted him in extending this principle to an independent kingdom. In this way also these letters may be seen as foreshadowing *Intellecto* because Honorius III does not appear to have held different views on the status of Hungary from those of his predecessor. Whereas the text of the decretal is free from any feudal reference, Honorius cited his wish to exhibit in this case his "paternal affection". The phrase may have been merely *pro forma*, but it is fully consistent with the articulated view of Innocent III.[72]

We must, therefore, reject the suggestion that the letters of 1205 and *Intellecto* emerged from a feudal context. On the contrary, their significance lies in part in the total absence of the language of feudalism. It was in Hungary that for the first time the popes upheld the principle of the inalienability of the regalia within an independent secular monarchy.[73]

Pennsylvania State University

72 See *Reg.* 1.270 (Hageneder and Haidacher, *Register*, I/ 270); Potthast, no. 290; *Reg.* 1.271 (Hageneder and Haidacher, *Register* I/ 271); Potthast, no. 285. *Reg.* 1.511 (Hageneder and Haidacher, *Register* I/ 511); Potthast, no. 565. *Reg.* 2.96; Potthast, no. 748. *Reg.* 5.103; Potthast, no. 3820. *Reg.* 6.8; Potthast, no. 1845. *Reg.* 10.39; Potthast, no. 3073. *Reg.* 14.156; Potthast, no. 4378.

73 Since this article was written Walter Ullmann has published a study which attempts to show the concept of the inalienability of regalian rights was invoked by the papacy much earlier than is commonly believed, specifically in the correspondence of Gregory VII with Hungary; "A Note on Inalienability in Gregory VII," *Studi gregoriani* 9 (1972) 117-40. His argument depends upon a critical reading of a remark of Pope Gregory to the Hungarian King Salomon: "... tu tamen in ceteris quoque a regia virtute et moribus longe discedens ius et honorem sancti PETRI quantum ad te imminuisti et alienasti, dum eius regnum a rege Teutonicorum in beneficium, sicut audivimus, suscepisti." See *Die Register Gregors VII.* 2.145 (*Lib.* II, *ep.* 13). Applying a juristic interpretation to this passage Professor Ullmann has concluded that Gregory was rebuking the king for having alienated a public right of rulership and that the Pope was drawing upon pre-existing tradition in invoking the inalienability principle. I would suggest to the contrary that the passage is more straightforward particularly when we understand *alienare* to mean, as it often may, "to neglect", "to discard", or "to set at variance." It may thus be rendered: "Nevertheless, you also departing greatly in other respects from royal virtue and manners have impaired and neglected the right and honor of St. Peter as far as you could since, as we have heard, you have received his [St. Peter's] kingdom as a benefice from the king of the Germans." (*Cf.* the translation of E. Emerton which ignores this problem: *The Correspondence of Pope Gregory VII* (New York, 1932), p. 48). The *ius et honor sancti Petri* should be understood specifically as the putative right of the papacy to bestow the kingdom as a benefice and the correlative superior dignity implicit in the bestowal itself. It is this right and dignity which Salomon injured and disregarded, but he did not give away public rights of rulership. A secular monarch whose role was merely that of steward or custodian of the property of St. Peter, to employ Professor Ullmann's terms, could not alienate the right to bestow the kingdom as a benefice since this right was not in his custody. One cannot give away what one does not have. Conceivably the pope might alienate such rights, but kings could only infringe or neglect to observe them. In short the king of Hungary's offense to which Gregory objected was not an alienation of the *iura regni* pertaining either to Salomon or to St. Peter. This letter of Gregory VII, so important in other ways, has little bearing on the development of the inalienability principle.

APOCALYPTICISM IN THE MIDDLE AGES:
AN HISTORIOGRAPHICAL SKETCH

Bernard McGinn

I F, as some theories of history suggest, the historiography of a problem is essential to the understanding of the problem itself, the recent publication of two important studies on medieval apocalypticism indicates that the time is ripe for a consideration of where the past century of scholarship has led in the interpretation of this phenomenon. The works of Miss Marjorie Reeves, *The Influence of Prophecy in the Later Middle Ages: A Study in Joachimism* (Oxford, 1969) and *The Figurae of Joachim of Fiore* (Oxford: Oxford-Warburg Series, 1972), the latter in collaboration with the late Miss Beatrice Hirsch-Reich, are the fruit of over thirty years of research and study. Their publication is of major moment for medieval intellectual history and invites us to consider the significance of apocalypticism from a more ample historiographical viewpoint than has hitherto been the case.

While several bibliographical and historiographical surveys devoted to Joachim of Fiore (*c*. 1135-1202) are in existence,[1] there is almost nothing which attempts to deal with wider questions of apocalypticism *per se* in the medieval period. There are many reasons why this is so. A glance at any of the survey articles on Joachim is enough to demonstrate the extent and complexity of the studies involved; and, of course, no evaluation of these interpretations is possible without a good

---

1 The best survey is that of M. Bloomfield, "Joachim of Flora. A Critical Survey of his Canon, Teachings, Sources, Biography, and Influence," *Traditio* 13 (1957) 249-311. *Cf*. also F. Russo, *Bibliografia Gioachimita* (Florence, 1954) and "Rassegna bibliografica Gioachimita (1958-67)," *Cîteaux* 19 (1968) 206-14, as well as E. Mikkers, "Neuere Literatur über Joachim von Fiore," *Cîteaux* 9 (1958) 286-93. Russo's *Bibliografia* has been critically reviewed by B. Hirsch-Reich, "Eine Bibliographie über Joachim von Floris und dessen Nachwirkung," *Recherches de théologie ancienne et médiévale* 24 (1957) 27-44.

knowledge of the sources upon which they are based. But these sources themselves offer difficulties of unusual proportions. In terms of the availability of many texts only in manuscript form, the antiquity and inaccessibility of some printed editions,[2] and complicated questions concerning the authenticity and ascription of various works, it is difficult for the scholar to gain the type of control over the sources which would allow him some security in evaluating the interpretations.

The delimitation of the topic chronologically and methodologically also encounters difficulties of a formidable nature. As far as chronological boundaries are concerned, the restriction of the present essay to the period 600-1400 A.D. is partly arbitrary, but also partly defensible as marking out a coherent period with its own characteristics. While most of the eschatological themes of the Middle Ages were inherited from the Christian past, it is quite clear that by 600 A.D. the context in which they operated was quite a different one from that of the Patristic world. Similarly, with the appearance of the Hussite movement in the first half of the fifteenth century, it may be argued that a significantly different and truly revolutionary form of apocalyptic movement has entered the scene.[3] Despite the considerable overlap at each end, there is coherence to the period.

Theoretical limitations, difficult to follow through as they may be in practice, must also be made. "Eschatology" in itself would be too broad a term for the topic under review. All medieval thinkers were eschatological in one sense or another, and to try to survey everything that has been written about their attitudes towards the nature of sacred history and the revelation of the last things would be a formidable task indeed. Furthermore, the general category of eschatological thought encroaches on a number of other broad concerns, especially those of millenarianism and messianism, to such an extent that to write a history of the students of eschatology in the Middle Ages could become so diffuse as to be almost arbitrary.

This is the reason for the restriction of this study to the narrower phenomenon of apocalypticism. General eschatology becomes apocalyptic when it announces details of the future course of history and the imminence of its divinely appointed end in a manner that manifestly goes beyond the mere attempt to interpret the Scriptures.

---

2 Joachim's three major works, the *Concordia novi ac veteris testamenti* (Venice, 1519), the *Expositio in Apocalypsim* and the *Psalterium decem chordarum* (Venice, 1527) have fortunately been photographically reprinted by the Minerva G.M.B.H. (Frankfurt, 1964-65).

3 Following B. Töpfer, *Das kommende Reich des Friedens* (Berlin, 1964), pp. 308-9.

New and more precise descriptions of the last events are incorporated, frequently from a new revelatory source (the Sibyl was a popular one); and traditional eschatological imagery is made more vital by being applied directly to current historical events. In many cases those involved in such activity seem to have a sense of personal mission different from traditional teaching and preaching; they receive the reputation of prophets, those in control of the future.

Defined in this way, apocalypticism can be said to include the more radical aspects of the two terms frequently associated with it in modern writing — millenarianism and messianism. Millenarianism, in the broad sense used by some,[4] would include apocalyptic as a particular species of its genus; but since we are restricting ourselves to the medieval period, and since these broad definitions frequently include unresolved problems of methodology, millenarianism will be understood here in the original sense of chiliasm, i.e., as related to the belief in the thousand-year reign of Christ and the saints on earth spoken of in Apoc. 20: 4-6, and therefore merely as one part of the Christian doctrine of the last things. The same may be said about messianism. Broad definitions tend to make it virtually synonymous with millenarianism; but since in the medieval tradition the Second Coming of Christ, or the appearance of various secondary messianic figures (e.g., the Last World Emperor) is only part of the scenario of the last events, it will be understood here only as pertaining to the role played by Christ and Christ-like figures at the end of time.

It is true that when the times were bad — when physical or moral catastrophes seemed about to overwhelm Christianity — there were many who did not hesitate to speak of the approaching end of history. But it is the fervor with which such predictions are made and the centrality that they hold in an author's thought which determine whether or not he can be described as an apocalyptic. There is a considerable difference between the customary bow to traditional eschatology that one may find in many medieval authors and the burning conviction of the nearness of the end that is present in others. Thus there is a definite tradition in western medieval thought, commencing with the assimilation of certain Byzantine Sibylline texts, fertilized by some of the major developments of the eleventh and twelfth centuries (especially

---

4   *E.g.*, G. Guariglia, *Prophetismus und Heilserwartung- Bewegungen* (Horn-Vienna, 1959), pp. 22-59; E. J. Hobsbawn, *Primitive Rebels* (New York, 1965), pp. 57-9; and N. Cohn, "Medieval Millenarianism," S. L. Thrupp, ed., *Millenial Dreams in Action* (New York, 1970), p. 31.

the Gregorian Reform and the Crusades), reaching a high point in the thought of Joachim of Fiore, but having its most pronounced effects in the history of the influence of Joachitism in the thirteenth and fourteenth centuries, which can be aptly characterized as apocalyptic in the sense explained above.

Our subject is not medieval apocalypticism in itself, but the history of its historians. The task is one of such dimensions that only the major figures and the most significant lines of development can be discussed. Much has been omitted; but it is to be hoped that a sketch of the main lines will also prove useful for interpreting details not discussed here. What follows is an attempt to provide the context within which any work on medieval apocalyptic is to be read.

I

Critical study of apocalypticism in medieval thought was scarcely possible before the nineteenth-century revolution in scientific historical method, and it is significant that its first major monument was a product of one of the most important currents of the theology of the middle part of the century, the Tübingen School of Ferdinand Christian Baur (1792-1860). Baur is rightly considered the "Father of Modern Church History", and it is a sign of his perspicacity as an historian of the Church that the prize competition established by the Protestant faculty of Tübingen for the school year 1856-57 concerned the determination of the apocalyptic views of Joachim of Fiore by means of a discrimination between his authentic works and those mistakenly ascribed to him. Earlier historians had cast doubts on some of the works traditionally included in Joachim's corpus; but it was the winner of this prize, a theological student from Stuttgart, Karl Friderich, who first definitively proved the spurious character of the important *Super Hieremiam prophetam* and *Scriptum super Esaiam*, and began the still continuing task of establishing the origins and the context of the many pseudonymous works that complicate the history of medieval apocalyptic.[5]

The problems of the thought of the Calabrian Abbot and the authenticity of the works circulating under his name also attracted the at-

5 "Friderich's kritische Untersuchung der dem Abt Joachim von Floris zugeschriebenen Commentare zu Jesejas und Jeremias, mitgeteilt von D. Baur," *Zeitschrift für wissenschaftliche Theologie* 2 (1859) 349-63, 449-514.

tention of French scholars. The rationalist savant, Ernest Renan (1823-92), in his 1866 article, "Joachim di Flore et l'évangile éternel",[6] gave the first significant assessment of Joachim's relation to one of the more radical expressions of thirteenth-century apocalypticism, the crisis of the "Eternal Gospel" at the University of Paris in 1254-56. Other French interest in medieval apocalyptic of this era centered around the "Legend of the Year 1000", i.e., the assertion that belief that the world would end in 1000 A.D. had introduced widespread terror shortly before the actual date. Based upon some tenth-century sources indicating belief in the near approach of the end (though few of them have anything to do with the actual date of 1000) and formulated for the first time by the Church historian Cardinal Baronius in the sixteenth century, the legend was widely accepted in nineteenth-century France. Critics were not lacking who pointed out, among other things, that there was no uniform chronology at the time and hence little agreement about which year actually was the thousandth after the Incarnation, and that the late tenth century does not seem any richer in apocalyptic expectation than the two preceeding centuries.[7]

Despite this interest, it was Germany and not France which was the most important center of the earliest studies of apocalypticism. The first comprehensive survey of the field came from the pen of Johann Joseph von Döllinger (1799-1890), the founder of Catholic Church history in nineteenth-century Germany. Even after a century of scholarship, Döllinger's essay, "Der Weissagungsglaube und das Prophetentum in der christlichen Zeit", is still one of the few general attempts to cover the whole medieval period.[8] Döllinger's work is notable not only for the wide range of material which he utilized, but also for his pioneering attempt to work out a typology of medieval prophecy into religious, dynastic, national, and cosmopolitan categories.

---

6 *Revue des deux mondes* 64 (1866) 94-142. Translated in *Studies in Religious History* (New York, 1887), pp. 210-304.

7 See F. Plaine, "Les prétendues terreurs de l'an mil," *Revue des questions historiques* 13 (1873) 145-64; and especially, J. Roy, *L'an mil. Formation de la légende de l'an mil; état de la France de l'an 950 à l'an 1050* (Paris, 1885), especially pp. 169-91. For a modern survey of the question, see A. Vasiliev, "Medieval Ideas of the End of the World: West and East," *Byzantion* 16 (1942-43) 462 ff. It is unfortunate to see the legend, even if in attenuated and qualified fashion, being given a new lease on life by such a scholar as H. Focillon in his *L'an mil.* See chap. 1 of the English translation, *The Year 1000* (New York, 1969), pp. 39-72.

8 First published in 1871 and reprinted in his *Kleinere Schriften* (Stuttgart, 1890), pp. 451-557, the work has been translated into English as *Prophecies and the Prophetic Spirit in the Christian Era* (London, 1873). Döllinger also edited a part of Peter John Olivi's *Postilla in Apocalypsim* in his *Beiträge zur Sektengeschichte des Mittelalters* 2 (Munich, 1890), pp. 526-85.

Friderich, Renan, and von Döllinger represent three attitudes —
liberal Protestant, rationalist anti-clerical, and Catholic — which were
important motivating forces behind the interest in medieval apocalyptic
at this time. They were by no means the only forces. Historians of
heresy in the Middle Ages, such as the Italian Felice Tocco, were also
interested in apocalyptic material, and so was the hyper-critical wing of
German scholarship which was such a distinctive part of the latter
nineteenth century. In 1874 W. Preger, in the best traditions of this approach, proved the inauthenticity of the three major works of Joachim,
the *Expositio super Apocalypsim*, the *Concordia novi ac veteris testamenti*, and
the *Psalterium decem chordarum*.[9] Another major motivation behind
apocalyptic studies was German nationalism, especially in its imperial
form. As several recent commentators have noted,[10] it was only in the
nineteenth century that the legend connected with the sleeping emperor
of the Kyffhäuser mountain began to play a large part in German
national consciousness. The political significance of this legend in the
period of Germany's struggle for unification was great; it was enhanced
and given academic respectability by such works as that of W. von
Giesebrecht, *Geschichte der deutschen Kaiserzeit* (1st ed., Braunschweig,
1855). The fusion of the theme of the Last World Emperor with that of
the return of the heroic Barbarossa was not so much a function of
medieval prophecy as of the political interests of the nineteenth century; but it did provide an impetus for the study of one aspect of
medieval apocalyptic, as the works of G. Voigt, G. von Zezschwitz, and
A. von Gutschmid indicate.[11]

The years 1885-1890 can be said to mark the transition from the
period of early and sporadic interest in apocalypticism to one of a full
flowering of scholarly concern that was to last until the end of the First
World War.[12] For quality of scholarship, as well as for sheer productivity, the generation of 1885-1920 is at least the equal of those that have
succeeded it.

9   "Das Evangelium Aeternum und Joachim von Floris," *Abhandlungen hist. Klasse der bayerischen
Akademie der Wissenschaften* 12,3 (1874) 1-41.
10   Notably P. Munz, *Frederick Barbarossa: A Study in Medieval Politics* (Ithaca, 1969), chap. 1: "The
Kyfhäusser Legend," pp. 3-22; and P. J. Alexander, "Byzantium and the Migration of Literary
Motifs: The Legend of the Last Roman Emperor," *Mediaevalia et humanistica* N.S. 2 (London and
Cleveland, 1971) 49-54.
11   Voigt, "Die deutsche Kaisersage," *Historische Zeitschrift* 26 (1871) 131-87; von Zezschwitz, *Vom
römischen Kaisertum deutscher Nation: Ein mittelalterliches Drama, nebst Untersuchungen über die byzantinischen
Quellen der deutschen Kaisersage* (Leipzig, 1877); and the important review of this by von Gutschmid in
the *Historische Zeitschrift* for 1879, reprinted in his *Kleine Schriften* 5 (Leipzig, 1894), pp. 495-506.

German historians dominated the field in an almost overwhelming manner. The reasons are not hard to find. The most obvious was the development of the *Monumenta Germaniae historica* as not only the most important national source collection for medieval history, but also as the rigorous training school for a generation of scholars.[13] Three of the historians of the period began that intimate association between the study of medieval apocalypticism and the history of the MGH which has lasted down to the present day: Oswald Holder-Egger (1851-1911), a pupil of Georg Waitz and distinguished editor, was a long-time Associate (*Mitarbeiter*) seriously considered for the Presidency of the Institute in the early 1900's; and Ernst Sackur (1862-1901) and Ernst Bernheim (1859-1942) were Associates on the *Libelli de lite* in the 1890's. The impulse given to German medievalists by the *Monumenta*, however, was enhanced by the sectarian interests of German Catholic historians as they attempted to recover from the blow of Döllinger's defection after the First Vatican Council and to escape from the defensive stance into which they had been forced by Bismarck's *Kulturkampf*. The collaboration of two gifted Catholic historians of the period, the Dominican Heinrich Denifle (1844-1905), and the Jesuit (later Cardinal) Franz Ehrle (1845-1934), was responsible for the *Archiv für Literatur- und Kirchengeschichte des Mittelalters*,[14] still a most important source for materials for the history of thirteenth-century apocalyptic.

If the preponderant position of German medieval scholarship at the turn of the century had much to do with its domination in the field of apocalyptic studies, there were also theological factors of note that were probably scarcely less influential, though perhaps not as directly evident. It is hard to think it purely fortuitous that the same generation that discovered the consistent eschatological dimensions of the New Testament should also have shown such regard for the medieval manifestations of radical thought about the last things. For the most part, the medieval historians have left no explicit references to the influence that this shift in Biblical and theological studies may have exer-

---

12   D. Douie in her sketch of the historiography of the Spiritual Franciscans called 1884 an *annus mirabilis* on the basis of the appearance of works by Tocco, Richard and Renan. *Cf. The Nature and Effect of the Heresy of the Fraticelli* (Manchester, 1932), p. 277.

13   D. Knowles remarks: "... [it] gave German medievalists the lead among European historians which even two disastrous wars have not taken from them;" *Cf.* "The *Monumenta Germaniae historica*" in *Great Historical Enterprises* (London, 1962), p. 95.

14   Seven volumes were published between 1885 and 1900. On the work of these two men, *cf.* M. Grabmann, "Heinrich Denifle O.P. und Kardinal Franz Ehrle S.J.," *Philosophisches Jahrbuch* 56 (1946) 9-26.

cised upon their work; but the community of interest between the two areas is manifest in the person of Wilhelm Bousset (1865-1920). Primarily known as a Biblical exegete, Bousset extended his researches in eschatology into later periods in a manner which displayed his immense erudition and opened up new possibilities for the interpretation of the medieval materials. Following the lead of the Old Testament studies of H. Gunkel, he viewed the history of Christian eschatology in the light of the insights that he had gained from the study of the history of religions. A good example of this is to be found in his interpretation of the Antichrist legend as a development from the Babylonian creation myth transformed into an expectation of the last things.[15] Such explanations may seem oversimplified today, but at the turn of the century the approach was an original one. Whatever one may think of Bousset's particular theories, the value of his learned discussions of the history and transmission of eschatological texts cannot be denied.[16]

The only contemporary of Bousset who shared an approach influenced by the history of religions was the Frenchman Paul Alphandéry (1875-1932), one of the early editors of the *Revue d'histoire des religions*. His major field of concern was the history of heretical movements and his writings of apocalyptic interest include studies on the influence of prophecy in medieval sects, on the Antichrist legend, and on the eschatological dimensions of the Crusades.[17] Alphandéry was a learned, if tendentious, historian; neither he nor Bousset had a notable effect on their contemporaries or immediate successors. Historians of medieval apocalypticism have on the whole not paid sufficient attention to the insights and methods offered by the history of religions.

The impressiveness of many of the other achievements of this generation cannot be denied. The appearance of the first volume of the *Archiv*

---

15 *Der Antichrist in der Ueberlieferung des Judentums, des Neuen Testaments, und der alten Kirche* (Göttingen, 1895); English translation, *The Antichrist Legend* (London, 1896), especially pp. 13-15, and 144. See also his article "Antichrist" in the *Hastings Encyclopedia of Religion and Ethics* 1 (New York, 1908), pp. 578-81.

16 "Beiträge zur Geschichte der Eschatologie," *Zeitschrift für Kirchengeschichte* 20 (1899) 103-31, 261-90, especially for medieval Byzantine apocalyptic; and *Die Offenbarung Johannis* (Göttingen, 1906, 6th ed.), pp. 49-119, for the history of exegesis of the Book of Revelation.

17 "De quelques faits de prophétisme dans les sectes latines antérieures au Joachimisme," *Revue d'histoire des religions* 52 (1905) 177-218; "Mahomet-Antichrist dans le moyen âge latin," *Mélanges Hartwig Derenbourg, 1844-1908* (Paris, 1909), pp. 261-77; and "Les citations bibliques chez les historiens de la première croisade," *Revue d'histoire des religions* 99 (1929) 139-57. A posthumus work on the Crusades was put together by his pupil A. Dupront, *La chrétienté et l'idée de croisade* (Paris, 1954).

für Literatur- und Kirchengeschichte in 1885, containing Denifle's article, "Das Evangelium aeternum und die Commission zu Anagni", his edition of the *Protocoll* of Anagni,[18] and the first part of Ehrle's article, "Die Spiritualen, ihr Verhältnis zum Franciscanerorden und zu den Fraticellen" (which edited material from Angelo of Clareno, one of the more important Joachites), marked the coming of age of critical studies on the history of the apocalyptic thought of the thirteenth-century Franciscans. Ehrle pursued his researches into the Spiritual Franciscans in the second volume (1886) with a partial edition and study of Angelo's *Historia septem tribulationum*, and an article entitled "Zur Vorgeschichte des Concils von Vienne". The indefatigable Jesuit continued his work on the events leading up to the Council of Vienne in the third volume (1887), and also published the first real study of Peter John Olivi (1248-97), the most significant apocalyptic thinker of the thirteenth century.[19] Ehrle completed his studies in the fourth volume (1888), having amassed just under a thousand pages of texts and commentaries which were to provide a major impetus to the growth of interest in thirteenth-century apocalypticism and to the early history of the Franciscan order. During the same years, the first of the modern Franciscan periodicals, the *Miscellanea Francescana*, began publication at Foligno in 1886; in 1908 it was joined by the weightier *Archivum Franciscanum historicum* published by the fathers of Quaracchi. Both journals have continued to provide outlets for a wide variety of articles and editions important for the later stages of medieval apocalyptic. Many pioneer studies of Franciscan history of this period still have relevance for the modern scholar.[20]

The work of Denifle and Ehrle was followed by more than two decades in which O. Holder-Egger almost eclipsed their productivity. The Sibylline and Joachite texts which he edited in his "Italienische Prophetieen des 13. Jahrhunderts" [21] made available prophetic works which spoke to a much wider world of political and ecclesiastical con-

---

18 The document drawn up in 1255 by the Commission formed by Pope Alexander IV to study the orthodoxy of Joachim's writings and that of the *Evangelium aeternum* of Gerardo di Borgo San Donino.

19 "Petrus Johannis Olivi, sein Leben und seine Schriften," 409-552.

20 Especially, E. Balthazar, *Geschichte der Armutsstreites im Franziskanerorden bis zum Konzil von Vienne (1311)* (Münster, 1911); F. Callaey, *L'idéalisme franciscain spirituel au XIVᵉ siècle: Etude sur Ubertin de Casale* (Louvain, 1911); H. Hefele, *Die Bettelorden und das religiöse Volksleben Ober- und Mittelitaliens im XIII. Jahrhunderts* (Leipzig, 1910); and L. Oliger, "Documenta inedita ad historiam Fraticellorum spectantia," *Archivum Franciscanum historicum* 3-6 (1910-13).

21 *Neues Archiv der Gesellschaft für ältere deutsche Geschichtskunde* 15 (1890) 143-78; 30 (1904-05) 323-86; and 33 (1907-08) 97-187.

cerns than those directly dealing with the crisis over absolute poverty in the Franciscan order. His masterly edition of Salimbene's *Chronica* (MGH, *Scriptores* 32 (1905-13)) presented the world with a superb version of the most important narrative source for thirteenth-century Joachitism. At the same time that these editions of thirteenth- and fourteenth-century texts were being issued in such profusion, the earlier medieval period was not neglected. Some works of the twelfth-century author Gerhoch of Reichersberg appeared in the MGH's *Libelli de lite* edited by the able Ernst Sackur,[22] who also enriched the tale of available early medieval texts by his editions and learned discussions of the Tiburtine Sibyl, the Pseudo-Methodius, and the tract of Adso of Liège on the Antichrist. This work still remains central to the history of medieval apocalypticism prior to the eleventh century.[23]

Denifle, Ehrle, Holder-Egger, and Sackur all made immeasurable contributions to the advancement of our knowledge of medieval apocalyptic, but none of them attempted to produce an over-all interpretation of the field. Such studies, however, were not lacking between 1885 and 1920. Three works deserve our attention. German interest in the history of the legends associated with the figure of the emperor continued to grow in the decades following the unification of 1870. Historians such as H. Grauert pursued the topic,[24] but the true summary work did not appear until 1895. Franz Kampers (1868-1929), in his *Kaiserprophetieen und Kaisersagen im Mittelalter*, produced that *rara avis* of historical study — a popular book which fully deserved its renown. Kampers' control of the complex sources of his material and his ability to construct a readable (if occasionally forced and overblown) account of the development of the imperial legends make this still the best book for the medieval period,[25] despite the author's own subsequent researches and the work of such historians as G. Schultheiss, K. Hampe, and E. Kantorowicz.

Perhaps the key to Kampers' success was in his adherence to a chronological framework, since the two contemporary attempts to survey the whole of medieval apocalyptic adopted a thematic approach that contributed greatly to their deficiencies. Ernst Wadstein's *Die*

---

22 *Libelli de lite* 3 (1897): *De investigatione Antichristi*, Liber I (pp. 304-95); and the *De quarta vigilia noctis* (pp. 503-25).

23 *Sibyllinische Texte und Forschungen* (Halle, 1898).

24 "Zur deutschen Kaisersage," *Historisches Jahrbuch* 13 (1892) 100-43.

25 The work was reissued in a more popular form the following year as *Die deutsche Kaiseridee im Prophetie und Sage*.

eschatologischen Ideengruppen (Leipzig, 1896) considers the Antichrist, the end of the world, and the last judgment in the first part, and various aspects of chiliasm in the second. The book is filled with information, but the author's sweeping generalizations and unfortunate characterizations result from trying to do too much on too narrow a base of information. More successful (perhaps because less pretentious) was Ernst Bernheim's *Mittelalterliche Zeitanschauungen in ihrem Einfluss auf Politik und Geschichtsschreibung*, Teil I: *Die Zeitanschauungen* (Tübingen, 1918). The author, a former Associate of the MGH and theorist of the nature of historical method,[26] taught at Greifswald from 1883 to 1921 where he directed a number of theses on topics related to medieval apocalypticism. Perhaps it is the fate of any general interpretation, but the works of Wadstein and Bernheim have definitely not lasted in the same way that the more technical and limited studies of their contemporaries have. The latter are the real monuments of that generation of German historians whose end coincides so neatly with the conclusion of the first great apocalyptic event of our own century.

The end of the First World War can be said to mark a major shift in the historiography of medieval apocalypticism. One group of scholars swiftly left the scene; even the few that managed to bridge the gap had done most of their original work in the earlier period. Two characteristics of the scholarship after 1920 distinguish it from the era just examined. First of all, Germany lost its position of unquestioned domination in this field of medieval study. It is true that German contribution to the area was still of great importance, and that Herbert Grundmann (1902-70), the President of the MGH, was perhaps the foremost expert of the period; but the growth of Italian scholarship on Joachim of Fiore after World War I, the proliferation of Franciscan studies, the increasing interest in aspects of medieval heresy, as well as other tendencies, all worked to reduce the centrality of Germany's position. The second characteristic of the past fifty years has been a greater variation of viewpoints than was evident in the earlier time. A marked similarity of approach, founded upon the traditions of German institutional and intellectual history, dominated the generation from 1885 to 1920 (with the exception of Bousset and Alphandéry); after 1920 the historiographical options become more varied.

Karl Burdach (1859-1936) began his monumental study of later medieval thought, *Vom Mittelalter zur Reformation*, in 1912. Various sec-

---

26   *E.g.*, *Lehrbuch der historischen Methode* (Leipzig, 1889).

tions of the fourth volume, *Das Briefwechsel Cola's da Rienzo* (1912-29), contribute to the study of medieval apocalypticism. Burdach's erudition was formidable, and the edition of the letters of Rienzo and the pseudo-Joachite text, *Oraculum Cyrilli cum expositione Abbatis Joachim*,[27] is of great value; but the interpretation of Joachim as a forerunner of the Renaissance has found little favor with other students and does scant justice to the importance of the Calabrian in the context of the thought of his time.

While Burdach's work was in progress, a young scholar named Herbert Grundmann published his Leipzig dissertation, *Studien über Joachim von Floris*, in 1927. As the author has remarked in the preface to the 1966 reprint of the book, there are many things in the work which could be criticized or corrected on the basis of later research (much of it his own);[28] but this does not take away from the fact that Grundmann's *Studien* was the first successful general analysis of the main lines of Joachim's thought. In placing the Abbot within the context of medieval apocalyptic thought, as well as in its deft analysis of his exegetical and historical theories, it remains one of the fundamental works on the greatest figure in medieval prophecy of the end.

Studies in the history of apocalyptic were to owe much to Grundmann during the following four decades. He turned his attention to Joachim's heirs in the thirteenth and fourteenth centuries, and in a series of articles helped to clear up complicated questions of the origin and transmission of texts and the influence of apocalyptic themes in the late medieval period.[29] Grundmann then widened his scope in the direction of the general study of heresy. His most noted work, *Religiöse Bewegungen im Mittelalter* (1935; the second edition of 1961 adds an important "Neue Beiträge"), which considered various aspects of Apostolic Poverty movements, the Beguines, and the Free Spirit movement, was a pioneer effort in the social interpretation of medieval heresy. Unfortunately, this magisterial work has little of direct relevance to apocalyptic as such, though it does suggest a mode of in-

27 By P. Puir, *Vom Mittelalter zur Reformation* 2.4, pp. 223-343.
28 (Darmstadt, 1966), p. vii.
29 "Ueber den Apokalypsen-Kommentare des Minoriten Alexanders," *Zentralblatt für Bibliothekswesen* 45 (1928) 714-23; an important review of L.A.Paton, *Les prophéties de Merlin* in the *Göttingische gelehrte Anziegen* 190 (1928) 562-83; "Kleine Beiträge über Joachim von Floris," *Zeitschrift für Kirchengeschichte* 48 (1929) 137-65; "Liber de Flore. Eine Schrift der Franziskaner-Spiritualen aus dem Anfang des 14. Jahrhunderts," *Historisches Jahrbuch* 49 (1929) 33-91; "Die Papstprophetien des Mittelalters," *Archiv für Kulturgeschichte* 19 (1929) 77-159; and "Dante und Joachim von Floris, zu *Paradiso* X-XII," *Deutsches Dante-Jahrbuch* 14 (1932) 210-56.

terpretation which Grundmann himself apparently chose not to pursue, for when he returned to the study of Joachim in the 1950's and 1960's,[30] he did not attempt an analysis of the social context of Joachim's thought and its influence, but restricted himself to questions of intellectual and political history. Perhaps he thought that in the case of Joachim a social interpretation would not prove fruitful, but he made no explicit pronouncements on the reasons for this abstention. During his term as President of the MGH (1959-70), Professor Grundmann actively encouraged the publication of texts of eschatological interest in the series.[31]

Grundmann's immediate predecessor in the President's chair of the German Institute, Friederich Baethgen, also took some interest in apocalypticism, as his semi-popular survey of the history of the figure of the Angelic Pope, *Der Engelpapst: Idee und Erscheinung* (Leipzig, 1943), indicates. The only writer to rival Grundmann in output, however, was Ernst Benz, a noted historian of religion. *Ecclesia spiritualis* (Stuttgart, 1934), his major work in this area, is not a satisfactory book. Popular in style, without textual references to support many of the claims that are made, it is an extended history of the Spiritual Franciscans that begins with a survey of the ideas of Joachim. Benz's overriding concern is to demonstrate that the Spirituals represented a return to a purely apocalyptic, anti-institutional vision of the Church in conformity with primitive Christianity and inalterably in opposition to the papal Church of the medieval period.[32] It cannot be denied that this view reflects certain aspects of the Spiritual movement; indeed, Benz based his work upon a series of earlier articles of a more solid and specialized nature;[33] but so obsessive is his concern to stress just how radical Joachim and his Franciscan followers really were, that the argument is often forced and

---

30 *Neue Forschungen über Joachim von Fiore* (Marburg, 1950); "Zur Biographie Joachims von Fiore und Rainers von Ponza," *Deutsches Archiv für Erforschung des Mittelalters* 16 (1960) 437-546; "Kirchenfreiheit und Kaisermacht um 1190 in der Sicht Joachims von Fiore," 19 (1963) 353-96; and "Lex und Sacramentum bei Joachim von Fiore," *Lex et Sacramentum im Mittelalter*, ed. P. Wilpert (*Miscellanea mediaevalia*, Band 6) (Berlin, 1969), pp. 31-48.

31 These have appeared in the subsection "Quellen zur Geistesgeschichte des Mittelalters" begun in 1955. They include vol. 1, Alexander Minorita, *Expositio in Apocalypsim*, ed. by A. Wachtel (1955); and vol. 4, Rupertus Tuitiensis, *De victoria verbi Dei*, ed. by R. Haacke (1970). Wachtel has also promised an edition of the important pseudo-Joachite work, *Super Hieremiam prophetam*.

32 *Cf.* "Einleitung," especially 2-3.

33 "Joachim-Studien," *Zeitschrift für Kirchengeschichte* 50 (1931) 24-111, 51 (1932) 415-55, 53 (1934) 52-116; "Die Geschichtstheologie der Franziskaner-Spiritualen des 13. und 14. Jahrhunderts nach neuen Quellen," 52 (1933) 90-121; and "Die Kategorien der eschatologischen Zeitbewusstseins," *Deutsche Vierteljahrschrift für Literaturwissenschaft und Geistesgeschichte* 11 (1933) 200-29.

incorrect on key points.[34] Benz's stark contrast of good and evil views of
the Church in the thirteenth century is inadequate to deal with the
complexities and mixed motivation which the history of the period exposes to us.

Grundmann had already hinted at the significance of the twelfth-
century German apocalyptic writers, particularly Rupert of Deutz (d.
1130), Anselm of Havelberg (d. 1158), and Gerhoch of Reichersberg (d.
1169); but the first author to demonstrate their importance in the
evolution of the exegesis of the Book of Revelation in the Middle Ages
was Wilhelm Kamlah whose *Apokalypse und Geschichtstheologie. Die mittelalterliche Auslegung der Apokalypse vor Joachim von Fiore* (Berlin, 1935) is
still virtually the only book to treat this problem in detail. Kamlah's
work may be unfortunate in its decision to prescind from the social and
political context of the views discussed, but its usefulness cannot be
denied.

The rich mine of material on the twelfth-century predecessors of
Joachim has been further pursued in the scholarship of the past forty
years, just as Joachim himself has not been neglected.[35] No definitive
work has yet appeared on Anselm of Havelberg,[36] but important studies
of Rupert[37] and Gerhoch[38] have been completed in recent years. Three
other twelfth-century thinkers whose writings include material of
significance for the history of apocalyptic have also attracted attention.
Otto of Freising (d. 1159), because of his association with the imperial

34   *E.g.*, his summary of Joachim's views on pp. 46-8 oversimplifies the complex question of the
Abbot's attitude towards the Church of the Second Age to such an extent that it is almost a
caricature.

35   Another writer who contributed to Joachim studies at this time was J. Huck whose *Joachim
von Floris und die Joachitische Literatur* (Freiburg-im-Breisgau, 1938) made valuable texts available for
the first time, but whose discussion of the career and ideas of the Abbot was not successful. Two
other German authors of the period also helped stimulate interest in twelfth-century theories of
history, Alois Dempf in his important *Sacrum imperium* (Munich-Berlin, 1929), and Johannes Spörl in
Grundformen hochmittelalterliche Geschichtsanschauungen (Munich, 1935). The former book contains an
extensive interpretation of the medieval apocalyptic tradition.

36   See, however, the articles of M. van Lee, G. Schreiber, K. Fina, and M. Fitzthum in the
Analecta Praemonstratensia, and the recent survey of W. Edyvean, *Anselm of Havelberg and the Theology
of History* (Rome, 1972).

37   M. Magrassi, *Teologia e storia nel pensiero di Ruperto di Deutz* (Rome, 1959); W. Kahles, *Geschichte
als Liturgie: Die Geschichtstheologie des Rupertus von Deutz* (Münster, 1960); and H. Grundmann, "Der
Brand von Deutz 1128 in der Darstellung Abt Rupertus von Deutz," *Deutsches Archiv für Erforschung
des Mittelalters* 22 (1966) 385-471.

38   D. van den Eynde, *L'œuvre littéraire de Géroch de Reichersberg* (Rome, 1957); E. Meuthen, *Kirche
und Heilsgeschichte bei Gerhoh van Reichersberg* (Leiden-Cologne, 1959); and P. Classen, *Gerhoch von
Reichersberg: Eine Biographie* (Wiesbaden, 1960).

ideal, has long been a favorite subject with German medievalists. As far
as his eschatological theories are concerned, in the present century the
most important studies have been those of J. Schmidlin, P. Brezzi, J.
Koch, and J. Mohr.[39] Hildegard of Bingen (d. 1179) has also been written about fairly extensively; B. Widmer's *Heilsordnung und Zeitgeschehen
in der Mystik Hildegards von Bingen* (Basel-Stuttgart, 1955) is the best
recent monograph. A single study exists of the historical and
eschatological views of the great early Scholastic Hugh of St. Victor (d.
1141).[40] While the rediscovery of twelfth-century apocalyptic has been
an important area of recent study, no good survey book exists and it is
obvious that much work remains to be done.

The past fifteen years in Germany have been on the whole the most
stimulating period since the middle thirties. This period has seen not
only the final studies of Grundmann, but also a number of other
significant contributions to the history of apocalyptic. Hanno Helbling
attempted a philosophical analysis of the changes introduced into the
Western consciousness of time by Joachim and his radical followers.
Unfortunately, his book, *Saeculum humanum: Ansätze zu einem Versuch über
spätmittelalterliches Geschichtsdenken* (Naples, 1958), while it makes some
penetrating points, is a premature effort that lacks the rigor of method
and mastery of text which would be needed to prove his position. Amos
Funkenstein studied Patristic and early medieval views of history in his
*Heilsplan und natürliche Entwicklung: Gegenwartsbestimmung im Geschichts-
denken des Mittelalters* (Munich, 1965), but his thesis that the eleventh and
twelfth centuries were marked by the rise of an evolutionary view of
history contrasted to both the previous Augustinian tradition and the
subsequent Joachite one seems too dialectically procrustean to be taken
at face value.[41] Among other authors, Arno Borst in his massive *Der
Turmbau von Babel* (Stuttgart, 1957-63) has given summary accounts of
medieval apocalyptic thinkers.[42] A survey of the sources, content, and
influence of the tenth-century text on the Antichrist by Adso also ap-

39 J. Schmidlin, "Die Eschatologie Ottos von Freising," *Zeitschrift für katholischen Theologie* 29
(1905) 445-81; and *Die geschichtsphilosophische und kirchenpolitische Weltanschauung Ottos von Freising*
(Freiburg-im-Breisgau, 1906); P. Brezzi, "Ottone di Frisinga," *Bollettino dell'Istituto storico italiano per il
medio evo* 54 (1939) 129-328; J. Koch, "Die Grundlagen der Geschichtsphilosophie Ottos von
Freising," *Studien zur historischen Theologie: Festgabe Franz Seppelt* (Munich, 1953), pp. 79 ff.; and
W. Mohr, "Zum Geschichtsbild Ottos von Freising," *Perennitas. Pater Thomas Michaels O.S.B. zum 70.
Geburtstag* (Münster, 1963), pp. 274-93.
40 W. A. Schneider, *Geschichte und Geschichtsphilosophie bei Hugo von St. Viktor* (Münster, 1933).
41 *E.g.*, the remarks on pp. 115-21.
42 In Band II/2 (1959).

peared during this period from the pen of Robert Konrad, *De ortu et tempore Antichristi. Antichristvorstellung und Geschichtsbild des Abtes Adso von Montier-en-Der* (Kallmünz, 1964).

The most interesting new development on the German front, however, has been the appearance of the East German Marxist school of the history of medieval radical movements. The most prolific member of this group is Ernst Werner who has collaborated on a number of studies of medieval sects appearing under the auspices of the *Institut für Erforschung der mittelalterlichen Sektenwesens*.[43] Some of what Werner has written is so heavily ideological that it is difficult for a non-Marxist historian to think that it can tell us much about the Middle Ages, especially when it contains serious errors concerning the material in question;[44] but at least one of his articles offers an illuminating view on some old problems. "Messianische Bewegungen im Mittelalter"[45] attempts to determine a typology of messianism in the medieval period and the social factors that conditioned it. Werner makes it evident that his commitment to dialectical materialism is at the basis of his analysis;[46] but the typologies are useful and thought-provoking, whatever one's attitude towards the underlying ideology may be.

For the history of apocalypticism, however, the most important name in the East German group is that of Bernhard Töpfer, whose reputation rests chiefly upon the most thorough general survey of medieval apocalyptic to appear in many decades, *Das kommende Reich des Friedens* (Berlin, 1964). A full-length review would be necessary to do justice to this work, hence the following remarks are only a programmatic way of framing the problems raised by this kind of interpretation. Töpfer, it appears, can be read on two levels: on the one, as the scholar who has mastered the literature and its problems and strives to create a coherent and convincing picture of the development of medieval apocalyptic, he is frequently most convincing; on the other, as the Marxist theorist seeking to display the true meaning of the history he sketches, he is far less convincing, if convincing at all. Naturally, the two levels interact in

---

43 T. Büttner and E. Werner, *Circumcellionen und Adamiten. Zwei Formen mittelalterlichen Häresie* (Berlin, 1959); and M. Erbstösser and E. Werner, *Ideologische Probleme der mittelalterlichen Plebejertums. Die freigeistige Häresie und ihre sozialen Würzeln* (Berlin, 1960). His own *Pauperes Christi* appeared independently at Leipzig in 1956.

44 *E.g.*, "Popular Ideologies in Late Medieval Europe: Taborite Chiliasm and its Antecedents," *Comparative Studies in History and Society* 2.3 (1960) 344-65, especially what he has to say about Joachim on pp. 349-50.

45 *Zeitschrift für Geschichtswissenschaft* 10 (1962) 371-96, 598-622.

46 *E.g.*, p. 622.

many ways, but the distinction is not a facile one, especially since the
rigid Marxist material usually appears in an almost tacked-on fashion at
the end of the various chapters. Thus, while Töpfer's views on individual problems are almost always well-informed, and usually well-
balanced, and while we can applaud his refusal to ascribe the epithet
"revolutionary" to every apocalyptic movement of the Middle Ages, we
can sincerely question whether the *deus ex machina* of economic determination really explains as much about medieval apocalyptic as the
author claims it does.

It is obvious that German scholarship since 1920 has been impressive
in its fecundity and originality, but a glance at writing in other
languages indicates that it has lost the domination it enjoyed before the
First World War. Spurred on by an understandable national pride, and
all too frequently by the scarcely-veiled desire to defend orthodoxy,
Italian historians plunged into Joachim studies with gusto after 1920. If
it may be said that the general tendency of German studies has been to
highlight the radical and heterodox features of the Abbot's thought,
then, with the necessary qualifications, it may also be asserted that
Italian treatments have tended to move in the other direction.

The most important early name is that of Ernesto Buonaiuti (1881-
1946). A student of the history of early Christianity, he was commissioned by the Istituto Storico Italiano per il Medio Evo to edit some
of the unpublished works of Joachim for the *Fonti per la storia d'Italia*
series. The edition of the *Tractatus super quatuor evangelia*, one of
Joachim's last works, was published in 1930,[47] followed by the *De articulis fidei* and some sermons in 1936. Buonaiuti's interpretation of
Joachim is summarized in a small book, *Gioacchino da Fiore. I tempi, la
vita, il messaggio* (Rome, 1931), and in a long series of articles issued between 1928 and 1946. Strongly influenced by the Modernist movement
within the Catholic Church, Buonaiuti wished to demonstrate Joachim's
orthodoxy, but in a rather distinctive way. Joachim is truly "orthodox"
because his eschatological and ethical concerns placed him in opposition to nascent Scholasticism, a phenomenon which Buonaiuti saw
as harmful to true Christianity.[48] One cannot help but think that for
Buonaiuti Joachim has become something of a stick with which to
belabor the Neoscholastic Catholicism to which he was opposed; but it

---

47 Buonaiuti's skill as an editor was criticized by E. Franceschini, "Il codice padavano An-
toniano XIV, 322, e il testo del *Tractatus super quatuor evangelia* di Gioacchino da Fiore," *Aevum* 9
(1935) 481-92; and C. Ottaviano in a review in *Archivio di filosofia* 1 (1931) 73-82.
48 *E.g.*, p. li of the "Introduzione" to the *De articulis fidei*.

is important to point out that the Italian author did continue to show the relevance of history of religions to the investigation of medieval apocalyptic and did much to stimulate the interest of Italian historians in the thought and influence of the Abbot of Fiore.

A group of scholars soon rose to a more traditional defense of Joachim's orthodoxy. Monsignor Leone Tondelli (1883-1953) had the good fortune to discover a manuscript which he identified as the *Liber figurarum* (a book of drawings illustrating Joachim's thought mentioned by some early writers) in Reggio-Emilia in 1937. He published an edition of this in 1940. A second edition, making use of further manuscripts and the assistance of Marjorie Reeves and Beatrice Hirsch-Reich, was issued in 1953. Along with this facsimile, Tondelli published a lengthy if somewhat disjointed and repetitious study of Joachim and his influence on Dante. Again and again he returned to the defense of the Catholic orthodoxy of the Abbot.

There were Italian scholars, such as Carmelo Ottaviano, the editor of the pseudo-Joachimite *Liber contra Lombardum* (1934), who were willing to admit the heretical features of the Abbot's thought, but the brunt of the Italian effort has been to confess a material heresy in Joachim's Trinitarian views while defending the orthodoxy of his theories of history. Francesco Foberti even went so far as to see the condemnation of Joachim's views on the Trinity at the Fourth Lateran Council as a Cistercian plot against the renegade Cistercian Joachim.[49] Francesco Russo, on the other hand, one of the most prolific authors that the history of Joachim studies has produced, adheres to the main line of the Italian interpretation. His *Bibliografia Gioachimita* (Florence, 1954), while deficient in many respects as critics have pointed out, is still a useful tool for the continuing study of Joachim's thought. His interpretation, to be found in a mass of articles and the summary book, *Gioacchino da Fiore e le fondazioni florensi in Calabria* (Naples, 1958), is more interesting on the history of the order that Joachim founded than on the Abbot himself. The most recent Italian scholar to concern himself with Joachim in an extensive manner is Antonio Crocco. His knowledge of the text of Joachim's writings is impressive, and his penetration of the Abbot's Trinitarian views is perhaps the best currently available; but the defense that he offers of the orthodoxy of Joachim's theories labors under the same weaknesses that will be discussed below in the case of the works of Miss Reeves, viz., the danger of missing the point about the

---

49   *Cf.* his *Gioacchino da Fiore e il Gioacchinismo antico e moderno* (Padua, 1942), p. 98.

true significance of the thought of the Calabrian in the context of the medieval church.[50]

The other focus of Italian interest in apocalypticism has been a development of the studies on heresy begun in the last century by Tocco. Raffaelo Morghen has been a notable figure in this area of Italian historiography in the era since 1920. In terms of his contribution to the history of apocalyptic, the general survey with selected texts published in 1961, *La crisi dell'età medioevale*, deserves to be noted;[51] but probably his most valuable accomplishment has been his work as President of the Istituto Storico Italiano per il Medio Evo in attracting scholars to study these problems and in providing an outlet for their researches. The late A. Frugoni, who edited Joachim's *Adversus Judaeos* for the *Fonti* in 1957, published a series of studies on the career of Pope Celestine V (who held office from July to December of 1294), the Spirituals' candidate for the *Pastor angelicus*.[52] In 1955 Raoul Manselli published his *La "Lectura super Apocalypsim" di Pietro di Giovanni Olivi: Ricerche sull'eschatologismo medioevale* under the auspices of the Istituto, the first general history of medieval apocalyptic in many decades. Unlike the accounts of Wadstein and Bernheim, but like the more detailed subsequent study of Töpfer, Manselli adopted a chronological format: three general chapters discuss the evolution of eschatological views from Augustine to Peter John Olivi, the last two concentrate on Olivi, particularly on the *Lectura super Apocalypsim* of which Manselli intends to produce an edition. There are no startling revelations in this book, but the outline is clear and the positions adopted usually moderate. Manselli has also been interested in Arnald of Villanova (*c.* 1238-1311), an astrologer, physician, and apocalyptic writer associated with the Spiritual movement. Besides his articles devoted to Arnald,[53] he has

---

50   His works include *Gioacchino da Fiore* (Naples, 1960); *L'età dello Spirito Santo e l'ecclesia spiritualis in Gioacchino da Fiore* (Naples, 1964); and *Simbologia Gioachimita e simbologia Dantesca* (Naples, 1964). Among his important articles are "Profilo storico del Gioacchinismo dell'Anno dell'Alleluja a Cola da Rienzo," *Sophia* 24 (1956) 203-11; "La formazione dottrinale di Gioacchino da Fiore e le Fonti della sua teologia trinitaria," *Sophia* 23 (1955) 192-96; and "La teologia trinitaria di Gioacchino da Fiore," *Sophia* 25 (1957) 222-32.

51   An expanded version of the texts which Morghen appended to illustrate this summary history is now available from F. Bolgiani and R. Manselli, *Antologia di testi di teologia della storia.* 1: *Cristianesimo antico e medioevale* (Turin, 1965).

52   *Celestiniana. Istituto storico... Studi storici*, fasc. 6-7 (Rome, 1953).

53   "La religiosità d'Arnaldo da Villanova," *Bollettino dell'Istituto storico...* 62 (1950) 123-58; "Arnaldo da Villanova, diplomatico, medico, teologo e riformatore religioso alle soglie del secolo XIV," *Humanitas* (Brescia) 8 (1953) 268-79; and "Arnaldo da Villanova e i Papi del suo tempo," *Studi romani* 7 (1959) 146-61.

produced a valuable survey of the intellectual and social ferment surrounding the Catalan author in his *Spirituali e beghini in Provenza*.[54] A measure of the place that later medieval apocalypticism holds in recent Italian scholarship can be seen from the papers of the "Third Conference for Studies on Medieval Spirituality" held at Todi in 1960 and published in 1962 under the title *L'attesa dell'età nuova nella spiritualità dalla fine del medioevo*. The collection includes studies by Morghen, Manselli, Frugoni, Frater Ilarino da Milano (a noted Franciscan student of heresy), Tullio Gregory, who has studied the reaction of Scholasticism to the eschatological tradition,[55] and a few foreign students.

Interest in the early history of the Franciscans, evident in the period from 1885 to 1920, also continued to be a prime avenue into the history of medieval apocalyptic for many scholars in the post-World War I period. The learned L. Oliger published further articles on the Spirituals;[56] and a number of other students, such as G. Bondatti, E. Donckel, A. Wachtel, V. Doucet, and J. Ratzinger also made valuable additions to our knowledge of apocalypticism in the Franciscan order.[57] J. M. Pou y Marti's *Visionarios, beguinos y fraticelas catalanes, siglos XIII-XV* (Vich, 1930) contributed to the story of apocalyptic among Spanish Franciscans and related groups. The period since 1920 has also seen the communication of interest in the person of St. Francis to a wider historical audience, especially in the English-speaking world. This development, though begun at the end of the nineteenth century through such works as Paul Sabatier's *Vie de Saint François d'Assise* (Paris, 1894, with numerous later editions and translations), bore its richest fruit for serious historical scholarship in the post-World War I period.

It was through the back door of Franciscan studies that English historians first became interested in the apocalyptic material that had

---

54 *Istituto storico... Studi storici*, fasc. 31-4 (Rome, 1959).

55 See "Escatologia e Aristotelismo nella scolastica medioevale," *Giornale critico della filosofia italiana* 10 (1961) 163-74; and "Sull'escatologia di Bonaventura e Tommaso d'Aquino," *Studi medievali*, 3rd Series, 6 (1965) 79-94.

56 Especially "Beiträge zur Geschichte der Spiritualen, Fratizellen und Clarener im Mittelalter," *Zeitschrift für Kirchengeschichte* 4 (1927) 215-42; and "Spirituels," *Dictionnaire de théologie catholique* 14.2 (Paris, 1941) 2522-49.

57 Bondatti, *Gioachinismo e Francescanismo nel Dugento* (S. Maria degli Angeli, 1924); Donckel, "Studien über die Prophezeiung des fr. Telesphorus von Cosenza, O.F.M.," *Archivum Franciscanum historicum* 26 (1933) 29-104, 282-314; Wachtel, "Die weltgeschichtliche Apokalypse-Auslegung des Minoriten Alexander von Bremen," *Franziskaner Studien* 24 (1937) 201 ff., 305 ff.; V. Doucet, "Angelus Clarinus ad Alvarium Pelagium," *Archivum Franciscanum historicum* 39 (1946) 63-200; and J. Ratzinger, *Die Geschichtstheologie des heiligen Bonaventuras* (Munich, 1959), with an English translation entitled *The Theology of History in St. Bonaventure* (Chicago, 1971).

already been so intensively studied on the continent for over half a century. The popular historian G. G. Coulton (1858-1947), in dependence on the work of Holder-Egger, translated sections of Salimbene into English and commented on the world of thirteenth-century religion in his *From St. Francis to Dante* (London, 1907); but the real founder of Franciscan studies in England was A. G. Little, whose work has been continued by his son-in-law, John Moorman, the bishop of Ripon.[58] The first work in English to deal explicitly with the apocalyptic theories of the Franciscans was Decima Douie's *The Nature and Effect of the Heresy of the Fraticelli* (Manchester, 1932). It gives a full account of the various Spiritual leaders and their theories, especially Angelo of Clareno (c. 1255-1337), Peter John Olivi, and Ubertino of Casale (c. 1259-1335). Outdated in places by subsequent research, its deft appreciation of the personalities of the great Spirituals is its most lasting achievement. In recent years the literature in English on the Spiritual Franciscans has seen the publication of two first-rate books: R. Brooke's *Early Franciscan Government* (Cambridge, 1959) deals chiefly with the institutional development of the order, but does provide some information on the beginning of the Spiritual crisis; and M. Lambert's *Franciscan Poverty* (London, 1961), a history of the treatment of the concept of poverty in the order from Francis down to the condemnation of 1323, is the best account available in any language and an indispensable book for Franciscan apocalypticism.

In the 1930's English scholars also began to give some attention to the Calabrian master of the Spirituals. Henry Bett included a brief introduction entitled *Joachim of Flora* (London, 1931) in his "Great Medieval Churchmen" series, and it was during this same period that Miss Marjorie Reeves began her work on the reputation of the Calabrian. Since her 1932 thesis was never published, the scholarly world had to wait until the 1950's before the fruits of the labors of Miss Reeves became known. In the meantime, she had been joined at Oxford by the German scholar, Beatrice Hirsch-Reich, whose interests closely paralleled her own. Their part in the second edition of the *Liber figurarum* has already been noted, and many of their early articles deal with the history of this text and the defense of its ascription to Joachim and his immediate circle.[59] Miss Reeves also studied the influence of

---

58 Moorman's *A History of the Franciscan Order* (Oxford, 1968) is a conservative summary of the order down to 1517. It has little that relates directly to apocalyptic questions, but provides a useful background.

59 M. Reeves, "The *Liber figurarum* of Joachim of Fiore," *Mediaeval and Renaissance Studies* 2

Joachim's thought on a variety of religious orders, edited one of
Joachim's minor writings with Miss Hirsch-Reich (the *De septem sigillis*),[60]
and collaborated with the American scholar Morton Bloomfield in an
article on "The Penetration of Joachimism into Northern Europe".[61]
Miss Hirsch-Reich, besides her work on the bibliography of Joachim
studies and on the manuscript tradition of his works, wrote on the Abbot's Trinitarian theories and on his attitude towards the Jews.[62]

The study of medieval heretical or dissident movements has also continued to provide an important part of the wider context within which
apocalyptic literature and movements have been investigated in the
English-speaking world. Norman Cohn's *The Pursuit of the Millenium*
(London, 1957; 3rd enlarged edition 1970) is one of the most notable
examples of this channel of access, as is Gordon Leff's two-volume
Heresy in the Later Middle Ages (Manchester, 1967). Cohn's work,
something of a best-seller as far as recent medieval history is concerned,
is original and provocative, though frequently superficial (the third
edition is notably more cautious than the first two). Leff is thorough (at
least on the question of apocalyptic) and on the whole conservative in
outlook. To spell this out in greater detail, it should be noted that
Cohn's attempt to determine the economic and psychological conditions
that facilitated the growth of radical messianic theories from the Middle
Ages down to the twentieth century is at times very insightful, but any
keen student of medieval apocalyptic will soon become aware that the
author treats of only a select part of the available material and only insofar as it fits his scheme. Cohn's experiment in what might be termed
medieval social psychology is one of the most original contributions of
recent years to the investigation of the apocalypticism of the Middle
Ages, but there are too many weaknesses to make his book more than a
pioneering essay. The imprecision of his use of the term messianism, his
lack of rigorous source criticism, and the blindness to the effect that

(1950) 57-81; "The *Arbores* of Joachim of Fiore," *Studies in Italian Medieval History Presented to Miss E. M. Jamison* (British School of Rome, Paper 34, Rome, 1956), pp. 124-36; M. Reeves and B. Hirsch-Reich, "The *Figurae* of Joachim, Genuine and Spurious Collections," *Mediaeval and Renaissance Studies* 3 (1954) 170-99; and B. Hirsch-Reich, "Das Figurenbuch Joachims von Floris," *Recherches de théologie ancienne et médiévale* 24 (1954) 144-47.

60 *Recherches de théologie...* 21 (1951) 211-57.

61 *Speculum* 29 (1957) 772-93. Among the other important articles of Miss Reeves is "Joachimist Influences on the Idea of the Last World Emperor," *Traditio* 17 (1961) 323-70.

62 "Die Quelle der Trinitätskreise von Joachim von Floris und Dante," *Sophia* 22 (1954) 170-78; and "Joachim von Fiore und das Judentum," *Judentum im Mittelalter*, ed. P. Wilpert (*Miscellanea mediaevalia*, Band 4) (Berlin, 1966), pp. 228-63.

counter-examples might have upon his proposed thesis regarding the genesis of messianic movements (e.g., in the light of Cohn's views the Black Death should have provoked the *ne plus ultra* of medieval messianism) are serious deficiencies in his interpretation.

Professor Leff's aims are more limited. His two chapters on "Poverty and Prophecy"[63] provide the best general introduction to Franciscan apocalypticism in English (Lambert deals with the narrower theme of apostolic poverty). The limitations of Leff's study are equally obvious: it is still framed in terms of the influence of apocalypticism on the Franciscan order alone, and consists mainly of a summary of previous research.

The spread of interest in medieval apocalyptic to the English-speaking world has also borne fruit on the other side of the Atlantic in the past two decades. Mention has already been made of Bloomfield's collaboration with Reeves and of his masterly survey of the scholarship on Joachim up to 1957. The same author, himself primarily a student of medieval literature, has indicated the importance of apocalypticism to the understanding of late medieval literature in his book *Piers Plowman as a Fourteenth-Century Apocalypse* (New Brunswick, 1961). Interest in Byzantine apocalyptic literature, almost abandoned among western scholars since the days of Sackur and Bousset, has lately been given new life by the work of the American Byzantinist, Paul J. Alexander. Most significant among his works for historians of Latin apocalypticism is his edition and study of the Greek original of the Tiburtine Sibyl.[64] Finally, the past few years have seen a heightening of interest in the Joachite tradition among American medievalists, as the articles of E. R. Daniel among others indicate.[65]

Our survey of the historiography of medieval apocalypticism may seem lacking by its failure to give thus far much consideration to French literature on the topic. Medieval studies in French, dominant in so many fields, have on the whole been sporadic in their consideration of apocalypticism. The works of P. Alphandéry in the early period have already been noted; another early twentieth-century writer deserving

---

63   1.51-255.

64   *The Oracle of Baalbeck. The Tiburtine Sibyl in Greek Dress* (Dumbarton Oaks Studies 10; Washington, 1967). See also besides the article referred to in n. 9, "Historiens byzantins et croyances eschatologiques," *Actes du XIIᵉ congrès international d'études byzantines* (Belgrade, 1964) 2.1-8; and especially the valuable methodological survey "Medieval Apocalypses as Historical Sources," *American Historical Review* 73 (1968) 997-1018.

65   *E.g.,* "Apocalyptic Conversion: The Joachite Alternative to the Crusades," *Traditio* 25 (1969) 127-54.

mention is Paul Fournier who published his *Etudes sur Joachim de Flore et ses doctrines* in 1909. Fournier's thesis, trying to show that Joachim's Trinitarian views were dependent on those of Gilbert of Poitiers (d. 1154), has been generally rejected by later scholarship. In succeeding years, a few French-language historians did turn their attention to Joachim,[66] but never in great numbers. The most significant work done since that of Alphandéry has come from the pen of Jeanne Bignami-Odier who has produced valuable manuscript studies and an important book on the fourteenth-century writer John of Roquetaillade.[67]

In recent years some of the noted French historians of medieval theology have turned their eyes towards the problems of apocalypticism. M.-D. Chenu in his great book *La théologie au douzième siècle* (Paris, 1957) made a remarkable contribution to determining the social context of many aspects of twelfth-century thought. Although he does treat of Joachim and his predecessors,[68] it is obvious that he is more interested in, and more successful with, the evangelic renewal than he is with apocalypticism as such. We still await a good treatment of the social roots of medieval apocalypticism.

Henri de Lubac has devoted attention to Joachim in his *Exégèse médiévale*,[69] and has also briefly discussed aspects of the earlier twelfth-century apocalyptic thinkers. De Lubac's analysis of Joachim is one of the most comprehensive and perceptive in recent literature, though it is restricted to intellectual history. He cuts through many of the needless oppositions of earlier Joachim scholarship with an admirable insight, showing the Abbot's originality in terms of his theory of exegesis, as well as the radical implications of this originality, despite his orthodox intentions. Perhaps it is the sympathy that de Lubac has for the authentic religious genius of the Calabrian Abbot that helps to make this such an excellent introduction. Altogether, Grundmann, Kamlah, and de Lubac have given us some sense of the genius of Joachim in the area of exegesis at least; we still await the studies that will do the same for the more difficult areas of his theory of history and his views of the Trinity.

66 *E.g.*, E. Jordan, "Joachim de Flore," *Dictionnaire de théologie catholique* 8.2 (Paris, 1925) 1425-38; and the odd book of E. Anitchkof, *Joachim de Flore et les milieux courtois* (Rome, 1931).

67 *Etudes sur Jean de Roquetaillade* (Paris, 1952). Among her articles are "Notes sur deux manuscrits de la Bibliothèque du Vatican contenant des traités inédits de Joachim de Flore," *Mélanges d'archéologie et d'histoire* 54 (1937) 211-47; and "Les visions de Robert d'Uzes, O.P.," *Archivum Fratrum Praedicatorum* 25 (1955) 258-310.

68 Especially in chapters 3, 10, and 11.

69 2.1 (Paris, 1961), chap. 6, pp. 437-558.

II

On the basis of the preceding historiographical analysis, however summary, it may be possible to evaluate the immense contributions and the serious problems presented by the works of Miss Reeves, *Prophecy in the Later Middle Ages* and *The Figurae of Joachim of Fiore*. The earlier and more general book must engage our attention first.

Between the thematic surveys of Wadstein and Bernheim and the chronological accounts of Manselli and Töpfer, Miss Reeves adopts a middle course. *Prophecy in the Later Middle Ages* is divided into four thematic sections: "The Reputation of the Abbot Joachim", "New Spiritual Men", "Antichrist and the Last World Emperor", and "Angelic Pope and *Renovatio Mundi*". Each section, however, is pursued in chronological fashion. This makes for occasional awkwardness (especially in the splitting up of the treatment of individual authors), but given the amount of material handled, it was an intelligent compromise. The time scale is broad, for one of the signal achievements of the book is to have extended the horizon of Joachim studies through the Renaissance and Reformation down to the seventeenth century. The following remarks relate chiefly to the pre-1400 aspects of the themes with which Miss Reeves deals, but it must be said at the outset that the reader can only applaud the breadth of a treatment that contributes almost as much to Renaissance studies as it does to medieval history.

One of the difficulties in the study of medieval apocalypticism, as mentioned previously, is the fact that so much of the material is still available only in manuscript form. Miss Reeves has an immense knowledge of the manuscript tradition, and her decisions about intricate questions of date and provenance of texts are sound and helpful. A rewarding bonus of *Prophecy in the Later Middle Ages* is the thirty pages of appendices outlining the most important manuscript evidence for: a) "The Genuine and Spurious Works of Joachim", b) "Some Short Prophecies Attributed to Joachim", and c) "Examples of Prophetic Anthologies". While not as extensive as the lists in Russo, those given here are both more accurate and more helpful — for the first time historians of medieval thought have been given what amounts to a map of the *terra incognita* of the manuscript material for Joachim and the Joachite tradition. The advantages of this for future work in the field can scarcely be overestimated.

"The Reputation of the Abbot Joachim" traces the views taken towards the Calabrian from the time of his contemporaries down to that of Daniel Papebroch (1628-1714), the Bollandist editor of his life.

Homo catholicus or heretic, saint or villain, visionary or charlatan: judgments on Joachim were usually violently opposed to each other. The treatment of Joachim in the eyes of his contemporaries is excellent; but the intellectual reconstruction of his thought in the chapter entitled "Joachim's View of History" (pp. 16-36), valuable in its handling of the place that visionary experiences played in the evolution of the Abbot's thought, offers some problems. Aside from secondary questions of the dating of some works,[70] the careful delineation of the dependence of Joachim's view of history on his theology of the Trinity is to some extent marred by a failure to treat of the role that his revolutionary views on scriptural interpretation had in this total picture.[71] Perhaps the author thought that it would be hard to improve upon the accounts of Grundmann and de Lubac here, but some attempt at least might have been made to relate the third key to the Abbot's thought, his new theory of the senses of Scripture, to his Trinitarian and historical views.

The knowledge of the thirteenth-century influence of Joachim in this section is impressive, but in one important regard at least Miss Reeves does not prove her case. There is no real evidence that the famous outbreak of the Flagellents at Perugia in 1260 was inspired by Joachite motives,[72] despite the assertion of this in a number of authors. The Oxford scholar's manner of argument here is at variance from her usual careful interpretation of text.[73] After two valuable chapters on "The Diffusion of Joachimist Works in the Later Middle Ages" and "Joachim's Double Reputation in the Sixteenth and Seventeenth Centuries", she summarizes her views on the nature of his orthodoxy. Since this raises one of the fundamental problems of present-day Joachim studies, comments on her interpretation will be postponed until this brief sketch of the content is completed.

The remaining three parts study the history of various themes within the Joachite tradition. Not all of these were present in the works of the Abbot himself (e.g., that of the Last World Emperor), but all became

---

70   On pp. 25-26 we are told that the *De vita sancti Benedicti* is "... probably early", by which Miss Reeves seems to mean before 1182; but C. Baraut in his edition of the text gave good reasons for dating it to 1186-87; *cf.* "Un tratado inédito de Joaquin de Fiore," *Analecta sacra Tarraconensia* 24 (1951) 39. H. Grundmann has also accepted this dating in his "Zur Biographie Joachims von Fiore...," 493.

71   A point I have also tried to make in "The Abbot and the Doctors: Scholastic Reactions to the Radical Eschatology of Joachim of Fiore," *Church History* 40 (1971) 31.

72   *Cf.* R. Manselli, "L'anno 1260 fu anno Gioachinnitico?," *Il movimento dei disciplinati* (Perugia, 1960), pp. 99-108. This important collection of papers is not referred to by Miss Reeves.

73   *E.g.*, "Certainly the date 1260 was *in the air* and this was the Joachimist date. It was *in the air, perhaps*, because of the circulation of the Tables of Concords; more likely, because simple little verses like the one we have quoted were *flying around.*" (p. 54; my italics).

significant in the shifting currents of late medieval apocalyptic. The longest section deals with the "New Spiritual Men", i.e., the religious groups which successively claimed to be the fulfillment of the two orders that Joachim had prophesied would dominate the Age of the Spirit. In 1951 Miss Reeves challenged the traditional view that the *Super Hieremiam prophetam*, one of the most important works falsely attributed to Joachim, originated in Franciscan circles by asserting an origin from a hitherto unexplored group of Joachites among the Florensian and Cistercian monasteries in southern Italy.[74] B. Töpfer was not convinced by her arguments and preferred the traditional view;[75] Reeves reaffirms her case in the present book (pp. 151-58). Without going into the complexities of the problem, it seems that valid arguments can be found on both sides, so that in our present state of knowledge a definitive decision cannot be made. Perhaps when Wachtel's projected edition of the *Super Hieremiam* is completed we will be in a better position to make a judgment. In another controversial area, viz., the extent of Olivi's dependence on Joachim, Reeves's case for a strong dependence (pp. 196-98) is more convincing than R. Manselli's arguments for a more restricted one.[76] Finally, the sketch of Joachim's influence on the Observantine Franciscans, the Augustinian Friars, and the Jesuits is a part of the author's special contributions to the history of apocalypticism.

In the third and fourth parts Miss Reeves was obviously faced with the dilemma of deciding whether or not to include a discussion of the pre-Joachim development of the figures of the Antichrist, the Last World Emperor, and the Angelic Pope. The compromise adopted is not a triumph. We are treated to a brief account of the earlier history of the idea of the World Emperor in the beginning of part 3 (pp. 295-303), but there is no discussion at all of the rich history of the Antichrist, or of such things as the twelfth-century roots of the Angelic Pope in Gerhoch of Reichersberg.[77] Moreover, the review of pre-twelfth-century apocalyptic, largely dependent on Cohn, leaves much to be desired.[78]

---

74   "The Abbot Joachim's Disciples in the Cistercian Order," *Sophia* 19 (1951) 355-71.

75   *Das kommende Reich des Friedens*, pp. 108-24.

76   *La Lectura super Apocalypsim*, pp. 165 ff., 186-87.

77   See Töpfer, pp. 30-1, for some hints regarding this.

78   *E.g.*, (1) R. Schmidt's fine article, "*Aetates mundi*. Die Weltalter als Gliederungsprinzip der Geschichte," *Zeitschrift für Kirchengeschichte* 67 (1955-56) 288-317, is never utilized in the discussion of the theory of the World Ages; (2) Augustine's complex position deserves a fuller treatment; and (3) on the question of the relation of the Last World Emperor and the Crusades, Cohn is followed rather than the solid work of C. Erdmann, "Endkaiserglaube und Kreuzzugsgedanke," *Zeitschrift für Kirchengeschichte* 51 (1932) 384-414.

The simple dichotomy of optimism versus pessimism is a questionable tool for the investigation of a thousand years of thought. Nevertheless, it is only fair to point out that Miss Reeves did not intend to make any original contribution to early medieval apocalyptic in the present book.

All in all, the latter half of the book is most impressive. The discussion of the dialectic of the French and German versions of imperial prophecy in the later Middle Ages is far more complete than that in Kampers' work, and the handling of the concept of *renovatio mundi* as a common theme of the medieval and renaissance versions of the Joachite movement is one of the most original parts of the book. In a sense, Miss Reeves has succeeded where Burdach failed — she has shown, on the basis of a careful study of a multitude of authors both famous and obscure, the lines of connection between the ideas of the Calabrian Abbot and important aspects of renaissance thought. A significant shift has occurred, however, for the emphasis is no longer on Joachim as a predecessor of a new dawn in human history, but rather on the "medieval" character of this aspect of the Renaissance. As Miss Reeves puts it:

> Humanist hopes fastened eagerly on medieval symbols of the Golden Age and in a quite extraordinary way the new discoveries, new learning, new printing, new religious orders, fell into the patterns as fulfillments of old expectations and portents of the new age dawning. Nowhere, perhaps, are medieval and humanist thought so closely linked as in this view of history (p. 507).

The wealth of new material that Miss Reeves's *Prophecy in the Later Middle Ages* has made available to students of medieval apocalyptic will be perhaps its most enduring achievement. This success, however, must be seen against the shadow of a number of serious problems raised by the interpretive viewpoint which the author has chosen. Miss Reeves is so concerned with the war of tracts and prophecies — the apocalyptic "Battle of the Books" — that there is a danger that one may come to think that medieval prophecy of the end was little more. The social dimensions of the ideas in question, while never denied, are rarely given serious attention. Thus the possible connections between Joachim and the Amalrician sect are not discussed, but merely dismissed with the comment that there is yet "... no clear means of determining whether or no there was any relationship between them" (p. 473); and it is noteworthy that the chapter on thirteenth-century popular apocalyptic movements (pp. 243-50) is among the weakest in the book. The chapter on "Radical Views of *Renovatio Mundi*" (pp. 473-504) is even more revealing. The fourteenth- and fifteenth-century sects, including the important Taborites, are dismissed in seven pages, while the bulk of the treatment is given over to sixteenth-century feuds, largely bookish in nature. Nevertheless, it is true that to date there are really no successful interpretations of the social and political roots of medieval apocalypticism. Miss Reeves's neglect of this dimension confronts present historiography with a nagging question of considerable import for the vitality of studies in medieval apocalypticism — is a social and political interpretation impossible given the nature of our sources, or does it merely demand a shift of perspective and the development of new and more nuanced skills on the part of the interpreters?

The second major problem raised by the book concerns the concluding chapter of the first part, "Orthodox or Heterodox?" (pp. 126-32). No one today doubts that the Trinitarian errors condemned at the Fourth Lateran Council were really Joachim's. The Abbot's doctrine of the Trinity was a personal and on the whole confused protest (based upon certain theological traditions active in the latter half of the twelfth century) against the triumph of Peter Lombard. The most interesting thing about it is not its degree of error or orthodoxy, but the effect it had upon the growth of Joachim's vision of history and the degree to which it exposes late twelfth-century theological tensions. Miss Reeves has several perceptive comments on this theological context (e.g., pp. 30-32, 45), but does not pursue the problem in depth.

On the more fundamental question of the "orthodoxy" of Joachim's historical theories, it seems that the author wants to have her cake and eat it too. In many places, particularly when discussing *renovatio mundi*, she is willing to admit that the ideas of Joachim (and not merely of the later Joachites) exercised a decisive influence on changing previous Christian conceptions of the structure of history (e.g., pp. 14, 59, 291-92, 305, and 501-04); but in her treatment of the Abbot himself she absolves him of the charge of heresy and mutes the radical nature of his conception of the Third Age. Over and over again she emphasizes that the survival of the transformed papacy into the Age of the Spirit and the fact that no new institutions are announced for this era (e.g., pp. 132, 303, 395-96, and 507) are sufficient proof that the Abbot was really orthodox. Is orthodoxy a matter of intent or of effect? Obviously the former, in medieval terms at least. But is the medieval concept of orthodoxy really the best instrument that a twentieth-century historian has at his disposal to illuminate the significance of Joachim's thought?

The problem of Joachim's system is not how it measures up to some particular historical definition of orthodoxy (be it thirteen or twentieth century); but how it relates to the social, cultural, and ecclesiastical background that forms the horizon of notions of orthodoxy themselves. Hence the problem would be better framed if we were to ask ourselves about the nature of the effect of the Abbot's thought upon the thirteenth-century church considered in all its fulness. An adequate reply to this kind of question would, I believe, indicate that he was far more radical, that is, favorable to serious intellectual, social, and institutional changes, than Miss Reeves would lead us to believe.

Joachim was in many ways a part of the great movement for the reform of the church which had been active in western society since the mid-eleventh century. His originality in terms of the reform tradition lay in his emphasis upon the direction from which reform was to come. For the Abbot of Fiore reform was not by means of a return to the past, a *renovatio* of the pristine state of the church in morals, laws, and institutions. Though others had stressed the breaking-in of the future as an important element in reform ideology (notably Anselm of Havelberg), it was Joachim who provided the most complete theory of a *renovatio*, forward-looking and perfective, that was to take place in a new and better age to come.[79] But Joachim's future-oriented reform program must be seen within the context of the late twelfth- and thirteenth-century church which, having failed to achieve the ideals advanced by the eleventh-century reformers, increasingly accepted a pragmatic utilization of institutions of effective government (e.g., bureaucratic organization, the use of highly-trained personnel, especially Canonists, and better organized systems of taxation and judicial process) as the model of ecclesiastical order. This model was threatened in a most serious way by the apocalyptic vision of the reformed church present in the writings of Joachim. The Abbot of Fiore's ideas and the reality of the institutional structure of the church of Innocent III and his successors could not avoid being at loggerheads. The clash of his theory of reform and the institutional context in which it found itself is clear in Joachim's own works; it would become explicit in terms of social and political action as the Abbot's ideas were taken up by various groups who came to believe that the Third Age had already dawned and that the ecclesiastical organization of the time was a force blocking its realization. Had Joachim been resurrected to

79 Miss Reeves is well aware of the importance of this dimension in the thought of the Joachites at least. As she says of Arnald of Villanova in n. 2 on p. 317: "In my view Arnald's Joachimism consisted in the conjunction of the proclamation of Antichrist and the call to *renovatio*. His plan for reform has an eschatological setting."

dispute with these disciples, he might have argued about the judgment of fact involved, but he could scarcely have objected to the theory since in essence it was his own. Orthodox or heterodox, Joachim was fundamentally radical.

Because Miss Reeves continues to use the orthodoxy-heterodoxy model as an interpretive tool for assessing Joachim, the more radical features of his thought tend to become obscured. Among the critical areas involved are the status of the papacy, the sacraments, and of the clerical order in the Age of the Spirit. There is a rather full, though perhaps one-sided, account of the first, a brief reference to the second, and almost nothing on the third of these points.[80] Twice the author gives series of texts from the Abbot that stress the survival of the papacy into the age to come, despite whatever changes it may undergo (pp. 132, 395-97), but the meaning of these texts must always be viewed in the light of other texts that seem to indicate such a reduced role for the papacy that one is justified in speaking of a fundamental change.[81] Joachim studies stand in need of a full monograph on his views of the papacy, one that will correlate both types of texts. Suffice it to say that Miss Reeves has by no means solved all the objections of those scholars who lay greater stress upon the latter series, just as they cannot deny the existence and import of the series which she emphasizes. One also might have hoped that Miss Reeves would have dealt with the place of the sacraments in the Age of the Spirit. She merely refers us to Msgr. Tondelli's arguments, without indicating the strength of the case that has been made for the lack of the necessity of the sacraments in the spiritual church to come (p. 130).[82]

In the light of the ideological opposition between Joachim and the church of his time, it is significant that Miss Reeves does not discuss any threat that the Abbot's thought might have posed to the domination of the clerical order.[83] Medieval clerisy, threatened by lay movements from below, retrenched its control and intensified its repressive agencies in the thirteenth and fourteenth centuries. Joachim claimed that the clerical order would survive in the new age, but the leadership of the church was to pass into the hands of the monastic *viri spirituales*.

80 Grundmann briefly treated all three in his *Studien...*, pp. 112-18.
81 De Lubac, pp. 480-84; Grundmann, pp. 115-18; and Töpfer, pp. 72-6; all list such texts. For a summary of the positions, *cf.* Bloomfield, "Joachim of Flora," 266-7.
82 Stressed by Grundmann, p. 114; and Töpfer, pp. 57-8.
83 Something that the members of the Papal Commission at Anagni were aware of; see the text from their *Protocoll* quoted on p. 188.

Assuredly, this leadership was not to be a domination of the external institutions of the church (such would be impossible in the Age of the Spirit), and this is why the Spirituals of the Franciscan order — here in true harmony with Joachim's thought — were so dismayed that they were not allowed the independence to carry on their new life pointing to such spiritual hegemony once they were convinced that the Third Age was at hand. The Spirituals and their Curial and Conventual opponents were living in different time-dimensions with differing conceptions of the church, and the blame must be laid at least partially at the feet of Joachim.

Was Joachim also responsible for the *Liber figurarum*, that collection of striking illustrations of the Joachimite vision of history which since its identification in 1937 has continued to provoke discussion and argument? This is the central question addressed in the second major contribution of Miss Reeves (with the able assistance of her colleague Miss Hirsch-Reich). While *The Figurae of Joachim of Fiore* is a less ambitious work than *Prophecy in the Later Middle Ages*, it is scarcely less important to the current state of historiography on medieval apocalypticism. Over the objections of such Italian scholars as F. Foberti and F. Russo,[84] the authors provide a convincing case for the authenticity of the *Liber* (pp. 75-98), as well as a description of its history; but this is not all that the more recent book has to offer.

The major portion of this sumptuous and detailed volume is taken up with a careful study of the sources, meaning, and influence of the diagrams found in the *Liber figurarum* and frequently alluded to or present in other works of Joachim. There is no necessity to dwell upon these individual figures in detail, save to indicate that they form an invaluable resource for the study of the thought of Joachim and his successors, especially in the two areas where they involve questions of more general concern.

The first of these areas forms the summation of a theme that Miss Reeves has been at pains to highlight for many years. The customary view of Joachim's theory of history lays much stress upon his doctrine of the three ages (actually, the Abbot tends to use the term *status* rather than *aetas* to describe them, a point that may be of real significance). This view fails to do justice to the complexity of the Calabrian's various patterns of history. Miss Reeves long ago reminded us of the continuity

---

84 Foberti, *Gioacchino da Fiore e il Gioacchinismo*, pp. 227-63; and Russo, "Il Libro delle Figure attribuito a Giacchino da Fiore," *Miscellanea Francescana* 41 (1941) 326-44.

of a pattern of the two *aetates* of the Old and the New Testament, as well as the three *status* of Father, Son, and Holy Spirit in the thought of Joachim;[85] and there are other patterns too, especially of five, seven, and twelve. The Oxford scholar has continued to argue that the persistence of the two-fold pattern shows Joachim's close relation with traditional medieval apocalyptic — in one sense, at least, Joachim did not intend to break with tradition. But the fundamental question raised by this important observation does not concern the existence of the schema itself, but that of its coherence with the other schemata. Is Joachim a consistent thinker?

In the present book a more complete case is advanced for the consistency of Joachim's schemata than has been thus far available (pp. 7-11), but one is still left with some doubts. The mixture of patterns, especially the all-important two's and three's, is an indication both of the logical inconsistency of Joachim and of the unique place that he holds in the history of medieval apocalyptic. If the pattern of two's may be said to represent his debt to the past and the starting point of his speculations, the pattern of three's indicates the transformation that was his real contribution to apocalypticism — his own creation out of the vivid experience of history of the latter part of the twelfth century.

Furthermore, the second major issue raised by *The Figurae of Joachim of Fiore* buttresses this case. In an earlier work Miss Reeves had described Joachim as a picture thinker[86] — the full meaning of this remark is well brought out in the present book. Joachim's somewhat confused verbal attempts to portray his vision of history cry out for visual presentation; indeed, it seems that the visual images (trees, circles, eagles, the Alpha and Omega, and the ten-stringed psaltery, etc.) were frequently prior to verbal presentations in the development of Joachim's thought. In the polymorphic richness of such symbolism to make the kind of judgments of separation that the two-fold pattern is "historical" and the three-fold one "mystical" seems to partake of the character of a category confusion.[87] What Miss Reeves has uncovered in terms of her stress on the symbolic nature of Joachim's thought on the one hand is to some degree taken away by the invocation of non-symbolic categories of interpretation on the other. Nonetheless, this should not be allowed to obscure the importance of the emphasis on

85 *E.g.*, "The *Liber Figurarum* of Joachim of Fiore," 71-2, 75-7.

86 *Op. cit.*, 67-74.

87 Found in Miss Reeve's early work; *e.g.*, pp. 75-9; and also in this most recent one, *e.g.*, pp. 11, 155, 164, and 247.

Joachim's symbolism. Miss Reeves has indicated a most important direction for future work in the Abbot, and in medieval apocalyptic in general. In Joachim we are witnesses to a powerful example of the symbolic mentality at work, and it is high time to invoke the rich resources of contemporary philosophical and theological analysis of symbolism as tools in the investigation of his thought.[88] The recognition of the symbolic nature of apocalyptic imagery is not a new one, even in the case of Joachim; what the work of Miss Reeves has done is to give us a new and much richer presentation of the intricacies of Joachim's symbolic world.

Finally, in both books Miss Reeves draws our attention back to an obvious fact that we sometimes are prone to forget — the centrality of prophecy to western medieval apocalypticism. The final sentence of *Prophecy in the Later Middle Ages* puts it thus:

> Perhaps we might say that only when intelligent and educated men ceased to take prophecy seriously were the Middle Ages truly at an end. The contention here is that this change hinges on a change in our whole attitude to history and to our own participation in it (p. 508).

This is a profound observation, but its converse is equally true: we are still much given to prediction and prophecy in western society, even if in altered fashion. The man with the power to predict the future remains an authority with us, even after the beginning of the eighteenth century, the Age of Enlightenment, when Miss Reeves closes her study. Rather than turn to Scripture and private illumination as the sources for his special knowledge, he has used the rational vision of man and nature, the doctrine of evolution, or current technological planning as the sources for his prophetic message. Perhaps science fiction and the blueprints for the future of society that issue from our "think-tanks" are the twentieth-century equivalents of the low- and high-brow apocalyptic prophecies of the centuries studied by Miss Reeves. The sense of the prophetic role current in popular Christianity has in the past few years tended to become increasingly related to present witness to the action of the word of God in history in contrast to the medieval understanding which centered upon the expectation of the future. These permutations suggest that an analysis of the prophetic role understood in the latter sense, viz., as the man who is thought to have control over the future, might show this to be a distinctive theme of

88 I have in mind here such studies as Paul Ricoeur's *The Symbolism of Evil* (New York, 1967).

western intellectual and social history that has merely changed clothes in a secularized world. It is only another of the rich possibilities that the work of Miss Marjorie Reeves has opened up for us.

The role of this historiographical survey has been to sketch the past, not (in apocalyptic fashion) to predict the future. Obviously, the views and even possibly the prejudices of the author have been evident throughout. Were I to adopt the role of prophet, the single prediction that I should like to make would be that the most promising direction for future work in this area lies in openness to the contributions of new approaches in historical method as well as to the methods and findings of related disciplines. History of religions (and its related anthropological studies), the nuanced social analysis practiced so well by some contemporary historians,[89] and philosophical and theological study of the symbolic mentality all have important riches to offer to the historians of medieval apocalypticism. May the promise of their contribution be more successful in its fulfillment than the predictions of the apocalypticists themselves.[90]

University of Chicago

---

89 *E.g.*, as utilized by Eric Hobsbawm in his study of some modern forms of archaic millenarianism in *Primitive Rebels*, chaps. 4-6.

90 As this article was going to press a new major study on medieval apocalyptic appeared, namely H. D. Rauh, *Das Bild des Antichrist im Mittelälter: von Tyconius zum deutschen Symbolismus* (Münster, 1973).

THE ECCLESIASTICAL PILGRIMS OF THE *CANTERBURY TALES*:
A STUDY IN ETHOLOGY

George J. Engelhardt

T HE *General Prologue* of the *Canterbury Tales* is an ethologue that reflects the medieval mixed congregation of elect and reprobate, good and bad, *homines spirituales* and *homines animales* — those perfect in ethos and those defective in ethos. This ethologue, which implies the dual vision of this world expressed in the complementary medieval traditions of the dignity of man and the *contemptus mundi*, is in turn implemented by the individual tales of the Canterbury sequence. These premises have been explained in a previous study published in *Mediaeval Studies* 36 (1974): "The Lay Pilgrims of the *Canterbury Tales*: A Study in Ethology". That study is complemented by the present study, which treats of those pilgrims associated with the medieval Church.

The Clerk of Oxford embodies the ethos of a perfect clerk. The talent of nature and of grace that he received gratis from God he has through years of genial study transformed into the talent of knowledge which he now bestows freely and happily upon others. Unlike the Man of Law, he is not exploiting this talent to acquire for himself and his heirs "that wealth which often blinds/ The minds of the powerful and bends the honor/ Of majesty, lessens the laws, and delays justice". Rather he is accumulating

> The riches of the mind, which the man who has once received
> Is poor no more, but once enriched, always abounds;
> The love of which is upright, the possession noble, the use
> Beneficial, the distribution more beneficial, the fruit abounding.
> This is the wealth of heaven, the celestial treasure, the overflowing
> Grace that enriches the learned, which, prodigal itself, wishes
> Its possessors to be bountiful and scorns the avaricious.
> Locked up, it perishes; spread abroad, it returns. If not made public,
> It falls away. Going forth, it gains much force.
> Rust does not consume this wealth nor fire

Devour it nor the purloining of a thief lessen it, shipwreck
Submerge it, the robber carry it off, the foe plunder it.[1]

This clerk, then, is the opposite of the *aulicus clericus* in both senses of that epithet. The years of discipline that have elapsed since he went through the trivium have removed him far from those instant savants of noble station who "in a moment of time become masters even before they are disciples".[2] Not "so worldly for to have office", he is not driven by avarice or ambition to frequent the houses of the great in quest of promotion within or without the Church. Instead he trusts to the bounty of friends, submitting to the spirit of the ancient canon that assigns whatever a clerk has to the poor: a clerk, therefore, who accepts a stipend of the Church when he can sustain himself by the bounty of kinsmen is sacrilegiously depriving the poor of that which is theirs.[3] This cheerful poverty confirms the inward humility and outward mildness of the Clerk. Although he has mastered the high style of the *ars dictandi* with which notaries addressed kings in Latin, he can graciously speak to lesser men with a plainness accommodated to their rank and understanding.[4] Although he will use in his turn the same rime royal as the Man of Law, he has no occasion to simulate the art that dissimulates art. His innocence is attested by the economy of his speech. The custody of the mouth that manifests itself in virtuous taciturnity or in a gentle voice succinctly uttering sound thoughts was an established sign of humility.[5] Since parsimony of speech was commonly taken to be a sign of wisdom as well, it is affected by the Man of Law (1.309, 313), who, furthermore, demands a handsome fee for every word expended on his clients. The Clerk, on the contrary, who teaches as gladly as he learns, bestows his talent like the apostolic *hilaris dator*.[6] He is, accordingly, an appropriate spokesman for the perfect patience, the *patientia hilaris*, of Griselda. Her tale, derived by the Clerk not from merchants but from the "worthy clerk" Petrarch, fulfills the Host's request for "som myrie tale" in a fashion no less pregnant than the "sobre cheere" of the

---

1   Alan of Lille, *Anticlaudianus* 7.229-31, 233-44. All translations are my own.

2   Jerome, *Letters* 69.9; Bernard of Clairvaux, *De moribus et officio episcoporum* 7. Note that Chaucer has not felt it necessary to make his complete clerk formally perfect: Chaucer does not expressly say that the Clerk had received this or that degree.

3   Peter Cantor, *Verbum abbreviatum* 48 (PL 205.152); Gratian, C.1 q.2 c.6-7; C.16 q.1 c.68.

4   4.16-20; *Ad Herennium* 4.12.17; Ludwig Rockinger, ed., *Briefsteller und Formelbücher des eilften bis vierzehnten Jahrhunderts* 1 (Munich, 1863; rpt. New York, 1961), pp. 55, 434-35.

5   1.304-07; 4.2-4. Benedict, *Regula monachorum* 7.

6   John of Salisbury, *Policraticus* 7.15; Geoffrey of Vinsauf, *Documentum* 2.2.62-69, ed. E. Faral in *Les arts poétiques du XIIᵉ et du XIIIᵉ siècle* (Paris, 1924), pp. 283-84.

Sergeant gratifies the demands for sobriety that elicited the tale of woeful Constance.

Griselda abides not in the incipient or proficient grade, but in the perfection, of patience. Her response to her husband when he proposes to deprive her of her second child is typical: "Right gladly wolde I dyen, yow to plese."[7] She endures "with humble herte and glad visage" all the tribulations devised by his compulsive curiosity.[8] It is precisely because her patience is perfect that the Clerk, like Petrarch, can interpret her conduct tropologically as an argument a fortiori for the submission of the human will to the will of God. Transcending the misogyny that had vitiated the clerical tradition since pagan antiquity, the Clerk exposes Griselda to the inhumanity only of a husband — not of two mothers-in-law. He recognizes

> Though clerkes preise wommen but a lite,
> Ther kan no man in humblesse hym acquite
> As womman kan, ne kan been half so trewe
> As wommen been, but it be falle of newe. (4.935-38)

The last clause, however, may allude to the noble wives whose "crabbed eloquence", irking poets no less than husbands, the Man of Law undertook to muffle and whose "heigh prudence" — so different from the prudence of Griselda (4.1022), but so like the perverse discretion of the obsessed Walter — the Clerk invokes in his ironic envoy.[9] It was against the noble husband that the ribald narrator of Boccaccio's novella had delivered his final quip: "Whom it would perchance not ill have suited to have hit upon one that, when he had chased her forth from the house in a shirt, would have made another so shake her skin that there would have issued therefrom a 'bella roba'." It is rather to the noble wives that the moral Clerk addresses his jocose epilogue, ironically simulating for the moment a "lusty herte, fressh and grene", quite removed from that gravity of age which prompted the tropology of Petrarch, now "buryed in Ytaille" like Griselda and her patience. Unlike these noble

---

7   4.665. Note also 4.603, 832, 843, 949, 967, 1013, 1016, 1045.

8   4.949. Thus Boccaccio: "with the face not only dry but cheerful (col viso non solamente asciutto ma lieto)," *Opere*, ed. Bruno Maier (Bologna, 1967), p. 722; Petrarch: "alacritas" (3.53; 6.42), *Sources and Analogues of Chaucer's Canterbury Tales*, ed. W. F. Bryan and Germaine Dempster (Chicago, 1941; rpt. New York, 1958), pp. 314, 28.

9   Traditionally the virtue of prudence addresses itself to the past, present and future. Walter's prudence is perverse because (1) before marriage he is preoccupied with the present (4.78-84), (2) after marriage, with the future. Walter's false prudence thus contrasts with the "alacrity" of Griselda, alacrity being a concomitant of true prudence: see Hugh of St. Victor, *De fructibus carnis et spiritus* 12 (PL 176.1002).

wives and unlike the imperfect heroine of the Sergeant, Griselda is poor
and lowly. Unlike the exiled queen, whom the Man of Law expressly
exempts even at sea from the misery of poverty, Griselda leaves her
father's house with nothing and returns with nothing: "'Naked out of
my fadres hous,' quod she,/ 'I cam, and naked moot I turne agayn'"
(4.871-72). Her abrupt translation from the "litel oxes stalle" to
marquisate might have inflated another with the arrogance of the up-
start; yet, presumably, it was this poor and humble upbringing that
made her capable of perfect patience (4.1037-43).

When the Clerk chose to repeat a tale which he twice reminds his
audience Petrarch had written "with heigh stile" (4.41,1148), he might
seem to have ignored the Host's charge:

> Youre termes, youre colours, and youre figures,
> Keepe hem in stoor til so be that ye endite
> Heigh style, as whan that men to kynges write.
> Speketh so pleyn at this tyme, we yow preye,
> That we may understonde what ye seye.[10]

Yet neither the Italian novella of Boccaccio nor the Latin "mythologia"
that Petrarch, "changing or adding a few words here and there", was
moved to "reweave with another pen (*stilo alio*)" — a pen other than
that "stilus" with which Boccaccio had published this tale years before
— can lay claim to the high style because they employ those "polite ter-
mes of sweit rhetore" or those colors — those figures of speech or
thought and those tropes — which contribute to the high or grave
style.[11] Whether or not Chaucer misread "stilo alto" for the Petrarchan
"stilo alio", he and his Clerk could categorize the tale as grave or high
because it treats of two noble persons, one by birth, one by virtue,
enacting a "sweet story" that evokes "the noblest part of human

---

10   4.16-20. *Cf.* Geoffrey of Vinsauf, *Poetria nova* 1061-97, ed. Faral, pp. 230-31.

11   Petrarch, *Opera* 1 (Basel, 1554; rpt. Ridgewood, N.J., 1965), pp. 600, 606; Robert Henryson,
Morall Fabillis, Prol. 3 in *Poems*, ed. Charles Elliott (Oxford, 1963, rpt. 1968), p.1; *Ad Herennium* 4.8.11.
In the *Ad Herennium*, a Latin art of rhetoric composed in the first century B.C. and well known in
the Middle Ages as the *Rhetorica secunda* and the *Rhetorica nova*, the anonymous author compares the
"exornationes" of words and thoughts to colors (4.11.16). These *exornationes* correspond to the
figures of speech, the tropes, and the figures of thought of later Latin rhetorical theory. In
medieval theory the tropes are comprised under the *ornatus difficilis* or *ornata difficultas* (designations
deriving from the ancient *exornatio*, which in turn derives from the Greek κόσμος 'ornament' or
κατασκευή 'gear'; *cf. paratus*, Geoffrey of Vinsauf, *Poetria nova* 949, 957). These tropes are called difficult or grave (*gravis*) because they are hard for the poet to invent. When used judiciously, they
facilitate the reader's understanding; however, he will find them hard to understand when far-
fetched, "peregrina vel abdita" (*Poetria nova* 830-43, 945-48, 1074-76).

feeling", commiseration.[12] Neither does the Clerk, adding more words to Petrarch than Petrarch added to Boccaccio, deviate from the economy of language proper to a clerk, since these dilatations, the apostrophe to the "stormy peple", for example, or the last speech of Griselda, are not otiose but edifying and pathetic. Finally, the tale is hard, yet not because it draws upon the recondite tropes of the *ornatus difficilis*, rather because it records a constancy so hard to sustain, though gladly sustained by a poor country girl ("rusticana muliercula"), that many readers, finding it difficult for themselves, have thought it, as Petrarch testifies, impossible for all.[13]

The theme of martyrdom reappears in the tale told by the Prioress. Her ethos may be epitomized by the formula *praelatus puer*, which in turn is subsumed under the *momentaneus sacerdos* signalized by Jerome.[14] As a feminine variant of the instant priest or boy prelate, the Prioress has been thrust upon her convent *prece vel pretio*, by the wealth or influence of her family.[15] Thus she has been elevated simoniacally to an ecclesiastic position that enables her to avoid the tribulations of marriage and the servitude of a wife while enjoying the worldly perquisites that accrue to the lady of a manor.[16] Her motive for entering the religious life has been no more canonical than her ingress to that life or her instant progress in it. Her character is at once a parody on the Pauline *hilaris dator*, the cheerful giver that God loves, and the eulogistic paradox of the *puer senex*, the child that exceeds his elders in wisdom. As a prioress, she is a prelate required by that office to teach her subordinates, yet she cannot gladly teach that which she has not gladly learned during many years of cheerful preparation. As a simoniac whose place in the Church has been purchased, she cannot freely share the grace that may not be bought. She is spiritually rude despite her formalistic acquirements in provincial French or in the table manners prescribed by Ovid for rustic girls aspiring to become urbane courtesans. Although physically mature, "For, hardily, she was nat undergrowe" (1.156), she is still a child, not so much in humility (Matt. 18: 4), however, as in sense (1 Cor. 14: 20) and in sexuality. Hence her

---

12 Petrarch, *Opera* 1.600, 606; *Ad Herennium* 4.8.11; Geoffrey of Vinsauf, *Documentum* 2.3.145, ed. Faral, p. 312.

13 Petrarch, *Opera* 1.606-07.

14 Jerome, *Letters* 69.9.4-6, cited by Gratian, D.48; Peter Cantor, *Verbum abbreviatum* 61 (PL 205.185-89).

15 For the formula "prece vel pretio", see, *e.g.*, 9.6; 10.167, 784.

16 *Cf.* Gratian, D.53.

hypocoristic name, Madame Eglantine, ironically apposite to a neophyte
"newly planted" in a nunnery. So puerile is her understanding of
charity that she refines for little dogs, or abandons to the forays of
mice, the grain that properly should feed the deserving poor.[17] For her,
men have no attraction. They are either great bullies that beat small
hounds or faceless appurtenances like her priest. Therefore the formula
Amor vincit omnia that spells out the "crowned A" inscribed on her
brooch cannot pertain to carnal love, common to all and all conquering
— πάνδημος Ἔρως καὶ πανδαμάτωρ — against which Gower posed this
question to the world: "What honor shall the victor have,/ If love of
woman can vanquish him?"[18] Madame Eglantine intends the motto to
suggest rather the love of the Christian virgin that macerates the flesh,
the love of the Christian confessor that spurns the world, and, per-
fecting all, the love of the Christian martyr, stronger than death and
symbolized by the papal ring. Evoking the fortitude of charity, that love
transfigures the natural softness of woman memorialized in the
etymology of her common name, *mulier mollis*, and endues her with the
valor unto death of the strong woman or *mulier fortis*, the Scriptural type
of the Virgin Mary and the bride of Christ in his union with the
Church.[19] To the literate contemporary, moreover, the formula implies
by subaudition the paronomastic variant *Labor vincit omnia*, a proverb
importing the necessity of the active mode of life which is coterminous
with this present existence.[20]

   The tale of the Prioress may be construed as a fantasy in which this
self-professed "child of twelf month oold" (7.484) assumes the persona
of the "litel clergeon": an innocent who is something of a *puer senex* like
St. Nicholas, "For he so yong to Crist dide reverence" (7.515); a
widow's son just as she is a daughter of Mother Church bereft in this
world of her eternal spouse; a virgin, confessor, and martyr, whose
chastity is symbolized by a gem of the same hue as the gauds of her
rosary.[21] The Jews "Sustened by a lord ... For foule usure and lucre of

   17   *Cf.* Jerome, *Letters* 58.6.4.
   18   *Vox clamantis* 5.1.19-20; *cf.* 5.3.147: "Sic amor omne domat, quicquid natura creavit";
Helinand, *Sermones* 20 (PL 212.648).
   19   Ambrose, *Exhortatio virginitatis* 12.81 (PL 16.360); Honor, *Gemma animae* 1.216 (PL 172.609);
Philip of Harveng, *De institutione clericorum* 1.21 (PL 203.691-92); Helinand, *Sermones* 20, 25
(PL 212.646-52, 692).
   20   *Cf.* Vergil, *Georgica*, ed. Will Richter (Munich, 1957), pp. 139-40, n. 145 f.; Alan of Lille, *Anticlaudianus* 3.100; Nigel Wireker, *Speculum stultorum*, trans. Graydon W. Regenos (Austin, 1959),
p. 73n.
   21   1.159; 7.609.

vileynye" (7.490-91) represent the well connected men with whom she is litigating over the redemption of her convent's liberties — a redemption to which the hymn *Alma redemptoris* may allude.[22] The "greyn" laid by the Virgin upon the child's tongue symbolizes, like the *coccus* grain, the blood of martyrs that is the seed of the Church.[23] It attests that the martyrdom of the child is an acceptable sacrifice, well pleasing to Mary and her Son. Martyrdom is the supreme act in the active mode of life. In martyrdom the grains that moan amid the chaff — "grana inter paleas gementia" — cheerfully give the ultimate witness of their faith.[24] The active mode of life, which is superseded at death by the contemplative life of the blest, was commonly symbolized by the proverbial industry of the ant, who gathers grain in summer so that he does not starve in winter.[25] When the "greyn" is taken by the abbot from the tongue of the child, he and his tongue are released from their labors here below — from the anthem which he constantly sings, living and dying, as confessor and martyr. Henceforth he will sing the new song amidst the virgins that follow the Lamb. Then the sweet savor of faith and good works signified by the grain of salt laid upon the tongue in Baptism shall be perfected in the refection of the Church Triumphant.[26]

In this fantasy the Prioress imagines herself "entuning" her love for the Virgin and her convent's privileges in defiance of the predators even to the point of death. Then at last the ecclesiastical superiors, who until then had suffered her to sing, will consign her body to eternal rest from the labors of her song. Then the temporal authorities will, like the provost of her tale, smite the adversaries. Then the cry will be heard that Gower would fancy he had heard when divine justice, humbling Richard, exalted Bolingbroke: "Omnia vincit Amor." [27]

The song that the Prioress imagines herself singing unto death is the plaint of litigation. Her imperfect faith (1 Cor. 6: 7) is oriented less to the clemency of the Virgin than to the rigor of the provost and his law. Behind her smiling "ful symple and coy" there dwells not the proverbial sagaciousness that "smiles quietly" but the litigious tongue insinuated in the equivocal line "Hire gretteste ooth was but by Seinte

22   *Cf.* John of Salisbury, *Historia pontificalis* 45.

23   Tertullian, *Apologeticus adversus gentes pro christianis* 50: "semen est sanguis Christianorum"; Raban Maur, *De universo* 21.15 (PL 111.570): "cocco martyrum".

24   Augustine, *In Joannis evangelium* 7.1; *cf.* the "granum sinapis" Matt. 17:19, Gregory, *Moralia* Pref. 6.

25   Alan of Lille, *Summa de arte praedicatoria* 7 (PL 210.127).

26   7.579-85; Rev. 14:3-4; Theodulf of Orléans, *De ordine baptismi* 5 (PL 105.225-26).

27   *Cronica tripertita* Pref. 7.

Loy" (1.120), a verse foreshadowing the equivocal oath of the false
canon: "For of yow have I pitee, by Seint Gile!" (8.1185).[28] Her mouth,
"ful smal, and therto softe and reed", is less disposed by its wisdom to
admonish others in spiritual song (Col. 3: 16) than to prick them with
words as "egre" as the eglantine, the "brembul flour" (7.745-47) from
which she is named — not the bramble from which the virginal rose
springs to emulate the Immaculate Rose that knew no sin, but the
"spina rosans" impatient of a man's touch, the "esglantiers" hedging
the Rose where *Dangiers* lurks in the garden of the *Roman de la Rose.* The
amiable port exhibited by the Prioress hardly radiates the perfection of
Christian patience which, in the words of the thirteenth-century
Richard of Thetford, "smiles amid abuse like a drunken man" — or like
Griselda. It simulates instead the cheer of court that chivalry had accommodated from Christian fortitude, an obligatory joyfulness that
Gurnemanz enjoins upon the simple Parzival: "sît manlîch und wol
gemuot" (172.7). If it suggests that blitheness of demeanor which Venus
prescribes for the servant of love in Lydgate's *Temple of Glas* (1173-79),
Madame Eglantine must nevertheless not be enrolled among the
maidens

> That conseiles in hir tender youþe
> And in childhode (as it is oft[e] couþe)
> Yrendred were into religioun
> Or þei hade yeris of discresioun,
> That al her life cannot but complein,
> In wide copis perfeccion to feine:
> Ful couertli to curen al her smert
> And shew þe contrarie outward of her hert. (199-206)

However much Damysel Corteyseye may be mirrored in her fair sem-
blance, it is Damysel Symplesse who presides there in the "ful symple"
smile which with its trace of native rudeness discourages, like Damysel
Symplesse in the allegorical *Abbey of the Holy Ghost,* too much affability
from strangers and from men.[29]

This ironic struggle between a simoniacal nun and her sacrilegious
adversaries, postulated here to explain the ethological function of the
Prioress's Tale and to suggest a motivation for her pilgrimage to the tomb
of the martyred Becket, is enacted once again in the tale told by her

---

28   Ecclus. 21:23: "tacite ridebit" (ἡσυχῇ μειδιάσει).

29   Guillaume de Lorris, *Roman de la Rose* 2798; Alan of Lille, *Anticlaudianus* 5.494; Gower, *Confessio amantis* 5.10. Latin verses; *Vox clamantis* 4.15.659; *cf.* 6.21.1358. *Middle English Religious Prose,* ed.
N. F. Blake (London, 1972), p. 96.

mentor, the Second Nun. The Second Nun is not described in the *General Prologue*. She styles herself an "unworthy sone of Eve" (8.62) in what may be a pregnant substitution for the generic formula "homo miserae condicionis".[30] Whether she would have been endowed by the poet with a stalwart physique, somewhat like Dangiers, big and fiery-eyed, if not black and bristled, or, antilogically, with a diminutive frame can only be surmised.[31] Perhaps her portraiture might have shown her to be as "swift and bisy", "round and hool", and "brennynge" in a mundane sense as she imagines her protagonist, "Cecilie the white", to have been in the transmundane (8.113-18). Nevertheless, the persona which she has chosen to assume in her tale is that of the spiritual Amazon or virago, the *conjunx virgo* Cecilia. Thus the tales told by each of the women in the pilgrimage — the Wife of Bath, the Prioress, and the Second Nun — are fantasies in which they project the character they fancy for themselves. The ethos of each woman, furthermore, is skewed with its own distortion to the Biblical ethos of the *mulier fortis*.

The Church, of whom the virile woman is a type, preserves her chastity by refusing to sell herself in simony.[32] The Second Nun, although indifferent to the kind of simony by which the Prioress has been thrust upon the Church, is nonetheless determined to resist the sacrilege now threatening their convent. The prioress transforms her sacrilegious adversaries into Asiatic Jews, but these, like the thirteenth-century Jews of Lincoln to whom they are compared, would be con-flated in the Prioress' foreshortened view of history with the Jews that persecuted the infant Church in the first epoch of the Christian era. The other antagonist of the primitive Church, the Roman tyrant, provides the Second Nun with the grotesque mask under which she reviles the foes of her convent while arrogating to the Prioress and herself that crown which the justice of God is reserving for those who fight the good fight with Pauline sobriety.[33] The exorcism offered by the Second Nun, however, pretends to an efficacy less immediate than that of the Prioress. In the tale of each nun, the victim, despite a "nekke ycorven", is miraculously granted a stay of death, during which the "litel clergeon" continues to sing and the married virgin to preach. In the *Prioress's Tale* this respite enables the provost to detect and punish the murder. In the *Second Nun's Tale* the murderer is the prefect himself,

---

30 *Carmina burana* 26.1.2-3n, ed. Alfons Hilka and Otto Schumann (Heidelberg, 1930), 1.45, 2.39.

31 Guillaume de Lorris, *Roman de la Rose* 2906-08.

32 Geoffrey of Vendôme, *Epistolae* 4.16 (PL 157.159-60).

33 8.220-21, 388; 2 Tim. 4:7-8.

and Cecilia employs the suspension of death not to requite her tor-
mentors but to insure that, when the time of persecution has passed,
her house shall remain in perpetuity — thus fortified against sacrilege
— the Church of St. Cecilia.

In the spiritual dominance which this married virgin maintains over
her husband and his brother, the Second Nun shadows forth her ascendancy over the Prioress and the Nun's Priest. In the fortitude with
which the valiant Cecilia withstands the tyrant, the Second Nun en-
visions the kind of response that she commends for herself and her
pupil to the menace of sacrilegious violence. Yet the Second Nun in her
version of the manly woman may well have slipped into the sin of pride.
The "rude" derision with which she permits her magisterial exemplar
to scold and flout the "nyce" prefect hardly seems to express the
Pauline servant of the Lord mildly and humbly educating his adversaries.[34] Rather it suggests that the counsel of the Second Nun may
prove to be not so much "the wey to blynde" (8.92) as a pitfall (Matt.
15: 14) for the Prioress, whose inner eyes are no more discerning than
the "outter yën" (8.498) of the Roman idolator. Thus the Second Nun
hopes for a crumb from the table of her Master while her mistress feeds
"wastel-breed" to little dogs.[35] Both look for a miracle that requires not
the eyes of the heart but merely the eyes of the body to be seen.[36]

For the sweet priest, Sir John, making his pilgrimage upon a foul but
serviceable jade, the menace to the convent assumes a modality more in
keeping with his vantage of cheerful and serene patience. The grand
reduces itself to the humble, the heroic and tragic to the mock heroic
and mock elegiac. Hagiography defers to the animal tale, and the
violence suited to the primitive age of tyrants and miracles gives way to
guile, that alternative mode of injustice and retaliation which is more
consonant with the hypocrisy and false peace of the contemporary
epoch. In this milieu the antagonist emerges not as a truculent Jew or
ferocious gentile, but as "A col-fox, ful of sly iniquitee" (7.3215), whose
red pelt is tipped with demonic black (3.1383) and whose violence is
coated with flattery, a figure that evokes the simoniac of Biblical
tropology or the barratrous lawyer of *Vox clamantis* 6.3.207 or the
sacrilegious Herod of Luke 13: 32.[37] A cock serves as protagonist, a trite
figure for the vigilant prelate, resplendently individuated now and aptly

---

34 Augustine, *Sermones* 88.18.20-21 (PL 38.549-50); Gratian, C.23 q.4 c.8.
35 1.146-47; 8.59-61. Matt. 15:26-27.
36 Augustine, *Sermones* 88.1.1-6.6 (PL 38.539-42).
37 Humbert, *Adversus simoniacos* 2.22-23 (PL 143.1095-98).

distinguished with a French name. A singer like the "litel clergeon", he is compared ambiguously to a mermaid, the creature that from waist down is fish.

Chanticleer does not represent the narrator Priest. This royal fowl stands rather for the Prioress. The fairest of the seven sisters and his paramour, the soft-sided Pertelote — whose name is an aphetic variant of the Old French *apertelet* 'bold' — is intended somewhat archly to suggest the austere Second Nun, in whose heroics the Priest discerns the specious sin of foolhardiness which is inducing the Second Nun and the Prioress to tempt God as they respond with grandiose simplicity to the anti-Pelagian doctrine, signalized by Bradwardine in his *Sermo epinicius*, that God is the author of victory.[38] The poor, continent widow, who provides the setting for the tale, is a familiar type of the Church Militant. In the contrast of her drab yard, enclosed with sticks and ditch, to the regality displayed by Chanticleer and his sisters, the Priest satirizes the courtly affectations of the Prioress. In the service that Chanticleer renders to Venus "Moore for delit than world to multiplye" (7.3345), the Priest parodies the devotion of this sexless woman, who has renounced physical propagation and withdrawn from the world, not to engage in spiritual propagation, but to enjoy the privileges of a chatelaine while shunning the burdens of a wife. When Chanticleer deploys the learned authors in his disputation with Pertelote and recoils from the fox through natural antipathy, he demonstrates the use of reason and common sense which the Priest commends to the Prioress. When, however, gazing on the beautiful face of Pertelote, he confuses the very passage in Ecclesiasticus that warns man not to look upon a woman's beauty lest she confound him,[39] he exemplifies the surrender of reason to passion, the submission of the spirit to the flesh, manifested by the Prioress when she prefers the counsel of the Nun to the counsel of the Priest and rejects the authentic virtue advocated by the man in favor of the infirmity simulating fortitude urged by the woman. Thus the interplay of Chanticleer and Pertelote incorporates that medieval tropology by which man symbolizes the reason or the spirit, woman the passions or the flesh, man giving his name to virtue or fortitude, woman yielding hers to infirmity or frailty.[40] The Priest exploits this tropology, which associates the *homo animalis* with woman and the *homo spiritualis* with man, when he assigns

38   Cf. *Ad Herennium* 4.25.35.
39   7.3160-66. Ecclus. 25:28-30, 33.
40   10.331-32.

to Pertelote, and hence to the Secund Nun, the merely natural explanation of dreams. The brash contempt with which she dismisses any spiritual interpretation of Chanticleer's dream reflects the specious fortitude of the virago. As the advocate of true fortitude, the benign Priest conforms rather to the serpentine prudence and dovelike simplicity with which the apostles were sent among wolves (Matt. 10: 16). When at last the kind wit or common sense of Chanticleer reasserts itself, enabling him to recognize not only time but opportunity — when, accordingly, he can retort the flattery of the fox upon the fox and so escape, he enacts the strategy by which the Priest would rescue the Prioress from her folly. Encouraged by the Nun, she has conceived a course of litigation that both deem not only licit but glorious. In the judgment of the Priest it is not only inexpedient, it is unsafe.[41] Madame Eglantine is playing into the hands of her enemies. Having never seen a fox, she is conniving blindly and imprudently in her own discomfiture. To escape from this peril she must now feign submission to her foes while encouraging them to provoke by their flagrance the counteraction of Church and people symbolized by the chase. Only thus may love conquer — not the melodramatic love of the Prioress and her chaplain, but, despite its variability, the common love of the people expressed in their clamor.[42] Yet the very sequence in which the tales of the Prioress, the Nun's Priest, and the Second Nun are disposed suggests that such masculine counsel is not to be heeded. The common sense of the *Nun's Priest's Tale* in no measure abates the heroics with which the robust Nun proceeds to invigorate her legend of the conjugal virgin. The Prioress and her chaplain, persisting in the delusion that they are virile women, will have no more use for the sweet reasonableness of the mild Priest than for that brawn of his which elicits from the banal mentality of the Host the jest no less inept than stale of the "trede-foul" (7.3450-59).[43] The puerile Eglantine will profit no more from wise counsel than Kenelm, who "nas but seven yeer oold,/ And therfore litel tale hath he toold/ Of any dreem" (7.3117-19).

Despite the intractability of those whom he serves, the Nun's Priest conforms to the ethos prescribed for the confessor and counselor.[44] He is wise unto good and simple unto evil (Rom. 16: 19), prudent as the ser-

---

41 For the canonical use of such traditional τελικὰ κεφάλαια, see, *e.g.*, Gratian, C.22 q.5 c.18. For litigation, see Gratian, C.14 q.1 c.1.

42 *Cf.* Gower, *Cronica tripertita* 3.372, 473.

43 *Cf.* 7.3448 and Gower, *Vox clamantis* 4.14.603.

44 *De claustro animae* 2.12 (PL 176.1059); Peter Cantor, *Verbum abbreviatum* 144 (PL 205.344).

pent, simple as the dove (Matt. 10: 16). The ethical precisian may judge, nevertheless, that his conduct does not square with the dictum of Jerome: "Have the simplicity of the dove not to fashion snares for anyone and the cunning of the serpent not to be tripped up by the traps of others. It differs little in sinfulness whether a Christian can deceive or be deceived."[45] Yet the onus lies rather upon the Prioress. If, like the serpent, she did not permit herself to be blinded by the wiles of her adversaries and the foolish counsel of her chaplain, she would, like the dove, need no recourse to guile. If she had been as truly charitable and the Secund Nun as truly wise as Sir John is truly meek, if Charity, Wisdom, and Meekness had ruled in her convent as they rule in the medieval tropology of Nabugodonozor and his three bailiffs, then the King might well have heard neither noise nor plaint while peace and rest prevailed in soul and comfort in life. Since, however, the Prioress has, through false simplicity, allowed herself to become entrapped, the Priest must as a practical counselor with no alternative but to choose the lesser of two evils seek to extricate her by deceiving her foes with her foes' stratagem. If the Prioress, renouncing the fantasies of a neophyte and the litigiousness of the world, had in the spirit of the counsel given by the apostle to the well educated youth endeavored rather to educate her adversaries with gentleness — ἐν πραΰτητι — until they who were themselves entrapped in the snares of the devil should return to their senses and the will of God, then the gentle Priest, who had learned as a servant of God, a laborer without prelatic pride, to endure ill gently, would not have been impelled, educating her with gentleness, to counter her undisciplined predilection for the profane babblings of the courts with a foolish-seeming fable of a fox and cock and hen. Then, like the Parson (10.35-36), he could have sown pure wheat.[46]

Thus the "sweete preest", although concerned with giving pleasure, is

---

45 Jerome, *Letters* 58.6.4; *cf.* Gratian, C.22 q.2 C.21-22.

46 2 Tim. 2:14-26; Joseph Knabenbauer, S.J., *Commentarius in S. Pauli Apostoli Epistolas* 5 (Paris, 1913), pp. 315-25. Chaucer refers to this passage in the *Parson's Tale* 10.630, where "he that ofte chideth" is likened to "the develes child"; in a previous passage, 10.612-18, flatterers are called the "develes norices, that norissen his children with milk of losengerie" and "the develes chapelleyns, that syngen evere *Placebo*". The Second Nun, who fosters the Prioress' puerile litigiousness, is described in the *General Prologue* 1.164 as "hir chapeleyne".

Although Chaucer and the Nun's Priest would venerate the saints, the Second Nun's misemployment of St. Cecilia's legend would presumably incur the stricture of St. Paul against "old wives' tales" ("aniles fabulas") 1 Tim. 4:7, where a formula similar to that of 2 Tim. 2:16 is used. *Cf.* also 2 Tim. 4:3-5 (cited by the Parson 10.32-34), where the Greek "nephe" ("sobrius esto") recalls the "ananēpsōsin" ("resipiscant" 'return to senses, sobriety of mind') of 2 Tim. 2:26. For the tropology of Nabugodonozor, see *Middle English Religious Prose*, ed. Blake, p. 93.

not excessive in this concern like the complaisant man or the flatterer. Sir John complies with the "affability" prescribed for the true confessor. Always keeping in mind that which is good and beneficial in human intercourse, "this goodly man" now and then will give some measure of pain to secure in the event more felicity for those to whom he ministers. Toward Madame Eglantine as toward all he comports himself like a sensible friend, yet without the passion and sentiment of friendship, pleasing or displeasing not because he loves or hates but because he is what he is. Impelled by a habit so consonant with man's true nature as this mode of friendship, he appeals not to the law by which men litigate but to the law of nature residing in kind wit and good sense.[47]

Like the Prioress, the Monk conforms to the generic ethos of the *praelatus puer* or *momentaneus sacerdos*. Both are scions of the gentry whom simony, dispensing with the discipline due the neophyte, has thrust upon the Church as instant masters. Each has comfortably withdrawn from the world the better to enjoy the world. The Prioress plays the lady while sidestepping the burdens of the wife; the Monk pursues the knightly pleasures of the chase while avoiding the military obligations of knighthood. Like her small hounds, his greyhounds devour literally the alms of the needy, the bread of their brothers in Christ.[48] This venatic love is a mark of the traditional *praelatus puer*, whose ear is attuned rather to the un-Aaronic tintinnabulation of his bridle than to the tolling of the chapel bell.[49] It brands the Monk as a variant of the uncanonical *clericus venator* — a variant all the more reprehensible because monastic.[50] The inconsonance of such an ethos with the demands of monastic ascesis had long been recognized. The decretals record the commonplace ascribed to Ambrose: "Do you suppose, brothers, that he fasts who at the first ray of dawn does not wake for church, does not seek eagerly the hallowed precincts of the blessed mar-

---

47 For the flatterer, the complaisant man, and the "sensible friend" (ἐπιειχὴς φίλος) without passion, see Aristotle, *Nicomachean Ethics* 4.6, cited by St. Thomas in his discussion of "amicitia sive affabilitas", *Summa theologiae* 2.2.114. For the implications of ἐπιειχής, see R. Gauthier and Y. Jolif, *L'éthique à Nicomaque* 2 (Louvain, 1958), pp. 431-33, 533-35; Thomas Aquinas, *ST* 2.2.80.1. For the Greek πραότης "mansuetudo", *i.e.*, "meekness", "mildness", "gentleness", "debonairetee", see Gauthier and Jolif, 2.301; *Parson's Tale* 10.654-60.

48 Jerome, *Letters* 58.6.4.

49 10.432-36; Bernard of Clairvaux, *De moribus et officio episcoporum* 2.7; *Sermones super Cantica canticorum* 33.15; Gratian, D.43 c.1. See also my "The *De contemptu mundi* of Bernardus Morvalensis-Book Three: A Study in Commonplace," *Mediaeval Studies* 29 (1967) 256-58.

50 X, 5.24.

tyrs, but rising, gathers the servants, disposes the nets, leads out the dogs, wanders all over the woods and forest?"[51] It is not the oil of happiness, the grace of charity, that has fattened the head that shines like glass.[52] The Monk's face has been anointed rather by the sin of voracity — "edacitatis vitio" — which has made him fat-witted, his hundred tragedies notwithstanding.[53] His love knot no more associates him with the bond of love and perfection — "vinculum caritatis" (Hos. 11: 4), "vinculum perfectionis" (Col. 3: 14) — than the inscription "Amor vincit omnia" certifies in the Prioress a sense of the love that conquers death. A dissociable man, for whom it is not good or pleasant, like precious ointment on the head, to dwell together with his brethren in one (Ps. 132: 1-2), he prefers to range abroad with horse and hounds, while an agreeable appointment as outrider permits him to circumvent the ancient stricture against the roving monk or *gyrovagus*. For the stolid audacity with which he declines to revere monastic tradition or discipline, he might seem to be a bold man. His projecting eyes, "eyen stepe" (1.201), that bespeak fell malice in medieval physiognomy, rolling — like a wild man's — in a head that steams like a demonic furnace, may well conjure up the image of the Wild Huntsman.[54] But the Monk is no apparition, not even "a forpyned goost" (1.205). His mount is not a coal-black steed but a damsel's palfrey, comfortably colored a berry-brown.[55] His quarry is not the boar but the hare. The Monk, then, is no more a "manly man" (1.167) in any spiritual or physical acceptation than the Prioress is a manly woman. Since he is no less puerile than she and therefore no less asexual, the stock jest of the "trede-fowel" is wasted upon him (7.1941-62).

When this monk undertakes to bewail in tragic manner the fall of illustrious men, he might seem to be actuated by the canonical precept

---

51 Gratian, D.86 c.13.

52 Alan of Lille, *Distinctiones dictionum theologicalium*, s.v. oleum (PL 210.881).

53 Gratian, D.44 c.12.

54 For "eyen stepe", see *Three Prose Versions of the Secreta secretorum*, ed. Steele, p. 115; *OED*, s.v. "steep"; *cf.* Peter Cantor, *Verbum abbreviatum* 11: "signa sua habet superbia, ut non lateat (ut oculos sublimes)", (PL 205.52). For "rollynge" eyes, see *Secreta secretorum*, ed. Steele, p. 225; that such eyes could in physiognomy signify a lecher only serves to emphasize ironically the asexuality of the Monk. *Cf.* Martianus Capella, *De nuptiis Philologiae et Mercurii* 4.328; Hugh of St. Victor, *De institutione novitiorum* 12 (PL 176.941). For the "Wild Hunt", see *Early Middle English Verse and Prose*, ed. J. A. W. Bennett and G. V. Smithers, 2nd ed. (Oxford, 1968), p. 204.

55 The beard, kirtle, and mantle of the pacific king in *Wynnere and Wastoure* 90-91 are "bery-brown"; *cf.* the *Cook's Tale* 1.4368-69. The imagery is not softened as Voznesenky presents Peter the Great in *The Skull Ballad*: "like a nag, gaunt, / Having become black, like anthracite. / On his face rush the eyes, / Like a wheel-spinning motor-cycle."

that monks should not preach but should lament the misery and iniquity of the human condition in this contemptible world.[56] Yet he is mourning neither for the world nor for himself. Instead, this man, whom God has endowed with the talent to become an abbot, is attempting under the guise of this protracted tragic tally to exculpate the pusillanimity and the sloth that have betrayed, physically and spiritually, his proper virtue and manhood. This *praelatus puer* is professing in effect that he has chosen to remain a child and to advance no further in prelacy lest he incur, elated with pride, the judgment set down by Paul for the neophyte made bishop, the ruin of the devil with which the Monk commences his lugubrious catalogue.[57] Yet he is in fact merely echoing — to "noon audience" (7.2801), divine or human — the ineffectual defense offered by every unprofitable servant that hides his talent in the earth or wraps it in a handkerchief.[58]

The ethos of the *praelatus puer* gives rise to a second ethos that may be designated by a term borrowed from Greek ethology: *argos* 'functionless' (*a-ergos*).[59] This epithet is applicable to the Monk since he refuses to assume a function (*ergon*) in keeping with his birth, talent, or profession. "To been an abbot able" (1.167), he is content with the sinecure of outrider, expending on hares the capacity for domination betokened by "his eyen stepe". This formula and this physiognomic trait are shared by the Host. True to his surname Bailly,

> A semely man oure Hooste was withalle
> For to han been a marchal in an halle.
> A large man he was with eyen stepe. (1.751-53)

Otherwise the "manly man" is quite dissimilar from him who lacked nothing of manhood (1.756). Where the Monk lets pass the Host exceeds. Harry Bailly does not hide his talent; he ventures a talent that he never received. Proffering himself as guide, judge, ruler, and "governour" (cf. 7.1940) of the pilgrims because "Fayn wolde I doon yow myrthe, wiste I how" (1.766), he betrays his kinship with the classical *periergos* or "overdoer", who in pursuance of kindness and good will assumes a function that is beyond his means.[60] Inasmuch as this good will is not immune to pique, the Host betrays a second kinship — with

---

56   Gratian, C.16, q.1 c.4.
57   1 Tim. 3:6; Jerome, *Letters* 69.9.4-6.
58   Jerome, *Commentaria in Matheum* 25:25.
59   Gauthier and Jolif, 2.55, 288-90. *Cf. De claustro animae* 2.12 (PL 176.1058-59); Thomas Aquinas, *ST* 2.2.185.2.
60   Theophrastus, *Characters* 13.1-2.

the medieval *surquiders* or "overweener".[61] Like the *periergos* who eagerly takes it upon himself to guide a journey by way of a short cut (then cannot find where he is) or the *surquiders* who is prompt to offer counsel (urging people to begin such things as they can never end well), the Host undertakes to be the "gyde" of a diversion that will shorten the way (1.791) to and from Canterbury.[62] If this diversion should go astray, if the Host should fail in his quest of good will, he (and not Chaucer) will be responsible.

The *Surquiders* in the allegory of the *Mirour de l'omme* is accompanied by the *Derisour* and his servant, *Malapert*. Something of each persists in the ethos of the Host. As if in travesty of the precept that a jest should accord with the person involved, he mocks the sexless Monk and the well tempered Priest with the same stale joke of the "tredefowel".[63] "Wys and wel ytaught" in his own estimation (1.755) and therefore by his own nomination suited to be master of the pilgrimage, he bristles like Surquiders at the least touch of criticism, for his wisdom is not meek but bold.[64] When the Parson rebukes him for his blasphemous oaths, he ridicules him as a Lollard. When the Pardoner touches upon his sinfulness, he offers to cut off the relics of the Pardoner's manhood. In the boldness of his speech (1.755), he outdoes Malapert, not only divulging the derelictions of the Cook but encouraging the Canon's Yeoman to "discover" that which he should hide.[65] He may even slander the innocent, not from malice like Malapert, but like the complaisant man, the *areskos*, to be sociable.[66] To gratify the Merchant, who has duped all but the Shipman with his tale of January and May, the Host parades the faults of his wife, who in reality may have been as blameless as the shrewish wife of the Merchant was imaginary.

Indecent and injurious, the jocularity of the Host goes beyond the temperate mean. It exceeds the licit office (*ergon*) of verbal play in social intercourse. Its intrinsic scurrility cannot be extenuated by the palliative of jocose intent, to the banal formula of which — "non serio sed joco" — the Host habitually resorts (1.4355 ; 7.1963-64). The humorless Monk, on the contrary, has "no lust to pleye" with jests or tales (7.2806). Yet the gravity of his mien is affected only to compensate

61   10.403; Gower, *Mirour de l'omme* 1441-1728.
62   Theophrastus, *Characters* 13.6; Gower, *Mirour de l'omme* 1477-80.
63   For the ensuing discussion of "play" ("ludus"), see Thomas Aquinas, *ST* 2.2.168.2-4.
64   Gower, *Mirour de l'omme* 1512-22; *cf.* Jas. 3:1, 13.
65   8.696; Gower, *Mirour de l'omme* 1687-89.
66   Theophrastus, *Characters* 5; Gauthier and Jolif, 2.305.

for his addiction to another kind of play that nullifies the gravity of his mind. Having made the sport of hunting the purpose of his life, setting the pleasure it affords above the rule of St. Maur or St. Benedict, he exceeds the rule of reason in active play, while, deficient himself in playful speech and unreceptive to the playful speech of others, he falls short of that rule in verbal play.

Like the Monk and Prioress, the Friar, Summoner, and Pardoner are simoniacs. These two groups, however, represent divergent forms of simony. The Monk and Prioress are purchasers, the Friar, Summoner, and Pardoner are vendors, of the grace that God gives gratuitously. The Monk and Prioress, furthermore, are well born, while the latter three are base born.

The ethos to which the Friar belongs had been described centuries before by Jerome in a formula that became canonic: "negotiatorem clericum, ex inope divitem et ex ignobili gloriosum".[67] He is a huckster of low birth who uses the ministry of the poor to enrich or promote himself. As a *quaestuarius* seeking his reward not at the journey's end but on the way, he is a mercenary whose characterization is aptly linked by rime with that of the Merchant.[68] To compensate for his vulgar origin, he vaunts an exotic name in its Anglo-Norman form, Huberd — the name of the kite that confesses the fox in the *Roman de Renart* — a name that may have been current in England for the scavenging magpie, from which it is extended antonomastically in a well known English lyric to the scavenging man in the moon: "Hupe forþ, Hubert, hosede pye!" To enhance his specious courtesy (1.249-50), he affects a Frenchified pronunciation of English. With a spurious custody of the tongue, he mimics the lisp that betokens the venal preacher in medieval tropology. Although as strong as any agrestic champion, he thus womanizes his voice to cajole a clientele of puerile women, perverting the rhetorical principle that accommodates the manner of delivery to the kind of audience.[69] Yet in his false reverence or "respect of persons" no less

---

67 Jerome, *Letters* 52.5.3; Gratian, D.88 c.9.

68   10.781; Robert of Basevorn, *Forma praedicandi* 5 in *Artes praedicandi*, ed. Th.-M. Charland, O.P. (Paris, 1936), p. 243.

69   1.264-65: "Somewhat he lipsed, for his wantownesse, / To make his Englissh sweete upon his tonge." The lisping may refer to an affectation of French pronunciation, in which *s* was lost before *l n m j v f b d g* in the eleventh century (becoming *d* before *l n* in Anglo-Norman) and before the voiceless stops in the thirteenth. See also Cato, *Distichs* 3.4; Quintilian, *Institutio oratoria* 11.3.24; Seneca, *Epistles* 115.2; Alan of Lille, *Liber poenitentialis* (PL 210.283). If Hubert is taken as the name of the man in the moon in the medieval lyric, then, since the man in the moon is commonly identified in folklore with Cain, and since Cain, *i.e.*, Caim, is used as a medieval acronym for the four orders of friars, the name Hubert may by metalepsis signify a friar.

than in the very wantonness of his merry demeanor, he betrays vestiges of that boorish provenance (*rusticitas*) which the adulteration of his speech is supposed to dissemble.[70] While he abuses the indiscriminate hospitality of rural franklins and urban matrons, he avoids the sun that browns the honest laborer, thus reserving for his neck a delicate pallor that the poet invidiously compares to the royal flower of France.[71] The copious alms that he wheedles from all, from unshod widow or affluent wife, and purloins for himself could not be less canonically bestowed on any strolling player, for in singing, playing on a rote, or wrestling he excels every mime.[72] Spurning the poor from whom he sprang and whom his order was founded to serve, he rationalizes this dissociability with scruples (1.243-47) travestying the very Pauline maxim — "Evil company corrupts good morals" (1 Cor. 15: 33) — that impelled Jerome to shun such hucksters as the Friar himself. Like any peddlar he carries trinkets — "knyves and pynnes" (1.233-34) — stuffed in his tippet, but such trinkets are also the traditional gauds, the trumpery gifts or *munuscula*, with which the bawd in medieval story, like the "magpie" Urraca in the *Book of Good Love* (919), insinuates her services — services which, like all services, the Friar renders first and foremost to himself. In supplying with dowers the poor maidens whom he thus seduced just as in visiting the rich who are sick, he parodies the corporal works of mercy. Unlike the effete Monk or Prioress, he is sexually vigorous. Lust, not logic, makes his eyes twinkle.[73]

The Friar is a self-serving prodigal who begs not to hoard like the avaricious, but to defray the exorbitant costs of his vanity and licentiousness. The motive for his venality is a libertinism that mocks in its wanton mirth the sober hilarity of such cheerful givers as Francis of Assisi. The primary instrument of this venality is the confessional. Its mode is adulation. As a sweet, pleasant, and easy dispenser of penance, the Friar simulates the properties of the true confessor realized in the "sweete preest", the "goodly man sir John". As a sociable "brother", the Friar prefers the fellowship of sinners to the natural equality of the virtuous.[74] As a complaisant counselor, he compounds his own habituation to sin with the inurement of those whom he has been

70 Jerome, *Letters* 22.29.6. Peter Cantor, *Verbum abbreviatum* 66 (PL 205.199-202).

71 For the *pauper delicatus*, see *De claustro animae* 2.18 (PL 176.1070-72).

72 Gratian, D.86 c.7-8.

73 *Cf. Three Prose Versions of the Secreta secretorum*, ed. Steele, p. 233; Alan of Lille, *Anticlaudianus* 3.21; Ambrose, *Hexameron* 6.9.55.

74 10.755-57. Gregory, *Moralia* 21.22; 26.45; *Pastoral Care* 2.6.

licensed to save. Whether roving with his bagman in quest of purchase and rent or perverting love-days into occasions of profit, he revives the ancient sacrilege and adulation of Judas, who bore about, and filched from, the purse of the apostles (John 12: 6), betrayed Christ with the kiss of peace, and sold Him for "a good pitaunce" (1.224).[75]

The Friar's antagonist, the Summoner, the scabrous servant of an archdeacon, reverts to the simoniacal servant of Eliseus, the leprous Giezi (4 Kings 5: 20-27). He is opposed to the Friar as in the medieval taxonomy of sin detraction is opposed to adulation.[76] In the flattering Friar the respect of persons (*acceptio personarum*) obscures the communion of equality that virtuous living restores to fallen nature. In the Summoner the taking of bribes (*acceptio munerum*) thwarts the anathema of excommunication. In the antagonism of their tales, however, each simonist detracts from the other with diabolic malice, imputing to his corrival a reprobate sense which a reprobate stupor permits neither to recognize in himself.[77] Thus the charge laid by the Friar on the summoner of his tale:

> And right as Judas hadde purses smale,
> And was a theef, right swich a theef was he;
> His maister hadde but half his duetee.
> He was, if I shal yeven hym his laude,
> A theef, and eek a somnour, and a baude. (3.1350-54)

redounds on the Friar himself, while the Giezite in his story projects the friar as a mock-Eliseus (3.2116) who claims for himself a faculty for revelation exceeding the visionary powers accorded by Scriptural truth to the master of Giezi.[78] The Summoner, again, transmits to the friar of his tale the selfsame irascibility and lecherousness with which he is infected (1.626; 3.1804), and the Friar, who will cheerfully cajole even a widow's mite, displays the summoner of his tale extorting a widow's curse, an imprecation feared by vulgar superstition no less than the anathema.[79] Meanwhile in life both simonists are busy enriching themselves from the dowry of the widowed Church itself and from the patrimony of the Crucifixion as they hurry toward their common heritage.[80]

75   10.616. Peter Cantor; *Verbum abbreviatum* 43, 45, 153 (PL 205.135, 142, 366).
76   10.614.
77   10.486.
78   *Cf.* 3.1851-58; 4 Kings 4:27.
79   *The Fox and the Wolf* 201-02 in *Early Middle English Verse and Prose*, ed. Bennett and Smithers, p. 73.
80   Bernard of Clairvaux, *De consideratione* 4.4.12.

The Summoner rides on the pilgrimage crowned with a garland like the reprobates crowned with roses whom the Book of Wisdom (1-2) bequeaths to the devil because they make a covenant with death and do not spare the widow nor refrain from detraction, but lie in wait for the just man and test him with contumely. As they call death to themselves like a lover calling his love ("amicam" 1.16), so the Summoner bears "a stif burdoun" to the Pardoner's song, "Com hider, love, to me!" (1.672-73).

The reprobate sense in its ultimate ignominy is manifested by the character of the Pardoner. Like the pagan idolaters at the first coming of Christ whom divine wrath abandoned to the nameless passions — "passiones ignominiae" — of unnatural vice (Rom. 1: 18-32), this medieval idolater, whose god is gain (Eph. 5: 3-6), has consummated his idolatry with sodomy. Outdoing even his pagan forebears who exchanged the truth of God for a lie, he has changed the pardon of Christ, the gratuitous redemption of the Saviour, into a commodity.[81] In divine retribution he is suffered to carry about with him no relics truer than those relics of his desiccated manhood — the dry genitals symbolic of simony — which the Host with a banality gross but no longer inept would enshrine in fitting corruption.[82] Where the hand usurps the function of the mouth and abuses the purpose of the offertory, it is appropriate that the members of generation should desist from the uses of nature and that unnatural vice should subserve corruption.[83] When threatened, the Pardoner, like his friend and compeer, the Summoner, responds with wrath. Yet the anger provoked in the Pardoner by the menace of the Host is significantly different from the anger to which the

81   It must not be assumed that the Pardoner intends his audience to make a distinction between his pardons — "myn hooly pardoun" (6.906) — and the pardon of Christ (6.916-18). It is his practice to pass off his pardons as authentic grants of indulgence, and the medieval grant of indulgence drew upon the Church's treasury of merits and good works stored up by Christ as well as by the Virgin Mary and the saints — by the Head of the Mystical Body of Christ as well as by the members.

The term absolution refers properly to the forgiveness of the guilt of sin by the confessor. The relaxation of the penance imposed by the confessor, *i.e.*, the payment of the debt of temporal punishment through the grant of indulgence that draws upon the Church's treasury after the guilt of sin has been forgiven by the confessor, is properly designated as "solutio". The Pardoner's use of the terms "absolucion" and "assoille" may suggest that he is accustomed to pass himself off upon his "lewed" audience (1.701-06); 6.392) not merely as a pardoner but also as a confessor — as one who could not only pardon but absolve. Yet only an ordained priest could confess, *i.e.*, absolve.

82   10.139; Jean de Meun, *Roman de la Rose* 7081; Gerhoch of Reichersberg, *Adversus simoniacos* 27 (PL 194.1365).

83   6.398-99, 444-45; Hugh of St. Victor, *De institutione novitiorum* 12 (PL 176.941); Gratian, D.92 c.1.

challenge of the Friar stirs the Summoner. Each person responds with anger to a mode of injury, but the mode is determined by his ethos. It is the guile (*fraus*) with which the Friar turns against the Summoner his own weapon, detraction, that enrages the Summoner. The Pardoner is agitated by the threat of physical violence (*vis*), a threat to which as an effeminate man he is especially vulnerable.[84]

The timeworn traits of the effeminate mien — the shaven face, the pumiced skin assiduously cultivated by generations of fops — accrue to the Pardoner by default of nature: "No berd hadde he, ne nevere sholde have;/ As smothe it was as it were late shave" (1.689-90).[85] One such feature, the uncovered head, long affected by effeminate clerics, has become in the Pardoner a sign of newfangledness:

> But hood, for jolitee, wered he noon,
> For it was trussed up in his walet.
> Hym thoughte he rood al of the newe jet;
> Dischevelee, save his cappe, he rood al bare. (1.680-84).[86]

The avidity for the novel is a vice traditionally associated with the shameless insolence or irreverence of the *illusor*.[87]

The stereotype of the *illusor* determines the riotous existence of the young prodigals in the *Pardoner's Tale*. They play at dice. They play with women. They mock with "vileynye" the poor old man.[88] They mock with oaths the Ancient of Days. They delude one another, they delude themselves, and they are deluded by God.[89] Proposing to make league against Death, they make instead a covenant with hell.[90] Because of their reprobate sense they no longer remember that death can be overcome only by dying to sin in the sepulture of Baptism with Christ, who took on a mortal body that in it He might slay death.[91] Rather they cherish drunkenness, the "sepulture of mannes resoun" (10.822). Craving novelty, they ignore the newness of Christ and cleave to the inveteracy of sin. In the figure of the poor old man an aged body yearns for its inhumation in Mother Earth just as the pilgrim soul sighs for its

---

84　3.1431; 10.799; Cicero, *De officiis* 1.13.41.

85　Helinand, *Sermones* 18 (PL 212.633).

86　Helinand, *Sermones* 18 (PL 212.633).

87　*Cf.* Plato, *Laws* 7.797. For the definition of "insolence", see Alan of Lille, *Summa de arte praedicatoria* 10 (PL 210.133).

88　Isa. 3:4-5; Wisd. 2:10.

89　Prov. 3:34.

90　*Cf.* Isa. 28:15.

91　Augustine, *Sermones* 88.1.

fatherland in heaven.[92] This inclination to the earth is literal and natural in the old man's earthly body. It is metaphorical and culpable in the young men's earthy spirits. The old body seeks death that eludes it temporarily. The young *illusores* find death temporarily that will elude them eternally (10.211-16). Their youthful spirits, suffused with a pride of life that makes them oblivious of their spiritual order, incite the young revelers with an illusory love of neighbor to "seke" physical Death (6.694, 772) so that young folk may the longer enjoy the life of sin which is spiritual death. Ironically, they slay only themselves, body and soul, accelerating their physical death, confirming their spiritual death. Having spurned regeneration, they yield their lives spiritually and physically to corruption. False thieves themselves, betraying one another to the false thief Death whom they conspired to slay, they are each "of his assent" (6.758). Willfully ignorant like the *illusores* that shall come in the last days (2 Pet. 3: 3-5), they have misconstrued the portent of the plague. The wrath with which they now confront the challenge of Death or any impediment to their pleasures they shall project upon their vision of the incommutable Judge at the Day of Wrath.[93] Then they shall be bound in the same faggot as the spurious sower of seed, the Pardoner, the vessel of corruption masquerading as a vehicle of regeneration in his own quest for the wages of sin.[94]

The irreverence, the reprobate sense, the unnatural vice, and the plenitude of evil that pervaded the world at the first coming of Christ were considered in the medieval conceptualization of history to prefigure the iniquity that shall abound when charity grows cold in the last tribulation before the second advent. The effeminacy of the Pardoner is therefore portentous. The histrionics of his homiletic delivery — the neck stretched forth in the manner of a crane, the "bekking" east and west of an un-Paracletic dove sitting on a workaday barn — mimic grotesquely the proud and petulant gestures of the women that precipitated the ruin of Judah when that kingdom was ruled by *illusores* — a ruin that prefigures anagogically the *anomia* of the final tribulation.[95] Like them and like Sodom the Pardoner has "preached" his sin.[96] He has flaunted his cupidity in his discourse to the pilgrims. He

---

92 Augustine, *In Joannis evangelium* 6:2. The term "oold man" corresponds to the Latin *senex*, not to the Pauline *vetus homo* 'former man'.

93 Gregory, *Moralia* 32.9.

94 Matt. 13:24-43. See my "The *De contemptu mundi* of Bernardus Morvalensis, Part One: A Study in Commonplace," *Mediaeval Studies* 22 (1960) 127.

95 Isa. 3:16; 28:14; 29:20.

96 Isa. 3:9: "et peccatum suum quasi Sodoma praedicaverunt nec absconderunt."

has mirrored himself in the *illusores* of his tale. Even his initial gesture — calling for a cup of ale — aligns him with the *histriones*, the common players, barred by canon law from Church revenue. A self-proclaimed fellow of the perpetually juvenile that busily use the creatures as in youth, he proffers an exemplum "Of yonge folk that haunteden folye".[97] A eunuch who has chosen despite Christ to persist as a dry tree,[98] he tells a tale of a tree at the root of which waits the death that Christ came to slay in the advent of mercy. In one respect, however, he falls short of the unreserved impudence that foreshadows the advent of wrath. Nowhere does he allude to his homosexuality. Rather he veils this perversion, however transparently, under repeated protestations of heterosexuality (3.166; 6.453). From this reticence, presumably, Chaucer wishes his audience to infer that the Day of Wrath, though drawing near, is not yet imminent. When it is, the reprobate will seek death and will not find it (Rev. 9: 6).

The ethos of the Canon — the canon of the Yeoman's tale as well as the canon of the pilgrimage — has for its archetype the perjurer-conjurer. This archetype is especially incompatible with the ethos prescribed for a man of religion since the archetype incorporates two vices opposed to religion.[99] Magic is a mode of superstition. Superstition is opposed to religion because it offers divine worship to a creature rather than the Creator. Magic seeks knowledge not from God but from the operation of demons through pacts tacitly or expressly made with them. It is therefore vain, false, and illicit. Like superstition, magic exceeds the virtuous mean by transcending that mean through deviation. Such an excess is imputed by the Yeoman to his master — the misuse of a transcendent wit:

> He is to wys, in feith, as I bileeve.
> That that is overdoon, it wol nat preeve
> Aright, as clerkes seyn; it is a vice.
> Wherfore in that I holde hym lewed and nyce.
> For whan a man hath over-greet a wit,
> Ful oft hym happeth to mysusen it. (8.644-49)

Perjury is a mode of irreligion. It is contrary to religion through defect since it exhibits not reverence but contempt of God when it calls Him

---

97   3.187; 6.464; Wisd. 2:6.

98   Wisd. 3:14; Isa. 56:3-5.

99   Thomas Aquinas, *ST* 2.2.92, 96, 98. Conjuring and perjury are linked respectively to the first and second commandments — see *John Gaytryge's Sermon* in *Middle English Religious Prose*, ed. Blake, p. 78.

to witness that which is vain or false or illicit. Since irreligion and superstition are opposed to religion, they are consequently opposed to justice, of which religion is a potential part, a moral virtue annexed to justice. Magic and perjury are, then, especially inconsonant with the function of a canon regular, whose very title in both its parts signifies the order indispensable to justice.

The garb of the Canon, the black cloak over a white surplice, indicates that he is, like the canon of the tale, a canon regular, more particularly, an Augustinian canon; yet the slovenliness of the garb betrays the addiction of its wearer to the science of alchemy.[100] Though harder on the complexion, this "elvysshe craft" (8.751, 842) is no more respectable than catoptromancy (8.668).[101] It is as vain and false as any kind of superstition. Neither canon, to be sure, has recourse openly and crudely to so quaint a device as conjuration; yet the Yeoman slyly likens the strange names used in alchemy to the incantations of the *ars notoria* (8.860-61). He avers that he has all but seen the fiend materialize in the explosions incidental to alchemy (8.916-17), and he constantly disparages the canon of his tale as a fiend in human form. Such an alchemist may not, perhaps, overtly or expressly use his materials as signs to elicit demonic operation, yet neither does he employ these chemicals as natural causes that can produce their proper and lawful effects. He is attempting instead to secure through these materials effects other than the proper and lawful effects which they have the natural power to produce. He aspires to transcend the natural causality in which the will of God is expressed. He therefore "maketh God his adversarie", purposing to work "in contrarie of his wil" (8.1476-78). Thus the occult "Elixer" personified by the Yeoman (8.862-72), which he vainly seeks in order to achieve this perversion of causality, is not a natural cause proper to true science. It is tantamount, tacitly if not expressly, to the signs devoid of natural efficacy by which demons are invoked in the arts of superstition.

When such a canon essays the role of perjurer-conjurer, he incurs not only the enmity of God but the animosity of victims whose gullibility is actuated by the same deadly sin of avarice that motivates his perjury, his trickery, and his subtlety.[102] Like the goldsmith turned alchemist in the *Mirour de l'omme* (25513-36), he defrauds these victims of

---

100 *Cf.* Gower, *Vox clamantis* 4.8.359-66.
101 John of Salisbury, *Policraticus* 2.28.
102 "Gullibility" is equivalent to the French *sotie* (Gower, *Mirour de l'omme* 25278, 25596); hence 8.1341 "sotted". "Innocence" (8.897, 1076) = *sotie*, not the integral part of justice, "scilicet declinare

the gold and silver that he has pledged to repay with interest. To avoid his creditors, he takes flight, wandering about like the monastic *gyrovagus*, lurking in lanes (8.658) like Lyer in *Piers Plowman* (B 2.216), until he becomes as elusive as "that slidynge science" itself (8.682, 732).

Like a merchant, such a canon ventures gold and silver to turn a profit (8.946-50), yet the gold and silver that both venture is often not their own. In the end the perjury and subtlety and trickery of such a canon will force him to seek the sanctuary of a church like the *marchant pelerin* in the *Mirour de l'omme* (25849-72), or the sanctuary of a pilgrimage, like the Canterbury Merchant, or the sanctuary of the "suburbes" and the "hernes", like the Yeoman's master.

The Yeoman's protestation that he is telling a tale not of his lord but of another canon "That kan an hundred foold moore subtiltee" (8.1091) resembles the Merchant's avowal: "but of myn owene soore,/ For soory herte, I telle may namoore" (4.1243-44). Each is intended as a patent dissimulation. The Merchant wishes to be identified with January. The Yeoman expects the odium investing the canon of his tale to redound upon his master. In each instance the narrator hopes to conceal his true motivation. The absconding Merchant would like the pilgrims to think that he has joined them to seek a respite not from his creditors but from a shrewish wife. The splenetic Yeoman wants to extenuate the malevolence of his calumny. The question whether the canon of his tale and his master are two distinct canons or one and the same is nugatory. The tenor of the Yeoman's entire diatribe inculcates that all alchemists are of one piece. Like the tricky tradesmen denounced by Gower, "Trestout sont d'une escole apris" (*Mirour de l'omme* 25500).

The Canon's Yeoman, the sorcerer's apprentice and faithful servant turned informer, may be said to exceed his master in injustice, for to the superstition and irreligion imbibed from the Canon he now adds on his own another vice opposed to justice, detraction. The momentary convert, seizing upon false occasion to vent the spleen accumulated during the Scriptural seven years of labor and famine (8.720), makes a travesty of that moral virtue annexed to justice which is called vindication when, abetted by the Host, he exposes to strangers the sins

a malo, ad quod pertinet innocentia" (Thomas Aquinas, *ST* 2.2.80.1). "Perjurie", "Tricherie" (*cf.* 8.1069 "trecherie"), and "Soubtilité" are servants of "Covoitise", the first daughter of Avarice in *Mirour de l'omme* 6313-588; see also 25177-980. The recurring use of the term "subtiltee" in the *Canon's Yeoman's Tale* is equivocal: while signifying ostensibly the knowledge (*queintise*) of alchemical arcana, it signifies implicitly the cunning (*queintise*) of guile.

unknown to them of his master.[103] In his exposé of the alchemist he simulates the method of true science, "adinveniendo vel addiscendo", appealing to his own experience and to authority.[104] Yet his citations are as farcical as his adventures. His disavowal of malicious intent to the "worshipful chanons religious" (8.992-1011) reads almost like a parody of the paramythic formula addressed in earnest by Gower to the mendicant friars.[105] The plausible explanation offered by Gower for the shortage of money in England — that the guile of the Lombard bankers "is one of the principal causes why our land is too barren" of gold and silver coins (*Mirour de l'omme* 25448-49) — echoes absurdly in the Yeoman's asseveration that alchemy is "The cause grettest of swich scarsetee" (8.1393). His own explanation why he cannot supply the blush required by convention to palliate calumny — "for fumes diverse/ Of metals, whiche ye han herd me reherce,/ Consumed and wasted han my reednesse" (8.1098-1100) — is not even specious.

The figures of the perjurer and conjurer had served conjointly in the medieval tradition of the *contemptus mundi* as portents of the last epoch. In the *Canterbury Tales*, where the sense of impending doom is not urgent, the vices of the canons are not so ominous. The superstition and the irreligion of each have been attenuated by the poet. As alchemist, neither canon explicitly — only tacitly — courts demonic cooperation. As perjurer, neither is shown by the poet expressly invoking divine witness to confirm his promise to repay the gold and silver borrowed from his clients. Yet the reader is invited to infer that both canons habitually had recourse to such attestation from the ubiquity of oaths throughout the *Canon's Yeoman's Prologue* and *Tale* and from the facility with which the canon of the tale employs execration to confirm the price of his "receite" or assert the "trouthe" of his character (8.1046, 1361). It is, however, the skew of their censor, the ludicrously vindicatory Yeoman himself, that most diminishes the portentousness of the alchemical canons.

This tempered expectation of the last epoch is consonant with the mixed ethologue of good and bad prefacing the *Canterbury Tales*. A sense of imminent doom would have called rather for an unrelieved ethologue, spelling out rank by rank the universal evil that shall abound throughout the world when Christ comes to judge the living and the

---

103   Thomas Aquinas, *ST* 2.2.80.1. For false occasion, see Gower, *Mirour de l'omme* 6351.
104   Thomas Aquinas, *ST* 2.2.96.1.
105   Gower, *Vox clamantis* 4.16.677-98; cf. *Mirour de l'omme* 25213-36.

dead. The mixed ethologue, redolent of human dignity through its good characters and eliciting with the bad the contempt of the world, is more appropriate to the mixed congregation and still maturing iniquity of the *pax Christiana*. The *contemptus mundi* and the *dignitas humanae naturae* share as parenetic genres a common theme — conversion to God. This conversion is sustained by the baptized Christian through penance. A manual of confession, therefore, is a fitting work to conclude a pilgrimage that exemplifies both the imperfection and perfection of human nature. The most suitable pilgrim to deliver this tractate on repentance is the perfect priest, who, while he rides humbly among the least, shows the spiritual way to his fellow pilgrims in keeping with the allegorical interpretation of his title: *presbyter* 'praebens iter'.[106]

The ethos of the perfect priest embodied in the Parson is derived from the application of a Scriptural parable. As a true shepherd he walks, ministering to his flock on foot, not riding like the masters and hunters of this world. As a true shepherd, content like the patriarchs to be not a king of men but a shepherd of his flock, he lords it over vices, not over brethren whom he serves as pattern of the flock.[107] Shunning the elation of pharisaic pride, he undertakes the conversion of others in the works of mercy only when he has converted himself to God in works of justice. As a true shepherd he is not mercenary. Like the Pauline *hilaris dator* and the Clerk of Oxford, he spends his talent gladly and well, devoutly teaching and preaching what he has learned by study and practice. He is not a pluralist. He reverts to none of the sins of the *aulicus clericus*. He loves not with the world's love but with charity patient and beneficent. With humility and discipline he watches over God's peace in the sheepfold of his soul and the sheepfold of his flock.[108]

The Parson and the Plowman are brothers in Christ. The Plowman is not of the earth earthy. He is a spiritual man like the perfect men of the Canterbury ethologue. He is the brother of the Parson because every man reborn in Christ who cooperates with the Spirit in the works of charity is restored to the equality in which God created all men.[109] Faithful to the love of God and the love of man in God and for God, the Plowman is therefore the opposite of the fierce peasant, the *ferus rusticus*, whose bestiality Gower excoriates in the *Vox clamantis* 5.9-10.

106 Bernard of Cluny, *De contemptu mundi* 2.246; *cf.* Gregory, *Pastoral Care* 1.1.
107 Gregory, *Pastoral Care* 2.6.
108 Anselm of Canterbury, *Homiliae* 15 (PL 158.670-73); *De claustro animae* 2.12 (PL 176.1059-60).
109 10.516; 755-57; Gregory, *Moralia* 21.22-24; Gower, *Vox clamantis* 6.14.1017-24.

This untamed peasant is for Gower the elemental *homo animalis*. Upon him more strictly than upon the members of any other class the rule of our first father is entailed. By the sweat of his face he must labor to feed the gentlemen of this world. When he aspires to their leisure, they like their fathers in the better days now past must drive him back to the servile labor divinely ordained to curb his pride. This penal labor is transformed by Chaucer's Plowman into an instrument of grace by which he claims his share of human dignity. Thus Chaucer's Plowman attests to the dignity of human nature and to the humanity of Chaucer himself. Gower's peasant epitomizes the contemptibility of this world.

Loyola, Chicago

MEDIEVAL RUSSIA, THE MONGOLS, AND THE WEST: NOVGOROD'S RELATIONS WITH THE BALTIC, 1100-1350

Thomas S. Noonan

ONE of the most popular generalizations about medieval Russia is that it was isolated from the rest of Europe by the Mongol conquest. According to this interpretation, two centuries of Mongol rule put an end to Russia's lively contacts with the West and thus retarded Russia's normal historical development. Russia did not experience a Renaissance, a Reformation, or other "European" phenomena because the Mongol yoke had isolated it from the West. It has also been argued that even after Mongol rule was overthrown in the fifteenth century, Muscovy was preoccupied with the defense of its frontiers from the constant raids launched by the Mongol successor states at Kazan, the Crimea, and elsewhere. Hence, the Mongols contributed both directly and indirectly to the comparative backwardness of the sixteenth- and seventeenth-century Muscovite state. While medieval Europe underwent a marked transformation, Russia was overrun by the Mongols, cut off from European developments, and deprived of Western influences.[1]

---

1   A concise statement of this viewpoint can be found in Sidney Harcave, *Russia: A History* (Philadelphia-New York, 1964), p. 36: "Still further changes resulted from the Mongol-imposed isolation from the West. Before the coming of the Mongols, Russia had established many ties with the West and had achieved a level of civilization which compared favorably with that of contemporary England and Germany. But, restrained from Western contacts, the country fell behind in comparative progress; while the West was entering the age of complex urban life, of universities, of Humanistic literature and Renaissance art, Russian civilization remained static or retrogressed." For a similar evaluation of the Mongol yoke seen Hans von Eckardt, *Russia* (New York, 1932), p. 23; Michael T. Florinsky, *Russia: A Short History* (New York, 1969), p. 54; Janko Lavrin, *Russia, Slavdom and the Western World* (London, 1969), pp. 18-19; Roger Portal, *The Slavs* (London, 1969), p. 53; Warren B. Walsh, *Russia and the Soviet Union* (Ann Arbor, 1958), p. 51; Francis Dvornik, *The Slavs: Their Early History and Civilization* (Boston, 1956), pp. 254-5; B. H. Sumner, *Survey of Russian History* (London, 1947), p. 175; and, Nikolay Andreyev, "Pagan and Christian Elements in Old Russia,"

This version of the Mongol yoke is no doubt popular because it facilitates an explanation of westernization in Russia. In somewhat exaggerated terms, there is an implicit suggestion that Peter the Great restored the ties which the successors of Ghengis Khan had torn asunder. Even those authors who do not treat the Mongols as wild barbarians contribute to this interpretation. Professor Vernadsky, for example, attempted to evaluate the Mongol impact on Russia by contrasting pre-Mongol Kievan Russia with post-Mongol Muscovite Russia.[2] While Vernadsky did not claim that all differences were due to the Mongols, this very framework along with his sharp contrasts between Kievan and Muscovite Russia definitely create the impression that Mongol rule had a profound and lasting influence upon the course of Russian history. In fact, authors of quite different persuasions can agree that Mongol rule had a great impact upon Russia's relations with the West. For those who sympathize with Russia, the responsibility for Russia's apparent backwardness can be put upon an outside agent. The Mongols, not the Russians, created the cleavage between Russia and the West. Critics of Russia, past and present, can emphasize Mongol influences and evoke images of oriental despots and an "Asiatic" social structure. Russia thus becomes the western extension of "Eastern" society, deficient in those values and attitudes which supposedly characterize Western civilization. The adaptability of the Mongol yoke thesis is probably one of the primary reasons for its popularity.

Many objections have been raised against the popular conception of the Mongol impact. Some authors attempt to refute specific examples of alleged Mongol influence within Russia; the Mongol impact as a whole is undermined by attacking individual manifestations of possible Mongol influence.[3] Others emphasize the fact that the end of Mongol rule in Western Russia preceded its demise in Eastern Russia by about one century. The Ukraine and Belorussia became part of the

---

Slavic Review 21 (1962) 20-1. The famous pre-revolutionary historian, V. O. Kliuchevsky, ignored the question of Mongol influence due to his internalist approach to Russian history. Nevertheless, Kliuchevsky remarked (*A History of Russia* 2 (London, 1911), p. 119) that while sixteenth-century Muscovy had to concentrate upon the defense of its frontiers against Tartar raids, "the peoples of the West were progressing rapidly in industry, in trade, in social life, and in the arts and sciences."

2 George Vernadsky, *The Mongols and Russia* (New Haven, 1953), pp. 333-90.

3 The arguments against Mongol influence are summarized in Nicholas V. Riasanovsky, *A History of Russia* (New York, 1969), pp. 78-83, and Jesse D. Clarkson, *A History of Russia* (New York, 1961), pp. 67-70. Various interpretations of the Mongol impact upon Russia are reviewed in B. D. Grekov, A. Iu. Iakubovskii, *Zolotaia Orda i ee padenie* (Moscow-Leningrad, 1950), pp. 247-58; Vernadsky, *The Mongols*, pp. 333-5; and V. V. Kargalov, *Vneshne-politicheskie faktory razvitiia feodal'noi Rusi: Feodal'naia Rus' i kochevniki* (Moscow, 1967), pp. 218-61.

Lithuanian-Polish state and were thus politically separated from other Russian lands.[4] At an even more fundamental level, it can be argued that the popular conception of Mongol rule often assumes that western and central Europe provide a model for historical development with which other areas can be compared and measured. The Mongol conquest offers the most convenient and obvious explanation for the fact that Russia does not appear to conform with this model: an external force interfered with Russia's normal progression and prevented its Western-like transformation. Russia's divergence from the model was, in this sense, "unnatural" because it was produced by foreign domination.

The "Europe-centric" approach to history as well as the very existence of a European model can be criticized although that is not our purpose here.[5] Instead, another basic objection to the popular view of the Mongol yoke will be discussed, namely the implicit assumption it makes about Russian attitudes. There is a presumption that medieval Russia wished to participate in the transformation of Europe but was prevented by the Mongols. Russia supposedly desired interaction with European society but, due to the Mongols, it did not have the opportunity. Medieval Russia underwent an unwilling and involuntary separation from western and central Europe.

Was Russia's apparent isolation from the West either unwilling or involuntary? Many scholars have argued that the religious differences between Orthodox Russia and Catholic Europe created a major cultural barrier between Russia and the West.[6] Medieval Russia, from

4 Paul Miliukov, Charles Seignobos, L. Eisenmann, *History of Russia* 1: *From the Beginnings to the Empire of Peter the Great* (New York, 1968), pp. 97-100; S. F. Platonov, *History of Russia* (New York, 1925), p. 76.

5 For a recent discussion of these and other related questions see Henry L. Roberts, "Russia and the West: A Comparison and Contrast," *Slavic Review* 23 (1964) 1-12. Karl Wittfogel ("Russia and the East: A Comparison and Contrast," *Slavic Review* 22 (1963) 627-43), on the other hand, uses the Mongol conquest in an effort to connect medieval Russia with his model of oriental despotism.

6 Riasanovsky, *A History*, p. 39, writes: "It must be kept in mind that Christianity came to Russia from Byzantium, not from Rome. Although at the time [of Russia's conversion in 989] this distinction did not have its later significance and although the break between the Eastern and Western Churches occurred only in 1054, the Russian allegiance to Byzantium determined or helped to determine much of the subsequent history of the country. It meant that Russia remained outside the Roman Catholic Church, and this in turn not only deprived Russia of what that Church itself had to offer, but also contributed in a major way to the relative isolation of Russia from the rest of Europe and its Latin civilization. It helped notably to inspire Russian suspicions of the West and the tragic enmity between the Russians and the Poles." Similar views have been expressed by Omeljan Pritsak, John S. Reshetar, Jr., "The Ukraine and the Dialectics of Nation-Building," *Slavic Review* 22

this point of view, consciously rejected the non-Orthodox society of western and central Europe and all the developments connected with it. Russia did not wish to be transformed along with the rest of Europe or to experience a Renaissance, Reformation, and other Western phenomena. Russia was not receptive to European influences because it made a fundamental distinction between the Orthodox and Catholic worlds. While Russia's isolation from the West is sometimes attributed to both the Mongol yoke and the religious differences,[7] the religious explanation, if true, undermines the assumption that Russia was receptive to Western influences but was cut off from them by Mongol rule. Medieval Russia's isolation becomes primarily self-imposed rather than the product of foreign domination. The Mongols might have had a significant internal impact upon Russia, but this impact had no necessary connection with the problem of Russia and the West. Consequently, an evaluation of the supposed Mongol isolation of medieval Russia must take into account Russian attitudes toward the West and Russia's receptivity to foreign influences. In other words, the coincidence of Mongol rule with the initial period of Russia's apparent divergence from the West may have suggested a very misleading causal relationship.

While medieval Russia's receptivity to Western influences cannot be measured with any degree of accuracy, it is possible to determine, with some reliability, medieval Russian attitudes toward the West. These attitudes, in turn, can help to answer the question of whether Russia's supposed isolation and backwardness were the results of the Mongol yoke or a conscious effort to insulate Russia from a western society which was deliberately rejected on religious grounds.

In evaluating Russian attitudes, several factors should be kept in mind. A time period must be selected which includes part or all of the pre-Mongol and Mongol eras in Russian history. Ever since the schism between the Eastern and Western churches in 1054, the Russian church

---

(1963) 224-5; Lavrin, *Russia*, p. 17; Ivar Spector, *An Introduction to Russian History and Culture* (New York, 1965), p. 23; G. P. Fedotov, *The Russian Religious Mind* 1: *Kievan Christianity* (Cambridge, Mass., 1946), p. 21; Dvornik, *The Slavs*, pp. 243-5; John Lawrence, *A History of Russia* (New York, 1965), pp. 32-3; and Herbert J. Muller, *The Uses of the Past* (New York, 1954), p. 284. Also see Dmitri Obolensky, "Russia's Byzantine Heritage," *Oxford Slavonic Papers* 1 (1950) 37-63.

7 Walsh, *Russia*, p. 52, states: "Perhaps the salient feature was that neither the Renaissance nor the Protestant Reformation even reached Russia. This was partly because the Russian Orthodox Church so willed it, and partly because of the Tatars." Also see Lavrin, *Russia*, p. 17; W. H. Parker, *An Historical Geography of Russia* (London, 1968), p. 67; Spector, *An Introduction*, p. 23; and R. D. Charques, *A Short History of Russia* (New York, 1958), pp. 29, 47-8.

adopted an increasingly antagonistic attitude toward the Catholic West.[8] The distinction between Russia and the West which the Orthodox church propagated preceded the Mongol yoke and continued to develop independent of Mongol policies. The Mongols, at most, may have only strengthened existing attitudes. In order to examine the impact of religious differences in shaping Russian attitudes toward the West, it is necessary to consider the period when the Russian church first emphasized these differences. We should also remember that after the mid-fourteenth century Moscow promoted Orthodox unity and anti-Catholic feelings for its own political purposes.[9] Moscow deliberately exacerbated anti-western attitudes in order to enhance its own position vis-à-vis Poland and Lithuania. While Moscow may have simply capitalized on current attitudes toward the West, our task should be to examine the importance of these attitudes before they became intertwined with the Muscovite conflict against Poland and Lithuania.

It is also necessary to consider an area of Russia which had extensive contacts with the West and was not isolated from it. The attitudes found in such an area form the best indication of how medieval Russia viewed the West. In other words, the selection of a region whose attitudes toward the West were not influenced in some way by the Mongol yoke provides the best means for judging the influence of Orthodoxy in creating these attitudes. By eliminating one variable, we can better examine the importance of the other. If the area chosen rejected the West for religious reasons, the relative importance of the Mongol yoke and Orthodoxy in areas which had only minimal ties with Russia's western neighbors can be better evaluated.

Given the temporal and spatial considerations discussed above, Novgorod's relations with the Baltic during the period 1100-1350 provide an excellent opportunity for studying medieval Russian at-

---

8 The early anti-Catholic tendencies in the medieval Russian church are examined in A. Popov, *Istoriko-literaturnyi obzor drevnerusskikh polemicheskikh sochinenii protiv latinian (XI-XV vv.)* (Moscow, 1875); A. Pavlov, *Kriticheskie opyty po istorii drevneishei grekorusskoi polemiki protiv latinian* (St. Petersburg, 1878); and A. Sobolevskii, "Otnoshenie drevnei Rusi k razdeleniiu tserkvei," *Izvestiia Imperatorskoi Akademii Nauk*, 1914, no. 2. Specific examples of anti-Catholic attitudes from the pre-Mongol period are noted in Henryk Paszkiewicz, *The Origins of Russia* (New York, 1954), pp. 97-98; Henry Paszkiewicz, *The Making of the Russian Nation* (London, 1963), pp. 39-40, especially nn. 137-140; and Fedotov, *Russian Religious Mind*, p. 188. Significantly, Francis Dvornik (*The Slavs in European History and Civilization* (New Brunswick, 1962), p. 213) dates Russia's anti-Western attitudes to the early thirteenth century and suggests some connection with the contemporaneous activities of German knights and merchants in the eastern Baltic.

9 *Cf.* the discussion in A. E. Presniakov, *The Formation of the Great Russian State* (Chicago, 1970), pp. 255-61.

titudes toward the West and evaluating the relationship between these attitudes and Russia's apparent isolation from the West. Novgorod and its unruly subordinate city of Pskov were never isolated from the rest of Europe by the Mongol yoke.[10] In fact, the Mongols seem to have encouraged Novgorod's trade with the Baltic since the profits of this commerce could be exploited through the tribute imposed upon Novgorod. One Khan even instructed Novgorod not to permit obstructions in its trade route with Riga.[11] Novgorod's attitudes toward the West were thus unaffected by any Mongol-imposed isolation. Do these attitudes suggest that physical and political isolation were responsible for Russia's seeming divergence from the West?

What was Novgorod's attitude toward the culture of its non-Orthodox Baltic neighbors? Novgorod and Pskov had extensive political and economic relations with their Baltic neighbors. As a result, there has been a tendency to equate Novgorod's foreign contacts with some usually vague pro-western orientation. In one recent formulation of this theme, westward-looking Novgorod is contrasted with eastward-looking Moscow.[12] Therefore, we must ask whether extensive foreign ties, particularly a lively foreign trade with the Baltic, made Novgorod predisposed or receptive to Western influences. Did Novgorod's political and economic relations create a feeling of community with the West? Did a pro-Western orientation exist in Novgorod?

Contacts with the Baltic brought Novgorod and Pskov into close contact with Finns, Germans, Scandinavians, and Balts, with pagans and Catholics, and with less advanced and equally advanced peoples. Novgorod's relations with the Estonian Chud', Latvians, Swedes, Germans, and Lithuanians involved peoples and societies which were themselves quite diverse. Did Novgorod tend to view all these peoples as an

10   For the history of medieval Novgorod and Pskov see A. I. Nikitskii, *Istoriia ekonomicheskogo byta Velikogo Novgoroda* (Moscow, 1893); A. Nikitskii, *Ocherk vnutrennei istorii Pskova* (St. Petersburg, 1873); A. I. Nikitskii, *Ocherk vnutrennei istorii tserkvi v Velikom Novgorode* (St. Petersburg, 1879); Nikolai Kostomarov, *Severnorusskaia narodopravstva vo vremena udel'no-vechevogo uklada* (*Istoriia Novgoroda, Pskova i Viatki*) 2 vols. (St. Petersburg, 1886); and Konrad Onasch, *Gross-Nowgorod* (Vienna-Munich, 1969). A good bibliography of Soviet works can be found in B. M. Apriatkin, *Ukazatel' literatury po istorii Novgorodskogo kraia, vyshedshei v 1917-1958 gg.* (Novgorod, 1959). This was updated to 1960 in *Novgorodskii istoricheskii sbornik* 10 (1961) 263-75. Some subsequent studies of note are V. L. Ianin, *Novgorodskie posadniki* (Moscow, 1962); A. L. Khoroshkevich, *Torgovlia Velikogo Novgoroda s Pribaltikoi i zapadnoi Evropoi v XIV-XV vekakh* (Moscow, 1963); L. V. Cherepnin, *Novgorodskie berestianye gramoty kak istoricheskii istochnik* (Moscow, 1969); and *Ledovoe Poboishche 1242 g.* (Moscow-Leningrad, 1966).

11   *Gramoty Velikogo Novgoroda i Pskova*, ed. S. N. Valk (Moscow-Leningrad, 1949), no. 30, p. 57 (hereafter abbreviated *GVNP*).

12   James H. Billington, *The Icon and the Axe* (New York, 1967), p. 80.

undifferentiated part of the non-Orthodox world? Did it have different
attitudes toward pagans and Catholics? Is there any indication that the
level of their culture determined Novgorod's attitude toward them?

Since the period under study involves both the pre-Mongol and
Mongol eras, any change in attitudes over a period of time would be
significant. Did the Mongol yoke seem to alter Novgorod's perception of
its neighbors in any demonstrable way? Were Novgorod's attitudes
toward its Baltic neighbors consistent over time and independent of
Mongol role? The terminal date of 1350 also excludes the possibility
that Muscovite attitudes will influence our findings. Did Novgorod see a
fundamental division between the Orthodox and non-Orthodox worlds
long before Moscow championed Orthodox solidarity in order to
weaken its western opponents?

In evaluating Novgorod's attitudes toward its western neighbors, the
lives of saints and related church works have been excluded due to
their inherent bias toward all of Russia's non-Orthodox neighbors.
While the anti-Western references found in these works are important,[13] it is even more significant to examine the extent to which the
church influenced the attitudes of Novgorodian society as a whole.
Charters and trade treaties testify to Novgorod's relations with the West
but they tell us very little of Novgorod's attitude. Consequently, our
best source for medieval Novgorodian attitudes toward the West are
the chronicles of Novgorod and Pskov.[14] Although compiled by

13 One example of such references concerns the questions raised by the twelfth-century Novgorod priest, Kirik, about the need to rebaptize Latins who became Orthodox and the appropriate
penalties for women who brought their sick children to pagan magicians and who visited Catholic
priests in the German church. In response to Kirik's queries, it was decided that the penance for
visiting a Catholic priest was identical with that for going to a pagan magician and that those who
went to the Catholic priest were considered in the same category as Orthodox who secretly kept
their pagan beliefs (Metropolitan Makarii, Istoriia russkoi tserkvi 3 (St. Petersburg, 1888), pp. 224-5,
236). Fedotov (Russian Religious Mind, p. 189) argues that since some Novgorod women apparently
took their children to pagan magicians and visited Catholic priests, "Kievan Russia was remote
from religious fanaticism." There are also fifteenth-century tales which report the deserved death
of a Novgorod official who in 1179 helped German merchants construct a Catholic church in Novgorod as well as the destruction of an icon within this Catholic church (S. O. Shmidt, "Predaniia o
chudesakh pri postroike novgorodskoi ropaty," Istoriko-arkheologicheskii Sbornik (Moscow, 1962) 319-
25). Since this study omits non-Novgorod sources, no emphasis has been placed upon the statement
of Henry of Livonia that Prince Vladimir Mstislavich was expelled from Pskov because his daughter
married the brother of the archbishop of Riga (Heinrici chronicon Livoniae, ed. Leonid Arbusow -
Albert Bauer (Hannover, 1955), chap. XV, 13. There is an English translation by James A. Brun-
dage, The Chronicle of Henry of Livonia (Madison, 1961)).

14 The following Novgorod and Pskov chronicles have been published: "Novgorodskaia pervaia letopis' mladshego izvoda," = N1LMI, and "Novgorodskaia pervaia letopis' starshego izvoda,"
=N1LSI, both found in Novgorodskaia pervaia letopis' starshego i mladshego izvoda, ed. A. N. Nasonov

churchmen, the Novgorod and Pskov chronicles are by no means narrow ecclesiastical sources. They can be more aptly characterized as semi-official records of events which were considered important in the history of both cities.[15] The chroniclers of Novgorod and Pskov were very much interested in secular events both within their own lands and elsewhere. Thus, the numerous chroniclers who composed a variety of entries during some two and one half centuries reflect, if imperfectly, Novgorod's values and attitudes. Given the absence of other sources, these chronicles constitute the best indication of how Novgorod viewed its western neighbors.

*
* *

Despite their close and constant contacts with the Baltic, neither Novgorod nor Pskov demonstrated any interest in the internal affairs of their western neighbors. This was true even when these affairs had a profound impact upon Novgorod. One striking example of this phenomenon is the absolute silence concerning the German conquest of Livonia in the early thirteenth century. There is no reference either to the establishment of the Livonian Order or to its subsequent conquest of various Latvian and Estonian tribes. Instead, the chronicles suddenly note that Novgorod and Pskov came into conflict with the Germans along their western borders.[16] No attempt was made to explain why the Germans appeared there or where they came from.

(Moscow-Leningrad, 1950); "Novgorodskaia vtoraia letopis'," = N2L, in *Polnoe Sobranie Russkikh Letopisei* = PSRL, 3 (St. Petersburg, 1841) and PSRL 30 (Moscow, 1965); "Novgorodskaia tret'ia letopis'," = N3L, in PSRL 3; "Novgorodskaia chetvertaia letopis'," = N4L, in PSRL 4 (St. Petersburg, 1848) and PSRL 4, Chast' pervaia, Vypusk 1, 2, 3 (Petrograd-Leningrad, 1915-1929); "Novgorodskaia piataia letopis'," = N5L, in PSRL 4, Chast' vtoraia, Vypusk 1 (Petrograd, 1917); "Pskovskaia pervaia letopis'," = P1L, in *Pskovskie letopisi* = PL, ed. A. N. Nasonov, 1 (Moscow-Leningrad, 1940) and PSRL 4; "Pskovskaia vtoraia letopis'," = P2L, in PL 2 (Moscow, 1955) and PSRL 5 (St. Petersburg, 1851); "Pskovskaia tret'ia letopis'," = P3L, in PL 2; and "Sofiiskaia pervaia letopis'," = S1L, in PSRL 5 and PSRL 5, Vypusk 1 (Leningrad, 1925). There is an English translation of N1LSI and parts of N1LMI in *The Chronicle of Novgorod, 1016-1471*, tr. Robert Michell and Nevill Forbes (London, 1914) = CN.

15 The basic studies of medieval Russian chronicle-writing are: A. A. Shakhmatov, *Obozrenie russkikh letopisnykh svodov XIV-XVI vv.* (Moscow-Leningrad, 1938); M. D. Priselkov, *Istoriia russkogo letopisaniia XI-XV vv.* (Leningrad, 1940); D. S. Likhachev, *Russkie letopisi i ikh kul'turno-istoricheskoe znachenie* (Moscow-Leningrad, 1947); and A. N. Nasonov, *Istoriia russkogo letopisaniia XI-nachala XVIII veka* (Moscow, 1969). A good list of studies and editions of the Novgorod and Pskov chronicles published before 1960 can be found in R. P. Dmitrieva, *Bibliografiia russkogo letopisaniia* (Moscow-Leningrad, 1962), pp. 333-5, 337-8, 343. Also see N. G. Berezhkov, *Khronologiia russkogo letopisaniia* (Moscow, 1963).

16 See the account of the 1217 Novgorod raid against the Chud' land in N1LSI, N1LMI, P3L, CN. The Chud' called upon the Germans for help and a brief skirmish took place between the Nov-

Other examples of Novgorod's disinterest in its neighbors' internal affairs can be cited. Novgorod's Baltic neighbors were divided among themselves, a situation which strengthened Novgorod's political position considerably. Presumably their antagonisms and rivalries were of considerable interest in Novgorod. However, the bitter conflict between the Germans and the Danes in Livonia and Estonia is never mentioned. In fact, the Danish presence in Estonia is not even specifically indicated until the Novgorod-Danish treaty of 1302,[17] and the previous century of Danish activity in the southeastern Baltic went unrecorded in Novgorod. The Livonian Order, the archbishop of Riga, and the Riga merchants were frequently at odds and occasionally pursued conflicting policies. There is no hint of these strained relations; the Novgorod and Pskov chronicles give the impression that complete unity and harmony reigned among their German neighbors.

The German and Danish conquest of the southeastern Baltic met strong resistance, and there were numerous Latvian and Estonian revolts against the foreign crusaders. Since these revolts involved both the political situation on Novgorod's frontiers and pagan opposition to Latin Christianity, we should expect that Novgorod and Pskov would be interested in these events. However, only the 1344 uprising of the Estonian Chud' and their subsequent defeat are noted and then in very matter-of-fact terms.[18] Thus, internal conflicts and tensions between the Germans and the native population failed to elicit any real interest in either Novgorod or Pskov.

The silence of the chronicles about some of the most significant developments in Livonia and Estonia is even more remarkable when we remember that in the twelfth and early thirteenth centuries Novgorod made sporadic raids into the Chud' lands aimed at collecting booty and plunder.[19] The Livonian crusade ended Novgorod's westward expansion

---

gorod and German forces. After this, the German presence in Livonia and Estonia is taken for granted. It should also be noted that the Novgorod chronicles contain comparatively little information about Novgorod's Baltic trade. The Variazhskaia (Varangian) Church is mentioned in 1152 (*N1LSI, N1LMI, CN*) and 1181 (*N1LSI, N1LMI, CN*). The overseas merchants (*zamor'stii, zamor'skyi*) erected the Holy Friday Church in 1156 (*N1LSI, N1LMI, CN*). Novgorod merchants are reported in the Baltic during 1130, 1134, and 1142 (*N1LSI, N1LMI, CN*). The attack on Novgorod merchants in Gotland during 1189 led to a temporary rupture in Novgorod's Baltic trade (*N1LSI, N1LMI, CN*).

17 *GVNP* no. 35, p. 64. Also see *N1LSI, N1LMI, CN* under 1302.

18 *N1LMI, S1L, CN* under 1344.

19 See *N1LSI, N1LMI, N2L, S1L, CN, P1L, P2L, N4L* under 1111, 1112, 1113, 1116; *N1LSI, N1LMI, N4L, S1L, CN* under 1130, 1131, 1133; *N1LSI, N1LMI, N4L, CN* under 1179; *N1LSI, N1LMI, N4L, S1L, CN* under 1191; *N1LSI, N1LMI, S1L, CN* under 1192; *N1LSI, N1LMI, P3L, CN* under 1212, 1214. Chud' raids against Novgorod and Pskov were reported in *N1LSI, N1LMI, CN* under 1176, and *N1LSI, N1LMI, N4L, S1L, CN* under 1189, 1190.

and initiated a series of major German campaigns against the Novgorod lands.[20] Given Novgorod's concern with this area, it is difficult to explain why there was no explanation of how it came under German and Danish rule or what happened to it subsequently.

The absence of information about the internal developments in Livonia and Estonia cannot be attributed to ignorance in Novgorod and Pskov. It is inconceivable that they were unaware of what was happening along their western borders, especially with the frequent visits of merchants back and forth across these frontiers. Another reason must be sought to explain why the history of its Baltic neighbors went unrecorded, if not unnoticed, in Novgorod and Pskov. Some indication of the Novgorod and Pskov attitude emerges when we examine the information about German-Lithuanian relations. The Livonian and Teutonic knights were constantly at war with the Lithuanians. Their pressure seriously weakened Lithuania and ultimately led to the Lithuanian union with Poland. This conflict between two neighbors, each of whom individually posed a major threat to Novgorod and Pskov, should have attracted some attention, but there is no evidence that it did. With only one exception, every German-Lithuanian war recorded in the chronicles also involved Novgorod and/ or Pskov.[21] In other words, these German-Lithuanian wars gained significance only because of Russian participation and not because they involved two of Novgorod's often hostile neighbors. The history of its Baltic neighbors was deemed unimportant unless Novgorod and Pskov were involved.

The same criterion of involvement was applied in the treatment of the Lithuanians and Latvians. In the period under consideration, the Lithuanians gradually formed a powerful state which extended its influence throughout the West Russian lands. The emergence of Lithuania as the dominant force in the vast area bounded by Novgorod in the north, Smolensk in the east, and Kiev in the south should have

---

20   Livonian conflicts with Novgorod and Pskov are noted in *N1LSI, N1LMI, P3L, CN* under 1217; *N1LSI, N1LMI, N4L, P3L, CN* under 1219, 1222, 1223; *N1LSI, N1LMI, CN* under 1224; *N1LMI, N1LSI, N4L, P3L, CN* under 1233; *N1LSI, N1LMI, N4L, P3L, CN* under 1234; *N1LSI, N1LMI, N4L, S1L, P1L, P2L, P3L, CN* under 1239, 1240, 1241, 1242; *N1LSI, N1LMI, N4L, CN* under 1253; *N1LSI, N1LMI, N4L, S1L, P3L, CN* under 1262; *N1LSI, N1LMI, N4L, S1L, P1L, CN* under 1268; *N4L* under 1266; *S1L* under 1267; *N1LSI, N1LMI, S1L, P2L, CN* under 1267, 1269; *N4L, S1L, P3L* under 1271, 1272; *N1LSI, N1LMI, N4L, S1L, P1L, P2L, CN* under 1298, 1299; *N4L, S1L, P1L, P2L, P3L* under 1323; *N4L, S1L, P1L, P2L, P3L* under 1341; *N1LMI, N4L, S1L, P1L, P2L, P3L, CN* under 1341, 1342; *N1LMI, N4L, S1L, P1L, P2L, P3L, CN* under 1343; *N4L, P1L, P2L, P3L* under 1348, 1349.

21   *N4L, S1L* under 1347. Novgorod and/or Pskov allied with the Lithuanians against the Germans in 1222 and 1262 (*N1LSI, N1LMI, N4L, S1L, P3L, CN*). Novgorod and Pskov allied with the Germans against the Lithuanians in 1237 (*N1LSI, N1LMI, CN*).

created considerable interest within Novgorod and Pskov since Lithuanian developments often had a direct and immediate impact upon Novgorod. In fact, only two internal events within Lithuania are mentioned: the deaths of Grand Princes Mindovg (Mindaugas) in 1263 and Gedimin (Gediminas) in 1341.[22] The murder of Mindovg probably was noted because it sparked a bloody civil war within Lithuania. Voishelg, a son of Mindovg who had converted to Orthodoxy, participated in these internecine conflicts which also forced many Lithuanians, including Prince Dovmont, to seek refuge in Pskov. Dovmont converted to Orthodoxy and later was revered as one of Pskov's greatest princes. Mindovg's death and the resultant civil strife in Lithuania were considered noteworthy only because of Voishelg and Dovmont. The former is depicted as a champion of Orthodoxy, while the latter became a military hero in Pskov.[23] The death of Gedimin is probably noted either because Khan Uzbeg died the same year, or, as is more likely, because his demise was followed by another civil war in Lithuania which had repercussions in Novgorod and other Russian areas.[24] Between these two events, 1263 and 1342, nothing of importance apparently took place in Lithuania which was worth recording. Novgorod and Pskov were interested in their Baltic neighbors only when these neighbors came into contact or conflict with them.

The criterion of involvement also explains why the Latvians are almost completely ignored.[25] Neither Novgorod nor Pskov ever made a concerted attempt to subjugate the Latvians while the Latvians never seriously threatened the Novgorod lands. Consequently, there was little or no reason to mention the Latvian tribes even though they had lived side by side with Novgorod for hundreds of years, and both Russians and Latvians experienced the effects of the Livonian crusade and the rise of Lithuania. While Novgorod and Pskov recorded their contacts

22 *N1LSI, N1LMI, N4L, S1L, CN* under 1263; *N1LMI, S1L, CN* under 1341. Lithuanian raids against Novgorod and Pskov are reported in *N1LSI, N1LMI, S1L, CN* under 1183; *N1LSI, N1LMI, CN* under 1198; *N1LSI, N1LMI, N4L, S1L, CN* under 1200; *N1LSI, N1LMI, CN* under 1210; *N1LSI, N1LMI, N4L, P3L, CN* under 1213; *N1LSI, N1LMI, CN* under 1217, 1223, 1224; *N1LSI, N1LMI, N4L, CN* under 1225, 1229, 1234; *P1L, P2L, P3L* under 1236, 1238, 1239, 1247; *N1LSI, N1LMI, N4L, S1L, CN* under 1245, 1246, 1258, 1323; *N1LSI, N1LMI, N4L, CN* under 1253; *N1LMI, N4L, S1L, CN* under 1285, 1335, 1346, 1347; *P1L, P2L* under 1348. Novgorod raids against the Lithuanians are noted in *N1LSI, N1LMI, N4L, S1L, P1L, P3L, CN* under 1266, 1267.

23 *N1LSI, N1LMI, N4L, S1L, P1L, P2L, P3L, CN* under 1265, 1266.

24 *N1LMI, N4L, S1L, CN* under 1345.

25 See *N1LSI, N1LMI, CN* under 1200; *P1L, P2L, P3L* under 1284; and *N4L, S1L, P1L, P2L, P3L* under 1341 for three references to relations with the Latvians.

and conflicts with the peoples of the southeastern Baltic, they very clearly had no interest in the internal history of these neighboring peoples. Such questions might concern the Russian princes who defended Novgorod's borders and the Novgorod merchants who travelled to Riga, but they obviously were not considered of sufficient interest or importance to record for posterity.

The disregard of internal developments in the southeastern Baltic cannot be explained by some local Novgorod and Pskov parochialism. The Novgorod and Pskov chronicles contain considerable information about the affairs of other areas. As long as Kiev remained a major city, the Novgorod chroniclers recorded most of the noteworthy political events in its history as well as the efforts by various Russian princes to gain control of Kiev.[26] Other major developments in southern Russia also received attention.[27] The emergence of the Vladimir-Suzdal area and the activities of the Suzdalian princes both within their principality and beyond are noted by the Novgorod sources.[28] The first Mongol expedition into southern Russia, which culminated in the crushing defeat of a Russian-Cuman force on the Kalka River in 1223, is described in great detail.[29] It is significant that this isolated battle in the distant steppe with an unknown enemy who afterwards disappeared for almost fifteen years received such lengthy treatment while the emergence of the Livonian Order and the Lithuanian state along Novgorod's own bor-

26 There are references to the ascension and death of Prince Vladimir Monomakh (N1LSI, N1LMI, CN under 1113, 1125), to the death of his son and successor in Kiev, Mstislav (N1LSI, N1LMI, CN under 1132), to the death of Prince Iaropolk (N1LSI, CN under 1139), to the princely conflicts following Vsevolod's death (N1LSI, N1LMI, CN under 1146), to Iuri Dolgoruki's capture of Kiev (N1LSI, N1LMI, CN under 1149), to further princely conflicts for Kiev (N1LSI, N1LMI, CN under 1151, 1154, 1155), to the death of Iuri Dolgoruki (N1LSI, N1LMI, CN under 1157), to the struggles for the Kievan throne (N1LSI, N1LMI, CN under 1158, 1159), to the activities of various princes in Kiev (N1LSI, N1LMI, CN under 1167, 1168, 1170, 1171, 1173, 1174), to the capture of Kiev by the Olgovichi and Cumans (N1LSI, N1LMI, CN under 1203), and to the Mongol conquest of Kiev in 1240 (P1L under 1239; P3L, S1L under 1240).

27 Russian-Cuman relations are noted under 1103, 1106, 1111, 1135, 1167, 1203, 1224, and 1235 (N1LSI, N1LMI, CN). The Novgorod chronicles also record high waters along the Dnieper and its tributaries in 1109, fires in Kiev, Chernigov, and Smolensk in 1111, the death of Polotsk princes in 1101 and 1128, the death of a Pereiaslavl prince in 1114, a campaign against Galich in 1145, the murder of Prince Igor in 1147, the various civil wars among the Russian princes in 1160, 1195, 1214, 1218, 1219, and 1235, princely movements from one city to another in 1179 and 1232, and an anti-princely uprising in Smolensk during 1186 (N1LSI, N1LMI, CN).

28 The Novgorod chronicles made frequent references to the campaigns of Yuri Dolgoruki, Andrei Bogolubskii, and Vsevelod III: 1139, 1147, 1148, 1149, 1151, 1155, 1157, 1174, 1176, 1177, 1183, 1205, 1210 (N1LSI, N1LMI, CN). Novgorod's relations with the Suzdalian princes are also discussed in some detail.

29 N1LSI, N1LMI, CN under 1224.

ders, events which directly affected Novgorod for centuries, were never systematically described.

The Mongol conquest of Russia in 1237-1240, unlike the German and Danish conquest of the Baltic, is recorded in the Novgorod sources.[30] During the first century of Mongol rule, Novgorod seems fairly well informed about Russian-Mongol relations. We read of Russian princes who were killed at the Khan's court, of the numerous trips of various Russian princes to Sarai, of the appearance of Mongol representatives in the Russian lands, and of notable events within the Golden Horde.[31] The continuing internecine conflicts among the Russian princes as well as other developments elsewhere in Russia also received attention.[32]

Novgorod was very much interested in certain external events, many of which affected it much less than internal events within the southeastern Baltic. But, there can be no doubt that this interest was confined to the Russian lands and their history, regardless of the impact upon Novgorod. Novgorod's lack of interest in the history of its Baltic neighbors can best be explained by the fact that they were not part of the Russian lands. Novgorod was almost exclusively concerned with events in Russia and it did not show any interest in what happened in non-Russian areas, even those adjoining Novgorod's own territories.

Novgorod's basic orientation can be seen in the use of the expression "Russian land" (*Rus'skaia zemlia*) by the Novgorod and Pskov chroniclers. For example: the princes of the Russian land fought the Cumans,[33] the Cumans ravaged the Russian land,[34] conflicts among Russian princes divide the Russian land,[35] Mongol forces ravage the Russian land,[36] Prince Alexander Nevskii is honored because he worked

30   *Ibid.* under 1236, 1238.

31   Russians died at Sarai in 1245, 1246, 1272, 1319, 1326 (*N1LMI, N1LSI, CN*) and 1292, 1339 (*N1LMI, CN*). Trips by Russian princes to and from the Khan's court are noted in 1242, 1246, 1250, 1262, 1263, 1270, 1302, 1314, 1315, 1318, 1322, 1325, 1327, 1328, 1331, 1332 (*N1LSI, N1LMI, CN*) and 1334, 1336, 1337, 1338, 1339, 1340, 1342 (*N1LMI, CN*). Mongol activities in Russia were noted in 1251, 1257, 1259, 1269, 1318, 1322, 1325, and 1327 (*N1LMI, N1LSI, CN*). The chroniclers recorded events within the Golden Horde in 1291, 1341, and 1342 (*N1LMI, CN*).

32   Inter-princely conflicts were noted in 1282 (*N1LMI, CN*) and 1304, 1314, 1318, 1320, 1321, and 1322 (*N1LSI, N1LMI, CN*). The Novgorod chroniclers also recorded the death of Grand Prince Alexander Nevskii (*N1LSI, N1LMI, CN* under 1263), the death of Grand Prince Andrei Alexandrovich (*N1LSI, N1LMI, CN* under 1304), fires in Moscow, Vologda, and Vitebsk (*N1LMI, CN* under 1335), a fire in Moscow (*N1LMI, CN* under 1337), the death of Ivan Kalita (*N1LMI, CN* under 1340), and the murder of Prince Gleb of Briansk (*N1LMI, CN* under 1340).

33   *N1LSI, N1LMI, CN* under 1103.

34   *Ibid.* under 1224.

35   *Ibid.* under 1238.

36   *Ibid.* under 1245, 1327.

for Novgorod and all the Russian land,[37] the Metropolitan of Kiev has jurisdiction over the Russian land,[38] and the entire Russian land suffers from a famine.[39] While the Novgorod chroniclers make a distinction between Novgorod and the rest of Russia in such phrases as "going to Rus'" from Novgorod or "coming from Rus'" to Novgorod,[40] it seems clear, nevertheless, that Novgorod saw itself as part of the Russian land. The misfortunes and calamities of Russia are those of Novgorod as well. Novgorod was very much interested in the history of the Russian lands because it associated itself with these lands.

What made Novgorod part of the Russian land? During the period under discussion, no united Russian state existed. Furthermore, Novgorod had fought to obtain independence from Kiev in the twelfth century and it continuously resisted Muscovite control before succumbing to Moscow in the second half of the fifteenth century. Novgorod's ties with the Russian land were not based on a desire for political unification. Novgorod did not wish to be part of any Russian state, whether centered in Kiev or Moscow. Novgorod's association with the Russian land appears to have had a primarily religious basis. The Russian land had been baptized by St. Vladimir in the late tenth century.[41] The Russian land thus became a Christian land and it came to include all those areas inhabited by a Russian Orthodox population and/or ruled by a Russian Orthodox prince. Given the absence of a Russian state, the disintegration of the Russian land into hostile principalities, and the domination of these principalities by the Mongols and Lithuanians, it was a common faith which created and maintained a basic sense of community.[42]

Orthodoxy distinguished the Russian lands from the territories of the non-Orthodox neighboring peoples and provided the foundation for

---

37 *N1LSI, CN* under 1263.

38 *N1LSI, N1LMI, CN* under 1270.

39 *N1LMI* under 1230.

40 *N1LSI, N1LMI, CN* under 1135, 1149, 1165, 1180, 1181, 1211, 1218.

41 *N1LMI* under 989: "Krestisia Volodimir' i vsia zemlia Ruskaia..."; *P1L* under 989: "Krestisia vsia zemlia Ruskaia..."; *P2L* 10: "Volodimir', izhe kresti vsiu Rouskouiu zemliu."; *P3L* under 989: "Krestisia vsia Ruskaia zemlia..."; *N1LMI* under 1240: "na pamiat' sviatogo kniazia Vladimera, krestivshago Ruskuiu zemliu...."

42 The "Tale of the Downfall of the Russian Land" (*Slovo o pogibeli russkoi zemli*), a non-Novgorod source dating to shortly after the Mongol conquest, clearly expresses the idea of the religious unity of the Russian land. For a discussion of the *Slovo*, the use of the term *Rus'skaia zemlia*, and medieval Russia's predominantly religious sense of community see Paszkiewicz, *The Making*, pp. 51-6, 203-44. There is an English translation of the *Slovo* in Serge A. Zenkovsky, ed., *Medieval Russia's Epics, Chronicles, and Tales* (New York, 1963), pp. 173-4.

the idea that the politically disunited Russian lands shared a common
bond. This sense of religious unity transcended political differences and
separated the Russian lands from adjoining non-Orthodox areas.
Novgorod's concern with other Russian lands therefore coincided with
its Orthodox orientation. Novgorod recorded events taking place in
other areas of Russia because these were Orthodox lands and thus part
of the same Orthodox community as Novgorod. It has already been
noted that the Battle of Kalka in 1223 and the Mongol conquest of 1237-
1240 received far greater attention than the Catholic conquest of the
pagan Latvians and Estonians or the rise of the pagan Lithuanian state.
The former events concerned the Russian-Orthodox lands to which
Novgorod belonged while the latter involved the affairs of non-
Orthodox peoples.

The distinction between the Orthodox and non-Orthodox worlds
also explains why the fall of Constantinople to Western crusaders in
1204 is described at great length.[43] The fact that this account was
borrowed from a Greek source is of less importance than its inclusion
in a Novgorod chronicle. The "Frankish" capture of the divinely-
protected center of Orthodoxy was of infinitely greater significance
than the conquest of the nearby pagan Estonian and Latvian population
by the Catholic Germans and Danes. Conflicts within the non-Orthodox
world were of no real importance to Novgorod's Orthodox community.
On the other hand, the fall of the capital of the Orthodox world was an
event of the first magnitude.

The distinction between the Orthodox and non-Orthodox worlds
which determined Novgorod's attitude toward other areas also characterized Novgorod's approach to religious affairs. Novgorod was very
much concerned with Orthodoxy while it ignored the pagan and
Catholic faiths of its Baltic neighbors. There are numerous references
to the appointments, activities, and deaths of the Russian metropolitans
and many Russian bishops.[44] The construction of Orthodox churches in
other Russian cities was noted.[45] The martyrdom of Prince Mikhail of
Chernigov at the court of Batu in 1245 is described in considerable
detail.[46] A lengthy account of the fall of Constantinople in 1204 was

43 *N1LSI, N1LMI, CN* under 1204.
44 *Ibid.* under 1104, 1105, 1111, 1114, 1149, 1159, 1166, 1167, 1233, 1237, 1263, 1326, 1329;
N1LMI, CN under 1281, 1340, 1343.
45 *N1LSI, N1LMI, CN* under 1123, 1145.
46 *Ibid.* under 1245.

deliberately inserted into a Novgorod chronicle.[47] The use of Orthodox churches in Volynia for Catholic services was denounced.[48]

Even more important than the many specific references concerning the Orthodox religion is the whole context in which Russia's history is placed. Russia is a Christian country whose fortunes are determined by God. God punishes Novgorod and the other Russian lands for their sins. The failures and misfortunes of Novgorod's and Russia's enemies are the result of divine judgement.[49] In fact, Christian often becomes a synonym for Russian. God prevents Christian (Russian) princes and peoples from fighting one another.[50] Foreign invaders kill Christians (Russians).[51] These same invaders suffer divine retribution because they shed Christian (Russian) blood.[52] The constant association of Russian and Christian is another indication of Novgorod's basic orientation. As a part of the Russian (Orthodox Christian) land, Novgorod was vitally interested in the history of other Russian (Orthodox Christian) peoples.

Given this basic orientation toward the Russian Orthodox lands, it is not surprising that the Novgorod and Pskov chroniclers completely ignore the paganism of their Chud' and Lithuanian neighbors. Since these pagans were considered godless, they belonged to the non-Christian (non-Russian) world. There is no attempt to explain or even denounce Lithuania's paganism. Tales of false idols, sacred trees, abominable rites, and pagan temples are conspicuous by their absence. Similarly, the Chud' are treated simply as pagans without any description of their pagan practices. The only account of the Chud' religion dates to 1071 and seeks to show that the Christian God is superior to the gods of a Chud' magician.[53] This story, which is also found in the *Russian Primary Chronicle*,[54] forms part of a long tendentious attack on

---

47   *Ibid.* under 1204.

48   *N1LMI, CN* under 1349.

49   *N1LSI, N1LMI, CN* under 1128, 1158, 1161, 1164, 1169, 1194, 1203, 1215, 1219, 1224, 1225, 1230, 1234, 1237, 1238, 1240, 1242, 1251, 1258, 1259, 1263, 1265, 1266, 1267, 1268, 1301, 1303, 1315, 1331; *N1LMI, CN* under 1291, 1299, 1343, 1348.

50   *N1LSI, N1LMI, CN* under 1180, 1198, 1235, 1255, 1270.

51   *Ibid.* under 1224, 1234, 1238, 1245, 1293, 1322.

52   *Ibid.* under 1224, 1253, 1265, 1266. For other references to Christians see *ibid.* under 1179, 1192, 1220, 1230, 1254, 1259, 1310, 1337, 1340, 1196.

53   *N1LMI* under 1071. A Novgorod man sought the aid of a Chud' magician. However, the magician could not summon his gods until the Novgorod man had removed the cross he was wearing. The magician explained that his gods were afraid of the symbol of the heavenly God.

54   *Lavrent'evskaia Letopis', PSRL* 1 (Moscow, 1962) under 1071; *Ipat'evskaia Letopis', PSRL* 2 (St. Petersburg, 1908) under 1071; *The Russian Primary Chronicle, Laurentian Text,* tr. and ed. Samuel H. Cross and Olgerd Sherbowitz-Wetzor (Cambridge, Mass., 1953) under 1071.

pagan priests and paganism designed to demonstrate the superiority of Orthodox Christianity. As such, its purpose was to undermine the strength of paganism within Russia, not to describe the Chud' religion. Aside from this one exception, there is no information about the paganism of the Chud' and Lithuanians. Novgorod's Christian-Russian orientation meant that it has no interest in non-Christian religions. The pagan beliefs and rites of its neighbors were of no concern to Novgorod.

Novgorod also ignored the Catholic religion of its German, Swedish, and Danish neighbors. Catholic doctrines, rites, and beliefs are never mentioned and no attempt is even made to indicate possible theological errors or errant practices. Despite the fact that these peoples were also Christians, Novgorod clearly distinguished between its own Orthodox faith and the Catholicism of its neighbors. The Catholics were never referred to as Christians but as Latins, Germans, and Swedes. Only the Russians are considered Christians.

The fundamental distinction between Orthodoxy and Catholicism becomes even clearer when we consider specific incidents. Voishelg was baptized into the "true Christian religion", namely Orthodoxy.[55] When the Catholic Poles used Orthodox churches in Volynia for their "Latin" services, the chronicler noted that these (Catholic) services were detested by God.[56] The Novgorod sources also report that when King Magnus of Sweden invaded the Neva region in 1348, he challenged Novgorod to a religious debate in order to determine *which faith* was better. Novgorod informed Magnus that he should get in touch with the Patriarch at Constantinople whence Russia received Orthodoxy if he wished to debate the relative merits of their respective faiths.[57] The chronicler also noted that Magnus began to baptize the Izhera people into "his own faith" (*v'' svoiu veru*).

While Novgorod was obviously more interested in its trade route to the Baltic via the Neva River than in religious debates, the Novgorod

---

55 *N1LSI, N1LMI, CN* under 1265: "po pravoi vere" and "posna istinnuiu veru krestiian'skuiu."

56 *N1LMI, CN* under 1349: "a tserkvi sviatyia pretvorischa na latyn'skoe bogumerz''skoe sluzhenie."

57 *Ibid.* under 1348: "ch'ia budet vera luch'shi." See John L. I. Fennell, "The Campaign of King Magnus Eriksson against Novgorod in 1348: An Examination of the Sources," *Jahrbücher für Geschichte Osteuropas* 14 (1966) 1-9. Ever since the second half of the twelfth century, Novgorod had come into conflict with Sweden for control of the Neva River area and the lands surrounding Lake Ladoga: see *N1LSI, N1LMI, S1L, CN* under 1164, 1240, 1256; *N1LM, S1L, CN* under 1283; *N1LMI, CN* under 1284; *N1LMI, N4L, S1L, CN* under 1292, 1293; *N1LMI, S1L, CN* under 1295; *N1LSI, N1LMI, N4L, S1L, CN* under 1300, 1301, 1311, 1314, 1317, 1322, 1323, 1337, 1338, 1339, 1347, 1348, 1350.

account of Magnus' challenge clearly indicates a well perceived difference between Orthodoxy and Catholicism. Novgorod's evasive response is very disappointing since the unwillingness to debate deprives us of a formal exposition of Novgorod's attitude on the differences between Latin and Orthodox Christianity. The Novgorod chronicler does not even utilize Magnus' challenge as a device to denounce Catholicism and affirm the superiority of Orthodoxy. Nevertheless, it is clear from these incidents that Christian meant Orthodox Christian and that the Catholics, like the pagans, had a different faith from the Russians.

The fact that pagans and Catholics belonged to the non-Orthodox world may explain why the Novgorod and Pskov chroniclers use the same adjectives for the Cumans, Mongols, Lithuanians, and Germans. All four are referred to as pagan and godless.[58] From a Christian point of view, the Cumans, Mongols, and Lithuanians were pagan and godless. While the Germans were called pagan and godless in the heat of battle, it is striking that such terms were never applied to Russian (Orthodox) princes regardless of their misdeeds. While Russians may have been sinners, their Christianity was never questioned. This was not the case with the Germans. Catholics were apparently not considered true Christians. Like the Cumans, Mongols, and Lithuanians, they too were pagan and godless.

The use of the word *Nemtsy* provides further evidence of Novgorod's attitude toward its Catholic neighbors. The Livonian knights are usually described as *Nemtsy*.[59] While *Nemtsy* in modern Russian means Germans, the term is sometimes used in the medieval Novgorod sources to designate the Swedes.[60] To avoid confusion between various *Nemtsy*, one Novgorod chronicler even mentioned Swedish *Nemtsy* in order to distinguish them from ordinary German *Nemtsy*.[61] The broad use of the

---

58   For references to cursed, pagan, heathen, lawless, and godless Cumans see *N1LSI, N1LMI, CN* under 1203, 1218, 1224, 1235. The Mongols are called pagan, godless, lawless, and accursed: *N1LSI, N1LMI, CN* under 1236, 1238, 1245, 1259, 1339, 1341, 1342, 1343; *P1L* under 1239. Pagan, accursed, and godless Lithuanians are noted in *N1LSI, N1LMI, CN* under 1213, 1234, 1237, 1265, 1266, 1341; *P1L* under 1266. The Livonian knights are referred to as pagan Germans, pagan Latins, and godless: *P1L*, 3, 4, under 1242, 1299; *P2L*, 13, 17, 18; *P3L* under 1242, 1267, 1271, 1299; *S1L, N4L* under 1271. Accursed Swedes are mentioned in *N1LSI, N1LMI, CN* under 1300.

59   *N1LSI, N1LMI, CN* under 1217, 1219, 1224, 1228, 1233, 1234, 1237, 1240, 1241, 1242, 1253, 1268, 1269, 1298, 1326, 1328, 1335, 1342, 1343.

60   *Ibid.* under 1283, 1284, 1311, 1313, 1314, 1317, 1322, 1337, 1338, 1348, 1350; *N3L* under 1347; *N4L* under 1301, 1322, 1338, 1347, 1350; *S1L* under 1283, 1292, 1293, 1311, 1317, 1318, 1322, 1337, 1338, 1347.

61   *S1L* under 1292, 1295, 1300. By the seventeenth century, *Nemtsy* came to mean western Europeans in general.

term *Nemtsy* suggests a tendency to lump together all non-Slavic
Catholics of the Baltic (Germans, Swedes, Danes) even though the
political differences among them were well known in Novgorod. The
Nemtsy belong to the Germanic and Nordic branch of the larger Latin
(Catholic) world.

The use of the term *latin'skyi iazyk"* in the Novgorod treaties is also
very revealing. The 1189-1199 trade treaty with the Germans was made
"with the ambassador Arbud, with all the German sons, with the
Gotlanders, and with the entire *latin'skym' iazykom'*".[62] Novgorod's 1262-
1263 treaty was concluded "with the German ambassador Shivord, with
the Lubeck ambassador Ol"sten, and with the entire *latin'skym
iazykom'*".[63] The proposed 1269 treaty was for the "German sons, and
the Gotlanders, and the entire *latinskogo iazyka* ...".[64] The final 1269
agreement noted that the Riga and Lubeck representatives had come
"for their merchants of the *latinskogo iazyka*".[65] The same terminology
was used in the 1301 treaty with Lubeck, Gotland, and Riga.[66] Since
iazyk" usually means language, tongue, or people, many historians and
linguists believe that it does not refer to faith in this phrase. However,
their chief objection is to the interpretation of *Rus'skyi iazyk"* as the
Russian faith, i.e., Orthodoxy.[67] Without becoming involved in the controversy concerning *Rus'skyi iazyk"*, it seems clear that *latin'skyi iazyk"*, as
used in the Novgorod treaties, designates German merchants of the
Latin faith who were otherwise not specified in these treaties. Consequently, *latin'skyi iazyk"* is a collective term for German merchants
trading with Novgorod who are distinguished from other merchants
due their Latin or Catholic religion. The important point is that
these merchants are specifically identified by their religion. Novgorod's
treaties were made with Lubeck, Riga, Gotland and all the German
Latins, not with all the German peoples or the entire German land.
From Novgorod's point of view, German merchants as a whole were
most readily characterized by their Latin religion.[68]

Given the conscious distinction between its own Russian Orthodox
society and the non-Russian non-Orthodox societies of its pagan and

---

62 *GVNP* no. 28, pp. 55-6.
63 *Ibid.* no. 29, pp. 56-7.
64 *Ibid.* no. 31, pp. 58-61.
65 *Ibid.* no. 32, p. 62.
66 *Ibid.* no. 34, pp. 63-4.
67 This question is discussed in Paszkiewicz, *The Making*, pp. 44-51.
68 *Latin'skyi iazyk"* may also indicate that, for the medieval Russians, it was most significant that
Catholics used Latin in their religious services.

Catholic neighbors, one might expect that Orthodox missionary activities among the non-Orthodox peoples of the Baltic would receive considerable attention. In fact, there is a surprising silence about the spread of Orthodoxy into the non-Orthodox neighboring lands, a silence which is all the more remarkable since Orthodoxy did spread beyond the political borders of Novgorod and Pskov. Novgorod's relations with the Estonian Chud' are depicted solely in terms of raids against the Chud' land which were designed to collect plunder and tribute. However, Henry of Livonia, the chronicler of the German conquest of Livonia, specifically mentions the conversion of some Estonians and Latvians to Orthodoxy.[69] Since Orthodoxy must have been introduced into the Estonian land and possibly into the Latvian land from Novgorod and Pskov, it is hard to explain why their partial conversion was never mentioned, not even in passing. Perhaps this omission can be attributed in part to the fact that Estonia and Latvia lay outside the Russian land. Perhaps the militant crusading spirit was alien to Russian Orthodoxy of the time.

The conversion of several Lithuanian princes to Orthodoxy is recorded but, with the exception of Voishelg, all these princes served in either Novgorod or Pskov and their conversion thus became a condition of their political position rather than an example of Orthodox missionary work. Dovmont fled Lithuania and served as Prince of Pskov for the rest of his life.[70] Olgerd's son, Alexei, was baptized at the insistence of Pskov.[71] Narimont, the brother of Olgerd, accepted Orthodoxy in order to secure the Novgorod territories which his father, Gedimin, had forced the Novgorod archbishop to place under a Lithuanian prince.[72]

Voishelg is the only Lithuanian prince whose conversion was presented as a genuine religious act occurring within Lithuania. According to the chronicle account, Voishelg was so devout that he journeyed to the Holy Mount in order to become a monk, refused to abandon his faith upon returning to Lithuania, and built his own monastery where he remained until the murder of his father, Mindovg. But, Voishelg probably attracted Novgorod's attention only because he left the

---

69 *Heinrici chronicon Livoniae*, chap. XI, 7; chap. XIV, 2; chap. XVII, 3; chap. XX, 3.
70 See n. 23.
71 *P1L, P2L, P3L* under 1341.
72 *N1LMI, CN, N3L, N4L, S1L* under 1331, 1333.

monastery in order to avenge his father's death. This act of revenge is
portrayed by the chronicler as divine punishment of the pagan
Lithuanians for having killed Christians (Russians).[73] Voishelg becomes
the Christian champion who brings God's retribution upon the pagan
Lithuanians who have raided and ravaged the Novgorod and Pskov
lands. The truly genuine conversion of Voishelg is significant primarily
because it provides a more suitable background for his later actions. A
convert to Orthodoxy was a much more appropriate instrument of
God's wrath against the enemies of Novgorod than a pagan Lithuanian
prince. Had Voishelg remained in his monastery and accepted his pagan
father's murder in a spirit of Christian resignation, he would have
probably never been mentioned since he no longer symbolized divine
retribution for Lithuanian attacks on Novgorod.

Even if we accept the sincerity of Voishelg's conversion and believe
that this alone attracted the notice of the Novgorod chronicler, it
becomes difficult to explain why the spread of Orthodoxy within
Lithuania during the next century is completely ignored. The only indication of this development is found in one reference to the existence
of an Orthodox church in Vilnus.[74] Furthermore, this sole reference
comes from a chronicle that contains considerable non-Novgorod
materials from this period and occurs as a passing comment in a brief
description of one episode in the power struggle which succeeded
Gedimin's death. Thus, even this single reference is accidental and
seemingly connected with the chronicle writing of East Russia rather
than Novgorod. All the evidence concerning the spread of Orthodoxy
into the non-Orthodox lands bordering on Novgorod comes from non-
Novgorod sources.

While Novgorod had almost no interest in the spread of Orthodoxy
outside the Russian lands, there was concern with any evidence of
Catholic missionary work within the Russian and particularly the
Novgorod lands. The use of Orthodox churches in Volynia for Catholic
services has already been noted.[75] The Novgorod chroniclers record the
presence of a bishop in the Swedish forces which attacked the Neva
area in 1240.[76] The chroniclers also note that the 1348 Swedish campaign in the same region included an attempt to convert the Izhera
people to Catholicism.[77] Thus, Novgorod's world had an invisible but

---

73 See n. 23.
74 *S1L* under 1347.
75 See n. 56.
76 *N1LSI, N1LMI, CN* under 1240.
77 *N1LMI, CN* under 1348.

nevertheless clearly defined border. Events beyond these borders, even when they concerned the spread of Orthodoxy, were not recorded. Any Catholic religious activity within these borders was noted.

The proposed 1339 agreement between Novgorod and Sweden illustrates the significance of this religious frontier. This draft treaty provided for the murder of pagan Korelians who had fled from one side to the other. However, Novgorod specifically exempted those Korelians who accepted Orthodoxy.[78] Pagan Korelians who fled from Swedish territories to those of Novgorod merely crossed a political frontier. They were killed. Those who fled and then were baptized crossed from the non-Orthodox world into the Orthodox world and thus had their lives spared. Orthodoxy apparently formed the essential criterion in Novgorod's attitude toward the peoples of other areas.

The case of the Korelian fugitives demonstrates that the distinction between Russian and non-Russian had more of a religious than an ethnic basis. A Lithuanian prince who converted to Orthodoxy became, by this act, a member of the Russian-Christian community. Novgorod and the Grand Prince of Vladimir-Suzdal' may have opposed the presence of a Lithuanian prince in Pskov but their objections were based on political considerations, on the danger that this situation might increase Pskov's autonomy from Novgorod or lead Pskov into the Lithuanian sphere of influence.

Only in cases of dire emergency did Pskov request the aid of a pagan Lithuanian prince and, once the immediate danger subsided, these princes were required to convert if they were to remain in Pskov. The best example of this principle occurred when Pskov invited the Lithuanian Olgerd to defend it from German attacks in 1342. Pskov wanted Olgerd to stay as its prince and therefore it insisted that he convert to Orthodoxy. Instead, Olgerd left one of his sons, Andrei, in Pskov and Andrei was duly baptized.[79] Novgorod may have accused Pskov of renouncing the overlordship of Novgorod and the Grand Prince because it called upon Lithuanian aid,[80] but Pskov was never reproached for abandoning the Christian faith. A Lithuanian Orthodox prince was judged in the very same way as any other Russian prince: did his actions protect the interests of Novgorod and Pskov without interfering in their internal affairs? Lithuanians, Germans, Korelians, and Chud" could

---

78 *Ibid.* under 1339.
79 See n. 71.
80 *NıLMI, CN* under 1342.

thus all become part of the Russian community upon conversion to Orthodoxy. The crucial and fundamental distinction was religious, Orthodox vs. non-Orthodox, not ethnic, East Slavic vs. non-Slavic.

*

* *

Pre-Mongol Kievan Russia with its numerous international contacts and relatively advanced society appears quite different from post-Mongol Muscovite Russia. This has created a widespread belief that the Mongols were responsible for the divergence between pre-Mongol and post-Mongol Russia. Although specific examples of Mongol influence upon Russia have been discounted by some, there remains the problem of why Kievan Russia seems to be part of Europe while Muscovite Russia does not. The real difficulty lies in the implicit assumption that had it not been for the Mongols, medieval Russia would have progressed along the same general lines as the rest of Europe. In other words, it was the absence of contacts rather than of desire which created the estrangement between Russia and the West. This assumption presupposes a certain degree of Russian receptivity to Western influence and some willingness to borrow and adopt Western ways. The purpose of this paper has been to inquire whether such receptivity and willingness existed within Russia.

Novgorod's relations with the Baltic during the period 1100-1350 suggest very strongly that it was religion and not the Mongol yoke which created the divergence between medieval Russia and the West. Novgorod consistently associated itself with the Orthodox faith and the Orthodox Russian lands and it had no interest in the neighboring non-Orthodox societies. Extensive political and economic ties did not alter this attitude in any perceptible way. Neither did it make any difference whether these neighboring societies were pagan or Catholic. Both were rejected because they were non-Orthodox. The fundamental distinction between the Orthodox and non-Orthodox worlds had no relationship with the Mongol yoke. The distinction existed in Novgorod which was an area that had never been isolated from the West by the Mongols.

Novgorod's two-dimensional religious attitude was probably reinforced by its very relations with the West. The Livonian Order represented more than a threat to Novgorod's territories and its political independence. It endangered Novgorod's Orthodox faith. There could be no doubt that, as in Livonia, the German conquest of Novgorod would be followed by Novgorod's forced conversion to the

Catholic faith. The Swedes also desired to baptize Novgorod into the "true Christian faith".[81] Thus, Novgorod's relations with the Baltic involved a crucial religious aspect that was absent in Novgorod's relations with other Russian lands. Novgorod's conflicts with the West assumed many of the characteristics of a religious war in defense of the true Orthodox faith.

Was Novgorod's attitude toward the West representative of medieval Russian attitudes or was Novgorod the exception? Since there is no reason to believe that Novgorod's attitudes in this respect were unique, we must assume that other Russian areas also perceived the fundamental distinction between their Orthodox society and that of the non-Orthodox West. This distinction was introduced into Russia by the Greek clergy and was strengthened by Russian conflicts with the non-Orthodox West. It is hard to see how the Mongols played any appreciable role in these developments. Consequently, the popular belief that the Mongols isolated medieval Russia from the West and created Russia's apparent backwardness needs to be reevaluated. The Mongols did not cause an unwilling or involuntary separation between medieval Russia and the West: medieval Russia had begun to reject the Western (non-Orthodox) world before the Mongols ever came to Russia. The Mongols can be accused of many things but it does not appear that they isolated Russia from the West any more than they isolated China from its neighbors. Medieval Russia, of its own free choice, did not wish to conform to the Western model of historical development nor share in the transformation which characterized the alien non-Orthodox society of western and central Europe.

University of Minnesota

---

81   See Fennell, "The Campaign of King Magnus," 1 n.1, on the religious aims of the 1348 campaign.

WOMEN IN THE MIDDLE AGES:
A WORKING BIBLIOGRAPHY

Carolly Erickson and Kathleen Casey

THE recent growth of research in the field of medieval women's studies has been hampered by bibliographic problems. The following list[1] attempts to acknowledge the new orientations that have emerged in the last decade while preserving the most valuable older works. Well-established research themes such as courtly love, education, witchcraft, and the religious life have been underemphasized; most exclusively literary studies have been omitted, and biographical works have been kept to a minimum. Those that are listed were chosen for the light they throw on issues transcending the concerns of an exceptional individual.

Because of space limitations, many useful titles have not been included, either because their emphasis is a field other than history or because their main chronological or thematic focus lies outside the medieval period. Among these are John T. Noonan, Jr., *Power to Dissolve: Lawyers and Marriages in the Courts of the Roman Curia* (Cambridge, Mass.: Harvard University Press, 1972); Peter Laslett, *The World We Have Lost* (New York: Charles Scribner's Sons, 1965); *La femme*: Recueils de la Société Jean Bodin pour l'histoire comparative des institutions 12 (Brussels: Librairie Encyclopédique, 1962), and Doris Mary Stenton, *The English Woman in History* (New York: Macmillan, 1957). On the other hand, the chronological or thematic "Middle Ages" have in a few cases been prolonged to accommodate ambiguities. The humanist Christine de Pisan, for example, appears in the list because much of her work extends the discussion of medieval philosophical and social themes.

1 The generous bibliographical assistance of Cynthia Truant and Paul Gordon is gratefully acknowledged.

Additional bibliography can be found in Francis Lee Utley, *The Crooked Rib, an Analytical Index to the Argument about Women in English and Scots Literature to the End of the Year 1568* (Columbus: Ohio State University Press, 1944), in Lutz K. Berner, "Recent Research on the History of the Family in Western Europe," *Journal of Marriage and the Family* 35 (August, 1973) 395-405, and in Mary R. Beard, *Women as Force in History. A Study in Traditions and Realities* (New York: Macmillan, 1946).

1 POPULATION DATA

Ariès, Philippe. "Sur les origines de la contraception en France," *Population* 8 (July-Sept., 1953) 465-472.

Bousquet, G.-H. "L'Islam et la limitation volontaire des naissances. Brèves réflexions sur un grand problème social," *Population* 5 (Jan.-March, 1950) 121-128.

Brissaud, Y.-B. "L'infanticide à la fin du moyen âge, ses motivations psychologiques et sa répression," *Revue historique de droit français et étranger*, 4th Series, 50 (1972) 229-256.

Coleman, Emily R. "L'infanticide dans le Haut Moyen Age?," *Annales: Economies, Sociétés, Civilisations* 29 (March-Apr., 1974) 315-335.

Dupâquier, J. et Lachiver, M. "Sur les débuts de la contraception en France ou les deux malthusianismes," *Annales: Economies, Sociétés, Civilisations* 24 (Nov.-Dec., 1969) 1391-1406.

Hallam, H. E. "Some Thirteenth-Century Censuses," *Economic History Review*, 2nd series, 10 (April, 1958) 340-361.

Herlihy, David. "The Tuscan Town in the Quattrocento: A Demographic Profile," *Medievalia et humanistica*, N.S. 1 (1970) 81-109.

— —. "Mapping Households in Medieval Italy," *Catholic Historical Review* 58 (1972) 1-24.

Hopkins, Keith. "Contraception in the Roman Empire," *Comparative Studies in Society and History* 8 (October, 1965) 124-151.

Krause, J. "The Medieval Household: Large or Small?" *Economic History Review*, 2nd Series, 9 (April, 1957) 420-432.

Noonan, John T., Jr. "Abortion and the Catholic Church: A Summary History," *Natural Law Forum* 12 (1967) 85-131.

— —. *Contraception — A History of Its Treatment by the Catholic Theologians and Canonists.* Cambridge, Mass.: Belknap Press of Harvard University Press, 1966. 561 pp.

— —, ed. *The Morality of Abortion; Legal and Historical Perspectives.* Cambridge, Mass.: Harvard University Press, [1970]. 276 pp.

Patlagean, Evelyne. "Sur la limitation de la fécondité dans la haute époque byzantine," *Annales: Economies, Sociétés, Civilisations* 24 (Nov.-Dec., 1969) 1353-1369.

Pounds, Norman J. G. "Overpopulation in France and the Low Countries in the Later Middle Ages," *Journal of Social History* 3 (Spring, 1970) 225-247.

Riquet, Michel. "Christianisme et population," *Population* 4 (Oct.-Dec., 1949) 615-630.

Russell, Josiah Cox. *British Medieval Population*. Albuquerque: University of New Mexico Press, 1948. 389 pp.

— —. "Population in Europe 500-1500" in *The Fontana Economic History of Europe*, ed. C. Cipolla. London: Collins-Fontana Books, 1972. Pp. 25-70.

2 HEALTH AND WELFARE

Aveling, James H. *English Midwives: Their History and Prospects*. London: J. and J. Churchill, 1872. 187 pp.

Bolton, H. Carrington. "The Early Practice of Medicine by Women," *Journal of Science* 18 (February, 1881) 57-70.

Bullough, Vern L. "Medieval Medical and Scientific Views of Women," *Viator: Medieval and Renaissance Studies* 4 (1973) 485-501.

Hughes, Muriel Joy. *Women Healers in Medieval Life and Literature*. New York: King's Crown Press, 1943. 180 pp.

Mead, Kate Campbell Hurd. *A History of Women in Medicine*. Haddam, Conn.: Haddam Press, 1938. 569 pp.

Roussier, Jules. "Opinions anciennes sur les grossesses prolongées (antiquité, moyen âge)" in *Etudes d'histoire du droit privé offertes à Pierre Petot*, ed. Pierre-Clément Timbal. Paris: Recueil Sirey, 1959. Pp. 473-480.

Still, George F. *The History of Paediatrics. The Progress of the Study of Diseases of Children up to the End of the XVIIIth Century*. London: Oxford University Press, 1931. 526 pp.

Thorndike, Lynn. "Further Consideration of the *Experimenta, Speculum astronomiae,* and *De secretis mulierum* Ascribed to Albertus Magnus," *Speculum* 30 (July, 1955) 413-443.

3 MARRIAGE ALLIANCE AND DESCENT

Baecker, Louis de. *Le droit de la femme dans l'antiquité, son devoir au moyen âge, d'après des manuscrits de la Bibliothèque nationale*. Paris: [A. Claudin], 1880. 172 pp.

Baldwin, John W. "A Campaign to Reduce Clerical Celibacy at the Turn of the Twelfth and Thirteenth Centuries" in *Etudes d'histoire du droit canonique dédiées à Gabriel Le Bras*, ed. Pierre-Clément Timbal. Paris: Sirey, 1965. Vol. 2. Pp. 1041-1053.

Bechstein, Susanne. "Die Frauen in Hohenlohe im mittelalterlichen Vormundschaftsrecht," *Württembergisch Franken* 50 (1966) 268-275.

Belmartino, Susana M. "Estructura de la familia y 'edades sociales' en la aristocracia de Leon y Castilla según las fuentes literarias y historiográficas (siglos X-XIII)," *Cuadernos de historia de España* 47-48 (1968) 256-328.

Benedetto, Maria Ada. *Ricerche sui rapporti patrimoniali tra coniugi nello stato sabaudo. A proposito della questione dotale di Filiberta di Savoia-Nemours*. (Università di Torino. Memorie dell'Istituto Giuridico, ser. 2, no. 96.) Turin: G. Giappichelli, 1957. 218 pp.

Bertrand, Rafael O. "Un capítulo de la política matrimonial de los Papas," *Cuadernos de historia de España* 18 (1952) 71-129.

Bezard, Yvonne. *La vie rurale, dans le sud de la région parisienne, de 1450 à 1560.* Paris: Firmin-Didot, 1929. 382 pp.

Bridel, L. *La femme et le droit; étude historique sur la condition des femmes.* Paris: F. Pichon, 1884. 148 pp.

Brooke, C. N. L. "Gregorian Reform in Action: Clerical Marriage in England, 1050-1200," *Cambridge Historical Journal* 12 (1956) 1-21.

— —, "Married Men among the English Higher Clergy, 1066-1200," *Cambridge Historical Journal* 12 (1956) 187-188.

Bullough, D. A. "Early Medieval Social Groupings: The Terminology of Kinship," *Past and Present* 45 (1969) 3-18.

Bussi, Emilio. "La donazione nel suo svolgimento storico, gli elementi romani e cristiani nelle forme della donazione medioevale" in *Cristianesimo e diritto romano.* (Pubblicazioni della Università Cattolica del Sacro Cuore, Scienze giuridiche, 2nd Series, 43.) Milan: Società editrice "Vita e Pensiero", 1935. Pp. 171-294.

Cam, Helen. *Liberties and Communities in Medieval England: Collected Studies in Local Administration and Topography.* New York: Barnes and Noble, 1963. Chap. 8, pp. 124-135, "Pedigrees of Villeins and Freemen in the Thirteenth Century".

Champeaux, Ernest. "*Jus sanguinis*, trois façons de calculer la parenté au Moyen âge," *Revue historique de droit français et étranger*, 4th Series, 12 (1933) 241-290.

Chojnacki, Stanley. "Dowries and Kinsmen in Early Renaissance Venice," *Journal of Interdisciplinary History* 4 (Winter, 1974-1975). In press.

Coleman, Emily R. "Medieval Marriage Characteristics: A Neglected Factor in the History of Medieval Serfdom," *Journal of Interdisciplinary History* 2 (Autumn, 1971) 205-219.

Cordier, E. "Le droit de famille aux Pyrénées," *Revue historique de droit français et étranger*, 1st Series, 5 (1859) 257-396.

Crouzel, Henri. *L'église primitive face au divorce, du premier au cinquième siècle.* (Théologie historique 13.) Paris: Beauchesne, [1971]. 410 pp.

Daudet, Pierre. *Etudes sur l'histoire de la juridiction matrimoniale. Les origines carolingiennes de la compétence exclusive de l'église (France et Germanie).* Paris: Recueil Sirey, 1933. 183 pp.

— —, *Etudes sur l'histoire de la juridiction matrimoniale. L'établissement de la compétence de l'église en matière de divorce et de consanguinité. France — X^e-XIIe siècles.* Paris: Recueil Sirey, 1941. 159 pp.

Dauvillier, Jean. *Le mariage dans le droit classique de l'église, depuis le décret de Gratien (1140) jusqu'à la mort de Clément V (1314).* Paris: Recueil Sirey, 1933. 517 pp.

— —, "Pierre le Chantre et la dispense de mariage non consommé" in *Etudes d'histoire du droit privé offertes à Pierre Petot*, ed. Pierre-Clément Timbal. Paris: Recueil Sirey, 1959. Pp. 97-106.

Decker, Raymond G. "Institutional Authority versus Personal Responsibility in the Marriage Section of Gratian's 'A Concordance of Discordant Canons'," *The Jurist* 32 (Fall, 1972) 51-65.

Delpini, Francesco. *Divorzio e separazione dei coniugi nel diritto romano e nella dottrina della chiesa fino al secolo V.* (Scrinium theologicum 5.) Turin: [Marietti], 1956. 138 pp.

Drew, Katherine Fischer. "The Germanic Family of the *Leges Burgundionum*," *Medievalia et humanistica* 15 (1963) 5-14.

Dumas, Auguste. *Etude sur le droit romain en pays de droit écrit. La condition des gens mariés dans la famille périgourdine au XVᵉ et au XVIᵉ siècles.* Paris, 1908. 342 pp.

Eames, Elizabeth. "Mariage et concubinage légal en Norvège à l'époque des Vikings," *Annales de Normandie* 2 (1952) 195-208.

Engdahl, David E. "English Marriage Conflicts Law before the Time of Bracton," *The American Journal of Comparative Law* 15 (1966-67) 109-135.

Esmein, Adhémar. *Le mariage en droit canonique.* Paris: Larose et Forcel, 1891. 2 vols.

Faith, Rosamund J. "Peasant Families and Inheritance Customs in Medieval England," *Agricultural History Review* 14 (1966) 77-95.

Falk, Ze'ev W. *Jewish Matrimonial Law in the Middle Ages.* (Scripta Judaica 6.) London: Oxford University Press, 1966. 154 pp.

Frank, Roberta. "Marriage in Twelfth- and Thirteenth-Century Iceland," *Viator: Medieval and Renaissance Studies* 4 (1973) 473-484.

Fraser, J. "The Alleged Matriarchy of the Picts" in *Medieval Studies in Memory of Gertrude Schoepperle Loomis*, ed. Roger Loomis. Paris: Champion; New York: Columbia University Press, 1927. Pp. 407-412.

Friedberg, Emil. *Das Recht der Eheschliessung in seiner geschichtlichen Entwicklung.* Leipzig: B. Tauchnitz, 1865. 827 pp.

Furnivall, F. J., ed. *Child-Marriages, Divorces, and Ratifications (and etc.) in the Diocese of Chester, A.D. 1561-6* (Early English Text Society, Original Series 108.) London: Kegan Paul, Trench, Trübner and Co., 1897. 256 pp.

Ganshof, François-Louis. "Note sur quelques textes invoqués en faveur de l'existence d'une tutelle de la femme en droit franc" in *Etudes d'histoire du droit privé offertes à Pierre Petot*, ed. Pierre-Clément Timbal. Paris: Recueil Sirey, 1959. Pp. 183-190.

Gaudemet, Jean. "Droit canonique et droit romain. A propos de l'erreur sur la personne en matière de mariage (C. XXIX, qu. 1)," *Studia Gratiana* 9 (1966) 45-64.

Gellinek, Christian. "Marriage by Consent in Literary Sources of Medieval Germany," *Studia Gratiana* 12 (*Collectanea Stephan Kuttner* 2) (1967) 555-579.

Girard, René. "Marriage in Avignon in the Second Half of the Fifteenth Century," *Speculum* 28 (July, 1953) 485-498.

Guilhiermoz, Paul. "Le droit de renonciation de la femme noble, lors de la dissolution de la communauté, dans l'ancienne coutume de Paris," *Bibliothèque de l'Ecole des chartes* 44 (1883) 489-500.

Haskell, Ann S. "The Paston Women on Marriage in Fifteenth-Century England," *Viator: Medieval and Renaissance Studies* 4 (1973) 459-471.

Helmholz, Richard. *Marriage Litigation in Medieval England.* Cambridge: The University Press. In press.

Herlihy, David. "Family Solidarity in Medieval Italian History," *Explorations in Economic History* 7 (Fall-Winter, 1969-70) 173-184.

— —. "Land, Family and Women in Continental Europe, 701-1200," *Traditio* 18 (1962) 89-120.

Holub, Joseph. "Les 'Agiles'. Les effets juridiques du mariage contracté entre nobles et non-nobles dans l'ancien droit hongrois," *Revue historique de droit français et étranger*, 4th Series, 33 (1955) 83-98.

— —. "La *Quarta puellaris* dans l'ancien droit hongrois" in *Studi in memoria di Aldo Albertoni.* (Studi di diritto privato, italiano e straniero diretti da Mario Rotondi, 19.) Padua, 1938. Vol. 3. Pp. 277-297.

Howard, George Elliott. *A History of Matrimonial Institutions.* 3 vols. Chicago: University of Chicago Press, 1904.

Hughes, Diane Owen. "Urban Growth and Family Structure in Medieval Genoa," *Past and Present* 66 (February, 1975) 3-28.

Imbert, Jean. "Le régime matrimonial de la coutume de la cité de Metz" in *Etudes d'histoire du droit privé offertes à Pierre Petot*, ed. Pierre-Clément Timbal. Paris: Recueil Sirey, 1959. Pp. 289-300.

Kalifa, Simon. "Singularités matrimoniales chez les anciens Germains: le rapt et le droit de la femme à disposer d'elle-même," *Revue historique de droit français et étranger*, 4th Series, 48 (1970) 199-225.

Kittel, Margaret Ruth. *Married Women in Thirteenth-Century England: A Study in Common Law.* Dissertation, Univ. of California, Berkeley, 1973.

Lafon, Jacques. *Les époux bordelais (1450-1550): régimes matrimoniaux et mutations sociales.* Paris: S.E.V.P.E.N., 1972. 345 pp.

Lancaster, Lorraine. "Kinship in Anglo-Saxon Society," *British Journal of Sociology* 9 (1958) 230-250, 359-377.

Laribière, Geneviève. "Le mariage à Toulouse aux XIVe et XVe siècles," *Annales du Midi* 79 (October, 1967) 335-361.

Le Bras, Gabriel. "Le mariage dans la théologie et le droit de l'église du XIe au XIIIe siècle," *Cahiers de civilisation médiévale* 11 (Apr.-June, 1968) 191-202.

— —. "Observations sur le mariage dans le Corpus Justinien et dans le droit classique de l'église" in *Etudes offertes à Jean Macqueron.* Aix-en-Provence, no publ., 1970. Pp. 425-429.

Lesinski, Bogdan. "Le statut de la femme en Pologne au moyen âge d'après le *Jus Terrestre*," *Revue historique de droit français et étranger*, 4th Series, 36 (1958) 34-58.

Lettmann, Reinhard. *Die Diskussion über die klandestinen Ehen und die Einführung einer zur Gültigkeit Verpflichtenden Eheschliessungsform auf dem Konzil von Trient: eine kanonistische Untersuchung.* (Münsterische Beiträge zur Theologie 31.) Münster i. Westf.: Aschendorff, 1967. 195 pp.

Leyser, K. "Maternal Kin in Early Medieval Germany. A Reply," *Past and Present* 49 (November, 1970) 126-134.

Lingenthal, K. E. Zachariae von. "A Medieval Procedural Form for Marriage Annulment Cases," *The American Journal of Legal History* 10 (January, 1966) 76-81.

Lugli, Vittorio. *I trattatisti della famiglia nel Quattrocento.* (Biblioteca filologica e letteraria 2.) Bologna-Modena: A. F. Formiggini, 1909. 126 pp.

Lynch, John E. "Marriage and Celibacy of the Clergy: The Discipline of the Western Church. An Historico-Canonical Synopsis," *The Jurist* 32 (Fall-Winter, 1972) 14-38, 189-212.

McLaughlin, T. P. "The Formation of the Marriage Bond According to the *Summa Parisiensis*," *Mediaeval Studies* 15 (1953) 208-212.

— —, "The Prohibition of Marriage against Canons in the Early Twelfth Century," *Mediaeval Studies* 3 (1941) 94-100.

Merzbacher, Friedrich. "Die Eheschliessung durch Stellvertreter nach altem und geltendem kanonischen Recht" in *Ecclesia et ius. Festgabe für Audomar Scheuermann zum 60. Geburtstag.* Eds. Karl Sieper et al. Munich: F. Schöningh, 1968. Pp. 455-466.

Metz, René and Schlick, Jean, eds. *Le lien matrimonial. Colloque du Cerdic, Strasbourg, 21-23 mai 1970.* (Hommes et église 1.) Strasbourg: no publ., 1970, 244 pp.

Metz, René. "Recherches sur la condition de la femme selon Gratien," *Studia Gratiana* 12 (*Collectanea Stephan Kuttner* 2) (1967) 377-396.

— —, "Recherches sur le statut de la femme en droit canonique: bilan historique et perspectives d'avenir: problèmes de méthodes," *L'année canonique* 12 (1968) 85-113.

Mistruzzi de Frisinga, Charles. "La succession nobiliaire féminine en Italie dans le droit et dans l'histoire," appendix to Ida Auda-Gioanet, *Une randonnée à travers l'histoire d'Orient: les Comnènes et les Anges.* Rome: F. Ferrari, 1953. 144 pp.

Noonan, John T., Jr. "Freedom, Experimentation and Permanence in the Canon Law on Marriage" in *Law for Liberty*, ed. James E. Biechler. Baltimore: Helicon, 1967. Pp. 52-68.

— —, "Marriage in the Middle Ages: Power to Choose," *Viator: Medieval and Renaissance Studies* 4 (1973) 419-434.

Orabona, Luciano. "Il matrimonio cristiano nell'età precostantiniana," *Studi romani* 16 (1968) 7-16.

Painter, Sidney. "The Family and the Feudal System in Twelfth-Century England," *Speculum* 35 (January, 1960) 1-16.

Parmisano, Fabian. "Love and Marriage in the Middle Ages," *New Blackfriars* 50 (1969) 599-608, 649-660.

Pesendorfer, Marianne. "Das Ehehindernis in der gesetzlichen Verwandtschaft (c. 1059 und c. 1080). Zur Frage der Anknüpfung an die staatliche Rechtsordnung und einiger damit im Zusammenhang stehenden Probleme des kanonischen Rechts," *Österreichisches Archiv für Kirchenrecht* 20 (1969) 199-225.

Petot, Pierre. "Licence de mariage et formariage des serfs dans les coutumes françaises au moyen âge," *Czasopismo prawno-historyczne, Annales d'histoire du droit* 2 (1949) 199-208.

— —, "Les meubles des époux au moyen âge d'après les coutumes françaises," *Revue internationale des droits de l'antiquité* 3 (*Mélanges Fernand de Visscher* 2) (1949) 213-230.

Phillpotts, Bertha S. *Kindred and Clan in the Middle Ages and After. A Study in the Sociology of the Teutonic Races.* Cambridge: University Press, 1913. 302 pp.

Poumarède, Jacques. *Les successions dans le sud-ouest de la France au Moyen Age.* (Publications de l'Université des sciences sociales de Toulouse. Centre d'histoire juridique. Série historique 1.) Paris: Presses universitaires de France, 1972. 341 pp.

Raftis, J. Ambrose. *Tenure and Mobility: Studies in the Social History of the Mediaeval English Village.* (Pontifical Institute of Mediaeval Studies, Studies and Texts 8.) Toronto: Pontifical Institute of Mediaeval Studies, 1964. 309 pp.

Richardson, Henry G. "The Marriage of Isabelle of Angoulême. A Problem of Canon Law," *Studia Gratiana* 12 (*Collectanea Stephan Kuttner* 2) (1967) 397-423.

Ritzer, Korbinian. *Le mariage dans les églises chrétiennes du Ier au XIe siècle.* Paris: Cerf, 1970. 494 pp.

Rossi, Guido. *Le statut juridique de la femme dans l'histoire du droit italien. Epoque médiévale et moderne.* Milan: A. Giuffrè, 1958. [2], 20 pp.

Rousset, Paul. "La femme et la famille dans l'*Histoire ecclésiastique* d'Orderic Vital," *Zeitschrift für schweizerische Kirchengeschichte* 63 (1969) 58-66.

Sheehan, Michael M. "The Formation and Stability of Marriage in Fourteenth-Century England: Evidence of an Ely Register," *Mediaeval Studies* 33 (1971) 228-263.

— —, "The Influence of Canon Law on the Property Rights of Married Women in England," *Mediaeval Studies* 25 (1963) 109-124.

— —, *The Will in Medieval England.* (Pontifical Institute of Mediaeval Studies, Studies and Texts 6.) Toronto: Pontifical Institute of Mediaeval Studies, 1963. 359 pp.

Smith, Charles E. *Papal Enforcement of Some Medieval Marriage Laws.* Baton Rouge, La.: Louisiana State University Press, 1940. 230 pp.

Stammler, Rudolf. *Ueber die Stellung der Frauen im alten deutschen Recht.* Berlin: C. Habel, 1877. 39 pp.

Stockmeier, P. "Scheidung und Wiederverheiratung in der alten Kirche," *Theologische Quartalschrift* 151 (1971) 39-51.

Timbal, Pierre-Clément. "La belle-mère, le gendre et le facteur; un mariage parisien au XIVe siècle" in *Etudes d'histoire du droit privé offertes à Pierre Petot,* ed. Timbal. Paris: Recueil Sirey, 1959. Pp. 543-552.

Trani, G. "Le 'Retour à la table,' une tentative coutumière pour maintenir le patrimoine familial," *Revue historique de droit français et étranger*, 4th Series, 49 (1971) 65-94.

Vaccari, Pietro. "Aspetti singolari dell'istituto del matrimonio nell'Italia meridionale," *Archivio storico pugliese* 6 (1953) 43-49.

Vismara, Giulio. "L'unità della famiglia nella storia del diritto in Italia," *Studia et documenta historiae et iuris* 22 (1956) 228-265.

Vogel, Cyrille. "L'âge des époux chrétiens au moment de contracter mariage, d'après les inscriptions paléochrétiennes," *Revue de droit canonique* 16 (1966) 355-366.

Weinberger, Stephen. "Peasant Households in Provence: ca. 800-1100," *Speculum* 48 (April, 1973) 247-257.

Whitelock, Dorothy, ed. and trans. *Anglo-Saxon Wills*. Cambridge: The University Press, 1930. 244 pp.

Wojnar, M. M. "Legal Relationship and Guardianship as Matrimonial Impediments," *The Jurist* 30 (1970) 343-355, 456-498.

Yver, Jean. *Egalité entre héritiers et exclusion des enfants dotés, essai de géographie coutumière*. Paris: Recueil Sirey, 1966. 310 pp.

4 Socialization

Gardiner, Dorothy Kempe. *English Girlhood at School. A Study of Women's Education through Twelve Centuries*. London: Oxford University Press, 1929. 501 pp.

Gaudier, M. "De l'éducation des femmes au xive siècle, étude historique," *Annales de l'académie de Macon* 9 (1870) 30-42.

Heinrich, Sister Mary Pia. *The Canonesses and Education in the Early Middle Ages*. Washington, D.C.: [Catholic University Press], 1924, 218 pp.

Hentsch, Alice A. *De la littérature didactique du moyen âge s'adressant spécialement aux femmes*. Cahors: A. Coueslant, 1903. 238 pp.

Jourdain, Charles. "Mémoire sur l'éducation des femmes au moyen âge," *Mémoires de l'Académie des Inscriptions et Belles-Lettres*, 2nd Series, 28 (1874) 79-133.

Kösterus, Friedrich. *Frauenbildung im Mittelalter: eine culturhistorische Studie*. Würzburg: Woerl, 1877. 40 pp.

5 Production and Consumption

Abram, Annie. "Women Traders in Medieval London," *Economic Journal* 26 (1916) 276-285.

Bonds, William N. "Genoese Noblewomen and Gold Thread Manufacturing," *Medievalia et humanistica* 17 (1966) 79-81.

Briganti, Antonio. *La donna e il diritto statutario in Perugia. La donna commerciante (secoli XIII e XIV)*. Perugia: Guerra, 1911. 77 pp.

Dale, Marian K. "The London Silkwomen of the Fifteenth Century," *Economic History Review* 4 (October, 1933), 324-335.

Dixon, E. "Craftswomen in the *Livre des métiers*," *Economic Journal* 5 (1895) 209-228.

Eames, Elizabeth. "La part de la femme dans l'administration du domaine et les travaux agraires en Norvège à l'époque des Vikings," *Annales de Normandie* 3 (1953) 115-124.

Fagniez, Gustave. *Etudes sur l'industrie et la classe industrielle à Paris, au XIIIe et au XIVe siècle.* (Bibliothèque de l'Ecole des hautes études. Sciences philologiques et historiques 33.) Paris: F. Vieweg, 1877. 426 pp.

Franklin, Alfred. *Les corporations ouvrières de Paris, du XIIe au XVIIIe siècle, histoire, statuts, armoiries, d'après des documents originaux ou inédits.* Paris: Firmin-Didot, 1884. 13 fasc.

Höppner, Martin. *Die Frauenarbeit in Paris im Mittelalter.* Göttingen, 1921. 123 pp.

Origo, Iris. *The Merchant of Prato.* (Bedford Historical Series 16.) London: Jonathan Cape, [1960]. 380 pp.

Piponnier, Françoise. *Costume et vie sociale: la cour d'Anjou XIVe-XVe siècle.* Paris: Mouton, 1970. 429 pp.

Smith, Joshua Toumin, ed. *English Gilds. The Original Ordinances of More than One Hundred Early English Gilds etc.* (Early English Text Society, Original Series 40.) London: Oxford University Press, 1870. 483 pp.

6 COMMUNITIES

Bateson, Mary. "Origin and Early History of Double Monasteries," *Transactions of the Royal Historical Society*, N.S. 13 (1899) 137-198.

Bernards, Matthäus. "Zur Seelsorge in den Frauenklöstern des Hochmittelalters," *Revue bénédictine* 66 (1956) 256-268.

Boyd Catherine. *A Cistercian Nunnery in Mediaeval Italy: The Story of Rifreddo in Saluzzo, 1220-1300.* Cambridge, Mass.: Harvard University Press, 1943. 189 pp.

Eckenstein, Lina. *Woman under Monasticism; Chapters on Saint-Lore and Convent Life between A.D. 500 and A.D. 1500.* Cambridge: University Press, 1896. 496 pp.

Grauwen, W. M. "De vrouwelijke religieuzen in de Orden van de 12^e en 13^e eeuw," *Analecta Praemonstratensia* 44 (1968) 100-105.

Hugo, Thomas. *The Mediaeval Nunneries of the County of Somerset, and Diocese of Bath and Wells; Together with the Annals of Their Impropriated Benefices, from the Earliest Times to the Death of Queen Mary.* London: Taunton, 1867. 628 pp.

Krenig, Ernst G. "Mittelalterliche Frauenklöster nach den Konstitutionen von Cîteaux, unter besonderer Berücksichtigung fränkischer Nonnenkonvente," *Analecta sacri ordinis cisterciensis* 10 (1954) 1-105.

Manselli, Raoul. *Spirituali e Beghini in Provenza.* (Istituto storico italiano per il medio evo. Studi storici 31-34.) Rome: Nella sede dell'Istituto, 1959. 355 pp.

McDonnell, E. W. *The Beguines and Beghards in Medieval Culture, with Special Emphasis on the Belgian Scene.* New Brunswick, N.J.: Rutgers University Press, 1954. 643 pp.

McLaughlin, T. P. "Abelard's Rule for Religious Women," *Mediaeval Studies* 18 (1956) 241-292.

Neumann, Eva G. *Rheinisches Beginen- und Begardenwesen.* (Mainzer Abhandlungen zur mittleren und neueren Geschichte 4.) Meisenheim: Anton Hain KG, 1960. 205 pp.

Persoons, E. and Lourdaux, W. "De statuten van de Vrouwenkloosters aangesloten bij het kapittel van Windesheim," *Archief voor de geschiedenis van de katholieke Kerk in Nederland* 9 (1967) 231-244.

Phillips, Dayton. *Beguines in Medieval Strasburg: A Study of the Social Aspect of Beguine Life.* Ann Arbor: Edward Brothers, 1941. 252 pp.

Power, Eileen. *Medieval English Nunneries.* (Cambridge Studies in Medieval Life and Thought.) Cambridge: University Press, 1922. 724 pp.

Ridder, C. B. de. "Quelques mots sur l'origine des beguines," *Annales d'histoire ecclésiastique belgique* 12 (1875) 5-21.

Wemter, Ernst M. "Die Beginen im mittelalterlichen Preussenlande," *Zeitschrift für die Geschichte und Altertumskunde Ermlands* 33 (1969) 41-52.

7 SEXUAL ETHIC

Albertario, Emilio. "Di alcuni riferimenti al matrimonio e al possesso in S. Agostino" in his *Studi di diritto romano.* Milan: A Giuffrè, 1933. Vol. 1, chap. 12. 229-248.

Bouvet, Francisque. *De la confession et du célibat des prêtres: ou, La politique du pape.* Paris: Comptoir des imprimeurs-unis, 1845. 532 pp.

Broudéhoux, Jean Paul. *Mariage et famille chez Clément d'Alexandrie.* Paris: Beauchesne, [1970]. 238 pp.

Browe, Peter. *Beiträge zur Sexualethik des Mittelalters.* Breslau: Müller and Seifert, 1932. 143 pp.

Crouzel, Henri. *Virginité et mariage selon Origène.* (Bresdlauer Studien zur Historischen Theologie 23.) Paris: Desclée de Brouwer, 1963. 217 pp.

Dervieu. "Le lit et le berceau au moyen âge," *Bulletin monumental* 81 (1912) 387-415.

Devereux, Robert. "Eleventh-Century Muslim Views on Women, Marriage, Love and Sex," *Central Asiatic Journal* 11 (1966) 134-140.

Emmen, A. "Verginità e matrimonio nella valutazione dell'Olivi," *Studi francescani* 64 (1967) 11-57.

Flandrin, Jean-Louis. "Contraception, mariage et relations amoureuses dans l'Occident chrétien," *Annales: Economies, Sociétés, Civilisations* 24 (Nov.-Dec., 1969) 1370-1390.

Gryson, Roger. *Les origines du célibat ecclésiastique du premier au septième siècle.* (Recherches et synthèses. Section d'histoire 2.) Gembloux: Duculot, 1970. 228 pp.

Hair, P. E. H. "Bridal Pregnancy in Earlier Rural England Further Examined," *Population Studies* 24 (March, 1970), 59-70.

— —. "Bridal Pregnancy in Rural England in Earlier Centuries," *Population Studies* 20 (November, 1966) 233-243.

Laeuchli, Samuel. *Power and Sexuality: The Emergence of Canon Law at the Synod of Elvira.* Philadelphia: Temple University Press, 1972. 143 pp.

Lancashire, Ian. "Sexual Innuendo in *The Reeve's Tale*," *The Chaucer Review* 6 (Winter, 1970) 159-170.

McNeill, John T. and Gamer, Helena M. *Medieval Handbooks of Penance.* (Records of Civilization, Sources and Studies 29.) New York: Columbia University Press, 1938. 476 pp.

Noonan, John T., Jr. "Marital Affection in the Canonists," *Studia Gratiana* 12 (*Collectanea Stephan Kuttner* 2) (1967) 479-509.

Rordorf, Willy. "Marriage in the New Testament and in the Early Church," *Journal of Ecclesiastical History* 20 (October, 1969) 193-210.

Vaccari, Pietro. "La tradizione canonica del 'debitum' coniugale e la posizione di Graziano," *Studia Gratiana* 1 (1953) 533-547.

8 THE IMAGE OF WOMEN

Abbot, Nabia. "Women and the State in Early Islam," *Journal of Near Eastern Studies* 1 (Jan.-Oct., 1942) 106-126.

Allworthy, Thomas B. *Women in the Apostolic Church.* Cambridge: W. Heffer and Sons, 1917. 147 pp.

Badel, P. "Raison 'Fille de Dieu' et le rationalisme de Jean de Meun" in *Mélanges offerts à Jean Frappier de langue et littérature du moyen âge et de la renaissance.* (Publications romanes et françaises 112.) Geneva: Librairie Droz, 1970. Vol. 1. 41-52.

Baer, Richard A. *Philo's Use of the Categories Male and Female.* (Arbeiten zur Literatur und Geschichte des hellenistischen Judentums 3.) Leiden: E. J. Brill, 1970. 116 pp.

Benton, John F. "Clio and Venus: An Historical View of Medieval Love" in *The Meaning of Courtly Love*, ed. F. X. Newman. Albany: State University of New York Press, 1968. 19-42.

Bernards, Matthäus. *Speculum Virginum; Geistigkeit und Seelenleben der Frau im Hochmittelalter.* Cologne: Böhlau, 1955. 262 pp.

Bezzola, Reto R. "La transformation des mœurs et le rôle de la femme dans la classe féodale du xie au xiie siècle" in his *Les origines et la formation de la littérature courtoise en Occident (500-1200).* (Bibliothèque de l'Ecole des hautes études. Sciences historiques et philologiques 313.) Paris: Champion, 1960. Part 2, vol. 2. 461-484.

Bolton, W. F. "*The Wife's Lament* and *The Husband's Message*: A Reconsideration Revisited," *Archiv für das Studium der neueren Sprachen und Literaturen* 205 (February, 1969) 337-351.

Brunelli, Giuseppe A. "De la 'Ballade de l'espouse' aux aphrodisiaques du legs de l'Orfèvre (Villon, 'Le Testament,' 1378-1405 et 1118-1125)," *Revue belge de philologie et d'histoire* 35 (1957) 763-770.

— —. "Jean Castel et le 'Mirouer des dames'," *Le moyen âge* 62 (1956) 93-117.

Bücher, Karl. *Die Frauenfrage im Mittelalter.* Tübingen: H. Laupp'sche Buchhandlung, 1910. 92 pp.

Cabane, Abbé Auguste. *Essais d'études religieuses. La femme avant et depuis l'Evangile. Origines de la bienfaisance chrétienne.* Montpellier: Grollier et fils, 1884. 300 pp.

Caird, G. B. "Paul and Women's Liberty," *Bulletin of the John Rylands Library* 54 (Spring, 1972) 268-281.

Caluwé, Jacques de. "La conception de l'amour dans le lai d'Eliduc de Marie de France," *Le moyen âge* 77 (1971) 53-77.

Casey, Kathleen L. "The Cheshire Cat: Reconstructing the Experience of Medieval Women" in *Liberating Women's History. Theoretical and Critical Essays*, ed. Bernice A. Carroll. Urbana: University of Illinois Press. In press.

Delhaye, Philippe. "Le dossier anti-matrimonial de l'*Adversus Jovinianum* et son influence sur quelques écrits latins du xiie siècle," *Mediaeval Studies* 13 (1951) 65-86.

Denomy, Alex J. "An Inquiry into the Origins of Courtly Love," *Mediaeval Studies* 6 (1944) 175-260.

Donahue, Charles. "The Valkyries and the Irish War-Goddesses," *Publications of the Modern Language Association* 56 (March, 1941) 1-12.

Dove, Mary. "Gawain and the *Blasme des Femmes* Tradition," *Medium aevum* 41 (1972) 20-26.

Epstein, Isidore. "The Jewish Woman in the *Responsa* (900 C.E.-1500 C.E.)" in *The Jewish Library*, ed. Leo Jung. New York: Jewish Library Publications, 1934. Vol. 3. 123-152.

Erickson, Carolly. "The View of Women," *The Medieval Vision*. London-New York: Oxford University Press, 1975.

Evans, Joan. *Dress in Mediaeval France*. Oxford: Clarendon Press, 1952. 94 pp.

Finke, Heinrich. *Die Frau im Mittelalter*. Kempten: Kösel, 1913. 190 pp.

Friedman, Lionel J. "'Jean de Meun,' Antifeminism and 'Bourgeois Realism'," *Modern Philology* 57 (August, 1959) 13-23.

Goyau, Lucie Faure. *Christianisme et culture féminine*. Paris: Perrin et Cie., 1918. 270 pp.

Grisay, Auguste, et al. *Les dénominations de la femme dans les anciens texte littéraires français*. Gembloux: Duculot, 1969. 259 pp.

Harris, Joseph. "'Maiden in the Mor Lay' and the Medieval Magdalene Tradition," *The Journal of Medieval and Renaissance Studies* 1 (1971) 59-87.

Healy, Sister Emma Thérèse. *Woman According to Saint Bonaventure*. New York: Georgian Press, 1956. 275 pp.

Hennessy, W. M. "The Ancient Irish Goddesses of War," *Revue celtique* 1 (1870) 32-55.

Herlihy, David. *Women in Medieval Society*. Houston: University of St. Thomas, 1971.

Jacobius, Helene. *Die Erziehung des Edelfraüleins im alten Frankreich nach Dichtungen des XII., XIII. und XIV. Jahrhunderts.* (Beiheft zur *Zeitschrift für romanische Philologie* 16.) Halle: M. Niemeyer, 1908. 80 pp.

Jonin, Pierre. *Les personnages féminins dans les romans français de Tristan au XIIe siècle. Etude des influences contemporaines.* (Publication des Annales de la

Faculté des Lettres, Aix-en-Provence, nouv. sér., no. 22.) Gap: Ophrys, 1958. 528 pp.

Karnein, Alfred. *De Amore deutsch; der Tractatus des Andreas Capellanus in der Übersetzung Johann Hartliebs.* (Münchener Texte und Untersuchungen zur deutschen Literatur des Mittelalters 28.) Munich: Beck, 1970. 283 pp.

Kaufman, Michael. "Spare Ribs: The Conception of Woman in the Middle Ages and the Renaissance," *Soundings* 56 (Summer, 1973) 139-163.

Keidel, George C., ed. *The Evangile aux femmes — An Old-French Satire on Women.* Baltimore: Friedenwald, 1895. 93 pp.

Kelly, Douglas. "Courtly Love in Perspective: The Hierarchy of Love in Andreas Capellanus," *Traditio* 24 (1968) 119-147.

Leclercq, J. "Un témoin de l'antiféminisme au moyen âge," *Revue bénédictine* 80 (1970) 304-309.

McRobbie, Kenneth. "Women and Love: Some Aspects of Competition in Late Medieval Society," *Mosaic* 5 (Winter, 1972) 139-168.

Moller, Herbert. "The Social Causation of the Courtly Love Complex," *Comparative Studies in Society and History* 1 (1959) 137-163.

Monfrin, J. "Poème anglo-normand sur le mariage, les vices et les vertus, par Henri (xiiie siècle)" in *Mélanges offerts à Jean Frappier de langue et littérature du moyen âge et de la renaissance.* (Publications romanes et françaises 112.) Geneva: Librairie Droz, 1970. Vol. 2. 845-866.

Moore, John C. "Love in Twelfth-Century France: A Failure in Synthesis," *Traditio* 24 (1968) 429-443.

Murray, Robert. "Mary, the Second Eve in the Early Syriac Fathers," *Eastern Churches Review* 3 (Autumn, 1971) 372-384.

Murtaugh, Daniel M. "Women and Geoffrey Chaucer," *English Literary History* 38 (December, 1971) 473-492.

Neubauer, A. "Textes hébraico-italiens concernant les femmes," *Atti della Reale Accademia dei Lincei, Rendiconti,* 4th Series, 7 (2nd Semester, 1891) 181-192, 347-355.

Newman, F. X., ed. *The Meaning of Courtly Love.* Albany: State University of New York Press, 1968. 102 pp.

Odegaard, Charles E. "The Empress Engelberge," *Speculum* 26 (1951) 77-103.

Origo, Iris. "Eve or Mary? The Tuscan Women of the Fifteenth Century, as Seen by San Bernardino of Siena," *Cornhill Magazine,* Vol. 173, no. 1034 (Winter, 1962-1963) 65-84.

Paulus, Niklaus. "Mittelalterliche Stimmen über den Eheorden," *Historisch-politische Blätter für das katholische Deutschland"* 141 (1908) 1008-1024.

Portmann, Marie-Louise. *Die Darstellung der Frau in der Geschichtschreibung des früheren Mittelalters.* (Basler Beiträge zur Geschichtswissenschaft 69.) Basel: Helbing und Lichtenhahan, 1958. 147 pp.

Power, Eileen. "The Position of Women" in *The Legacy of the Middle Ages,* eds. C. G. Crump and E. F. Jacob. Oxford: Clarendon Press, 1926. 401-433.

Renier, Rodolfo. *Il tipo estetico della donna nel medio evo.* Ancona: A. G. Morelli, 1885. 192 pp.

Schneider, Annerose. "Zum Bild von der Frau in der Chronistik des früheren Mittelalters," *Forschungen und Fortschritte* 35 (April, 1961) 112-114.

Tupper, Frederick. *Types of Society in Medieval Literature*. New York: H. Holt, 1926. 167 pp.

Vadet, Jean-Claude. *L'esprit courtois en Orient dans les cinq premiers siècles de l'Hégire*. Paris: G.-P. Maisonneuve et Larose, 1968. 490 pp.

Vogelsang, Thilo. *Die Frau als Herrscherin im hohen Mittelalter*. (Göttinger Bausteine zur Geschichtswissenschaft 7.) Göttingen: "Musterschmidt" Wissenschaftlicher Verlag, 1954. 91 pp.

Wulff, August. *Die frauenfeindlichen Dichtungen in den romanischen Literaturen des Mittelalters bis zum Ende des XIII. Jahrhunderts*. (Romanische Arbeiten 4.) Halle: E. Niemeyer, 1914. 199 pp.

9 BIOGRAPHICAL STUDIES

Bainton, Roland H. "Katherine Zell," *Medievalia et humanistica*, N.S. 1 (1970) 3-28.

Briand, Abbé Émile. *Histoire de Sainte Radegonde, reine de France, et des sanctuaires et pèlerinages en son honneur*. Paris: Oudin, 1898. 536 pp.

Buckler, Georgina. *Anna Comnena: A Study*. London: Oxford University Press, 1929. 558 pp.

Bullock-Davies, Constance. "Marie, Abbess of Shaftesbury, and Her Brothers," *English Historical Review* 80 (April, 1965) 314-322.

Butler, Mary M. *Hrotsvitha: The Theatricality of Her Plays*. New York: Philosophical Library, 1960. 234 pp.

Caix de Saint-Aymour, Amédée. *Anne de Russie, reine de France et comtesse de Valois au XIᵉ siècle*. 2nd ed. Paris: H. Champion, 1896. 116 pp.

Campbell, Miles W. "Queen Emma and Aelfgifu of Northampton: Canute the Great's Women," *Mediaeval Scandinavia* 4 (1971) 66-79.

Caraman, Philip G. *St. Angela. The Life of Angela Merici, Foundress of the Ursulines, 1474-1540*. New York: Farrar, Strauss, 1964. 188 pp.

Chalon, Louis. "A propos des filles du Cid," *Le moyen âge* 73 (1967) 217-237.

Fahy, Conor. "The Marriage of Edward IV and Elizabeth Woodville: A New Italian Source," *English Historical Review* 76 (October, 1961) 660-667.

Favier, Marguerite. *Christine de Pisan: Muse des cours souveraines*. Lausanne: Rencontre, 1967. 224 pp.

Fischer, Hermann. *Die heilige Hildegard von Bingen, die erste deutsche Naturforscherin und Ärztin, ihr Leben und Werk*. (Münchener Beiträge zur Geschichte und Literatur der Naturwissenschaften und Medizin 7, 8.) Munich: Münchner Drucke, 1927. 162 pp.

Geraud, Hercule. "Ingeburge de Danemark, reine de France, 1193-1236," *Bibliothèque de l'Ecole des chartes* 6 (1844) 3-27, 93-118.

Gilson, Etienne. *Heloise and Abelard*. Trans. L. K. Shook. Chicago: H. Regnery Company, 1951. 194 pp.

Griffiths, Ralph A. "The Trial of Eleanor Cobham: An Episode in the Fall of

Duke Humphrey of Gloucester," *Bulletin of the John Rylands Library* 51 (Spring, 1969) 381-399.

Harvey, Nancy Lenz. *Elizabeth of York : The Mother of Henry VIII.* New York: Macmillan, [1973]. 241 pp.

Hudson, William Henry. "Hrotsvitha of Gandersheim," *English Historical Review* 3 (July, 1888), 431-457.

Jeandet, Yette. *Héloise. L'amour et l'absolu.* Lausanne: Editions Rencontre, 1966. 256 pp.

Laigle, Mathilde. *Le "Livre des Trois Vertus" de Christine de Pisan et son milieu historique et littéraire.* (Bibliothèque du XVe siècle 16.) Paris: H. Champion, 1912. 375 pp.

Ledóchowska, Teresa. *Angèle Merici et la Compagnie de Ste.-Ursule à la lumière des documents.* Rome-Milan-Ancona, 1968. 2 vols.

Levi della Vida, Giorgio. "La corrispondenza di Berta di Toscana col califfo Muktafi," *Rivista storica italiana* 66 (1954) 21-38.

Lightbody, Charles W. *The Judgements of Joan; Joan of Arc, a Study in Cultural History.* Cambridge, Mass.: Harvard University Press, 1961. 189 pp.

Mickel, Emanuel J., Jr. "A Reconsideration of the *Lais* of Marie de France," *Speculum* 46 (January, 1971) 39-65.

Pernoud, Régine. *Joan of Arc, by Herself and Her Witnesses.* Trans. Edward Hyams. London: Macdonald, [1964]. 287 pp.

— —. *La reine Blanche.* Paris: A. Michel, 1972. 366 pp.

Pinet, Marie Josèphe. *Christine de Pisan, 1364-1430: étude biographique et littéraire.* (Bibliothèque du XVe siècle 35.) Paris: H. Champion, 1927. 463 pp.

Richard, Jules-Marie. *Une petite-nièce de saint Louis: Mahaut, Comtesse d'Artois et de Bourgogne (1302-1329), étude sur la vie privée, les arts et l'industrie en Artois et à Paris au commencement du XIVe siècle.* Paris: H. Champion, 1887. 456 pp.

Santy, Sernin. *La Comtesse de Die, sa vie, ses œuvres complètes, les fêtes données en son honneur, avec tous les documents.* Paris: [Picard], 1893. 146 pp.

Schmelzeis, Johann Philipp. *Das Leben und Wirken der Heiligen Hildegardis.* Freiburg im Breisgau-Leipzig: Herder'sche Verlag, 1879. 616 pp.

Soranzo, Giovanni. "Orisini Orsino, Adriana di Mila sua madre, e Giulia Farnese sua moglie, nei loro rapporti con Papa Alessandro VI," *Archivi,* 2nd Series, 26 (1959) 119-150.

Stabińska, Jadwiga. *Królowa Jadwiga.* Cracow: Znak, 1969. 146 pp.

Sticca, Sandro. "Hrotswitha's 'Dulcitius' and Christian Symbolism," *Mediaeval Studies* 32 (1970) 108-127.

Thomassy, Marie-Joseph-Raymond. *Essai sur les écrits politiques de Christine de Pisan, suivi d'une notice littéraire et de pièces inédites.* Paris: Debécourt, 1838. 199 pp.

Vacandard, M. "Le divorce de Louis le Jeune," *Revue des questions historiques* 42 (April, 1890) 408-432.

Willard, Charity C. "Isabel of Portugal and the French Translation of the 'Triunfo de las Doñas'," *Revue belge de philologie et d'histoire* 43 (1965) 961-969.

— —. "The Manuscript Tradition of the *Livres des trois vertus* and Christine de Pisan's Audience," *Journal of the History of Ideas* 27 (July-Sept., 1966) 433-444.

10 GENERAL

Aubenas, Roger. *La sorcière et l'inquisiteur. Episode de l'Inquisition en Provence, 1439.* (Archives de Provence 1.) Aix-en-Provence: Archives de Provence, 1956. 81 pp.

Besançon, Alain. "Le premier livre de 'La Sorcière'," *Annales: Economies, Sociétés, Civilisations* 26 (Jan.-Feb., 1971) 186-204.

Busoni, Philippe, ed. *Chefs-d'œuvre poétiques des dames françaises depuis le XIIIe siècle jusqu'au XIXe.* Paris: Paulin, 1841. 372 pp.

Campbell, J. A. "Virgins Consecrated to God in Rome during the First Centuries," *American Catholic Quarterly Review* 25 (1900) 766-799.

Clay, Rotha M. *The Hermits and Anchorites of England.* London: Methuen & Co. Ltd., 1914. 272 pp.

Corcos, Fernand. *Les femmes en guerre.* Paris: Editions Montaigne, 1927. 190 pp.

Daniélou, Jean. *The Ministry of Women in the Early Church.* Trans. the Rt. Revd. Glyn Simon. London: Faith Press, 1961. 31 pp.

Dietrick, Ellen B. *Women in the Early Christian Ministry.* Philadelphia: Alfred J. Ferris, 1897. 148 pp.

Duchesne, L. "Lovocat et Catihern," *Revue de Bretagne et de Vendée* 57 (1885) 5-21.

Eckenstein, Lina. *The Women of Early Christianity.* Revised by Celia Roscoe. London: Faith Press, 1935. 159 pp.

Facinger, Marion F. "A Study of Medieval Queenship: Capetian France 987-1237," *Studies in Medieval and Renaissance History* 5 (1968) 3-48.

Flahiff, George B. "*Deus non vult*: A Critic of the Third Crusade," *Mediaeval Studies* 9 (1947) 162-188.

Forbes, Thomas R. *The Midwife and the Witch.* New Haven: Yale University Press, 1966. 196 pp.

Galametz, Brant de. "Les fiancées volontaires et l'asile dans le mariage," *Bulletin de la Société d'émulation d'Abbeville* 9 (1904) 188-199.

Gide, Paul. *Etude sur la condition privée de la femme dans le droit ancien et moderne et en particulier sur le Sénatus-Consulte Velléien.* 2d ed., with notes by A. Esmein. Paris: Larose et Forcel, 1885. 588 pp.

Gist, Margaret A. *Love and War in the Middle English Romances.* Philadelphia: University of Pennsylvania Press, 1947. 214 pp.

Gryson, R. "L'attitude de l'église ancienne vis-à-vis du ministère des femmes," *Collectanea Mechliniensia* 53 (1958) 352-363.

— —. *Le ministère des femmes dans l'église ancienne.* (Recherches et synthèses. Section d'histoire 4.) Gembloux: Duculot, 1972. 203 pp.

Haskagen, J. "Spannungen in der Frauenkultur auf der Hohe des Mittelalters," *Theologische Quartalschrift* 129 (1949) 93-100.

Henriques, Fernando. *Prostitution and Society: A Survey, Primitive, Classical and Oriental*. New York: Citadel Press, [1963]. 438 pp.

Herlihy, David. "Some Psychological and Social Roots of Violence in the Tuscan Cities" in *Violence and Civil Disorder in Italian Cities, 1200-1500*, ed. Lauro Martines. (UCLA Center for Medieval and Renaissance Studies, Contributions 5.) Berkeley: University of California Press, 1972. 129-154.

— —. "Vieillir à Florence au Quattrocento," *Annales: Economies, Sociétés, Civilisations* 24 (Nov.-Dec., 1969) 1338-1352.

Huyghebaert, Nicolas. "Les femmes laïques dans la vie religieuse des xie et xiie siècles dans la province ecclésiastique de Reims" in *I laici nella "Societas christiana." dei secoli XI e XII*. (Pubblicazioni dell'Università Cattolica del Sacro Cuore, Serie Terza, 5. Miscellanea del Centro di studi medioevali 5.) Milan: Società editrice Vita e Pensiero, 1968. 346-389.

Jones, William R. "Political Uses of Sorcery in Medieval Europe," *The Historian* 34 (August, 1972) 670-687.

Kittredge, George L. *Witchcraft in Old and New England*. Cambridge, Mass.: Harvard University Press, 1929. 641 pp.

Koch, Gottfried. "Die Frau im mittelalterlichen Katharismus und Waldensertum," *Studi medievali*, 3rd Series, 5 (1964) 741-774.

— —, *Frauenfrage und Ketzertum im Mittelalter. Die Frauenbewegung im Rahmen des Katharismus und des Waldensertums und ihre sozialen Wurzeln (12.-14. Jahrhundert)*. (Forschungen zur mittelalterlichen Geschichte 9.) Berlin: Akademie-Verlag, 1962. 210 pp.

Laboulaye, Edouard de. *Recherches sur la condition civile et politique des femmes*. Paris: A. Durand, 1843. 528 pp.

Labriolle, Pierre de. "Appendice à la question du *Mulieres in ecclesia taceant*," *Bulletin d'ancienne littérature et d'archéologie chrétiennes* 1 (1911) 292-298.

— —. *La crise montaniste*. Paris: E. Leroux, 1913. 607 pp.

— —. "Le 'mariage spirituel' dans l'antiquité chrétienne," *Revue historique* 137 (May-June, 1921) 204-225.

— —. *Les sources de l'histoire du Montanisme, textes grecs, latins, syriaques*. (Collectanea Friburgensia 24.) Fribourg: Librairie de l'Université, 1913. 282 pp.

Langlois, Charles. *La vie en France au moyen âge d'après quelques moralistes du temps*. Paris: Hachette. 1908, 359 pp.

Lea, Henry C. *Materials toward a History of Witchcraft*. Arranged and edited by Arthur C. Howland. Philadelphia: University of Pennsylvania Press, 1939. 3 vols.

Lehmann, Andrée. *Le rôle de la femme dans l'histoire de France au moyen âge*. Paris: Berger-Levrault, 1952. 526 pp.

— —. *Le rôle de la femme dans l'histoire de la Gaule*. Paris: Presses Universitaires de France, 1944. 150 pp.

Marignan, Albert. *Etude sur le manuscrit de "l'Hortus deliciarum"*. Strasbourg: Heitz, 1910. 83 pp.

Michelet, Jules. *La sorcière*. Paris: E. Dentu, 1862. 460 pp.

Midelfort, H. C. Erik. "Recent Witch Hunting Research, or Where Do We Go from Here?" *Papers of the Bibliographical Society of America* 62 (3rd Quarter, 1968) 373-420.

Monter, E. William, ed. *European Witchcraft.* New York: Wiley, 1969. 177 pp.

Morris, Joan. *The Lady Was a Bishop: The Hidden History of Women with Clerical Ordination and the Jurisdiction of Bishops.* New York: Macmillan, 1973. 192 pp.

Moulin, Jeanine, ed. *La poésie féminine.* Paris: Seghers, 1966. 2 vols. Vol. 1: *La poésie féminine du XII*ᵉ *au XIX*ᵉ *siècle.*

Myers, A. R. "The Captivity of a Royal Witch: The Household Accounts of Queen Joan of Navarre, 1419-21," *Bulletin of the John Rylands Library* 24 (October, 1940) 263-284.

Perella, Nicolas J. *The Kiss Sacred and Profane. An Interpretative History of Kiss Symbolism and Related Religio-Erotic Themes.* Berkeley: University of California Press, 1969. 356 pp.

Peruzzi, Candida. "Un processo di stregoneria a Todi nel 400," *Lares* 21 (Jan.-June, 1955) 1-17.

Petit-Dutaillis, Charles. *Documents nouveaux sur les mœurs populaires et le droit de vengeance dans les Pays-Bas au XV*ᵉ *siècle.* (Bibliothèque du xvᵉ siècle 9.) Paris: H. Champion, 1908. 226 pp.

Posner, Arthur. "Literature for Jewish Women in Medieval and Later Times" in *The Jewish Library*, ed. Leo Jung. New York: Jewish Library Publ. Co., 1934. Vol. 3. 213-243.

Range, Joan A. "Legal Exclusion of Women from Church Office," *The Jurist* 34 (Winter-Spring, 1974) 112-127.

Reynolds, Roger E. "*Virgines subintroductae* in Celtic Christianity," *Harvard Theological Review* 61 (October, 1968) 547-566.

Rokseth, Yvonne. "Les femmes musiciennes du xııᵉ au xıvᵉ siècle," *Romania* 61 (October, 1935) 464-480.

Soggin, Jan Alberto. "Il matrimonio presso i Valdesi prima della Riforma (1170-1532)," *Il diritto ecclesiastico* 64 (1953) 31-95.

— —. "Uno scritto sul matrimonio dei Valdesi prima della Riforma," *Atti della Accademia Nazionale dei Lincei, Rendiconti, Classe di scienze, morali, storiche e filologiche*, 8th Series, 6 (July-Oct., 1951) 400-404.

— —. "Uno scritto sul matrimonio dei Valdesi prima della Riforma; Epilegomena," *Atti della Accademia Nazionale dei Lincei, Rendiconti, Classe di scienze, morali, storiche e filologiche*, 8th Series, 14 (May-June, 1959) 259-262.

Strauss und Torney, Lulu von. *Deutsches Frauenleben in der Zeit der Sachsenkaiser und Hohenstaufen.* Jena: E. Diederichs, 1927. 81 pp.

Weigand, R. "Das Scheidungsproblem in der mittelalterlichen Kanonistik," *Theologische Quartalschrift* 151 (1971) 52-60.

Weinhold, Karl. *Die deutschen Frauen in dem Mittelalter.* Vienna: Carl Gerhold, 1851. 496 pp.

Werner, Ernst. "Die Stellung der Katharer zur Frau," *Studi medievali*, 3rd Series, 2 (1961) 295-301.

— —. "Zur Frauenfrage und zum Frauenkult im Mittelalter: Robert V. Arbrissel und Fontevrault," *Forschungen und Fortschritte* 29 (September, 1955) 267-276.

Willson, H. B. "Nemt, vrowe, disen kranz," *Medium aevum* 34 (1965) 189-202.

Wilpert, Joseph. *Die gottgeweihten Jungfrauen in den ersten Jahrhunderten der Kirche.* Freiburg-im-Breisgau, 1892. 105 pp.

Wright, Thomas. *A History of Domestic Manners and Sentiments in England During the Middle Ages.* London: Chapman and Hall, 1862. 502 pp.

— —. *The Homes of Other Days: A History of Domestic Manners and Sentiments in England from the Earliest Known Period to Modern Times.* London: Trübner and Co., 1871. 511 pp.

Zerbst, Fritz. *The Office of Woman in the Church.* Translated by A. G. Merkens. St. Louis: Concordia, 1955. 128 pp.

Zscharnack, Leopold. *Der Dienst der Frau in den ersten Jahrhunderten der christlichen Kirche.* Göttingen, 1902. 192 pp.

Berkeley, California
State University of New York, Binghamton

OFFICE AND JUSTICE:
LOUIS XI AND THE PARLEMENT OF PARIS
(1465-1467)*

Christopher W. Stocker

On more than one occasion, remarked Philippe de Commines in his memoires, Louis XI confided that if he had lost his hold on Paris during the war of the *Ligue du bien public* of 1465, he was ready to flee to Switzerland or Milan.[1] Although the coalition of rebellious nobles lacked the resources to mount either an all-out assault or a protracted siege, Louis nevertheless did come perilously close to losing his capital. For within Paris the leaguers had a fifth column working to convince the Parisians to open the gates of the city voluntarily to the nobles. It appears from the accounts of contemporary witnesses that the king's enemies were particularly successful in recruiting adherents among the *bourgeoisie aisée* and the legists, that is, from the notables of the city.[2] This was the result of a vigorous propaganda campaign that mingled threats of violent reprisals should the Parisians not admit the leaguers within the walls voluntarily, with promises of royal offices for leaguer supporters and better government for the realm as a whole.[3]

Among the notables whose backing the leaguers endeavored to secure were the magistrates of the Parlement. The *parlementaires* oc-

* The research upon which this paper is based was made possible by a grant-in-aid from the American Council of Learned Societies.

[1] *Mémoires*, ed. Joseph Calmette (Paris, 1924-1925), 1.57. It is not my intention to rehearse here the history of the *Ligue du bien public*, the most thorough treatment of which is still that of Henri Stein: *Charles de France, frère de Louis XI* (Paris, 1921), pp. 45-135. For what transpired in Paris I have relied chiefly upon the "Journal Parisien de Jean de Maupoint," ed. G. Fagniez, *Mémoires de la Société de l'histoire de Paris et de l'Ile-de-France* 4 (1887) 54-101; Jean de Roye, *Chronique scandaleuse*, ed. B. de Mandrot (Paris, 1894-1896), 1.87-141; and the *Dépêches des ambassadeurs milanais en France sous Louis XI et François Sforza*, ed. B. de Mandrot and Charles Samaran, 3 (Paris, 1920), 4 (Paris, 1923).

[2] Stein, 104.

[3] Maupoint, 64-65; Commines, 55; Stein, 105.

cupied a particularly important place in Parisian society and they had a great deal of influence in the affairs of the city. Socially they enjoyed a variety of privileges, exemptions, immunities and honorific distinctions in virtue of the office they held. Moreover, as individuals several were furthering their status by acquiring lands and seigneuries in the Parisian countryside, an activity that attests to their wealth as well as to their ambition.[4] Politically, the magistrates belonged to the local governing elite. The Parlement itself by this time had taken on the responsibility for many facets of local administration: police, housing, sanitation, communication, education and the supervision of religious, moral and economic behavior. Over and above their administrative work as a *corps*, individual members of the Parlement periodically held office at the *hôtel de ville*, which was now almost completely in the hands of the legists of Paris.[5] It is obvious why the leaders of the league sent a special deputation to the Parlement in 1465. A favorable pronouncement from this body could have been expected to influence others and would thus have made it more likely that Paris would open its gates to the leaguers.

Although our sources are tantalizingly vague on the matter, it would appear that no small number of *parlementaires* looked favorably upon the enterprise of the disgruntled nobles. The surest indication of their sympathy is the fact that on 29 August Louis XI issued orders that the Parlement cease meeting as a body, a move that must have been intended to forestall any formal decision by the court on the question then being debated in the *hôtel de ville* of whether or not the leaders of the league should be admitted within the city. Louis XI apparently had reason to believe that the Parlement might say yes.[6]

4 On the privileges of the magistracy see Edouard Maugis, *Histoire du Parlement de Paris, de l'avènement des rois Valois à la mort d'Henri IV* (Paris, 1913-1916), 1.517-729. On their penetration into the surrounding region see, most recently, Guy Fourquin, *Les campagnes de la région parisienne à la fin du moyen âge* (Paris, 1964), pp. 465-74, 482-83.

5 On legists, magistrates and municipal government, note the tabulation of *prévôts des marchands* and *échevins* in Bibliothèque Nationale [hereinafter abbreviated B.N.], MS. Fr. 11746. See also Felix Aubert, "Le Parlement et la ville de Paris au XVIe siècle," *Revue des études historiques* 62 (1906) 225-47, 337-57. When the leaders of the league demanded meetings with representatives of the city, they asked the Parlement, the University, the cathedral chapter of Notre Dame and the *corps de ville* each to elect three men; of the twelve elected seven were lawyers or judicial officers and each one of the four corporate groups named at least one legist in its contingent of three (Maupoint, 63).

6 Archives Nationales [hereinafter abbreviated A.N.], U 113, fol. 2; Stein, 104, 539. Curiously, the re-opening of the Parlement in October 1465 (while Louis XI was negotiating with the princes) was later taken as evidence that he had the support of the magistrates at the time of the league (Maugis, 1.632, 634).

In spite of this apparent disaffection within the court in 1465, historians of the Parlement, who usually pay considerable attention to the political interests and activities of the magistrates, have virtually neglected this particular episode. Because the registers of the court covering the period between November 1462 and November 1469 are missing, no serious attempt has ever been made to fathom the grievances of the magistrates at the time of the *Ligue du bien public*. Even the oldest collections of extracts from the original registers contain at most only a few brief passages from this period, certainly not enough to convey the concerns of the magistrates at the time.[7] The events of 1465 and the subsequent actions of both Louis XI and the magistrates do, however, suggest two likely reasons for their equivocal behavior during the critical months of July and August. Some of the magistrates may have favored the league simply because they were or had been clients of noblemen who figured prominently in the enterprise. Some others, no doubt, were influenced by the political program the leaguers presented in the propaganda campaign they aimed at the citizenry of Paris.

The first explanation was actually suggested by a contemporary, Commines, and there is doubtless some truth in it.[8] Clientage relations between lawyers and powerful princes had a decided influence upon both the provision to office in the Parlement and upon the political behavior of the magistrates in the fifteenth century. Consider, for example, the fate of the clients of the dukes of Burgundy during the convulsions that shook the kingdom in the early fifteenth century. In 1417 several *parlementaires* who were known supporters of Duke John the Fearless were removed from their offices. But in 1418 the duke was able to retaliate by dismissing the Parlement and then reconstructing it to include his own followers. When Charles VII returned to Paris in 1436 he, in turn, reconstituted the Parlement, dropping several "Burgundians" and replacing them with men from his Parlement in exile at Poitiers. At the same time, however, he had to agree to let Duke Philip the Good name twelve members of the Parlement in the future, and Philip used this alienated royal prerogative to look after his own legists.[9] When Louis XI came to the throne in 1461, after having spent

---

7 The only extracts I have found with any material at all from this period are A.N. U 113 and MS. 14434 in the Bibliothèque Royale in Brussels.

8 Commines, 51.

9 *Journal de Clément de Fauquembergue*, ed. A. Tuetey and Henri Lacaille (Paris, 1903-1909), 1.40, 141; Maugis, 1.57-60, 62-68; Roland Delachenal, "Une clause de la Paix d'Arras: les counseilleurs bourguignons dans le Parlement de Charles VII," *Bulletin de la Société de l'histoire de Paris et de l'Ile-de-France* 18 (1891) 76-83.

five years as a guest of Philip the Good, a number of his first appointments to the Parlement, not surprisingly, went to legists whose families had past connections with the dukes of Burgundy.[10]

The count of Charolais, son of Duke Philip the Good, was one of the leaders of the *Ligue du bien public*. His leadership and the resources which he and his father furnished the coalition helped give the league a decidedly "Burgundian" character. Given the previous episodes of Burgundian interference in the royal administration and the "Burgundian" character of the rising in 1465, it should not come as much of a surprise to learn that the most prominent member of the Parlement alleged to have supported the league in 1465, the *Premier Président* Mahieu de Nanterre, came from an old legist family of Paris that had in the past been associated with the dukes of Burgundy.[11] There were other magistrates in the court with Burgundian political connections and perhaps some or all of them felt that loyalty and obedience to their erstwhile patron was absolutely necessary for their own political survival. Then, too, other prominent leaguers besides the duke of Burgundy must have had allies within the Parlement since that body presumably also numbered among its personnel legists who had formerly been pensioned as lawyers or procurators by other league nobles to handle their legal matters at the Parlement.[12]

There is reason to believe, however, that more than the private political allegiances of what was undoubtedly a minority of the magistrates lay behind the court's equivocal behavior in 1465. The leaguers did purport to stand for the public good, and in their appeals for support they did present the inhabitants of Paris with a political program calculated to make the notables of Paris declare in favor of the rebellion. It is true that the basic issue the nobles seized upon was extremely simplistic — the bad government of Louis XI and the need for a thorough housecleaning of his administration.[13] But in so doing they

---

10 *Avocat du roi* Guillaume de Ganay and councillors Jean de Longueil, Guillaume Aguenin, Jean Boucher and Aymé Le Viste, all installed in 1461.

11 *Journal de Clément de Fauquembergue*, 2.219; John Bartier, *Légistes et gens de finances au XVe siècle* ("Académie Royale de Belgique: Mémoires," vol. 1, no. 2; Brussels, 1957), pp. 384-86; Delachenal, 79. On the "Burgundian" character of the *Ligue du bien public*, see Stein, 104.

12 All prominent nobles retained *avocats* and procurators at the Parlement with an annual pension, customarily renewed. See, for example, the listing of the legal advisors of Duke Francis II of Brittany (B. A. Pocquet du Haut-Jussé, "Le conseil des ducs de Bretagne, 1459-1463," *Bibliothèque de l'Ecole des Chartes* 116 (1958) 165); of those of Philip the Good of Burgundy (Stein, 517); and of those of the dukes of Orléans (B.N. Pièces originales 2161-2164 (dossier 48873), nos. 776, 829, 913, 942-43, 968-69, 986).

13 See, for example, the letters and manifestoes summarized or printed in Stein, 68-69 and 518-

touched upon two matters that must have been of particular interest to
the members of the Parlement: the reform of the administration of
justice and the return to office of several prominent personages whom
Louis XI arbitrarily removed at his accession, either out of spite or
because he wanted to reward favorites and cronies. Office and justice
were the larger political issues.

The leaguers denounced corruption and neglect in the judicial
administration of Louis XI repeatedly from the inception of their
rebellion to the very end of the military campaigns, and they insisted
that provision for judicial reform be written into the Treaty of Con-
flans.[14] They themselves, however, produced no specific reform
proposals at any time. They eventually left this task to a thirty-six man
commission (established by the treaty) which was supposed to introduce
whatever administrative reforms were necessary. Several members of
the Parlement were included in this committee, so one might expect its
work to reflect in some way the interests of the court on the matter of
judicial reform. But the commission produced no reform measures that
were ever officially promulgated. An outbreak of the plague compelled
the commission to move from its original meeting place, and this in-
terruption of its work, along with the demobilization of the princes' armies, allowed Louis XI to dismiss the reformers before they could
produce the expected reforms.[15]

The leaguers' denunciation of the bad councillors of Louis XI raised
another issue that concerned the Parlement. The appointment of better
administrators and, more specifically, the reappointment of the officers
unjustly deprived of their positions at Louis' accession was another in-
sistent demand in the leaguer program for administrative reform.[16] The

19, and in J. Quicherat, "Lettres, mémoires et autres documents relatifs à la guerre du bien public
en l'année 1465," *Documents historiques inédits*, ed. J. Champollion-Figeac, 2 (Paris, 1843), pp. 196-97,
297-99, 384-85. The most articulate spokesman for the cause of reform and for the enterprise of
1465 was the bishop of Lisieux, Thomas Basin, whose justification for the rising is contained in his
Histoire de Louis XI, ed. and trans. Charles Samaran (Paris, 1933), bk. 2, ch. 1-3.

14   Articles 12-14 (*Ordonnances des rois de France de la troisième race* (Paris, 1723-1849) 16.381-83).

15   Maupoint, 75-80; Roye, 1.161-62; Léopold Delisle, "Documents parisiens de la Bibliothèque
de Berne," *Mémoires de la Société de l'histoire de Paris et de l'Ile-de-France* 23 (1896) 256-62. The Milanese
ambassador reported that the commission was also empowered to make provision to royal offices
(*Dépêches des ambassadeurs milanais* 4.37).

16   It was made in a list of demands presented to Louis XI on 12 September (Maupoint, 74-75)
and was acknowledged explicitly by Louis XI when he made changes in the composition of the
judicial administration early in November (Quicherat, 403-5; Roye, 1.138-39). See also Basin, bk. 1,
ch. 6-7; Quicherat, 384-85; Roye, 2.169-70; and Henri de Surirey de Saint-Remy, *Jean II de Bourbon,
Duc de Bourbonnais et d'Auvergne* (Paris, 1944), p. 115.

league contended that the self-seekers and favorites who had obtained offices from Louis XI upon his accession at the expense of the good servitors of Charles VII were to blame for most of the ills in the administration. While the leaguers themselves did not go beyond demanding personnel changes and the appointment of good and honest administrators in the future, their initiative provided those Parisians having a particular interest in these questions with an opportunity to make their interests known to Louis XI, too. The king's administrators were such a group and they were particularly interested in two problems underlying the specific questions raised by the nobles, namely the procedures for appointing to royal offices and the guarantee of tenure in office.[17]

What they wanted can readily be deduced from the concessions that Louis XI was forced to grant the Parisians in the autumn of 1465 in the course of his negotiations for a final settlement with the leaders of the league.[18] At that time he made a number of changes in the personnel of his administration and he promised to change the method of nomination to judicial office. Later on, he acceded to their wishes for greater security of tenure. The importance of these questions to both Louis XI and the Parisians is evident in the king's earlier attempts to regain the support of the Parisians without giving ground on any of these three points, and on the refusal of the Parisian notables to succumb to his alternative proposals.[19] Unlike reform of the administration of justice, which could be put off until interest in it subsided enough that it could finally be ignored, these problems about office-holding could not be left unsettled if Louis XI expected to assure himself of the loyalty of his Parisian subjects.

The first of his concessions to the Parisians, the one specifically requested by the leaders of the league, was the restoration to their offices of a number of administrators who had been removed at the ac-

---

17 Commines, 51.

18 There is no evidence of direct negotiations between Louis XI and the Parlement over the demands of the latter. But the king was compelled to bring members of some of the prominent corporate bodies of the city, the Parlement included, into his council for the negotiations with the nobles. This may have provided the occasion and the means for the Parisians involved to have pressed their demands (Maupoint, 74-77, 80, 91-95).

19 He initially hoped to deter them from siding with his enemies by trying to show that the real motive of his opponents was personal gain and not solicitude for the common good (Quicherat, 213-14), and then by making fiscal and other material concessions to the Parisians (*Dépêches des ambassadeurs milanais* 3.284; Maupoint, 58-60).

cession of Louis XI.[20] When this operation was nearly completed, Louis XI made his capitulation to the Parlement on the matter of its recruitment. On 12 November he wrote the court announcing that he intended to restore an old recruitment procedure, favored by the magistrates but neglected for some time. This was the election of members by the magistrates themselves. Henceforth when an office became vacant the court was to elect three individuals of known capability, and from the list the king would select one for the office.[21] It was another two years before Louis XI openly acknowledged the interests of the magistrates in the matter of tenure. On 27 October 1467 he informed the Parlement that henceforth no holder of a royal office would be removed arbitrarily. The only occasions upon which a royal office could change hands were to be the death of the holder, his voluntary resignation of the office, or his forfeiture of the office declared by the appropriate judicial authorities following the proper legal procedures.[22] Although not directly a result of the political disturbance of 1465, this measure was introduced just as another coalition of nobles threatened to begin a military campaign and once again move upon Paris, a situation highly reminiscent of that of 1465.[23] There can be little doubt that Louis XI, mindful of the near disaster of 1465, made this extreme concession in an effort to attach the magistrates and other office-holders firmly to his side before the new coalition of nobles could enlist their support.[24]

Of these three concerns — judicial reform, recruitment procedures, and security of tenure — the last has since 1465 received by far the most attention. Not only was it the only one specifically singled out by Commines, but its primary importance was attested to by Louis XI him-

---

20   *Dépêches des ambassadeurs milanais* 3.100-1; Roye, 1.126, 138-40; Maupoint, 91-95. The text of the royal letter reinstating Guillaume Jouvenal as chancellor has been published by Quicherat (403-5).

21   *Ordonnances des rois de France* 16.441. This was essentially a reissue of an article in an ordinance issued by Charles VII in 1446 (*ibid.* 13.472). Two months later Louis XI extended this procedure to the Parlement of Toulouse (B.N. MS. Fr. 22407, fol. 19r) and he seems to have done so to the Parlement of Bordeaux as well (*Lettres de Louis XI*, ed. J. Vaesen and E. Charavay (Paris, 1883-1909), 3.85). For a recent evaluation of election to judicial office at the turn of the fifteenth century, see Françoise Autrand, "Offices et officiers royaux en France sous Charles VI," *Revue historique* 242 (1969) 313-19.

22   *Ordonnances des rois de France* 17.25-27.

23   Stein, 206 ff.

24   The purpose of the edict, as announced in the preamble, was "to extirpate their doubt and provide security for them in our service so that they might have cause to act and persevere in our service as they ought."

self. In 1482, shortly before his death, he prepared a sort of political testament for his son, the future Charles VIII, in which he commanded the youth not to upset the composition of the administration when he came to the throne, using his own experience to illustrate why the existing personnel should be confirmed in office. The troubles of 1465, Louis explained, were a direct result of the administrative juggling that he performed in 1461. By paying no heed to the demand of royal office-holders for security in their offices he drove them into opposition and nearly lost his throne.[25]

Louis' political testament, with its explanation of the *Ligue du bien public* as the retribution for the mistakes he made in 1461, was cited in influential and widely circulated works written in the sixteenth century, notably Jean Bodin's *Six livres de la République* and Charles Loyseau's *Cinq livres des offices*. Both jurists were primarily interested in the ordinance of 1467 assuring the security of the office-holder against arbitrary removal. Each linked Louis' promise in 1467 directly to the rising of 1465, and reiterated the argument of Louis XI that the rising of 1465 was in turn linked directly to the dismissal of office-holders in 1461.[26] These important works thus served to perpetuate the view that the problem of tenure was what lay behind the troubles in 1465, a view which Louis XI himself had borrowed from the propaganda of the league for his political testament.

As it happens we are not compelled to rely solely upon this indirect evidence in order to reconstruct the aims and desires of the magistrates at the time of the *Ligue du bien public*. Bound into a fifteenth-century compendium now in the Bibliothèque de l'Arsenal in Paris is a copy of

---

25 *Ordonnances des rois de France* 19.58-59.

26 Bodin: "... venant à la couronne [Louis XI] desappointa tout à coup les anciens serviteurs de son père, qui le manierent si bien qu'il fut à un poinct pres de quitter, comme il confessa depuis, ou de perdre sa couronne et son estat; et craignant que son fils ne tombast au mesme precipice, il luy enjoignit de ne changer ceux qu'il avoit avancés: Et non content, il fit ordonnance par laquelle il declaira tous les offices perpetuels: et ceux qui en seryent pourveus, n'en pourroyent estre destituées, que par resignation, mort ou forfaiture," *Les six livres de la République* (Lyons, 1579), p. 416. Loyseau: "Louis XI ... à son avènement changea la plupart des principaux officiers du Royaume, que fut l'une des principales causes de cette mémorable guerre civile, nommée Bien Public: ce qu'ayant bien reconnu, il ordonne en l'an 1467 que désormais les officiers de France ne pourroient etre destituez sans forfeiture jugée. Même connuissant par expérience la grand utilité de cette sienne ordonnance, et craignant qu'après son décèz elle ne fut non plus observée que celle de Philippe le Bel, il s'avisa quinze ans après qu'elle fut faite, et étant au lict de la mort, de la faire jurer par Charles VIII, son fils et successor, luy remontrant (dit l'histoire) que l'observation d'icelle feroit une des grandes assurances de son Estat: et non content de la luy avoir fait jurer, il envoya tout à l'instant au Parlement l'acte du serment pour y être publié et enregistré," *Oeuvres* (Paris, 1660), p. 30.

368 C. W. STOCKER

a letter of instruction addressed by the Parlement to three of its members who had been delegated to remonstrate with Louis XI in the name of the court. The letter appears to be the text of the statement the three were to present to him. To all intents and purposes, therefore, it is the equivalent of a remonstrance of the Parlement. Although the copy is undated and the situation that occasioned its preparation is not mentioned in the text, on the basis of internal evidence it is possible to place the time of its composition with certainty between May 1466 and October 1467. It is reasonably safe to assume, therefore, that the grievances presented in this letter were also the matters of greatest concern to the magistrates at the time of the *Ligue du bien public*.[27]

The letter is made up of twenty-five articles grouped into five numbered sections, each of which (excepting the last) focuses upon a single clearly defined problem. The first section is the longest. Its ten articles all touch in one way or another upon the increasing use made by Louis XI of an informal and special judicial agency known as the Grand Conseil. The Grand Conseil was not a settled court like the Parlement. It was a tribunal composed of a small number of judges commissioned to meet with the king on an *ad hoc* basis to hear judicial disputes that had been evoked from the established courts, particularly the Parlement.[28]

The six articles of the second section protested strongly against another form of interference with the judicial activity of the court

27 Bibliothèque de l'Arsenal, MS. 2450, fols. 290-297v. This copy of the letter was made by Germain Chartelier, a notary at the *greffe* of the Parlement from 1479 to 1493. It is bound together with several other extracts and copies made by Chartelier of material taken primarily from the registers of the Parlement. This particular item seems to have been copied from the registers of the *greffe civile*. For a more detailed description of the whole *recueil* see H. Martin, *Catalogue des manuscrits des bibliothèques de France: Bibliothèque de l'Arsenal* 3 (Paris, 1887), pp. 8-10.

The copy of the letter does not contain a date, but the letter must have been prepared sometime between May 1466 and late autumn, 1467, since one of the three magistrates to whom it was addressed, President Adam Cousinot, only obtained his office in May 1466, while the *greffier* at the Parlement who signed the letter, Jean Cheneteau, left the office of *greffier* to take an office of councillor in the Parlement in December 1467 (B.N. MS. Fr. 32140, fol. 178). Thus the preparation of this remonstrance could well have been connected with the meetings of the reform commission in 1466. One of the three addressees, President Le Sellier, was a member of that commission (Delisle, "Documents parisiens," p. 262). It is also possible, however, that a reference in a letter of Louis XI dated 26 July 1467 (*Ordonnances des rois de France* 17.2-7) to a recent protest from the magistracy is in fact a reference to the presentation of this remonstrance, which could well mean that the remonstrance was drawn up in 1467. This letter of Louis XI is in fact a direct reply to one particular item mentioned in the remonstrance, the payment of the wages of the magistrates (below, p. 370).

28 The emergence and early history of the Grand Conseil has been traced by Noel Valois in the introduction to his *Inventaire des arrêts du Conseil d'Etat: règne de Henri IV* (Paris, 1886). For the theoretical foundations of this form of royal intervention in the operation of the judicial bureaucracy see below pp. 378-79.

equally objectionable to the magistrates. Apparently Louis XI had been permitting persons with lawsuits pending before the Parlement to obtain letters from the royal chancery ordering the magistrates to suspend or alter the normal routine for processing these suits. Such intervention was, of course, invariably to the advantage of the litigants who had solicited it. The magistrates singled out in the letter six specific forms of procedural interference as samples of the king's ill-advised tampering with the established judicial process.

The third topic, the nomination to office in the Parlement, was dealt with very briefly. The magistrates simply requested that Louis XI implement the ordinance of November 1465, intended to restore elective recruitment. The fourth section was devoted to problems arising out of the payment of the wages of the magistrates. Some time ago Edouard Maugis pointed out that no single issue caused more debates, remonstrances and confrontations between the king and the Parlement than that of wage payments.[29] This was because payments were invariably in arrears and often were not made in full even then. So it is no surprise to find the matter raised in this letter.

There were two problems regarding wage payments that worried the magistrates: the reassignment to other purposes of those revenues originally allocated to furnish their wages, and the size of the total allocation itself. To furnish the revenue necessary to pay the magistrates for their services, the king customarily set aside the profits from the sale of salt at certain specified royal salt depots. But in order to meet the financial obligations that he had incurred in the accords he made with individual leaguer princes in 1465, Louis XI had been compelled to alienate to them the revenues from some of the salt depots customarily reserved for the payment of the magistrates. This amputation of the resources which produced their salaries, coupled with a slowdown in the sales of salt, left the magistrates short two months of their pay from the previous year. The size of the current allocation was itself a problem because Louis had been dipping into the funds that were supposed to be used to pay the regular wages of the whole court in order to establish supplementary pensions for a few select members of the court, and because he had been giving certain members of the court permission to collect wage payments for periods when they were not in attendance at the Parlement, payments which also had to come from those funds. This latter privilege was in open contravention of the

29 Maugis, 1.460.

established usage whereby the magistrates were paid their daily wage allotment for only those days on which they were in attendance at the Palais.

Having learned shortly before they prepared this remonstrance that the sum set aside for their wages for the current session was only 28,000 *livres*, although to meet the additional pensions it should have amounted to over 31,000 *livres*, the magistrates duly protested that they could not leave their "patrimonies, their own affairs and ... their benefices [in the church]" to serve the king unless their wages were paid in full, and requested Louis XI to arrange to have the proper sum assigned upon sources of revenue "in safe places of assured receipt."[30]

Although the remonstrance itself said nothing more specific about pensions and nothing at all about the payment of wages to absentees, it is evident that those members of the Parlement who did not benefit from these two special favors must have launched formal complaints about these abuses twice in this period, once in 1465 and again in 1467. For on 12 November 1465, the same day that he announced his intention to restore elective recruitment, Louis XI promised that all ordinary wage assignations would be met before he authorized any special payments for favored members of the court.[31] Again, on 26 July 1467, he made a similar promise, this time referring in vague terms to a recent complaint that the magistrates had made to him on this score.[32]

The letter of instruction concluded with two single items, a request that Louis XI stop remitting the customary fines against those who made appeals from the decisions of lower courts that were not upheld in the appellate courts, and an explanation of the Parlement's refusal to install two men (not named) whom the king had recently given offices there. The offices they were given, apparently, were two clerical councillorships that Louis XI had earlier promised to suppress in order to equalize the number of lay and clerical councillorships in the Parlement.[33]

From this brief summary of the remonstrance it would appear, rather surprisingly in view of what the other evidence seemed to suggest, that the major concern of the magistrates at the time of the *Ligue du bien*

30 Article 22.
31 *Ordonnances des rois de France* 16.439-40.
32 *Ibid.*, 17.2-7, and above, n. 27.
33 Councillorships in the Parlement were designated as lay or clerical, and were supposed to be held by legists of the appropriate status. At the time of Louis' accession there were 42 clerical councillorships and 38 lay councillorships and he decided there should be 40 of each (Maugis, 1.82).

public was the proper structure and functioning of the judicial administration, rather than matters related to tenure or recruitment. The explanation of the points at issue in 1465 and the circumstances which lay behind them offered by Louis XI and repeated by Bodin and Loyseau is hardly to be found in the letter the Parlement forwarded to the king in 1466 or 1467. The treatment it accords the recruitment and tenure question is quite different. To be sure, the magistrates, like the nobles who entered the *Ligue du bien public*, professed their concern over the provision of ill-qualified men to judicial office. But the root of the problem, as traced in this account, was that the king was at the mercy of office-seekers able, because of their proximity to him, to take advantage of his willingness to make provisions to office on the basis of their requests. Caught by surprise, not sufficiently informed of the character or professional competence of the candidates put forward, betrayed by chancery officials who could be pressured or cajoled into preparing unauthorized letters of provision, or worn down by the persistence of those imploring him, in other words, extremely vulnerable, Louis XI had to let others initiate the provision to royal offices.[34] The magistrates thus took the position that the real problem in the recruitment of the judiciary was too little direct royal initiative, rather than too much, as many critics of Louis XI would have it.

The view that Louis XI was a harassed king, unable to say "no" because he was uninformed or because there was too much pressure on him, a king who appears to have lost the initiative in recruiting his administration, if indeed he ever possessed it, is certainly at variance with the usual portrait of this ruler. Can it be taken seriously as a valid picture of how he made provision to office in the years after 1461? It was of course thoroughly conventional and very much safer for critics of the regime to put the blame for ills in the government elsewhere than upon the shoulders of the king. Usually they singled out for their attacks bad councillors and administrators who kept the truth from him, advanced their own interests while in office, and misused his authority for their own advantage in ways he could not always detect or correct. And one would expect a cautious approach of just this sort to cloak a remonstrance critical of a king as jealous of his authority and vengeful as Louis XI. But conventional though the approach taken in the remonstrance may be, it does contain more than a grain of truth. Royal offices

---

34 So they defended elective recruitment with the argument that it would "obvier à ce que led. Seigneur par importunité de requérans ne mectre à ladicte court gens non expers ni expérimentez en justice," (article 18).

had for a long time openly been given in response to the entreaties of courtiers and royal familiars. This was the easiest way for the king to find enough names for the mounting number of positions he had to fill. And, too, the strength of his position depended in part upon his success in satisfying the great nobles, one of whose demands and expectations was a liberal distribution of royal offices to their own dependents and clients.[35] Doubtless the magistrates were correct, as well, in laying some of the blame upon the connivance of the officers of the chancery in Paris, whose activities, we know, often enough escaped royal control.[36]

Certainly what documentation we have of the provision to royal office during the reign of Louis XI does support the argument advanced in the remonstrance. Those around the king did use their familiarity to press candidates for offices upon him, and he very obviously had to bow before some of this pressure.[37] Among the papers of Jean Bourré, one of his chief aides, there are a number of written petitions for office that office-seekers forwarded to Bourré which testify plainly to the practice of solicitation from below.[38] Moreover, Louis XI himself admitted in letters sent to the Parlement both before and after the *Ligue du bien public* (in 1464 and again in 1469) that he had habitually issued provision to offices in response to the entreaties of office-seekers, reserving for them offices not yet vacant or sometimes even indiscriminately, though accidentally, assigning them offices still occupied.[39] And in the famous letter of 1467, which purported to assure royal office-holders of their tenure and prevent arbitrary dismissals, Louis XI stated specifically that his arbitrary removal of officers in the past was strictly inadvertent and should be attributed to the zeal of those unscrupulous persons who took advantage of the fact that he was not fully informed and asked for offices that were already filled.

35   C. Stocker, "Office as Maintenance in Renaissance France," *Canadian Journal of History* 6 (1971) 24-25.

36   On the problem that fifteenth-century monarchs had in policing the operation of the chancery and preventing the unauthorized preparation and signing of royal letters see G. Tessier, "L'audience du sceau," *Bibliothèque de l'Ecole des Chartes* 109 (1951) 51-95. The character and conduct of the chancery officers of Louis XI was roundly censured by the Estates General of 1484 (Jehan Masselin, *Journal des Etats-Généraux de France tenus à Tours en 1484*, ed. Adhelm Bernier (Paris, 1835), pp. 682, 684-85).

37   *E.g.*, B.N. MS. Fr. 20491, fol. 48; MS. Fr. 20490, fol. 43; *Lettres de Louis XI* 4.241; B.N. MS. Fr. 2912, fol. 63; B.N. MS. Fr. 2811, fol. 156; B.N. Pièces originales (dossier 18654), no. 20.

38   These *placets*, which Bourré was to advance to Louis XI, are scattered through B.N. MS. 20485-20495, and are especially numerous in the last.

39   Letter of 14 June 1464 (*Lettres de Louis XI* 2.189); letter of 22 October 1469 (*Ordonnances des rois de France* 17.260).

It seems clear, then, that the magistrates viewed the issue of abuses in the nomination to judicial office in much the same way that Louis XI himself did, that is as fundamentally an administrative problem growing out of inadequacies in the procedures employed for making provision to office. Reduced to its essentials, the problem was how to cope with the inevitable pressure of solicitation for office when the king was not in a position to evaluate the quality of the candidates proposed or even to know for certain if the requested office was vacant.

Not surprisingly, the solutions proposed by Louis XI and the Parlement, though different, were both administrative solutions. The magistrates proposed elective nomination in the court and defended it with the argument that no one knew better than the magistrates themselves the names of jurists particularly well-qualified to hold judicial offices, since no one saw as many capable and enterprising practitioners as they did. They stated explicitly that by handing over the initiative to the knowledgeable and impartial judges in the Parlement, the king could no longer be duped into giving offices inadvertently to incompetents. The solution advanced by Louis XI in the famous letter on irremovability of 1467 was also an administrative solution. He instructed the Parlement to refuse to seat anyone with letters to offices that were not actually vacant. In other words the court itself was to exercise the function of *contrôle* over such provisions; however, it was not to initiate those provisions. This anticipates Louis' solution to the problem of multiple provisions set forth in the letter of 1469, referred to above. Here, too, the administrative solution was to give the magistrates a form of *contrôle* by making it their responsibility to settle the disputed office upon the candidate whose letters were drawn up after the office actually became vacant, a solution that left Louis XI in control of the actual nomination when the time came to fill an office, but still allowed him to promise *expectatives* and thus rid himself of pressures from persistent seekers of office.[40]

What, though, of the question of tenure, linked by Louis XI, Bodin and Loyseau to the dismissals of 1461, and alleged by Commines to have

---

40 "Comme depuis nostre avènement à la couronne, plusieurs mutations ayent esté faictes en noz offices, laquelle chose est en la pluspart advenue à la poursuite et subjection d'aucuns et nous non advertiz duement; par quoy, ainsy que entendu avons et bien cognoissons estre vraysemblable, plusieurs de noz officiers, doubtant cheoir audict inconvenient de mutation et de destitution, n'ont pas tel zèle et ferveur à nostre service qu'ilz auroient..." Obviously he did not expect an end to surprises of this sort. But with this proposal there was now a procedure to deal with them when they happened.

been a major interest of the magistracy in 1465? It may not necessarily be correct to assume that, because this was nowhere mentioned specifically in the remonstrance, the matter of security in office was not a very important consideration of the magistrates at this time. For if the cause of arbitrary dismissals was primarily the carelessness of the king when he gave in to those who pestered him for offices, as they both said was the case, then by giving the magistrates the initiative in provision to office (through the restoration of elective recruitment) the major threat to the security of the office-holder would disappear. For inasmuch as the magistrates could be expected to have full knowledge of which offices were vacant and which were not, if they were to initiate nominations there would be little likelihood of provision being made to an office that was still occupied. Election, in other words, could solve the tenure problem as well as the recruitment problem and perhaps the magistrates simply did not deem it necessary to spell this out any more explicitly.

The other possible explanation of their failure to do so is that they were not as concerned about the matter as is sometimes imagined. The fact is, there simply were no great dismissals of members of the court either in 1461 or at any point prior to the uprising in 1465. Upon his accession Louis XI did change the ranking of some of the presidents of the *Grand'Chambre* and did dismiss the *gens du roi* (the *procureur-général* and the two *avocats du roi* who defended the interests of the crown), but these latter could be considered the king's own men in the court in a way that the councillors themselves could not. Other than that, the Parlement was confirmed in 1461 as it stood.[41] The disappearance of the registers of the court makes it impossible to determine whether his actions between 1462 and 1469 jeopardized the tenure of the magistrates or caused them any particular concern on this score. Fragmentary extracts from original registers now lost furnish only one instance, that early in 1465, when the king threatened to remove a councillor of the Parlement. On two occasions when there was no recognized vacancy Louis promised to award the next office to become vacant to specific individuals, but on neither occasion did he attempt to remove an officer forcibly in order to make room for the beneficiary. In fact, in one of the two cases Louis XI created an extraordinary office for the new ap-

41 Maugis, 1.80-81 and 3.332, 336; *Ordonnances des rois de France* 15.13-14. It was, however, rumored that Louis XI did at one time entertain the idea of making quite substantial changes in the composition of the Parlement (Georges Chastellain, *Oeuvres*, ed. Kervyn de Lettenhove (Brussels, 1863-1866), 4.39-41; "Fragment d'une chronique du règne de Louis XI," ed. A. Coulon, *Ecole française de Rome: Mélanges d'archéologie et d'histoire* 15 (1895) 137-38).

pointee to hold until an ordinary office should become vacant through normal means.[42]

Before proceeding to the issue that lay at the heart of the remonstrance, judicial reform, an explanation of why Louis XI took such pains to connect the disaffection of the administrators with the tenure question, and in particular with the dismissals of 1461 should be offered. The political testament ceases to be puzzling as soon as one realizes that it cannot be taken at face value. The main point it makes — that as a result of the dismissals of 1461 and the revolt of 1465 Louis XI learned that he must not arbitrarily dismiss his office-holders — is completely at variance with what we know of Louis' actions after 1465. His subsequent handling of the provision to offices leaves no doubt that if he learned anything at all from the experience of the *Ligue du bien public*, it was not that he must refrain from depriving royal officers of their offices, but precisely the opposite. Henceforth he would have to take a greater interest in the provision to office than he had done previously, doing whatever was necessary to assure himself that those who occupied royal offices were completely trustworthy and unshakably loyal to him personally. This included removing from office anyone of whose personal fidelity he was not certain. In the case of the Parlement of Paris, it appears that the arbitrary promotions and dismissals which caused the greatest anxiety within the magistracy all came after, not before, 1465.[43] This new awareness on the part of the king also manifested itself in his insistence upon the fidelity of the officer, which he asserted directly in the 1469 letter to the Parlement concerning multiple provisions,[44] and again in his political testament. In the latter document Louis' openly stated belief that the personal fidelity of the individual was the primary consideration in the staffing of the administration is in fact given as the reason why he insisted upon the confirmation of his own officers in their offices after his death.[45]

42 A.N. U 113, fol. 1; B.N. MS. N.a.fr. 8037, fol. 72v.

43 Maugis, 1.80-100; B. de Mandròt, "Jacques d'Armagnac, duc de Nemours, 1433-1477," *Revue historique* 44 (1890) 295-307; *Lettres de Louis XI* 8.26. When the Parlement balked at some of his appointments and at these dismissals he told them, "C'est à nous de faire et disposer de noz offices et estaz à notre plaisir, et ainsi sommes délibérez le faire" (*ibid.*, 7.231-32) and "quant vous aurez des offices, vous en pourvoyerez voz gens, car des miennes j'en veus faire à mon appetit, et non pas au vostre; et ne plus en tuez plus la teste, car je le veux ainsi" (*ibid.*, 8.315).

44 "Nous désirons, quant ladicte vacation escherra, y estre pourveu de gens souffisans et à nous féables..." (*Ordonnances des rois de France* 17.260). It is significant that whereas the 1464 letter to the Parlement instructed the magistrates to seat whichever candidate for the disputed office had the earliest letters of provision, this letter instructs them to give the office to the most recent provision, the one issued after the office was known to be vacant.

45 "Nous lui avons aussi par exprès commande, ordonné et enjoinct que quant il plaira à Dieu

The reason Louis XI should have taken the trouble to falsify deliberately the lesson he learned from the events of 1465 was suggested some time ago by Maugis. What Louis XI wanted most of all, as he neared death, was to make certain that his son and heir retained all the administrators whom the old king had brought into the royal administration in the latter years of his reign. These particular individuals were men Louis XI felt could be trusted to preserve the authority of the monarchy after his passing. Knowing that Charles would be pressured to dismiss his father's favorites and reinstate those who had been removed from office, Louis felt that he had to make as forceful and convincing a case for the retention of the incumbent administration as he could.[46] What could be a better way to make his point (or a more traditional one for that matter) than by citing for the instruction of the Dauphin a "lesson of history", one that would appear particularly convincing inasmuch as the instructor avowed that he himself had learnt it the hard way. It is as a piece of political advice, not as a serious attempt to understand the opposition of his office-holders in 1465, that the political testament of Louis XI must be read.

Judging from the priority that it was accorded in the remonstrance, judicial reform, rather than tenure and recruitment procedures, was the uppermost concern of the magistrates at the time of the *Ligue du bien public*, and it is to this question that we must now turn. This hitherto rather neglected interest of the magistracy emerges quite clearly in the initial sections, also the longest, of the document. Although the magistrates made very plain their complete agreement with the leaguers that the administration of justice needed to be reformed, they did not see the problem in quite the same light as did the nobles. The latter generally attributed the abuses in the judicial administration of Louis XI to his appointment of bad men to judicial office, that is, to the moral character of the justiciars. The magistrates, who could hardly assent to this proposition, ascribed the perversion of royal justice to procedural problems, not to the poor quality of the judiciary. Reduced

---

qu'il parvienne à ladicte couronne de France, qu'il entretienne es charges et offices qu'il trouvera estre lesdits seigneurs de nostre sang et lignaige, les autres seigneurs, barons, gouverneurs, chevaliers, escuiers, capitaines et chiefz de guerre, et tous autres ayant charge, garde et conduicte de gens, villes, places et forteresses, et les officiers ayans offices tant de judicature que autres de quelque manière et condicion que lesditz officiers et charges soient, sans aucunement les changer, muer, descharger ne desappoincter, ne aucun d'eulx, sinon toutes voyes qu'il feust et soit trouve qu'ilz ou les aucuns d'eulz feussent et soient autres que bons et loyaulx..." (*Ordonnances des rois de France* 19.58).

46   Maugis, 1.80, 96.

to its essentials, the argument of the magistrates was that justice was less likely to be corrupted when dispensed by regularly established judicial agencies following traditional administrative practices, than when it was left to casual agencies like the Grand Conseil, or when ordinary agencies were compelled to abandon established usages and procedures and follow instructions or commands given by the king.

In developing this antithesis the magistrates laid considerable stress upon the importance of the environment in which judges had to function. They pointed to two conditions they believed necessary if the magistrate were to work properly: first, he had to be left alone, away from political pressure,[47] and second, he had to be settled in one place, notably a place where he could consult with other learned jurists and where he had access to law books, copies of old laws and ordinances, and records of past judicial decisions.[48] With the first condition they showed their displeasure at Louis' habit of commanding that the Parlement alter or suspend normal procedures in order to favor certain parties, and with both they took a slap at the Grand Conseil. Fluctuating in composition, itinerant with the king and small enough to be overawed by him, this assemblage was pointedly contrasted to the Parlement of Paris, an established *corps* composed of a permanent and large body of judges, established in one place where judicial records and other expert judicial counsel abounded.[49]

47   "Et que justice vraye et parfaicte doit estre libéralement faicte et distribuée, s'est assavoir les jugemens des hommes faiz en couraige et entendement franc sans contraincte. Et que autrement le faire ne seroit pas jugement car ung jugement ou sentence de Raison sont ditz l'oppinion du juge par qui le jugement est fait, et pour ce ung jugement fait par constraincte ne peut estre dit jugement. *Quia judicia debent esse libera* et non pas faiz a l'apétit ou volunté de l'une des parties" (article 11).

48   "... Sans etre translatés de lieu en autre, et est leur administraction telle que requiert l'omme estre solitaire, ne paré et quieté, et avoir lieu où soit l'usaige et fréquentation de gens clercs, de livres, registres, ordonnances et constitucions" (article 3).

49   "Et conviendra exposer aud. Seigneur l'institution de ladicte court de parlement qui a esté instituée par ses prédécesseurs ou nombre des gens qui y sont afin que plus meurement et par grande deliberacion les jugemens des causes et matières des subgetz du royaume y feussent faiz et bonne justice à chacun administrée et les droiz du Roy gardez. Et depuis lad court ainsi instituée le royaume a tousiours esté renommé et recommandé par tout le monde Chrétien et Sarrazin de bonne et entière justice qui est la plus grant gloire qui puisse estre donné au Roy. Et que lad. court est ordonné et establié pour congnoistre en souveraineté des causes d'appel des appellacions interiectées des juges subgetz de ce Royaume et autrement, et aussi pour congnoistre ordinairement du demaine du Roy, des causes des pers de France, des régales et autres qui de leur nature et condicion si pour la grandeur d'icelle et selon les ordonnances royalux y doivent estre traictés," (article 1); "et n'est lad. court de Parlement instituée et establie et non sans cause en la ville de Paris pour ce que en icelle y a grant nombre de gens de conseil," (article 2); "et pour ce que les Roys le temps passé ont tousjours eu singulièrement l'euil à l'entretènement de lad. court, ont voulu et or-

The magistrates supported the argument in favor of fixity and centralization by citing another benefit in addition to the assurance of the impartiality of the judge that this provided. It was much easier, they said, for litigants to find the expert legal help they needed when they went to court if the Parlement was settled permanently in one place. For in such a place, as was already the case in Paris, there would be a large community of lawyers and *procureurs*. But when judges moved about, they argued, it was very difficult for litigants to find professional legal assistance. And even if they did happen to find a lawyer or *procureur* at some spot where the itinerant judges paused, as soon as the tribunal resumed its peregrinations the litigants were deprived of that aid and had to search for counsel all over again somewhere else.[50] This was no small problem because, in their view, without good professional counsel a litigant could easily be victimized by an unscrupulous adversary who did not in fact have the law on his side. Justice, they implied, depended upon good lawyers as well as upon good judges. And good lawyers only congregated where judicial institutions were settled.

In spite of their opposition to procedural meddling and evocations, the remonstrance contains no formal challenge to the *right* of Louis XI to interfere in the administration of justice. The reason, very simply, is that the Parlement had no theoretical grounds for doing so. Legal theory and customary usage stood against it. The king was the source of the justice administered in his name; judicial authority over his subjects reposed, as it were, in his person. While practical necessities obliged him to delegate most of his judicial business to royal officials established for that particular purpose, he could never delegate all the judicial authority that inhered in his royal person, however many judges or courts he established. His judicial authority was inexhaustible; but more than that, the justice which remained in his person after all the delegations were made, the *justice retenue* as it was called, was his truly sovereign justice, higher than that exercised by any of his delegates. In his presence there could be no other justice, and indeed no other judges. This conception was given vivid illustration in the ceremony of the *lit de justice*, during which the king entered the Parlement to take his place in the seat reserved for him. From there he could impress his will upon the magistrates, all of whose judicial

*

donné que gens notables clercs et expers en fait de justice et en grant nombre feussent mis en icelle afin que la justice souveraine de ce royaume feust mieux conduicté et administrée au bien et honneur du Roy et de ses subgetz...' (article 4).

50   Articles 2, 5 and 6.

authority upon such occasions may be said to have flowed back into his person. It was this same conception that justified his "interference" in the normal routine of the judicial administration and provided the theoretical underpinning for the establishment of the informal Grand Conseil for settling, in close contact with the king himself, cases evoked from other jurisdictions.[51]

Since, therefore, the magistrates could not challenge the *right* of the king to intervene in the operation of the judicial administration, they preferred to sidestep theoretical issues in favor of practical considerations, hoping in that way to shift the discussion from the legal to the moral plane. In the remonstrance the essential question thus became not what the king could or could not do, but what he should or should not do. Taking the same tack that they had used on the recruitment question, the *parlementaires* laid the blame for Louis' interference in the administration of royal justice upon those private individuals who wheedled and coaxed him into making use of the *justice retenue*.[52] Once again the ill to be reformed was seen as an almost inevitable consequence of the king's helplessness in the face of those in his entourage who would take advantage of his ignorance to further their own selfish ambition and interest. The magistrates were careful to point out that the only persons who sought special intercession of this sort were individuals who knew that they would otherwise lose their lawsuits. It was to evade the law that they appealed to the *justice retenue*.[53]

Not surprisingly, the remedy that the Parlement advocated for this ill was essentially the same as the one advanced to meet problems arising out of solicitation for offices. To put an end to abuses in the administration of justice they asked Louis XI to refrain voluntarily from exerting his judicial authority to its fullest limit. Instead he should trust his judges and the established legal procedures which they and their predecessors were accustomed to use. This parallels exactly the magistrates' request that he not press to its limits his authority to initiate provisions to office, but entrust the judges with that responsibility by supporting the established procedure of elective recruitment.[54] Whatever the king's theoretical powers as justiciar, in practice

51 Roger Doucet, *Les institutions de la France au XVIe siècle* 1 (Paris, 1948), pp. 89-90 and 175.

52 Articles 8, 14-16.

53 "Et peut on clerement congnoistre que ceulx qui procurent telz renvoiz et evocacions ne le font que pour fouyr à justice, travailler et molester leurs parties adverses.." (article 8).

54 The magistrates did cite past practices and past ordinances whereby the predecessors of Louis XI did bind themselves to abide by procedures favored by the Parlement (articles 4, 7, 10).

justice would be better if the judicial officials were left to work on their own, for they were far less easily victimized by private parties than he.

What should be emphasized over all is that the magistrates did not press for structural or procedural innovations within the administration, and certainly not for more political authority for the Parlement as a *corps*.[55] The reform of royal justice was their deepest concern, and judicial reform would best be achieved by maintaining the Parlement of Paris in what they argued was its traditional position of judicial authority, that is, by conserving the administrative structure that had already grown up. The essential feature of that structure was the existence of a single court for dispensing the king's sovereign justice. And this one sovereign court[56] was to remain fixed in one place, Paris, where there was already a large enough number of professional jurists to meet the needs of all litigants, and where it was possible to accumulate opinions and written records for the instruction of the judges.

The thrust of this argument quite clearly is that the more completely the administration of justice was centralized and bureaucratized, the more probably its integrity would be preserved. This is a rather remarkable piece of judicial reasoning and tactical strategy, for it required no little boldness on the part of magistracy to trumpet as a virtue characteristics of the judicial administration that had already produced consequences thoroughly disliked by the populace at large. Centralized and bureaucratic justice, as rendered by the Parlement, was slow and complicated. Its procedures and its reasoning were utterly incomprehensible to those who, themselves not lawyers by training, were dependent upon and often exploited by the *gens de loi*. Just how much of a problem the trammels of bureaucratic procedure had become is evident from the repeated attempts of Louis' immediate predecessor and successors to reform judicial procedure and police the activities of lawyers and judges.[56] Nor did others outside the Parlement who were interested in judicial reform have as much enthusiasm for the idea of a single sovereign court as did the magistrates. The late fifteenth century saw the creation of several provincial parlements, undertaken in part as a reform of royal justice responding to the wish of the king's subjects in peripheral or newly incorporated provinces to have the king's sovereign

55 Article 16 contains the phrase "le roy et sa cour souverain." The magistrates also used the term in a remonstrance against evocations in 1489 (A.N.X^la 9323, no. 85).

56 These reforms were embodied in the great ordinances of 1446, 1453, 1493 and 1499 (*Ordonnances des rois de France* 13.471-82; 14.284-314; 20.386-411; 21.177-207.

justice more accessible to them.[57] And whereas the magistrates argued vigorously against the king's use of his *justice retenue* because it led to corruption in the administration of justice, others could still see the *justice retenue* as a means to combat some of the ills within the increasingly complex, impersonal and insufficiently policed judicial administration. Even at the end of the fifteenth century the memory of Saint Louis hearing the complaints of his ordinary subjects under the great oak in the forest of Vincennes was strong enough to inspire Charles VIII to institute pleas at the palace in his presence and to plan special assizes, also in his presence, to be held at various points where he would pause during his travels through the realm.[58] What is of interest here in such a reform program is not its soundness or practicality as a solution to the problem of improving the quality of royal justice, but rather the indication it gives of the persistence of an old and completely different (and to the king more attractive) idea of reform in the administration of justice.

What drove the magistrates to put forth a program of judicial reform that was not only so different but so much less "popular" than the proposals of the leaguers or the reform programs enunciated in the reign of Charles VIII? The remonstrance itself cannot, of course, supply the answer, but it does indicate the direction in which the answer probably lies. The characteristic that most clearly distinguishes the reform proposals of the magistrates from the other programs is the great emphasis laid upon the preservation of the judicial function and authority of the Parlement of Paris, so this particular concern is the obvious item to consider first in speculating upon the motives of the magistracy. There are a number of plausible reasons why the Parlement's position as the sole repository of the king's sovereign justice was of concern to the magistrates, all touching upon specific interests acquired by the magistrates as office-holders. First of all, it must be remembered that their offices conferred upon the magistrates a number of material and honorific distinctions which, taken together, made office in the Parlement a considerable dignity, an "estate" of no mean worth. The privileged "estate" of the magistrate found its justification in the very nature, or quality, of the activity which he engaged upon

57 See, for example, the argument advanced in the defense of the judicial sovereignty of the Parlement of Dijon, against the claims of the Parlement of Paris, in an ordinance of 14 March 1478 (*ibid.*, 18.369). The background of the establishment of the first provincial parlements is explained in F. Lot and R. Fawtier, *Histoire des institutions françaises au Moyen Age* 2 (Paris, 1958), pp. 472-500.

58 Commines, 3.305; *Lettres de Charles VIII*, ed. P. Pelicier, 5 (Paris, 1905), pp. 158-59, 167-69.

because of the office he held: dispensing the king's sovereign justice.[59] Important as the privileges and distinctions associated with office-holding were, these were not the sole benefits conferred upon the magistrates as office-holders in the Parlement. Yet more might seem at stake when the judicial authority of the court was threatened. It was the Parlement's position as the king's sovereign court that gave the magistrates responsibility for examining, criticizing and registering royal legislation, a responsibility that provided the court with an opportunity to engage in political debate with the king and his closest aides.[60] Every innovation or move to tinker with the administration which infringed upon the judicial sovereignty of the court and so loosened the close identification of office in the Parlement with the sovereign justice of the king might well have been seen at the Palais as potentially weakening the validity of the justification for the privileges and distinctions attached to these offices or as potentially undercutting the court's broader administrative and political responsibilities, or both.[61]

It may be that their interest in elective recruitment and their opposition to non-resident members drawing full salary from the king were themselves, at least in part, manifestations of the magistrates' concern over the erosion of the judicial authority of the Parlement. Whatever else it was, the giving of offices in the Parlement to ill-qualified or perennially absent magistrates was an indication to the Parlement that in the king's mind the judicial function attached to the office was less important than the usefulness of that office as a source of material support for a favored servitor.[62] And such an attitude was hardly likely to enhance the dignity founded upon the function of the office. So they could well have construed such provisions, too, as a potential threat to the value of their offices, anchored as so much of it was in that dignity.

The fate of the Chambre des Comptes, an institution that through most of the fourteenth century rivalled if indeed it did not surpass the Parlement in political significance and prestige, would have given sub-

59   Above, n. 4.
60   On the judicial foundation of the political activity of the Parlement see, most recently, J. H. Shennan, *The Parlement of Paris* (London, 1968), ch. 5, esp. pp. 156-57. Maugis (1.517-631) provides the best historical survey of the political activity of the Parlement through the sixteenth century.
61   This argument is elaborated more fully in my article, "The Politics of the Parlement of Paris in 1525," *French Historical Studies* 8 (1973) 191-212.
62   Stocker, "Office as Maintenance," *passim.*

stance to such a concern. The magistrates could hardly have failed to notice that beginning in the fifteenth century more and more provisions to office in the Chambre des Comptes had been dictated by the king's concern to furnish loyal aides with maintenance, with the result that this body was filling up with administrative pluralists and non-residents who drew salaries there but served the king on other business. Nor could it have escaped their notice that the administrative importance and the prestige of the Chambre des Comptes were not what they had once been.[63]

Other important action undertaken by the Parlement in the fifteenth century is certainly consistent with the views on office and justice the remonstrance of 1466-67 seems to indicate had grown up within the magistracy. It was in this era that for the first time the Parlement did not cease to function during the interval between the death of one king and the coronation of his successor, defying a usage of long standing that upon the death of a king the tenure and authority of all royal office-holders ceased until and unless they were confirmed in their offices by his successors. And this was also the period in which the presidents of the Parlement began wearing the red robes of their judicial office during the royal funeral ceremony, a usage in striking contrast to the wearing of mourning attire by the other officials of the late king. The refusal both to suspend their activity and to wear mourning on these occasions was intended to demonstrate something about the nature of justice and of judicial office. They were vivid illustrations of the idea that the judicial function of royalty was an eternal thing, distinct from the individual who embodied that function in his lifetime as king.[64] Unlike the human occupant of the royal office, the magistrates were to argue explicitly in 1483, royal justice never dies.[65] The argument clearly implies that those who held judicial office, the magistrates of the Parlement, were the servants first and foremost of this sempiternal function of royalty, undying justice, before they were the servants of the individual who embodied that function during his mortal lifetime. What the magistrates were in fact affirming in these actions was their loyalty to the Parlement as an administrative institution, and more abstractly, their loyalty to the judicial function itself, a bond that could

---

63 Idem, *Offices and Officers in the Parlement of Paris, 1483-1515* (Diss. Cornell, 1965), pp. 287-93.

64 On the Parlement's decision to continue in session after the death of the king in 1461 and in 1483, and on this funerary usage, see Ralph Giesey, *The Royal Funeral Ceremony in Renaissance France* (Geneva, 1960), pp. 54-59, 185-86.

65 A.N. X[la] 1490, fol. 389.

under certain circumstances supersede the personal bond that united them to the king as servitors to their lord. One of those circumstances was the *Ligue du bien public* of 1465. The remonstrance of 1466-67, although focused on other matters pertaining to justice and office-holding, points in the same direction.

It is no accident that the magistrates should have developed and articulated these views at the time they did. These ceremonial and verbal expressions followed closely upon the heels of a progression of extensive changes that profoundly modified the structure of late medieval judicial administration in the direction of further centralization and bureaucratization. Only during the fourteenth and fifteenth centuries did the judicial administration of the king in the *bailliages* and *séné-chaussées* largely become the business of judicial specialists with professional legal training who looked on judicial administration as the substance of a career and might belong to emerging local dynasties of legists and judicial office-holders. Before then the tasks of judicial administration were either farmed out, primarily as financial opportunities, or else entrusted to other royal agents, usually military or financial, as a mere adjunct to their primary administrative responsibilities.[66] In Paris, where careerism and some specialization by function existed considerably earlier, there were significant changes of a different sort. The sheer quantity of judicial business to come before the Parlement, as well as before the local court for the *prévôté* of Paris (the Châtelet), increased considerably during the same period[67] and two new courts were established in Paris near the end of the fourteenth century, the Cour des Aides and the Cour du Trésor.[68] This concentration of judicial business in Paris was to create new opportunities for aspiring legists both inside and outside the city. Provincial legists, who knew very well that the best place to get ahead was Paris because of the unique opportunities for advancement there,[69] moved to Paris. In so doing they contributed significantly to the growth of a new social

---

66 Bernard Guenée, *Tribunaux et gens de justice dans le bailliage de Senlis à la fin du Moyen Age* (Strasbourg, 1963), pp. 135-66, and esp. 376-77.

67 *Ibid.*, pp. 513-27.

68 Gustave Dupont-Ferrier, *Nouvelles études sur les institutions financières de la France à la fin du Moyen Age: les origines et le premier siècle de la Chambre ou Cour des Aides de Paris* (Paris, 1933) and *Les origines et le premier siècle de la Court du Trésor* (Paris, 1936).

69 Jean Jouvenal, a native of Troyes who came to Paris in the late fourteenth century to practice law and was to found one of the great *robe* dynasties of the fifteenth century, told his son "that if he'd known almost any other town in the world where he'd been able to learn more of worth and of honour than Paris, he'd have gone there", quoted by P. S. Lewis, *Later Medieval France* (London, 1968), p. 177.

"milieu" in the capital, the existence of which was to transform the pattern of recruitment for the Parlement. More and more appointees to the court would in the fifteenth century come out of this milieu of lesser judicial officers, lawyers, procurators and notaries in Paris that administrative expansion had spawned.[70]

In addition to this, and related directly to it, the conception of office-holding itself underwent an important refinement. Until well into the fourteenth century the Parlement of Paris was dissolved at the end of each session and reconstituted anew at the beginning of the next. This could hardly encourage legists to develop expectations of life-long careers as office-holders in the Parlement. However, by the second half of the fourteenth century the Parlement had come to be thought of as a permanent body, permanent within the life of the reigning king at least, the membership of which was retained as a matter of course from one session to the next.[71] And not only that, but the idea that an officer should remain in possession of his office unless guilty of a particularly flagrant action gained increasing currency during the fifteenth century. This happened even in spite of plausible juridic arguments against it[72] and in spite of the frequent interruptions of careers in royal administration brought about by the civil wars of the reigns of Charles VI and Charles VII, whose repercussions on the tenure of royal office extended, as already noted, even into the reign of Louis XI. These obstacles were not great enough to prevent either the development of a careerist mentality among legists or the appearance of office-holding dynasties in Paris.

All of the above developments undoubtedly contributed to the formation of that perception of judicial administration by the magistracy that has been described and analyzed above. They encouraged the magistrates to become more professionally conscious and prepared them to envision the holding of judicial office for the king as a career activity even for their children after them. They spurred legists to develop an indentification with the institution in which they served and

70 This process will be illustrated at greater length in a study I am currently preparing of the recruitment and composition of the court between 1461 and 1526.

71 Maugis, 1.1-2; Jacques Kubler, *Recherches sur la fonction publique sous l'ancien régime: l'origine de la perpétuité des offices royaux* (Nancy, 1958), pp. 71-74; J. Viard, "La cour et ses 'Parlements' au XIVᵉ siècle," *Bibliothèque de l'Ecole des Chartes* 79 (1918) 60-65. The study of Raymond Cazelles, *La société politique et la crise de la royauté sous Philippe de Valois* (Paris, 1958) illustrates how closely administrative careerism was tied to the political fortunes of princely patrons, and hence how insecure it was, in the fourteenth century.

72 See most recently, Autrand, "Offices et officiers," esp. pp. 325-28.

the task which they performed. And from such an attitude to the belief that royal justice was purest when left to the duly constituted judicial office-holders is not a very long step, particularly when the protection of the dignity of the office and its holder was at issue.

The remonstrance of 1466-67 was, therefore, more than a simple reaction to problems growing out of the actions of Louis XI, particularly the somewhat exaggerated "purge" of the administration in 1461. To be understood fully, the agitation of the magistracy should be seen in the broader context of the expansion and transformation of royal judicial administration in France during the late fourteenth and fifteenth centuries. If so, one would expect both the general approach to judicial reform adopted in the remonstrance of 1466-67 and the specific proposals advanced in it to be taken up again by the Parlement even after the last reverberations of the *Ligue du bien public* had died away. Such was the case. Evocations, recruitment procedures, wage inequalities, the use of offices for maintenance, the reliance of the king upon the Grand Conseil and *ad hoc* judicial tribunals, and his interference with the routine procedures of the court were all fundamental issues in confrontations between the Parlement and the crown in the period after 1465. To cite just two specific examples, a remonstrance prepared by the Parlement in 1489 on the subject of evocations from the Parlement is highly reminiscent, not only in its argument but even in its phraseology, of the remonstrance of 1466-67,[73] and every one of the above mentioned issues was raised again in the great reform manifesto presented by the court to Louise of Savoy during the captivity of Francis I in 1525.[74] Thus it is not the uniqueness of the demands of the remonstrance of 1466-67 that invests this document with its greatest significance; on the contrary, this letter is especially worthy of note because it is the earliest precise statement from the magistrates of what were to be fundamental political interests of the "renaissance" Parlement.

University of British Columbia

73　A.N. X[1a] 9323, no. 85. Maugis published this remonstrance with some abridgements and summations in his history of the Parlement (1.374-79).

74　My study of the activity of the Parlement in 1525 (above, n. 61) contains a detailed examination of this remonstrance.

CURSUS IN MIDDLE ENGLISH:
A TALKYNG OF ÞE LOUE OF GOD RECONSIDERED

Lois K. Smedick

In a recent article Sherman M. Kuhn has raised again the question of cursus in English.[1] His own examination of the Old English Bede and of other Old English writings has led him to challenge the view that the "late Latin rhetorical device" was used by vernacular writers before the Conquest: "The so-called cursus in Old English literature is nothing more than a part of the natural rhythm of the language" (p. 206). Kuhn suggests further that if methods like his own were used to test what passes for cursus in Middle English and other writings, similar conclusions might be reached for these writings as well. Some years ago I undertook such a study of the fourteenth-century rhythmical prose text, *A Talkyng of þe Loue of God*, the rhythm of which had been associated with the cursus by Margery Morgan.[2] Since my conclusions support Professor Kuhn's suggestion, it may be useful to publish them at this time.

The introduction of the Vernon version (MS. Bodley 3938) of *A Talkyng* describes the style of the treatise in this way:

> Men schal fynden lihtliche þis tretys in
> Cadence. After þe bigynninge. ȝif hit beo
> riht poynted: & Rymed in sum stude. To
> beo more louesum. to hem þat hit reden.[3]

---

1 "Cursus in Old English: Rhetorical Ornament or Linguistic Phenomenon?," *Speculum* 47 (1972) 188-206.

2 See my unpublished doctoral dissertation, "*A Talkyng of þe Loue of God*" *and the Rhythm of Meditation* (Bryn Mawr, 1967). Ms. Morgan discusses the Middle English text in two articles, "*A Talking of the Love of God* and the Continuity of Stylistic Tradition in Middle English Prose Meditations," *RES*, N.S. 3 (1952) 97-116 and "A Treatise in Cadence," *MLR* 47 (1952) 156-164, wherein the connection with cursus is explicitly made.

3 *A Talkyng of þe Loue of God*, ed. M. Salvina Westra (The Hague, 1950), p. 2.

The term "cadence" has been variously construed with reference to this text and to other Middle English writings, the range of meaning being indicated by the *Middle English Dictionary* definition: "rhythm of prose or poetry; rhetorical periods; the use of rhythm or rhetorical periods".[4] Ms. Morgan noted that "cadence" was sometimes loosely used to signify the style associated with formal letter-writing, as prescribed by the handbooks of dictamen. The rhythm of *A Talkyng*, she therefore proposed, may be attributable in part to imitation of the Latin cursus, "probably rightly regarded as the most distinctive feature of official writing in the later mediaeval period" (p. 158). As regards the scribe's enigmatic remark about pointing or punctuating, perhaps it refers to the association of the paragraph sign (in the Vernon text) with the most definite pauses, and hence with the cursus that may be expected to precede.[5]

It would seem a simple matter to scan the text, paying particular attention to the marks of finality, in order to establish whether or not Ms. Morgan's hypothesis is correct. Yet certain problems arise: What degree of license is to be allowed in recognition of forms of cursus? How are possibly variant pronunciations to be handled, in particular, the accentuation of Romance loan-words and the pronunciation, or not, of final *-e*? Judgements about sentence-stress also, of course, affect scansion. Is *Móder sone féyrest*, like *in wó forte dwélle*, a possible instance of cursus planus? Or is it not proper to treat *sone* as the second element of a quasi-compound, and hence to reduce its stress? Finally, and perhaps most importantly, what frequency of forms of the cursus will serve to establish imitation — the corollary being, how significant an element in the obvious rhythm of the Middle English text are the patterns of stress cultivated for Latin clause-endings?

Regarding the first question, degree of license in form, Kuhn has noted (p. 203) in connection with Ælfric's "rhythmical prose", that the amount of cursus one finds there depends greatly upon "whether one is a strict or a loose constructionist". Precisely, and so for vernacular writings in general. Several years ago Margaret Schlauch examined the *Kunstprosa* of Chaucer's translation of *De consolatione philosophiae*, and analyzed all sixteen cola of one passage as exemplifying cursus, whether planus, tardus, or velox, or modified forms thereof.[6] A more strict con-

---

4   *MED*, ed. Hans Kurath and Sherman M. Kuhn, Part C.1 (Ann Arbor, 1959), p. 7.

5   "A Treatise," 157-63. See n. 15 below.

6   "The Art of Chaucer's Prose," in *Chaucer and Chaucerians*, ed. D. S. Brewer (London, 1966), pp. 156-58.

structionism, by eliminating the "choriambic" variation (planus minus its final unaccented syllable) would diminish the number of cursus-forms by a quarter. Exclusion of endings with an extra unaccented syllable would reduce the number still further, to 50 percent of the total. Since it has been held by Kuhn and others that the rhythms of cursus are inherent in the language, reduction beyond a certain point invites scepticism about rhetorical deliberateness. It would seem most prudent, therefore, to restrict consideration to the three types of endings regularly recognized: the cursus planus, a paroxytone followed by a trisyllabic paroxytone (.../x x/x); the cursus tardus, a paroxytone followed by a tetrasyllabic proparoxytone (.../x x/x x); and the cursus velox, a proparoxytone followed by a tetrasyllabic paroxytone (.../x x\x/x), with the possibility of secondary accent on the fourth to last syllable. Mathieu G. Nicolau, who studied the subject extensively in relation to Latin prose, formulated the basic rule thus: the first accented word of the clausula must have as many post-tonic unaccented syllables as the second word has pre-tonic unaccented syllables.[7] Hence there will always be an even number of unaccented syllables between the last two accents, and these syllables will be evenly divided between the last two accented words. Since the substitution of shorter words in combination for the required tri- or tetrasyllables is not unknown even among Latin writers, it seems reasonable to assume the same license for English texts, but probably not to the point of considering a sequence of monosyllables as potential cursus. Variant placement of caesura (which in the basic forms is simply a matter of word-division) may also be tolerated, at least in preliminary analyses. Some scholars have argued for the possibility of additional unaccented syllables, on the principle of resolution as in verse. The allowance of this freedom, however, diminishes the already slim margin between deliberately and accidentally cadenced prose, that is, prose cadenced without rhetorical intention.

A fourth type of cursus has been recognized, with some mediaeval precedent, and named by modern scholars: the "dispondaicus" or "trispondaicus". Here, a paroxytone would be followed by a tetra-syllabic paroxytone (.../x \x/x), as in a favourite clausula of Cicero's: *esse videatur*. The fact seems to be that this ending was tolerated rather than prescribed, and that it is more frequent in "arhythmical" than in rhythmical texts, although certain eleventh- and twelfth-century

---

7 "Notes sur l'histoire du 'cursus' rythmique," *Bulletin Du Cange, Archivum latinitatis medii aevi* 7 (1932) 37. Nicolau's comprehensive study, *L'origine du 'cursus' rythmique et les débuts de l'accent d'intensité en latin* (Paris, 1930), has formed the basis for my summary.

theoretical treatises approve an eight-syllable paroxytone in conclusion, such as *excommunicationis*. One argument against the trispondaicus is that it does not have the symmetry observed by Nicolau, as regards post-tonic and pre-tonic syllables. (The same argument might be offered, of course, against displacement of caesura in the other three forms, as well as against introduction of an extra syllable between the two accents.) In my analysis, phrases alternating stress with lack of stress, whether twice or three times, have been classified together under the heading "Dispondaicus or trispondaicus", while phrases having the accentual pattern /x x x/x (caesura varies) have been classified as a possible variant of the regular planus.

In addition to the question of license in recognition of forms, I have mentioned particular problems of pronunciation. As has been shown, forms of cursus are distinguished from one another, and from endings that do not belong to the scheme, according to the number of un-stressed or lightly stressed syllables that follow each of the two main accents preceding the close of phrase, clause, or sentence. Accordingly, any decision as to the frequency of cursus in a particular text necessarily depends upon the placing of accents, both primary and secondary, and the counting of unaccented syllables in the words in-volved. In order to scan a text properly, then, one must know the habits of accentuation of its author (or of the person who cast the text in its present style) and the circumstances under which he was accustomed to pronounce the unaccented syllables that are historically possible. For a dated and localized Middle English text, both of these factors can be determined with a fair degree of certainty; yet it is the very margin of uncertainty that becomes crucial when an attempt is made to classify rhythmical endings. The exploitation of multiple forms, deliberate use of archaisms to achieve a desired rhythm, the cancellation of word-accent that may result from lack of sentence-stress — all of these possibilities complicate the scansion. Rhyme or rhythmical pattern may suggest the pronunciation of a word in some contexts, but this in-formation should not be generalized for occurrences of the same word under different conditions. Later history of the word is a better guide. In scanning *A Talkyng* for cursus, I have attempted to adhere closely to normal accentuation as outlined by, for example, Lorenz Morsbach and Karl Brunner.[8] Every primary accent is given rhythmical value, and

---

8   For a fuller discussion of the various problems, especially the accentuation of Romance loan-words and pronunciation of final -*e*, see Smedick, *Rhythm*, ch. 4, pp. 137-67, and appendix, pp. 231-38. Ian Robinson, *Chaucer's Prosody* (Cambridge, 1971), pp. 82-131, provides a recent survey of opinion on these problems with particular reference to Chaucer.

every word is assumed to have a primary accent except those words, mostly monosyllables, which in consequence of habitual lack of emphasis have dropped to the level of proclitics or enclitics. This group includes articles, prepositions, conjunctions, pronouns, and adjectives and adverbs with a formal function. A certain amount of leeway is surely permissible here, as well as in the accentuation of auxiliary verbs and of forms of the verb "to be" generally. Rhythmical value may also on occasion be allotted to a possible secondary accent, especially in a longer Romance loan-word.

In the matter of unstressed syllables, I have assumed pronunciation unless there is strong external evidence to the contrary. Final -e, whether historical or analogical but pronounced, presents a special problem here for two reasons: opinion regarding the chronology of its disappearance is not uniform; and the possibility of facultative use of obsolete or obsolescent -e must be considered, given the exigencies of cursus, especially the necessity of a final unstressed syllable in all forms. (Ms. Schlauch's recognition of the choriambic ending may be seen to proceed from the frequency of the stressed final syllable in Middle English phrases.[9]) My practice has been to assume the pronunciation generally acknowledged normal (for time and place) within the phrase, that is, the silencing of -e's there; but to posit the facultative use of -e at the end.[10]

My third main question had to do with the frequency of cursus-forms necessary to establish or at least imply deliberate use. This is a thorny problem involving both the origin and distribution of the cursus as a rhetorical device, and also the extent to which cursus is a natural part of the Latin language and even of English. Nicolau links the emergence of cursus with the transition in Latin from an accent of pitch to one of stress, a transition which he places in the third century A.D.[11] Any text composed during or after that century, until the practice went out of fashion at the end of the Middle Ages (even later, according to some accounts), may show regular use of cursus. That the device was not, as some persons have believed, a revival or innovation on the part of the

9 See Schlauch, p. 156: "As unaccented final -e's disappeared in Chaucer's time, *cursus planus* tended to become choriambic (that is, / x x / or 4-1), for instance in the writings of Richard Rolle of Hampole."

10 Alliterative verse supplies a kind of parallel for the interiors of phrases and Chaucer's verse for the ends. For a discussion of -e in the alliterative long line, see Marie Borroff, *Sir Gawain and the Green Knight* (New Haven, 1962), pp. 182-89.

11 *L'origine*, p. 82.

eleventh- or twelfth-century papal chancery seems to be indicated by the continuity of the traditional teaching from the third century. The statements relative to rhythmical endings form only part of a coherent system, including rules for punctuation, that was transmitted more or less intact from the earlier to the later Middle Ages. But although any Latin prose from the third century on, and vernacular prose imitative of Latin, may be cadenced according to the teaching of the Latin rhetoricians and grammarians, nevertheless the later mediaeval regularization of cursus, its adoption by the papal chancery, and the subsequent proliferation of handbooks with simple instructions make likely a more strict adherence to the three basic patterns from about the thirteenth century. *A Talkyng*, dated in the third quarter of the fourteenth century by its latest editor, was composed, it seems, when adherence to the rules of dictamen, including conspicuously the doctrine of cursus, was at a height: "... though the Roman Cursus was in papal letters best used during the pontificate of Innocent III, it was most widely used in the fourteenth century. By that time a knowledge of it had spread to every court in Europe."[12] That the text might reflect current Latin practice is therefore not unlikely; the fact of influence remains to be proved.

Professor Kuhn maintains, as noted above, that cursus is merely part of the natural rhythm of, at least, Old English. His own study offers considerable support of that claim. While Nicolau sets a minimum of 60 percent endings conforming to cursus for an inference of deliberate use,[13] Kuhn by cautious count finds 72.5 percent such endings in an Old English boundary description (p. 196) — as rhetorically "arhythmical" a text as one might hope to find. Comparative data, even including computer calculation of probabilities, appear to be the only way of setting a reasonable minimum for a particular language at a particular time. Of course, if Nicolau is correct in this third-century date, control texts in early English may be hard to come by, given the ever-present example of Patristic writings, for instance, or of the Roman liturgy. If instead of comparing the endings in arhythmical and rhythmical texts, one looks within a single text at the interiors of phrases as contrasted to the ends, there is still the possibility of a natural contrast between in-

12 Noel Denholm-Young, "The Cursus in England," *Oxford Essays in Medieval History Presented to Herbert Edward Salter* (Oxford, 1934), p. 90.

13 *L'origine*, p. 38; if the trispondaicus is included, the minimum percentage ought to be 65, according to Nicolau.

terior and end-rhythm, of which the Latin cadences may be only a formalization. Then too, in a heavily punctuated text like *A Talkyng*, there scarcely seems to be an interior. Moreover, adept practitioners of cursus were capable of constructing overlapping cadences: *Interpretes barbaros sustinemus multotiens*,[14] wherein the second and third words form a velox, and the third and fourth words a tardus. Compare, from *A Talkyng* (p. 26), *þat leuere is menskeliche to ʒiuen þen quedliche. to wiþ holden.*, a possible sequence of three overlapping planus phrases, the last one extended by an extra syllable: *menskeliche to ʒiuen, ʒiuen þen quedliche, quedliche to wiþ holden*. The scribe's punctuation, in this instance, serves to draw attention to the possibility of cursus in mid-phrase.

In recognition of all of these complexities, I offer the following findings as but one contribution to the accumulation of data relevant to cursus in English.

For my original analysis, I selected eighteen passages distributed throughout the treatise *A Talkyng of þe Loue of God*, including sections based on earlier texts (*Þe Wohunge of ure Lauerd, On wel swuðe God Ureisun of God Almihti*) and sections for which no ancestor has been found. The phrase- and clause-endings, as indicated by punctuation in the Vernon manuscript, were classified under six headings on the basis of arrangement of stressed and unstressed syllables. Besides the three forms of cursus (planus, tardus, velox), the categories include the questionable trispondaicus or dispondaicus, the stressed ending, and a miscellaneous category, "Other", which comprises chiefly instances of clashing stress. The last two categories are open to objection as being over-inclusive or insufficiently distinguishing. For just as cursus embraces three distinct patterns of stress, all ending in one or more light syllables, so there is a variety of patterns having the common characteristic of final stress; and non-final clashing accent, the predominant "other" pattern, may come in different places within the phrase, thus producing another heterogeneous group of patterns. But my study attempted first to discover the extent of cursus, and hence observed only in a general way the two basic departures from the rhythm of cursus: failure to space stress, and allowance of a final stressed monosyllable or oxytone.

Before examining the passages in detail, it may be well to make some general observations. First of all, the stressed ending may be made to predominate merely by not allowing the pronunciation of *-e*, since the

14 Richard de Bury, *Philobiblon*, ed. Michael Maclagan (Oxford, 1960), p. 48.

already large number of phrases ending in a stressed syllable would be thereby more than doubled. A second important consideration is the treatment of possessives and common adjectives and adverbs. The decision for or against an instance of clashing stress usually depends upon whether or not such words as "my", "thy", "our", "all", "dear", "so" receive strong accent. Following the principles already outlined, I have in general assigned stress except where emphasis on the questionable word seemed to distort the meaning of the phrase. This procedure puts more endings in the "Other" column than our modern habits of accentuation would probably justify, but there is no reason to assume that juxtaposed accents offended the ear of mediaeval Englishmen.

Occasionally, the manuscript punctuation has been set aside in pursuit of cursus. The majority of the punctuated phrases contain two major stresses, thus providing scope for the three forms of cursus. Where a one-stress phrase occurs, I have considered the possibility of combining it with an adjacent phrase, especially if the latter also has only one major stress. Likewise, I have occasionally added punctuation when a segment is unusually long and has a natural pause part way through. One liberty that others may be inclined to take should perhaps be mentioned here. A stressed ending followed by a two-stress phrase, in particular one with a subordinate first stress, will sometimes form a velox, for example: *al þat þou wolt: ouer al be forþed*. (*A Talkyng*, p. 56). Punctuation must, of course, be ignored, but a natural pause at the same point will usually dominate over any other possible caesura. I do not include such occurrences in the count of cursus because this departure from manuscript punctuation seems to me more radical.

It should suffice, to demonstrate the method followed, to reproduce here only a portion of the eighteen tables that were compiled. The seven that follow, like the original eighteen, represent all parts of the text, that is, sections traced to earlier versions of the material as well as "new" sections. In the tables, for typographical convenience, the punctus elevatus is represented by a colon, and the paragraph sign by the double virgule.

Table I

In the first passage selected there is a concentration of planus cadences part way through that might seem to suggest a degree of deliberateness. And it is interesting to note that four planus endings are followed by the punctus elevatus, a mark of punctuation indicating a

TABLE I

Planus	Tardus	Velox	Dispondaicus or trispondaicus	Stressed	Other
þer of þi blisse:				Whose euere wol haue part.	
heer of þi pyne.				he mot dele wiþ þe.	
ne felauschupe worþi:					Nis he nouȝt good felawe.
as i.þe biȝete.				þat nul scoten i þe los.	
after his euene.			Hym bi houeþ scoten.		
			He mot þi steppes folwe.	þat wol be þi felawe louynde lord:	
þorw sore and þorw sorwe. in peyne and in pouert.				and þolyng of wo.	
Wiþ schome and wiþ schenschupe ȝif hit so falleþ. ?					
Ne trowe no mon wiþ ese. to steyȝe to þe sterres:			& lastinde winnes:		for to clymbe to þi weole.
			þin endeles blisse.		Ne bugge wiþ delyces:
whi wiþ armes of loue.			ne cluppe I.þe so faste:		A. swete lord Ihesu.
þat no þing from þi loue.			departe myn herte://		

pause with rising inflection, hence a kind of emphasis through suspense.[15] The percentage of cursus is not particularly high: thirteen or fourteen (with revised punctuation) possible instances among twenty-eight phrases, or a maximum of 50 percent. Moreover, at least seven of these instances are questionable. Should not *þi*, for example, receive stress in such a phrase as *for to clymbe to þi weole*, since divine *weole* is being specified? (In the first two phrases listed as planus, the contrast between *þer* and *heer* seems to draw stress away from *þi*.) Similarly, some readers might choose to emphasize *mon* rather than *no* in the admonition *Ne trowe no mon wiþ ese. to steyȝe to þe sterres*:

Table II

A relatively high percentage of the endings in the second passage either clearly are of the planus pattern or may be made so by suppression of stress on *all, þi(n), vre,* or *þis*. To this number may be added two tardus cadences and two or three (allowing an extra syllable) velox, for a maximum total of twenty endings conforming to cursus among a possible thirty, therefore 67 percent. (Although a further mark of punctuation seems warranted in the long segment beginning *Nartou lodesterre* ..., there is no clear break at which it might be inserted.) There are very few stressed endings and also few endings with clashing stress, unless a number of the questionable planus phrases are transferred. A passage of this sort coming in the midst of others with markedly different distribution of rhythms seems to raise in a persuasive way the possibility of conscious striving for cursus. But there is a special factor to be considered here: five of the twenty endings classed as cursus have the pattern "... and ...": *seilen and faren* (planus), *þe cure and þe cumfort* (planus), *In help & in Meyntenaunce* (tardus or, with Romance accentuation, velox), *Moder and Mayden* (planus), *schomeliche and lihtliche* (planus). In my original study, I noted (pp. 183f.) that pairs of words linked by "and" often produce cursus, particularly if the variation of an additional syllable is admitted. The reason for the high incidence of cursus in this situation is clear: "and" supplies one of the two necessary separating syllables between the two main stresses; then any additional unstressed syllable sets up potential cursus, that will be realized if one (planus) or two (tardus) unstressed syllables — or three syllables, provided the middle one may bear emphasis (velox) — follow the second stress:

15 Concerning the relationship between punctuation and cursus, see Smedick, *Rhythm*, ch. 3, pp. 90-136.

TABLE II

Planus	Tardus	Velox	Dispondaicus or trispondaicus	Stressed	Other
A Milde Marie Moder of Merci.					
	socour of serweful.				
and cumfort of care.					
					Þou þat art qween of Angeles.
		Nartou lodesterre to alle þo þat in þe séé of þis worldes Anguissche			
seilen and faren.					
Ladi of all schaftes.					
to whom is bi takene.					
þe cure and þe cumfort.					
of hem þat hem felen.					
			caytif wrecches.//		
					ȝe þat in hor owne eȝen.
seon hem self wrecches.					
and sechen þin helpe.					
			wiþ trust hope of herte:		
				in þin aduocatye is put.	
þe cause of vre sunnes.					
				to stonden at domes day	
			vr aller lugges mooder.		
					of vre soule hele.//
	In help & in Meyntenaunce.				
Þenk heer on þis wrecche.					
			þat falleþ þe to fote.		
Moder and Mayden.					
in hope of þin helpe.					
		Pese me ladi for þi muchele merci.			
cryinde reuþely after þi grace.					
			to þi derworþe sone.		
þat Ichaue wiþ sunne schomeliche and lihtliche.					
				so fele tyme a gulte.//	

/	and	/	stressed ending
/	»	/ x	trispondaicus or ending of velox, depending on what precedes
/	»	/ x x	"other" ending
/	»	/ x/ x	"other" ending or trispondaicus, if accent falls on penultimate

/	»	x/	stressed
/	»	x/ x	planus
/	»	x/ x x	tardus
/	»	x/ x/ x	tardus plus one syllable or velox, if accent falls on penultimate

./	»	x x/	stressed
/	»	x x/ x	planus plus one syllable, or trispondaicus
/	»	x x/ x x	tardus plus one syllable
/	»	x x/ x/ x	tardus plus one syllable after each stress, or velox plus one syllable

/ x	»	/	stressed
/ x	»	/ x	planus
/ x	»	/ x x	tardus
/ x	»	/ x/ x	tardus plus one syllable or velox

/ x	»	x/	stressed
/ x	»	x/ x	planus plus one syllable, or trispondaicus
/ x	»	x/ x x	tardus plus one syllable
/ x	»	x/ x/ x	tardus plus one syllable after each stress, or velox plus one syllable

etc.

Kuhn noticed the phenomenon (p. 199) in relation to synonymous pairs, or tautologies, in the Old English Bede: an unstressed "and" between words of the common pattern / x or x/ x produces planus, including the variant with extra unstressed syllable. Fijn van Draat, whose study of the Bede tautologies serves as a kind of starting point for Kuhn's reconsideration, seems to put cart before horse in attributing the tautological phrases to conscious attempt at cursus, rather than seeing cursus as a natural result of using pairs to translate a single word. Returning to our text, one may note that without the pairs the proportion of cursus drops to a less remarkable 50 percent. It may also be noted that the litany-like phrases of address to Mary, with *of* functioning rhythmically as *and* does, account for one third of this percentage.

Table III

Again, the frequency of planus endings hinges upon treatment of relatively less important words — possessives and the commonly used adjective *deore*. If these words are scanned as unstressed, nineteen phrases among the forty-two in the selection may qualify as planus. With one velox the proportion of cursus would be 48 percent. Ten of the possible planus endings could be questioned, however, on the basis of suppression of stress. In my classification I have attempted to be guided by the semantic value of the words in their context. As before (first selection), it might be tempting to posit some connection between the more emphatic marks of punctuation — punctus elevatus, punctus interrogativus, and the composite punctus versus — and occurrence of cursus, but the evidence is less than conclusive. While seven possible instances of planus are followed by what the editor considers elevatus, the same mark closes four phrases that are probably trispondaic, and the question marks and "periods" are distributed almost entirely among the last three, or non-cursus, columns. Only one out of eight occurrences in these columns follows a possible, though not probable, instance of cursus.

Table IV

Of the sixteen phrases, if *for serwe.* and *or for roupe.* are combined into one two-stress unit, in accordance with the normal phrasing, three seem definitely to be planus and five more may be so (excluding the one counted as tardus). Further repunctuating, within the clause beginning *þat þe blod* ..., would interrupt a velox and is therefore not suggested. With one tardus and one velox the percentage of endings conforming to cursus, 63, slightly exceeds Nicolau's minimum. There are no stressed endings, which is unusual. Trispondaic cadences occur with about normal frequency.

Table V

Here the number of likely cursus is very low. Among fifty-two phrases, if *þen þin.* and *as Ich wene.* are combined (repunctuation of the clause beginning *þat I neuere...* does not affect the overall number), a maximum of sixteen, or 31 percent, may be scanned as planus, with one alternatively tardus. All but one of the cursus endings are subject to question. In the latter part of the selection, the stressed ending predominates.

TABLE III

Planus	Tardus	Velox	Dispondaicus or trispondaicus	Stressed	Other
stured is to wrappe: pat al nis offendet:				Allas Allas my lord god. and no ping ne haue I me last.	
					or eny good wille.//
3if I ha wrapped pe sone.			pat scholde me helpe.		
who schal pese me wip pe sone.			nis pe moder erred:		hou is pe sone quemed.∞//
				And 3if pe Mooder be wrop.	
			3if pe sone me hate.∞// But deore lord of Merci.	3if pe Moder beo my fo.∞//	pat art al merci. And pou his deore Mooder.
And wherto schulde merci. 3if gultus ne weore.//			pat art ful of grace.∞//	3if I haue ow bope a gult.	
?		Or who schal me geten pe Moderloue.	ne be 3e ful of Merci:		
?					Schal pe Malice of my euel. passen oure goodnesse: Or alle myne sunnes: ben more pen oure Milce.//
?				Ne art pou lord bi come mon.	
? ? ?					and taken hast vr kuynde. and pou my deore ladi. bi comen art his Mooder:.//
in heuene & in corpe: for resun of sunful.			And hast al pi menske.		
			and wreche to slaken.//		
?			pat hard dep and schendful:	pou lord bi come mon. and a Mylde Maidenes barn.	
pe swerd of pi peyne: purlede pi soule.			wip maydenes menske:		poledest for pyn enemys.// And pou his deore Mooder.

TABLE IV

Planus	Tardus	Velox	Dispondaicus or trispondaicus	Stressed	Other
for serwe. or for rouþe.			But what tonge may tellen. what herte may þenken.		of þat harde boffetyng.
?	þat horlyng and defoulyng.				at þi furste takyng.//
þat þou þoledest schomelich.					brouȝte helle houndes.
			whon þat ludas scariot.		
?			wiþ treson þe to taken.		And hou heo þe bounden. so egerlyck & so faste.
& bringe til heore princes.					
?					
?		þat þe blod sprong out at þe fynger nayles:			
As holy halwen hit siggen. & writen is in boke.//					

TABLE V

Planus	Tardus	Velox	Dispondaicus or trispondaicus	Stressed	Other
			A: Ihesu now þei driuen.		þe blunte vnruide nayles: þorw þi feire hondes.
				and þi frely feet.// Nou bersteþ þi skin.	
þi senwes and þi bones: for reuþe of þi mones.//				Min herte cleueþ in my brest:	
			A Ihesu swetyng. wher is eny wepyng. wher is welle of teres.		
to lauen on my leores. þat I neuere bi day. stunte nor be nihte					nou I.seo þi feire lymes.
þe blood of þi woundes. ?				so reuþli I.dihte.//	springes so breme.
			þat virgyne clene:	and stremeþ on þi white skin. so reuþe to sene. by Moder lokeþ þeron.	
þen þin. as ich wene.//					hir serwe sit þe sarre.
				A: now þei setten vp þe cros. & setten vp þe Roode treo: & þi bodi al be bled. hongeþ þer onne.// A: Ihesu now þei setten þe eros.	
in to þe morteis.				þi loyntes sturten out of liþ.	
?				þi woundes ritten a brod.	þi bones al to scateren.
?				lord þat þe was wo bi gon.	for goled so wyde:
?			in þat ilke tyde//	whon þou heddest al bled.	A: my deore lemmon.
					þou wox al druye. and gonne þhirste sore.
þei boden þe to drinken Eysel and galle.				but whon þou tastedest þerof.	
þow woldest no more.// ?			whon þou heng on roode.	teken al þyn oþer wo. þei bouteden vppon þe.	A: my swete lemmon.
?				as hit weore a lomb.	
(?)			louȝ whon þe to bisemare. grennynde foule.	so mylde and so meke.	wiþ scharpe sc:

Tables VI and VII

The remaining two selections are comparable to the preceding one in low percentage of cursus. In selection VI, a maximum of five planus occurs, and one velox, among nineteen endings (including one produced by insertion of a point), or 32 percent cursus. In selection VII, if one mark of punctuation is added, within the clause beginning *þat sittest ...*, and if the mark before the final one-stress phrase is ignored, or better, shifted back two words, twelve out of thirty-two endings (38 percent) may qualify as cursus — eleven planus, one velox. The segment *For hit is.* might be added to *so wonder muchel.* to produce an additional velox, especially since punctuation between the verb and what follows seems superfluous. It may be noted that, as in my fifth selection, cursus is concentrated in one part of each of these passages, with the stressed ending predominating in the rest.

In this sampling, as in the more extensive one from which it is drawn, the maximum percentages of endings conforming to cursus range from a low in the 30's to a high in the 60's — only slightly higher, that is, than Nicolau's minimum for claiming deliberate use of cursus. No correlation becomes apparent between section of text and concentration of the prescribed patterns. Each of the four divisions from which sample passages were selected (the preface was excluded) has passages representative of the low and high maxima. Averaging of the percentages shows that somewhat less than half (44 percent), at most, of all the endings may be scanned as cursus. And this is an average of maximum percentages; the number of likely instances, still with allowance of variant caesura and an extra unaccented syllable, is considerably lower: one hundred and sixty-eight out of five hundred and fifty-four phrases (repunctuated), or 30 percent. Almost as many endings are likely to have been stressed: one hundred and fifty-four, or 28 percent. Even if the more than one hundred phrases classified as di- or trispondaicus are considered possible instances of cursus, the total percentage, 51, is below the minimum. Moreover, very few of the endings are either tardus or velox; the planus seems to be the only pattern of the three that could possibly have been followed deliberately.[16]

---

16 *Cf.* Kuhn's remarks concerning the dominance of planus in van Draat's "best examples" of cursus from the Old English Bede, "Cursus," 199. From his own analysis of the Old English "boundary paragraph", however, Kuhn infers that planus does not necessarily always dominate in that language, although it is the form most easily obtained in Latin.

TABLE VI

Planus	Tardus	Velox	Dispondaicus or trispondaicus	Stressed	Other
?		euer to ben in blisse.	A.swete ladi Marie.		muchel is þat menske.
? ? ?			such a sones Mooder:		wiþ al hol Maydenhod.
			and Maydenes menske. And hast him so in baun doun.		
				al þat þou wolt:	and al at þi wille: þat he wole.
			ouer al be forþed.	And forte schewen vs þis. he streihte þe his Riht Arm.	
			as he heng on Roode.	And bouwede touward þe his derworþe hed. As ȝif he seide to þe. Mooder al þat þou wolt:	
?					schal ben at þi wille.⫽

TABLE VII

Planus	Tardus	Velox	Dispondaicus or trispondaicus	Stressed	Other
?				Swete Ihesu my leoue lyf.	my lemmon so deore.
and louely of chere.				Feir swetely and freo.	
?				and serue þe here:	Let me beo þi seruaunt.
?		Swete Ihesu my lyues loue.		sitte þe neere.//	þat I.may in þi blisse.
þat sittest so heiʒe / in heuene a boue.//					
What schal I seyen.//				What schal I.don.//	
			For hit is.so wonder muchel.		What schal I.þenken in þi loue.
wiþ outen eny bigynnynge.				þat þou me formedest furst.	
				and madest lyk þi self of nouʒt.//	
				And eft ʒit.	
?			in þe middel worchyng.		hit is so muchel.
				þat wiþ þi bodiliche lyf.	
				þou hast me siþen longe I souʒt.	
				And wiþ þi deþ þat was so hard:	
			vppon þe Roode.	so deore bouʒt.	
				þen wiþ herte may be bouʒt.	And heiʒtest me more mony fold:
				For al þi self al one al weldinde lord.	
				verrey god.	
				and soþfast mon	
in bodi.and in soule.//					

Many of the punctuated segments are not, strictly speaking, endings, as the term would be understood in the scanning of Latin rhythmical prose. But distribution of cursus in the English text is not such that percentages would be substantially altered by restricting scanning to actual endings. For example, a composite mark of finality (one including [//], on which the paragraph sign may be superimposed) occurs seventy-four times in the eighteen selections analyzed. But only twenty probable instances of cursus directly precede such a mark, or with the trispondaicus included, twenty-nine. Hence more than half the time, at least, the composite period or question mark is associated with rhythms other than cursus. As Kuhn remarks (p. 204 n. 68), concerning a study of Ælfric's rhythms, to find as much cursus within clauses as at clause-ends is to demonstrate a lack of cursus, in the view of some authorities.[17]

Whatever the Vernon editor or scribe may have meant by *Cadence*, it does not appear that the rhythmical effects of *A Talkyng of þe Loue of God* may be linked in any conclusive way with the Latin cursus. I would suggest that rhythmical patterning, like the other "reiterative figures of sound" to be discovered in the text, may be better analyzed in the context of the poetic function of language in general.[18] In my original study, I pointed to the clustering of like rhythms — a kind of stanzaic patterning — as a more significant element than the dominance of a particular rhythm, or set of rhythms such as the cursus. This stanzaic patterning, if such it may be called, can scarcely be considered apart from the whole intricate parallelism not only of sound but also of sense, in the more lyrical stretches of *A Talkyng* and related texts.

University of Windsor

---

17 Kuhn is here referring to the study by Frances Randall Lipp, "Ælfric's Old English Prose Style," *SP* 66 (1969) 698-718. Since Ms. Lipp's recognition of cursus-forms differs in important particulars from my own, it would not be appropriate simply to compare her percentages with mine. But it may be noted here that only one third of the "half-lines" analyzed from Ælfric's *Life of St. Oswald* conform, by her rules, to planus, tardus, or velox, with planus by far the most frequent of the three.

18 See Roman Jakobson, "Closing Statement: Linguistics and Poetics" in *Style in Language*, ed. Thomas A. Sebeok (Cambridge, 1960), especially pp. 358-59 and 368-69, wherein Jakobson discusses the insights of Gerard Manley Hopkins on the subject of poetic language and poetic structure.

ORDER AND RIGHT REASON IN AQUINAS' ETHICS

Frank J. Yartz

I<small>N</small> his *Commentary on the Nicomachean Ethics of Aristotle*, St. Thomas Aquinas speaks of two general types of order. One type of order reason discovers; another reason makes.[1] The order that reason discovers in nature is studied in metaphysics and natural philosophy. The other type of order, that which reason makes, is classified according to the area in which the order is made: (1) that made in the arrangement of concepts is the concern of logic; (2) that established in the operations of the will is an ethical consideration; (3) that made in external things, the subject matter of the mechanical arts. The second type of order listed is virtue, a good habit.[2] Establishment of certain patterns of action in the operation of man's will determines the "order" of one's life.[3]

---

1 Thomas Aquinas, *Commentary on the Nicomachean Ethics* 1, lect. 1, 1: "Ordo autem quadrupliciter ad rationem comparatur. Est enim quidam ordo quem ratio non facit, sed solum considerat, sicut est ordo rerum naturalium. Alius autem est ordo, quem ratio considerando facit in proprio actu, puta cum ordinat conceptus suos adinvicem, et signa conceptuum, quia sunt voces significativae. Tertius autem est ordo quem ratio considerando facit in operationibus voluntatis. Quartus autem est ordo quem ratio considerando facit in exterioribus rebus, quarum ipsa est causa, sicut in arca et domo... Nam ad philosophiam naturalem pertinet considerare ordinem rerum quem ratio humana considerat sed non facit; ita quod sub naturali philosophia comprehendamus et metaphysicam. Ordo autem quem ratio considerando facit in proprio actu, pertinet ad rationalem philosophiam, cujus est considerare ordinem partium orationis adinvicem... Ordo autem actionum voluntariarum pertinet ad considerationem moralis philosophiae. Ordo autem quem ratio considerando facit in rebus exterioribus constitutis per rationem humanam, pertinet ad artes mechanicas."

2 *Summa theologiae* 1-2, 49, 2 ad 1: "... dispositio ordinem quendam importat... Unde non dicitur aliquis disponi per qualitatem nisi in ordine ad aliquid; et si addatur bene vel male, quod pertinet ad rationem habitus, oportet quod attendatur ordo ad naturam, quae est finis." See also *ST* 1-2, 55, 2 ad 1: "Facit autem virtus operationem ordinatam; et ideo ipsa virtus est quaedam dispositio ordinata in anima..." Habit is an *ordo*; habit is also virtuous if it is good. Virtue then can be looked at as an order. Now the virtues established in the will have special influence on man's activity, for Aquinas says, "cujus ratio est quia voluntas movet omnes alias potentias, quae aliqualiter sunt rationales, ad suos actus...' (*ST* 1-2, 56, 3c).

3 *Cf.* Frank J. Yartz, *Order and Moral Perfection* (Diss. St. Louis, 1968), pp. 64 ff.

A closer look at St. Thomas Aquinas' description of "ethical order" as that which reason makes in the operations of the will brings to light some serious questions. Whose reason must be followed for moral living? Is the reason of anyone else better than mine? Does the reason of each person determine the order that will be followed? Additionally, does the order that is discovered in nature relate to the order made? St. Thomas surely distinguishes the two in the passage cited from the *Commentary*, but does he make a complete separation of them? The answer to these questions will determine the sense in which Thomas Aquinas' ethic is subjective or objective.

The purpose of this paper, then, is to study order and reason — especially, right reason. In fact, the only way to discover the true nature of right reason for Thomas Aquinas is through his theory of order. Important relationships that exist between order and right reason will be analyzed subsequently under three main divisions. First, an interpretation of right reason already popular with Thomists will be brought forth. Second, it will be shown that this interpretation which reflects the true order-theory of Aquinas rests on the notion that reason (as well as order) is concrete as well as abstract in nature. Third, the notion that reason (intellect)-and-will in its role of commanding the sense appetites is crucial — although not the only factor involved in the essence of the abstract notion of right reason.

I. Right Reason: An Interpretation

St. Thomas stresses the importance of reason in his discussion of human acts. An act not performed in the light of reason is not an human act. "Reason is the first principle of all human acts and whatever other principles of human acts may be found, they obey reason in a certain fashion ..."[4] Further, Thomas Aquinas insists that what is against the order of reason is properly against the nature of man as man; what is according to reason is according to the nature of man as man.[5] Thus in the order of reason is contained what man ought to do to be a morally good person. A good act is one that is in accord with right reason, the standard of morality:

---

4 *ST* 1-2, 58, 2 c: "... omnium humanorum operum principium primum ratio est: et quae-cumque alia principia humanorum operum inveniantur, quodammodo rationi obediunt..."

5 *ST* 1-2, 71, 2 c: "... Et ideo id quod est contra ordinem rationis, proprie est contra naturam hominis, inquantum est homo; quod autem est secundum rationem est secundum naturam hominis, inquantum est homo."

The good for any thing whatever consists in the fact that its action is in agreement with its form. Now the form proper to man is that which makes him a rational animal. Consequently, it must be that a man's action is good from the fact that it is in accord with right reason. For the perversion of reason is repugnant to the nature of reason.[6]

Possibly the best way to approach an understanding of the above passage is to go through some of the important uses of the word "reason" for Aquinas.[7] We find St. Thomas using the word "reason" to refer to the intellect of an individual person: "ratio proprie accepta nullo modo potest esse alia potentia ab intellectu in nobis."[8] Also, Thomas Aquinas tells of reasons in the mind of God: "... necesse est quod ratio ordinis rerum in finem in mente divina praeexistat ..."[9] Both of these meanings are involved as essential elements in the description of reason as the norm of morality. A person through his capacity for reasoning (having a form which allows for the operation of reasoning) discovers his relations to God and other creatures in the universe and in view of these relations decides what is a good act or an evil act. Vernon Bourke in his Aquinas Lecture, *St. Thomas and the Greek Moralists*, says:

Man is, according to St. Thomas, a member of a definite species, formally characterized by the possession of a reasoning intellect. This is a matter of metaphysics: the perfection, even in the area of operations, of any being is to be in act to the fullest extent in accord with the formal act of its being. The *ratio hominis* is at once a principle of the species man, and a principle of rightness in human thought and voluntary action. In the order of the acts of reasoning, terminating in right judgments, man's intellect does not work in a vacuum. The speculative reason judges rightly when it is conformed to the existing nature of its real objects. Practical reasoning, on the other hand, is ruled, or rectified, by the judgments of speculative reason. The rightness, or wrongness, of a practical judgment — and of the resultant moral act — is determined, not by a direct comparison of the proposed act with the natures of things, but by the conformity, or nonconformity, of practical reasoning with speculative reasoning, through which the real order is primarily known. Existing things regulate speculative reason; speculative reason, thus rectified, regulates practical reasoning.[10]

---

6 In 2 *Ethic.* lect. 2, ed. Pirotta, p. 89, no. 257: "Cujus ratio est, quia bonum cujusque rei est in hoc, quod sua operatio sit conveniens suae formae. Propria autem forma hominis est secundum quam est animal rationale. Unde oportet quod operatio hominis sit bona ex hoc, quod est secundum rationem rectam. Perversitas enim rationis repugnat naturae rationis..."
7 *Cf.* C. Peghaire, *Intellectus et ratio selon S. Thomas* (Ottawa, 1926).
8 *De Veritate* 15, 1 c.
9 *ST* 1, 22, 1 c.
10 V. Bourke, *St. Thomas and the Greek Moralists* (Milwaukee, 1947), p. 23.

The speculative intellect, called reason by St. Thomas Aquinas, is absolute in the sense it is considered to be righted when it obeys its own laws, that is, the laws of logic.[11] The practical intellect is righted when, following the laws of the speculative reason, it works from actually intended ends.[12] Both aspects of reason work together in the attempt of man to discover his relations to the world and creatures in it.

Thus, in the philosophy of St. Thomas Aquinas, reason as the standard of morality does not only refer to reason *qua* intellect, whether speculative or practical, but it has a much broader meaning. It is through reason (intellect) that man discovers his reason (order) in nature and acts out of deference for this relationship (order) in which he finds himself.

II. REASON: CONCRETE AND ABSTRACT

Discussion of the interpretation of *recta ratio* given has brought to light that the meanings of certain words important to the discussion converge. *Ratio* is an *ordo*. Order means relation, unity, distinction, individuality.[13] There cannot be order if there are not distinct individual

---

11 *ST* 1-2, 56, 3 c: "Et ideo intellectus, secundum quod habet ordinem ad voluntatem, potest esse subjectum virtutis simpliciter dictae... Cum enim prudentia sit 'recta ratio agibilium,' requiritur ad prudentiam quod homo se bene habeat ad principia hujus rationis agendorum, quae sunt fines; ad quos bene se habet homo per rectitudinem voluntatis, sicut ad principia speculabilium per naturale lumen intellectus agentis. Et ideo sicut subjectum scientiae, quae est 'ratio recta speculabilium,' est intellectus speculativus in ordine ad intellectum agentem; ita subjectum prudentiae est intellectus practicus in ordine ad voluntatem rectam."

12 *Ibid.* See also J. De Finance, *Ethica generalis* (Rome, 1959), p. 131: "Ut natura, ratio sicut omnis natura, inclinatur ad proprium bonum. Valor qui ei, ut sic consideratae, refertur, est valor alicujus *satisfactionis rationalis*, ut delectationis sciendi vel pulchra contemplandi. Qui valor nobilis quidem est, sed nondum moralis. Adhuc statur formaliter in ordine delectabilis, utut exquisiti generis. Adhuc statur in linea dynamismi *naturalis* voluntatis, cujus horizon est *beatitudo*. Ut ratio, ratio absolutum intendit. Unde, cum se exercet ut ratio seu plene rationabiliter iudicat (quando est recta), judicat de valoribus referendo *exercite* obiectum non ad fines aliarum tendentiarum, neque ad suum ut est natura, sed ad suum ut est ratio, id est ad Absolutum seu Ideale (practicum), quod est quasi horizon voluntatis ut est rationalis et *Valor absolute valens*. Se imponit nempe *propter seipsum*, propter suam intrinsecam perfectionem et non propter aliud, secus non esset Ideale rationis ut est ratio (seu voluntatis ut est rationalis), sed ut alicui fini particulari inservit."

13 In 1 *Sent.* 20, 1, 3, 1 c: "Ordo in ratione sua includit tria, scilicet rationem prioris et posterioris, unde secundum omnes illos modos potest dici esse ordo aliquorum, secundum quos aliquis altero prius dicitur et secundum locum et secundum tempus et secundum omnia huiusmodo. Includit etiam tertio rationem ordinis ex qua etiam ordo in speciem contrahitur. Unde unus est ordo secundum locum, alius secundum dignitatem, alius secundum originem, et sic de aliis." Also *De potentia Dei* 7, 9, ad 7: "... ipsa relatio quae nihil est aliud quam ordo unius creaturae ad aliam aliud habet inquantum est accidens, et aliud inquantum est relatio vel ordo."

things. There cannot be order, if the individuals are not related, that is, if in some sense they cannot be looked at as a unity.

The word "order" can be used in two senses, abstract and concrete:

> Order can be taken in two ways. Either to signify degree only, so those who belong to one grade are said to be of one order or to signify the relation which is between the various degrees, so the ordination is called order and in this way is taken abstractly ... In the first way order is taken concretely, so that an ordered degree is called an order ...[14]

The term "rank" means an order. A person who has achieved a certain honor for excellence in an academic endeavor is said to fall into a certain rank, class, or order. This is the concrete usage of the term "order". The abstract usage refers to the relationship among different ranks or grades.

Insofar as *ratio* is an *ordo, ratio* can be used in the abstract as well as concrete sense. Not making this distinction has caused much confusion in efforts at interpreting St. Thomas Aquinas' meaning of *recta ratio*. The problem becomes especially acute for us because our language is not as flexible as the Latin. While in the Latin the sense of order as abstract is more prevalent, in English the concrete usage seems to predominate.

The notions "right" and "reason" can be taken in either an abstract or a concrete sense. In Thomas Aquinas "right" does not merely mean "correct" in contrast to "incorrect", that is, illogical reasoning (concrete usage). Reason does not mean merely a faculty or power man has (concrete usage). In fact, if only the concrete usage prevails, "right reason" would mean only "logical usage of the faculty of reason". But the concrete sense of the word does not seem sufficient to describe what Thomas Aquinas means by a standard or norm of morality. Lehu comes close to the concrete usage in his claim that reason is a dictate of the power of human reason.[15] Bourke's interpretation rests on the abstract usage in which "reason" and "right" mean more than correct usage of

---

14 In 2 *Sent.* 9, 1, 1, ad 2: "... ordo potest sumi dupliciter: vel secundum quod nominat unum gradum tantum, sicut qui sunt unius gradus, dicuntur unius ordinis; et sic ordo est pars hierarchiae: vel secundum quod nominat relationem quae est inter diversos gradus, ut ordo dicatur ipsa ordinatio; et sic sumitur quasi abstracte, et sic ponitur in definitione hierarchiae; primo autem modo sumitur concretive, ut dicatur ordo unus gradus ordinatus." See also A. Kalberer, *St. Thomas's Notion of Order* (Diss. Toronto, 1946).

15 L. Lehu, *La raison règle de la moralité d'après saint Thomas* (Paris, 1930). See also L. Hamel, "Controversia Lehu-Elter-Lottin circa regulam moralitatis secundum S. Thomam," *Antonianum* 7 (1932) 377-84. A view that supports the theory of V. Bourke (*St. Thomas*) is M. L. Martinez, *Recta Ratio according to St. Thomas* (Diss. St. Louis, 1950): "Only reason which has been 'righted' can serve properly as the rule of human acts in general ... reason cannot be thus made right except in

a power. Such an interpretation squares with the fact that for Aquinas morality is not just concerned with the individual as set apart from other persons and things. In fact it falls into the spirit of the order-theory of Aquinas stressed before. It puts morality into a social context. In this context man as the individual perfects himself. Material beings are of such a nature that there must be many of them; in their multitude they mirror God more perfectly. Thomas Aquinas stresses this in book 3, chapter 97 of his *Summa contra gentiles*. Many activities cannot be carried out by one individual alone; man needs others to help him perfect himself. To become morally perfect, then, man must acquire habits (virtues). Through these the various powers in him become unified. By this unification within himself man relates better to (becomes more unified with) his family, church, state — society.

III. Reason, Will, and Sense Appetites

So far the value and extent of the expansion of *ratio* as an *ordo* has been stressed. It stretches out to include reason in things and reason in the mind of God. But it must not be forgotten that *ratio* can be contracted to mean "intellect", a power of the soul. In the following discussion of the command of reason-and-will over the sense appetites this later notion of *ratio* will be of considerable significance. However, since all the meanings of *ratio* can be said to "share in" or "participate in" each other, we cannot even in this discussion totally disregard what has been said earlier.

Now Thomas Aquinas claims "... reason directs not only the passions of the sense appetite, but also the operations of the intellectual appetite, that is, the will, which is not a subject of a passion ..."[16] and "the will moves to their acts all other powers that are in some way rational ... Hence, if a man actually wills well, this is a result of having a good will."[17] Two questions are brought to light in view of what Aquinas

reference to, in correlation with, a man's appetites... Acts of prudence and art, under the guidance of *recta ratio*, both imply and reveal a rightness of order among all the powers, sensible and intellectual, of the human agent... All beings seek unity, and it is in this theory of *recta ratio* that St. Thomas shows us one of the principal ways in which rational creatures may achieve this unity. We thus see how unfounded is the fear that to make reason the rule of conduct is to fail to render its due to man's whole nature and its existential situation" (pp. xxi-xxii).

16   *ST* 1-2, 59, 4 c: "Ratio autem ordinat non solum passiones appetitus sensitivi, sed etiam ordinat operationes appetitus intellectivi, qui est voluntas, quae non est subjectum passionis."

17   *ST* 1-2, 56, 3 c: "Cujus ratio est, quia voluntas movet omnes alias potentias, quae aliqualiter

says: (1) what kind of causality does reason exert over the will? (2) can the sense appetites exert any power or influence over the will? Remember, Thomas Aquinas claims that the will (in its relations to the intellect) commands or orders the sense appetite. This ordering is, of course, the ideal way things should come about, but one does not have to go very far to find an example in which the sense appetites are not ordered at all.

Before taking up the first point, a parenthesis should be opened up regarding the intellectualism and/ or voluntarism in the texts just cited. Aquinas asserts a domination of the will over the sense appetites and also stresses that reason commands the will.[18] However, the nature of the relationship of intellect to will in Aquinas indicates he is not a fully bloomed intellectualist or voluntarist. George Klubertanz is correct, I think, in maintaining Aquinas does not fall into either category:

> ... I do not think St. Thomas is an "intellectualist". I say this, not because I think that he is a voluntarist but rather because I think that the "intellectualist-voluntarist" disjunction marks a fork in a road St. Thomas never entered.[19]

Let us now proceed to the first question: what kind of causal power does reason exert over the will? Reason (intellect) does not move the will as an efficient cause:

> The object moves, by determining the act, after the manner of a formal principle, whereby in natural things actions are specified, as heating by heat. Now the first formal principle is universal being and truth, which is the object of the intellect. And therefore by this kind of motion the intellect moves the will, as presenting the object to it.[20]

Good, which is the proper object of the will, is all that can move the rational appetite. In one sense, then, the intellect can be said to move the will necessarily — nothing else could move the will. But there is

sunt rationales, ad suos actus... et ideo quod homo actu bene agat, contingit ex hoc quod homo habet bonam voluntatem." See also In 2 *Ethic.*, lect. 5, ed. Pirotta, no. 292.

18 In view of passages cited in n. 17, one would think Aquinas is voluntarist, but when we read him in other places such as *ST* 1-2, 3, 5 c, Aquinas could just as well be called an intellectualist. Certainly the intellect and the will depend on each other in their operations.

19 G. P. Klubertanz, "The Empiricism of Thomistic Ethics," *Proceedings of the American Catholic Philosophical Association* 31 (1957) 20.

20 *ST* 1-2, 9, 1 c: "Objectum movet determinando actum ad modum principii formalis, a quo in rebus naturalibus actio specificatur, sicut calefactio a calore. Primum autem principium formale est ens et verum universale, quod est objectum intellectus, et ideo isto modo motionis intellectus movet voluntatem, sicut praesentans ei objectum suum."

another sense in which the intellect does not move the will necessarily. If it did, the will could not be said to be free. The intellect does not move the will to choose any particular good. The will is free to accept or to reject any particular good presented to it. The good presented by the intellect alone can move the will, but this is true in general only, for the intellect cannot dictate which specific good is to move the will or rational appetite.

Thus, when Thomas Aquinas claims that reason directs (orders) the operations of the will, he does not mean to say that the will must accept the direction of the intellect. The direction of reason is not an efficient cause. Consequently, man never has to will to live a moral life.

To study the influence of the intellect-and-will over the sense appetites is to see only one half of the picture; the other half regards the influence the passions can exert over the intellect and will. A strong movement of the sense appetite (such as in the case of anger) can blind the rational faculties and, consequently, our judgments are impeded.[21] This blinding takes place before the deliberation of reason. Therefore, Thomas Aquinas in his *Commentary on the Nicomachean Ethics of Aristotle* is careful to qualify the kind of order he claims reason makes in the operations of the will (ethical order) as that made *in deliberating*.[22] But it must be pointed out that the passions affect the intellect-and-will *indirectly* and in two ways:

> A passion of the sense appetite cannot directly influence or move the will, but it can do so indirectly, and this in two ways. In one way by reason of a certain abstraction; for since all the powers of the soul are rooted in the one essence of the soul, it is inevitable that when one potency is intent in its act, another potency will be inhibited in its act or even entirely impeded from its act ... In another way on the side of the object of the will, which is the good apprehended by reason. For the judgment and apprehension of reason is impeded because of the vehemence and the unusual apprehension of the imagination and the judgment of the virtus aestimativa, as is evident in madmen.[23]

---

21 *De malo* 3, 9 c: "... ex aliqua corporali transmutatione ligatur usus rationis, ut vel totaliter nihil consideret, vel quod non libere considerari possit, sicut patet in dormientibus et phreneticis. Per passiones autem fit aliqua immutatio circa corpus, ita quod interdum aliqui propter iram et concupiscentiam vel aliquam hujusmodi passionem in insaniam inciderunt. Et ideo quando hujusmodi passiones sunt fortes, per ipsam transmutationem corporalem ligant quodammodo rationem, ut liberum judicium de particularibus agendis non habeat."

22 See n. 1.

23 *ST* 1-2, 77, 1 c: "... passio appetitus sensitivi non potest directe trahere aut movere voluntatem, sed indirecte potest; et hoc dupliciter: uno quidem modo secundum quandam abstractionem; cum enim omnes potentiae animae in una essentia animae radicentur, necesse est quod

The above text needs further elucidation. It has been said already that the good-in-general alone can move the will (as a formal cause). To say this is to keep in line with the notion that the lower stratum can only be moved by the higher stratum:

> To the will also is the sensitive appetite subject in execution, which is accomplished by the power. For in other animals movement follows at once the concupiscible and irascible appetites. For instance, the sheep, fearing the wolf, flees at once, because it has no superior counteracting appetite. On the contrary, man is not moved at once according to the irascible and concupiscible appetites; but he awaits the command of the will, which is the superior appetite. For wherever there is order among a number of motive powers, the second moves only by virtue of the first; and so the lower appetite is not sufficient to cause movement, unless the higher appetite consents. And this is what the Philosopher says..., namely that *the higher appetite moves the lower appetite, as the higher sphere moves the lower.* In this way, therefore, the irascible and concupiscible are subject to reason.[24]

Now in one passage, it seems as though Thomas Aquinas maintains the sense appetite cannot move the will, for the sense appetite is a lower power than the will and only the higher power is able to move the lower power. Yet Thomas Aquinas does say that passions move the will *ex parte objecti*. What is the extent of the command of the will? And how is it possible for the appetites to move the will, if they can move it at all? As an answer to the difficulty presented, let us consider the following:

> The will can then be moved by the passion insofar as, through the apprehension of reason, the object of the will is presented to the will

quando una potentia intenditur in suo actu, altera in suo actu remittatur, vel etiam totaliter impediatur... Et secundum hunc modum per quandam distractionem, quando motus appetitus sensitivi fortificatur secundum quamcumque passionem, necesse est quod remittatur vel totaliter impediatur motus proprius appetitus rationalis, qui est voluntas. Alio modo ex parte objecti voluntatis, quod est bonum ratione apprehensum. Impeditur enim judicium et apprehensio rationis propter vehementem et inordinatam apprehensionem imaginationis et judicium virtutis aestimativae, ut patet in amentibus."

24 *ST* 1, 81, 3 c: "Voluntati etiam subjacet appetitus sensitivus quantum ad executionem, quae fit per vim motivam. In aliis enim animalibus statim ad appetitum concupiscibilis et irascibilis sequitur motus; sicut ovis timens lupum statim fugit: quia non est in eis aliquis superior appetitus, qui repugnet. Sed homo non statim movetur secundum appetitum irascibilis et concupiscibilis; sed expectatur imperium voluntatis, quod est appetitus superior. In omnibus enim potentiis motivis ordinatis, secundum movens non movet nisi virtute primi moventis. Unde appetitus inferior non sufficit movere nisi appetitus superior consentiat. Et hoc est quod Philosophus dicit ... quod 'appetitus superior movet appetitum inferiorem, sicut sphaera superior inferiorem.' Hoc ergo modo irascibilis et concupiscibilis rationi subduntur."

precisely as the object of the passion. Thus, the object is presented to the will not merely in the cold light of its participation in the universal good, but as disposing the subject through the sensory appetite.[25]

While the will is said to command or order the lower powers in man, it does not always do so as has already been implied. *Indirectly* the will can be influenced by the passions. This word *indirectly* means that the intellect in reverting to the singular can influence the good presented to the will. This good "is presented to the will not merely in the cold light of its participations in the universal good" and thus it influences the command of the will.[26] In a sense, then, the passions can be said to control the will, but this is not done by the passions *qua* passions, but rather the object of the will as "colored" by the passions.

(It should be noted that we have just described only one way in which the passions can move the will *ex parte objecti*. There are two other ways already referred to in the texts cited. Reason can be impeded by a strong emotion, which prevents one from functioning in a normal way. Bodily transmutations can also account for a coloring of the object presented to the will.[27])

Three things have thus far been accomplished. (1) It has been shown that the intellect (reason) orders the operations of the will. The intellect presents the will with a good as a plan for acting. The will is free to accept or to reject any specific good presented. (2) The will has been described as the faculty that commands. It commands the other powers of the soul. Here its command of the sense appetites, the passions, is central. (3) According to the order-theory of Thomas Aquinas, the will must command the other powers (in a cooperation with the intellect or reason that is essential to the will's operation). It is of a higher nature than the sense powers. It is only the higher that can command the lower. To say that the passions *indirectly* influence the intellect-and-will's operation does not do violence to this theory of order.

Now we are faced with another question: what happens to the passions when the will commands them? Two possibilities are involved

---

25   R. Baker, *The Thomistic Theory of the Passions and Their Influence Upon the Will* (Notre Dame, Ind., 1941), p. 107. The central aim of this thesis is summarized in the following passage: "Just as the phantasms of sense serve as instruments of intellectual cognition, so the passions of the sense appetite seem to be invaluable dispositive instruments used by the human will in its proper activity" (*ibid.*, p. 138). Baker, however, does not consider the Thomistic order-theory in his discussion of the passions and the will.

26   *Ibid.*

27   See n. 21 and 23.

here. (1) The will can make them completely inactive. If this happens, then the main feature of being morally good is to transcend the passions to become as pure an intellect as you possibly can. Thomas Aquinas reminds us that the Stoics do say this. Virtue for them is identical with knowledge. To become knowledgeable means to become moral. And furthermore knowing involves separating oneself from things dealing with the senses.

(2) The other possibility is to integrate the passions so that they act in accord with the other powers of the soul. Here ethical order is not a transcendence of the passions, an escaping of the bodily appetites in the literal sense of the word, but rather involves becoming more complete as a man in that one makes the passions operate as they should. In the words of Thomas Aquinas:

> If by passions we mean inordinate affections as the Stoics held, then it is clear that perfect virtue is without the passions. But if by passions we mean all movements of the sense appetites, then it is plain that moral virtues which are about the passions as their proper objects, cannot be without the passions. The reason for this is that otherwise it would follow that moral virtue would make the sense appetite wholly inactive. Now it is not the role of virtue to free the powers subject to reason from their activity, but to make them carry out the commands of reason by exercising their own acts.[28]

*

* *

The conclusion of this paper can be set forth in three points. (1) The universe is not just comprised of various ranks of creatures. Order does not mean a finality in which relations of ends among themselves are not evidenced. Order, in fact, means relation. Thomas Gilbey says:

> (St. Thomas) did not regard the material world as if it were a volcano whose rumblings threatened the architecture of reason and religion erected on the crust of past eruptions. It was a *continuatio* of the spiritual into the material and a *communicatio* between them, an evolutionary surge from the first to the last day of creation. Man's *ratio* shared in the *ratio* of the universe; both derived from the *ratio divina*.[29]

28 *ST* 1-2, 59, 5 c: "Respondeo dicendum quod si passiones dicamus inordinatas affectiones, sicut Stoici posuerunt, sic manifestum est quod virtus perfecta est sine passionibus. Si vero passiones dicamus omnes motus appetitus sensitivi, sic planum est quod virtutes morales, quae sunt circa passiones sicut circa propriam materiam, sine passionibus esse non possunt. Cujus ratio est, quia secundum hoc sequeretur quod virtus moralis faceret appetitum sensitivum omnino otiosum. Non autem ad virtutem pertinet quod ea quae sunt subjecta rationi, a propriis actibus vacent; sed quod exequantur imperium rationis, proprios actus agendo."

29 T. Gilbey, *Principality and Polity* (New York, 1958), p. 110. Words in parentheses are mine.

Thomas Aquinas' world, then, is a dynamic one.

(2) Vernon Bourke's theory of right reason features Aquinas' notion of *ordo* as a relation. A comparison of Bourke's theory with that of others (such as Lehu's) indicates that while Lehu does not seem to be aware of the fact that the word reason in the pertinent texts regarding *recta ratio* means more than just intellect, Bourke's theory implies at every turn the notion of reason as an *ordo* and, moreover, *ordo* as a relation. Possibly the reason for all the confusion and misunderstanding about *recta ratio* stems from the fact that both *recta* and *ratio* are *concrete* as well as *abstract* words. And, of course, in translation the sense of the words gets lost.

(3) *Recta ratio* involves the ordering of the sense appetites by the intellect-and-will. The creation of this order is essential to leading the good life.

(4) Early in the paper the some questions were brought up: whose reason must be followed in moral living? mine? someone else's? does the reason of each person determine the order to be followed? does the order as discovered in nature relate in any way to the order made?

The paper has provided a basis for answering these questions. Reason according to Thomas Aquinas opens out to include more than just "my reason" or "the reason of any other individual". It includes the participation in and relationship of my reason to that of the plan of the entire universe. Thus the order made (ethical order) should come about in relation to that discovered, if man is to perform morally good actions.

Loyola, Chicago

BEDE, A HISPERIC ETYMOLOGY,
AND EARLY SEA POETRY

Alan K. Brown

I

THE fourth chapter of Bede's major calendrical treatise has a passage which escapes rather startlingly from its context of basic definitions of duodecimal fractions:

> Si in quattuor [partiri vis], quarta pars quadrantis nomen, residuae tres dodrantis accipiunt. Et huius disciplinae regula solvitur quod plerosque turbat imperitos; quia Philippus in expositione beati Iob, aestum maris Oceani cotidie bis venire describens, adiunxerit hunc: *unius aequinoctialis horae dodrante transmisso tardius sine intermissione sive die venire sive nocte.*[1]

> The word for a fourth part is *quadrans*, and for the remaining three fourths it is *dodrans*. And the rule of this *mathesis*[2] can be used to solve a problem which has been confusing a number of unskillful persons, namely that in his commentary upon Job, while picturing the twice-daily arrival of the Ocean tide, Philippus has added that it "arrives unfailingly, day or night, later by the passing of the *dodrans* of an equinoctial [i.e. mean or standard] hour."

All that is clear from this remark is that unnamed persons have been confused or misled about the use of the word *dodrans* "three fourths", and that their difficulty can be cleared up by a mere mention of the proper definition, in the context of a passage quoted from the Philippus commentary upon Job.

But what is the difficulty? Bede's editor has suggested tentatively that Philippus is being attacked for having slightly understated the average

---

1 Charles W. Jones, ed., *Bedae opera de temporibus* (Cambridge, Mass., 1943), p. 185/35-41.

2 I take it that Bede is playing upon the common equation *disciplina: mathesis* and the relationship between the latter word and *mathematica*, so that the *imperiti* are in effect accused of lacking both common learning and common arithmetic.

daily retardation of the tides as three fourths of an hour instead of the slightly more accurate figure of four fifths which Bede himself used.[3] This is an ingenious explanation; however, it is unlikely to be the correct one, since it is not Philippus who is at the focus of Bede's criticism but rather some moderns who through ignorance (*imperiti* is sarcastic slight understatement) have failed to understand the word. Even if we were to suppose that these unknown persons had been interpreting Philippus' *dodrans* as though it referred to a larger fraction than three quarters (and of course the actual tidal retardation is about five sixths of an hour, even larger than Bede's figure), the same objection would apply. And in any case, it is difficult to see why Bede's criticism is injected into a terse chapter on fundamental duodecimal reckoning, instead of being mentioned in his much later chapter devoted especially to the tides.[4]

The form and the tone of Bede's remark show instead that it must be meant to correct some gross contextual error in his contemporaries' understanding of *dodrans*. Now, a peculiar homonym of this word, another *dodrans*, is found in early Insular Latin writings, where it seems to have the meaning "flood" or "tide" or sometimes "sea".[5] The resemblance of these senses to the content of the Philippus passage quoted by Bede seems unlikely to be an accident, and I think that it will seem likely, almost as soon as stated, that Bede had this homonym in mind and meant to show that it was an absurd error. The explanation, though not spelled out, clearly would be that the phrase *dodrante transmisso* was misunderstood in its context as meaning that the tide arrives "with the *dodrans* sent across" or better "having crossed" (the most familiar sense of *transmittere* in contexts where the sea is mentioned), "by the passing of the *dodrans*", so that those unfamiliar with the word could take it to be something that arrives ahead of or with the high or the rising tide. As will be seen, this deduction can be made more precise.

Whether Bede could really have meant to offer this explanation for the Insular Latin word *dodrans*, and whether the explanation is at all a

3 Jones, p. 335.

4 Where Bede actually does attack Philippus (or his sources) for the error of stating that the tide arrives everywhere at the same time: cap. 29 (Jones, p. 234); and see n. 21 below.

5 These are the senses usually deduced for the word by modern editors. I note that in a new edition of *The Hisperica Famina* (Toronto: Pontifical Institute of Mediaeval Studies, 1974) — to which I have had access by the kindness of the editor of *Mediaeval Studies* — approximately this range of meanings, "flood", "tide", "billows" or "water", is given in the commentary, but that the translation uses the sense "tidal wave" suggested by the *Revised Medieval Latin Word-List* for this passage (see nn. 6 and 35) and recommended by the present article.

possible one, are questions that go hand in hand. At the same time, since Bede is a supremely gifted and reliable contemporary witness, it is necessary to distinguish sharply between the absurdity of the posited error and the plausibility of the explanation (if it is Bede's) which posits it. The other explanations which have been advanced for the word in recent times — e.g., that Insular *dodrans* really refers to the three-quarters full moon which might somehow be related to a monthly higher tide, or that it means the sea because the sea was believed to cover three fourths of the earth[6] — are full of doubtful assumptions and stand isolated, tending to cancel each other out.

On the other hand, the etymology suggested by Bede's quoting the Philippus passage, some twelve hundred and fifty years ago, bears a striking resemblance to a number of explanations that in recent years have been advanced for other items of the so-called Hisperic vocabulary of Insular Latinity. What Wallace M. Lindsay referred to as "that peculiarly Hisperic word (of various spellings) *thermopylae* 'crag'" is believed to rest upon a failure to understand the proper name in a certain passage of Orosius' histories.[7] The late Father Paul Grosjean detected two equally outlandish developments: first, that *arca* and its various derivatives as used in the Hisperica Famina and by Aldhelm and other Insular writers seem to represent a naive deduction from a phrase of Jerome's on Matthew 23, *et armaria et arcae habent libros*;[8] second, that the amazing Hisperic word *gurgustus* "fish" can only be the result of a failure to understand *gurgustium piscium* of the Vulgate Job 40: 26.[9] (Indeed, since these same words are quoted but not explained in the Philippus commentary, it would be possible that Hisperic *dodrans* and *gurgustus* arose from almost the same passage in the same Bible commentary.)

Bede's conservative Latin style is usually felt to lie at the opposite pole from the extravagant vocabulary employed by many of his fellow

---

6   These are the explanations, respectively, attributed to Stowasser by R. Ehwald, *Aldhelmi opera*, MGH, *Auctores Antiquissimi* 15 (Berlin, 1919), p. 526 n. (I have not had access to Stowasser's Hisperica Famina commentary), and of F. J. E. Raby, *The Oxford Book of Medieval Latin Verse* (Oxford, 1959), p. 458. But was three quarters more often mentioned than any other large fraction? Further suggestions: *dodrans* "nine twelfths", hence the ninth wave (R. E. Latham, *Revised Medieval Latin Word-List from British and Irish Sources* (London, 1965), s.v.); "three quarters", hence a connection with the triangular shape of the earth (J. D. Pheifer, *Old English Glosses in the Epinal-Erfurt Glossary* (Oxford, 1974), p. 80).

7   Paul Grosjean, "Confusa Caligo," *Celtica* 3 (1956) 43-44, 49, 66.

8   *Ibid.*, 68; PL 26.837.

9   *Ibid.*, 44.

islanders, and if he did once use *lar* as a poetic synonym for "fire", he probably failed to recognize the Hisperic origin of the false etymology.[10] However, despite his own habitual avoidance of the Insular ornate style, he once praised his near-contemporary Aldhelm as a writer *sermone nitidus*.[11] The present case would thus be the first in which Bede has been found to animadvert openly against a Hispericism, and it is interesting that he appears to attack Insular *dodrans* not as an obscure inherited word but as an item of living learning. (He himself, with only a brief acknowledgement of barbarism — *placuit appellare* —, adopted those necessary words of the tidal vocabulary *malina* and *ledo*, which some unknown tongue had bestowed on the late Latin of western Europe.[12]) The style of the attack, its mixture of anonymity for the perpetrators of the error and of cutting sarcasm for the mistake, is the same which Bede uses elsewhere in dealing with blunders committed by a modern Spaniard, Isidore of Seville,[13] and in puncturing an Irish commentator's unfortunate comparison between a prophet and a bladder filled with wind.[14]

Bede's criticism of Insular *dodrans*, though expressed so tersely that its point seems to have been missed in modern times, may have found its target among his contemporaries as easily as he seems to have expected; the word is hard to document after his time, whereas some other Hispericisms such as *thermopylae* descended to the Carolingians. He gives us no new direct indications of what isolated circles can have allowed such outrageous misunderstandings of the commonest writings to become enshrined in words. However, the answer, and a good deal of other information, is at hand in the writings emanating from the Celtic, mostly Irish, monastic schools and from closely related Anglo-Saxon traditions.

Philippus upon Job, a commentary apparently dating in some form or another from the fifth century,[15] was far better known to the early

10   *Metrical Life of Cuthbert*, line 335, ed. Werner Jaeger, *Palaestra* 198 (Leipzig, 1935), p. 83.

11   *Historia ecclesiastica* 5.18; the apparent praise has provoked the derision even of his editor Charles Plummer (2 (Oxford, 1896), pp. 312-13).

12   *De temporum ratione*, cap. 29, ed. Jones, pp. 234/41-42 and notes, p. 364.

13   *Cf.* Jones, p. 131.

14   PL 93.73D; the nationality of the commentator is discovered by Bernhard Bischoff, *Mittelalterliche Studien: Ausgewählte Aufsätze* 1 (Stuttgart, 1966), p. 267.

15   To judge from Gennadius, the author was a disciple of Jerome's, and possibly Gaulish; a short passage from the commentary is attributed to Jerome by Faustus of Riez. The edition is being prepared by the Rev. Irénée Fransen, O.S.B., to whose kindness I owe some much-needed guidance past the current extreme confusion and differences of opinion involving the printed texts.

Irish and English[16] than it has been in modern times.[17] It will be necessary therefore to quote more of the context dealing with the tides than Bede needed for his audience. The passage is to Job 38: 16, *Numquid ingressus es profundum maris, et in novissimis abyssi deambulasti?*

... Ubi alii dixerunt *Numquid ingressus es fontem maris?* initium atque originem unde ipsum mare quasi de matrice emanet[18] dicere videtur; quod Oceani perenni cursu ac recursu[19] fieri novimus, feruntque hoc atque confirmant, quod illa immensa effusio maris Oceani per omnium regionum ac patriarum[20] fluvios itura, uno puncto temporis fiat; quam nos tamen scimus[21] omnium dierum ac noctium alternante successu[22] per horas viginti quattuor bis[23] venire, atque unius horae aequinoctialis dodrante transmisso, tardius sine intermissione sive die venire sive nocte, per quinque vero[24] aequinoctiales horas refluo[25] aestu violentoque impetu sive in opertis[26] tantum sive etiam retrusis[27] magnorum quoque fluminum cursibus ad superiora conscendere ... Proinde incredibile <credibile?>[28] videri potest quod in eodem mari velut fons quidam tantarum aquarum ebulliat, de cuius profunditate et subiacente[29] abysso ... aquae illae immensae in[30] superficiem profundantur, et rursum recurrentes in eosdem

16 Three texts in eighth-century Insular scripts survive, and there are other manuscripts as early or nearly so. Many attempts have been made to identify one or another of the recensions with a Job commentary mentioned by Bede among his own works, *Historia ecclesiastica* 5.24. The tidal lore is quoted by the early Irish *De ordine creaturarum* (PL 86.936), with a related passage in the Lismore Augustine's *De mirabilibus sacrae scripturae* (PL 35.2159).

17 Pending the appearance of Father Fransen's edition, the most accessible text is that of the shorter of the two principal recensions: PL 26.796-97 for the passage cited (not 752 as Jones), reprinted from Erasmus' edition of the works of Jerome (Basel, 1516; 7, fol. 109), to which most of the variants in the notes below refer. The longer recension was printed at Basel in 1527 by Johannes Sichardus, apparently from a lost Fulda manuscript (p. 173A for this passage), and from another text in the fourth volume of Hervagius' edition of the works of Bede (Basel, n.d., pp. 821-22). Not all of the variations are noted below.

18 de matrice, de mari Oceano emanat *in the shorter recension. Hervagius*, quod *before* ipsum.

19 ac recursu *omitted by Hervagius*.

20 provinciarum *shorter recension* (patriarum *Bede*).

21 At *for* quam *shorter rec.* Bede reflects the wording in his correction of Philippus' major error about the tides (n. 4 above): "Scimus enim *nos*," he says half-sarcastically, "qui diversum Britannici maris litoris incolimus," that the tide does no such thing.

22 alternatis successibus *shorter rec.*

23 bis *not shorter rec. as printed*.

24 vero *not shorter rec.*; sex *wrongly for* quinque *Sichardus*.

25 refluitura *shorter rec.*

26 in adopertis *Sichardus*, ardor peritis *Hervagius*, in opertis *shorter rec.* Perhaps *adopertis* "covered" (by points, bends or the like) in contrast with *retrusis* "shut off" (by a bar). The suggestion of *apertis*, mentioned in my translation, is not legitimate here.

27 retusis *Hervagius and shorter rec.*

28 credibile *Hervagius*.

29 sufficiente *shorter rec.*

30 aquae immensae in illam *Hervagius*; aquae illae in *shorter rec.*

profundissimos sinus decidant[31] praecipitesque descendant,[32] et a Deo sibi constituta lege perpetua ab imis semper ebulliant atque iterum in ima decurrant.

Hast thou entered into the depths of the sea, and walked in the ends of the abyss? Where others [the Old Latin translation] have said *Hast thou entered the fount of the sea?* — meaning, evidently, the source and spring whence the sea itself rises as if out of a womb; which we know to be the case by the constant flood and ebb of Ocean, and they both assert and confirm it from the fact that this enormous outflow of the Ocean sea on its way into the rivers of all the lands takes place within a single unit of time. Yet as we ourselves know, it arrives twice during the twenty-four hours' alternation of day and night, arriving unfailingly, day or night, later by the passing of three fourths of an equinoctial hour; and throughout five equinoctial hours runs in a returning flood and a fierce rush up into the courses of great rivers, whether those which are covered [*or* open? *apertis*] only, or even those which are shut off ... So that it may appear [not?] unbelievable that there is a sort of spring of all these waters that gushes out within the sea — out of whose depth, and the abyss beneath, ... these immeasurable waters pour forth up onto the surface and on their return plunge back down into the same bottomless gulfs; continually, by that eternal law which God hath established unto Himself, arising up out of the depths and descending again into the same.

Two impressions are strongest here. First, this passage must be one of the main sources of the long-continued medieval belief that tides arise out of the abyss through a spring or spiracle in the sea bottom — here called also a sea womb, in the imagery of an adjoining passage in Job; I shall return to this point. Second, besides the general notion of vastness, the emphasis is upon the violent rush of the tide up into the rivers of the lands; great rivers, even those with closed or hidden lower courses, are especially mentioned. If it were necessary to establish a meaning for *dodrans* from this context alone — and according to the hypothesis, that is exactly what happened — the guess would be "wave of the oncoming tide", particularly its most striking manifestation, the regular tidal waves, or so called bores or eagres, which race up into such Atlantic estuaries as the Garonne, Rance, Seine and Severn. The bore is well known to reach impressive and sometimes destructive heights in those channels which are partly blocked to the sea by various configurations of bends and bars; so that Philippus' observation is quite exact.

31 fines incidant *Sichardus*.
32 discedant *shorter rec.*

II

The hypothesis must be tested against the relatively few documentations of Insular *dodrans*. One may as well start with the Hisperica Famina themselves, texts which, undatable and barely translatable as they are, seem to represent the central school tradition of obscure Latinity which gives Insular style its outré flavor.[33] *Dodrans* occurs in the so called A text in a set-piece description of the sea, a topic handled according to the same outline though with different words in the fragmentary D text. We are told first (A 383-392) of the sea in storm (388, 389), beating on the shores (383, 384, 385, 391), stirring the sands of the bottom (386), tossing to the skies (387, 390), sinking ships (392). Next is a short (393-95) picture of the sea at rest. After an equally short introduction (396-98) to the twice-daily rhythm of the tides

> Gemellum neptunius collocat ritum fluctus;
> Protinus spumaticum pollet in litora adsisam;
> Refluamque prisco plicat recessam utero;

in which we seem to recognize the sea-womb of Job and its commentary (recurring at 424, *internum aequoris ... uterum*, parallel to the D text, lines 8 and 24), we come to a longer section (399-415) which contrasts the violence of what seems to be a spring tide (*mallina*) with the quiet of the neaps (*lido*) when ships may sail. The foaming, swelling *mallina* regularly (399, *solita flectit ... discurrimina*) attacks and plucks at the muddy shores (399-401); it drowns the vast channels with its swelling *dodrans* (402, *Vastaque tumente dodrante inundat freta*), it washes ashore driftwood (?) and seaweed (403-404), tears shellfish from the rocks (405-406), casts many species of sea-monsters on the sands (407), and beats upon the *termopilae*, the cliffs and crags, of the shore (408).[34]

What is to be made of this strange identification between a regular spring tide, accompanied by its *dodrans*, and a more general disturbance of the sea? The modern term *tidal wave* assigns the same false cause to cataclysmic surges, and has actually been applied to the *dodrans* of this passage.[35] The same suggestion of the sea's gaining upon the land is briefly given — together with a valuable link to another branch of the Insular tradition — by the macaronic and Hisperic hymn Adelphus

---

33   This is of course the late Father Grosjean's view.
34   F. J. H. Jenkinson, ed., *The Hisperica Famina* (Cambridge, 1908), pp. 13-15; D text, pp. 43-44.
35   J. H. Baxter and Charles Johnson, *Medieval Latin Word-List from British and Irish Sources* (London, 1934), p. 141. (Entry dated "550"; *cf.* list of sources, p. x.)

Adelphe: *Blebomen agialus nicate dodrantibus*, glossed in the St.-Omer text *Videmus, litus vincitur adsissis*. The last word, also belonging to the rich and recondite tidal vocabulary of the time, is glossed in its turn by an Old Breton word which contains the usual Breton and Welsh term for "high tide" and the prefix *ad-* "again, back";[36] the meaning might conceivably be "spring tide". It is true that a river bore, though a very limited phenomenon, can be a frightening and impressive one, especially at the springs.

Two texts whose authors and dates are known use *dodrans* in connection with the dangers of the stormy sea. Toward the year 600 of our era, Columbanus speaks of the fame of Rome reaching Ireland *trans euriporum rheuma, trans delfinum dorsa, trans turgescentem dodrantem*: across the currents of narrow seas, over the backs of sea monsters, and (rising to some sort of climax) past the swelling *dodrans* (which is surely more than a mere "flood" or current).[37] About a century later, Aldhelm, a West Saxon who had been schooled by an Irishman, uses the word in a passage critical of Irish learning and apparently meant as a deliberately overblown pastiche of his early reading: the recipient of his letter has returned across the Irish Sea, *caerula trans ponti glauca, inormesque dodrantium glareas atque spumiferas limphae obstirpationes, circili carina procellosum sulcante salum*, etc.[38] The "vast gravels of *dodrantes*" are presumably the sea bottom revealed by the foaming sea-walls (waves, *hafgerðingar*) of the next phrase (cf., of course, *Aeneid* 1.105-107).

A rhythm by one of Aldhelm's disciples has some similar phrasing (99-100, *Necnon marina cerula Glomerantur in glarea, Qua inruit inruptio*, etc.), and would also suggest a meaning like "enormous wave":

> Per pelagi itinera
>   Salsa spumabant equora,
> Cum bulliret brumalibus
>   Undosus vortex fluctibus;
> Oceanus cum molibus
>   Atque diris dodrantibus
> Pulsabat promontoria
>   Suffragante victoria:

---

36 *Revue celtique* 11 (1890-91) 86-87; Jenkinson, p. 61; Léon Fleuriot, *Dictionnaire des gloses en vieux breton* (Paris, 1964), pp. 54, 236-37, etc.

37 Ed. G. S. M. Walker, *Scriptores Latini Hiberniae* 2 (Dublin, 1957), p. 48/29-30. *Delphines* with the meaning "sea-monsters" (not dolphins) is thoroughly Hisperic.

38 Ed. Ehwald, p. 489/13-14.

> Sic turgescebat trucibus
> > Pontus ventorum flatibus
> Infligendo flaminibus
> > Scopulosis marginibus.[39]

Along the ocean-ways the salt seas foamed, as the watery maelstrom boiled with wintery currents; Ocean beat victoriously with its combers and awful *dodrantes* upon the headlands: so the main swelled with fierce wind gusts striking in blasts upon the rocky shores.

The poem describes a storm on land, the sea-passage having apparently been added merely for the sake of its vocabulary; indeed, its imitative tone shows once again that these northern islanders had made a regular school topic of their storms, currents and cliffs, deliberately adding to the classical commonplaces they had inherited from the tideless Mediterranean.

One other literary use of *dodrans* has less to do with the sea's slowly gaining upon the lands than with the dark wave rising up to overwhelm them. An anonymous seventh-century Irish commentator's remark, recovered by Professor Bernhard Bischoff,[40] makes a surprising identification: *"Effudit eas" id est ut in Dilu<v>io fecit vel in dodran<te>*: the Flood. What may well have been an influential context is one of the Deluge stanzas of the poem attributed to St. Columba:

> Invehunt nubes pontias
> > Ex fontibus brumalias
> Tribus profundioribus
> > Oceani dodrantibus
> Maris, coeli climatibus
> > Caeruleis turbinibus[41]

(F. J. E. Raby:) The clouds carry the wintry floods from the fountains of the sea (*pontias*), the three deeper floods (*dodrantibus*) of Ocean, to the regions of heaven in azure whirlwinds.[42] (Or better, perhaps, "from the realms of sea and sky".)

And another portion of the Hisperica Famina has a similar ring:

> Trina mormoreus pastricat trophea nothus;
> Quod spumaticum rapuit tolo diluuium;
> Pollentemque tonuit rapere dodrantem;
> Ac corporeas perculit tactu effigies

---

39 Ehwald, p. 526/103-14.
40 *Mittelalterliche Studien* 1 (see n. 14 above), p. 240.
41 *Revue celtique* 5 (1881-83) 209; *Oxford Book of Medieval Latin Verse*, p. 62.
42 *Ibid.*, p. 458.

— i.e. (loosely) the south sea-wind snatched the foaming Flood and its swelling *dodrans* and destroyed all creatures.[43] These contexts suggest that in terms of the account in Genesis, the *dodrans* is applied to that aspect of the Flood which came between the opened springs of the deep and the storms (or cataracts) of heaven, and was driven and swept up over the land by the storm-winds.[44]

However, the most powerful influence upon all of these Insular writers is not the book of Genesis, but inescapably those lines nearly adjoining our earlier passage from the book of Job: *Who shut up the sea with doors when it brake forth as if it had issued out of the womb ... and set bars and doors, and said, Hitherto shalt thou come, but no further: and here shall thy swelling waves be stayed*. The Philippus commentary makes the connection:

> Hunc ergo "maris processum" effusionem aquarum dicere mihi videtur qui de occultis venarum terrae sinibus emanabat, et operiebat omnem faciem terrae; quod in Diluvio manifestius factum legimus, ubi dicitur: *Et omnes fontes abyssi magnae aperti sunt*. Proinde vulvam maris terrae sinum aestimo ...
>
> So I think this coming forth of the sea means the outpouring of waters that issued from hidden channels deep underground and covered the whole face of the earth [during the Creation], which we more plainly read of as happening in the Flood: *And all the springs of the great abyss were opened*. Hence I take the sea-womb to be the depths of the earth ...

The anonymous Irishman who identified *dodrans* and Deluge evidently took his wording from this passage;[45] and, as Bede's method of attack should have led us to expect, the other writers who use the word seem to have been thoroughly familiar with the adjoining Philippus passages which stress the same explanation for the Flood as for the tides of Ocean.

III

The literary evidence, then, suggests a background and a range of meaning for Insular Latin *dodrans* which are entirely compatible with the suggested origin out of the Philippus commentary. To learn more,

---

43 Jenkinson, p. 17/489-92.

44 In the Irish Augustine (seventh century) there is a clear consideration of the Flood's meteorology — in the literal sense only, as the author is careful to say in ruling out consideration of the waters above the firmament. There is a mention of contemporary inroads by the sea, tearing headlands away from the main, in the same context (PL 35.2156-58).

45 Bischoff suggested the influence of Jerome's wording in his commentary upon the same topic, *et eliquat in dulcem pluviarum saporem*; but obviously Philippus' wording is incomparably closer.

we turn to what has usually been regarded as an entirely different literature.

In Old English glossaries of the early eighth century (including later copies of the same material), *dodrans* is rendered by the vernacular term *egur, eagor*, whose meaning is also rather cloudy.[46] Its literary employment, however, brings us at once to the description of the Flood in the poetic paraphrase of Genesis:

> Drihten sende
> regn from roderum and eac rume let
> willeburnan on woruld þringan
> of ædra gehwære, egorstreamas
> swearte swogan. Sæs up stigon
> ofer stæðweallas.[47]

The Lord sent rain from heaven and also caused great springs to burst forth from every vein of earth, the *egor*-currents, dark, to roar; the seas rose up over the shore-walls (cliffs).

In the same context, the compound or metaphor *egorhere* "army or host of the *egor*" appears twice: the host of the *egor* slew all earth's offspring;[48] and

> Ic eow treowa þæs
> mine selle, þæt ic on middangeard
> næfre egorhere eft gelæde
> wæter ofer widland.[49]

I give you My promise that never again shall I bring the *egor*-host onto the earth, the water over the continents.

We may take it that the use of this word stands under the influence of Insular Latin *dodrans*, since it is extremely unlikely that the Latin-Old

---

46   The dictionaries' definitions seem, in fact, to depend more on the supposed senses of *dodrans* than upon the Old English contexts. An egregious case is the entry *egor* in the J. Bosworth and T. N. Toller *Anglo-Saxon Dictionary* (Oxford, 1898), p. 244, with the definition "nine ounces or inches, a span", which rests upon nothing more than the fact that in earlier dictionaries and one old glossary (Cotton Cleopatra) the original Latin sense of *dodrans* was assumed. Documentations: Erfurt Glossary *aegur* and Corpus Glossary *egur*, ed. J. D. Pheifer, no. 316, and W. M. Lindsay, D343; Cotton Cleopatra *egor*, ed. T. Wright and R. Wülcker, *Anglo-Saxon and Old English Vocabularies* (London, 1884), I 386/29 and 474/4; applied to Aldhelm's letter to Ehfrid, A. W. Napier, ed., *Old English Glosses, Chiefly Unpublished* (Oxford, 1900), no. 13/1; added to *malina* in the composite Harley Glossary, ed. R. T. Oliphant (The Hague, 1966), D811, and Wright and Wülcker, 225/11.

47   G. P. Krapp and E. V. K. Dobbie, eds., *The Junius Manuscript*, ASPR 1 (New York, 1931), p. 43/1371-76.

48   *Ibid.*, p. 44/1402-3.

49   *Ibid.*, p. 47/1535-38.

English glosses established the equivalence of the two terms from the context of the Genesis poem, or that Germanic mythology afforded a primeval flood with exactly this name.[50]

The other occurrences of the Old English word seem to add to the resemblance, though they do not make the sense much more precise. In *Beowulf*, the context is a heroic swimming contest:

> þær git eagorstream earmum þehton,
> mæton merestræta, mundum brugdon,
> glidon ofer garsecg. Geofon yþum weol,
>   wintrys wylm[um];[51]

... where you two topped the *eagor*-current with your arms, spanned the seaways, plied your hands, slid over the deep; Ocean surged with waves, with winter's billows ...

Andreas, a poem whose phrasing many a reader has felt to be imitative of *Beowulf*'s, uses the same compound of *eagor* four times in connection with the sea, but only once with a comparable effect of danger or of hyperbole:

> Frecne þuhton
> egle ealada, eagorstreamas
> beoton bordstæðu, brun oft oncwæð
> yð oðerre, hwilum upp astod
> of brimes bosme on bates fæðm,
> egesa ofer yðlid.

Awful, terrible the seaways seemed; the *eagor*-currents beat the ship's sides (?), dark wave often answered wave, sometimes rose up out of the sea's bosom into the boat's lap, a terror over the vessel.[52]

The other three occurrences in the same poem may, for all that their contexts suggest, be simply poetic diction for "the sea". In the Old English Metres of Boethius (the poetic paraphrase closely associated with King Alfred) the same *eagorstream* compound has become so pallid that it serves as a name for the sea still further displaced so as to refer to the element Water.[53] However, we return to the very specific sense

---

50   Vernacular poetry, even when written down, was not glossed in Latin (the procedure would have seemed nonsensical). A supposed connection between *eagor* and Ægir, a figure of Norse mythology, was shown to be impossible by the *Oxford English Dictionary* (see below).

51   Ed. Fr. Klaeber (Boston, 1950), p. 20/513-16.

52   Lines 440-45, ed. K. R. Brooks (Oxford, 1961), p. 15 and notes; Krapp and Dobbie, eds., *The Vercelli Book*, ASPR 2 (New York, 1932), p. 15. I have repunctuated.

53   Along with several other sea terms used in the same way. Metre 20/115, 122; Krapp and Dobbie, eds., *The Paris Psalter and the Meters of Boethius*, ASPR 5 (New York, 1932), pp. 180-81.

attested by the Genesis poem when we find the simple *egor* as an interlinear gloss explaining *Cataclysmus*, the Flood, in a Latin description
of a tidal wave.[54]

There is a later English word, now spelled *eagre* or *eager*, which is used
of the tidal bores of such rivers as the Severn and the Trent and is
thoroughly well attested in that sense since the twelfth century, nearly
as far back as the recordings of Old English *eagor*.[55] The *Oxford Dictionary
of English Etymology* is relatively favorable to the modern English word's
being the continuation of *eagor*,[56] if the latter was a compound of Old
English *ēa* "river; water" and some element beginning with *g* — for
which, however, no convincing suggestion has yet been advanced.[57]

It is not hard to do so. There is an Old English *gyru* "mud, fen",
plural *gyrwas* "fens, fen-dwellers", another form of which may appear as
gerae (for *gyrae*?) glossing *congregatio aquarum* and *rivi aggerum* (the waters
of Egypt, Isaiah 19: 6).[58] With *gyru* the dictionaries compare *gor* "filth,
excrement, guts", which may well be an unmutated form; the Modern
English descendant, *gore*, has a sense which suggests a semantic development found in a number of Old English words — from "outflow,
falling liquid, drop (etc.)" to "blood". If Old English *gyru* has a basic
sense of "overflowed land", then a compound with *gor, ēa-gor*, might
well mean "river-overflowings". I do not offer this etymology as certain, but it is quite plausible, and thus adds to the likelihood that *eagor*
is the same word as *eagre* and has always meant a tidal bore. This

54   A. W. Napier (see n. 46), no. 7/159, p. 159. The context (Ehwald, p. 267/3-5) is: "ferventis
oceani flustra et spumantis cataclismi caerula cum proprios egrederentur terminos et quasi divinae
potestatis censura Diluvii irruptionem minaretur seu in antiquam chaos omnia redire cogerentur,"
etc. (it will be noticed that the comparison with the Flood is repeated). Unlike his source Jerome,
Aldhelm does not make it clear that St. Hilarion's wave was caused by an earthquake. A Latin gloss
with the English reads *genus fluctus*, which may be picked up from *frementes fluctus* two lines below in
Aldhelm, or may be an early manifestation of the notion "tidal wave".

55   William of Malmesbury gives a somewhat sensational but very clear description of the
Severn bore under the Latinized spelling *higra*.

56   And thereby reverses its predecessor the *Oxford English Dictionary*, which did not consider the
possibility of a compound containing an initial (hard) *g*-, and which showed all other etymological
proposals (including some which still appear in various dictionaries) to be impossible phonologically.

57   The possibility of a compound first arose after the publication of the Oxford English Dictionary's entry, and as part of the suggestion of an *ēa-gār* "water-spear", on the analogy of the
word *bore*; *cf.* Ernest Weekley, *An Etymological Dictionary of Modern English* (1921), *s.v.* As the *Oxford
Dictionary of English Etymology* remarks, the idea lacks any sort of confirmation. Old English *æg-*, the
apparent first element of one or two compounds referring to the sea, is phonologically impossible
in *eagre*, and not necessarily directly related to *eagor*; it may be a by-form of another word.

58   H. D. Meritt, *Old English Glosses, a Collection* (New York, 1945) 55/8, from St. Gall MS. 229; in a
Continental copy, Insular *y* and *e* can easily have become confused.

meaning would then make it clear why *eagor* was chosen as the translation of *dodrans*-Deluge: we are once again among the terms of the Philippus commentary, with its identical cause for the Flood and for the twice daily Ocean tide, rushing violently with its *dodrans* (as some thought) up into the rivers of the world.

IV

By now, I suppose, it has been shown rather thoroughly that Bede knew the true origin of Insular Latin *dodrans*. It is also possible to assign a meaning to the word: "tidal wave" in all of the senses in which the phrase has been popularly used, including both waves and bores (eagres) actually produced by the rising tide, and rare cataclysmic inundations really caused — so the experts are always reminding us — by seismic events, in which case "tidal wave" is a misnomer. It can, however, be traced back into the late Middle Ages, in the form of the peculiar French phrase *raz de marée*. It seems odd that this false notion should have occurred both in early and in later times in northwestern Europe, and nowhere but there; odd, that is, unless it should turn out that no coincidence is involved, but that the concept has descended from the early Irish monks who studied the few books at hand in their cells above the Atlantic, and wrote poetry which drew upon their reading and their surroundings. However, if that should be the case, we seem to have nearly forgotten nowadays that the universal flood arrived in a tidal wave.

A result of this investigation is that a connection has been discovered — I believe for the first time — between an element of Old English literature and the style of the earliest Latin poetry of the islands. In this case the Latin schools demonstrably influenced the vernacular, and no doubt Old English sea poetry reflects other subtle topical influences of the same sort. A fuller appreciation of these effects, however, is likely to depend upon wider understanding of the unity of early Insular literary culture, including poetry in the Old Irish and Old Norse vernaculars. Two or three such poems come readily to mind, as well as some widespread themes such as that of the three dreadful waves.

The Ohio State University

THE WORKING METHOD OF A THIRTEENTH-CENTURY FRENCH NOTARY: THE EXAMPLE OF GIRAUD AMALRIC AND THE *COMMENDA* CONTRACT

John H. Pryor

THE first manuscript of the series II in the Archives Communales de la Ville de Marseille is the oldest extant French notarial cartulary. Of paper, with a parchment cover, the leaves approximately 30 cms. × 19.5 cms., this cartulary was written in the spring of 1248 by the notary of Marseilles, Giraud Amalric.[1] Amongst the thirteenth-century Marseillese notaries whose cartularies are extant, Amalric alone had his practice in the commercial centre of Marseilles: on the waterfront, alongside the tables of the money changers. Because he was a notary serving the commercial community of Marseilles, there were times when Amalric became particularly hard pressed with work, especially in March and April when large numbers of merchants departed on spring voyages to Outremer, the Maghreb, the kingdom of Sicily, and elsewhere. Between 17 March and 17 April 1248, Amalric wrote *notae* for 528 contracts: an average of 23 on each day on which he worked. On 30 and 31 March he wrote *notae* for 97 contracts. It would obviously have been impossible for him to have redacted on the spot *instrumenta* in completed form on parchment *cartae* for all these contracts. However, in the courts of Marseilles, *notae* were regarded as equally as efficacious a form of proof of contract as *instrumenta*, and therefore many of Amalric's clients did not require that he redact *instrumenta* for them.[2]

---

1   The cartulary was edited by Louis Blancard in part 2 of his *Documents inédits sur le comm   · de Marseille au moyen-âge*, 2 vols. (Marseilles, 1884-1885). One of the first works in an extremely difficult field, Blancard's edition is now outdated and historians, particularly historians of law, diplomatic, and the notariate, should be extremely wary in their use of it.

2   Régine Pernoud, ed., *Les statuts municipaux de Marseille*, Collection de textes pour servir à l'histoire de Provence publiée sous les auspices de S.A.S. le Prince de Monaco (Monaco-Paris, 1939), lib. 2, c. 16, par. 16 (p. 95): "Item decernimus quod omne debitum quod ex causa licita debeatur, super quo facta erit carta vel nota publica per manum notarii habentis auctoritatem officii tabellionatus a communi Massilie inscriptis celebratum presumatur, omni questione remota;..."

When receiving in the first instance the details of contracts from the parties involved, Amalric attempted neither to redact *instrumenta* on the spot nor, in most cases, even to write out the *notae* in their full form. Instead he used a working method which enabled him to cope with the volume of work by writing down in the first instance only the essential, economic details of a contract. Both completion of the *notae* and redaction of *instrumenta* were normally left until later.

Of the 1031 *notae* which Amalric wrote in his cartulary of 1248, 466 were for *commenda* contracts: that best known of medieval commercial contracts. These *notae* for *commenda* contracts demonstrate Amalric's working method extremely well. But before examining Amalric's method for writing *notae* for *commenda* contracts, the basic features of the *commenda* should be recapitulated:

1. a sedentary investor, generally known as the *commendator*, delivered capital into the possession of a travelling associate, generally known as the *tractator* but at Marseilles as the *commandatarius*;

2. the *tractator* might or might not contribute capital of his own to that of the *commendator*;

3. the *commendator* might make certain specifications concerning the management of the enterprise or direct the *tractator* to invest the *commenda* in certain specified commodities;

4. the *tractator* carried the capital away, generally overseas, to trade with it;

5. on expiration of the time or voyages agreed upon, the *tractator* returned to render account and divide the proceeds with the *commendator*. In certain circumstances the *tractator* could remit the proceeds to the *commendator* without personally making the return voyage;

6. after allowing for expenses and deducting the capital originally invested, profit was divided according to a ratio agreed upon in the contract. Any loss was born entirely by the *commendator* unless the *tractator* had also invested capital, in which case they bore liability for loss pro rata as they had invested.

*

*   *

On occasions, the script of *notae* written by Amalric for *commenda* contracts runs continuously through all the various clauses from beginning to end of the *notae* in their full, completed form. In such cases Amalric appears to have written out the full *notae* in the first instance: at the time when he received the details of the *commenda* contracts from the parties themselves. Such, for example, was the case in the *nota* given at Plate 2, no. 6 in which Amalric wrote:

Debet[3] Eodem die et loco. Ego Petrus de Cavallaria de Arelate confiteor et
   recognosco tibi Bertrando Borello
      de Arelate, me habuisse et recepisse in comanda a te, XXV libras
      monete miscue modo curribilis
   in Massilia, que sunt L libre raimondensium, implicatas in draparia et
      verdeto et in aliis co-
   munibus implicitis meis. Renuncians inde excepcioni non numerate
      et non tradite michi pecunie. Cum qua co-
   manda ibo, Deo dante, in proximo viagio quod facturus sum apud Pisis
      in galea Poncii Merueis,
   et inde revertar in hanc terram in dicta galea vel in alio ligno, ad for-
      tunam Dei et usum maris,
   et tuum resegum, et ad quartam partem lucri. Quam comandam
      promicto tibi per stipulacionem bene et fideliter porta-
   re tenere et custodire, et cum ea mercari et negociari prout melius
      potero vel scivero, et to-
   tum capitale et lucrum reducere in posse tui vel tuorum, et veritatem
      inde tibi dicere et fidem porta-
   re per totum. Obligans inde tibi et tuis omnia bona mea presencia et
      futura. Renuncians induciis XX
   dierum et quatuor mensium et omni alii dilacioni et iuri et excep-
      cioni per quam contra predicta venire possem.
            Factum fuit inde publicum instrumentum.
      Testes: Giraudus Manent, Durantus Carreria, Rainerius de Ulmo.

This *nota* followed the standard form used by Amalric for *notae* for *commenda* contracts. One should notice in particular that the clauses from *Quam comandam* onwards were standard to all *notae* for *commenda* contracts because they were unaffected by the economics of each individual contract. They concerned the obligations of the *tractator* and were the same irrespective of the value of the *commenda*, the type of investment, or the particular voyage in question. Consequently Amalric could omit these clauses in the first instance and thus save himself much time when working under pressure. In fact, he appears to have written out all the clauses uninterruptedly only when informed from the very beginning that the parties required *instrumenta*. In every case in which the clauses were written out uninterruptedly the notation "Factum fuit inde publicum instrumentum" was subscribed below the *nota*.

---

3 *Debet* indicated that the fee for the *nota* had not yet been paid. *Solutum* indicated that it had been paid.

However, when the parties did not require *instrumenta* as proof of contract, Amalric omitted those clauses which were extra to the economic details of the particular *commenda* contract in question. He simply wrote down the names of the parties, the value of the *commenda*, the type of investment, and the voyage to be made. Then leaving a space of about two inches blank, he wrote down the names of the witnesses to the contract and any clauses relevant to the obligations of the *commendator* or guarantors. Thus in the *nota* given at Plate 3, no. 9 he wrote:

Debet Eodem die et loco. Ego Jacobus Benedictus confiteor et recognosco tibi
        Guillelmo Guilaberto de Sancto Antonino, civi
    Massilie, me habuisse et recepisse in comanda a te XXX libras monete
        miscue modo curribilis in
    Massilia, implicatas in LXXXV bisanciis sarracenatis Acconis mundis et
        expeditis de doa-
    na et dacita et omnibus avariis. Renuncians inde excepcioni non
        numerate et non tradite michi pecunie.
    Cum qua comanda ibo, Deo dante, in proximo viagio quod facturus
        sum apud Ciprum in nave Sig
    sui que dicitur Signus.

                  in pipere

BLANK

                  vel sucaro
                  vel lana
                  capellorum
Testes: Gauterius Descmonte, Petrus de Molinis, Bernardus de Conchis.

In some cases such spaces left blank by Amalric remained completely unused thereafter.[4] The outcome of the *commendae* in question is unknown since the parties did not afterwards request that Amalric add anything further to the *notae*.

In the right-hand margin of such spaces left blank, Amalric occasionally wrote brief notes to remind himself of unusual clauses which the parties had included in their contract and which would have to be included in an *instrumentum* should one be redacted at any time in the future. For example, in the right-hand margin of the blank space of the *nota* given above (no. 9), Amalric wrote "in pipere vel sucaro vel lana capellorum". This referred to the types of goods in which the *tractator* was required to invest the *commenda*. Normally *tractatores* had a free hand to invest *commendae* in whatever way they considered most lucrative; however, *commendatores* occasionally demanded investment in cer-

4 See also Plate 3, no. 11.

PLATE I

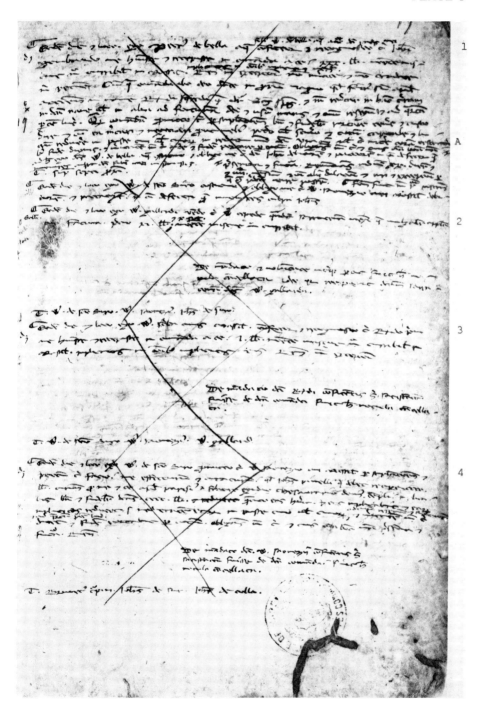

Cartulary of Giraud Amalric of 1248, fol. 17r

PLATE II

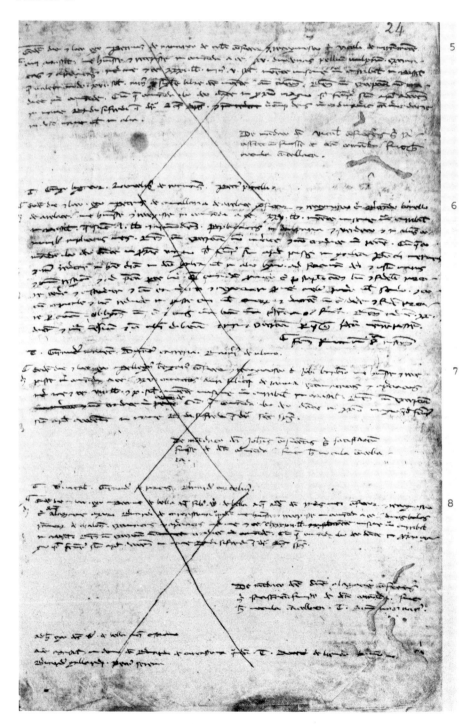

Cartulary of Giraud Amalric of 1248, fol. 24r

PLATE III

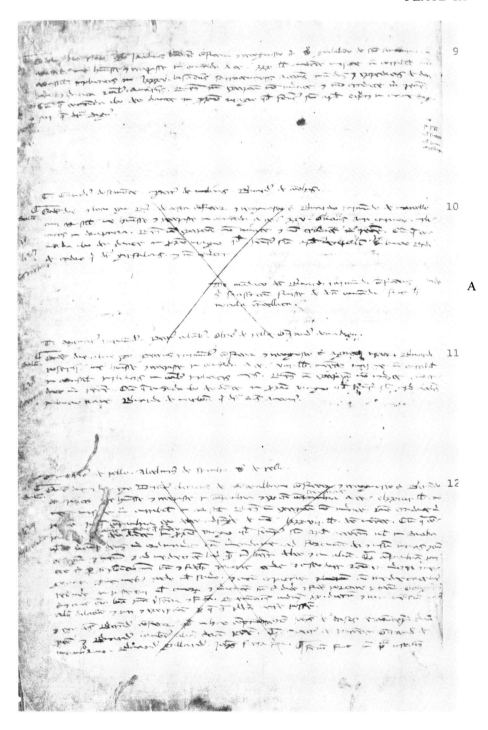

Cartulary of Giraud Amalric of 1248, fol. 60v

tain specified goods. This *commenda*, valued at £30 of mixed money[5] and invested in Sarracenate besants of Acre[6] for a voyage to Acre, was to be invested by the *tractator* in pepper, sugar, or the type of short wool used for making hats.[7] Since the *nota* was never completed, we do not know whether he ever managed to do so successfully.

A second type of short notation recorded the fact that the *tractator* had been given permission to remit the *commenda* proceeds to the *commendator* without having to make the return voyage in person. When a *tractator* had been given permission to do this, if Amalric did not intend to write out the full text of the *nota* in the first instance, he simply wrote the word *mitere* in the right hand margin of the blank space which he left below the text of the *nota* as he had thus far written it out.[8] If and when he later added those clauses which he had omitted in the first instance, the notation *mitere* reminded him to include the clause *vel tibi mictere coram testibus fide dignis*. Once having added this clause, together with the others, Amalric cancelled the word *mitere* in the margin. For example, in Plate 1, no. 1, at pt. A, the word *mitere* can be seen cancelled in the right hand margin of what was the blank space before the additional clauses were added. Laterally opposite the cancelled *mitere* can be seen the full clause for which the notation had served as a reminder and which Amalric included when he eventually added to the *nota* those clauses which he had originally omitted. The promise which the tractator made to return the *commenda* to the *commendator* was thus made to read: "Quam comandam promicto tibi per stipulacionem ... et totum capitale et lucrum reducere in posse tui vel tuorum in reditu meo dicti viagii vel tibi mitere coram testibus fide dignis, et veritatem inde tibi dicere..."

When a *tractator* or *commendator* was not content with Amalric's *nota* as proof of contract, he could ask that an *instrumentum* be redacted from the *nota*. As seen above, he might ask for it at the time when Amalric first received the details of the *commenda* contract from the parties and in such cases Amalric wrote out the full text of the *nota* in the first instance. However, even when neither party had requested an *in-*

---

5 Mixed money (*moneta miscua*): a combination of all the various currencies circulating at Marseilles, evaluated at a particular rate against any one currency.

6 Sarracenate besants of Acre (*bisancii sarracenati Acconis*): imitations of Muslim besants, struck at Acre. As distinct from "Sarracen besants" which were the true Muslim coins.

7 *Lana capellorum*: see A.-M. Bautier, "Contribution à un vocabulaire économique du Midi de la France," *Revue du Cange. Archivum Latinitatis medii aevi* 28 (1958) 120.

8 Plate 3, no. 10, at pt. A.

strumentum in the first instance and Amalric had therefore omitted the unnecessary clauses, a request for an *instrumentum* might be made to Amalric later. A *commendator* might make such a request if he had to take legal action against a *tractator* who had failed to make proper restitution of the proceeds of a *commenda*. Before redacting the *instrumentum*, Amalric returned to the *nota* and completed all the clauses omitted in the first instance. The fact that these clauses were added later is often easily discernible because the ink or pen used was different. On occasions Amalric had left too large a space blank and there was still space remaining after he had finished completing the *nota*. However, more often, he had not left enough space blank and the extra clauses had to be crowded in and around the names of the witnesses with the lines of writing becoming progressively more cramped as Amalric advanced. Such was the case in the *nota* given at Plate 1, no. 1, where it is exceptionally clear that the clauses from *Quam comandam* onwards were crammed in afterwards:[9]

Debet Eodem die et loco. Ego Petrus de Bella Aqua (filius Guillelmi de Bella
        Aqua, auctoritate dicti patris mei), confiteor et recognosco tibi
        Johanni
    Gombaudo, me habuisse et recepisse in comanda a te, XXX libras
        monete mis-
    cue modo curribilis in Massilia, (implicatas in omnibus implicitis meis).
        Renuncians inde excepcioni non numerate et non tradite
    michi pecunie. Cum qua comanda ibo, Deo dante, in proximo viagio
        quod facturus sum apud
    Acconem in nave Raymundi Sifredi que dicitur Sanctus Spiritus, et inde
        revertar in hanc terram
    in dicta nave vel in alia, ad fortunam Dei et usum maris et tuum
        resegum et ad quartam
    partem lucri.[10] Quam comandam promicto tibi per stipulacionem bene
        et fideliter portare tenere et custo-
    dire et cum ea mercari et negociari prout melius potero vel scivero et
        totum capitale et lu-
    crum reducere in posse tui vel tuorum in reditu meo dicti viagii vel tibi
        mitere coram testi- *mitere*

9 In this text, and in those following, parentheses indicate insertions presumably made by the notary at the time of writing. Italics indicate a cancellation made by the notary. Square brackets indicate either interpolation by the present author or missing or illegible passages reconstructed.

10 Compare the clauses from here to *venire possem* with those written out uninterruptedly in the first instance of writing a *nota* for a *commenda* contract as in the *nota* at Plate 2, no. 6 (above, p. 435).

bus fide dignis, et veritatem inde tibi dicere et fidem portare per totum.
Obligans inde tibi et tuis omnia bona mea # (# presencia et futura.
Renuncians induciis XX dierum et quatuor mensium et omni alii
dilacioni et iuri et excepcioni per quam contra predicta venire
possem).
Factum fuit inde publicum instrumentum.
Ad hec ego dictus Guillelmus de Bella Aqua constituo et obligo me tibi
dicto Johanni debitorem et pacatorem in omni defectu quam
invenires culpa dicti filii mei in premissis.
Testes: supra scripti proximi.

Note that even though Amalric attempted to squeeze all the additional
clauses in before the guarantee clause of the *tractator's* father (*Guillelmus
de Bella Aqua*), he had left insufficient space for them and was obliged to
complete them below it. A *signum remissionis* was used to indicate the
position of those clauses added below the guarantee clause.

Once having added to a *nota* all clauses that he wished to, Amalric
cancelled the *nota* by drawing a diagonal cross through it and noting the
fact that an *instrumentum* had been redacted from it ("Factum fuit inde
publicum instrumentum"). The statutes of Marseilles demanded that all
notaries note in their cartularies the reasons wherefore they cancelled
any *nota*. When, as in the case discussed above, a notary cancelled a *nota*
because he had redacted an *instrumentum* from it onto a *carta*, he could
make the cancellation without need for witnesses. However, when a
notary cancelled a *nota* because the debt recorded in it had been paid or
the contract or obligation recorded in it had been fulfilled, the cancellation could only be made at the wish of the parties and before witnesses.[11]

In those cases where a *commenda* voyage was satisfactorily completed
before either party had had Amalric redact an *instrumentum* from the
nota, Amalric cancelled the *nota* by again drawing a diagonal cross
through it and, in accordance with the demand of the statutes, indicating the reason for the cancellation. Such cancellations invariably
declared that the *nota* was cancelled because the *commendator* had
received satisfaction from the *tractator*:

De mandato dicti Raymundi [the *commendator*] confitentis sibi satisfactum
fuisse de dicta comanda fuit hec notula cancellata.[12]

The *tractator* need not necessarily have completed a voyage with the *commenda*. There might be many reasons why the parties might wish to can-

---

11 Pernoud, ed., *Les statuts municipaux de Marseille*, lib. 1, c. 28, par. 19 (p. 42).
12 Plate 1, no. 3. *Cf.* nos. 5, 7, 8, and 10.

cel a *nota* recording a contract. For example, a *nota* on fol. 8r of Amalric's cartulary, which recorded a contract for a *commenda* valued at £51 of mixed money for a voyage to Ceuta, was cancelled on the same day as it was written ("Eodem die et loco. De mandato dicti Mathei [the *commendator*] confitentis sibi satisfactum fuisse de dicta comanda fuit hec notula cancellata"). Presumably, the *tractator* had not completed a voyage to Ceuta and back in a single day. Apparently the parties simply changed their minds about the *commenda* contract and decided not to go through with it. They therefore asked Amalric to cancel the *nota*. On the other hand, some *notae* were cancelled long after they were written and in such cases we may assume that the *tractatores* had in fact completed extensive voyages. In most cases Amalric did not give the dates of cancellations of *notae*; however, in eight cases in which he did, the average time elapsed was about two years.[13]

When a *nota* was cancelled because the *commenda* contract had been satisfactorily fulfilled, an *instrumentum* could not thereafter be redacted from that *nota*. In no case does cancellation of a *nota* by virtue of satisfactory fulfillment of a *commenda* contract occur together with cancellation of it by virtue of redaction of an *instrumentum*. Conversely, when an *instrumentum* had been redacted, the *tractator* could no longer be released from his obligations under the *commenda* contract simply by cancelling the *nota*. A separate notarial act became required. One *nota* for such a release from obligation is found on fol. 93v of Amalric's cartulary:

Solutum Eodem die et loco. Ego Otho Angossola confiteor et recognosco tibi
    Bertrando Davino quod
        tu venisti mecum ad rectum computum et veram racionem de illa
        comanda de mastego
        quam ego tibi feci, diu est, in viagio quod fecisti apud Bogiam, et de
        omnibus aliis comandis quas,
        quam a me tam a Nicolao Angossola, habuisti usque in hodiernum
        diem, et satisfe-

---

13 | Folio | Nota written | Dest. of Voyage | Nota cancelled |
|---|---|---|---|
| 22v | 18 March 1248 | Acre | 11 May 1251 |
| 27r | 27 March 1248 | Messina | 11 May 1251 |
| 31r | 28 March 1248 | Acre | 22 March 1249 |
| 31v | 28 March 1248 | Acre | 22 March 1249 |
| 33r | 30 March 1248 | Sicily | 6 April 1250 |
| 36v | 30 March 1248 | Ceuta | 2 September 1250 |
| 39r | 30 March 1248 | Acre | 31 March 1250 |
| 75v | 15 April 1248 | Acre | 24 March 1251 |

cisti michi plenarie de dictis comandis. Renuncians inde excepcioni
    dictarum comandarum michi a te
non satisfactarum. Faciens inde tibi finem et remissionem et pactum
    perpetuum de non
petendo aliquid ulterius a te vel a tuis occasione dictarum coman-
    darum.
Testes: Petrus Guinardus, Bernardus Caper Bonis, Petrus Anglicus.

*
* *

Amalric noted that *instrumenta* had been redacted from all *notae*, but
only from those *notae*, which he had completed and rendered into their
full form. This was true whether he wrote out the full *notae* uninterruptedly in the first instance or whether he completed them later. In
both cases, it might well be asked why he went to the bother of completing the *notae* at all? Rehearsal of all the clauses was understandable
in those few cases where an unusual clause, such as a remission clause
or one requiring that the *tractator* invest in certain specified goods, was
to be included. But in most cases the clauses which Amalric added in
order to complete the *notae* were completely standard as given above (p.
435).[14] The explanation for Amalric's apparent excess of zeal is found
by comparing his working method with that of later notaries of Marseilles.

    Later in the thirteenth century, notaries at Marseilles kept two types
of cartulary. In the first they wrote down *notae* when asked to do so in
the first instance. These first cartularies were elongated and of a shape
designed to facilitate the notary's carrying them in his hand (approximately 30 cms. × 11 cms.). The notaries carried these cartularies
with them when they went to receive the details of contracts at the
homes and businesses of their clients. Unlike the first type, the second
type of cartulary was not intended to be portable. These cartularies
were of the same dimensions as Amalric's of 1248: approximately 30
cms. × 20 cms. They were kept at the notaries' offices or homes and in
them extended drafts in completed form (*extensa*) were made from the
notae before the *instrumenta* were finally redacted on parchment *cartae*.
In the Archives Départementales des Bouches-du-Rhône there are six
cartularies of the first type which belonged to the notary Pascal de
Meyrargues and which date from the period 1287-1300 (série 381 E

---

14 60% of completed *notae* have the clauses precisely in this form. 25% differ only in having a
remission clause while only 15% are significantly different in any way.

(*L'étude Malauzat*), nos. 7-12). On the other hand, four cartularies of the same notary in the Archives Communales de la Ville de Marseille are of the second type (série II, nos. 22-25). There are *notae* for two *commenda* contracts in one of the cartularies of the first type for which there are the corresponding *extensa* in one of the cartularies of the second type. Let us look at the *nota* for one of these *commenda* contracts:[15]

Arch. Dép. des B.-du-R., série 381 E, no. 10, fol. 86r

> Eodem die. Ego J[ordanus] L[au]geriu[s]
> civis Massilie, confiteor tibi [Giraude], uxori
> Johannis de Sancto Maximino, presenti, me a te
> habuisse in comanda, tres centos turonenses grossos
> argenti, *qui* cum quibus *proinde* debeo mercari et implicari
> in Maresma in hiis quibus melius potero, (et abinde in antea), ad
> utilitatem meam et tuam, et ad fortunam Dei
> et usum maris, et ad quartam partem lucri.
> Et promito tibi et tuis dictum capitale et lucrum
> ponere in posse tuo et tuorum. Sub obligacione etc.
> Renuncians etc. *Iurans*
> Actum in domo Johannis Garcie.
> Testes: Petrus Candelerii,
>   Guillelmus de Barcinonia,
>   Rostagnus Arquerii

The completed *extensum* which was written up from this *nota* is found in Arch. Comm. de la Ville de Marseille, série II, no. 22, fol. 80r:

> In nomine Domini amen. Anno incarnacionis eiusdem millesimo CC
>   XCV [XCVI], indictione IX, VIII idus marcii. Noverint universi
> quod ego Jordanus Laugerius, marinarius civis Massilie, bona fide et
>   sine dolo confiteor et in veritate sollempniter
> recognosco tibi Giraude, uxori Johannis de Sancto Maximino,
>   presenti stipulanti et recipienti, et tuis,
> me a te habuisse et recepisse numeracione continua in comanda et
>   nomine et ex causa comande, tres centos
> turonenses grossos argenti. In quibus renuncio excepcioni· *dicte*
>   *comande* (eorundem turonensium argenti) non habitorum a te et
>   non receptorum.
> Quam commandam dictorum CCC turonensium portare debeo, Deo
>   dante, (ex pacto habito inter me et te) ad lucrandum et negocian-
>   dum in viagio

---

15 See also Arch. Dép. des B.-du-R., série 381 E, no. 10, fol. 41r and Arch. Comm. de la Ville de Mar., série II, no. 22, fol. 64r.

Maresme quod facturus sum modo in gualea Stephani de Sancto
   Paulo vocata Sancta Katerina, et abinde
ubicunque Deus michi ministraverit, ad fortunam Dei et usum maris,
   et ad tuum resegium, et ad quartam partem
lucri dictorum CCC turonensium michi dandam. Et promitto tibi,
   dicte Giraude presenti stipulanti et recipienti, et tuis,
predictam commandam bene et fideliter tractare custodire et im-
   plicare ut melius potero et scivero ad utilitatem
et comodum tui et mei, et illam comandam seu dictos CCC turonenses
   argenteos implicatam vel eos implicatos,
ac totum capitale et lucrum ipsius commande, reducere Massilie in
   dicta galea *vel i* in potestate tui vel
tuorum fideliter, et veritatem tibi inde dicam per totum et bonam
   fidem portabo. Alioquin promito tibi et tuis per stipulacionem dare restituere et resarcire ultra dictam commandam omnes
   sumptus et expensas dampna disturbia gravamina
et interesse, quos que et quas pro petendis dictis comanda et lucro
   eiusdem a me faceres sustineres vel
incurreres, *quoque modo* (aut tui), in curia vel extra litigando vel aliter
   quoque modo. De quibus promitto tibi et tuis credere solo simplici
verbo tantum. Pro quibus omnibus et singulis supradictis obligo tibi
   et tuis omnia bona mea habita et habenda. Renunsians inde
induciis XX dierum et quatuor mensium et omni alii iuri. Actum in
   domo quadam heredum Johannis Garcie condam,
presentibus Petro Candelerii, Rostagno Arquerii, et Guillelmo de Bar-
   cinonia, testibus ad hec
vocatis et rogatis, et me Paschale de Mayranegis notario publico
   Massilie comitatuumque Provincie et Forcalquerii, qui
mandato precibus et requisicionibus utriusque partis hanc cartam
   scripsi etc.
            Sumptum est instrumentum.

In 1248, Amalric's practice had been to complete the *notae* in his cartulary before redacting *instrumenta* from them. By 1278, the date of the
next extant Marseillese notarial cartulary, practice had changed and
notaries made an entirely separate draft in a second cartulary before
redacting *instrumenta*. As in the above case, nothing further was added
to the text of the *nota* after the first instance. When an *extensum* was
written out, the notary cancelled the *nota* by drawing a diagonal cross
through it, but it was against the *extensum* that the notary recorded the
redaction of an *instrumentum*. (In the above case: "Sumptum est instrumentum.") Some notaries did not even call the register in which
they wrote *notae* in the first instance a cartulary (*cartularium*). Guillaume
Faraud considered the register in which he wrote out *extensa* as his *car-*

tularium and wrote the phrase *in cartulario est* at the foot of a *nota* after he had made an *extensum* from it.[16] This change of method and use of an entirely new type of cartulary for *notae* was characterized by the use by later notaries of a cartulary for *extensa* of the same dimensions as that in which Amalric had written *notae* in 1248. It was because Amalric had not used a second cartulary for *extensa*, and in fact had never written out *extensa* at all, that he had needed to complete the *notae* before redacting *instrumenta*. In a sense, his cartulary had been for both *notae* and *extensa* and the former had become the latter by the mere process of completion. However, the completed form of *notae* as used by Amalric was not as fully expanded as the form of true *extensa*. Comparison of the form of Amalric's completed *notae* with that of contemporary *instrumenta* for *commenda* contracts written by other notaries, makes this point immediately apparent. To begin with, the protocol and eschatocol of Amalric's *notae* were never written out in full form, as they always were in both *extensa* and *instrumenta*. Whereas to redact *instrumenta* from *extensa* was simply a matter of transcription, Amalric's working method left expansion and revision of the text to be made between the stages of the completed *notae* and of the *instrumenta*. Three factors indicate that Amalric did not write out *extensa* but rather made the necessary revisions and expansions to his *notae* mentally: firstly, his cartulary was of the same physical dimensions as those used by later notaries for *extensa*; secondly, he often went to considerable trouble to complete the text of *notae* before redacting *instrumenta*; and thirdly, it was against his *notae* that he recorded the fact that *instrumenta* had been redacted. Apparently this working method to which Amalric's cartulary testifies came to be considered unsatisfactory and was replaced by one in which the work of revision and expansion of *notae* was accomplished in writing rather than mentally. In fact Amalric's cartulary is of an entirely different genre from the extant cartularies of later notaries of Marseilles. It has much more in common with the well known Genoese cartularies of the twelfth century.

University of Sydney

---

16 Compare the *notae* and *extensa* for the same two *commenda* contracts in Arch. Dép. des B.-du-R., série 381 E, no. 1, fols. 6r and 27r and Arch. Comm. de la Ville de Mar., série II, no. 2, fols. 52r and 55r.

PAPALISM AND CONCILIARISM
IN ANTONIO ROSELLI'S *MONARCHIA*[1]

J. A. F. Thomson

I N recent years there has been a considerable amount of new study of mediaeval political thought, and more particularly of the intellectual basis of the conciliar movement and its connexion with older traditions of canonist teaching. The general tendency of this study has been to see the high-water mark of conciliar ideas being reached at the time of the Council of Constance, after which debates on ecclesiology tended to become a sterile reiteration of old positions in the renewed crisis between Papacy and Council at Basel. Dr. Anthony Black, however, has drawn attention to the fact that the writers of the Basel period took an interest in theories of constitutionalism and monarchy, and that they formulated their ideas in specifically political and secular forms, and has thereby suggested that the main interest of these writers lies in the more definitely political aspects of their work.[2] This is obviously a fair opinion, if one's concern is primarily with the development of political thought and with placing these writers in the context of a changing philosophy of the state, but at the same time it would appear to be worthwhile to examine the ecclesiology of the period, to see what light it throws on attitudes to the Papacy in the years following the great crisis of 1378-1417. As far as the popes were concerned, the problem was one of trying to reassert traditional claims to the plenitude of power and reconcile this with the obvious fact that only the action of the Council of Constance, and the denial there of such papal superiority, had brought about the reunion of the Church under an unchallenged pope.

1   I am grateful to Dr. A. J. Black for reading an earlier draft of this paper and making a number of suggestions for its improvement.

2   A. J. Black, "The Political Ideas of Conciliarism and Papalism, 1430-1450," *Journal of Ecclesiastical History* 20 (1969) 45-65; *Monarchy and Community* (Cambridge, 1970).

One work which illustrates this problem clearly is the *Monarchia sive Tractatus de potestate imperatoris et papae* by Antonio Roselli of Arezzo. The author was not, by absolute standards, a great political thinker, and even by comparison with some of his contemporaries, such as Nicholas of Cusa or Juan Turrecremata, he is certainly a second ranker. In one way, however, his range is wider than the latter's, because Turrecremata does not propound any theory of power outside the ecclesiastical sphere although, of course, he had no necessity to do so. Roselli's treatise is not a neglected masterpiece of political theory, and it is easy to explain the lack of interest which historians have taken in it. It is lengthy and verbose, extending to some three hundred folio pages in the most recent edition, that published in Hanover in 1611,[3] the style is inelegant and there is much reiteration of argument. The ideas in it, however, are put forward with subtlety and precision, which reveal the acuteness of the author's mind and his concern to make his position absolutely clear. Only one important modern study has concentrated on the work,[4] and valuable though it is, it does not cover all aspects of Roselli's thought. It sets his theories in the context of his life and career, which made an important contribution to his writings, and notes how the work can be related to earlier and to contemporary studies of monarchy, but it does not discuss the way in which the historical circumstances of the time created problems for a man whose sympathies lay firmly with the Papacy in its attempts to recover its power. However much he might uphold papal tendencies to absolutism, he still felt it necessary to recognise the validity of the actions taken at Constance. What makes this attitude the more significant is the position that Roselli held at the time when the work was written, because in the early 1430's he was a consistorial advocate at the Curia and in that capacity was responsible for drafting the bull *Deus novit* of 13 September 1433 which attacked the radical theses of the fathers at Basel.[5] It seems likely that such reservations as Roselli had about the nature of the papal plenitude of power may well have been shared by others in the Roman court, and

---

3 M. Goldast, *Monarchia S. Romani Inperii sive Tractatus de iurisdictione imperiali seu regia & pontificia seu sacerdotali* 1 (Hanover, 1611), pp. 252-556 (cited as Goldast).

4 K. Eckermann, *Studien zur Geschichte des monarchischen Gedankens im 15. Jahrhundert, Abhandlungen zur mittleren und neueren Geschichte*, Heft 73 (Berlin, 1933) (cited as Eckermann).

5 Eckermann, pp. 33-36; A. Stoecklin, "Das Ende der mittelalterlichen Konzilsbewegung," *Zeitschrift für schweizerische Kirchengeschichte* 37 (1943) 24. The first version of the *Monarchia* dates from 1433, the same year as *Deus novit* (Black, *Monarchy and Community*, p. 58). Roselli subsequently revised it, but the general tone of the work does not appear to have been altered (Eckermann, pp. 49-50).

it is noteworthy that his position at the Curia was not disturbed after he had written the *Monarchia*.[6]

Certainly there were many places in the work where supporters of papal absolutism would find Roselli's views congenial. It was necessary for a man's salvation for him to be within the hierarchical Church as well as within the Imperium.[7] At the same time the very way in which monarchy was also regarded as something holy could by implication represent a willingness to abandon the most extreme claims of papalist writing. On the other hand, when he considers the vital text which was cited on behalf of the Petrine primacy (*super hanc petram*, Matt. 16: 18) he interprets the rock as Christ rather than as Peter, a view which is more normally found in writers who were critical of papal power. He did make some attempt to reconcile conflicting views by seeing Peter as a secondary foundation, through whom power was transmitted to the other apostles and to their successors.[8]

There is much of the work which is of little concern to the student of conciliarism. Roselli spends much time in purely academic consideration of matters which were no longer live issues in the sphere of practical politics, particularly in his discussions of the origins of imperial power and of whether the pope was superior to the emperor. At a time when increasing common interests were driving the papacy and the empire into a reconciliation, Roselli's lengthy consideration of their respective claims to authority possesses little save an erudite irrelevance to mundane matters, though in this he does not stand apart from his contemporaries.[9] His attitudes to secular power are totally theoretical in the way in which he concentrates on the position of the emperor, and claims that all secular princes come under him in temporal matters, apart from the king of Sicily, who is subject to the pope in the temporal as well as in the spiritual sphere. In this he is completely in the legist tradition, looking back to the Empire of antiquity with its universal character, and he pays no attention to emerging national sentiment.[10] There is some evidence of him drawing theoretical conclusions from an observation of practice in ecclesiastical matters, as in his discussion of

---

6 Eckermann, p. 26.

7 Goldast, p. 312: "Deus constituit divinam et humanam monarchiam, et extra istam Ecclesiam et sanctam monarchiam, in qua consistit Ecclesia tota militans, non est salus." The power of the monarch was seen as subordinate to that of the pope, who possessed the power of both swords. (See below, p. 449.)

8 Eckermann, pp. 115-17; Goldast, pp. 318-19.

9 Eckermann, p. 94.

10 Goldast, p. 509; Eckermann, pp. 56, 72, 90-91.

the question of priestly celibacy, where he argues that chastity is not essential for priestly orders, although it is for monks. Here he defends his case by reference to the marriage of priests in the Greek Church.[11] In various places one finds references to historical precedents, as in the discussion of the power of the emperor to depose popes, where reference is made to the Synod of Sutri of 1046, and in the consideration of whether it is permissible for a pope to renounce his dignity, Roselli cites the case of Celestine V, and notes that despite his renunciation he was subsequently canonised.[12]

When one is examining Roselli's attitude to the conciliar movement, the crucial sections of the *Monarchia* to which one must refer are the second and third books, dealing respectively with papal power and with councils.[13] It is clear in these that he could not dismiss the actions of the Council of Constance as unimportant and that he was too honest to evade the theoretical issue which was posed by them. The impression which is left after reading the work is one of a man faced with a basic problem of intellectual integrity, of how he could reconcile a belief in the rightfulness of papal claims to power with the recognition of the practical necessity of accepting the validity of the actions taken by the Councils of Pisa and Constance if the titles of the popes of his own time were to be regarded as authentic. His acute awareness of the problems posed by the Great Schism is clear from the references which he makes to it, some of which will be cited later in this paper.

It is clear, however, that Roselli distinguished between upholding the rights of the Papacy as an institution and defending the men who occupied the supreme position in the Church, whose characters he was prepared to criticise. When discussing the method by which a pope should be chosen, he maintained that one pope should not be able to nominate his successor, "since today this office is not conferred on a man of holy life, but rather on blood and kindred."[14] But although he has no illusions about the characters of the popes, this does not prevent his outlook from being strongly papalist — this is clearly indicated in the list of powers which he declares are reserved to the pope. He appropriates to him what the civil lawyers claimed for the prince:

---

11 Goldast, p. 497. One may suspect that the negotiations between the Eastern Church and Eugenius IV just at the time when Roselli was writing may have prompted him to refer to this practice. For these, see J. Gill, *The Council of Florence* (Cambridge, 1961), pp. 51-54.

12 Goldast, pp. 287, 339.

13 *Ibid.*, pp. 301-79 (book 2), 379-446 (book 3).

14 *Ibid.*, p. 322. One suspects that this may be an allusion to the reliance placed by Martin V on Cardinal Prospero Colonna.

"Whatever pleases him has the force of law." He demonstrates that he is far from any Gelasian view of Church-State relations when he says: "He alone has both swords."[15] Even though he is concerned with vindicating princely authority as well as papal, and however much his arguments follow the line that parallels exist between secular and spiritual society, there is no doubt that he places the Papacy firmly at the head.[16] However, as befitted a trained canonist, Roselli was well aware that the law allowed for certain circumstances when action could be taken against a pope, and notably if he lapsed into heresy. The Decretist text *Si papa* (Dist. XL, c. 6) had provided for such action, and subsequent commentators on the *Decretum* had built largely upon it.[17] Equally it had been accepted from the time of such twelfth-century commentators as Rufinus and Stephen of Tournai that schism should be coupled with heresy as a crime for which the pope could be deposed. In the thirteenth century Joannes Teutonicus had been prepared to extend the right of deposition to cases where the pope was guilty of any notorious crime, at the end of the century John of Paris quoted this gloss on the subject, and at the beginning of the fifteenth century Zabarella repeated the same view.[18]

It is noteworthy how Roselli regards these arguments. As far as schism was concerned he was willing to justify the actions of the Councils of Pisa and Constance, and in the section of his work dealing with the Papacy he seems to regard persistence in schism, and failure to fulfil a promise to resign, as actions which gave rise to suspicion of heresy: "At the time of the sacrilege of the schism, a pope, who had sworn and vowed to renounce the papacy, to restore holy union, but who after a warning did not trouble to fulfil his oaths, but despised them and long persisted in his obstinacy, was condemned by the Council of Constance and earlier by the Council of Pisa. The reason for this was that after he had been warned about fulfilling his vows, he was suspected of persisting in the sin of heresy, therefore he was deservedly deposed and condemned."[19] In this passage Roselli does not make it clear to which of the rival popes he is alluding, but slightly earlier in the work, in his consideration of whether it was lawful for a pope to renounce his office, he

15 *Ibid.*, pp. 525, 535.
16 For Roselli's sympathy with imperialist authority, Eckermann, pp. 45-46; for the development of ideas of a parallel hierarchy, Black, *Monarchy and Community*, pp. 58-59.
17 This is fully discussed by B. Tierney, *Foundations of the Conciliar Theory* (Cambridge, 1955), pp. 8-9, 57-67, 214-15.
18 *Ibid.*, pp. 57-58, 65, 173, 228 n. 2.
19 Goldast, p. 348.

mentions the promise which Gregory XII had made to resign in order
to restore unity to the Church, and his subsequent failure to fulfil it
forthwith.[20] Obviously the circumstances of the Schism, and the failure
of the popes to work for unity in accordance with the pledges they had
made before their elections, played an important part in forming
Roselli's attitude, though he also employed logical categories to define
the relationship between schism and heresy, describing the former as
the genus and the latter as the species.[21] Later in the work, when he is
discussing the powers of councils, he returns, at least by implication, to
the events of Pisa and Constance, and justifies the actions of those who
had deserted their popes to call together an assembly, on the grounds
that one or both of the contending claimants might be schismatics, and
that if they were, they had no powers of censure which might be
feared.[22]

When he turns from schism to persistent crime the author does not
explain at this point how the latter could be regarded as tantamount to
heresy, but later he produces an ingenious argument which enables him
to justify action being taken in such a case, while still affirming that no
one had power to judge the pope for offences other than heresy: "...
even if the pope had committed countless murders with his own hands,
he could be judged by no one." However, although the pope cannot be
judged for scandalous conduct as such, even if it is notorious, if when
he is accused of a crime which is contrary to divine or natural law he
denies that it is a crime, such an assertion would be heretical, and
would therefore render him liable to judgment.[23] It seems fairly clear
that in this situation, Roselli is adapting the theory of deposition for
heresy in order to accommodate it to other circumstances, and that
because he regarded schism as a major threat to the Church, he was
willing to admit that extraordinary measures could be taken to deal
with it, even to the extent of accepting the deposition of a lawful pope.
Those who do not work for peace separate themselves from Christ, and
such, "even if one of them were the true pope, could be deposed by the
council as manifest heretics and schismatics." In order to extirpate the

---

20 *Ibid.*, p. 337.

21 *Ibid.*, p. 352.

22 *Ibid.*, pp. 401-2.

23 *Ibid.*, pp. 443-44. This view was also adopted, in a work dating from about 1440, by the
Spanish writer Rodrigo Sanchez de Arevalo, a far more rigorous papalist than Roselli. He, however, held that a heretic pope was automatically deposed by God and that the action of the council
was merely the declaration of the deposition as fact, and not a judicial decision. See R. H. Trame,
Rodrigo Sanchez de Arevalo, 1404-1470 (Washington, D.C., 1958), p. 41.

schism, which is a cause of scandal, it was possible to depose even a pope who had been canonically elected.[24]

At this point Roselli does not specifically mention the Council of Constance, but it seems apparent that he had it in mind. By accepting the point of view that the deposition of even a lawful pope was preferable to the continuation of the schism, and that it was legally permissible, as an emergency measure, he was able to accept a practical solution to the problems which had arisen during the years of crisis. Not least, he was able to avoid the problem of a council having to decide which of two rival contenders for the Papacy was the lawful one, the problem which had existed in practical terms at Constance. As Professor Tierney has pointed out, at the time of the promulgation of the decree *Haec Sancta* in 1415 it was impossible to say who was and who was not the true pope.[25] But if it was possible for a council to depose all claimants, when it was doubtful who had the best title, this meant that the restoration of unity was regarded as the prime function of the council, and as something which could override the claims of even a lawful pope. This had been precisely the situation which had existed at Constance, and it seems clear that Roselli's theory had its origin in a recognition of the practical implications of what the council had done, and in the desire to accommodate it to recent historical fact.

A close examination of the text of the *Monarchia*, however, suggests that between the rival claimants Roselli had a preference for the Pisan line of popes, and if this were the case it would be reasonable to infer that he accepted the validity of the council which had established it. He refers to the actions of the Council of Constance in deposing *Iohannem vicesimum tertium et Benedictum tertium decimum, sic in sua obedientia nuncupatum.*[26] That Roselli wrote *in sua obedientia* and *nuncupatum* and not *in suis obedientiis* and *nuncupatos* makes it probable that the qualification is applied only to Benedict XIII and not to John XXIII. Unfortunately there is no certain indication of Roselli's attitude to the Roman line of popes, though there is certainly implied criticism of Gregory XII's failure to resign earlier than he did,[27] and the apparent acceptance of the Pisan succession seems to be implied in the comparison between Benedict XIII and John XXIII mentioned above. If his preference was

24 Goldast, p. 354.

25 B. Tierney, "Hermeneutics and History: The Problem of *Haec Sancta*," in *Essays in Medieval History Presented to Bertie Wilkinson*, ed. T. A. Sandquist and M. R. Powicke (Toronto, 1969), p. 361. The most recent bibliographical survey of attitudes to the Council of Constance is in R. Bäumer, "Die Bedeutung des Konstanzer Konzils für die Geschichte der Kirche," *Annuarium historiae conciliorum* 4 (1972) 26-45.

26 Goldast, p. 437.

27 *Ibid.*, p. 337.

for the Pisan line, this would probably be in accord with contemporary curial opinion. If one judges by the fifteenth-century versions of the *Liber pontificalis*, it seems to have been fairly normal to dismiss the Avignon line as antipopes, and one should also note that in the time of Martin V curial opinion seems to have favoured the Pisan succession over the Roman. The supplications registers of the pontificate distinguish between *Felicis recordationis domini Innocentius VII ... et Gregorius XII in suis obedientiis sic nuncupati* and *Alexander V predecessor noster ... et deinde Baldassar tunc Johannes papa XXIII qui dicto predecessore ab hac luce sublato in papatu immediate successit.*[28] The contrast is too pointed to be accidental, so it seems clear that the curia recognised a need for accepting the validity of conciliar action, on which Martin V's title depended, and that such recognition was granted to Pisa as well as to Constance. As Roselli was serving as a curial official at the time when he was writing the *Monarchia*, it seems likely that the work may reflect much of curial opinion.

The passages cited hitherto show how Roselli was prepared to give some retrospective justification to the actions of the Council of Constance, which he described both as *sanctum concilium* and *sacrum concilium.*[29] There were, however, other issues, such as the very nature of councils, the right of a council to meet in defiance of papal wishes, a question with considerable practical implications in the early 1430's, and the problems which arose when there were no doubts as to the legality of the pope's title.

Roselli's definition of a council comes at the start of book 3: "I define a council thus, that a council is a general gathering of the faithful who come, especially of bishops, summoned and constituted by authority of the supreme pontiff, or sometimes supported by the authority of Christ or of the very council itself."[30] The fact that Roselli admits the possibility of a council being self-authenticating illustrates how far conciliar ideas had penetrated into the attitudes even of men whose sympathies were essentially papalist. The contrast is clear between him and the greatest spokesman of papal claims of the fifteenth century, writing a little later, Juan Turrecremata. "A universal council of the catholic Church is a gathering of the greater prelates of the

---

28 K. A. Fink, "Zur Beurteilung des grossen abendländischen Schismas," *Zeitschrift für Kirchengeschichte* 73 (1962) 341-42.

29 Goldast, pp. 288, 414. There does not appear to be any distinction of meaning between 'sacrum' and 'sanctum' in Roselli's mind.

30 *Ibid.*, p. 379

Church, summoned by special authority of the Roman pontiff to treat solemnly with common purpose of anything in the Christian religion, under the presidency of the pope in person or of some other in his place."[31] Turrecremata lays greater stress on the role of the pope, and also is more explicit in limiting membership of the council to the greater prelates, presumably as a reaction to the extension of voting rights to others by the Council of Basel.

The question of how the council was to be summoned involved considerable discussion, and it was indeed one of the key issues. A general council could not be convoked without authority, and if it were called without the licence of the pope it would be headless and *quoddam monstrum contra naturam aliorum conciliorum*. This view appears to be strongly papalist, but Roselli perceived the difficulties: here was *perplexitas*, in the situation when the pope did not wish to summon a council lest it might give some judgment on the pope himself, in one of the issues where the council possessed jurisdictional power over the pope. Such papal action could nullify this power which the council had.[32] In a situation of schism the difficulty would be even worse, because when the council should be judge between two contenders, the man who was in possession of the papacy might not wish to call it, and others would not have the power. On a number of occasions Roselli refers to the circumstances of the Schism when two men possessed actual but divided power, Urban having support from Italy, Germany, England, Hungary and Illyricum, and Clement the allegiance of France, Spain, Scotland and the island of Sicily.[33] In such circumstances, neither pope could authorise a council, or alternatively one claimant could forbid his adherents to attend another assembly.[34]

Yet a further occasion when difficulty arises is when a pope wishes to dissolve a council which he has summoned, and here again it is clear that Roselli was concerned with a practical issue, one indeed which was in dispute at the time of writing, as Eugenius IV tried to dissolve the Council of Basel. It is more likely that it was this which turned the author's thoughts to this problem than the attempted dissolution of the Council of Constance by John XXIII, which he does not mention,

31 Eckermann, p. 125.

32 Goldast, pp. 362-63.

33 *Ibid.*, p. 388. A somewhat shorter list of the countries is given earlier (*ibid.*, pp. 363-64), and in another place the alignments are given at the time of Benedict XIII and John XXIII (with no mention of Gregory XII) (*ibid.*, p. 288).

34 *Ibid.*, p. 364.

although it is possible that this also could have been in his mind. Here
again Roselli declares the right of men to rise against a heretical pope.
The power given to the pope is for the edification and not for the
destruction of the Church, and there is an obligation on him to call a
council and give his authority to it, when neglect would lead to the state
of the Church being disturbed. In the final analysis it is possible for the
council to meet or to continue in existence without papal authorisation,
if the pope is notoriously a heretic or an apostate.[35] When there is no
pope, papal powers devolve on the universal Church, which may
declare its own assembly legitimate. Such a council would not be
headless, because Christ would be the head. In practical terms it is
possible for an inferior to supplement the defects of a superior, and the
cardinals, the emperor, or even any of the faithful, could call a council.
In a case of necessity, concerning the union of the Church, it is lawful
to have communication even with schismatics. Even without a legal sentence it is lawful to withdraw from an apostate pope, and for the faithful to take action against him.[36] In all these cases it seems fairly clear
that Roselli is looking back to the conditions of the Schism, and is
prepared to justify the action which was taken to settle it.

The Council of Constance had attempted to establish regular
meetings of general councils through the decree *Frequens*, and there are
a number of references to it in the *Monarchia*, where it is clear that
Roselli's views were more moderate than those of later papalist writers
such as Turrecremata, who denied that the pope was bound by the
decree and said that he could abrogate it.[37] In book 3, chapter 3 there is
an incidental reference, in which the validity of *Frequens* is neither
denied nor affirmed.[38] In chapter 25 however Roselli returns to a fuller
discussion of the decree, stating the case for both the papal and the conciliar positions, in his characteristic manner, before turning to a
resolution of the contradictions. The critical point on which the issue
turns is whether the council was concerned with a matter of faith, for
in such cases the will of the council should prevail, and the pope could
not dissolve it before it had dealt with this question. In this one sees
standard canonist opinion, but one should also note that at the time
when the work was being written, precisely such a question had arisen

35   *Ibid.*, pp. 366-67.
36   *Ibid.*, pp. 367-68, 371, 376. To illustrate the right of the subject in a case of secret apostasy
the example is given of the revolt of Baalam's ass against its master.
37   Eckermann, p. 140.
38   Goldast, p. 392: "... quia non dicit illa decretalis frequens quod potestas non sit in papa."

in relation to the Bohemian revolt, and it is hard to resist the conclusion that Roselli may have had some sympathy for the opposition of the Council of Basel to the pope, despite his own position as a curial of-ficial.[39] In this attitude he appears to have followed the ideas of Car-dinal Cesarini, who had been appointed as legate to suppress the Hussites and to preside over the Council of Basel by Martin V, and who had been confirmed in this position by Eugenius. The failure of the military action against Bohemia had led Cesarini to think that the coun-cil could provide the only solution of the Hussite question, and he made a vigorous plea to the pope to allow the council to continue. Later, of course, he was to break with Basel, as the attitudes of the council mem-bers hardened against the pope, and in one sense he may be regarded as a practical counterpart to Roselli's theoretical ideas, a man who ac-cepted the basic power of the pope but who also could see the value of conciliar action in certain circumstances.[40]

Other occasions when Roselli did not accept the papal power of dissolution were those when the pope had been called apostate and when two claimants were contending for the Papacy, for these were cases which concerned the good of the universal Church. After a lengthy discussion he returns to considering *Frequens*, and declares that since the statute concerned the good of the universal Church, and that if the statute were not preserved the good of the Church would suffer, the pope alone could not annul it. He appears to be thinking par-ticularly of the maintenance of ecclesiastical discipline, because in this passage he refers to the need of reforming the bad custom of clerks going about in secular attire.[41] On the other hand, if the dissolution of a council did not lead to heresy, or if there is no doubt over matters of faith, it would be lawful for the pope to dissolve a council, not-withstanding the terms of the decree. In this he does not seem to be en-tirely consistent with his earlier reference to questions of church discipline. If the pope wished to translate a council, the situation was similar to that of an intended dissolution.[42]

Another area where Roselli's awareness of historical events appears is in his consideration of papal elections. He discusses whether the elec-

39 One should note that at the time when Roselli was writing in 1432-3, there was a fairly general rallying of support to the Council, including that of Cardinal Capranica and of some curialists.

40 Eckermann, p. 140; Gill, pp. 46-48, 91, 94. There is a full study of Cesarini's attitude in P. de Vooght, *Les pouvoirs du concile et l'autorité du pape au concile de Constance* (Paris, 1965), pp. 105-36.

41 Goldast, pp. 427-31.

42 *Ibid.*, pp. 431-32.

tion of Urban VI was valid, although it was not held *capitulariter*, and decides that it was.[43] The length of time which he spends considering various forms of pressure which have been applied to the cardinals in times of election again clearly refers back to 1378, and he draws a number of subtle distinctions between different circumstances. In the case of 1378 he cites evidence from various legal sources to show the nullity of an enforced election, but declares that if violence had been used on behalf of one candidate and another was elected, the election was valid.[44] The need to validate Martin V's title appears also in his attitude to the electoral rights of the cardinals. Initially he declares that it is doubtful if a general council has the power to deprive them of these rights, because their powers derive from pope and council. On the other hand the pope, in virtue of his superiority to the council, can deprive them. This would seem to be whole-hearted papalism, but then Roselli argues that a special case exists in a case of schism, when trouble had arisen through the action of the cardinals. In such circumstances the council could withdraw the right of election from the college and make the choice itself.[45]

Such views are markedly less rigid than later papalist theory, and in this Roselli was typical of his age. A fellow curialist, also from Arezzo, Laurentius Aretinus, holds very similar opinions and is far more tolerant of conciliarist teaching than are later writers of the papal restoration, even though he holds that the pope can be limited only by God. His *Liber de ecclesiastica potestate* probably dates from the period 1438-40, a little later than the *Monarchia*.[46] In the latter half of the fifteenth century papalist theory became increasingly rigorous, and nothing is more indicative of this than the treatment meted out to Roselli's work. About 1496 it was attacked by the Dominican Heinrich Institor, one of whose criticisms was the use which Roselli made of doc-

43   *Ibid.*, p. 324.

44   *Ibid.*, pp. 327, 333.

45   *Ibid.*, p. 323. Roselli also touches on another contemporary electoral problem, when he raises the question of the status of a cardinal who had been named by a pope, who had then died before the full ceremonies of admission had been completed. Roselli seems to accept that he should be regarded as a cardinal and allowed to take part in the election, although in 1431 Eugenius IV had denied the title of cardinal to Domenico Capranica, because he had not yet received the red hat (*ibid.*, p. 326; L. Pastor, *History of the Popes* 1 (London, 1906), p. 264). Martin V had been concerned with this issue in 1426, when he provided that four cardinals who had been secretly nominated should be entitled to participate in the next papal election, if he should die before their appointments were published (*ibid.*, p. 261).

46   Eckermann, pp. 7-9, 11. It is perhaps curious that he was so prepared to accept conciliar ideas just at the time when papalist attitudes were hardening.

trines of popular sovereignty, which provided a basis for his conciliarism in certain circumstances. In 1540 it was placed on the Index at Antwerp and condemned by the inquisition at Toledo.[47] Even more noteworthy is the fact that the jurisconsult Filippo Decio, writing in 1511 in defence of the rebel assembly called to Pisa against Julius II, quoted Roselli with approval on the question of the council's right to assemble itself when the pope had failed to do so.[48] The passage of three quarters of a century between the writing of the work and its citation here had seen such a shift of attitudes in favour of the pope's absolute power that the papalist writing of 1433 could be regarded as anti-papal in 1511.

The great increase in the claims made for papal power came with Turrecremata's *Summa de ecclesia*, completed in 1449,[49] although a decade before this he had already been advocating the papal cause in stronger terms than Roselli's. It was he who first attacked the validity of *Haec Sancta* on new grounds, that it had been approved before the Council of Constance was truly ecumenical in character, being at that time an assembly only of John XXIII's obedience.[50] In his *Oratio de primatu* of 1439 he distinguished three phases in the history of the council, the calling of John XXIII's obedience, the accession to it of Gregory XII's, and the union to these of Benedict XIII's, and claimed that it was only after all three obediences were united that the council could be truly described as general.[51] Such an argument could not however apply in the case of *Frequens*, promulgated as it was in the last phase of the council, but there Turrecremata merely claimed that the pope had power to abolish it, and that when Martin V confirmed it he did not have power to bind his successors.[52] He regarded heresy as the sole reason for deposing a pope, and held that against a true pope in time of schism only peaceful persuasion could be used. As far as the actions of the Council of Constance were concerned, he regarded Gregory XII's

47 *Ibid.*, pp. 142-43, 158-60. Probably, however, Institor's attack was directed more seriously against imperialist tendencies in Roselli's work.

48 Goldast, 2 (Frankfurt, 1614), p. 1778 (*recte* 1678).

49 Black, *Monarchy and Community*, p. 53. Even Turrecremata was willing to admit that there might be occasions, such as a disputed papal election, when a council might be necessary to resolve a crisis, even if no issue of heresy were involved. He does, however, set rigid limits to such emergencies. See U. Horst, "Grenzen der päpstlichen Autorität: Konziliare Elemente in der Ekklesiologie des Johannes Torquemada," *Freiburger Zeitschrift für Philosophie und Theologie* 19 (1972) 361-88, esp. 373-76.

50 Eckermann, pp. 138-39; Vooght, *Les pouvoirs*, p. 146.

51 R. Bäumer, "Die Zahl der Allgemeinen Konzilien in der Sicht von Theologen des 15. und 16. Jahrhunderts," *Annuarium historiae conciliorum* 1 (1969) 298-99.

52 Eckermann, p. 140.

cession as voluntary, and dismissed the other two as not being true popes.[53] Later pro-papal theorists adopted this approach, as can be seen in Cajetan's defence of the pope in the early sixteenth century against the conciliarist Jacques Almain.[54]

There is little doubt that in the struggles between Eugenius IV and the Council of Basel papalist doctrine hardened, and that the violent actions of the council antagonised much moderate feeling in Christendom. Such a reaction might indeed have set in even without the new controversies, because the election of Eugenius IV by the traditional method could make him appear less dependent on the action of a council than Martin V could ever have been, and thereby placed him in a stronger position to assert papal independence of conciliar claims. His success too at the Council of Florence, where the arguments for papal primacy were accepted by the Greek Church, must have also served to strengthen the views of those who wished to emphasise papalist doctrine, because obviously the pope's party was the one which had the blessing of God in its work for union.[55] By contrast, the action of the Council of Basel in causing a new schism against a pope whose title was undoubted could only serve to rally to Eugenius those who regarded schism as one of the greatest disasters which the Church could suffer, including those who had defended the right of the council to act against a pope who had failed to heal such a split. But one should guard against viewing the Council of Basel with hindsight. In its early stages, when it was attempting to settle the pressing issue of Bohemia, it had not yet incurred the disfavour which later served to condemn the whole conciliar cause by association. It was at precisely this time that Roselli was writing, at a time when men such as Cesarini, Andrew of Escobar and Nicholas of Cusa, all later adherents of Eugenius, were still supporting the resistance of Basel,[56] and the ultimate interest of the *Monarchia* lies in the fact that it represents a stage in the development of papalist theory, when some compromise was still possible with conciliar ideas, before political pressures led to a new outbreak of theoretical polemics, which were to leave their mark on later ecclesiology.

University of Glasgow

---

53   *Ibid.*, p. 146.

54   For a general study of this controversy, see O. de la Brosse, *Le pape et le concile* (Paris, 1965), and for the employment of Turrecremata's distinctions between the different phases of the Council of Constance, *ibid.*, p. 302.

55   Some of the arguments put forward by the papal spokesmen at Florence are noted by Gill, *The Council of Florence*, pp. 273-74, 278-79, 284, 286. The definition of the papal primacy in the decree of union is printed by him also, *ibid.*, pp. 414-15.

56   The attitudes of these men are discussed by Vooght, *Les pouvoirs*, pp. 105-36 (Cesarini), 163-74 (Cusa), 174-79 (Escobar).

THE USES OF THE PROVERB
IN THE MIDDLE DUTCH POEM *REINAERTS HISTORIE*

Donald B. Sands

WHAT follows is not a compendium of proverbs, but an attempt to identify the various literary techniques served by a profusion of proverbs in one long narrative poem. That the employment of proverbs within a medieval work can attain to a degree of technical sophistication is an idea usually overlooked by editors and even by specialized studies devoted to the proverb. (Most of these concentrate on provenience and distribution and ignore the problems of rhetorical nuance and contextual ambiguity altogether.) Admittedly, the poem discussed is remarkably suited for the scrutiny here given it, but there must be other medieval works which could be analyzed in a similar manner. The present study might in fact prompt others to look at the proverbs in such works anew and draw conclusions concerning their function that have, for one reason or another, been heretofore overlooked.

*

*   *

The anonymous Flemish *Reinaerts Historie* (usually referred to as *RII*) was written some time during Chaucer's literary lifetime, perhaps around 1375.[1] It is a composite work. Lines 1 to 3481 amount to a retelling of an earlier poem called *Van den Vos Reinaerde* (dated variously from 1250 to 1275) and lines 3482 to 7794 constitute a continuation and

---

1 Still the handiest annotated text of *RII* is Ernst Martin, ed., *Reinaert / Willems Gedicht Van den Vos Reinaerde und die Umarbeitung und Fortsetzung Reynaerts Historie* (Paderborn, 1874). Line references in context are to the Martin edition.

conclusion of it.[2] The older poem (referred to as *RI*) is of dual authorship. It was begun by a certain Arnout and finished by a certain Willem.[3] About either man nothing is really known. Yet *RI* is quite of a piece; narrative motifs follow easily upon each other and were it not for mention of the two names in one of its manuscripts, no one would need suspect dual authorship. A similar stylistic and technical unity informs *RII*; a modern reader feels he has before him the product of one man's pen; and *RII* is the seminal work of much English and German Reynard material.[4] Via Caxton's 1481 translation of a prose version of it printed in Gouda in 1479, it has sired numerous individual English adaptations — curiously, most of them in the category of children's literature. Via its eventual translation into Low German verse (the Lübeck *Reinke de vos* of 1498) and Gottshed's 1750 translation of this into High German prose, it is the ultimate source of Goethe's "unheilige Weltbibel," his *Reineke Fuchs* of 1794. For purposes of the following discussion, the first part of *RII*, that deriving from the older poem by Arnout and Willem, is referred to as *RII*[a], the second part, the continuation and conclusion, as *RII*[b].

A tally of individual proverbs in *RII* comes to seventy-two. (Criteria for selection are those detailed by J. Allen Pfeffer: "human experience and reflection distilled in the form of a lucidly phrased, variable saying" of "known or unknown origin and of limited or wide prevalence" whose "currency must be attestable."[5] Hence, proverbial expressions — *sprichwörtliche Redewendungen* — and numerous non-attestable proverb-like utterances are excluded.) A significant feature is that only thirteen

2 The most heavily annotated edition of the earlier poem is J. W. Muller, ed., *Van den Vos Reinaerde*, 2 vols. (Leiden, 1939-1942). Diplomatic printings of the MSS. of both the early poems and its continuation are in W. Gs. Hellinga, ed., *Van den Vos Reynaerde / I Teksten* (Zwolle, 1952), where line numeration differs sightly from Martin's edition (see n. 1).

3 The initial lines of one MS. (the Dycker Handschrift now in Schloss Alfter near Bonn) say Willem was vexed so sorely by the fact that an episode concerning Reynard remained incomplete in Dutch — an episode "die arnout niet en hadde bescreuen" (which Arnout had not written out) — that he attempted the fox's biography himself. Beyond this one reference (line 6 in the MS.) all else concerning the authorship of *RI* is conjecture. *Cf.* Hermann Degering, ed., *Van den Vos Reynaerde nach einer Handschrift des XIV. Jahrhunderts im Besitze des Fürsten Salmreifferscheidt auf Dyck* (Münster, 1910).

4 For a discussion of the literary merits of *RII*, see my study "Reynard the Fox as *Picaro* and *Reinaerts Historie* as Picaresque Fiction," *The Journal of Narrative Technique* 1 (1971) 137-45. Coverage of the literary history of Reynard in the Low German areas is in my edition *The History of Reynard the Fox Translated and Printed by William Caxton in 1481* (Cambridge, Mass., 1963), pp. 14-30, and in N. F. Blake, ed., *The History of Reynard the Fox Translated from the Dutch Original by William Caxton*, EETS 263 (London, 1970), pp. xi-xxi.

5 *The Proverb in Goethe* (New York, 1948), p. 1 f.

of the proverbs appear in *RII*ᵃ (that is, in lines 1 to 3481) while fifty-nine appear in *RII*ᵇ (that is, in lines 3482 to 7794). In other words, there are nearly five times as many proverbs in *RII*ᵇ as there are in *RII*ᵃ. Even in Goethe's *Reineke*, there is in the second part (namely, in the seventh *Gesang* through the twelfth) a vastly greater number of proverbs than in the first. Pfeffer lists thirty-six in all, only nine of which are found in the portion that corresponds to *RII*ᵃ.[6] The data lead to the supposition that the *RII* poet used proverbs with an esthetic intention the *RI* poet either did not need to utilize or, more probably, was not really aware of. Predominant in *RII*ᵃ is a succession of narrative motifs. In *RII*ᵇ these give way to numerous, chiefly hypocritical speeches. It is in these that proverbs appear and primarily their function is not to reach the conscience or reason of the audience through folk-wisdom, but to reveal the facility with which folk-wisdom enters into the service of individual dishonesty.

In much *Märchen*-material, naive or not, the proverb can have two functions: it may serve as the narrator's justification, or that of one of his characters, for a particular turn in plot and it may serve as the means by which the narrator establishes rapport between himself and his audience. In the first, it is a narrative device, in the second, an instrument promoting audience belief. In neither is its traditional wisdom brought into question. Medieval romance, more or less, utilizes the proverb much as does the *Märchen*; but in *RII* no use of it is made to trigger an action or justify its motivation and in only five instances does the narrator obtrude, giving, in proverb form, his view of a situation. In the first three (all from *RII*ᵃ) one might assume that the narrator by means of a proverb is pointing a moral his audience would derive from what is happening. He says of Reynard, who fails to appear before court, "wie quaet doet, die scuwet dat licht" (63). He remarks, as Reynard leads the credulous Bruin to the split tree-trunk in Lantfreit's farmyard, "mer het is dicke also ghesciet/ dat hem die menich verblijt on niet" (697f.). He observes, as the various animals gather to make their accusations against an all but forsaken Reynard, "die crancste heeft die minste crode" (1911).[7] Throughout *RII*ᵇ the narrator does not

---

6   The *Reineke* proverbs: I, 15 f., 92, 170 f.; II, 98; III, 20; IV, 105; VI, 30, 31, 128, 254, 265 f.; VII, 88 f., 117; VIII, 83, 103 f., 117, 133 f., 141, 188, 209, 243, 299 f.; IX, 8, 24 f., 242, 291, 344; X, 177, 185, 195, 332; XI, 80, 81 f.; XII, 219 f., 266 f., 345.

7   "The weakest possess the least retinue." Martin (*Reinaert*, p. 389) suggests several senses for *crode*, the one most applicable to the context here being "Menge, Begleitung."

obtrude until the very end where Reynard emerges victorious in his trial by combat with Isegrim the wolf and wins thereby the support of king and queen. What the narrator says embodies a truism applicable to the whole of the beast epic: "die wel gaet, gheeft men eer ende lof:/ mer diet misgaet, daer vliet men of" (7393f.). As if to drive home the unsavory point, he repeats the same a few lines later and in fewer words: "diet wel gaet, die crijcht veel maghen" (7409). But these five proverbs are only the *overt* ones aimed at the audience by the narrator. He does indeed again obtrude, but in the persona of Reynard and, surprisingly, in Reynard's second long confession of his sins. Here proverbial wisdom attains an esthetically ambiguous quality because it is spoken by the arch rogue Reynard himself and because, as a secondary reaction, the audience inevitably wonders whether the omniscient narrator might not also be speaking.

Of the two long "confessions" in *RII* (1475-1669 and 3955-4263), the second is radically different from the first since it is the creation of the *RII* poet. Both are addressed by Reynard to Grimbart the badger, his sister's son and loyal confidant. But the first confession consists chiefly of Reynard's enumeration of his misdeeds against Bruin, Tibert, Isegrim, and other court favorites; there are two encapsulated *Schwänke* — Isegrim, as monk, caught and beaten when he becomes entangled in the bell rope of the monastery at Elmare and Isegrim duped into falling into a peasant's hen-house. There is only one proverb, and that is sarcastic and of a kind to be noted later. As Isegrim inches into the blackness along the hen-roost in the peasant's barn, Reynard urges him on with the words "men moet wel pinen om ghewin" (1642). The whole of the first confession is anti-clerical, hence somewhat narrowly satiric: Reynard begins with "confiteor tibi, pater, mater" and Grimbart retorts "wildi biechten, dat segghet mi/ in duutsche: so mach ict verstaen" (1498f.). In contrast, the second confession, even though it does possess encapsulated *Schwänke* and a degree of anticlericalism, progresses beyond into an angry denunciation of social greed and dishonesty. The poet in Reynard's persona, with the point of view of a detached and worldly social observer, talks "straight." Paradoxically, the lines create a narrator-audience nexus which in their potential impact might far surpass the few proverbial asides that the narrator as narrator addresses to his audience. Reynard admits transgressions, but observes "wie honich handelt, vingher lect" (4129). Deception is a fault, he concedes, but a necessary art of survival: "... dus moet men hier ende daer/ nu lieghen ende dan segghen waer" (4189f.). Telling the truth consistently is fatal: "want die altoos die waerheit sprake,/ enconde die straete nerghent bouwen" (4252f.).[8] At this point, fox and badger draw near the court and Reynard, prepared to make an attempt to lie his way out of the charge of murdering Cuwart the hare, speaks three proverbs in a row:

> men moet wel lieghen alst doet noot,
> ende daer na beteren bi rade.
> tot allen misdoen staet ghenade:
> ten is neimen, hi endwaelt bi tiden.
>
> 4260-63

The confession ends. There is little for the loyal Grimbart to say except to concede the wisdom of his uncle and admit "ghi sout selve sijn die paep" (4269).

There are, then, in *RII*, eleven proverbs addressed by the narrator to the audience — five directly, six ambiguously — whose import lies, not solely in their rhetorical effectiveness, but also in their truth. Six others fall into a similar category, those spoken by Grimbart the badger, who serves as a sort of choric figure, since he is the only prominent character who reacts to chicanery as a typical honest burgher ought to react. In defending Reynard against the deluge of accusations leveled at him by Isegrim, Grimbart says "dat viants mont sprect selden wel" (189). Later, when Courtois the hound accuses Reynard of stealing a *worst* (pudding) he himself had stolen, the badger excuses the act with "met recht so wart mens qualic quijt/ dat men qualic heeft ghewonnen" (269f.). At the end of Reynard's second confession, when the badger is less aghast at Reynard's sins than overwhelmed by his wisdom, he exclaims that the best scholars "dicke die wijste liede niet ensijn:/ die leken vervroedense bi wilen" (4102f.). He adds, by way of giving Reynard absolution for his past transgressions, "die doot is, moet bliven doot" (4116). As the pair then make their way into the crowd of hostile courtiers, Grimbart reassures his uncle with three proverbs on the wisdom of being bold in the face of danger:

> die blode endooch tot gheenre ure:
> den coenen helpt die aventure.
> een dach is beter dan sulc een jaer.
>
> 4285-87

Noble the lion and his unnamed queen are, in public, champions of order and morality. Their few essays at proverbial wisdom are pompous,

---

8 *Bowen* here means, in an idiomatic sense, "travel" and the line may be read "for those who ever spoke the truth could nowhere travel their way"; *cf.* Martin, *Reinaert*, p. 396.

dull, and, in the case of the queen, also ludicrous. When Noble tries to persuade Tibert to bring Reynard to court, the cat is apprehensive and demurs. Bruin the bear has been badly mauled and Tibert feels he might fare no better. The king urges him on with "het is menich die mit listen can/ meer dan sulc mit crachten doet" (1062f.). When Noble wishes to execute Reynard without legal formalities, the queen, both Francophile and stickler for protocol, rebukes her spouse with "sir, pour dieu, ne croies mie/ toutes choses que on vous die" (3665f.) and caps her demand with "alteram partem audite!/ sulc claect, die selve meest misdoet" (3678f.). With hollow profundity, the king says, when Reynard seems finally to be within the clutches of Isegrim and his henchmen, "so langhe gaet te water die cruuc,/ dat si breect end valt aen sticken" (4356f.). When Reynard, victorious in his combat with Isegrim, desires to address those loyal to him, both king and consort consent, saying

> tis reden, dat men den vrienden seit
> grote saken, daer macht aen leit,
> ende men des volghet haren rade.
>
> 7381-83

Here, with the king and queen, the proverb is not the purveyor of common human wisdom. As in the speeches of Polonius, it underscores vacuousness of character. It is the proverb as cliché.

But king and queen are of limited virulence. They do not even appear evil as do Reynard's archenemies, Isegrim, Bruin, and Tibert. Surprisingly, in the hundreds of lines of direct discourse allotted the three, there is only one proverb, and that is comic because it is spoken self-righteously and as a means to camouflage greed. As the hulking bear is obviously on the verge of being trapped within the tree-trunk in which the fox has convinced him there is a cache of honey, Bruin smugly reassures Reynard of his continence: "waendi dat ic bem onvoet?/ maet es tot alle spele goet" (723f.). In contrast, the three thoroughly genuine rogues to whom the *RII* poet gives the majority of his proverbs — Dame Rukenaw the she ape, her husband Martin, and the *Erzschelm* himself, Reynard — do not seem evil at all. We recognize them as anti-social manipulators, but, "immoral" though they are, their courage, loyalty to each other, and (within the right context) honesty make them somehow ethical figures, something which the "moral" animals are not. The relatively overwhelming number of proverbs allotted them (fifty-six) serve as tools of deception. Dame Rukenaw is at once hideously foul and supremely wise and the proverbs she speaks, like the sententious words of Chaucer's "loathly lady" in "The Wife of Bath's Tale", func-

tion as polemics. Her great moment in *RII* occurs when she champions
Reynard at the beginning of the second trial. She immediately thrusts at
her royal audience with a weapon of high potency — proverbial lore of
Biblical origin. She quotes Luke 6: 36, initially the Latin "estote
misericordes" (4776) and then the vernacular "weest ontfermich!"
(4777). This she reinforces with Matthew 7: 1, initially again the Latin
"nolite judicare,/ et non judicabimini" (4778f.) and then the vernacular
"oordeelt niemen, so enseldi/ selve oordeel liden gheen" (4780f.). She
thereupon relates the parable of the woman taken in adultery, after
which she adduces her third Biblical proverb (Matthew 7: 3): "sulc siet
in eens anders oghe een stro,/ die selve in sijn oghe een balc heeft"
(4792f.), which, just to be sure king and queen fathom its implications,
she paraphrases in plain words — "tis menich, die over een ander
gheeft/ een oordeel, ende hi is selve die quaetste" (4794f.). Biblical
allusion persists. She notes that the lowly shall be exalted and that God
shall receive those who desire him — "al valt een dicke, ende he int
laetste/ opstaet ende to ghenade coomt" (4796f.) and "god ontfaetse,
die sijns begheren" (4798). She caps her exordium, her portentous call
to justice in legal matters, with another and freer paraphrase of Matthew 7: 3:

> niemen ensel den anderen condempneren,
> al wist hi wat von sinen ghebreke,
> hi endede eerst of sijns selfs bleke.[9]
>   4800-02

Noble at first irately rejects her plea for a hearing with the curt remark
"hi [Reynard] strijct altoos sinen steert" (he is always stroking his tail —
that is, always deceiving). Rukenaw's rejoinder is a concatenation of six
proverbs, all of which together are, like the proverbs of Sancho Panza,
overwhelming in their aura of wisdom and none of which is particularly pertinent:

> dat swaerste moet noch meeste weghen.
> een sel sijn lief minnen to maten
> ende sijn leet te seer niet haten.
> ghestadicheit voecht wel den heren.
> tis misselic, hoe die saken verkeren.
> men sel den dach te seer niet

---

9   Line 4002: "unless he first be rid of his own blemish." Martin glosses *bleke* as "bleiche Farbe"
(*Reinaert*, p. 446 and again, questioningly, in an annotation, p. 398); but J. Verdam, *Middelneder-
landsch Handwoordenboek*, rev. by C. H. Ebbinge Wubben ('s-Gravenhage, 1949), enters a *blec* with the
gloss "vlek" [blemish].

loven noch laken, eer men siet
dat hi ten avont is ghecomen.
goet raet can dic den ghenen vromen
die hem met vlijt daer keret an.
4848-58

The deluge of wisdom silences the royal couple. The she-ape keeps the floor and eventually gives Reynard opportunity to contrive his own defense. Here the proverb is the rhetorical fillip given pure sophism, and yet, when Rukenaw, just before the trial by combat, feels she must bolster the flagging spirits of her "nephew" the fox, sheer inertia prompts her to cap encouragement proverbially: she says, sympathetically, "beter camp dan hals ontwe" (6796) and "const gaet dicwijl over cracht" (6851).[10]

Prior to Rukenaw's defense of Reynard before the court, her husband Martin encounters fox and badger and assures them of his support. The *RII* poet seems to intend in Martin a caricature of a papal emissary whose one faith lies in the power of money and patronage. He is a completely cynical figure and his proverbs (seven in number) are, in context, repellent. Justice, Martin admits, is difficult ("... trecht is elken swaer ghenoech" 4609) and to achieve or circumvent it, one needs, not an unbiased jury, but a friend ("een trou vrient is een hulpe groot" 4422) and, more particularly, a friend to whom personal loyalty is all and to whom the infraction of a moral code is immaterial ("een trouwe vrient sel lijf ende goet/ voor sinen vrient setten, alst noot doet" 4555f.). He notes that justice sometimes needs "help" ("want trecht heeft dicwijl hulpe noot" 4576), such help coming via a petition cushioned with money ("die bede is mitter ghiften coen" 4552); hence, learning the power of money is wisdom ("men sel den pennic houden leren/ ter noot dat onrecht mede to keren" 4553f.) and whoever does not use a friend and money to buy himself off as occasion demands is damned ("wel is die vrient ende tghelt verdoemt/ daer niemen troost of baet of coomt" 4557f.). Martin and Rukenaw, both creations of the *RII* poet, are more humanized than any other animals in the later of the two beast epics. Martin is conversant with the machinery of what appears to be a parody of ultramontane politics, Rukenaw with the nastier variety of petty court intrigue. The few speeches allotted them are larded with proverbial lore. One senses that if Rukenaw's proverbs echo the

---

10   Rukenaw speaks four other proverbs (4895, 4926 f., 4981, and 5004), but these are not properly hers since they are embedded in her tale of serpent and man seeking justice before a royal tribunal.

sophistical rhetoric of the time, those of her husband are a bitter summation of its *Realpolitik*. If so, as with Reynard's proverbs addressed to Grimbart, those spoken by Martin are actually dicta of the poet himself, who again assumes the persona of one of his characters in order to reveal truth as he sees it.

Reynard's proverbs, thirty in number and hence too numerous to quote here completely, are, with the exception of those addressed to Grimbart (and the narrator's audience), like the proverbs of Dame Rukenaw — hollow *Redeschmücke* and instruments of deceit. To a modern reader their righteousness can appear insufferable and their hypocrisy inspired. One exhorts to religious renewal. Reynard quotes Matthew 24: 44 — "et vos estote parati" (4458) — as he, in the guise of an eremite, tries to take the life of Lampreel the cony. Another enjoins legal impartiality. He cries "dat recht endoet niemen onghelijc" (4627) as he is about to inundate the royal tribunal with lies. Another warns against incompetents in authority. He says to king and queen that Isegrim, Bruin, and Tibert have dangerous ambitions and points up his argument with "waer esels crighen heerscappien/ daer siet ment selden wel ghedien" (5749f.) — and here the listeners (both the animal courtiers of the poem and the human audience of the narrator) are fully aware that the dig is as appropriate to the royal pair as to the trio of political intrigants. Several — hypocritically — underscore the prevalence of hypocrisy:

> want daer veel op eerden leeft,
> die van buten draghen schijn
> anders, dan sie van binnen sijn.
> 4310-12

Occasionally, Reynard's proverbs distinguish themselves from others in *RII* by becoming instruments of mocking sarcasm, something akin to the *Schadenfreude* of a good portion of medieval humor. When Bruin is firmly caught in Lantfreit's tree-trunk and is about to suffer a horrible beating at the hands of the local farmers, Reynard announces their approach and tells Bruin they will give him something to drink since he has enjoyed Lantfreit's honey so thoroughly (which he certainly has not), adding as mock justification "het is goet dat men die spise wel net" (764).[11] The cruelty of the remark is matched a few lines later when

---

11 "It is good that one wets well his food." In addition to the proverbial idea that drink ought to accompany food, there is here also the connotation, frequent in medieval Germanic narrative, of the dispensing of drink implying the imparting of blows; *cf*. Martin, *Reinaert*, p. 359 (note on *shinken* of *RI*, line 705).

Reynard finds Bruin on a riverbank where he has collapsed from
exhaustion and, presumably, loss of blood. Seeing that the scalp has
been torn from Bruin's head, the fox addresses him as "sir priester,
dieux vous saut" (957) and then asks "in wat oorden wildi u doen/ dat
ghi draecht dat rode caproen?" (969f.).[12]

The *RII* poet's use of a profusion of proverbs appears significant
when one considers what other materials he could have used to give
body to his narrative. He, like the *RI* poet, must have been, to use Martin's words, "seinem Stande nach ... wohl ein gelehrter, d. h. geistlich
gebildeter"[13] and could probably have padded the speeches of his
animals with learned "sentense", as Chaucer, for example, pads Pertelote's presentation of her "doctrine", and he could have drawn
heavily on the topoi of late medieval Latinity. He is, however, a very different poet from the man who put *RI* into its final form. He simply does
not possess the *RI* poet's flair for narrative technique. (His Reynard, in
fact, is quite a different fox from the Reynard of *RI*, who is primarily a
prankish folk figure; his Reynard is psychologically top-heavy, an
angry brooder over discrepancies between social appearance and inner
intention.) Instead of rapid lineal narrative, he offers us long, tongue-in-
cheek speeches and the multitude of proverbs he interlards them with
must have been immediately familiar to his audience; but the poet, for
the most part, does not establish audience consensus with them, except
for the few instances at the beginning and the end where he obtrudes
and except also for those instances where he quite likely transfers his
own view of things into the mouths of Grimbart, Martin, and, during
the second confession, Reynard himself. The majority of proverbs in
context render common folk wisdom ambiguous and questionable. Little by little, to the original audience of *RII*, they must have seemed to
reopen Pilate's question. They might even have driven home in the
aggregate that old saws mean nothing, however explicitly true they may
appear, unless behind both speaker and listener there lies some sort of
inner integrity.

University of Michigan

12   The remainder of Reynard's proverbs, most of which are also mere flourishes in dishonest
rhetoric, are found in the following lines: 2335, 3005, 3205, 3208, 3944-46, 3960f., 4310-12, 4458,
4627, 5680-82, 5684f., 5749f., 5883f., 5914, 6018, 6038f., 6356f., 6358f., 6433f., 6448f., 7273f.
13   *Reinaert*, p. xx.

MILITARY MANUALS IN
FIFTEENTH-CENTURY ENGLAND

Diane Bornstein

THROUGHOUT the fifteenth century, warfare was a major activity and interest of the aristocracy. Many knights took part in the Hundred Years War. Some served in Ireland, Wales, and Scotland. Those who remained at home often had to police the countryside; and some engaged in feuds, waging their own private wars. War was an avocation as well as a vocation. When knights were not engaged in battle, their favorite activity was the mock combat of the tournament. Since fighting was a major aristocratic interest, it is not surprising that military manuals were among the most popular works of the time.

The main source for the medieval military manuals was *De re militari* by Flavius Vegetius Renatus, a fourth-century Roman of high rank, given the title of count in some manuscripts.[1] Vegetius wrote his treatise at the end of the fourth century, some time after the first inroad of the Huns (375 A.D.), which marked the beginning of the Empire's fall. Hoping to save the Empire by reviving its military discipline, he collected and synthesized accounts of the military wisdom that had made ancient Rome great. He states that his main sources are Cato the Elder, Cornelius Celsus, Paternus, Frontinus, and the regulations of Augustus, Trajan, and Hadrian.

Medieval writers found Vegetius' four-book treatise to be a convenient and comprehensive military manual. Book 1 discusses the selection, discipline, and training of an army as well as methods of setting up camps. The program of physical training for the recruit includes running, marching, leaping, vaulting, swimming, throwing missive weapons, handling the sword, using the sling and loaded javelin, shooting with the bow and arrow, and carrying heavy burdens. Book 2

---

1 Thomas R. Philips, ed., *Roots of Strategy* (Harrisburg, Pa., 1940), pp. 68-69.

concerns the composition of the legion. Since this book had little practical value, medieval translators often abridged or omitted large sections of it. Book 3 on tactics and strategy deals with the proper size of an army, means of preserving its health, methods of preventing mutiny, military signals, marches, retreats, ambushes, the choice of a field of battle, preparations for a general engagement, reserves, maneuvers in action, dispositions for engaging troops, and general maxims. Book 4 takes up the attack and defense of fortifications. The last sixteen chapters, sometimes treated as book 5, concern naval warfare.

The earliest English version of *De re militari* was translated in 1408 for Thomas, Lord Berkeley, when he was fighting against the rebels led by Owen Glendower in Wales.[2] He was besieging Aberystwyth Castle, serving as general commander and engineer in the timber-works under the command of Prince Henry.[3] Consequently, Lord Berkeley had a practical and immediate reason for commissioning the translation.

The translator usually describes things in terms of contemporary warfare. In chapter 16 of book 1, he tells how a fully armed warrior can be hurt by a stone. The soldiers described are wearing plated armor and habergeons, whereas those in the original are armed in cuirasses. In chapter 22 of book 4, he speaks of the guns for shooting stones that are used in Wales and in the North, possibly thinking of Lord Berkeley, his patron, who was then fighting in Wales:

> Also grete gunnes that schete now a dayes stones of so gret peys that no wall may withstonde hem as haue ben wel schewed bothe in the northe contrey and eke in the werres of Wales. Suche gynnes ben mighte ynoʒe to distroye eny ordenaunce of tymber suche as somercastells beth and other of whiche we haue spoke bifore.[4]

His additions show that he was adapting the text for contemporary knights. Editors and translators of *De re militari* have had trouble interpreting the term *armatura*, which Vegetius merely speaks of as an important exercise. Our translator decided that fighting fully armed within the lists was the only proper exercise for a Christian knight, for

2 Henry N. MacCracken, "Vegetius in English," in *Anniversary Papers by Colleagues and Pupils of George Lyman Kittredge*, eds. E. S. Sheldon, W. A. Neilson, F. N. Robinson (Boston, 1913), p. 389.
3 Charles L. Kingsford, *Henry V, the Typical Medieval Hero* (New York, 1901), p. 56.
4 Pierpont Morgan Library, MS. M.775, fol. 110. I would like to thank the authorities of the Pierpont Morgan Library for giving me permission to quote this manuscript. There are eleven manuscripts of the 1408 Vegetius written for Lord Berkeley. The text is being edited for the Early English Text Society by Katherine Garvin of Cambridge, England.

all others defined as *armatura* were devised by devils, worshiped by the Romans in their false gods:

> Yonge knyghtes oughte to bene taughte and lernede of heme that bene doctours and techers of werkes of werre how they shulde fyght whene they bene full armed wyth in lyste, for that is called armatura ... But here undyrstond all ye that þis boke shall rede that the skyll þat I declare noghte more opynly this worde armature in þis. ffor there bene VIII manere of fyghtynges that bene called armatures which the Romaynes used, as ysaye sayth in the IX boke of his ethemologens in two and fyfty chapytre of the which there is none able ne lawfull to be used of none cristen knyght for that forseid armure þat is called fyghtyng within lyste and that in ryghtfull cause, for the remenante of fyghtynges were found upe be feyned and fals vycions and dremes þorouȝ illusyon of develles the which the romaynes worshiped in fals goddes, the which devylles with all here myghte wrought to shedyng of manes blude as thyng that is to heme moste plesaunt. Wherefore as thees clarkes seye, it longeth noght to cresten werreours to knowe ne to use the maner of fyghtes that be foundyn upe be the devyll and noght be god ne ryghtfull querrel. Neuer the lese the use and exercise that they hadden in tho unlawfull werres made here knyghtes the more sotyll and sly when they comen to openwerres in the felde.[5]

The translator shows an interesting mixture of hostility and admiration in his attitude toward the Romans. Christian knights also are criticized in this section. Vegetius speaks of the rewards given for excellence in *armatura*, a subject that leads the translator into a digression on the covetousness of contemporary Christian knights:

> For ye shall undyrstond that knyghtes that tyme reseyued none othir sonde [present] for here trauayle but lyuelode of corne for heme and there hors, and the skyll [reason] was this. For that tyme knyghtes werred for wynnyng of wyrshipe for encres of here comynalte and lokede none othir rewarde but here lyuelode, and in this were they more lawfully rewelled that were paynemis than nowe be oure crystene knyghtes that werreth noght fore none of the skylles but for cruelte of wrechyng or elles for couetise.[6]

Like Vegetius, the translator felt that the soldiers of his time needed moral exhortation as well as military discipline. He faithfully follows Vegetius' program of physical training as well as his battle strategy, which completely contradicts the romantic chivalric code of fair play

5 *Ibid.*, fols. 34-34v.
6 *Ibid.*, fol. 35.

and heroism. He highly recommends the use of ambushes. Rather than engage in battle at all, it is better to "tame thine enemy bi honger than bi fightinge." [7] The general maxims at the end of book 3 epitomize Vegetius' pragmatic philosophy. Although "occasion or sodeyne happe in batayle helpeth more some time than vertu or strengthe,"[8] he firmly believes in discipline, prudence, training, and good strategy.

While Vegetius' pragmatism would have been useful to many fifteenth-century knights, his imperialism, nationalism, and militarism would have been inspiring. In the Prologue to book 1 he tells us that the ancients gathered together "studies of hye craftes" for the benefit of the commonwealth. Chapter 1 makes it clear that military science is the "hye craft" of most value, for by "customeable vsage of dedes of armes the Romaynes hade the victorye of all other nacions."[9] Vegetius states that men grow soft in peacetime, and that military prowess must be cultivated since good warriors are the best asset of a country. The nationalistic, militaristic spirit that infuses *De re militari* is just what Lord Berkeley and Prince Henry would have wanted to instill into the men who were fighting in Wales and France. Consequently, this translation of Vegetius undoubtedly was most useful, both as a practical military manual and as a source of propaganda.

The author of *Knyghthode and Bataile*, a verse paraphrase of Vegetius written between 1457 and 1460, was inspired by the strife and turmoil of the Wars of the Roses. He was a patriotic parson of Calais and a faithful supporter of Henry VI. This poem tells us so much about the circumstances of the time that it can be considered an original political poem as well as a translation.

The first installment of the work was presented to King Henry in March 1458, during a temporary reconciliation or "love day" between the warring Yorkists and Lancastrians. In his Proem the author reflects the hopes for peace aroused by that love day. By the time the parson was writing part 3 of his poem, hopes for peace had been shattered. The Prologue to this section describes the fleeing of defeated Yorkists to their strongholds in Ireland, Wales, and Calais. The nobles are identified by their badges and heraldic signs: "the golden eagle and his briddys III" are Richard of York and his three sons; the silver bear signifies Warwick the Kingmaker; the white lion, John Mowbray, Duke of Norfolk; the antelope and panther, Henry VI.[10]

---

7   *Ibid.*, fol. 100.
8   *Ibid.*, fols. 99-100.
9   *Ibid.*, fol. 26.
10 R. Dyboski and Z. M. Arend, eds., *Knyghthode and Bataile* (London, 1935), pp. 37, 130-33. The

The poet considerably modifies Vegetius' ideal of the soldier, making him more of a medieval *preux chevalier* than a Roman *mīles*. In dealing with the requirements of a knight, he adds the feudal qualifications of birth and blood. In discussing reasons for rejecting a man, he turns Vegetius' *ignāvus* into "ignoble". Tourneying is included in his training program for young knights, who should be taught "shakyng uppon the Sarrasins that grenne" (l. 2997). In citing the qualities of the soldiers to be evaluated by a commander before he engages in battle, Vegetius emphasizes experience whereas the translator stresses courage. He omits the rules for a retreat as well as the statement that the main strength of an army is in its infantry, which apparently conflicted with his chivalric ideals. Finally the poet extensively changes the social and political thought of his source. He takes a few key ideas from Vegetius, such as the wisdom of old times, the importance of discipline, and the value of good soldiers to the state, but he omits Vegetius' outbursts of imperialistic nationalism and emphasizes the defensive role of the army:

> Certeyn it is, that knyghthode & bataile
> So stronge is it, that therby libertee
> Receyved is with encreste and availe;
> Therby the Croune is hol in Maiestee
> And uche persone in his dignitee,
> Chastised is therby rebellioun,
> Rewarded and defensed in renoun.[11]

In *Knyghthode and Bataile*, the imperialism and nationalism of Vegetius are thus transformed into a new kind of English nationalism. The poet wants to improve the performance of knights so that they can defend the realm and crush rebellion. He continually cries out against violence, treachery, and disorder and presents an ideal vision of England as a peaceful, unified country under a just, strong king.

We find a very different brand of nationalism in the *Boke of Noblesse* by William Worcester. Between 1438 and 1459 Worcester was secretary to Sir John Fastolf, who had been one of the leading English military captains in France. When Fastolf returned home to England in 1440, he must have had plenty of stories to tell and plenty of opinions to deliver

---

poem is listed as no. 3185 in Carleton Brown and Rossell Hope Robbins, *The Index of Middle English Verse* (New York, 1943), p. 506, and in R. H. Robbins and J. L. Cutler, *Supplement* (Lexington, 1965), p. 352.

11 *Ibid.*, p. 60.

about the Hundred Years War. As his secretary, Worcester would have heard many of these tales. Worcester was the son of a townsman in the Norfolk area and a household official rather than a soldier. Yet he apparently adopted the militaristic outlook of his employer, for an aggressive spirit of nationalism infuses the *Boke of Noblesse*.[12]

This work was a piece of propaganda meant to support the specific policy of engaging in war with France. It was originally written in the 1450's to induce Henry VI to follow his father's warlike policy toward France, remodeled to attract Yorkist patronage between 1461 and 1472, and slightly revised for presentation to Edward IV in 1475.[13] Worcester blames the peace for England's troubles, showing how things looked to defeated captains and their dependents after the loss of Normandy.

Worcester assembles material from ancient and contemporary sources to support his point of view. He uses a large number of historical anecdotes. Approximately one third of his work deals with Roman and ancient history. About one third concerns English history and events in the Hundred Years War; in these passages, Henry V is often the exemplary figure. Finally, about one third takes up the responsibilities of knights and commanders.

Worcester quotes Sir John Fastolf, his employer, regarding the value of a prudent "manly man" as opposed to a recklessly brave "hardy man". He states that noblemen should practice temperance, avoid extravagance in their dress, devote themselves to defending the church and the common people, and receive a good military training. They should not study law or engage in civil occupations, as some were beginning to do. His comments reveal social change and protest against it at the same time:

> But now of late daies, the grettir pite is, many one that ben descendid of noble bloode and borne to armes, as knightis sonnes, esquiers, and of othir gentille bloode, set him silfe to singuler practik, straunge facultees frome that fet, as to lerne the practique of law or custom of lande, or of civile matier, and so wastyn gretlie theire tyme in suche nedelese

---

12 Studies of William Worcester and his work can be found in the edition of his *Itineraries* by J. H. Harvey (Oxford, 1969), and the essay on his language by Norman Davis, "The Epistolary Usages of William Worcester," in *Medieval Literature and Civilization: Studies in Memory of G. N. Garmonsway*, eds. D. A. Pearsall and R. A. Waldron (London, 1969), pp. 249-74.

A study of Sir John Fastolf can be found in H. S. Bennett, *Six Medieval Men and Women* (Cambridge, 1955), pp. 30-68.

13 K. B. MacFarlane, "William Worcester: A Preliminary Survey," in *Studies Presented to Sir Hilary Jenkinson*, ed. J. Conway Davies (London, 1957), pp. 198-214.

besinesse, as to occupie courtis halding, to kepe and bere out a proude countenaunce at sessions and shiris halding, also there to embrace and rule among youre pore and simple comyns of bestialle contenaunce that lust to lyve in rest. And who can be a reuler and put hym forthe in suche matieris, he is, as the worlde goithe now, among alle astatis more set of than he that hathe despendid xxx or xl yeris of his daies in gret jubardies in youre antecessourys conquestis and werris. ... And that suche singuler practik shulde not be accustumed and occupied undewly withe suche men that be come of noble birthe, but he be the yonger brother, havyng not whereof to lyve honestly.[14]

Worcester uses the ideals of chivalry to justify a policy of militaristic nationalism. Although he admits the distinction between just and unjust wars and musters many arguments to prove that war with France was lawful, his very use of this doctrine shows how it could be perverted. Any war could be defended as a just war. Yet Worcester honestly believed that the peace was responsible for the country's troubles.

A contrasting attitude toward war appears in Christine de Pisan's *Livre des fais d'armes et de chevalerie*, translated as the *Book of Fayttes of Armes and of Chyvalrye* by William Caxton in 1489.[15] Except for the elimination of some insulting remarks about the English, Caxton made few changes in Christine's text. In this work the role of the army is seen as defensive, and the spirit of militarism is dominated by Christian, chivalric values. It is divided into four books. Most of book 1 is based on Vegetius' *De re militari*. Chapters 1 through 7 owe little to Vegetius, however, for their standpoint is purely medieval. Christine presents her own portrait of the ideal commander, a chivalrous knight who practices the virtues of justice, temperance, prudence, generosity, pity, and humility:

The maners and condicions which belongen to a good conestable ben these, that he be not testyf, hastif, hoot, fell, ne angry, But amesured and attemporat, rightful in iustice, benygne in conuersacion of hye mayntene

---

14 John G. Nichols, ed., *The Boke of Noblesse* (London, 1860), p. 77.

15 In the Epilogue, Caxton states that the "translacyon was finisshed the viij day of Iuyll the sayd yere [1489] & enprynted the xiiij day of Iuyll next folowyng & ful fynyshyd." *The Book of Fayttes of Armes and of Chyvalrye*, ed. A. T. P. Byles (London, 1937), p. 291. In *Caxton and His World* (London, 1969), N. F. Blake points out that if the "next following" refers to the year, then the book was not printed until 1490; but if it refers to the day, it was printed less than a week after the completion of the translation. This would have been possible if the printing and translation had proceeded simultaneously (p. 98). Blake describes the *Fayttes of Armes* as an allegory on chivalry and a knight's equipment. This description applies to Caxton's *Book of the Order of Chivalry* rather than to the *Fayttes of Armes*.

& of lytyl wordes, sadde in countenaunce, no greet dyseur of truffes, verytable in worde and promesse, hardy, sure, & diligent, not couetous, fiers to his enemyes, pyetous to them that be vainquissed, and to them that be vnder hym he be not lightly angry, ne be not moeued for lytyl occasion, ne byleue ouer hasteley for lityl apprence [evidence], ne yeue fayth to wordes which haue ne colour of trouthe, ne that he be not curyous of mygnotes, iolyetes, ne of iewellis, but be he habylled & arrayed rychely in harnoys & mountures, & contiene hym fiersly, ne he be not slouthful, sluggyssh, ne slepy, ne curyous in metes & festes in lyf delycate, & in serchyng alleway thestate & couuyne [plan] of his aduersaires, & be he subtyl, pourueyed & wyly to deffende hym fro theym, & wysely to assaile them, wel aduysed vpon their espies & watches, & that he knowe to gouuerne his owen peple & holde in ordre & drede, & to doo right where he ought to doo it. And that he be not ouer curyous to playe in noo games, to honoure the good and them that be worthy, & nygh to hym, & wel to rewarde theym that deserue it. And that he be large & lyberal in cas that it be requysyte, & that his comyn speche be of armes, of fayttes, of chyualrye, and of the valyaunces of good men. And that he kepe hym wel from avauntyng, & be he louyng hys prynce & trewe to hym, fauorable to wedowes, to orphans, & to the poure, ne make grete compt of a lityl trespace doon to his persone, and smale debate to pardone lightly to hym that repenteth, and aboue all other thyng to loue god & the chyrche & to sustene & helpe right.[16]

After drawing this portrait of the ideal constable, she selects passages from books 1 and 3 of *De re militari* to illustrate his abilities and functions. In addition, she supplements Vegetius' material on battle strategy with up-to-date information. In chapter 23 she describes how to arrange an army on a battlefield according to the practice of her own time, using as examples the Battle of Roosebeke (1382) when Charles VI of France defeated the rebellious Flemings led by Philip van Arteveldt, and the Battle of Hasbain (1408) when Jean sans Peur, Duke of Burgundy, defeated the men of Liège.[17] Chapters 1 through 11 of book 2 are based on the *Stratagemata* of Frontinus. In Chapter 11, Christine adds a saying of Charles V of France to those of several Roman generals. Chapters 12 and 13 are based on the *Facta et dicta memorabilia* by Valerius Maximus. For the rest of book 2, Christine uses Vegetius' material on sieges and naval warfare, supplementing this with information on contemporary practices in siegecraft. Books 3 and 4 are based mainly on books 3 and 4 of Honoré Bonet's *Arbre des batailes*.

16   *Fayttes of Armes*, pp. 23-24.
17   *Ibid.*, pp. 80-82.

Christine selects material on the legality of war, the duties of a knight, the payment of wages, military contracts, spoils of war, prisoners, the rights of non-combatants, safe-conducts, truces, letters of mark, trials by combat, and heraldry. Rules concerning these issues formed the law of arms of the late Middle Ages.[18]

The political and social thought of the *Fayttes of Armes* reflects a medieval point of view. A few themes are taken from Vegetius, such as his praise of the art of war and his complaints about its neglect in degenerate times. In the *Fayttes of Armes*, however, we find a Christian, chivalric spirit that is utterly foreign to *De re militari*. The *Fayttes of Armes* shows how the ideals of Christian chivalry tried to mitigate the practice of war. In considering the question of the validity of war, it states that a war waged to uphold justice, resist oppression, or oppose usurpation is just, but a war motivated by revenge or aggression is against the law of God. Furthermore, even when his cause is just, a prince should try to negotiate with his enemy and avoid a war. The work forbids the slaying of prisoners, sets forth the rights of the common people and non-combatants, and states that on a holy day men may only rightfully fight in self-defense. Trials by combat are described but are strongly condemned. Even when it comes to public warfare, responsibility is not removed from the conscience of the individual. The soul of a soldier may be saved if he fights for the Christian faith or for justice, but he jeopardizes it if he fights in an unjust war.

The military manuals written and translated in fifteenth-century England thus present a wide variety of attitudes toward war. All of them agree with Vegetius, their major source, regarding the importance of military training and the value of soldiers to the state. The authors of the prose Vegetius and the *Boke of Noblesse* also echo his imperialism and nationalism, adapting it to English conditions and directing it against the French. But in *Knyghthode and Bataile* and the *Fayttes of Armes*, we find civilian pleas for a protective army and peace. These pleas would finally be answered in the sixteenth century, when the imperialistic ventures of the Hundred Years War and the civil strife of the Wars of the Roses finally came to an end.

Queens College

---

18 M. H. Keen, *The Laws of War in the Late Middle Ages* (Toronto, 1965), pp. 17-19.

NOTES ON ANTOINE DE LA SALE'S
RECONFORT DE MME DU FRESNE

Thomas E. Vesce

I

LOS AND LARGESS IN THE FIRST TALE OF THE *RECONFORT DE MADAME DU FRESNE*

THE scene which Antoine de la Sale draws in the first of the two tales in the *Réconfort de Madame Du Fresne* is one which is reminiscent of the old French epic: the siege of a city. The place in question here is the city of Breth (Brest) which, according to the author, is enduring an attack by the Prince of Wales during one of the contests in those seemingly interminable Anglo-French struggles known as the Hundred Years War.

In order to bring about a cessation of hostilities, the English prince resorts to what was common practice and offers M. Du Chastel, the French king's captain-defender, a pact: if, within the space of a week, help did not arrive, the defenders of the fortress would give up their posts and retire from the place under safe conduct.[1] Conversely, if help does indeed come, the prince will give orders to raise the siege and leave the area peacefully.

An integral part of this convention was the giving up of hostages to the besiegers. After calling his council together, it becomes clear to Du Chastel that there would be no other hostage to give but his very own (and only) thirteen-year-old son. Seeing no other way to meet the obligations of his station, the captain surrenders his son and has the news carried to his sovereign.

---

1 *Cf.* J. Misrahi, "The Sources of the *Réconfort de Mme Du Fresne*" in *Mélanges de langue et de littérature du Moyen Age et de la Renaissance offerts à Jean Frappier*, ed. M. J. C. Payen and M. C. Rénier, 2 (Geneva, 1970), p. 823.

Much like the reluctant Louis of Carolingian poems, the king happens to be busy with other matters and cannot spare any arms or soldiers. He does, however, send a large ship laden with all kinds of provisions which, with God's help and in spite of wind, tide and blockade, reaches the defenders of Brest and brings them relief a full four days before the expiration of the truce.[2]

It would be logical to assume then, in view of this aid, that the prince will abide by the terms of his agreement, return young Du Chastel to his people, and move off to other conquests. Not so! The English lord does not consider the arrival of the ship as sufficient to meet the stipulations of the convention, and so refuses to yield.

When Du Chastel's herald informs him of this, "cruelle response", the captain convenes his council to review the situation:

> Lors assembla tous ses parens et amis qui là estoient et la responce du prince leur dist. Puis, d'un après l'autre demanda leurs oppinions, de laquelle sy dure responce chascum fust très fort esmerveilliez. Puis, l'un regardant l'autre et priant l'un l'autre de premièrement parler, fust l'un qui dist que croire ne povoit que le prince vaulsist aller contre son seelle, lequel contenoit de rendre le filz du seigneur du Chastel, comme en ostaige lui livroit, reservé cas naturel et de la voullenté de Dieu, sy vraiement que il fust secouru ou que par faulte de secours il rendeist la place. «Ores ne puelt-il raisonnablement dire que vous, Monseigneur, ne soyez secouru, et souverainement, des vivres parquoy vous vous rendiez.[3]»

Having thus assessed the predicament they are all in, the dumbfounded councilors further define Du Chastel's own particular role in it:

> Touteffoiz, conclurent que rendre la place, sans entier deshonneur, à loyalement conseillier, n'en veoient point la fachon.[4]

Students of French literature can but agree with the late Jean Misrahi that what will now take place "in the hearts of the seigneur du Chastel and his wife is indeed du Corneille avant l'heure."[5]

How shall the problem be resolved? Through monologues, prayers, meditation? These methods will be employed later on in literature by such as Corneille, Racine, even Shakespeare, but here in this edifying

---

2 *Cf. Antoine de la Salle: sa vie et ses ouvrages*, ed. Joseph Nève (Paris, 1903), pp. 110-111. (All references to the text are from this edition, hereafter cited as *Réconfort*).

3 *Réconfort*, p. 112.

4 *Ibid.*, p. 113.

5 Misrahi, p. 823.

tale of the fifteenth century, La Sale will use those techniques known to his predecessors of heroic epic and romance: he breaks off formal consideration of the problem *expositum* of the state's security to speak about the great private grief of M. et Mme Du Chastel.

When Mme Du Chastel asks why her husband cannot sleep that night, he turns around in bed to tell her of their personal dilemma.[6] La Sale recaps in the captain's woeful eight line speech all of the day's events which had previously taken some three pages to run through. This epic-chanter's recapitulation is used to introduce Mme Du Chastel's character to La Sale's audience. Having trusted in the covenants of the lordly men around her, Mme Du Chastel now comes to learn that her son will not be returned as promised, and the shock and disbelief all but overwhelm her: "lors la doulleur de son cuer tellement la destraint, que elle cuida bien rendre à Dieu son esperit."[7]

On the following day, the English prince's heralds make their prince's intentions all too clear to M. Du Chastel:

«Monseigneur le cappitaine, à vous nous mande le très excellent et puissant prince de Galles, nostre très redoubté seigneur, vous adviser, admonester et sommer, de vostre honneur et de vostre devoir, c'est de luy rendre ceste place demain à heure de tierce, se entre deux ne estes par mer ou par terre, par force d'armes, secouru, ainsi que contient au seelle de voz armes, dont le double est icy, lequel tira de son sain. Et se aultrement est, par nous, officiers d'armes et personnes publicques, vous fait signiffier que votre ostaige sera confisqué.»[8]

While Du Chastel readily admits that such was the agreement, he insists that, since the prince's forces could not prevent the ship from reaching the fortress, it is the prince who must yield. Still, the captain realizes that another method must be used to settle the issue, and so he proposes a trial by combat: "Et se il [le prince] voulloit dire que il eust meilleur raison que moy, devant juge compettant je luy oseroye bien dire et par mon corps monstrer.»"[9]

Here then the captain has reached the pinnacle: for his honor's sake, he can do no more but offer to put his own life on the line and have God decide which of the two of them is in the right. But La Sale will not have the prince respond in kind, for the English lord is not an adherent

6 *Réconfort*, pp. 113-114.
7 *Ibid.*, p. 114.
8 *Ibid.*, p. 115.
9 *Ibid.*, p. 116.

of the chivalric code like Du Chastel but is a man of the new ways, a
condottiere, who will press his advantage home to its mark, and failing
that, will wreak havoc on any and all in his path. For this lord, pledges
are nothing; success is everything.

Once more, like an honorable suzerain of olden times, Du Chastel
calls together his council. Once more, "n'y eust celui qui aultre conseil
lui vaulsist donner que le premier."[10] Honor requires holding firm to
the agreement's terms, and since aid has been received, it is the rigorous
prince who is faulting his word and honor.

Again that night in his chamber, the captain recapitulates the day's
events to his wife, and ends by saying:

> «Ha ! beau sires Dieu, ayez mercy de moy, et me delivrez de la mortel
> dolleur que mon coeur a, quant pour bien faire je pers mon honneur, ou
> suis de mon filz le vray bouchier que j'ay livré à mort.»[11]

Madame grieves with him but realizes finally that she must decide
what he is to do. So, asking his pardon for what she will tell him, Mme
Du Chastel declares that nature and God have made mothers more the
possessors of their children than fathers, since mothers are the ones
who carry their children in their bodies to then birth them in pain.[12] After expressing this pre-emptive right of women for their offspring which
is directly opposed to the principle of *paterfamilias*, so nurtured by
medieval society, Mme Du Chastel bravely abandons her son to God:

> Touteffoiz ores, pour tousjours mais, je l'abandonne ès mains de Dieu et
> vueil que jamais il ne me soit plus riens, ainssi que se jamaiz je ne le avoye
> veu, ains liberalement de cuer et franchement, sans force, contraint ne
> viollence aucune, vous donne, cede et transporte toute la naturelle amour,
> l'affection et le droit que mere puelt et doit avoir à son seul et très amé
> filz.[13]

Further along in this painful exercise of charity, Madame turns to the
question of her husband's honor and states firmly:

> Et vrayement, Monseigneur, il y a grant choiz. Nous sommes assez en
> aaige pour en [des fils] avoir, se à Dieu plaist; mais vostre honneur une foiz
> perdue, lasse, jamais plus ne la recouvrerez.[14]

---

10 *Ibid.*, p. 117.
11 *Ibid.*, p. 118.
12 *Ibid.*, pp. 120-121.
13 *Ibid.*, p. 121.
14 *Ibid.*, p. 121.

So she bids her husband to give up likewise their son to God's will and safeguard his honor by keeping to the terms of the pact.

From this point onwards, while Du Chastel still tries to convince the prince to keep his pledge and release his son, it is clear that the moral strength supplied him by his wife will enable Du Chastel to resist any infringement upon his honor which the prince may attempt, even to the point of losing his only heir. When the English heralds continue to press for the surrender of the French, Du Chastel is ready for their lord's insinuation that honor requires him to yield the city:

> je lui respons que de moy appeller faulseur de mon seelle, que saulve l'onneur de prince, faulsement et malvaisement il a menty.[15]

He further continues to say that a hand to hand combat could settle the matter and that he is indeed a worthy challenger for the royal prince, being "de toutes [l]es quatre lignes, digne et souffisant sur tel querelle respondre à tous roys."[16]

But Du Chastel knows that the prince has declined his first offer to duel with him and so he now proceeds to treat with the English lord on his own level by offering to pay ransom for his son's life.

While awaiting the return of his own herald with the prince's reply, Du Chastel plans a sortie in order to harass the prince and perhaps join his son in death. Seeing through his military purpose, Madame cries mercy and reasons with her husband not to deprive her of son and spouse on one and the same day.

The scene of leave-taking of Du Chastel from his household and fellow defenders is extremely poignant but, like an experienced storyteller who delays the climax of his tale, La Sale breaks off his description of the scene to tell instead how the French herald was received in the English camp. Every time the prince's envoys had visited Brest, Du Chastel had treated them with every courtesy. This one time that the French herald goes before the prince to get his answer, the prince has him restricted to the camp and then forced to accompany young Du Chastel to his death.[17] La Sale thus underscores the prince's rapaciousness.

When the execution squad is sighted by Du Chastel's men, he knows that he must give up his sortie, and so he comforts his wife who

15 *Ibid.*, p. 124.
16 *Ibid.*, p. 125.
17 *Ibid.*, pp. 128-129.

recovers from her swooning only when he assures her of his intentions to remain safe within the fortress.

La Sale now begins the description of the young boy's death, surely one of the most powerful scenes in the whole story. As the party draws nearer to Mount Reont, young Du Chastel realizes that he is not being delivered up to his father but is instead being led to his death, and so he taunts his captor:

«Ha! Thomas, mon amy, vous me menez morir, vous me menez morir! vous me menez morir; helas! vous me menez morir! Thomas, vous me menez morir! hellas! monsieur mon pere, je vois morir! hellas! madame ma mère, je vois morir, je vois morir! hellas, hellas, hellas, je vois morir, morir, morir, morir! »[18]

And thus does La Sale report the last words of a young boy, bursting with life, who must be sacrificed to the policies of state and the principle of honor in a scene which alone should guarantee the literary fame of the author. An eye-witness account of the boy's actual death is given to his father by the French herald who concluded that when he asked for the boy's body, the prince gave it to him but haughtily remarked that such was the penalty the son had to pay for his father's breach of faith.[19] The herald tells Du Chastel that he answered these terrible words with the lesson:

«A! Monseigneur, ... saulve vostre grâce, selon la sainte euvangille, nul pere doit porter l'iniquité du filz, ne nulz filz celle du pere. Mais misericorde doit resluire en nous, et especialement ès personnes des princes.»[20]

Du Chastel must now break the news of their son's death to his wife. After honorably burying the young boy and forbidding all news of this from being brought to Madame by anyone, he seizes the opportunity to discharge this heavy burden when he suggests to her at table that should the prince be cruel and refuse ransom, they must be resolute, for, "il seroit mort et martir au vray service de nostre souverain, dont arions en paradiz un angel qui prieroit pour nous."[21] Madame agrees, adding that such a fate would be better than knowing her son to be a slave on the Welsh estates of the prince.[22] Du Chastel then proceeds to

18 *Ibid.*, p. 134.
19 *Ibid.*, p. 135.
20 *Ibid.*, pp. 135-136.
21 *Ibid.*, p. 137.
22 *Ibid.*, p. 138.

reveal the truth to his wife who responds by commending her son's soul to God.

Were La Sale a cleric by profession, the story would no doubt have ended here with a resolution, reminiscent of so many hagiographic poems, ever to praise God for his mysterious workings. Such a declaration would be in sonorous harmony with the nine pages of moral exhortations which preface this tale from the Anglo-French Wars.

However, La Sale, the soldier-preceptor turned story-teller, could hardly be satisfied with such a tragic, if edifying, ending. Virtue may well be its own reward, but the lessons of wartime can sometimes brutalize the most uprighteous. La Sale, therefore, continues his tale for another two pages to relate that when the prince finally tired of the siege six days later, he informed Du Chastel of his intention to move off on condition that the French sell for gold some artillery pieces they had captured from the English.[23] Du Chastel's reply to the English heralds is to the point:

> «Dites, au faulx, malvais tirant Herodes, vostre sieur, et Judas à son seelle, que j'ay or et argent assez. Et avant en la mer les [pièces] getteroye que il s'en serveist jamaiz."[24]

In an ambush which Du Chastel then springs upon the retreating English, over a hundred prisoners are taken. Du Chastel chooses twelve of the highest nobility and dashes their hope of ransom by ordering them confessed and then hung from a gibbet on the highest tower of the fortress.[25] As for the other 106 prisoners, Du Chastel had their right eyes, ears and hands destroyed and chopped off but otherwise spared them since their prince did allow his herald to return with his son's body. In the face of this, as La Sale says, the English host cursed the day they had ever set eyes on Du Chastel's fortress.[26]

In his critique of this story, Erich Auerbach firmly states:

> It is precisely during the fifteenth century, the time when La Sale lived, that a change begins to make itself felt. ... But of the impending change, La Sale refuses to take notice. ... he saw many notable things, but all he ever noted in them was their courtly and knightly aspect.[27]

---

23 *Ibid.*, p. 138.
24 *Ibid.*, pp. 138-139.
25 *Ibid.*, pp. 139-140.
26 *Ibid.*, p. 140.
27 Erich Auerbach, *Mimesis* (Princeton, 1953), p. 244.

To this and other such judgments, the late Jean Misrahi answered succinctly: "Surely faithfulness to a trust is a matter of personal integrity, of moral character, and not merely of feudal mores."[28]

And so it would indeed appear, for in order to survive, the values which inform a literary work must speak to the needs and/ or ideals of all types of men in search of enlightenment. Without a doubt, the "heavy of the piece" here is the English prince, who, by the way, all critics have established was not the Black Prince.[29] But this judgment of this literary character, the English lord, can only be injurious to his reputation (*los*) if his actions are measured against those ethical and moral standards which have shaped western civilization. If, on the other hand, the prince is rated according to his class or caste, which is how Auerbach suggests La Sale proceeded, then he will be seen simply as a soldier who aims to achieve his objective. As such, the English prince must be given high marks when he tries by all means, even guile when force proves insufficient, to succeed.

In love and war, as is said so often, to the victor go the spoils. Du Chastel's position, already militarily inferior at the beginning of the story, becomes morally endangered while, at the same time, becoming more and more powerful empathically because of the forced sacrifice-to-be of his only son to temporary reversals of state. This is exactly what makes the story interesting for, certainly, any struggle between two captains, once heard, is much like any other. But when an individual's hope for eternity, as embodied in his offspring, is made subject to the state's survival because of adherence to a supposedly higher code of conduct, also supposedly binding on all persons of noble lineage, then sympathy is aroused, as is curiosity, and one watches to see whether chivalric ethics, so closely aligned with the norms of Christian conduct, will win out over the pragmatic issue of besting one's opponent.

The story, in brief, is not essentially a narrowly drawn account of the ill-destined son of Du Chastel, nor is it a skilful recreation of the storming of Brest by the English (which is unhistorical).[29] Rather, it seems more like a fine recounting of the myriad challenges for living morally; of choosing to follow one's principles or choosing to forego them. And contrary to Auerbach, La Sale's tale does indeed take note of the changing times in its final actions.

---

28 Misrahi, p. 823.
29 *Ibid.*, p. 824.

As the wheel of fortune has creaked forward to put Du Chastel in a favorable position against his enemies, his outrageous treatment of them is surely caused by his moral hurt as well as by the fact of his son's death. When the vanquished cried mercy, the gentlemanly code always provided that they be spared unless, of course, the struggle was previously announced "à outrage". And the ransom which a live captive could produce readily sanctioned this civilized mode of behavior.

Yet, who are those who practice this largess in La Sale's story? Have the knights been generous of word and deed, as prescribed by their caste? It would be easier to seek the practice of this virtue elsewhere in the exemplary character of Mme Du Chastel. Like a latter-day Guibourc, she is the one who truly defends the fortress of Brest and the established code of the *status quo* by giving generously of that which she holds most dear. In doing so, she rises head and shoulders above all the other characters in the tale for none can match her unselfishness. While the men about her quibble about their contracted word and call each other treacherous names, she alone is ready to demonstrate the force behind those pledges. While she is losing part of her life to maintain honor (*los*) for her husband and his cause, the others are seen trading on their high-blown philosophy of life. Antoine de la Sale could give no greater praise to womankind than to show Mme Du Chastel as the steadfast handmaiden of uprighteousness at the passing of chivalric honor among men. Indeed, it is Madame who carries the heavy and lordly banner of honor, and with it, the gratitude of all for her magnificent largess.

II

The Dual Purpose of the Second Tale of the *Reconfort de Madame Du Fresne*

In the second tale of the *Réconfort du Mme Du Fresne*,[1] Antoine de La Sale employs various means to achieve his stated purpose of providing comfort to the lady, his daughter, for whom he was moved to compose the piece. Of these, there are personal, newsworthy recollections of his 1415[2] expedition to Ceuta, involving conquest and conversion to the

---

1 "Le Réconfort de Mme Du Fresne" in *Antoine de la Salle: sa vie et ses ouvrages*, ed. Joseph Nève (Paris, 1903), pp. 141-55. Also *cf.* Fernand Desonay, "Le petit Jehan de Saintré: 1re partie; Antoine de la Sale, sa vie," *Revue du XVIe siècle* 14 (1927) 6-7.

2 *Cf. Réconfort*, p. 144.

faith; the recording of the psychological sensitivity of the Portuguese king who orders that he alone shall divulge the news of the death of one of his bravest soldiers to the man's aged mother; finally, the dramatics of the *dénouement* of these events between the prince and the bereaved mother.

In its architectonic structure, the second tale of the *Réconfort* is rather much like an exquisite medieval diptych (pp. 141-149, the expedition to Ceuta; pp. 149-154, the Portuguese Court), where one part hinges delicately upon another with each enhancing the overall effect of the whole. In piecing together the literary sections of his story, La Sale recreates actual truths of everyday life. This process is best exemplified perhaps in the scene when the Portuguese king advises:

> Vous savez [Madame]) qu'il est chose naturelle et vraye que la mort est la mains certaine quant, en quelle facon, ne comment. Les ungs ne voyent point leurs parfaiz aaiges; les aultres meurent de diverses maladies, les ung soudainement, au lit, à table et cheminant, en armes et aultrement, et les aultres par murtriers, par traittres et par justice, à cause de leur meffais, et en tant de aultres façons que de le dire seroit grant.[3]

The stoicism of this counsel was well practised during La Sale's times, as Huizinga has shown.[4] To be sure, there were ample reasons for this turn of mind: constant warfare; the vacillation of spiritual authority (pope vs. anti-pope, conciliar movements); the Black Death; the mere question of survival through bleak winters. Any one of these was enough to rob life of a sense of continuity so that, if one must die, the idea that such a death might serve a purpose could offer some solace. This could explain then the final consolatory words the king tenders the mother of his dead knight:

> Mais vostre filz est mort absoult de painne et coulpe, au service de nostre vray Dieu, comme bon chrestien et pour saulver la vie a son fils et maistre.[5]

So it would seem finally confirmed that if one must die, one should at least give up living for God's cause. Having done this, Madame's son will join the saints in eternal bliss like so many other dead crusaders before him. Of the saintly tales retold in the French literature before La

---

3 *Ibid.*, p. 151.
4 *Cf.* J. Huizinga, *The Waning of the Middle Ages* (Garden City, N.Y., 1954), pp. 138-51, chap. 11: "The Vision of Death".
5 *Réconfort*, p. 151.

Sale's day, Ste Eulalie was so loved by God that, acting upon her request, her physical body died and her soul went up to heaven.[6] All zealous followers of a master — the first Christians, contemporary Muslims and Christian crusaders — thought it blessed to be dealt with thus by their God.

Madame is so encouraged by the king's assurance of this reward for her faithful son that she asks for the details of his death. In acceding to these wishes, the king caps his account with the words:

> Mais tant Dieu l'ama et prist son service en gré, que vray martir il l'appela pour finer ses jours ainsy.[7]

In adding these final words to the speech of announcement and consolation which the king makes to his knight's mother, La Sale does not seem to take cognizance of the fact that the saintly hero, as exemplified by St Alexis, has left off his martyr's trappings to follow instead an awe-inspiring life in this world. Earlier, in the introduction to the *Réconfort*, La Sale did say that one must thank God always and constantly even though he provides "maintes fois plus à souffrir à ceulx que il ayme mieulx que aux aultres."[8] La Sale also cautions that nothing should be so esteemed as to be overly lamented for when lost:

> Et sur ce Dieux, de sa grâce, nous a donné ung souverain conseil par noz sains Peres. C'est que se nous voullons vivre lyement en ce monde et avoir paix en noz cuers, que nous ne ayons nulle grande et forte affection à quelque chose temporelle et transsitive, tant soit-elle grande, moyenne ne petite, car puis que celle chose se puelt muer ou perdre, tant selon ce que nous auerons le deuil et tristresse qui nous tourmentera très griefment. Et selonc ce que l'amour nous delicte follement et nous dist: Se tu as pere, mere, mary; et le mary, femme, enffans, freres, sœurs et aultres amis ou parens ou quelzconcques aultres biens transsitoires, quelz qu'ilz soient, ne y mettz ton cuer, tant que tu ne les puisses laissier ou perdre quand temps sera ou à Dieu plaira.[9]

---

6 *Cf. Les plus anciens monuments de la langue française*, ed. Eduard Koschwitz, 4th ed. (Leipzig, 1920), p. 4, "Prose de Sainte Eulalie", vv. 23-25:

> La domnizelle celle kose non contredist,
> Volt lo seule lazsier, si ruovet Krist.
> In figure de colomb volat a ciel.

7 *Réconfort*, p. 152.
8 *Réconfort*, p. 102.
9 *Ibid.*, p. 103.

While such a passage contains much wisdom, admirably suited for coping with the everyday business of living and dying, it does appear that La Sale is embracing the typology of a literary ethic of some three centuries previous. Seemingly, the purpose of the king's speech is to offer his condolences to a bereaved relative — a very humane activity which many engage in today. However, considered from a literary point of view, La Sale apparently is retreating into the past and, as Auerbach claims,[10] gives ample proof of being restricted to his medieval climate.

But it is also very clear that La Sale is no simple writer, given to flowery passages replete with exaggerations and omissions. Too many times in his present work does La Sale state that he will not relate the entire facts of a particular subject because "très longue chose seroit."[11] Again, it would be somewhat difficult to find many medieval authors who inform their audiences that "je viz la plus grande partie des choses ... [mais] pour venir à mon propos, je les abregeray à mon pouroir, car aussy je n'ay pas memoire, et très long chose seroit à voulloir du commencement jusques à la fin tout reciter."[12]

If then La Sale, the thoughtful stylist, is regressive in extolling a virtuous submissiveness to God's will, it may be in order to augment one of the two main purposes of his *exemplum*: the recounting of the Crusade for Ceuta. One has to recreate scenes of sacrifice, endurance, perseverance if one's goal is the generation of political and religious fervor required for the lasting victory and maintenance of state and church.

This second tale of La Sale's *Réconfort* is very deceptive in this respect. One can read it several times and wonder about its value. Is it historical? La Sale has been criticized often on this point,[13] even though he was not a chronicler by profession. Is it then a creative piece drawn from La Sale's imagination?[14] But La Sale, several, if not all critics would agree, was not completely oblivious to the events stirring around him. He participated in and observed many actions, collected facts and contrived to form them into several writings of importance for the

10 *Cf.* Erich Auerbach, *Mimesis* (Princeton, 1953), pp. 242-44.

11 *Réconfort*, p. 147.

12 *Ibid.*, p. 142.

13 *Cf.* J. Misrahi, "The Sources of the *Réconfort de Mme Du Fresne*" in *Mélanges de langue et de littérature du Moyen Age et de la Renaissance offerts à Jean Frappier*, ed. M. J. C. Payen and M. C. Rénier, 2 (Geneva, 1970), p. 825: "La Sale was, of course, a creative artist writing 'historical' fiction with just about as much care for historical accuracy as, for example, Dumas père."

14 *Cf.* W. Söderjhelm, *La nouvelle française* (Paris, 1910), pp. 91-92.

study of fifteenth-century French prose.[15] Three other writers, Commynes, Machiavelli, Guicciardini, who made their livings acting in and observing the body politic, all did the same thing as La Sale. Yet the literary reputations of these three seem to have survived much better perhaps because they have been deemed better schooled, or more controversial, or more profound. That other newsy collector of fact and fable, Froissart, also seems curiously to have earned wider critical interest than La Sale.

On the face of it then, La Sale presents his reader with a story about how the Portuguese Ceuta expedition fared, and how one of the Portuguese knights dies saving the life of his lord, and how his mother received this news, and finally, how tragedy strikes all, no matter how high in rank. The story is neatly related in a scant ten pages which scarcely recommends it for comment, for there have been other stories before like it.

But how then may the tenor of contemporary society be measured? Supposedly, the times in which La Sale lived were awash with change. A full scale cultural depression had Northern Europe in its grips although to the South, in the Sicily which La Sale had seen and enjoyed so long in the service of René d'Anjou, the Renaissance had gushed forth some hundred years and more. Still, in 1457, returned north at Vendeuil-suroise,[16] La Sale sits down and, in this consolatory piece, quietly makes appeal to another time, another place when sacrifices were expected of all worthy men. Throughout the report of the knight's death, there is the refrain that he died a martyr, "pour saulver la vye a son seigneur,"[17] which was as it should be according to the service due God.

Here then is one of the hinges which holds this admirable diptych together: all praise to him who believes in God's Word, fights for it (*Gottesdienst*) and for his temporal lord (*Königsdienst*) so that both may prosper. New winds may be sweeping through La Sale's Europe, cringing under the onslaughts of various *condottieri* and *Landsknechten* but is is time now that a basic premise of the law be exalted: to be laudable, might must be used properly. Madame's son died but a marvelous funeral awaits his body; much honor is bestowed on his memory

---

15   *Cf.* "Le petit Jehan de Saintré," p. 15.

16   *Cf.* Fernand Desonay, *Antoine de la Sale: aventureux et pédagogue* (Liège-Paris, 1940), p. 182. Desonay had placed this one year later in his article, "Le petit Jehan de Saintré," pp. 16, 28. But *cf.* Antoine de la Sale, *Le petit Jehan de Saintré*, ed. J. Misrahi and Ch. Knudson (Geneva, 1967), p. xiv, where the work is dated from 1457.

17   *Réconfort*, p. 152.

— a perpetual Mass is established by the king in his honor[18] — for the knight has given his life for the preservation of the values of an orderly society.

Seventy years after La Sale's *Réconfort,* another writer, one Jacques de Mailles, would put into words the deeds, gestes and triumphs of another paladin of society, le Chevalier de Bayard.[19] But this story will differ from La Sale's tale here because by then everyone will concede that Bayard, from whom François Ier received knighthood on the field of Marignan,[20] is the last of the true knights of old. On the other hand, La Sale's noble story can be considered as an appeal for the revival of earlier ideals — a Rolandian attempt to infuse new life into the basic virtues of courtly society for the continued glory of God and country.

Perhaps, now that the age of static Romanesque iconography was past and society was becoming accustomed more and more to the dynamic perspective of Renaissance frescoes, La Sale's message may have been too subtly stated and therefore lost on the rampant captains of his day. Yet this is not to deny La Sale a mastery of his own stylistic techniques which, somewhat left-handedly, even Auerbach would seem to admit when he says that La Sale's style "is not without its peculiar magnificence. It is a variety of the elevated style; but it is class-determined, it is non-humanist, non-classical, and entirely medieval."[21] If this is true, then it would follow that La Sale should be appreciated as an accomplished spokesman of his times, as yet not dominated by the revivified canons of classical humanism. Indeed, Fernand Desonay at the end of his critical biographical essay on La Sale states:

> Passé 1450, on ne croit plus guère à la viduité des veuves, à la vertu des orphelines, au désintéressement du chevalier ...
>
> Mais Antoine de La Sale, lui, est bien le suprême tenant de la chevalerie idéale ... Son œuvre littéraire, malgré des gaucheries et des naïvetés touchantes, — et à cause même de ces gaucheries et naïvetés, — est le fier testament d'un réactionnaire sans reproche. Homme du passé au seuil de la Renaissance, Antoine de La Sale n'a pas abdiqué. Il nous offre le témoignage, qui force le respect d'un écrivain tardif et attardé que n'a rien renié de son rêve de jeunesse.[22]

---

18 *Cf. Réconfort,* p. 154.

19 *Cf.* Loyal Serviteur (Jacques de Mailles), *Histoire du Seigneur de Bayart, transcription de l'édition parisienne de 1527* (Paris, 1927).

20 *Cf. ibid.,* p. 246. Also *cf.* Auguste Bailly, *François Ier* (Montreal, 1954), p. 66.

21 *Mimesis,* p. 243.

22 *Antoine de la Sale: aventureux et pédagogue,* pp. 169-70.

It must also not be forgotten that in his discussion of La Sale's contribution, Auerbach pays no attention at all to the second tale in the *Réconfort*, for the "first [tale]) is by far the more important."[23] In this he may well be following the lead of W. Söderjhelm (whose study Auerbach cites) who had begun his discussion of the *Réconfort* by stating the importance of the first tale to the development of the novella.[24] After examining almost all of the first tale (Söderjhelm says nothing at all about M. Du Chastel's revenge on the English enemy at the very end of the tale),[25] the Danish critic ends his evaluation of the second tale, "et l'histoire ... ne peut se mesurer avec la précédente en tant que témoignage d'un talent d'écrivain et de novelliste."[26]

Therefore, if Auerbach is correct in saying that La Sale's talent extends only to the apt representation of his own world, La Sale would seem to be an author to be highly prized because of this ability. Again, if as Söderjhelm claims, the second tale gives little support to the creative talents of its author, the work should then be greatly valued as a social document, a faithful mirror of the contemporary scene, much as Desonay has said La Sale fashioned in his *Petit Jehan de Saintré*, the work he wrote just before the *Réconfort*.[27]

It is true enough that the second tale in the *Réconfort* does not possess the dramatic power of the first but must every work of an author be alike? Apparently, after drawing the fine psychological cameos which constitute the first tale, La Sale wished to adapt the second part of his *Réconfort* more directly to his purpose: providing his daughter with a guide for overcoming her grief. At this time of his life, he was by profession a tutor and here, more particularly, he was a father whose daughter needed succoring. Söderjhelm admits, "ce qui caractérise le style d'Antoine de La Sale dans cet ouvrage, comme dans les précédents, c'est le naturel."[28] And Auerbach offers that "even though we may wish to make allowances because the author was an old man ... the same paratactic and slightly confused kind of composition is already to be found in the novel of little Jehan de Saintré, which was written some years earlier."[29] Yet both critics seem to set aside the real-life role La

23   *Mimesis*, p. 232.
24   *Cf. La nouvelle française*, p. 84.
25   *Cf. ibid.*, p. 91, where Söderjhelm ends his analysis with the scene in which Mme Du Chastel learns of her son's death, a full two and a half pages short of the end of the story. *Cf. Réconfort*, pp. 138-40.
26   *La nouvelle française*, p. 96.
27   "Le petit Jehan de Saintré," p. 20.
28   *La nouvelle française*, p. 93.
29   *Mimesis*, p. 243.

Sale was trying to fulfil here and which led him to compose the *Récon-fort*. In convincing his offspring to bear up under the problems life can offer, how more naturally should La Sale have proceeded than by interlacing his words with a moral here, a little story there, then a few more recollections, as would a man who had long experience with the caring for others' feelings. On balance, it seems patently clear that the second tale of the *Réconfort*, far from being unimportant, gives ample measure of La Sale's acumen, sensitivity and generous spirit, qualities which any universal man of the Renaissance would admire.

Mercy College, Dobbs Ferry, New York

THE SEATING OF THE BARONS IN PARLIAMENT, DECEMBER 1461[1]

Kenneth G. Madison

Portions of the Lords' Journals for the three parliamentary sessions in 1461, 1512, and 1536 have been discovered in the British Museum's Harley MS. 158.[2] Also, within this volume of parliamentary miscellanea, collected by Ralph Starkey and Sir Simonds D'Ewes,[3] are a number of lists giving the lords as they sat in several parliaments.[4] Although lists of

1 The research for this paper was made possible in part by a Foreign Travel Grant (1968) and a Research Initiation Grant (1970-1) from Iowa State University. Throughout this paper unless otherwise stated all biographical information is from G. E. C[okayne], *The Complete Peerage*, rev. ed., 13 vols. (London, 1910-59), and summonses to parliament are from House of Lords, *Matters Touching the Dignity of a Peer of the Realm* 4 (London, 1826), pp. 950-77.

2 These fragments are found in British Museum Harley MS. 158, fols. 129-129b, 141-142, and 143-144b, respectively. The Journal for 1461 has been discussed and printed in R. Virgoe, "A New Fragment of the Lords' Journal of 1461," *Bulletin of the Institute of Historical Research* 32 (1959) 83-7, while the fragments for 1512 and 1536 are printed with incorrect foliation in Nicholas H. Nicolas, *Report of Proceedings on the Claim to the Barony of L'Isle in the House of Lords* (London, 1829), pp. 418-26.

3 Cyril E. Wright, *Fontes Harleiani* (London, 1972), p. 373, gives Starkey and D'Ewes as previous owners of Harley MS. 158, while Andrew G. Watson, *The Library of Sir Simonds D'Ewes* (London, 1966), p. 320, states that no examples of the handwriting of these two antiquarians are found on any of the folios of this volume discussed in this paper; therefore, no direct relationship between these folios and them can be demonstrated.

4 The lists and the reigns to which they refer are: fols. 113-113b, 121, 121b, 124-124b, and 134b-135 — Henry VI; fols. 124b-124 — Edward IV; fols. 114-114b, and 124b-124 — Henry VIII; fols. 122-123 — Edward VI; fols. 130, and 130b-131 — Philip and Mary; and fols. 125-126, 127-128, and 133-133b — Elizabeth I. Varying in format these fourteen lists include seven with both spiritual and temporal lords, five with only the temporal lords, and two with only those lords of the rank of baron. Although just six lists are dated, they all seem to be attributable to a particular parliament by internal evidence, but the detailed examination of the lives of the listed lords necessary to date them is outside the scope of this work. A recent article, G. R. Elton, "The Early Journals of the House of Lords," *English Historical Review* 89 (1974) 484-85 and 509, presents the "lists of seating" dating through 1461 as indicating only that some sort of records of attendance were made and that such lists do not give the seating order of the lords. In a future article I plan to challenge this view through an analysis of these "lists of seating" and other relevant parliamentary documents.

the order of the lords' seating cannot replace the Lords' Journals, or copies of them, as sources of information concerning the activities of the upper house, such lists do provide additional insight into questions of attendance and precedence. One of these lists in Harley MS. 158 appears to be a record of the lords of the rank of baron made for one day of the parliament of 1461. Because of its relationship to the known two copies of fragments of the 1461 Lords' Journal,[5] it is of importance and is printed below.

This list, which was incorrectly headed 'Another note of barons as they sate in Henrye the Syxte tyme as followethe' by its mid-sixteenth-century copyist, is located on the far right-hand side of the top half of Harley MS. 158, fol. 124b and on the far right-hand side of the bottom half of fol. 124.[6] This rather strange arrangement is the result of some long past repairing of the folio now numbered 124-124b, when the bottom half of this page was reversed and then attached to its top half. The mistake made in the repair work seems not to have been previously noticed, because both sides of this folio are covered by the columns of three different lists of lords: first, beginning at the top of fol. 124 and ending on the bottom of fol. 124b, a double column list dated as 17 March 31 Henry VI [1453]; second, beginning at the top left-hand side of fol. 124b, a double column list from the parliament of 1539-40; and third, starting on the top right-hand side of fol. 124b, the single column list labelled 'Another note of barons ...'. The last two end on the bottom of fol. 124. The reversal of the bottom half of the folio 124-124b has, no doubt, obscured the value of the last list for the parliament of 1461.

Internal evidence proves this 'note of barons' should have been assigned to the parliament of 1461. Of the thirty-two barons listed, five — Ferrers of Chartley, Hastings, Herbert, Stafford of Southwick, and

---

5   William H. Dunham, Jr., *The Fane Fragment of the 1461 Lords' Journal* (New Haven, 1935), pp. 3-25, gives a transcription of B.M. Additional MS. 34218, fols. 100-103b, and Virgoe, pp. 86-7 for Harley MS. 158, fols. 129-129b.

6   The "note of barons" is in a mid-sixteenth-century secretary hand, which also appears in Harley MS. 158, fols. 124 (top) and 124b (bottom), and fols. 134b-135. These two lists are reputedly for the order of seating of the spiritual and temporal lords on 17 March 1453. With the exception of several minor spelling differences and the misdating of the latter to 1433, which was also the original date on the former, they are nearly identical. Possibly fols. 134b-135 is a fair copy made from fols. 124 (top) and 124b (bottom). The existence of the former list on fol. 124 probably caused the copyist, when he came across a second seating list which looked similar to the one he had already, to entitle the new one as "Another note of barons as they sate in Henrye the Syxte tyme as followethe". Examination of the handwriting of other lists mentioned in n. 4 has not produced any unquestionable assignment of them to the copyist of the "note of barons".

Wenlock — had been created barons on 26 July 1461.[7] Two of these baronies became extinct within a decade: Stafford of Southwick in August 1469 and Wenlock in 1471. Three parliaments, those of 1467, 1469, and 1470, of the five summoned between 1461 and 1471 may be ruled out because by May 1466, Lords Montague, Grey of Ruthin, and Rivers had been raised to the earldoms of Northumberland (1464), Kent (1465), and Rivers (1466) respectively.[8] In addition, Lords Clinton, Cobham, Grey of Powis, and Lovel were not summoned to these three parliaments.[9] The two sessions of the parliament of 1463-5, which was summoned on 22 December 1462, may be dismissed because neither Grey of Powis nor the new Lord Stourton was summoned to or attended it.[10] This leaves only Edward IV's first parliament, which he summoned on 23 May 1461, to meet on 6 July but which did not begin until 4 November 1461.

By comparing the 'note of barons' with the nine known lists of barons in the Lords' Journal of 1461, the relationship of the 'note' to the Journal is apparent.[11] The rosters of the barons for 2 and 5 December are quite similar to that of the 'note'. There are, though, several significant differences. The variances between the attendance list for 2 December and the 'note of barons' are reflected in the latter as: the change of

7   Three other barons, Cromwell, Montague, and Scales, were until recently thought to have been created barons by Edward IV sometime after 4 March 1461. But, John Benet's chronicle indicates that these three were made barons in the short parliamentary session of 28 January - 3 February 1461; John Benet, "John Benet's Chronicle for the years 1400 to 1462," ed. G. L. Harriss and M. A. Harriss, *Camden Miscellany* 24 (1972) 229. For Sir John Neville and Sir Anthony Wydeville's creations further evidence exists which dates from before May 1461. On 28 January 1461, Neville signed himself as "J. Montagu", *Proceedings and Ordinances of the Privy Council of England*, ed. N. H. Nicolas, 6 (Lincoln, 1837), p. 310. On 19 and 22 February 1461, his ennoblement is noted and he is referred to as "Lord Montagu" and "lord of Montan", *Calendar of the State Papers of Milan*, 1 (London, 1912), pp. 49 and 51. Two letters, dated 4 and 18 April 1461, to John Paston I regarding the battle of Towton mention Montague and Scales in the news of the battle, *The Paston Letters, A.D. 1422-1509*, ed. James Gairdner, 3 (London, 1904), pp. 267-69.

8   Other barons who became earls were Herbert, made earl of Pembroke on 8 September 1468, and Stafford of Southwick, created earl of Devon on 17 May 1469. Both along with Earl Rivers were to die in the summer of 1469.

9   The new Lord Clinton was never summoned. Cobham and Lovel were minors. Grey of Powis was not recognized as a lord of parliament after 1461 and never again is known to have attended parliament.

10   In fact, William, Lord Stourton, the thirty-five year old heir of John, Lord Stourton, who had died on 25 November 1462, was not to be called to parliament until 1469. Josiah C. Wedgwood, *History of Parliament, Biographies* (London, 1936), p. 819, wrongly states that William, Lord Stourton, was summoned to the parliaments of 1463-5 and 1467-8 and not to that of 1469.

11   A number of spelling differences in the "note" and the copies of the Journals exist, but owing to the carelessness of sixteenth-century copyists these differences do not preclude the likelihood that the "note" is derived from the Journal itself, or a copy of it.

placement of Lord Scrope of Bolton from below Lord Audley to above Lord Fitzhugh, the replacement of Lord Willoughby by Lord Lovel, the reversal of the order of Lords Wenlock and Cromwell, and the addition of Lord Scales to the bottom of the list. The differences between the 'note' and the entry for 5 December appear in the latter as: the disappearance of Lord Grey of Codnor, the reversal of the two Lords Scrope, and the insertion of Lord Dacre between Lords De La Warr and Scrope of Upsall. These differences not only date the 'note of barons' to either 3 or 4 December 1461, but also supply a few more clues regarding the keeping of the Lords' Journals up-to-date by the parliamentary clerk and the use of precedence by the barons at this time.

The clerk's revision as shown by the comparison of the 'note' with the Journal sheds more light on the day to day composition of this parliament. For example, the disappearance of Lord Willoughby from the 'note' and of Lord Grey of Codnor, who is on the 'note', from the Journal of 5 December was occasioned by the fact they were not expected to be in parliament in the near future. The inclusion on the 'note' of Lord Lovel in Willoughby's place and Lord Scales at the bottom of the list indicates that these two were either present, though attendance is not shown on the 'note', or available to attend.[12]

Whether in the fifteenth century the barons in parliament were ordered by some system of precedence or simply listed in random order has never been seriously discussed.[13] The evidence relative to this topic before 1461 is both sparse and contradictory, but the Lords' Journals of 1461 do provide some information in this regard. The most clear indication some consideration was being given to problems of precedence is the reversal of Lords Wenlock and Cromwell in the 'note'. Between 28 November and 2 December Wenlock sat directly above Cromwell, and then in the 'note' and the known Journals for 5 to 12 December he is found just below Cromwell. The reversing of these two lords undoubtedly was in recognition of the creation of Humphrey Bourchier as

12 See n. 23 for further adjustments in the placing of Lovel and Scales.
13 Luke O. Pike, *A Constitutional History of the House of Lords* (London, 1894), pp. 115 and 129, says Henry VI could give precedence to one baron over another but feels that before Henry VIII's reign it is not possible to prove that the barons are in a definite order. Wedgwood, *Hist. of Parl., Register*, pp. liii-lxxviii, ignores the question, except to say that the summonses on the Close Rolls are not in order by precedence or seniority (p. lvii). J. Enoch Powell and Keith Wallis, *The House of Lords in the Middle Ages* (London, 1968), pp. 512-13, say only that the 1461 Journal and the Close Rolls show the relative precedence between the five groups of lords in parliament, *i.e.* archbishops, bishops, earls, abbots, and barons. Not until their discussion of the parliament of 1515 (p. 547), do the authors examine precedence among the barons.

Lord Cromwell in the second session of the parliament of 1460-1,[14] some six months before Sir John Wenlock was rewarded with his barony for his part in the Yorkist seizure of the Lancastrian throne.

Although the upper two thirds of the various baronial lists for 1461 are in no perceptible order or precedence, the bottom one third is. Once Wenlock and Cromwell were reversed all of the barons from Lord Stourton through Lord Stafford of Southwick are in order by date of their respective creations. Examination of the date of creation of all of the baronies which were created after Stourton (13 May 1448) in the 'note' and in the 1461 Journal produces two groups of lords, who at first glance appear to have been summoned through their wives. The first, composed of Dacre, Willoughby, Abergavenny, Fitzwarin, and Scales, were all seated above Stourton. The second group sat below Stourton and included Barnes, Cromwell, and Ferrers of Chartley. In fact, though, only the first group was summoned in this fashion and received a higher precedence, for Barnes, Cromwell, and Ferrers were actually new creations.

Of the former group all five were recognized as having received a revived barony.[15] Richard Fiennes on 9 October 1459 had become Lord

---

14 "Benet's Chronicle," p. 229. The ennoblement of Bourchier along with Sir John Neville as Lord Montague and Sir Anthony Wydeville as Lord Scales in this parliamentary session may be construed as an attempt by the Yorkist leaders in London to reward two loyal followers and to attract a potential supporter; see K. G. Madison, The Wydevilles, 1086-1491 (Diss. Illinois, 1968), pp. 156-8.

15 The only other baron, who appears to have been ennobled after Stourton and attended parliament between 1448 and 1461 and was placed above Stourton, was Richard Grey, Lord Powis. Although he was never summoned, Powis appeared in parliament on 23 July 1455 and again on 1 and 2 December 1461; Rotuli parliamentorum 5.283, and Dunham, fols. 102-102b Powis' father, Sir Henry Grey, was the son of Joan, the eldest daughter and coheir of Edward, Lord Cherleton of Powis (d. 1421). Despite the claim of The Complete Peerage 3.162 and note b, that Joan had inherited the lordship of Powis, there is little direct evidence indicating that her son, Sir Henry Grey, was recognized as "Lord Powis". On 16 March 1447 Grey calling himself "lord of Powes" made a gift of some property to the college of St. Mary and St. Nicholas, Cambridge; Calendar of the Patent Rolls, 1452-1461 (London, 1901), p. 23. Grey's right to claim the title, "Lord Powis", appears disputed in five documents, dated 26 and 27 November 1448 relating to the restoration of property in Wales, in the Treasury of the Receipt of the Exchequer, Council and Privy Seal Records, P.R.O., E 28/78/29-33. In these council records Sir Henry Grey, John, Lord Tiptoft, and John, Lord Dudley, are described as "Lordes of Powes". The claims of Tiptoft and Dudley to Powis came from the former's marriage to Joyce, the younger daughter of Edward, Lord Cherleton of Powis, and the latter's marriage to Cherleton's widowed second wife, Elizabeth. Whatever Tiptoft and Dudley's position was, by 1455 they seem to have allowed Grey's nineteen year old son, Richard, to have the lordship. This recognition by the lords in parliament of Richard Grey's claim to Powis coupled with his position among the barons in 1461 may indicate he was considered as a baron before Stourton was ennobled in May 1448 and that the Greys were heirs to the barony of Cherleton of Powis, which could account for his seat above Stourton.

Dacre, his wife, Joan, being the granddaughter and heir general of Thomas, Lord Dacre, who had died in January 1458. On 26 May 1455, Richard Welles, who had been addressed as 'Lord Willoughby' in letters sent in Henry VI's name as early as 15 March 1454,[16] was summoned to parliament as Lord Willoughby in the right of his wife, Joan, the daughter and heir of Robert, Lord Willoughby, who had died three years earlier. In 1450 William Neville, who for the past twenty years had been styled 'Lord Abergavenny' was summoned to parliament in this title. Although Neville's wife, Elizabeth, was now dead, and their son and her heir, George, had become the heir to this barony, the son's rights were ignored, and the father was summoned in his stead. William Bourchier, third son of William Bourchier, count of Eu, and husband of Thomasine Hankeford, the granddaughter and ultimately the heir of Fulk Fitzwarin (d. 1431), was summoned as Lord Fitzwarin in 1449. No member of the Fitzwarin family had been summoned to a parliament since the death of Fulk Fitzwarin in 1337, nor had any of Fulk's descendents been styled 'Lord Fitzwarin'. The fact that William Bourchier, Lord Fitzwarin, is seated just two places above Stourton may imply that his barony might be dated from the death of his wife's grandfather in 1431 rather than from its first summons in Edward I's reign. Early in 1461 Anthony Wydeville was created Lord Scales as the husband of Thomasine, apparently the elder daughter and coheir of Thomas, seventh Lord Scales, who had been murdered in July 1460.[17] By 9 December 1461, Anthony, Lord Scales, was seated just below Grey of Wilton, thereby indicating this barony like the other four was not a new creation.

The placement of the latter group of three barons in the lists of 1461 below Stourton shows that these barons were then being treated as new creations. John Bourchier, fourth son of the count of Eu, was married to Margery, the daughter and heir of Sir Richard Berners. Richard Ber-

---

16 POPC 6.177, 186, and 217. He also according to the Close Rolls on 2 April 1454 witnessed Richard Neville, earl of Salisbury's, installation as chancellor, Rot. parl. 5.499-50, or Calendar of the Close Rolls, 1447-1454 (London, 1900), pp. 508-9.

17 According to a monumental brass in the church of East Grinstead, co. Sussex, Katherine, daughter of Thomas, Lord Scales, had died on 9 June 1505. She had been the wife of Sir Richard Grey (d. 1483) and Richard Lewkenor, esquire, of Brambley (d. 1503). Grey was the second son of Sir John Grey of Groby and Elizabeth Wydeville, who in 1464 had married Edward IV. Apparently the Wydevilles had provided for Katherine by marrying her to Grey so that all the Scales estates could go to Thomasine and Anthony Wydeville. For a transcription of the brass see Mrs. C. E. D. Davidson-Houston, "Sussex Monumental Brasses," Sussex Archaeological Collections 78 (1937) 68-70. Also see, Madison, The Wydevilles, 1086-1491, p. 158, n. 53.

ners, who had died in 1421, had been called 'Lord Berners' in Henry V's reign though he never was actually summoned to parliament. Nor had Margery's first husband, John Ferreby, been summoned. Bourchier was recognized as a baron by 17 April 1454[18] and summoned to parliament on 26 May 1455 in a title based on the source of his wealth, his wife's inheritance. In his case there simply was no pre-existing title to revive. The creation of Walter Devereux as Lord Ferrers of Chartley is in several ways similar to the Berners and Fitzwarin creations. Devereux was married to Anne Ferrers, daughter and heir of Sir William Ferrers, who like his father before him, was called 'Lord Ferrers' and yet had never been summoned to parliament. The only one of Anne's ancestors to be summoned was John de Ferrers, who had died in 1312. By 17 April 1454 Devereux was being addressed as 'Lord Ferrers of Chartley', though he was not summoned to parliament until 1461.[19] His position among the barons in 1461 shows at that time his barony was considered a new one, though under the Tudors it was treated like the Fitzwarin barony and given a higher precedence.[20] Humphrey Bourchier, third son of Henry, Viscount Bourchier and later earl of Essex, was married to Joan Stanhope, younger granddaughter and coheir of Ralph, third Lord Cromwell, who had died in 1456. When early in 1461 Humphrey Bourchier was created Lord Cromwell, the rights of his wife's widowed and childless elder sister were ignored. Since the new Lord Cromwell never received the precedence of the original barony, his creation is to be viewed as a totally new one.[21]

Study of the 'note of barons' and the Journal entries for 2 and 5 December reveals, beside the replacement of Willoughby by Lovel mentioned above, two other minor modifications of the list. These two changes involved the same five lords. The first alteration was the moving of one of the Lords Scrope to the position below Lord De La Warr. But the copyist was unsure as to which Lord Scrope belonged in this place. After identifying the lower Lord Scrope as 'of Bolton', then 'of Upsall', and finally 'of Bolton', the copyist of the 'note' labelled the upper Lord Scrope as 'of Upsall'. The reason he settled on this

18 POPC 6.177. Berners in 1461 was seated just above Lord Stanley, whose father had been summoned as a lord in 1456.

19 POPC 6.177.

20 In Henry VIII's reign the Ferrers barony was treated first as a new creation (1461) and then by the end of the parliament of 1515 and thereafter as the original creation (1299), Journals of the House of Lords 1 (London, n.d.) passim and Harley MS. 158, fols. 141b-142 and 143-143b.

21 Powell and Wallis, p. 509. For the correct date of Ralph, Lord Cromwell's, death, see Wedgwood, Hist. of Parl., Reg., p. 227 n. 8.

arrangement may have been a result of his knowlege of the baronial order in Tudor parliaments in which Scrope of Bolton usually occupied
approximately this position.[22] In any case his conclusion was erroneous
for according to the roster for 5 December Scrope of Bolton sat fifth in
order and Scrope of Upsall, ninth. The second change was the shifting
of Lord Dacre from above Lord Dudley on the 'note' to between Lords
De La Warr and Scrope of Upsall on 5 December. Originally, the
copyist of Harley MS. 158, fol. 129b had written Dacre above Dudley
and later inserted him after De La Warr.

All of these minor alterations, as well as others found in the Lords'
Journal,[23] denote modifications in the order of precedence. Probably
these changes occur as the consequence of claims of precedence by
various barons as seemingly was the case in the series of adjustments in
the order of the barons in the second session of the parliament of
1515.[24] What justifications were offered by a baron for a particular
place of precedence is not clear. Neither the place of a baron's name in
the list of summonses on the back of the Close Rolls nor the date of the
creation of his title supplies evidence explaining the ordering of the
barons created before 1460. New baronies created by Edward IV and
his successors were kept in order by seniority of creation.[25] The 'note of
barons' and the Lords' Journal of 1461 show that, while the order of
precedence had not solidified by then, the barons like the dukes and
earls had an interest in the concept of precedence. This interest was
fostered by the development of a hereditary parliamentary peerage, the

22   While the copyist may have been aware of some or all of the lists found in Harley MS. 158
(see n. 4 for these), he did have the list of spiritual and temporal lords for 31 Henry VIII, which appears with the "note of barons" on fols. 124b-124. In this Henrician parliament Scrope of Bolton is
the twelfth baron out of twenty-eight. Throughout the sixteenth century Scrope of Bolton was
placed in the Lords' Journals in this fashion, *LJ* 1-2 *passim*.

23   The others were: the reversal of Dudley and Dacre on 30 November, the shifts of Lovel
from below Beauchamp to below Rivers and of Scales from the bottom of the list to below Grey of
Wilton by 9 December, and the movement of Lovel, again, to below Fitzwarin on 11 December.

24   Powell and Wallis, p. 547.

25   According to a description of the opening of Henry VIII's first parliament in 1510, the temporal lords were arranged by "the anciency of their first creation or admission by Garter king-of-
arms", British Museum Additional MS. 5758, fols. 8-9, printed by Powell and Wallis, pp. 543-4. In
1539 when Henry VIII established the rules of precedence for the House of Lords, the lords were
to "sytt and be placed after ther Auncienties as it hathe ben accustomed"; Stat. 31 Hen. VIII, c. 10,
7. The lack of a definition of "anciety" led to continual adjustment of the list of barons throughout the Tudor period; see *LJ* 1.79, 316, and 522 and 2.193-7. Finally, in 1597 the House of Lords appointed a committee to examine the state of the ordering of the lords in the Journals, but nothing
came of this investigation, *LJ* 2.195. Even Sir Robert Cotton, the antiquarian, could not discover
any rules of precedence for barons dating before Henry VIII's reign; see his "Precedency of peers
determinable in Parlament" in British Museum Harley MS. 6849, fols. 109-109b.

increase in participation of all ranks of the secular lords in the government of England after 1421, and the involvement of many lords in the political upheavals of the second half of the fifteenth century.[26]

British Museum, Harley MS. 158, fol. 124*b* (top).[27]

Another note of barons/ as they sate in Henrye/ the Syxte tyme as/ followethe/

lorde of Seynt Jones
lorde grey of Ruthyn
       grey of Codnor
       clynton
       Audelley
       Scruope of upsall
       Dacre.
       Dudley
       laware   bolton
       Scroope of ~~bolton upsa~~ [tear]
       fytzhughe
         a
       Cobhm
       grey of wylton
       suddeley
         a
       beauchm [p?] [tear caused by wear and repair]
fol. 124 (bottom).
lorde lovell
       saye
       Ryvs
lorde of burgavennye
lorde fytzwarryn
       powis
       Stourton
       barnes

---

26 J. S. Roskell, "The Problem of the Attendance of the Lords in Medieval Parliaments," *BIHR* 29 (1956) 198-9, whose views on precedence are largely based on the activities of the earls and dukes, feels the barons attended parliament indifferently. He believes that the interest in precedence was a result of the recognition by the secular lords that a hereditary parliamentary peerage was coming into existence rather than because of a sense of duty on their part to attend parliament.

27 I wish to thank the Trustees of the British Museum for permission to print this document.

Stanley
mountague
cromwell
wentloke
Hastinge
fferrys
Herberte
Southwycke
Scales

Iowa State University

THE MEDIEVAL CARTULARY TRADITION
AND THE SURVIVAL OF ARCHIVAL MATERIAL AS REFLECTED IN THE ENGLISH HOSPITALLER CARTULARY OF 1442

Michael Gervers

Dᴜʀɪɴɢ the Middle Ages important religious institutions as well as noble families received and promulgated thousands of title deeds and other legal documents. To facilitate reference, these charters were periodically copied into a book, or series thereof, known as a register or cartulary. I should like to discuss here the development of the cartularies of the Order of St. John of Jerusalem, or Hospitallers, in England.

It has been generally accepted that when cartularies were written, the individual entries were copied directly from original deeds if such originals were extant. The results of my analysis of the Hospitaller archives are directly opposed to this belief, for they indicate that once a document was copied into a cartulary, the original was thereafter disregarded in subsequent cartulary revisions. Purely for the sake of speed, convenience and economy, the scribes preferred to base a revision directly on the already existing manuscript, rather than on original documents; obviously an easier solution than arranging and rearranging thousands of bulky originals. Only the interim documents which had accrued to the Order since the last cartulary was drawn up were copied from the originals during these revisions. The modern librarian revising a card catalogue works in much the same way.

The basis for my observations is the comprehensive Cartulary of the Order of St. John of Jerusalem in England, a Cotton MS. (Nero E. vi) in the British Museum. Begun in 1442, it contains 467 folios and was originally divided for administrative purposes into two distinct parts, a *prima* and *secunda camera*, the term *camera* referring in all likelihood to the muniment chambers at the head priory, Clerkenwell (now part of London) where the material for these two sections was stored. The *secunda camera* (fols. 289-467) can be considered as an entity in itself, since nearly all of the 957 documents inscribed therein pertain to Order holdings in Essex county.[1]

It is through the folios of the *secunda camera* that I shall broach the subject of the medieval cartulary tradition, that is to say the policy maintained through the centuries by the Order of using a preceding cartulary as the immediate source for its successor, without necessarily referring to original deeds even if they were available.

CHART I

Titulus	Sectional Division		Latest *A*	Latest *B*
Cressing-Witham - - - - - - - - - - - - Cressing-Witham		I	—	1397
	- - - - Maplestead	II	*c.* 1290	1383
	Chaureth	III	1304	1319
Maplestead - - - - - - - - - - - -	Hedingham Castle	IV	—	1356
	Bumpstead Helion	V	1292	—
	Miscellaneous	VI	*c.* 1290	1358
	- - - - Halstead	VII	1295	1394
Gestingthorpe - - - - -				
Odwell - - - - - - - - - - Gestingthorpe		VIII	*c.* 1300	1385
Sampford-in-Essex	Sampford	IX	*c.* 1300	—
Boblow	Boblow	X	*c.* 1260	—

A good deal of evidence is derived from the sequence and grouping of entries. As Chart I indicates, the *secunda camera* of the Cartulary is divided into six *tituli* or titles, each the name of a parish or manor in Essex where the Order held lands. Such topographical divisions are a common form of cartulary organization. With the pertinent *titulus* appearing at the top of each recto folio, the six are grouped in the following order: *Cressing-Witham, Maplestead, Gestingthorpe, Odwell, Sampford-in-Essex* and *Boblow*. The deeds entered under the last four *tituli* all have one thing in common: they pertain to the respective parish or manor mentioned. In the first two *tituli*, Cressing-Witham and Maplestead, the organization is otherwise. In addition to Cressing-Witham, entries pertaining to thirteen other parishes occur under that *titulus*; under Maplestead, no less than twenty-four. Together, these two *tituli* contain more than two thirds of the documents in the *secunda camera*. If the *secunda camera* was organized topographically, why did the organizers of the cartulary not assign a new *titulus* to each parish, and if

---

1 My critical edition of the *secunda camera* is scheduled to appear in the British Academy's *Records of Social and Economic History* series c. 1978.

it was organized according to administrative dependence, why were the last four *tituli* not included under that of Maplestead, the site of the local Essex preceptory upon which they depended? The answer lies in the derivative and cumulative nature of the Cartulary. In other words, the arrangement met with here is the result of a series of separate arrangements arrived at long before 1442 when this comprehensive cartulary was composed, yet modified by the scriptorium of 1442 into an admixture of topographical and administrative groupings corresponding to the present *tituli*.

Signs of the antecedent arrangements appeared in a consecutive list I prepared, noting topographical identity and date, of all the separate entries in the *secunda camera*. The list reflected two very distinct patterns. First, the Maplestead *titulus* appeared to be composed of six separate units, four of them clearly topographical (Chart I). These I named respectively by association of content as *Maplestead* (not to be confused with the *titulus* of the same name), *Chaureth, Hedingham Castle, Bumpstead Helion, Miscellaneous,*[2] and *Halstead.* Cressing-Witham excepted, the remaining *tituli*, representing but one topographical area, could not be further divided. Thus, the six *tituli* of the *secunda camera* could be redistributed to form ten sections, the material in these sections pertaining either topographically or administratively to the parish listed beside the section in Chart I.

Secondly, even more striking than the discovery of distinct topographical groups within the *tituli*, was the appearance within most sections of two groups of documents. The first group contains material dating from the twelfth century to the end of the thirteenth. These I shall refer to hereafter as the *A* documents. The second, which if it appears at all always comes at the end of a section, contains documents almost without exception from the fourteenth century. These are the *B* documents. Reference to both groups also appears in Chart I.

From the date of the latest *A* document in each section, for the most part between *c.* 1290 and *c.* 1300 with none being later than 1304, and from the appended nature of the *B* material, it seems highly probable

---

2   This section appears to be based on a cartulary written *c.* 1260 which contained documents pertaining to properties then administered by the Order's preceptory at Little Maplestead, Essex. During the reorganization of *c.* 1300 most of the material copied out of this cartulary was entered in the new cartulary according to topographical and family association. Those documents which could not be associated in this manner were copied into a section reserved for miscellaneous material, to which additional miscellaneous documents were added in subsequent copyings. Section VI corresponds chronologically to *Chaureth II*, itself reflected in the content of section III.

that the scribes of the *secunda camera* were copying from a cartulary or series thereof begun *c.* 1290 and completed shortly after the turn of the century, to which further additions, the *B* material, had been made sometime after 1397 (the date of the latest *B* entry).

Looking closely at the *A* and *B* documents, some other very obvious trends and distinctions appear. We have already seen that for the most part the sections are based on topographical units, often containing material pertaining to but one parish. Within those sections the documents have been arranged wherever possible according to family. Finally, some such groupings are further arranged chronologically. Each section, particularly the *A* material, is thus carefully organized topographically, genealogically and chronologically. The occasional fourteenth-century or *B* deed appears within the *A* divisions, but only when those *B* group deeds could be associated by family and parish with material in the *A* group. *B* documents concerning parishes to be found among the *A* deeds, but not concerning families within these parishes, were considered miscellaneous with respect to *A* and were copied in a group at the end of the *A* material.

It seems quite clear from the internal organization of the Cartulary of 1442, from the sections as opposed to the *tituli*, and from the arrangement of entries according to the divisions *A* and *B* described above, that the manuscript as we know it today was derived from a series of preceding arrangements which I have already referred to as the cartulary tradition.

Such is some of the major evidence apparent from the manuscript itself. It can be corroborated by two Hospitaller cartulary fragments containing documents pertaining solely to Order holdings in Essex county.

Stuck as a pastedown to the inside back cover of Peterhouse MS. 62 in Cambridge are the mutilated fragmentary remains of a single folio from a Hospitaller cartulary written *c.* 1200.[3] On it can be deciphered the remnants of fifteen deeds, all of which appear amongst the folios of the Cartulary of 1442. Twelve of these occur in section III (Chaureth) of the *secunda camera*. Chart II, a comparison of the consecutive arrangement of documents in both MSS., is telling. Although a certain amount of rearrangement is evident, the progression of *secunda camera* nos. 295-303 clearly reflects the order occurring in the Peterhouse fragment. I do not wish in any way to suggest that because of the similarity of sequence in

---

3 See M. Gervers, "An Early Cartulary Fragment of the Order of St. John of Jerusalem in England," *Journal of the Society of Archivists* 5 (1974) 8-24.

both MSS., the one was the direct source for the other. Rather, I suggest that the difference in sequence is indicative of an interim rearrangement which was to serve as the source upon which section III was based.

CHART II		CHART III			
Peterhouse *c.* 1200 (Chaureth I)	Cartulary of 1442	Chaureth I *c.* 1200	Chaureth II *c.* 1260	Cartulary of *c.* 1300	Cartulary of 1442
no. 1r	no. 295				
2r	296	5v U			U no. 312 (313)
3r	297	6v V	V	V	V 376 (---)
4r	299	7v W	X	—	W 231 (232)
5r	*p.c.*			X	X 455
6r	300			Y	Y 456
7r	*p.c.*			Z	Z 457
8r	301	No topographical arrangement	Topographical arrangement	Topographical & family arrangement	Topographical & family arrangement transferred
1v	321				
2v	(?)				
3v	302				
4v	417				
5v (U)	312				
6v (V)	376				
7v (W)	231				
8v	303				
(*p.c.* = *prima camera*)					

That four fifths of the Peterhouse entries are to be found in section III of the *secunda camera* is significant. The section itself is unique, for of the 185 documents copied into it, 115 date from before the year 1200. Since the only Hospitaller administrative centre in Essex between *c.* 1151 and *c.* 1225 was at a manor called Chaureth (Broxted parish, Dunmow Hundred)[4], it is evident that the twelfth-century Essex deeds in section III concern properties which came under the jurisdiction of that manor (hence the attribution of the section). What is more, the fact that twelve of the Peterhouse entries are to be found among these deeds is a clear indication that one of the indirect sources, and undoubtedly the basis of section III, was Peterhouse, or rather the cartulary of *c.* 1200 itself.

4 For evidence of the Order's administrative centre at Chaureth during this period see the article in n. 3, pp. 10-13.

From Chart II it is evident that Peterhouse nos. 3v and 8v occur one after the other in the Cartulary of 1442 as nos. 302 and 303. If it could be shown that the entries between Peterhouse nos. 3v and 8v had subsequently been removed from the arrangement of that MS. in order to be united according to topographical arrangement with other documents located elsewhere, but concerning corresponding parishes, then it could be argued that the later rearranged form of the Peterhouse fragment, in which nos. 302 and 303 would occur next to each other, was a direct source for section III of the *secunda camera*. Turning to numbers 417, 312 and 231 of the *secunda camera* (Peterhouse nos. 4v, 5v and 7v respectively), we find our assumption to be well based; each occurs in the present section III in a group of deeds concerning corresponding parishes. The only entry which does not comply in its present sequence is no. 376, equal to Peterhouse no. 6v. The exception strengthens the argument, for it turns out that when Peterhouse no. 6v, identified in Charts II and III as *V*, was removed from its original order in the Chaureth cartulary of *c.* 1200, it was copied next to another deed, *X*, concerning the same parish; which other deed was at an even later recopying removed and entered somewhere else (with *Y* and *Z*), leaving no. 376 once again by itself (see Chart III above).

The peregrinations of this one deed are extremely important, for they indicate that between the copying of the Chaureth cartulary *c.* 1200 and the copying which left section III in its present form (there is no miscellaneous *B* group here), there was an interim copying. They also indicate that the said interim copying, unlike that of *c.* 1200, was organized according to topographical association.

It is clear from the arrangement of entries in section III when that interim copying took place. Three distinct groups are apparent. First, there are the twelfth-century entries. There can be little doubt that these derive originally from the Chaureth cartulary of *c.* 1200.

Second, there are entries dating from *c.* 1220 to 1257, associated topographically with neighbouring twelfth-century documents by family. These, I believe, represent material from a later cartulary (appearing in Chart IV as *Chaureth II*), made up shortly after 1257, the date of the latest entry in this group. The date is significant, for it corresponds closely to the date 1262, when the Chapter General, the supreme governing body of the Order, decreed that each priory was to draw up a register of its holdings.[5] At the time of this interim copying,

---

5 *Cartulaire général de l'Ordre des Hospitaliers de S. Jean de Jérusalem: 1100-1310*, ed. J. Delaville le Roulx, 3 (Paris, 1899), p. 48; Jonathan Riley-Smith, *The Knights of St. John in Jerusalem and Cyprus, c. 1050-1310* (London, 1967), p. 362 and n. 3.

those thirteenth-century documents which could be associated topographically and by family with twelfth-century documents from the cartulary of *c.* 1200 were added according to what was to become an established principle in later copyings. The entries from the cartulary of *c.* 1200 which remained together in the Cartulary of 1442 were left together precisely because no association could be found between them and other documents during this interim copying when entries were for the first time being grouped according to parish and family.

CHART IV

The Development of Section III
CHAURETH

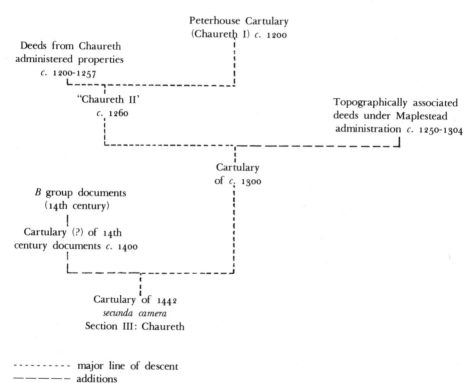

Peterhouse Cartulary
(Chaureth I) *c.* 1200

Deeds from Chaureth
administered properties
    c. 1200-1257

"Chaureth II'
    c. 1260

Topographically associated
deeds under Maplestead
administration *c.* 1250-1304

Cartulary
of *c.* 1300

B group documents
(14th century)

Cartulary (?) of 14th
century documents *c.* 1400

Cartulary of 1442
secunda camera
Section III: Chaureth

- - - - - - - - -   major line of descent
— — — — —   additions

The third group of deeds is represented by those dating from the second half of the thirteenth century, associated by place, but never by family with adjacent twelfth-century entries. This material is so obviously different both in dating and criterion for arrangement from the presumed later Chaureth additions discussed in group two, that there are good grounds for believing they were added at a different time. The latest of these deeds is dated 1304, hence the additions could not have been made before that time. This date coincides with the period *c.* 1290-1300 when all but two obviously later sections of the *secunda camera* appear to have been revised (Chart I, column *A*).

We may conclude from the arrangement of its content that section III of the Cartulary of 1442 derives from three different cartularies, each incorporating subsequent material pertinent to the overall administration of the topographical areas concerned. The first cartulary was that of *c.* 1200, containing grants dependent upon the Order's administrative centre at Chaureth. The second was a revision of the first, copied after 1257. The third, made soon after 1304, was the result of the general reorganization and recopying of the Order's Essex archives which went on at the turn of the fourteenth century. It is probable that that cartulary was the source from which the scribes of 1442 copied.

CHART V

The Development of Section IX
Sampford

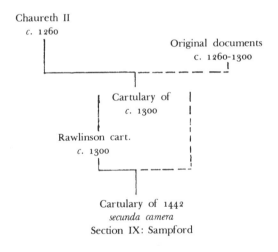

Chaureth II
c. 1260

Original documents
c. 1260-1300

Cartulary of
c. 1300

Rawlinson cart.
c. 1300

Cartulary of 1442
secunda camera
Section IX: Sampford

————— major line of descent
— — — — · additions

As in the case of the interim cartulary of *c.* 1260, *Chaureth II,* the evidence of a single section from the Cartulary of 1442 will suffice to illustrate another example of the Hospitaller cartulary tradition. That section is number IX, containing only 38 entries and pertaining to the parish of Sampford. Its development can be traced on Chart V. It is interesting for a number of reasons:

First, as Chart I shows, it corresponds exactly to the Sampford-in-Essex *titulus*.

Second, it contains a number of deeds dated *c.* 1225-1235 pertaining to land in Sampford which are grants to the Hospitallers in Chaureth, hence there can be no doubt that in the first half of the thirteenth century, Order lands in this parish were dependent upon the administrative centre at Chaureth, and that part of the content of the section would, therefore, have been transmitted through the interim Chaureth cartulary of *c.* 1260 (*Chaureth II*).

Third, only two of the thirty-eight entries have witness lists and they, obviously later additions, appear at the end of the section.

Since only the occasional witness list is missing from deeds in other sections of the *secunda camera*, it would be surprising if the scribe of 1442 had omitted the witnesses here, particularly when the last two deeds were copied with their witness lists intact. Without further evidence, one could assume with some degree of confidence that in 1442 the scribe was copying from a source from which the witness lists were already lacking.

By a stroke of historical coincidence, that source is still extant, and survives as a quire in MS. Rawlinson Essex 11 (fols. 1-8) from the Bodleian Library, Oxford. The sequence of Sampford deeds copied therein is exactly the same as that apparent in section IX of the *secunda camera*. The two final entries in that section which bear witness lists do not appear in the Rawlinson fragment, confirming our supposition that these were added to the Sampford section at some other time, or from a different source.

This analysis has covered but two of the ten sections in the *secunda camera*. Considered as a whole, these sections reflect the derivative nature of the cartulary, a factor corroborated by the existence of the two fragments of earlier cartularies. It is not the number of cartularies produced by the Order during its existence in England, however, that is of interest to us here, but rather that the scribes responsible for periodically revising these manuscripts based the revision on the organization and arrangement of the very manuscript they were revising. There is every indication, moreover, that they copied directly from the manuscript being revised, rather than from original documents, even if those documents were still extant at the time the copying took place. The only copying made from original documents would have been from those new deeds which had accrued to the Order between copyings.

Since accuracy was as essential in any legal document then as now, one might ask why the Hospitallers would have exposed themselves to the possibility of error in transcription by reproducing a copy rather than the original. The answer lies partly in the fact that it was easier and quicker, hence cheaper to work directly first from the manuscript being revised and adding interim material according to a set organizational plan, and partly from the fact that the cartulary was first and foremost designed to facilitate reference to the content of an archive. With the exception perhaps of the comprehensive Cartulary of 1442, written when most originals were probably no longer extant, these manuscripts were never intended to serve as legal documents in lieu of originals.

Before the Cartulary of 1442 was begun, and apart from the obviously interim material, we have no way of knowing to what extent originals of documents previously inscribed in cartularies were available at the time of successive cartulary copyings. Only one original deed is known to exist for the 957 entries in the *secunda camera*, and those few additional original Essex deeds which do exist do not have counterparts in the cartulary. As a result of destruction caused during the Peasants' Rebellion of 1381, when the Order's archives were burned, many if not most originals must already have been lacking in 1442.[6]

In the absence of original documents, a cartulary becomes a unique and priceless historical source for the material preserved therein. There are of course several drawbacks to the use of cartularies as unique sources. First, the material they contain is never a complete copy of the archive from whence they came. Documents were not only lost or misplaced, but the scribes themselves were selective about what they included.

Since some of those few extant original Essex deeds which are absent from the folios of the Cartulary of 1442 date from as early as the twelfth century, one wonders why, if they have survived to the present day, they were never included in one of the periodic cartulary revisions and thus preserved for posterity by the cartulary tradition. In answer to this question, it would seem that if a document were somehow omitted from the most nearly contemporary copying, it might forever remain outside the responsibility of the cartulary copyist.

---

6   A marginal note in Latin on fol. 3r of the Cartulary of 1442 reads in translation: "And be it remembered that the men of Kent, rebels against King Richard II, burnt charters and evidences of this hospital at Highbury and le Temple...."

The second obvious drawback to the use of cartularies as unique sources is that because they contain copies not only of originals, but also of copies of a series of preceding copies, they can never be counted on for accuracy.

While accuracy is the end-all of historical research, and while an original document is the preferred source, it should be remembered regarding cartulary copies that it is not only the content of the individual entry which is important, but also its position in the manuscript. Particularly in late medieval cartularies containing material from previous centuries, an analysis of the sequence of entries can provide a wealth of information concerning the developing organization, not only of the Order's archives, but also of its local administration. The present division of the Cartulary of 1442 into *tituli* is based upon the Hospitaller administration of its Essex properties in the mid-fifteenth century, just as the ten sectional divisions undoubtedly reflect administrative and organizational policies adhered to when those sections were devised *c.* 1300. The grouping of entries chronologically and topographically can be shown to reflect further administrative developments at the local level. Finally, the relative placement of each entry in the Cartulary is indicative of the relationship between the property concerned and Order administration at the time the Cartulary was written.

Although my observations are not intended to cover cartularies in general, it is doubtful that the methods of organization and transmission of archives described here were unique to the Hospitallers. Before any general conclusions can be made about such transmission, a similar analysis will have to be applied to other cartularies. Meanwhile, the evidence provided by the Hospitaller archives indicates that there is a pressing need to reevaluate and reinterpret the nature of cartulary and similar medieval copied sources.[7]

New York University

---

7   This article was originally presented as a paper at the Eighth Conference on Medieval Studies, sponsored by the Medieval Institute of Western Michigan University, 29 April - 2 May 1973.

THE EARL OF TOULOUSE:
A STRUCTURE OF HONOR

Robert Reilly

Such studies of *The Earl of Toulouse* as have been published are chiefly concerned with the sources from which it derives.[1] Of course, some studies have dealt with the theme or mythic pattern of the innocent persecuted wife as it occurs in the poem;[2] but no one has looked at it simply as a piece of literature, a fictional work which utilizes a distinct pattern of actions and words to present a particular idea in concrete form. It is exactly in this fashion that I should like to examine *The Earl of Toulouse*. Thus, by a study of the poem's structure, I hope to show that it is condioned by and presents in an affirmative manner an idealistic conception of honor.

The poem may easily be divided into four sections. This division is clear because the narrator announces a shift in the narrative at the ends of sections one and two:

> Leve we now þe Emperour in thoght:
> ...
> And to the Erle turne we agayn,[3]

The division after section three is not announced, but it seems to be appropriate on the same grounds, for the action again shifts from the Emperor to the Earl.

At this point I should like to give a summary of each section so that the subsequent discussion of their structural relationships will be clearer.

---

1   See Laura A. Hibbard, *Medieval Romance in England* (Oxford, 1924), pp. 35-43.

2   Edwin A. Greenlaw, "The Vows of Baldwin: A Study in Medieval Fiction," *PMLA* 21 (1906) 575-636.

3   "The Earl of Toulouse," ll. 163 and 166, in Walter H. French and Charles B. Hale, eds., *Middle English Metrical Romances* 1 (New York, 1964), pp. 383-419.

The initial section (ll. 1-165) is largely expository. It very briefly sketches the territorial dispute between the Earl of Toulouse and the Emperor of Almayn, describes each of the major characters, and narrates the battle in which the Earl is victorious. Both before and after the battle the Empress tells her husband that he is wrong and suggests that he be reconciled with the Earl.

The Earl's clandestine trip to see the Empress is presented in the second section (ll. 166-480). Saying that he has heard of her beauty and wishes to see it, the Earl puts himself completely in the hands of Sir Trylabas, a Turk he had captured during the battle with the Emperor. In exchange for his ransom and an additional sum of money, Sir Trylabas agrees to guide him to the Empress, and the Earl goes with him into Germany disguised as a hermit. When they arrive, Sir Trylabas asks the Empress to assist him in betraying the Earl, but she will have no part of that and insists that Sir Trylabas fulfill his bargain. After he sees her at Mass, the Earl decides to ask her for alms. This she gladly gives, concealing a ring among the coins. When he discovers the ring, the Earl annunciates his love for the first time, but he seems to regard it as a hopeless cause. As he starts home he is attacked by Sir Trylabas and two other knights; he kills them, but is then set upon by the local populace who force him to flee.

As the Earl gets home we return to the Empress. Section three (ll. 481-913) presents her involvement with the two knights appointed by the Emperor as her personal bodyguards. These two are much more interested in the body than the guarding. Although they pine for "love", their willingness to share the beloved leaves no doubt that the actual motivation is lust. Each in turn approaches the Empress with his proposition. Both are rejected, but each manages to extract a promise of silence from her. Together, they plot their revenge. An untried knight is induced to hide semi-naked behind the arras in the lady's bedroom as a joke. They contrive to find and kill him there, subsequently accusing the Empress of adultery. When the Emperor returns home he has little choice but to convene a parliament. This body indicts her, but proposes she be tried by combat if a champion can be found.

The messengers announcing the trial by combat go forth at the beginning of the final section (ll. 914-1224). The news quickly reaches the Earl, who decides he would help her if he could be sure she were without fault. He meets a merchant from Germany who tells him the date of the trial and assures him that the Empress is true to her husband. The Earl, disguised as a horse trader, goes into Germany with the merchant. He stays at an abbey where the Empress' uncle is abbot.

The abbot assures him again that the Empress has no guilt, that she has confessed her only fault — giving a ring to the Earl of Toulouse. Unwilling to have information at second hand, the Earl disguises himself as a monk. On the day of the trial he hears her confession. After he finds her true, he undertakes the trial, beats the two traitor knights, and forces them to confess their revengeful plot. This leads to his reconciliation with the Emperor. Three years later, upon the convenient death of the Emperor, the Earl is elected to the Imperium and marries the Empress. Their connubial bliss lasts 23 years and produces 15 children.

Even from this brief summary certain parallels and contrasts ought to be evident. The most obvious of these have to do with elements of the plot. Consider one contrast and one parallel. The contrast of relationship between the Earl and the Emperor at beginning and end is an extreme one. The intense opposition between them at the beginning results in open conflict. However, during the two central sections, one can almost forget the antagonism between the two men. At the end their facile reconciliation strains the imagination. Nevertheless, the introduction of this conventional sort of opposition and its structural placement at the beginning and end contributes in an important way to the unity of the poem. By returning to and resolving the conflict (no matter how unconvincingly) the poet provides a sense of fulfillment and completeness. The parallel is provided by the two trips of the Earl into Germany. While they clearly indicate the strength and persistence of his love for the Empress, they are so carefully made parallel in structure that they serve, by their repetition, to link parts two and four, again contributing to the poem's unity. On each trip the Earl has a guide whom he trusts. At line 230 he says to Sir Trylabas: "Y tryste to the as to my frende,/ Wythowte any stryfe." Later, when he is about to set off with the merchant, we are told, "For mekyll on hym was hys tryste" (l. 977). The Earl goes on each of these trips in disguise. The first time he clothes himself as a hermit; the second trip he trots off in the guise of a horse trader, complete with a string of seven steeds. Now there can be no doubt that the trips, as well as the disguises, are dictated by the plot; yet the repetition, in spite of its variation to hold interest, is so obvious that it must connect the two incidents in the mind of any attentive reader. As soon as this connection has been made, another link in the poem's unity has been forged. The contrast in the Emperor's relationship with the Earl, the parallel in the Earl's trips both use rather conventional elements for an identical purpose, to unify the whole work.

But there are more important parallels than these. Take, for example, the question of "right". It is introduced first in a negative way and then in a positive. Throughout the initial section it is made quite explicit that the Emperor is unjustly dealing with the Earl: "He had rafte owt of hys honde/Thre c poundys worth be yere of londe:" (ll. 28-29). Twice the Empress suggests to her husband that he rectify this injustice: "My dere lorde, y you pray/ Delyuyr the Erle hys ryght." (ll. 47-48) and "Hyt ys grete parell, sothe to telle,/ To be agayne þe ryght quarell." (ll. 142-143). This last statement, I believe, connects directly with the fourth section. There the question of right relates to the lady rather than to the Emperor. Whether she is in the right is not clear, at least to the Earl. Unlike the Emperor, the Earl will not undertake a battle in which he would "... be agayne þe ryght quarell." This attitude leads to his rather meticulous process of determining the lady's innocence before challenging the two treacherous knights.

This instance represents something much more sophisticated than the parallels and contrasts with which we began. There is, indeed, a parallel; the question of "right" is a motif presented at the beginning and returned to near the end. Yet this is no simple use of an obvious conventional parallel for the purpose of unification, because there is a profound contrast in the treatment of the motif. In the first section we are presented with an Emperor who quite willingly engages in combat even though he knows that his cause is unjust. Moreover, the purpose of this combat is material gain. Conversely, in the fourth section we are presented with an Earl who is completely unwilling to engage in a combat until he is thoroughly satisfied that the cause is just. Further, the purpose of this second combat is quite altruistic; for nothing in the preceding parts of the poem suggests that the Earl may expect either the love of the Empress or reconciliation with the Emperor as a result of the trial-by-combat. The secret way in which he disappears after defeating the two treacherous knights serves to assert his altruism dramatically. The parallelism of motif, coupled with the contrast of treatment, serves a more important purpose than unification; motif and treatment combine to define the concept of "right". That concept is roughly equivalent to justice. Coming as it does at the beginning and end, the concept of "right" serves as an intellectual frame for the central ideas of the work.

The two middle sections of the poem contain these central ideas; it is here that they are presented by the structure as comparison and contrast.

The situations in the second and third sections may not initially appear as parallel. However, if we reduce them to their elements some significant parallels are revealed. The action in each section is initiated by the lady's beauty. The Earl comes from a great distance solely to look upon this woman who has such a reputation for loveliness. The two knights, constantly in the presence of her beauty, desire to enjoy that beauty as fully as possible. Both the Earl and the two knights risk their lives on account of the lady. In each case she saves them from death (willingly in the Earl's case, by force of her "trouthe" in the case of the two knights). The major character in each section is the object of a treacherous plan; the Earl in part two, the Empress in part three. Section two is complete in itself, ending with the death of Sir Trylabas and the escape of the Earl. Section three, however, is incomplete since the resolution, with the salvation of the lady and punishment of the two knights, remains for the final section. The parallels and contrasts of situation in these two sections serve unmistakably to emphasize by very careful juxtaposition the similarities and differences of the various characters involved in the action.

In examining these similarities and differences of character, let us begin with the traitors, Sir Trylabas and the two knights. Sir Trylabas is direct. He takes an oath, but does not keep faith. The oath is couched in the strongest terms:

> Yn that couenaunt in þys place
>   My trowthe y plyght thee;
> Y schall holde thy forward gode
> To brynge the, wyth mylde mode,
>   In syght hur for to see;
> And therto wyll y kepe counsayle
> And neuyr more, wythowte fayle,
>   Agayne yow to bee;
> Y schall be trewe, by Goddys ore,
> To lose myn own lyfe therfore;
>   Hardely tryste to mee!   (ll. 218-228)

The very length of his oath emphasizes its serious import. Nevertheless, he twice offends against it, once in principle and once in practice: first by asking the Empress to help deliver the Earl to her husband, and later by directly attacking the Earl as he is going home. The two knights are not so direct, but just as treacherous. Certainly the responsibility of their office is a kind of oath which they betray by their unsuccessful attempts to seduce the Empress. These seduction attempts may be regarded as parallel to Sir Trylabas' suggestion that she help betray the Earl. In each case the Empress is presented with an immoral proposition which she rejects in the hope that the person making the proposition will reform. But she is doomed to disappointment; for Sir Trylabas renews his efforts against the Earl, and the two knights, in their frustration and insecurity, turn upon her. Indeed, this reversal, in which the seducers become accusers, is not only a betrayal, but an indictment of the trust which the Empress had reposed in them through her promise of silence. The traitors are alike because they violate their oaths, explicit or implicit, and because in each section there is both an intended treachery and an actual one.

With respect to the Earl and the Empress there are some important similarities. Each is betrayed because of a trust. The Earl trusts Sir Trylabas on the basis of the oath we have just considered. He says, "Y tryste to the as to my frende,/ Wythowte any stryfe." (ll. 230-231). The situation of the lady is quite similar, but with the complication that she makes a promise of secrecy to each of the knights before he reveals his purpose. The first knight says, "Lady, in yow ys all my tryste;" (l. 553) before he makes his proposition. Afterwards he says, "Yn me ye may full wele tryste ay;/ Y dud nothyng but yow to affray." (ll. 580-581). The second begins on much the same note, "'Madam', he seyde, 'now y am in tryste;'" (l. 637) but later he admits his guilt and begs for her mercy. After the propositions in both cases she accepts their word, agreeing to abide by her previous promise to keep counsel. Just as the Earl is jeopardized by his trust of Sir Trylabas, so the Empress is jeopardized by her belief in the two knights. This willingness to believe on the parts of Earl and Empress might be interpreted as rather naive. I think such an interpretation would be a mistake. The Earl, as a knight, is dedicated to the ideal of "trowthe"; he instinctively assumes that he will find the embodiment of the same ideal in his fellow knights; therefore he accepts Sir Trylabas' oath without the least suspicion. The lady is idealistic in a somewhat different sense. She believes that even a knight who has adulterous tendencies is capable of reform. Like the Earl, she assumes that the knight's statement is sufficient evidence of his intention. Both Earl and lady judge others by the standards which they set for themselves.

Those standards are indeed lofty ones. Fidelity ranks very high among them. The Earl is faithful to the Empress even though she has never spoken to him. True, she has given him a ring as some token of her mercy, but, while he is ecstatic at receiving it, he does not take it as a sign that their relationship is likely to develop. He says:

> Yf euyr y gete grace of þe Quene
> That any loue betwene vs bene,
>   Thys may be oure tokenyng.   (ll. 406-408)

Then he goes on to bemoan the fact that she has a husband. His fidelity moves him to the trial-by-combat, but again, expecting no amatory reward from her, he quietly disappears after her safety is assured. The Empress, on the other hand, is impeccably faithful to her husband. Twice she puts off her would-be seducers with scathing denunciations. Certainly there is no possibility that she might accept the Earl as a lover. She shows herself in the chapel as much for the benefit of Sir Trylabas, who must keep his bargain, as out of any pity for the Earl, who has come so far just to see her beauty. It is a bit incongruent that she even gives him the ring. Yet her doing so ultimately provides further evidence of her wifely fidelity when it becomes clear that this small act troubles her conscience so much that she must confess it, not only to the abbot, but to the Earl disguised as a monk.

So far we have been considering the similarities among the characters. The differences are equally enlightening. The contrast developed between the Earl and the two traitor knights is particularly pertinent. At first the Earl is motivated by what seems a rather whimsical desire to see the lady's beauty. After he sees her it becomes clear that his feelings have developed into love. Throughout the rest of the poem his actions have a kind of selflessness. At every point in the poem the Earl is indirect and circumspect. He does not approach the lady himself, but arranges through an intermediary to see her. He refuses to present himself as her champion, but defends her in disguise. Moreover, he is humble and undemanding. He is content to see the lady, overjoyed to receive her ring. True, he asks for the alms, but certainly that is a guise for approaching her, a guise which underlines his humility in her presence — he comes only as a beggar. The two knights represent the obverse of all these qualities. They are motivated by lust, not love. Altruism never occurs to them; they think only of their own very narrow self-interest. They are blatantly direct in their approach to the lady, bluntly suggesting that she save their lives by her love. "But ye do aftur my rede,/ Certenly, y am but dede:" (ll. 562-563). There is something demanding about their tone which suggests a kind of pride. They seem to think that in some way or other they are entitled to the favors of the lady. With respect to these four things, love, humility, directness, and demands, there is a complete contrast between the Earl and the two knights.

Perhaps the Empress can also be seen as the antithesis of the two knights. Her fidelity to her husband can be regarded both as honorable and as the highest kind of love. Surely her unqualified dismissal of the knights' propositions is a total rejection of lust. Her advice, to Sir

Trylabas that he keep his word and to each of the knights that he reform, leaves no doubt that she represents a force of moral improvement within the poem.

The structure, throughout the poem, but especially in the two central sections, is carefully contrived to display the significant similarities and differences found in the major characters. As the situations present these similarities and differences it becomes increasingly evident that a number of abstract qualities, both positive and negative, are represented through the speech and actions of the various characters.

At first glance, the negative characteristics might seem to have the upper hand, as they are presented by the larger number of characters. So, at the very beginning, we meet the Emperor, who unjustly fights against the Earl over a question of land. He is followed by Sir Trylabas, who not only intends injustice, but acts unjustly in direct opposition to his solemnly sworn oath. He mouths the words "trowthe" and "tryste", without the least intention of espousing their meanings. With the entrance of the two knights, injustice becomes absolute immorality, "trowthe" and "tryste" are so far perverted that they become the basis for a direct attack upon virtue. Thus, the negative characters present an ascending order of evil, an increasingly virulent opposition to goodness.

Nevertheless, for all their virulence, the evil characters never gain the ascendancy. For the Earl and the Empress are the embodiment of "trowthe" and "tryste". They are faithful, not only to their oaths, but also to the persons they believe in; the Earl to the Empress and she in turn to her husband. At the same time they unhesitatingly reject any participation in injustice or immorality. The Empress reproves her husband, forces Sir Trylabas to fulfill his oath, and scorns the advances of the two knights while urging them to reform. The Earl avoids any direct approach to the Empress, and cautiously evaluates her "right" before attempting the trial-by-combat.

Ultimately the victory goes to the Earl and the Empress. Their moral stature has enabled them to rescue one another from the jeopardy in which their devotion to "trowthe" had placed them. Poetic justice is satisfied — they are not only to live, but to live together. All the others die. The Earl has the pleasure of personally killing Sir Trylabas and of seeing that the two treacherous knights are burned for their treason. The Emperor, whose offense was mere avarice, is not killed, but he is afforded a rather brief life span.

We see, then, that the poem's structure, with its system of comparisons and contrasts, leads to further comparisons and contrasts of character, and ultimately to the abstract ideals represented by the characters. Moreover, the way in which the good characters triumph over the evil ones unequivocally suggests the poet's belief in the positive values and rejection of the negative ones. Injustice, infidelity, lack of trust and truth are condemned. Justice, fidelity, trust and truth are affirmed; taken together these four qualities form a concept of honor. Both the Earl and the Empress live by that concept. The poem unmistakably asserts that it is a concept worth living by, for men and for women, for lady as well as knight.

Rider College

THE ENTRAPMENT OF YVAIN

C. R. B. Combellack

CHRÉTIEN's first statement about the gateway that becomes Yvain's prison in *Le Chevalier au Lion*[1] is that it was very high and wide ("La porte fu moute haute et lee," 907). The castle wall might have been high and thick and the passage through it wide, but the gateway as a whole would be large partly because, since there are portcullises, there would have been some kind of gate building over the entrance. This gate is not merely a cut through a castle wall, with gates that swing inward or outward.

A portcullis was a vertically sliding *porte* or door hung over a gate entrance. Ordinarily it was a grating, not a solid door. It moved up and down in grooves. It and its counterweights hung from a pulley; its operators, stationed above the entrance, winched it up to open the gate; they fastened it and the counterweights to hold it above while the entrance was open; and ordinarily (though not always in this castle) the operators released it to fall.[2] The gate building might have consisted of several storeys. There might have been a second portcullis chamber (*chambre de herse*), especially since there was a second portcullis, but there had to be some kind of superstructure.

The action of the narrative implies portcullis machinery and operators, both for raising and on occasion for lowering the portcullises. When the would-be avengers of Esclados come to take the man trapped in the gateway (Yvain), they have the portcullises raised so that they can enter ("Puis firent treire a mont les portes,"[3] 1099). The men in

---

1 References are to Wendelin Foerster's "large" edition (Halle, 1887).

2 For a detailed illustration of a portcullis and portcullis machinery, with front and side views, see E. Viollet-le-Duc, *Dictionnaire raisonné de l'architecture française du XIᵉ au XVIᵉ siècle* 7 (Paris, 1875), p. 343.

3 *Portes* is loosely used, here in the plural of the sliding parts of the *porte*, the *portes colanz*.

the portcullis chamber would have been told to winch them up. And they must have been told to lower them after Esclados' funeral: Yvain watched until he saw the lady go back — saw Laudine go back into the castle — "Et que l'an ot fet avaler/ Anbedeus les portes colanz" (1518-9).

Chrétien never mentions the portcullis chamber, however, nor machinery for raising the portcullises, nor the men who would have worked the portcullises. A portcullis chamber might have machicolations in the floor for discharge of missiles onto enemies below; but that men in the chamber might see und overhear Yvain and Lunete below them, after Yvain is trapped, is a possibility that is ignored,[4] like the possibility that any one about the castle might have glanced in through the portcullis gratings.

There were two portcullises, one at each end of the passage through the gate. Chrétien describes the way the outer one works when Esclados and Yvain enter, and says a bit later that "Une autel porte avoit derriere/ Come cele devant estoit" (956-7). (The operation of the second one I shall consider later.)

Esclados and Yvain his pursuer come to the high wide gate. Large though it is, the gate has a narrow entrance ("estroite antree," 908). (Its width, which seems variable, I shall consider later.)

The portcullises are in raised position as the two knights approach. The passage is open at both ends, and so for the moment it would be like a tunnel or short corridor.

The gate is constructed just like a rattrap: "autresi feite/ Con l'arbaleste qui agueite/ Le rat" (913-5). The rattrap that waits for the rat would be a box trap, since trap and gateway resemble each other. Yvain will be caught in a room-sized box or cage as soon as the fall of the two portcullises has closed both ends. I have been told that rats are too smart to enter a closed box, and in any case resemblance to the gateway calls for the trap to be open at both ends until the rat enters (from either end, perhaps). It would be placed no doubt in a rat run where the rat's regular path would lead it to enter the box. Chrétien mentions only one entrance, describing the contrivance there to illustrate the contrivance in the gateway that will bring the portcullis down across the back of Yvain's horse. The intention clearly is not to take the rat alive, as Yvain is taken by accident, but to kill it with a knife

4 Or perhaps rejected when the place where Yvain finds himself trapped is improbably described in some manuscripts as a handsome room: "Qui tote estoit cielee a clos / Dorez et paintes les meisieres" (964-5).

blade as Yvain's horse is killed by the portcullis. Chrétien calls the knife an *espee* (916), and we can imagine it with some resemblance to a sword blade, solid and sharp. The blade is in its ambush ("an son aguet/ Desus," 916-7), in a position like that of the portcullis hanging above in the portcullis chamber; it comes loose and falls when anything touches the trigger or spring ("ele eschape lués et destant/ Que riens nule adoise a la clef," 918-9), however gently. The nature of the trigger soon becomes clear from what Chrétien says almost immediately about the gateway; for us, gateway and trap are mutually explanatory. The released blade strikes the rat below it (917). It must draw blood, though Chrétien does not say so. Perhaps it slices the rat in two, at the point where a saddle would be if rats wore saddles, for that seems to be what happens to Yvain's horse.

The trigger has its counterpart in the floor of the castle gateway. This is a device, an *engins* (925) consisting of two trebuchets which together hold up an iron portcullis (the outer one): "Einsi desoz la porte estoient/ Dui trabuchet qui sostenoient/ A mont une porte colant" (921-3). The description of the *porte colant* ("De fer esmolue et tranchant," 924) might be applied to a knife blade. If anything got onto ("montoit") the *engins*, the portcullis would descend from above (925-6). (Later, Yvain's horse "marcha le fust" (942) — stepped on the board — and so caused the portcullis to descend from above.) If the gateway entrance was floored with planks, as seems probable, any resemblance to ordinary plank flooring was deceptive.

A seesaw is one kind of trebuchet. The balancing of a beam or board or plank on a fulcrum gives a trebuchet two arms which can be made to move up and down alternately. With the surface of the trebuchet placed so as to be stepped on, the arm taking the weight of the entering rat or horse would sink downward from ground level as the other arm rose. The fulcrum would be below ground level too. A castle might well have a subterranean passage beneath a fortified gateway (especially for safe access to a barbican or for secret exit from the castle).

Trebuchets represented only one kind of ingenious use of weights and counterweights in mediaeval technology. Portcullises too were counterweighted. A castle might have over a moat a bascule bridge, weighted and counterweighted for raising and lowering. Small trebuchets were used for weighing such objects as gold coins, huge ones for hurling stones at the walls of invested castles. Though not all trebuchets in traps were planned for being stepped on,[5] some kinds

5 Gunnar Tilander, in *Remarques sur le Roman de Renart* (Göteborg, 1933) has from a mediaeval

were. Birds alighting to eat food placed on top of a cage might find themselves tumbled into the cage as the top tipped. Animals walking along a forest path might tread unwarily on one end of a concealed plank and be tumbled into a pit beneath.

Except for the trebuchets as a device to spring the trap, a doubly portcullised gateway was in fact a kind of large-scale version of the rat-trap Chrétien describes. Men really were sometimes caught in such gateways, and killed from above. When once the resemblance of man-trap and rattrap had suggested itself to an author's mind, the train of thought might easily lead him to imagine a castle gateway with trebuchets, unlike any castle gateway that ever was but a fine one for a romance.

An unusual but not unreal or impossible feature of the gateway is the fact that the outer portcullis at least (and by inference the second one also) seems to have been not a grating but a solid sheet of metal.[6] The weight of any portcullis might crush, but the grating type would plummet down like a row of fixed spears and would have stuck into the back of Yvain's horse. Yet the horse seems to be sliced in two, as with a knife, rather than stabbed. The *porte* descended; "S'ataint la sele et le cheval/ Derriere et tranche tot par mi" (946-7). Chrétien speaks of the half of the "cheval tranchié" (1093) which is visible in front of the gateway. And Yvain himself would have been cleaved through ("Toz eüst esté porfanduz," 940), if the portcullis had struck him instead of just grazing his back; it did cut ("trancha," 952) the spurs from his heels.[7] Solid portcullises seem also to be implied by Crhétien's statement that the crowds outside were certain what they would see when the gates were opened ("Lors cuidoient bien estre cert,/ ...," 1095 ff.); through gratings they could have looked and known instead of only feeling certain.[8] The simile of the rattrap with an *espee* may have led Chrétien to visualize

manuscript in the Bibliothèque Nationale an illustration showing a fox, with a noose around its middle, hanging upside down from one end of a trebuchet placed several feet above ground level. For more on trebuchets as traps, see Charles H. Livingston, "L'a. fr. Bu(c), et le fr. mod. *trébuchet, trébucher,*" *Revue de linguistique romane* 14 (1938) 237-56.

6   Solid portcullises were not common except for early ones in Italy (*La grande encyclopédie*, ed. A. Berthelot *et al.* 20 (Paris, n.d.), p. 18 *s.v.* "herse de forteresse").

7   The manuscripts offer several readings to describe the effect of the falling portcullis on whatever stepped on the device in the gateway. In Foerster's text of 1887 the text reads "esquachiez toz"; later he changed it to "detranchiez toz" (927).

8   Solid doors were sometimes used in addition to portcullises, but none are mentioned here; and the inference seems to be that "Quant li huis seroient overt" in 1096 means the drawing up of "les portes" in 1099.

portcullises that were as solid as sword blades and would cut like swords.

In the extant version of the Welsh counterpart of *Yvain* — *Chedwyl Iarlles y Ffynnawn*,[9] or *Owein* — the simile of the rattrap is missing and so are the trebuchets in the gateway. But Owein's horse, like Yvain's, is cut in two. Whatever the truth is of the relationship between *Owein* and *Yvain*, perhaps the cutting in two of Owein's horse is a vestige of rattrap-inspired solid portcullises made to fall when Owein's horse, in some earlier *Owein* or a predecessor of *Owein*, stepped on a trebuchet.

There could not be a perfect correspondence between the rattrap in *Yvain* and the gateway, because the number of animals that enter is different: one rat, two horses. Of the horses, one must pass safely under the outer portcullis that falls onto and kills the other horse. Chrétien deals with the complication. He puts a safe lane in the floor of the gateway for the one horse to use, right down the center. A three-lane passage is thus produced, with both the side lanes in effect mined. We may wonder why three lanes are chosen instead of two, one safe and one not. The reason just might be the result of some thought about how the mechanism would look and work. Chrétien wisely does not say how the trebuchets on each side held up the portcullis, but it would be with some variation of the way chains or ropes ordinarily held up a portcullis. The problem would be to have the *engins* below pull evenly on the portcullis above, which otherwise might stick in the grooves, as portcullises sometimes did. A single trebuchet in the center of the passage, fastened to the center of the portcullis, might work well but the connection between them would be remarkably conspicuous; a single trebuchet right or left would not pull evenly; two trebuchets, fastened each to the corner of the portcullis just above it, provides the answer. The two trebuchets could be made to act as a single pedal if they were connected by a rod or bar in the subterranean passage.

Esclados rides his horse down the safe central lane. As lord of the castle, he knows how his own gate is booby-trapped and so rides through it "sagemant" (933). But Yvain rides "folemant" (934), that is, ignorantly not in the center.

Chrétien explains how Yvain happens to be at one side. He is the pursuer, but he has so nearly caught up that he has reached forward and taken hold of the back of Esclados' saddle (936-7); this jockeylike position on his horse is what saves him from the portcullis. Clearly his

9   Ed. by R. L. Thomson (Dublin, 1968).

horse's nose cannot be just behind the other horse's tail. The two horses, though not running neck and neck, must be more or less side by side, and close together. And so Yvain's horse "marcha le fust/ Qui tenoit la porte de fer" (942-3).

One strange feature of the gateway is that the passage through seems to be now narrow and then again wider. As Esclados and Yvain approach and enter, it is so narrow that two men or two horses could not enter together, or meet and pass, without difficulty (908-12). But this is because of the trebuchets set in the floor, because it is made like a rattrap.[10] When the crowds come later to kill Yvain, "il n'i ot a celui triege/ Tandu ne trebuchet ne piege" (1101-2), and they all enter abreast. Zenker expressed approval of Foerster's suggested small door cut into a larger one as the solution to the problem of the width.[11] Yet Esclados and Yvain surely gallop together through a principal portcullised entrance, not through a wicket door or side gate with a miniature portcullis of its own. Or we can imagine a wide entrance temporarily blocked on each side and so made narrow, but then Esclados and Yvain would have been both funneled into the narrow safe central lane. The only sensible explanation is that when Chrétien said at first that the big gate had a narrow entrance, he was thinking only of the center lane which was as "estroiz" as a beaten path (929-31). The safe part of the entrance passage is narrowed or widened as the trebuchets are set or not set to operate.

Esclados fled on, and escaped through the second *porte* which was just like the one in front (956-60). The portcullis, the second one, fell behind him (960), behind him and behind his horse too. We know why his horse, in the safe center lane, did not activate the first portcullis to fall. But why did the second one descend at all, and why behind him?

It was not let down by human operators, if we accept Chrétien's suggestion when he says that both *portes* were alike (the sliding *portes*, with their mechanisms). Beneath the second portcullis there would have to be a second pair of trebuchets. Any animal entering the gateway from the castle side, like one entering it from outside, would have to stay in the safe center lane or tread upon a fatal trebuchet. But in the story the traffic here moves in only one direction. If Esclados stayed in the center lane, the second portcullis would stay aloft. But if for one

---

10 "Car ele estoit ... feite" like a rattrap, Foerster read eventually, adopting the *Car* of some manuscripts; "Qu'ele estoit" is the reading of 913 in the 1887 text. "Because" is certainly the idea.

11 Rudolf Zenker, "Ivain im Torverlies," *Zeitschrift für deutsches Altertum und deutsche Litteratur* 62 (1925) 50.

reason or another his horse swerved, it would indeed step onto a
trebuchet but at first only onto the inner end. By the time it reached the
other end of the plank, the end designed to sink under pressure, the
horse would be already well out from under the portcullis and of
course moving fast away. On demand, Chrétien could have explained
why the second portcullis fell and why it fell behind Esclados.

With the fall of the second portcullis, the trap is closed on Yvain.

Chrétien seems to have had a liking for technological gadgetry, at
least as an element of his literary style. The gateway with the trick
trebuchets is reminiscent of the marvelous secret door of the tower
described in *Cligés*. There may even be a verbal echo from one ar-
chitectural marvel to the other: no *huis ne fenestre* visible in the wall
where the door was,[12] no *huis ne fenestre* apparent through which Yvain
could escape from the gateway (1112). Like the electronic devices
Fleming gave to James Bond, Chrétien's are based on the technology of
the time and have an element of realism. He gave some thought to how
his would work, though authors have never been required to demonstrate feasibility in such matters. The humble simile of the rattrap is
particularly effective in its combination with the marvelous in the
description of the entrapment of Yvain.

Eugene, Oregon

12   *Cligés*, ed. W. Foerster (Halle, 1884), v. 5604.

THE TYPOLOGY OF THE WEEK
AND THE NUMERICAL STRUCTURE
OF THE OLD ENGLISH *GUTHLAC B*

Thomas D. Hill

Acording to the description of creation in Genesis, God created the world in six days and rested on the seventh. This account of the process of creation is of course the basis of both the Jewish and Christian liturgical year, but the circumstances of Christ's death and resurrection, as recounted in the gospels, profoundly affected the relationship of the Christian and Jewish liturgical structure. Christ was crucified on a Friday, which was the sixth day of the Jewish week, and arose, according to the gospels, on the first day after the Jewish Sabbath. Thus, in terms of the Jewish week, Christ arose and Christian worship commemorates his resurrection, on the first, or as Christian apologists put it, the eighth day of the week. The symbolic significance of this anomalous fact was extensively developed in patristic literature. The perpetually recurring cycle of the seven-day week was a natural and immediate symbol for the normal course of human history, while Christ's resurrection, as an event which prefigured the salvation of the just, obviously transcended history.[1] At the same time the seventh day, the day on which God rested after creating the world, was an immediate symbol of the heavenly rest.

These traditional associations are summarized by Bede in a homily on Matthew 27: 1-10:

> Sed aliud nobis memorabile mysterium tempore
> suae passionis sepulturae et resurrectionis intimare
> curauit. Sexta quippe feria crucifixus est sabbato

1   For a full discussion of the theme of the eighth day, see Jean Daniélou, *The Bible and Liturgy*, trans. anon. (Notre Dame, 1956), pp. 262-86. For an authoritative and readily accessible definition of Sunday as the first and eighth day, see Isidore, *Etymologiae*, ed. W. M. Lindsay (Oxford, 1911), 6.xviii.21.

quieuit in sepulchro dominica surrexit a mortuis
significans electis suis per sex huius saeculi
aetates inter pericula persecutionum bonis
operibus insudandum in alia autem uita
quasi in sabbato perpetuo requiem animarum
sperandum porro in die iudicii quasi in die
dominica corporum quoque immortalium
receptionem esse celebrandam in quibus deinceps
animae superno gaudio sine fine fruantur.[2]

In this paper I wish to argue that the *Guthlac B* poet was aware of the traditional typology of the week, and that this tradition is relevant for the formal structure of the poem. The history of Guthlac's "passion", his sickness and death, is presented as a series of seven days followed by the eighth on which Guthlac sends his soul in "wuldres dream" (1304). After Guthlac has first become sick, his disciple asks him what has happened, and Guthlac answers that he is about to die, and remarks:

Ne bið þæs lengra swice
sawelgedales þonne seofon niht
fyrstgemearces, þæt min feorh heonan
on þisse eahteþan ende geseceð
dæg scriþende.[3] (1034-38)

And as the poem makes clear, it is on the morning of the eighth day that Guthlac receives the sacrament and "sends" his soul to heaven.

Besides occurring in Felix's life of Guthlac, which is the source of *Guthlac B*,[4] this detail is paralleled elsewhere in saints' lives;[5] but it seems

---

2 *Opera homiletica* 2.7, ed. D. Hurst, CCSL 122.225-26; PL 94.134. The currency and accessibility of the homily is ensured by the fact that it was included in the *Liber homiliarum* of Paul the Deacon, 2.2. For a convenient listing of the contents of the "original" homiliary of Paul the Deacon see C. L. Smetana, "Aelfric and the Early Medieval Homiliary," *Traditio* 15 (1959) 165-80.

3 All quotations are from *The Exeter Book*, ed. George Philip Krapp and Elliott V. K. Dobbie (New York, 1936), by line numbers.

4 "Septem enim diebus dira egritudine decoctus octavo die ad extrema pervenit" (*Felix's Life of St. Guthlac*, ed. Bertram Colgrave (Cambridge, 1956), p. 152). Note that the Old English poet changes the Latin seven days followed by an eighth to seven nights followed by the eighth day. On the symbolism of the contrast between day and night in this context, see Bede, *Homilia* 2.7: "Et quidem aptissime quondam diem sequebatur nox quia homo a luce paradisi peccando lapsus in huius saeculi tenebras aerumnasque decidit aptissime nunc dies sequitur noctem quando per fidem resurrectionis a peccati tenebris et umbra mortis a lucem uitae Christo largiente reducimur" (p. 227). See also Joseph Harris' comment on the phrase "seuenistes fulle ant a day" in the Middle English lyric "Maiden in the Mor Lay" ("'Maiden in the Mor Lay' and the Medieval Magdalene Tradition," *JMRS* 1 (1970) 74-75).

5 Thus, for example, one of the exemplary narratives Gregory tells in his *Dialogues* concerns an episode in the life of the Bishop Severus. One time Severus came to the bed of a sick man who had

probable that the poet was aware of the significance of Guthlac's death and "ascension" on the eighth day, since the formal structure of the poem reflects the traditional pattern of six days of toil followed by a seventh day of rest. The poem is divided into sections by large capitals, and this sectional division reflects in all probability the formal divisions which the poet imposed on his work.[6] The text of *Guthlac B* as we have it is based on the fiftieth chapter of the *Vita Guthlaci*, which does not contain any such divisions. Again, these divisions are logically and rhetorically coherent, so that it is intrinsically improbable that a scribe or redactor could have imposed them on the poem.

In any case the first six "chapters" of *Guthlac B* concern the saint's life, work, and suffering on earth, while the seventh division opens with a description of Guthlac's soul ascending to enjoy the perpetual Sabbath of heaven:

> Da wæs Guðlaces gæst gelæded
> eadig on upweg. Englas feredun
> to þam longan gefean, lic colode,
> belifd under lyfte. (1305-08)

The poet of *Guthlac B*, then, is following his source in describing Guthlac's illness as lasting for seven days followed by the eighth on which Guthlac ascends to heaven, but he juxtaposes this traditional pattern with the equally familiar hebdomadal pattern of six followed by seven as a symbol of heavenly rest.

This numerical pattern, which involves essentially the conflation of two related numerical figures, is closely paralleled in a liturgical text, which was widely current in the Old English period. The "Benedictio in octavas Domini", which occurs in *The Pontifical of Egbert, The Gregorian Sacramentary, The Claudius Pontifical I,* and *The Leofric Missal,*[7] concludes

---

died in his sins, and Severus, who was greatly grieved, prayed God to revive this sinner. The sick man then came to life and told how devils had been on the point of leading him away. "Et dum per dies septem de perpetratis culpis poenitentiam aeger redivivus ageret, octava die laetus de corpore exivit" (*Dialogi* 1.12; PL 77.213).

6 These divisions, which are listed in the introduction of Krapp and Dobbie's edition of the *Exeter Book* lxxiv-lxxv, are a very striking feature of the manuscript, but the editors do not indicate them in their presentation of the text.

7 *The Pontifical of Egbert*, ed. W. Greenwald, The Surtees Society 27 (Edinburgh, 1853), p. 85 (10/11 c.; York); *The Gregorian Sacramentary*, ed. H. A. Wilson, Henry Bradshaw Society 49 (London, 1915), p. 304 (9 c.; Paris); *The Leofric Missal*, ed. F. E. Warren (Oxford, 1883), p. 66 (10 c.; Reims, Exeter); *The Claudius Pontificals*, ed. D. H. Turner, Henry Bradshaw Society 97 (Chichester, 1971), p. 34. For convenience of reference, I cite these works by their traditional titles although these are misleading in some respects. *The Gregorian Sacramentary* is Alcuin's revision of that work — the

with a prayer based on the mystical significance of number:

> Quo sic in senarii numeri perfectione in hoc saeculo vivatis, et in sep-
> tenario inter beatorum spirituum agmina requiescatis; quatinus in octavo
> resurrectione renovati, jubelei remissione ditati, ad gaudia sine fine man-
> sura perveniatis.[8]

It is simpler to discern the numerical pattern in *Guthlac B* and to cite
what are either sources or close analogues than to define its relationship to the poem as a whole. In part the problem derives from the
richness of the traditional associations of these numbers, but one can
discern something, I believe, of what the poet meant to express by his
use of the "language" of number. There are essentially two terms in
this numerical structure, the number six and the conflated numbers
seven and eight. The symbolic associations of both of these terms are
ambiguous and in both instances the ambiguity of the term reflects the
ambiguity of the portion of the poem with which it is associated. Thus
the number six is at the same time a symbol of perfection (as in the
"Benedictio in octavas Domini") and a symbol for the ordinary course
of human history with its inevitable concomitants of toil, suffering, and
death (as in the homily). The first six "fitts" of *Guthlac B* are concerned
with Guthlac's ministry, sickness, and death, and at the same time with
the extraordinary perfection of his life. Guthlac must suffer and die,
but nevertheless he has advanced so far in the spiritual life that he is
visited daily by an angel and can say with confidence that he is without
sin.[9] The ambiguity of the symbolic associations of the two conflated
numbers is less extreme, but here too the heavenly kingdom is
traditionally defined as perfect rest and perfect fulfillment — conceptions which, even if they are not mutually contradictory, reflect two
separate aspects of the joy of heaven. Seven is of course associated with

---

parenthesized indications of provenance and the date are from Klaus Gamber, *Codices liturgici latini
antiquiores*, 2nd ed. rev., Spicilegii Friburgensis Subsidia I (Fribourg, 1968) to which the reader is
referred for discussion and bibliography.

8   I quote from *The Pontifical of Egbert*, p. 85, since this seems to be one of the earliest instances
of this prayer in a specifically Old English liturgical text. The full version of the "Benedictio in octavas Domini" of which this prayer is a part is as follows: "Omnipotens Deus, cujus Unigenitus
hodierna die, ne legem solveret quam adimplere venerat, corporalem suscepit circumcisionem spirituali circumcisione mentes vestras ab omnibus vitiorum incentivis expurget, et suam in vos bene-
dictionem infundat. Amen. Et qui legem per Moysen dedit, ut per mediatorem nostrum bene-
dictionem daret, exuat vos mortificatione vitiorum, et faciat perseverare in novitate virtutum. Quo
sic..." (*ibid.*, p. 85). All of the various versions of this text which I have seen are essentially similar.

9   Thus Guthlac tells his servant that he is not afraid to die because "ne mæg synne on me/fac-
nes frumbearm fyrene gestælan, / lices leahtor" (1071-72).

the rest of the Sabbath and eight with the joy and fulfillment of the resurrection. Guthlac's soul ascends to heaven while his body remains on earth, but the marvels which accompany what one is tempted to call his "ascension" have very clear eschatological associations;[10] in one sense Guthlac's life reflects the course of human history and the scene of his death seems to anticipate the final resurrection. At any rate, the fact that Guthlac is entering a kingdom which involves both rest and fulfillment is suggested by the poets' association of this kingdom with both the numbers seven and eight.

If my argument seems reasonable, then the Old English poet who wrote *Guthlac B* was composing, like the presumed author of the Old Saxon *Heliand*, "per vitteas".[11] For the modern reader, medieval numerical symbolism, particularly in the context of a poem, seems arbitrary and mechanical, but for medieval artists and poets, number was a sign and almost a proof of the fact that God had created the world "in mensura, et numero, et pondere" (Sap. 11:21).[12] Thus the poet in imposing numerical structure on his work was in a sense imitating God as creator,[13] and if we can not share the medieval sense of the beauty and

---

10 For explicitly eschatological parallels to the radiance, the presence of angels, and the quaking of the earth which accompany the ascent of Guthlac's soul, see the Old English *Christ III* 1007-13 (describing the radiance of God and the presence of his angels at Judgement) and 976-81 (on the fall of mountains and cliffs) and *passim*. On this latter theme, *cf.* also Matthew 27:54.

11 The phrase is quoted from the Latin "preface" to the *Heliand* in which the author comments on the manner in which an ancient Saxon poet (presumably the *Heliand* poet) composed his verse: "Igitur a mundi creatione initium capiens, iuxta historiae veritatem quaeque excellentiora summatim decerpens, interdum quaedam ubi commodum duxit, mystico sensu depingens, ad finem totius veteris ac novi Testamenti interpretando more poetico satis faceta eloquentia perduxit. Quod opus tam lucide tamque eleganter iuxta idioma illius linguae composuit, ut audientibus ac intelligentibus non minimam sui decoris dulcedinem praestet. Iuxta morem vero illius poematis omne opus per vitteas distinxit, quas nos lectiones vel sententias possumus appellare (*Heliand und Genesis*, ed. Otto Behaghel, 7. Auflage, ed. Walther Mitza (Tübingen, 1957), p. 2). The problem of numerical structure in Old Saxon, Old High German and contemporaneous medieval Latin poetry has been the subject of considerable discussion (and controversy) among scholars in the field: see Johannes Rathofer, *Der Heliand: Theologischer Sinn als tektonische Form* (Cologne, 1962), pp. 301 ff.; Rathofer's conclusions have been challenged by Burkhard Taeger, *Zahlensymbolik bei Hraban, bei Hincmar und im Heliand? Studien zur Zahlensymbolik im Frühmittelalter*, Münchener Texte und Untersuchungen zur deutschen Literatur des Mittelalters 30 (Munich, 1970). See also Wolfgang Haubrichs, *Ordo als Form* (Tübingen, 1969).

12 This verse was a crucial text in the development of the tradition of medieval numerical symbolism. For a philosophically oriented discussion of this theme in the writings of at least one major figure, see W. J. Roche, "Measure, Weight and Number in Saint Augustine," *The New Scholasticism* 15 (1941) 350-76.

13 On the analogy between God as creator and man as artist, see Ambrose, *Hexaemeron* 1.27 (PL 14.137).

mystery of *Zahlensymbolik* we can at least appreciate the intellectual sophistication and the harmony of form and content which characterize this aspect of the achievement of the anonymous poet who composed *Guthlac B*.[14]

Cornell University

14   I am aware of course that the conclusion of *Guthlac B* is broken off and that it is at least possible that there were one or more additional "fitts" in the original. This possibility however does not affect my present argument, since I am only concerned with the numerical pattern which is explicit in the portion of the poem which we have. For discussion of the missing conclusion of *Guthlac B* see Krapp and Dobbie, pp. xxxi-xxxii and R. T. Farrell, "Some Remarks on the Exeter Book *Azarias*," *Medium aevum* 41 (1972) 1-8.

A NAME IN THE COTTON
MS. NERO A.X. ARTICLE 3

William Vantuono

THE photostat presented here reveals the name *J. Macy*[1] in the Cotton MS. Nero A.x. Article 3.[2] Parts of two folios have been enlarged and brought together. The one with the illuminated *N* is of fol. 62ᵛ of *Cleanness*. It is superimposed on fol. 114 of *Sir Gawain and the Green Knight*. Only the bottom of fol. 114 appears; there is an illuminated *S* near the top of this folio.

The illuminated letters in the MS. are blue, flourished with red, and the names I describe appear in red ink, not in the brown the scribe used in copying the poems. One will notice, trailing along the margin beneath the illuminated *N*, ornamental designs, interrupted by two downstrokes. After the second downstroke is a letter that resembles an *m*, followed by what looks like *acy*. The downstroke before *macy* may represent large *I* for *John*.

It seems unlikely that what looks like *macy* on fol. 62ᵛ of *Cleanness* is only a continuation of the illuminator's doodling because the squiggles on each side of the illuminated *N* are of a *u* shape. Besides, the writing at the very bottom of this composite photostat apparently reveals the name again in a spot that is separate from the illuminator's scroll work. This spot is at the bottom of fol. 114 of *Gawain*. Fol. 62ᵛ of *Cleanness*, set sideways, is superimposed over it so that the *macy* on the *Cleanness* folio

1   I wish to express my gratitude to Professor John Fisher of the University of Tennessee. His suggestions, advice, and encouragement did much to shape the final form of this research.

2   This unique MS. in the British Museum, containing *Pearl*, *Cleanness*, *Patience*, and *Sir Gawain and the Green Knight* in that order, has been reproduced in facsimile with an Introduction by Sir Israel Gollancz, EETS, O.S. 162 (London, 1923; rpt. London, 1971). The dialect is Northwest Midlands. According to Cyril E. Wright, *English Vernacular Hands from the Twelfth to the Fifteenth Centuries* (Oxford, 1960), p. 15, the MS. was written not later than A.D. 1400, on vellum: 17.3 × 12.3 cm.

appears directly above the *Macy* on the *Gawain* folio. The *M* of this *Macy* is quite clear, the *a* is tiny, the *c* is blotted beyond recognition, but the *y* is visible because of the curved downstroke at the end.

At first glance, the two names might seem to be by different hands, but they are both written in the red ink the illuminator used for making his designs. The fact that one appears at the end of scroll work alongside an illuminated *N* and the other appears at the bottom of a folio could help to account for the slight differences in appearance. For example, the *M* on the *Gawain* folio looks more like a majuscule than the *m* of *macy* on the *Cleanness* folio, and the *y* on the *Gawain* folio does not circle into an incomplete *o*, though one must consider that parts of many letters in this MS. are faded beyond recognition. Bits of evidence which indicate that the same hand was at work are the two little circles beneath the *M* on the *Gawain* folio. Similar circles are visible to the right of the name on the *Cleanness* folio.

Are the names revealed here merely accidental flourishes of the illuminator's pen? *Macy* seems to be written in a more haphazard manner on some other folios in the same position it occupies on fol. 62ᵛ of *Cleanness*. One may note, for example, the scroll work under the illuminated *P*'s of fol. 43 of *Pearl* and fol. 87 of *Patience*. What looks like the initials *JM* may be detected in the upper right-hand part of fol. 87, and the middle of the right-hand side of fol. 110 and the left-hand margin under the illuminated *T* of fol. 125 of *Gawain*. Do these other occurrences indicate that the illuminator only had a habit of making his flourishes in this way? Such a conclusion is implausible. Firstly, there are 48 illuminated letters in the MS. Would not similar "flourishes" appear more often than not? The looping lines, with circles adjacent to them, a recurring characteristic of the illuminator's ornamental designs, may be seen on almost every folio that contains an illuminated letter. Secondly, even if it is possible to detect what looks like the name or the initials in a half dozen or so more places, one may still conclude that the illuminator inserted the name at these points in a more concealed manner.

The appearance of *J. Macy* in the Cotton MS. gives no clear-cut answer as to what the name might mean, but there appear to be three possibilities: (1) the illuminator wrote his own name; (2) the illuminator wrote the name of the family for whom the MS. was made; (3) the illuminator wrote the name of the poet.

The first of these possibilities must receive precedence over the others. Illuminators did occasionally identify themselves. Herbert noted, for example, that the Dominican friar John Siferwas revealed himself as the illuminator of the *Sherborne Missal c.* 1400.[3] However, because there were so many Mascies in the Northwest Midlands of England in the late fourteenth century, it would be difficult to determine which *J. Macy* may be represented in the Cotton MS.

There are also examples of makers of MSS. identifying those to whom the work was to be presented. A marginal entry on fol. 76v of the manuscript which contains *St. Erkenwald,* British Museum Harleian 2250 dated *c.* 1470-80, reads: "Noverint universi per pre*sentes* nos Eesebyt bothe of dunnam in the comytye of Chester in the comythe."[4] Again, it would be difficult to determine which Mascy family may have been connected with the Cotton MS., since there were several of them in Cheshire in the fourteenth century. The castle of the main branch was located at Dunham-Massy, but by about 1350 the line of barons had come to an end.[5] In the fifteenth century, the Booths occupied the old family seat of the Barons of Dunham-Massy.

Although the third possibility would seem to be the least likely, it should not be dismissed, especially in view of the fact that three scholars, Ormerod Greenwood,[6] Barbara Nolan and David Farley-Hills,[7] have attempted to identify a Mascy as the *Pearl*-poet. Nolan suggested a cleric John de Massey, rector of Stockport in Cheshire, who died in 1376. However, if her arguments, which support Greenwood's thesis on numerology in *Pearl*, can be verified and linked to the name *J. Macy* in the photostat that accompanies this writing, I believe a more likely candidate for the *Pearl*-poet would be the John de Mascy of Sale, who was rector of Ashton-on-Mersey[8] between 1364 and 1401.

Nolan's identification is possible, but many scholars will argue that since the rector of Stockport died in 1376, he could not have been the poet because *Pearl* and *Gawain* were probably written after that date.[9]

---

3   John A. Herbert, *Illuminated Manuscripts* (London, 1911; rpt. New York, 1958), pp. 233-34.

4   See Henry L. Savage's introduction to his edition of *St. Erkenwald* (New Haven, 1926; rpt. Hamden, Conn., 1972), p. xi.

5   For information about this family and most of its branches, see George Ormerod's *The History of the County Palatine and City of Chester,* 3 vols. (London, 1819); 2nd ed. revised and enlarged by Thomas Helsby (London, 1882). Some Mascies also lived outside of Cheshire.

6   Ormerod Greenwood, in the introduction to his verse translation of *Sir Gawain and the Green Knight* (London, 1956), pp. 3-16, argued for a Hugh Mascy.

7   Barbara Nolan and David Farley-Hills, "The Authorship of *Pearl*: Two Notes," *The Review of English Studies* 22 (1971) 295-302.

8   See Raymond Richards, *Old Cheshire Churches* (London, 1947), p. 24, and Helsby, 1.558-64.

9   Conjectural dates of *c.* 1390 for *Gawain* and *c.* 1380 for *Pearl* are given by the *Middle English Dictionary,* eds. S. Kuhn *et al.*, 45 fascicles to L. 6 (Ann Arbor, 1954-). See the "Plan and Bibliography," pp. 42 and 64.

Therefore, the following information is offered in favor of John de Mascy of Sale, based on the fact that the name *J. Macy* does appear in the manuscript.

Ashton-on-Mersey in Northern Cheshire is east of the Wirral which is specifically mentioned in line 701 of *Gawain* after the knight crosses the Dee River from North Wales. It is also, like Sale, close to the Dunham-Massy castle. Dialectal evidence gathered so far does not rule out this area as the place of composition for the Cotton MS. poems. Though McIntosh believed *Gawain*, "as it stands in MS. Cotton Nero A.x. can only *fit* with reasonable propriety in a very small area either in SE Cheshire or just over the border in NE Staffordshire,"[10] as Davis stated, "Acceptance of so precise a location must await publication of the supporting documents."[11] Davis' observation that the language of the poet is not a simple and self-consistent local dialect seems most sensible. "His language is to some extent eclectic; yet the basis of it is no doubt, as most scholars have long believed, a dialect of the north-west midlands" (p. xxvii).

John de Mascy of Sale was a clerk in 1364, anxious to receive Major Orders:

> iiij. Id. Aug., at Heywod. John de Mascy of Sale, clerk, instituted to the church of Ascheton [Ashton on Mersey], at the presentation of Robert de Ascheton: Mandate. Obedience.[12]

Not content with the office of subdeacon that was conferred upon him in 1364, he desired quick promotions:

> Orders were not celebrated in the diocese on Saturday on which the Office "Sitientes" is sung. But John Mascy, Rector of Assheton, appeared before the Bishop at Heywode on that day seeking to be ordained Deacon, because otherwise he could not be ordained Priest within a year of his institution. The Bishop said he could not ordain him then, and that he was unable to celebrate any orders on holy Saturday next following.[13]

---

10   Angus McIntosh, "A New Approach to Middle English Dialectology," *English Studies* 44 (1963) 5.

11   *Sir Gawain and the Green Knight*, ed. J. R. R. Tolkien and E. V. Gordon, 2nd ed. rev. by Norman Davis (Oxford, 1967), p. xiv.

12   "The First Register of Bishop Robert de Stretton, 1358-1385," *Collections for a History of Staffordshire*, ed. by the William Salt Archaeological Society, N.S. 10.2' (London, 1907), p. 165.

13   "The Second Register of Bishop Robert de Stretton, A.D. 1360-1385," *WSAS*, N.S. 8 (London, 1905), p. 195.

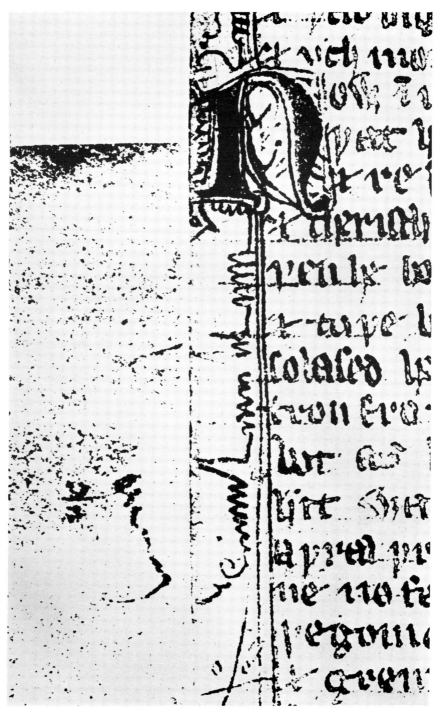

This composite photostat has been reproduced by permission of the British Library Board and the Council of the Early English Text Society. Represented is a 4× enlargement of writing in Cotton MS. Nero A.x. Article 3. Fol. 62ᵛ, set sideways, is superimposed over fol. 114 so that only the bottom of fol. 114 shows.

John was ordained deacon at the beginning of 1365 and priest toward the end of that same year.[14]

This same John de Mascy appears more than once between 1377 and 1389 in various documents. "In the 50 Edw. III, Geoffrey, the son of Sir John de Legh, and Cecily his wife, sued John de Mascy, parson of the Church of Assheton, for dower of a messuage and land, and 'two parts of a moiety of the Manor of Assheton, in Assheton, near Carington.'"[15] John appears in the double role of priest and civil servant, apparently on the side of justice, for as Helsby states, "Most likely Mascy was a trustee of Cecily's former husband, who may have been John de Carington? In any case, the parts in question did not, apparently then, belong to the Leghs."[16]

In the fifth year of the reign of Richard II, he appears as "Sire John de Mascy parson del Eglise de Assheton" in a document written in French relating to Richard and Robert de Mascy of Sale.[17] In the twelfth year of Richard's reign, his name appears again as rector of the Church of Assheton in a document written partly in Latin relating to Roger, the son of Robert de Mascy, and his wife Margaret, the daughter of William de Hulton.[18]

These records show that John de Mascy of Sale was active in civil affairs in the late fourteenth century and that he was involved in issues dealing with law. The internal evidence of *Pearl* indicates that the poet could have been that combination of cleric and nobleman, on the one hand fully cognizant of Biblical exegesis and the writings of the Church Fathers, and on the other well aware of the customs of his day. Everett and Hurnard are among those scholars who have pointed out the poet's use of legal terminology in *Pearl*.[19]

As I indicated earlier, the name *J. Macy* in the manuscript does not necessarily mean that *J. Macy* was the *Pearl*-poet. Most critics will probably feel that the name belongs either to the illuminator or to a family for whom the manuscript was written. However, in view of even the remote possibility that the illuminator wrote the name of the poet, it is hoped that the information presented here will be of interest to

14 *WSAS*, N.S. 8, pp. 196 and 198.
15 See Helsby's revision of Ormerod's *The History of the County Palatine* 1.558.
16 Helsby, 1.558.
17 Helsby, 1.563.
18 Helsby, 1.563-64.
19 Dorothy Everett and Naomi D. Hurnard, "Legal Phraseology in a Passage in *Pearl*," *Medium aevum* 16 (1947) 9-15.

scholars at the present time and may be useful to them in the future, for even if this study proves to be merely a stepping stone to the real identification of the poet, be he John de Mascy of Sale or someone else, this research will have served its purpose.[20]

Essex County College, New Jersey

20 While my typescript was with the printer, the editor of *Mediaeval Studies* kindly informed me of two recent articles by Clifford J. Peterson. In *"Pearl* and *St. Erkenwald*: Some Evidence for Authorship," *The Review of English Studies* 25, no. 97 (1974) 49-53, he noted what he considered to be an anagram for *I. d. Masse* in *St. Erkenwald*, similar to the one Barbara Nolan saw in *Pearl*. In no. 99 of the same volume, 257-66, Professor Peterson reviewed David Farley-Hills' suggestion that the *Pearl*-poet may have been the "maister Massy" Hoccleve praises in a short poem written between 1411-14, and then he sought to identify this "maister Massy' with a John Massey of Cotton in Cheshire. Nolan and Farley-Hills are cited in n. 7 of my present study. Peterson's finding of the anagram, if accepted, adds to the evidence that a *J. Mãscy* was the *Pearl*-poet. The possibility that this poet and Hoccleve's "maister Massy" were the same person becomes credible only if one considers that the man may still have been alive about a quarter of a century after *Pearl* was presumably written. See n. 9 of this study.

A NOTE REGARDING FOUR EARLY FELLOWS
OF ORIEL COLLEGE, OXFORD

L. T. Nau

THE Roman Rolls, which are preserved in the Public Record Office in London, contain two entries which concern four of the earliest Fellows of Oriel College, Oxford. These entries were used by Dr. Emden in his *Biographical Register*,[1] but their implications are not there brought out.

The first entry is a letter from Edward III to the pope requesting that Master John de Aston of Oriel be given the provision of an unnamed benefice which the pope had earlier conferred on another Oriel scholar, John de Laghton. The king asks that, since Laghton died before it took effect, the provision be transferred to Aston. The letter is dated 19 May 1332.

Dr. Emden refers to this letter in his notice of Laghton,[2] but draws the conclusion that in it the king was simply requesting a provision for Laghton; and in his notice of Aston he does not mention it at all.[3]

The second letter is very similar. On 28 May 1332, the king wrote to the pope asking that William de Leverton, S.T.B., be given the provision which William de Kirkham had been prevented from enjoying by his death. Both men are described as scholars of Oriel.

Dr. Emden refers to this letter too, in his notices of Kirkham and Leverton, but concludes that in this instance the king was requesting provisions for both Leverton and Kirkham.[4]

---

1 A. B. Emden, *A Biographical Register of the University of Oxford to 1500*, 3 vols. (Oxford, 1957-1959).

2 *Ibid.*, 2.1084.

3 *Ibid.*, 1.66-67. Although Dr. Emden did not connect Aston with the letter in the printed version of the *Register*, in his own copy of the work he pencilled in a note to the effect that Aston was a Fellow in 1332, citing the Roman Rolls, 12, m. 4, as his source. A photocopy of this annotated version of the *Registers* can be found in the Bodleian Library, Oxford.

4 *Ibid.*, 2.1138 (Leverton); 2.1056 (Kirkham).

The importance of the letters lies in the light they shed on the careers of these four early, possibly original, Fellows of Oriel. They show that Laghton, known from other sources to have been Rector of the college soon after its foundation,[5] was dead by the spring of 1332; that Aston was a Fellow nine years before the earliest date Richards and Shadwell had for him;[6] and that Leverton, the second Provost, was already a Fellow at least a few months before the death of the founder, Adam de Brome. Finally, they establish that William de Kirkham, a man of mature years, to judge by the use of the adjective *venerabilis*, and a Bachelor of Theology, was also an early Fellow of Oriel.[7]

A transcription of the two letters follows:

Public Record Office, C. 70/12, m. 4 (The Roman Rolls).

(*in the margin*:) pro magistro Johanne de Aston.

[1]   Pape Rex devota pedum oscula beatorum. Dum sanctitatis vestre munificenciam magistris pauperibus in universitate nostra Oxon. studentibus de graciis

[2]   provisoriis et inter ceteros quatuor clericis de domo nostra per celebris memorie dominum Edwardum nuper Regem Anglie patrem nostrum ad honorem virginis gloriose

[3]   in dicta universitate fundata ad preces nostras recolimus misericorditer patuisse, de tanti muneris exhibicione gaudentes plenas beatitudini vestre refe

[4]   rimus graciarum acciones. Verum pater, uno de quatuor clericis dicte domus nostre magistro Johanne de Laghton., cui dicta gracia vestra provisoria

[5]   facta extitit antequam effectum dicte provisionis optineret viam universe carnis ingresso, clemenciam vestram requirimus et rogamus, quatinus

[6]   in assecucione gracie predicte que in persona dicti Johannis morte preveniente locum habere non potuit, magistrum Johannem de Aston. eiusdem domus

[7]   nostre scolarem subrogare dignemini nostris si placet interventibus graciose. Conservet &c. Datum apud Wodestok. xix die Maii

5   *Oriel College Records*, ed. C. L. Shadwell and H. E. Salter (Oxford, 1926), p. 2.

6   G. C. Richards and C. L. Shadwell, *The Provosts and Fellows of Oriel College, Oxford* (Oxford, 1922), p. 5.

7   Though Richards and Shadwell do not list him as a Fellow of Oriel, Emden (2.1056) notes the connection, but not his death in 1332, or his degree.

(*in the margin:*) pro magistro Willelmo de Leverton.

[1]   Pape Rex devota pedum oscula beatorum. Dum sanctitatis vestre munificenciam magistris pauperibus in universitate nostra Oxon. studentibus de graciis provisoriis

[2]   et inter ceteros quatuor clericis de domo nostra per celebris memorie dominum Edwardum nuper Regem Anglie patrem nostrum ad honorem virginis gloriose in dicta

[3]   universitate fundata ad preces nostras recolimus misericorditer patuisse, de tanti muneris exhibicione gaudentes plenas beatitudini vestre referimus

[4]   graciarum acciones. Verum pater uno de quatuor clericis dicte domus nostre magistro Willelmo de Kirkham. cui dicta gracia vestra provisoria facta extitit antequam

[5]   effectum dicte provisionis optineret viam universe carnis ingresso, clemenciam vestram requirimus et rogamus quatinus venerabilem virum

[6]   magistrum Willelmum de Leverton. dicte domus nostre scholarem in sacra theologia bacularium in assecucione gracie predicte iuxta formam peticionis quam

[7]   sanctitati vestre pro eodem offerimus presentibus interclusam, subrogare dignemini nostris si placet interventibus graciose. Conservet &c. datum

[8]   apud Wodestok. xxviii die maii.

University of Toronto

THE BRITISH MUSEUM MS. *ARUNDEL 43*
MONOCHORD FRAGMENTS*

Denis Brearley and Thomas Wray

The following errata have been noted:

Page 161, lines 4-5	*Benedictburano*	READ	*Benedictọburano*
footnote 4	our Fragments ¹ and ².	READ	our Fragments **1** a
footnote 9	Musicae artis disclipina...,	READ	Musicae artis disciplina...,
page 162, line 8	sysrem	READ	system
footnote 10	*Grove* VI 112, 175.	READ	*Grove* VI 112, 175;
footnote 10	*Poluphonic*	READ	*Polyphonic*
page 163, line 18	*ae* and	READ	*ae*, and
page 164, line 11 of Latin text	a .c. circinum	READ	a .c. circinum
apparatus criticus	10 a.c.: ac	READ	10 *a* .c.: ac
page 165, line 7 up	E	READ	E♭
line 6 up	E	READ	E♭
line 5 up	or half	READ	or a half
line 3 up	let G ge	READ	let G be
last line	eight	READ	eighth
footnote 22	mereley	READ	merely
page 166, *sigla*	*Arundel 13*	READ	*Arundel 43*
line 1 of Latin text	.T.	READ	.Γ.
line 7 of Latin text	similiter (f. 67r)	READ	similiter// (f. 67r)
line 23 of Latin text	the "square b" should be underlined.		
apparatus criticus, note to line 8	8-9	READ	8
	c.d.		c d
apparatus criticus, note to line 8	.A.B.c.d.	READ	.A.B.**B**.c.d.
apparatus criticus	the note 8 *Hae* : heẹ should be added.		
	c.d.		c d
apparatus criticus, note to line 11	.A.B.C.c.d.	READ	.A.B.**B**.c.d.

* See *Mediaeval Studies* 36 (1974) 160-173.

apparatus criticus, note to line 16	17	READ	16
apparatus criticus, note to line 23	23	READ	23
apparatus criticus, note to line 23	.b.	READ	: .b.
page 167, line 27 of Latin text	VIII	READ	VIIII
line 33 of Latin text	a.T.	READ	a Γ.
line 35 of Latin text	A.C.	READ	A .C.
line 36 of Latin text	secundus in .b. rotundum	READ	secundus in .c., quartus finit. Ab .F. quaternorum passuum primus terminabit in .b. rotundum
line 38 of Latin text	sic	READ	hic
subheading in middle of page	FRAGMENT 2	READ	FRAGMENT **2**
line 5 of translation	in small letters	READ	with small letters
line 12 of translation	<T>	READ	<Γ>
line 15 of translation	T	READ	Γ
apparatus criticus, second note to l. 32	31	READ	32
apparatus criticus, third note to l. 32	33	READ	32
page 168, lines 1, 3, 12, 19	T	READ	Γ
page 169, running head	*13*	READ	*43*
line 2 of Latin text in the right hand column	in initio	READ	& in initio
page 170, footnote 27	3	READ	**3**

footnote 29 should read : See p. 162, par. 2.

footnote 33	his c	READ	his C^c
footnote 34	of 4	READ	of **4**
footnote 34	the scribe have	READ	the scribe would have
page 171, footnote 35	lower G	READ	lower G♭

footnote 35, the cross-reference should read : See p. 161, pars. 2 and 3, p. 162, par. 1.

Ottawa.

PUBLICATIONS
OF THE
PONTIFICAL INSTITUTE OF MEDIAEVAL STUDIES

9 *LES POÉSIES DE GUILHEM DE MONTANHAGOL*, Troubadour provençal du XIIIe siècle, éditées par Peter T. RICKETTS.
1964, pp. 175 $6.50

10 *LIFE AND WORKS OF CLAREMBALD OF ARRAS*, a Twelfth-Century Master of the School of Chartres, edited by Nicholas M. HARING.
1965, pp. 276 $9.50

11 *BERNARDI TRILIAE QUAESTIONES DE COGNITIONE ANIMAE SEPARATAE A CORPORE*. A critical edition of the Latin Text with an introduction and notes, edited by Stuart MARTIN.
1965, pp. x, 427 $11.00

12 *THE THEOLOGY OF THE HYPOSTATIC UNION IN THE EARLY THIRTEENTH CENTURY*, II: Alexander of Hales' Theology of the Hypostatic Union, by Walter H. PRINCIPE.
1967, pp. 254 $10.00

13 *THE COMMENTARIES ON BOETHIUS BY GILBERT OF POITIERS*, edited by Nicholas M. HARING.
1966, pp. xvi, 437 $11.00

14 *ST. THOMAS AQUINAS' QUAESTIONES DE ANIMA*. A "newly established" edition of the Latin Text with an introduction and notes, edited by James H. ROBB.
1968, pp. 282 $10.50

15 *EXCOMMUNICATION AND THE SECULAR ARM IN MEDIEVAL ENGLAND*. A study in legal procedure from the thirteenth to the sixteenth Century, by F. Donald LOGAN.
1968, pp. 239 $10.00

16 *STUDIES IN THE SERMONS OF STEPHEN LANGTON*, by Phyllis Barzillay ROBERTS.
1968, pp. 271 $10.50

17 *WORKS OF RICHARD OF CAMPSALL*. Vol. I: The text of twenty disputed questions on the *Prior Analytics* presented at Oxford ca. 1305, edited by E. A. SYNAN.
1968, pp. 326 $11.00

18 *LIBER POENITENTIALIS OF ROBERT OF FLAMBOROUGH*. A critical edition with introduction and notes, edited by J. J. Francis FIRTH.
1971, pp. xxviii, 364 $16.00

19 *THE THEOLOGY OF THE HYPOSTATIC UNION IN THE EARLY THIRTEENTH CENTURY*, III: Hugh of Saint-Cher's Theology of the Hypostatic Union, by Walter H. PRINCIPE.
1970, pp. 265 $11.00

20 *THE COMMENTARIES ON BOETHIUS*, by Thierry of Chartres and his School, edited by Nikolaus M. HARING.
1971, pp. 619 $20.00

21 *THE PROCESSIONS OF SARUM AND THE WESTERN CHURCH*, by Terence BAILEY.
1971, pp. xv, 208 $12.00

22 *LAND AND PEOPLE IN HOLYWELL-CUM-NEEDINGWORTH*: Structures of Tenure and Patterns of Social Organization in an East Midlands Village 1252-1457, by Edwin B. DEWINDT.
1972, pp. v, 299 $13.00

23 *THE HISTORICAL CONSTITUTION OF ST. BONAVENTURE'S PHILOSOPHY*, by John F. QUINN.
1973, pp. 981 $25.00

24 *GERHOCH OF REICHERSBERG*: Liber de Novitatibus Huius Temporis [epistola ad Adrianum Papam], by Nikolaus M. HARING.
1974, pp. 125 $6.00

25 *ARTS AND SCIENCES AT PADUA*. The *Studium* of Padua before 1350, by Nancy G. SIRAISI.
1974, pp. 199 $10.50

26 *LORDSHIP AND COMMUNITY*. Battle Abbey and its Banlieu, 1066-1538, by Eleanor SEARLE.
1974, pp. 479 $20.00

27 *COMMENTUM SEDULII SCOTTI IN MAIOREM DONATUM GRAMMATICUM*, by Denis BREARLEY.
1975, pp. 295 $14.00

28 *THE INTONATION FORMULAS OF WESTERN CHANT*, by Terence BAILEY.
1974, pp. 112 $6.00

29 *WARBOYS*: 200 years in the life of an English Mediaeval Village, by J. A. RAFTIS.
1974, pp. 267 $15.00

30 *THE LATIN POEMS OF RICHARD LEDREDE*, O.F.M., Bishop of Ossory, 1317-1360, edited from the Red Book of Ossory, by Edmund COLLEDGE.
1974, pp. 222 $14.50

31 *THE HISPERICA FAMINA: I. THE A-TEXT*. A new critical edition with English translation and philological commentary, by Michael W. HERREN.
1974, pp. 234 $11.50

32 *THE THEOLOGY OF THE HYPOSTATIC UNION IN THE EARLY THIRTEENTH CENTURY*, IV: Philip the Chancellor's Theology of the Hypostatic Union, by Walter H. PRINCIPE.
1975, pp. 234 $12.00

33 *FRIARS IN THE CATHEDRAL*: The First Franciscan Bishops, by Williell THOMSON.
1975, pp. 160 $10.00

MEDIAEVAL SOURCES IN TRANSLATION

1 *ON BEING AND ESSENCE* (Thomas Aquinas), translated with introduction and notes by A. A. MAURER.
Second revised edition, 1968, pp. 79 $1.75

2 *ON KINGSHIP, TO THE KING OF CYPRUS (ON THE GOVERNANCE OF RULERS)* (THOMAS AQUINAS), translated by G. B. PHELAN. Revised with an introduction and notes by I. Th. ESCHMANN.
1949, pp. XXXIX, 119 $1.75

3 *ON THE DIVISION AND METHODS OF THE SCIENCES* (THOMAS AQUINAS), translation of Questions Five and Six of the Commentary on the *De trinitate* of Boethius, with an introduction and notes by A. A. MAURER.
1963. New revised edition, pp. XL, 104 $1.75

4 *THE STORY OF ABELARD'S ADVERSITIES*, translated with notes by J. T. MUCKLE, and a preface by Etienne GILSON.
A new revised edition, 1964, pp. 80 $1.75

5 *THE FLEURY PLAY OF HEROD*, Text and Music, edited with translation from the Fleury manuscript, by Terence BAILEY.
1965, pp. 72 $1.75

6 *POETRIA NOVA OF GEOFFREY OF VINSAUF*, translated by Margaret F. NIMS.
1967, pp. 110 $2.25

7 *THE PLAY OF ANTICHRIST: A TWELFTH-CENTURY LUDUS DE ANTICHRISTO*, in translation together with a translation of ADSO's *LIBELLUS DE ANTICHRISTO*. Introduction, notes and translation by John WRIGHT.
1967, pp. 118 $2.25

8 *THE SCHOLAR'S GUIDE*. A translation of the Twelfth-Century *Disciplina clericalis* of PEDRO ALFONSO, by J. R. JONES and J. E. KELLER.
1969, pp. 117 $2.25

9 *ON ROYAL AND PAPAL POWER* (JOHN OF PARIS). Translated with an introduction by John WATT.
1971, pp. 261 $4.50

10 *THE FOUNTAIN OF PHILOSOPHY*, a translation of *Fons philosophiae* by GODFREY OF SAINT VICTOR, by E. A. SYNAN.
1972, pp. 89 $2.25

11 *BOOK WITHOUT A NAME*, a translation of PETRARCH's *Liber sine nomine*, by Norman P. ZACOUR.
1973, pp. 129 $3.25

12 *THE BOOK OF THE COVENANT* of JOSEPH KIMHI, a translation from the Hebrew, by Frank TALMAGE.
1972, pp. 88 $2.25

13 *KARLAMAGNUS SAGA*: The Saga of Charlemagne and his Heroes, I [Parts I-III], translated by Constance B. HIEATT.
1975, pp. 346 $8.00

14 *ALAN OF LILLE*: *Anticlaudianus* or the Good and Perfect Man, Translation and commentary by James J. SHERIDAN
1973, pp. 252 $5.50

15 *MASTER ECKHART*: Parisian *Questions and Prologues*, translated with an introduction and notes by A. A. MAURER.
1974, pp. 123 $3.50

16 *PORPHYRY THE PHOENICIAN. ISAGOGE*, by E. W. WARREN.
   1975, pp. 65 $3.25

17 *KARLAMAGNUS SAGA*: The Saga of Charlemagne and his Heroes, II [Part IV], translated by Constance B. HIEATT.
   (IN PROGRESS) $8.00

18 *THE LIFE OF COLA DI RIENZO*, translated with an introduction by John Wright.
   (IN PROGRESS) $5.00

SUBSIDIA MEDIAEVALIA

1 *A SURVEY OF THE VATICAN ARCHIVES AND OF ITS MEDIAEVAL HOLDINGS*, by
   Leonard E. BOYLE.
   1972, pp. 250 $9.00

2 *A CHECK-LIST OF MIDDLE ENGLISH PROSE WRITINGS OF SPIRITUAL GUID-
   ANCE*, by P. S. JOLLIFFE.
   1974, pp. 199 $11.50

3 *ASSART DATA AND LAND VALUES*. Two Studies in the East Midlands 1200-1350,
   by J. A. RAFTIS.
   1975, pp. 169 $8.50

4 *A CATALOGUE OF MEDIEVAL AND RENAISSANCE OPTICAL MANUSCRIPTS*, by
   David C. LINDBERG.
   1975, pp. 142 $7.50

5 *THE MEDIAEVAL LIAR*: A Catalogue of the *Insolubilia* Literature, by Paul V.
   SPADE.
   (IN PROGRESS) $7.00

6 *THE REGISTER OF RICHARD CLIFFORD, BISHOP OF WORCESTER*: A Calendar, by
   W. E. L. SMITH.
   (IN PROGRESS)

STANDARD EDITIONS AND MONOGRAPHS

ALGAZEL'S METAPHYSICS, Latin Text, edited by J. T. MUCKLE.
   1933, pp. XIX, 247 $4.50

BEING AND SOME PHILOSOPHERS, by Etienne GILSON.
   New enlarged edition. 1952, pp. XI, 235 $5.50

THE DOCTRINE OF BEING IN THE ARISTOTELIAN METAPHYSICS: A Study in the
   Greek Background of Mediaeval Thought, by Joseph OWENS with a preface by
   Etienne GILSON.
   1963, pp. 535 $11.00

SUMMA PARISIENSIS ON THE DECRETUM GRATIANI, edited by T. P. Mc-
   LAUGHLIN.
   1952, pp. XXXII, 272 $8.25

MÉLANGES OFFERTS À ÉTIENNE GILSON.
1959, pp. 704 $13.00

G. B. PHELAN: SELECTED PAPERS, edited by A. G. KIRN.
1967, pp. 249 $7.50

ST. THOMAS AQUINAS 1274-1974 COMMEMORATIVE STUDIES, editor-in-chief, Armand A. MAURER, with a foreword by Etienne GILSON.
1974, I. pp. 488, II. pp. 526   set $20.00

ESSAYS IN HONOUR OF ANTON CHARLES PEGIS, editor, J. Reginald O'DONNELL.
1974, pp. 395 $18.00

TORONTO MEDIEVAL LATIN TEXTS SERIES

1 *THREE LIVES OF ENGLISH SAINTS*, edited by Michael WINTERBOTTOM.
1972, pp. 94 $2.75

2 *THE GOSPEL OF NICODEMUS*, edited by H. C. KIM.
1973, pp. 54 $2.75

3 *PETER THE VENERABLE. SELECTED LETTERS*, edited by Janet MARTIN in collaboration with Giles CONSTABLE.
1974, pp. 107 $2.75

4 *A THIRTEENTH-CENTURY ANTHOLOGY OF RHETORICAL POEMS*, edited by Bruce HARBERT.
1975, pp. x, 78 $2.75

5 *TWO ALCUIN LETTER-BOOKS*, edited by Colin CHASE.
1975, pp. ix, 84 $2.75

All correspondence regarding articles should be addressed to:

Professor Virginia BROWN
Editor of Mediaeval Studies
59 Queen's Park Crescent East
Toronto, Ontario
Canada M5S 2C4

Mediaeval Studies *does not accept books for review.*

Subscription $14.00 yearly.

All correspondence regarding orders and subscriptions should be addressed to:
(from North America):

Walter M. HAYES, S.J.
Director of Publications
59 Queen's Park Crescent East
Toronto, Ontario
Canada M5S 2C4

(from elsewhere):

E. J. BRILL Ltd.
Oude Rijn 33a
Leiden
The Netherlands